Handbook of Regulation and Administrative Law

PUBLIC ADMINISTRATION AND PUBLIC POLICY

A Comprehensive Publication Program

Executive Editor

JACK RABIN
Professor of Public Administration and Public Policy
Division of Public Affairs
The Capital College
The Pennsylvania State University—Harrisburg
Middletown, Pennsylvania

1. *Public Administration as a Developing Discipline (in two parts),* Robert T. Golembiewski
2. *Comparative National Policies on Health Care,* Milton I. Roemer, M.D.
3. *Exclusionary Injustice: The Problem of Illegally Obtained Evidence,* Steven R. Schlesinger
4. *Personnel Management in Government: Politics and Process,* Jay M. Shafritz, Walter L. Balk, Albert C. Hyde, and David H. Rosenbloom
5. *Organization Development in Public Administration (in two parts),* edited by Robert T. Golembiewski and William B. Eddy
6. *Public Administration: A Comparative Perspective, Second Edition, Revised and Expanded,* Ferrel Heady
7. *Approaches to Planned Change (in two parts),* Robert T. Golembiewski
8. *Program Evaluation at HEW (in three parts),* edited by James G. Abert
9. *The States and the Metropolis,* Patricia S. Florestano and Vincent L. Marando
10. *Personnel Management in Government: Politics and Process, Second Edition, Revised and Expanded,* Jay M. Shafritz, Albert C. Hyde, and David H. Rosenbloom
11. *Changing Bureaucracies: Understanding the Organization Before Selecting the Approach,* William A. Medina
12. *Handbook on Public Budgeting and Financial Management,* edited by Jack Rabin and Thomas D. Lynch
13. *Encyclopedia of Policy Studies,* edited by Stuart S. Nagel
14. *Public Administration and Law: Bench v. Bureau in the United States,* David H. Rosenbloom
15. *Handbook on Public Personnel Administration and Labor Relations,* edited by Jack Rabin, Thomas Vocino, W. Bartley Hildreth, and Gerald J. Miller
16. *Public Budgeting and Finance: Behavioral, Theoretical, and Technical Perspectives,* edited by Robert T. Golembiewski and Jack Rabin
17. *Organizational Behavior and Public Management,* Debra W. Stewart and G. David Garson
18. *The Politics of Terrorism: Second Edition, Revised and Expanded,* edited by Michael Stohl

19. *Handbook of Organization Management,* edited by William B. Eddy
20. *Organization Theory and Management,* edited by Thomas D. Lynch
21. *Labor Relations in the Public Sector,* Richard C. Kearney
22. *Politics and Administration: Woodrow Wilson and American Public Administration,* edited by Jack Rabin and James S. Bowman
23. *Making and Managing Policy: Formulation, Analysis, Evaluation,* edited by G. Ronald Gilbert
24. *Public Administration: A Comparative Perspective, Third Edition, Revised,* Ferrel Heady
25. *Decision Making in the Public Sector,* edited by Lloyd G. Nigro
26. *Managing Administration,* edited by Jack Rabin, Samuel Humes, and Brian S. Morgan
27. *Public Personnel Update,* edited by Michael Cohen and Robert T. Golembiewski
28. *State and Local Government Administration,* edited by Jack Rabin and Don Dodd
29. *Public Administration: A Bibliographic Guide to the Literature,* Howard E. McCurdy
30. *Personnel Management in Government: Politics and Process, Third Edition, Revised and Expanded,* Jay M. Shafritz, Albert C. Hyde, and David H. Rosenbloom
31. *Handbook of Information Resource Management,* edited by Jack Rabin and Edward M. Jackowski
32. *Public Administration in Developed Democracies: A Comparative Study,* edited by Donald C. Rowat
33. *The Politics of Terrorism: Third Edition, Revised and Expanded,* edited by Michael Stohl
34. *Handbook on Human Services Administration,* edited by Jack Rabin and Marcia B. Steinhauer
35. *Handbook of Public Administration,* edited by Jack Rabin, W. Bartley Hildreth, and Gerald J. Miller
36. *Ethics for Bureaucrats: An Essay on Law and Values, Second Edition, Revised and Expanded,* John A. Rohr
37. *The Guide to the Foundations of Public Administration,* Daniel W. Martin
38. *Handbook of Strategic Management,* edited by Jack Rabin, Gerald J. Miller, and W. Bartley Hildreth
39. *Terrorism and Emergency Management: Policy and Administration,* William L. Waugh, Jr.
40. *Organizational Behavior and Public Management: Second Edition, Revised and Expanded,* Michael L. Vasu, Debra W. Stewart, and G. David Garson
41. *Handbook of Comparative and Development Public Administration,* edited by Ali Farazmand
42. *Public Administration: A Comparative Perspective, Fourth Edition,* Ferrel Heady
43. *Government Financial Management Theory,* Gerald J. Miller
44. *Personnel Management in Government: Politics and Process, Fourth Edition, Revised and Expanded,* Jay M. Shafritz, Norma M. Riccucci, David H. Rosenbloom, and Albert C. Hyde
45. *Public Productivity Handbook,* edited by Marc Holzer
46. *Handbook of Public Budgeting,* edited by Jack Rabin

47. *Labor Relations in the Public Sector: Second Edition, Revised and Expanded*, Richard C. Kearney
48. *Handbook of Organizational Consultation*, edited by Robert T. Golembiewski
49. *Handbook of Court Administration and Management*, edited by Steven W. Hays and Cole Blease Graham, Jr.
50. *Handbook of Comparative Public Budgeting and Financial Management*, edited by Thomas D. Lynch and Lawrence L. Martin
51. *Handbook of Organizational Behavior*, edited by Robert T. Golembiewski
52. *Handbook of Administrative Ethics*, edited by Terry L. Cooper
53. *Encyclopedia of Policy Studies: Second Edition, Revised and Expanded*, edited by Stuart S. Nagel
54. *Handbook of Regulation and Administrative Law*, edited by David H. Rosenbloom and Richard D. Schwartz

Additional Volumes in Preparation

Handbook of Bureaucracy, edited by Ali Farazmand

Handbook of Public Personnel Administration, edited by Jack Rabin, Thomas Vocino, W. Bartley Hildreth, and Gerald J. Miller

Handbook of Public Sector Labor Relations, edited by Jack Rabin, W. Bartley Hildreth, and Gerald J. Miller

ANNALS OF PUBLIC ADMINISTRATION

1. *Public Administration: History and Theory in Contemporary Perspective*, edited by Joseph A. Uveges, Jr.
2. *Public Administration Education in Transition*, edited by Thomas Vocino and Richard Heimovics
3. *Centenary Issues of the Pendleton Act of 1883*, edited by David H. Rosenbloom with the assistance of Mark A. Emmert
4. *Intergovernmental Relations in the 1980s*, edited by Richard H. Leach
5. *Criminal Justice Administration: Linking Practice and Research*, edited by William A. Jones, Jr.

Handbook of Regulation and Administrative Law

edited by

David H. Rosenbloom
School of Public Affairs
The American University
Washington, D.C.

Richard D. Schwartz
College of Law and Maxwell School
Syracuse University
Syracuse, New York

Marcel Dekker, Inc. New York•Basel•Hong Kong

Library of Congress Cataloging-in-Publication Data

Handbook of regulation and administrative law / [edited by] David H.
Rosenbloom, Richard D. Schwartz.
p. cm. — (Public administration and public policy ; 54)
Includes bibliographical references and index.
ISBN 0-8247-9167-3 (acid-free paper)
1. Administrative law—United States. 2. Administrative
procedure—United States. 3. Public administration—United States.
I. Rosenbloom, David H. II. Schwartz, Richard D.
III. Series.
KF5402.H36 1994
342.73'06—dc20
[347.3026] 93-45612
CIP

The publisher offers discounts on this book when ordered in bulk quantities. For more information, write to Special Sales/Professional Marketing at the address below.

This book is printed on acid-free paper.

MARCEL DEKKER, INC.
270 Madison Avenue, New York, New York 10016

Current printing (last digit):
10 9 8 7 6 5 4 3 2 1

PRINTED IN THE UNITED STATES OF AMERICA

Preface

The *Handbook of Regulation and Administrative Law* grew out of the editors' experience in team teaching a joint degree seminar for Master of Public Administration (MPA) and law (JD) students at Syracuse University during the 1980s. The year-long course was intended to integrate, or at least provide a bridge between, the two bodies of knowledge and thought that our students had studied. We quickly realized that the fields of public administration and law had progressed along separate tracks in their treatments of regulation and administrative law. Work in public administration emphasized management and policy, paying only scant attention to the legal framework for administrative procedure. Much of the legal scholarship, by contrast, focused on statutory and case law, while leaving matters of administrative organization and behavior largely undeveloped. Studies drawing substantially on both the public administrative and legal literatures were clearly the exception. The *Handbook* was conceived as an opportunity to forge a much stronger and more comprehensive link between administrative and legal analysis. We wanted a book that not only would be on the cutting edge of the study of regulation and administrative law, but that would also be suitable for students of both law and public administration.

We believe the *Handbook* achieves the high goals we established for it. The contributors are recognized experts who are able to cross the disciplinary boundaries of law, public administration, and policy. The topics they analyze make the book an invaluable compendium of state-of-the-art thinking on a full range of central subjects in the study of regulatory policy and administrative law.

Specifically, Part I presents a broad overview of the political, administrative, legal, and constitutional questions presented by the rise of the United States version of the administrative state. In Chapter 1, David H. Rosenbloom analyzes the relationship between the evolution of the administrative state and the development of administrative law in the United States. Chapter 2, by Samuel Krislov, discusses two of the main constitutional problems posed by the contemporary administrative state, namely, pressures on the separation of powers and issues of delegated power.

Part II focuses on trends in regulatory administration. Its chapters address social regulation (Gary C. Bryner), economic regulation (Marc Allen Eisner), state-level regulatory activity (Paul Teske), environmental regulation (Rosemary O'Leary), developments with regard to regulatory "takings" (Charles R. Wise), deregulation and reregulation (Paul Stephen Dempsey), and a review of the crucial legal issues, past and present, associated with administrative activity (Bernard Schwartz).

Part III starts with Kenneth F. Warren's comprehensive analysis of adjudication. The following chapter, by Jeffrey S. Lubbers, discusses the management of federal agency adjudication, a topic that has too often been ignored in the past. This section is rounded out by Robert A. Katzmann's study of the Federal Trade Commission's decision-making and antitrust policy during the 1980s. Katzmann's analysis illustrates the complexity of agency decision-making.

Part IV contains highly original analyses of rules and enforcement. Cornelius M. Kerwin's chapter on the management of agency rule-making is path-breaking, as are the chapters that follow on enforcement and the management of enforcement, by Robert A. Kagan and John T. Scholz

Part V contains two chapters dealing with aspects of administrative transparency. Robert G. Vaughn discusses federal information policy and administrative law and Robert Roberts analyzes regulatory bias and conflict of interest regulation.

Part VI considers three issues on the frontier of regulatory administration and administrative law: discretion (Martin Shapiro); administrative democracy (Gerald E. Frug), and bureaucracy and the public (Richard D. Schwartz). Together these chapters confront the prospects for making public administration comport more fully with our democratic constitutionalism.

To the best of our knowledge, the *Handbook of Regulation and Administrative Law* is the only interdisciplinary work of its kind. Because we anticipated that many readers would want to read the chapters separately for their topical coverage, we encouraged the authors to be comprehensive in fashioning contributions that could stand independently. Consequently, some overlap is present. Nevertheless, the *Handbook* was also compiled for those who will read it from cover to cover. While each part makes a substantial contribution, we believe that taken as a whole the volume is a coherent work that covers all the core subjects in the fields of regulatory administration and administrative law and substantially advances thinking about them.

A book of this magnitude generates many debts. We are very grateful to the contributors for their willingness to participate in the project and for their excellent chapters. Jack Rabin, Executive Editor of the Marcel Dekker, Inc., series on Public Administration and Public Policy, made the project possible and strongly supported the book throughout its development. Needless to say, without Jack and the contributors, there would be no book. Nor would we have undertaken such a project without the encouragement of our JD-MPA students. Ultimately, the book is in response to the challenges they posed. Syracuse University and The American University have facilitated the project in myriad valuable ways. Among the many colleagues who offered encouragement, insight and advice are James D. Carroll, Murray Comarow, Theodore Lowi, John Rohr, Victor Rosenblum, and members of Syracuse University's Center for the Study of Citizenship.

David H. Rosenbloom
Richard D. Schwartz

Contents

Contributors

Gary C. Bryner Associate Professor, Department of Political Science, Brigham Young University, Provo, Utah

Paul Stephen Dempsey Hughes Research Professor of Law and Director of the Transportation Law Program, College of Law, University of Denver, Denver, Colorado

Marc Allen Eisner Assistant Professor, Department of Government, Wesleyan University, Middletown, Connecticut

Gerald E. Frug Professor of Law, Harvard Law School, Cambridge, Massachusetts

Robert A. Kagan Professor, Department of Political Science and School of Law, University of California at Berkeley, Berkeley, California

Robert A. Katzmann Walsh Professor of Government and Professor of Law, Georgetown University; President, The Governance Institute; and Visiting Fellow, Brookings Institution, Washington, D.C.

Cornelius M. Kerwin Dean, School of Public Affairs, The American University, Washington, D.C.

Samuel Krislov Department of Political Science, University of Minnesota, Minneapolis, Minnesota

Jeffrey S. Lubbers Research Director, Administrative Conference of the United States, Washington, D.C.

Rosemary O'Leary Assistant Professor, Department of Public Administration, Syracuse University, Syracuse, New York

Robert Roberts Associate Professor, Department of Political Science, James Madison University, Harrisonburg, Virginia

David H. Rosenbloom Distinguished Professor of Public Administration, School of Public Affairs, The American University, Washington, D.C.

John T. Scholz Professor, Department of Political Science, State University of New York at Stony Brook, Stony Brook, New York

Bernard Schwartz Chapman Distinguished Professor of Law, The University of Tulsa College of Law, Tulsa, Oklahoma

Richard D. Schwartz Ernest I. White Professor of Law, College of Law, and Professor of Sociology and Social Sciences, Maxwell School, Syracuse University, Syracuse, New York

Martin Shapiro James W. and Isabel Coffroth Professor of Law, School of Law, University of California at Berkeley, Berkeley, California

Paul Teske Assistant Professor, Department of Political Science, State University of New York at Stony Brook, Stony Brook, New York

Robert G. Vaughn Professor of Law and A. Allen King Scholar, Washington College of Law, The American University, Washington, D.C.

Kenneth F. Warren Professor of Political Science and Public Policy, Saint Louis University, St. Louis, Missouri

Charles R. Wise Professor, School of Public and Environmental Affairs, Indiana University, Bloomington, Indiana

Handbook of Regulation and Administrative Law

I

OVERVIEW

1

The Evolution of the Administrative State and Transformations of Administrative Law

David H. Rosenbloom *The American University, Washington, D.C.*

In the traditional textbook model, bureaucracy is considered a permanent (and lamentable) fixture of government. Bureaucrats are viewed as entrenched, immovable obstacles to the policy and structural changes demanded by political officials and the publics they ostensibly represent. Those formally at the head of these command-and-control organizations find themselves unable to do either. But although bureaucracies generally are structurally stable, they are not impervious to direction and change. Several recent studies find greater bureaucratic responsiveness to political authorities and selected publics than has frequently been supposed (e.g., see the chapters by Kagan and Scholz, *infra*). Historically, public bureaucracies' purposes, cultures, procedures, technologies, and organizational formats have also changed.

In the United States, the administrative state itself has undergone several major transformations, and with each has come an important recasting of the law that governs the nation's public administration (see Stewart, 1975). Today, we may well be in another period of fundamental change. This chapter provides an historical backdrop for the *Handbook of Regulation and Administrative Law* by outlining the evolution of the American administrative state and the legal developments that have occurred in conjunction with it. It concludes that the American administrative state has, by stages, undergone democratization that makes it comport more fully with U.S. democratic constitutionalism. Specifically, the chapter explains why the nation first opted for top-down administration by politically insulated putative experts in scientific management, but later incorporated the principles of representativeness, rights, checks and balances, and (to a lesser extent) participation into its administrative processes. It also reviews the contemporary effort to make public administration more efficient and directly responsive to individuals' demand by basing it on market principles.

BUILDING THE ADMINISTRATIVE STATE, 1870–1920

The American administrative state began to develop rapidly in the period following the Civil War as constitutional, legal, and economic changes pointed toward a growing role for the federal government in society. Stephen Skowronek (1982) has copiously traced "the expansion of national administrative capacities" in the period from 1877 to 1920. The federal service and the army were substantially reformed. Federal administrative commissions were also developed to regulate businesses and economic practices. The structural changes were very real, but in some ways their guiding political ideology was even more fundamental.

The administrative changes were largely the products of two major political movements. During the period from the 1870s forward through most of the 1890s, there was a civil service reform movement that articulated a new—or arguably restorative—vision of government. It was later joined by the Progressive movement, which struggled to define the nation's political culture. The size, shape, and operation of the administrative state were not an end in itself, but rather a key to the broad political changes they sought.

The civil service reform movement has been persistently misrepresented in the American public administration literature. The reformers have been portrayed as locked in battle with political bosses and machine politicians in a struggle to enhance the morality and efficiency of the public service. But their overall aims were much wider and their specific reforms can be explained *only* in terms of their political objectives. What the reformers sought was nothing less than a fundamental change in the character of American politics and the quality of its leadership. The various state and local civil service reform associations published hundreds of pamphlets, and their members probably gave thousands of speeches. Time after time, they came back to the larger theme of reform. In the words of one of their leaders, Carl Schurz, "the question whether the Departments at Washington are managed well or badly is, in proportion to the whole problem, an insignificant question" (1913, vol. 2: 123).

In a word, the significant political question was "leadership." Schurz noted that the reformers wanted "to restore ability, high character, and true public spirit once more to their legitimate spheres in our public life, and to make active politics once more attractive to men of self-respect and high patriotic aspirations" (1893: 614). Another reformer, Dorman Eaton, clearly spelled out the political problem tackled by the reformers:

> [W]e have seen a class of politicians become powerful in high places, who have not taken (and who by nature are not qualified to take) any large part in the social and educational life of the people. Politics have tended more and more to become a trade, or separate occupation. High character and capacity have become disassociated from public life in the popular mind. (1880:392)

Eaton's view was hardly inconsequential. He was an architect of the Civil Service Act of 1883, also called the Pendleton Act after the senator who introduced it.

The act is best known for establishing the merit, or civil service, system in the federal service and for creating a central personnel agency, the Civil Service Commission, to oversee its further development and implementation. (A similar set of reforms was introduced in the early 1870s, but was abandoned in 1875.)

There is no need to review all of the Civil Service Act's provisions here. The statute's overall purpose was to deprive the political machines and their bosses of patronage. In the reformers' view, without patronage, the machines would starve, weaken, and ultimately die off. They would be replaced by leadership that, as Eaton put it, was by "nature" qualified to govern.

Had the Pendleton Act sought only to enhance efficiency, it would not have required that civil service exams be open and competitive. Competence can be guaranteed by simple pass exams. Patronage can be prevented only by exams that are open to all comers coupled with appointments in rank order of scores. The reformers learned this from the example of civil service reform in England. As Eaton observed, in addition to yielding "the best public servants," the open competitive exam "makes an end of patronage. . . . [I]t has been found to be the surest safeguard against both partisan coercion and official favoritism" (1880:365). But in the late 1880s, well before the advent and popularization of Frederick Taylor's *Scientific Management* (1917), neither the reformers nor anyone else could seriously have contended that exam scores would correlate strongly with levels of on-the-job performance. The act also contained a number of provisions intended to prevent partisan coercion of federal employees to engage in campaigning and funding activities.

During the 1890s, the civil service reform movement was subsumed by the Progressives, who sought a much wider array of political, economic, and social reforms. They were impelled by many ideals and concerns, but overall, the Progressive movement was largely a response to rapid industrialization, urbanization, and immigration. The Progressives' zeal and success were partly due to a sense that they were fighting for the soul of the nation. For instance, Woodrow Wilson, who spanned both the reform and Progressive movements, expressed his apprehension bluntly about the

> character of the nation which is being most deeply affected and modified by the enormous immigration which year after year pours into the country from Europe: our own temperate blood, schooled to self-possession and to the measured conduct of self-government is receiving a constant infusion and yearly experiencing a partial corruption of foreign blood: our own equable habits have been crossed with the feverish habits of the restless old world. We are unquestionably facing an ever-increasing difficulty of self-command with ever-deteriorating materials, possibly with degenerating fibre. (Rohr, 1986: 72).

Wilson apparently believed that "the only way in which we can preserve our nationality in its integrity and its old-time originative force in the face of growth and imported change is by concentrating it, by putting leaders forward vested with abundant authority in the conception and execution of policy" (Rohr, 1986: 231, note 61).

Why? Because immigration, coupled with the dynamics of political machines and increasing urbanization threatened to establish a dominant political culture that was very much at odds with what the Progressives favored. Richard Hofstadter has explained:

> [O]ut of the clash between the needs of the immigrants and the sentiments of the natives there emerged two thoroughly different systems of political ethics. . . . One, founded upon the indigenous Yankee–Protestant political traditions, and upon middle class life, assumed and demanded the constant, disinterested activity of the citizen in public affairs, argued that political life ought to be run, to a greater degree than it was, in accordance with general principles and abstract laws apart from and superior to personal needs, and expressed a common feeling that government should be in good part an effort to moralize the lives of individuals while economic life should be intimately related to the stimulation and development of individual character. The other system, founded upon the European background of the immigrants, upon their unfamiliarity with independent political action, their familiarity with hierarchy and authority, and upon the urgent needs that so often grew out of their migration, took for granted that the political life of the individual would arise out of family needs, interpreted political and civil relations chiefly in terms of personal obligations, and placed strong personal loyalties above allegiance to abstract codes of law or morals. (1955: 9)

But how could leadership be strengthened? In part, through political and electoral reforms intended to weaken the grip of machines on the political parties and their policy agendas. The short ballot, primary election, referendum, recall, and direct election of senators were of great importance in this regard. In part, too, by further promoting the civil service reform agenda of installing merit systems in local and state governments and strengthening regulations to take public employees out of partisan politics. At the federal level the proportion of employees who were under the merit system grew from approximately 41 percent in 1901 to almost 80 percent by 1930 (Skowronek, 1982: 71; Rosenbloom, 1971: 104). In 1907, President Theodore Roosevelt amended Civil Service Rule I by executive order to prohibit employees under the merit system from taking active "part in political management or in political campaigns" (Rosenbloom, 1971: 99). The Sixteenth Amendment (1913) made it far easier for the federal government to pay for its administrative growth.

The Progressive strategy to strengthen political leadership and weaken the influence of machines and immigrants further included taking whole areas of government out of politics. City management became both a new profession and design for urban governance. The 1916 version of the Model City Charter of the National Municipal League provided that "the city manager shall be the chief executive officer of the city. He shall be chosen by the council solely on the basis of his executive and administrative qualifications" (Mosher, 1976: 83). Further, "neither the council nor any of its committees or members shall dictate the appointment of any person to office or employment by the city manager, or in any manner interfere with the city manager or prevent him from exercising his own judgment in the appointment of officers and employees in the administrative service" (Mosher, 1976: 82).

The creation of "public authorities" were another means of taking government out of politics. Although the Port of London Authority, created in 1908, was apparently the first such structure, Jameson Doig (1984: 181) has shown that public authorities were a viable path to the "businesslike" administration strongly favored by Wilson and other Progressives. Eventually, public authorities such as the Port of New York Authority, established in 1921, removed vast areas of government from control by elected officials and public budgets.

THE IDEOLOGY OF REFORM–PROGRESSIVE PUBLIC ADMINISTRATION AND ADMINISTRATIVE REGULATION AND LAW

Both the civil service reformers and the Progressives faced strong opposition. Their administrative reforms were not democratic. Indeed, they were intended to weaken the connection between electoral politics and administration. Wilson was candid on this point: "civil service reform is . . . necessary for good government, but it is not democratic in idea. . . . It substitutes for the average man or 'the man of the people,' the man of the schools; that is, the instructed and fitted man" (Rohr, 1986: 231). Somehow, this disconnect between politics and administration had to be explained. The reform–Progressive public administrative ideology served this purpose.

Their ideology rested on three major tenets. First, there was a clear separation between politics and administration. The reformers insisted that of the great number of "places [in the civil service] very few are political. Political offices are those which are connected with devising and enforcing a policy which the people have approved at the polls" (Rosenbloom, 1971: 75). Wilson's famous 1887 essay on "The Study of Administration" relied on the theme that "administration lies outside the proper sphere of *politics*. Administrative questions are not political questions" (494). Frank Goodnow's classic, *Politics and Administration* (1900), argued that government had but two functions: expression of the people's will and the execution of it. Hence there was the need for Progressive electoral reforms to make for better expression and administrative reforms to improve execution. If public administration were not political, then it could be the domain of "instructed and fitted" administrators whose expertise should be insulated from electoral politics.

Second, public administration was a "field of business." Its dominant values were efficiency and economy. Consequently, as Leonard White put it in the first American public administration textbook, *Introduction to the Study of Public Administration* (1926: Preface), "the study of administration should start from the base of management rather than the foundation of law, and is therefore more absorbed in the affairs of the American Management Association than in the decisions of the courts." Later Luther Gulick would pronounce efficiency "axiom number one" for public administration (1937: 192).

Third, public administration could be a science. In Wilson's words, "there should be a science of administration which shall seek to straighten the paths of government, to make its business less unbusinesslike, to strengthen and purify its organization, and to crown its duties with dutifulness" (1887: 485). Wilson thought such an applied science could be adapted from European experience. However, the advent and popularization of Scientific Management in the early 1900s led public administration in the direction of becoming a design science, like engineering. Position classification, as codified in the Federal Position Classification Act of 1923, was a clear example. Early forerunners of today's Master of Public Administration programs, such as that of Syracuse University's Maxwell School in the 1920s, included courses on civil engineering.

By 1937, this public administrative ideology had developed into an "orthodoxy" in the United States. It is now regarded as "classical," though not functional. By the late 1940s, it was dismissed as intellectually and empirically flawed for its dependence on the politics–administration dichotomy and its inadequacies as a science (Dahl, 1947; Simon, 1947; Waldo, 1948; Appleby, 1949). Nevertheless, it continues to inform public administrative practice to an extent. As Dwight Waldo once noted, the orthodoxy was deeply ingrained in the U.S. political and administrative cultures (Waldo, 1961: 220). It has been substantially modified, but is difficult to replace entirely. In fact, as late as the mid-1970s, classical public administration was said to be "alive and well—and living in the White House" (Beam, 1978: 72–77).

The reform and Progressive movements had a very substantial impact on the directions taken in U.S. regulatory administration and administrative law. Their desire to take administration out of politics and to place it in the hands of "fitted" men made the independent commission a natural choice for the implementation of regulatory policies. The Interstate Commerce Commission (ICC), established in 1887, was the first modern example, eventually followed by the Federal Reserve Board (1913) and the Federal Trade Commission (FTC) (1914). At first, the ICC was housed in the Department of the Interior, but as John Rohr points out, "Two years after creating the commission, Congress conferred independent status upon it 'without a single hearing or a word of recorded debate' " (1986: 95). Among other features, the Interstate Commerce Act provided for five commissioners with six year overlapping terms. They could be removed by the president for "inefficiency, neglect of duty, or malfeasance in office." No more than three of the commissioners could be drawn from the same political party.

Substantively, Progressive regulation dealt primarily with various aspects of what is now called "market failure."[1] The ICC was seriously underpowered, but its purpose was to act as a surrogate for the market. The act required that railroad rates be "reasonable and just." However, in the 1897 case of *ICC v. Cincinnati, New Orleans and Texas Pacific Railroad Company* (167 U.S. 479), the Supreme Court held that the commission did not have the authority actually to set rates. The FTC, by contrast, was created to regulate the way markets functioned and to ensure that they remained competitive. It was authorized to combat deceptive practices, such as false advertising, and to prevent mergers or acquisitions that substantially reduce competition or promote monopolization. The Pure Food and Drug Act (1906), Meat Inspection Act (1907), the Federal Reserve Act (1913) sought to regulate the safety of specific products or services. All these forms of regulatory administration were substantially expanded at both the federal and state levels as time went on.

Legally, Progressive regulatory initiatives at the federal level presented a major challenge to the nation's longstanding tradition of judicial authority in the society and economy. As John Johnston observed, "During the nineteenth century, the American legal system was almost wholly dominated by the judicially administered common law" (1981: 10). The common law included rules governing such economic concerns as employment practices, laborers' rights to engage in collective action, and products liability. The growth of administrative law to regulate the economy would inevitably diminish the scope of the common law and the power of the judges who developed, interpreted, and applied it.

From a Progressive perspective, the common law appeared to be out of date and too slow to adjust to the rapid industrialization and urbanization that were transforming many of the practices within its ambit. For instance, the famous common law "fellow servant rule" made fellow employees, rather than employers, liable for many workplace injuries long after the small-scale apprenticeship production arrangements out of which it grew had been permanently eclipsed by industrialization. By and large, the common law also presented a barrier to modernizing labor relations in the face of vast changes in production practices (Rosenbloom and Shafritz, 1985: chapter 3). The doctrine of "privity" made sellers rather than producers liable to consumers for injurious products even though prepackaging and mechanical complexity made it impossible for retailers independently to evaluate the safety of the goods they sold. In this context, science itself seemed to underscore the need for new regulatory approaches. The legal historian Lawrence Friedman noted:

> The discovery of germs, invisible, insidious, hidden in every spot of filth, had a profound effect on the legal system. To a much greater extent than before [the 1890s], goods—including food—were packaged and sent long distances, to be marketed impersonally, in bulk, rather than to be felt, handled, and squeezed at the point of purchase. This meant that a person was dependent on others, on strangers, on far-off corporations, for necessities of life; that society was more than ever a complex cellular organism; these strangers, these distant others had the capacity to inflict catastrophic, irreparable harm. (1973: 458)

The common law's increasingly anachronistic quality was compounded by the legal culture. The law was treated as a body of abstract theoretical principles that often appeared to be divorced from reality. In this respect, it resembled much contemporary economic theory, with similar limitations as a basis for prescribing public policy successfully (see Etzioni, 1988). If judges were "influenced by everyday events and the currents of opinion, they were loath to admit it" (Johnson, 1981: 10). This is why the famous "Brandeis brief" in *Muller v. Oregon* (208 U.S. 412, 1908) appeared so revolutionary. As Johnson explains:

> Unlike past appellate arguments that relied upon case precedents, the . . . "Brandeis brief" . . . alluded strictly to legal authorities on only 3 of its 113 pages. Most of Brandeis's support for his position was drawn from government labor statistics, reports of factory inspectors, and testimony from psychological, economic and medical treatises. Sources such as these had rarely been called to the attention of the appellate courts before 1908, and never had any attorney drawn so heavily upon such extra-legal authorities in a single brief. (1981: 30)

The more deeply one probes the juxtaposition between the common law and Progressive administrative regulation, the clearer the conflict between them becomes. The common law was very deeply rooted in the contractarian conceptions of natural rights and the U.S. constitutional order. Rights to life, liberty, and property, if not "inalienable," certainly predated the constitutional regime. According to the civil contract, government's purpose was to protect them. The contractarian approach requires due process, both procedural and substantive, for the legitimate regulation of property rights. The Supreme Court's decision in the 1890 case of *Chicago, Milwaukee and St. Paul Railway Co. v. Minnesota* (134 U.S. 418: 458) may appear startling to a contemporary reader:

> The question of the reasonableness of a rate charge for transportation by a railroad company . . . is eminently a question for judicial investigations, requiring due process of law for its determination. If the company is deprived of the power of charging reasonable rates for the use of its property, and such deprivation takes place in the absence of an investigation by judicial machinery, it is deprived of the lawful use of its property, and thus, in substance and effect, of the property itself. . . .

Substantive due process was construed as "protection from arbitrary and unreasonable action" (*Black's Law Dictionary*, 1979) by dint of a legislative or administrative regulatory scheme. The Court's decision in *Lochner v. New York* (198 U.S. 45 [1905], 57–61) conveys the conjunction between the legal abstraction and contractarianism of the period exceedingly well:

> There is no reasonable ground for interfering with the liberty of person or the right of free contract, by determining the hours of labor, in the occupation of a baker. There is no contention that bakers as a class are not equal in intelligence and capacity to men in other trades or manual occupations, or that they are not able to assert their rights and care for themselves without the protecting arm of the State, interfering with their independence of judgment and of action. . . .
>
> Statutes of the nature of that under review, limiting the hours in which grown and intelligent men may labor to earn their living, are mere meddlesome interferences with the rights of the individual. . . .

Progressive administration, by contrast, relied heavily on utilitarianism and pragmatism. Woodrow Wilson's (1887) essay identified the values that would inform public administrative theory for the next half century or so:

> It is the object of administrative study to discover, first, what government can properly and successfully do, and, secondly, how it can do these proper things with the utmost possible efficiency and at the least possible cost either of money or of energy. (481)

If cost-effectiveness and expansive due process coincide, it is happenstance; frequently—probably *generally*—they do not. Wilson, who thought the United States had many positive lessons to learn from public administrative practice in authoritarian regimes, finessed the potential conflict between utilitarian administration and contractarian governance by insisting that there was a "difference between the province of constitutional law and the province of administrative function" (1887: 496). "The broad plans of governmental action are not administrative; the detailed execution of such plans is administrative" (Wilson, 1887: 496). But what if the administrative agency is charged with regulating the use of private property, such as a railway or a bakery, in the public interest? The conflict cannot be resolved in theory and has been an important tension underlying public administration ever since the reform–Progressive period.

Opposition by the legal community to the fledgling administrative state was rife. Approximately 200 regulatory measures were struck down by the courts during the "Lochner era" (Gunther, 1975: 565). The courts often employed the "derogation canon," which held that statutes contrary to the common law ought to be interpreted in the fashion least likely to interfere with it. Procedural due process was interpreted to require that administrative adjudicatory procedures meet common law rules of evidence. Agency findings of fact were not accepted as reliable by the courts, which might require administrative facts to be demonstrated de novo in trials. In 1914, Roscoe Pound spoke for much of the legal community in denouncing administrative adjudication as "executive justice" or "one of those reversions to justice without law" (Pound, 1914: 18). Although there were some important exceptions to such opposition, e.g., see *Texas and Pacific Railway Co. v. Abilene Cotton Oil Co.* (204 U.S. 426 [1907]), the legal community presented substantial barriers to the growth of administrative regulation and was able to make it far more costly and arduous. The contest came to a head during the New Deal, when the Great Depression seemed to signal the utter failure of laissez-faire economics while the court's hostility to greater federal administrative penetration of the economy posed a serious threat to judicial independence.

THE NEW DEAL, REGULATORY ADMINISTRATION, AND ADMINISTRATIVE LAW

Like the reformers and Progressives, the New Dealers substantially transformed public administrative thought and practice. However, the New Deal's impact was complex and filled with paradoxical outcomes for both administration and law.

Structural Changes

Administratively, broadly construed, there were several developments that left the federal government forever changed. First, in the face of the ongoing Great Depression, during which some 25% of the workforce was unemployed, the federal government assumed far greater responsibility for the nation's economy. In 1932, the electorate overwhelmingly rejected waiting for recovery in the laissez-faire mode as the market itself seemed to fail on a massive scale. Urbanization, industrialization, and unprofitability in farming combined to deprive the nation of its nineteenth-century "safety net"—the family farm to which one could return in hard times. Conceivably, the states could have responded to the crisis in some collective fashion, but since the problem was national in scope, it seemed to require federal action. Between 1933 and 1936, the following were among the federal agencies created to deal with structural and/or industry-wide problems: the Federal Home Loan Bank Board, the Commodity Credit Corporation, the Federal Deposit Insurance Corporation, the Federal Communications Commission, the Securities and Exchange Commission, and the National Labor Relations Board. By the end of the decade, these were joined by the Agricultural Marketing Service, the Civil Aeronautics Board, and others. The reach of the federal government was also extended by the Social Security Act (1935) and the Fair Labor Standards Act (1938). Other measures, including the National Industrial Recovery Act of 1933 and the Works Project Administration, were of great moment, if relatively short-lived.

Second, in conjunction with the new scope of federal administrative activity came massive growth in the executive branch. The number of agencies expanded rapidly. In 1933–1934, some 60 new agencies were created (Van Riper, 1958: 320). The number of federal civilian personnel, which stood at 610,000 in 1931, more than doubled to 1,438,000 by 1941 (U.S. Bureau of the Census and Social Science Research Council, 1951: 710). The relatively compact administrative state of the Progressive period began to sprawl into a "headless fourth branch" of government.

Third, the president was construed as the nation's administrative manager in chief. The President's Committee on Administrative Management, established in 1937, was the major proponent of this change. Also known as the Brownlow Committee, after its chair, Louis Brownlow, its other two members, Charles Merriam and Luther Gulick, were stalwarts of public administration in the orthodox vein. Gulick alone hit all the bases in his various writings:

(A) There is a dichotomy between politics and administration. He called politics and administration "two heterogeneous functions," "the combination of which cannot be undertaken within the structure of the administration without producing inefficiency" (Gulick, 1937 [1978 reprint]: 44).

(B) Administrative activity is best coordinated through "unity of command." "The rigid adherence to the principle of unity of command may have its absurdities; these are, however, unimportant in comparison with the certainty of confusion, inefficiency and irresponsibility which arise from the violation of the principle" (Gulick, 1937: 43).

(C) Efficiency, the preeminent value of public administration, can be achieved through science. "The fundamental objective of the science of administration is the accomplishment of the work in hand with the least expenditure of man-power and materials. Efficiency is thus axiom number one in the value scale of administration" (Gulick, 1937: 192).

(D) Administrative independence is not antithetical to democratic governance. "[D]emocracy is a way of government in which the common man is the final judge of what is good for him. [¶] Efficiency is one of the things that is good for him because it makes life richer and safer. That efficiency is to be secured more and more through the use of technical specialists. These specialists have no right to ask for, and must not be given freedom from supervisory control, but in establishing that control, a government which ignores the conditions of efficiency cannot expect to achieve efficiency" (Gulick, 1937: 45).

Each of these tenets provided a key piece of the Brownlow Committee's argument for president as administrative chief. John Rohr has zeroed in on its view of the politics–administration dichotomy:

> Applying the principles of scientific management, the committee drew a sharp distinction between policy and administration. This distinction found its institutional embodiment in Congress, where policy was made, and in the executive branch, where it was carried out. Thus, the budget would serve as "the means of control of the general policy of the Government by the Legislative Branch and the details of administration by the Executive." . . . By describing virtually every governmental activity as some kind of "administrative management"—personnel management, fiscal management, planning management, or administrative reorganization—the committee asserted the president's power over the government as a whole. . . .
>
> Lest anyone miss the point of the division of labor the committee has in mind, the report recommends that the "two new departments be set up *by law* to cover . . . [public welfare and public works] [sic], and that there be assigned to these departments *by the president* not only the appropriate new activities in these fields but also the old activities closely related thereto." Thus Congress will establish the departments and then graciously step aside while the president, in accordance with the principles of scientific management, assigns them their activities. (Rohr, 1986: 137–139)

The committee's argument for unity of command vested in the president was even more blunt:

> Stated in simple terms these canons of efficiency require the establishment of a responsible and effective chief executive as the center of energy, direction, and administrative management; the systematic organization of all activities in the hands of qualified personnel under the direction of the chief executive; and to aid him in this, the establishment of appropri-

> ate managerial and staff agencies. There must also be provision for planning, a complete fiscal system, and means for holding the Executive accountable for his program. (Mosher, 1976: 114)

Among other proposals, the committee sought the consolidation of the nonadjudicatory functions of the independent regulatory commissions within the executive departments. Yet there would be no threat to democracy because "the President is indeed the one and only national officer representative of the entire Nation" (Mosher, 1976: 111).

As suggested in the foregoing paragraph, efficiency remained a central value. The committee asserted that the efficiency of the federal executive branch was of worldwide importance: "Facing one of the most troubled periods in all the troubled history of mankind, we wish to set our affairs in the very best possible order to make the best use of all our national resources and to make good our democratic claims. If America fails, the hopes and dreams of democracy over all the world go down" (Mosher, 1976: 113).

In a somewhat convoluted argument, the committee asserted that greater administrative independence, coordinated through unity of command, would not only enhance efficiency, but would also promote accountability to Congress and the electorate:

> [A]ccountability often is obscured by the Congress itself in imposing upon the Executive in too great detail minute requirements for the organization and operation of the administrative machinery. Faced by such mandatory and detailed legislative requirements (whether in general law or in a rider on an appropriation bill), first the bureau chief, then the Secretary of the department, and then the President is absolved from part of his executive responsibility, and in consequence the Congress is foreclosed from adequately criticizing the conduct of the business.
>
> We have called attention to this difficulty with respect to fiscal accountability. We hold that once the Congress has made an appropriation . . . which it is free to withhold, the responsibility for the administration of the expenditures under that appropriation is and should be solely upon the Executive. (Mosher, 1976: 132)

The committee and the president behind it failed to achieve most of what they sought. Rohr notes that the committee's perspective was constitutionally flawed: "At the heart of the doctrine is a fundamental error that transforms the president from chief executive officer to sole executive officer" (Rohr, 1986: 139). The politics were equally bad as Peri Arnold points out: "By association with the simultaneous 'court packing' fight, the reorganization effort was tarred with the charge of Roosevelt seeking change to aggrandize power" (Arnold: 1986, 104). Nevertheless, in 1939, Congress gave the president some of the reorganization authority sought, and he quickly used it to create the Executive Office of the President. The latter, of course, has emerged as a central force in the federal executive branch. Yet, in 1947 Brownlow complained of congressional interference in administration in terms that will sound familiar to contemporary readers:

> The next step which we the people should take to meet the needs of the Presidency is to persuade the Congress not to yield to the constant temptation to interfere with the administration of the Executive Branch by needlessly detailed requirements for procedures in the execution of the laws it enacts; procedures sometimes so hampering that they almost have the effect of defeating the very purpose for which the Congress has enacted the law. The President is under the Constitutional obligation to "take Care that the Laws be faithfully executed," and if we mean to help the President to discharge this obligation we must be sure that his authority so to do is not usurped either by the Congress as a whole, by the House of Representatives or the Senate, and—most important of all—by particular committees of the Congress. (Brownlow, 1949: 116)

Value Changes

The Brownlow Committee relied heavily on a belief in administrative expertise and in a separation of politics from administration. However, the New Deal program also sought to build representation into its administrative decisionmaking. There were several reasons for this: Bolstering the legitimacy of greater administrative penetration of the economy and society; interest group pressures; cooptation; and commitment to democracy could be counted among them. Secretary of Labor Frances Perkins once averred that public participation in New Deal programs "is the modern substitute for the old town meeting and the old talk around the stove" (Rohr, 1986: 167). In any event, as James Q. Wilson noted, "The New Deal was perhaps the high water mark of at least the theory of bureaucratic clientelism. Not only did various sectors of society, notably agriculture, begin receiving massive subsidies, but the government proposed, through the National Industrial Recovery Act . . . , to cloak with public power a vast number of industrial groupings and trade associations" (Wilson, 1986: 437). In the late 1930s and early 1940s, a few limited measures were adopted to create greater equal employment opportunity for blacks in the federal service (Rosenbloom, 1977: chapter 3).

Notwithstanding uneven and problematic implementation, the idea of representative bureaucracy itself became important in American public administration (Krislov and Rosenbloom, 1981). Administrative expertise was not placed at the whim of interested publics, but neither was it seen fit to define the public interest without public input. Ultimately, of course, it is impossible to reconcile the desirability and expense of representativeness with the politics–administration dichotomy. If public administrators do not make policy (even if only in the choice of means), then public input is clearly irrelevant and potentially "meddlesome," as Woodrow Wilson put it (1887: 499). However, in a political culture like that of the United States, to the extent that administrative agencies do make policy, demands for participation, representation, and checks and balances will be placed upon them. In shattering the myth of apolitical administration, the New Deal opened the door to a continuing process of democratization of American Public administration.

A related outcome of the New Deal was to debunk the orthodoxy's claim to be scientific. At the same time that the Brownlow Committee was developing its Report, the Brookings Institution was preparing a report on governmental reorganization for a subcommittee headed by Senator Harry Byrd. Both institutional bias and personality conspired virtually to ensure that the two reports would be at odds in important ways. But the Brookings group was as well schooled in orthodox public administration as Brownlow's (Arnold, 1986: chapter 4). The significance of the disagreement was not lost on Lloyd Short, writing in the *American Political Science Review* in 1939: "The writer cannot refrain from expressing the regret which is shared by many that the divergent views of the President's committee and the Brookings Institution on certain matters should have been permitted to figure so prominently in congressional committee hearings and debates in the press" (Short, 1939: 66). The main disagreement was over the desirability of curtailing the Comptroller General's powers regarding preaudits and disallowances of expenditures. Brookings, whose client was Congress, favored maintaining this legislative official's powers (he heads the General Accounting Office), while Brownlow, representing the president, argued that they should be confined. If this was science, it certainly appeared to be in the service of politics and to be dubious science at best.

The dispute cracked the facade of a dominant paradigm that was soon to be intellectually destroyed. By the late 1940s, public administration was widely regarded in academic circles as a political process, and bureaucratic politics became a subject of analysis. Eventually, this development, along with the others reviewed here, would have a great impact on the future of American public administration and the directions taken in administrative regulation and law.

Legal Changes

The constitutional history of the New Deal is well known and need not be treated in detail here. Essentially, the Supreme Court and a substantial number of lower federal courts found each of the prongs of New Deal public administrative change offensive to the Constitution.

The effort to expand national control over the economy was resisted on two grounds. First, the Supreme Court read the commerce clause in a traditional and narrow fashion. The federal government could not regulate commerce that did not cross state lines unless it (1) involved products that became physically intermingled with such commerce, (2) entered a stream of commerce that did so, or (3) threatened the efficacy of a legitimate regulation of interstate commerce (Pritchett, 1977: 189–191). In addition, the definition of "commerce" itself was narrow by today's standards, and the commerce being regulated had to have a "direct" effect on interstate commerce. In *Carter v. Carter Coal Co.* (1936), the Supreme Court reasoned:

> The distinction between a direct and an indirect effect turns, not upon the magnitude of either the cause or the effect, but entirely upon the manner in which the effect has been brought about. If the production by one man of a single ton of coal intended for interstate sale and shipment . . . affects interstate commerce indirectly, the effect does not become direct by multiplying the tonnage, or increasing the number of men employed, or adding to the expense or complexities of the business, or by all combined. (298 U.S. 238, 308)

C. Herman Pritchett (1977: 193) observed that the opinion "illuminated as by a flash of lightning a judicial dream world of logical abstractions, where there was no difference between one ton of coal and a million tons of coal, where considerations of degree were not cognizable by the law. Production was local. A production crisis in every part of the country simultaneously could never add up to a national problem with which Congress could deal. . . ."

Second in *United States v. Butler* (1936), the Court invoked the Tenth Amendment as a limit on federal power. It found that the Agricultural Adjustment Act of 1933's scheme for making payments to farmers who adopted production controls for the sake of price stabilization had invaded powers reserved to the states (297 U.S. 1).

Expansion of executive power was opposed in *Schechter Poultry Co. v. U.S.* (295 U.S. 495 [1935]) and other cases on the grounds that "Congress is not permitted to abdicate or to transfer to others the essential functions with which it is . . . vested" (529). Consequently, legislative delegations to executive agencies would violate the separation of powers unless Congress "has itself established the standards of legal obligation, thus performing its essential legislative function" (530).

The judicial blow to representativeness was less stunning, but in the Carter case, the Court found that a delegation of legislative power to a majority of employed mine workers and the producers of over two-thirds of the nation's tonnage of coal to be "legislative delegation in its most obnoxious form; for it is not even delegation to an official or an official body, presumptively disinterested, but to private persons whose interests may be and often are adverse to the interests of others in the same business . . ." (298 U.S. 238 [1936], 311). Although representation of clientele interests does not require such delegation, it does presuppose that private parties will have an influence on policies adopted by executive branch agencies. In that case, as critics such as Theodore Lowi have pointed out, such programs make "conflict-of-interest a principle of government" (1969: 86).

Former Supreme Court Justice Robert Jackson called these and other judicial decisions an effort to "nullify the New Deal" (1941: chapter 4). President Roosevelt's response was to nullify the Supreme Court's opposition. After he sought legislation to expand the Court's size, Justice Owen Roberts (perhaps for other reasons) switched his voting from anti– to pro–New Deal, thereby turning what had frequently been a four-justice minority in favor of New Deal initiatives into a majority. Between 1937 and 1943, Roosevelt appointed a chief justice and eight associate justices, as well as many lower court judges. Soon, the constitutional law followed the election returns, so to speak. The commerce clause was reinterpreted so radically that in *Wickard v. Filburn* (1942), Congress could reach a farmer's 23 acres of wheat, "even if [the farmer's] activity be local and though it may not be regarded as commerce, . . . if it exerts a substantial economic effect on interstate commerce . . ." (317 U.S. 111 [1942]). The nondelegation doctrine, though never overruled, was never employed and, consequently, as Kenneth Davis noted, was "without practical force" (1975: 39). Nor was the Constitution interpreted as a barrier to making the federal bureaucracy more representative of the interests it regulated.

1946

The New Deal effort to increase federal administrative authority and to restructure the government had not reached completion when the nation's attention was diverted to World War II. With the creation of the Executive Office of the President (EOP) in 1939, the presidency was modernized and strengthened. However, the roles of Congress and the courts vis-à-vis the new executive and in the separation of powers remained poorly specified. The nagging question of how best to protect individuals' rights against the enlarged federal bureaucracy was also unanswered. In 1946, Congress returned its attention to these matters with a vengeance. It enacted four laws of fundamental, even "constitutional" import: the Legislative Reorganization Act, Tort Claims Act, Administrative Procedure Act (APA), and the Employment Act. Together, these statutes tied the administrative state more tightly to American democratic constitutionalism. Although 1946 was of consummate importance to public administrative practice at the federal level and theory generally, it has been studied in piecemeal fashion, rather than comprehensively. The treatment here will briefly outline the coherence and significance of the legislative events of 1946. Chronologically, the Employment Act came first, followed by the APA and then the reorganization (which included the Tort Claims Act). However, an explanation of the totality of Congress's accomplishment is best conveyed by beginning with the reorganization, which has been fundamental to interaction between the legislature and agencies ever since.

The Legislative Reorganization Act (August 2, 1946)

The New Deal, the judiciary's acceptance of broad delegations of legislative power to the executive after 1937, and the establishment of the EOP in the wake of the Brownlow Committee Report were governmental and political changes of great magnitude. Congress, the "First Branch," would play a less proactive and a more reactive role in future policymaking and regulatory activity. It would broadly delegate its authority to administrative agencies and then exercise oversight and a variety of controls to ensure that the administrators complied with its intentions.

Structural reorganization was viewed as a prerequisite for successful legislative oversight of the agencies. Congress had always engaged in oversight as part of the system of checks and balances, but it had generally done so haphazardly in response to scandals and crises, rather than on a continuous basis. The logic of change was explained by Senator Robert M. La Follette, Jr., cosponsor of the Reorganization Act:

> Congress lacks adequate facilities today for the continuous inspection and review of administrative action. The time has long since passed when we could anticipate every situation that might arise and provide for it in minute regulatory legislation.
>
> With the expansion of Federal functions during the twentieth century, Congress has perforce created many commissions and agencies to perform them and has delegated its rule-making power to them. But it has failed to provide any regular arrangements for follow-up in order to assure itself that administrative rules and regulations are in accord with the intent of the law. . . .
>
> In order to strengthen Congressional oversight of administrative performance, the Legislative Reorganization Act authorizes the standing committees of both houses to keep watch over the execution of the laws by the administrative agencies within their jurisdiction. Staffed with qualified specialists, these committees will conduct a continuous review of the activities of the agencies. . . . (La Follette, 1947)

The act sought to achieve these goals by reorganizing the committee system so that jurisdictions were clearer and less duplicative within each house, standardizing some aspects of committee procedure, creating a Legislative Reference Service in the Library of Congress, charging the Comptroller General with responsibility to conduct expenditure analyses of the agencies, providing for more committee staff, and authorizing that "each standing committee . . . shall exercise continuous watchfulness of the execution by the administrative agencies concerned of any laws, the subject matter of which is within the jurisdiction of such committee" (Sec. 136). The extent to which the act achieved its overall purposes is debatable.

The act was premised on the assumption that the relationship between standing committees and their subcommittees on the one side and administrative agencies on the other would not be harmonious. Committees, it was thought, would have sufficient incentives to engage in vigorous oversight. However, this has turned out to be the exception rather than the rule. Randall Ripley and Grace Franklin (1976: 175) explain that effective oversight requires the following: a committee chairperson devoted to serving other members of the committee; a relatively high level of subcommittee autonomy within the committee; sufficient and aggressive committee staff; committee members who are experienced and committed to oversight; and a general committee orientation toward overseeing rather than legislating. However, they note, "since few committees meet all of these conditions very often or for long periods of time the relative paucity of systematic oversight is easy to understand and explain" (Ripley and Franklin, 1976: 175).

Instead of exercising forceful oversight, subcommittees and committees frequently entered into relationships with agencies and concerned interest groups that have variously been called "subgovernments," "iron triangles," or "cozy triangles" (see Lowi, 1969, for the most influential discussion). The so-called military industrial complex, consisting of units in the Department of Defense, the congressional armed services committees, and defense contractors, is the archetypal case. Because Congress has so much constitutional authority vis-à-vis administrative agencies, subgovernments are resistant, if not impervious, to presidential control through political executives. For years, the latter were dismissed by political scientists as ineffective "birds of passage" in "a government of strangers" (Heclo, 1977). Regulatory agencies were not exempt from tendencies toward subsystem governance. The general sense that they were "captured" by the interests they ostensibly regulated contributed significantly to the movement toward deregulation that began in the late 1970s.

The Tort Claims Act

Title IV of the Legislative Reorganization Act is generally referred to as the "Tort Claims Act." Its purpose was consonant with the reorganization's larger purpose of making Congress more efficient. As La Follette explained, "Congress is overburdened by many . . . private matters which divert its attention from national policy-making and which it ought not to have to consider. . . . It serves as a tribunal for the settlement of private claims . . ." (1946: 46). The Tort Claims Act, which has been amended several times, authorized the heads of agencies to settle property damage and personal injury claims not exceeding $1,000, "where the United States, if a private person, would be liable to the claimant for such damage, loss, injury, or death . . ." (sec. 403 [a]). It also permitted suits by private parties in the federal district courts.

The Tort Claims Act was significant in several respects. First, it was a clear waiver of the government's common law immunity from civil suits for damages. Eventually, the government's willingness to be sued for ordinary torts undercut the logic of providing officials with immunity for breaches of individuals' constitutional rights. By the mid-1970s, the historical presumption of absolute immunity for constitutional torts had been replaced by qualified immunity only, thereby considerably extending the liability of public administrators at all governmental levels (Rosenbloom, 1983: chapter 6). Second, it was a recognition that government in the administrative state takes on some of the characteristics of an enterprise. With approximately 2 million civilian employees, spread throughout myriad departments, agencies, and bureaus in the United States and abroad, the potential for government agents wrongly to injure private individuals had become considerable. Third, in allowing tort claims to be resolved by the courts, the act inevitably improved the judiciary's vantage point regarding public administration. Deference to administrative expertise was no doubt tempered as the courts heard more allegations of injurious administrative failure. Even where the plaintiffs lost, as in the famous *Dalehite v. U.S.* (346 U.S. 15 [1953]) decision, the courts could not help but learn more about the limits of administrative expertise and capacity.

The Administrative Procedure Act (June 11, 1946)

Like the legislative reorganization, the APA, which has been likened to a bill of rights for the administrative state, was a major piece of the governmental realignment of 1946. As amended, the APA continues to provide the basic legal framework for much of the federal administrative process. It has proved elastic enough to accommodate vast changes in the substance of agency rulemaking, the scope of adjudication, and judicial outlooks regarding review of agency action.

The APA was predicated on two concerns of central importance to Congress's effort to establish a clearer role for itself in the post–New Deal administrative state. The rulemaking provisions of the APA were intended to ensure that agency rulemaking pursuant to delegations of legislative authority was open and at least marginally participatory. Standard procedures for notifying the public about new substantive rules or rule changes and permitting interested parties to comment did not democratize public administration, but they were a step in that direction. Their logic was to increase the attention of the interested public to the rulemaking activities of administrative agencies. Formal rulemaking, incorporating aspects of legislative and judicial processes, afforded a substantial opportunity for private parties to participate in administrative policymaking.

The APA establishes some ground rules for protecting individual rights against administrative action. Procedures for adjudication incorporate elements of constitutional due process, including notice, a fair procedure, and independent hearing examiners (or now administrative law judges). Again, congressional concern with the use of delegated authority was a central factor. Agencies operating under orthodox public administrative doctrine would be insulated from politics, self-assured in their exercise of administrative expertise in the service of efficiency and economy, and utilitarian rather than contractarian in their view of individuals' status. Whereas Rohr concluded that the Brownlow Committee was actually "indifferent to rights" (1986, 148), Senator McCarran supported the APA on the grounds that it "is a bill of rights for the hundreds of thousands of Americans whose affairs are controlled or regulated in one way or another by agencies of the Federal Government. It is designed to provide guarantees of due process in administrative procedure" (*Congressional Record*, March 12, 1946, 298). The APA's provisions for judicial review are intended to strike a balance between the need for administrative discretion and protection of individuals' property and other interests. The courts are authorized to "compel agency action unlawfully withheld or unreasonably delayed" and "hold unlawful and set aside agency action, findings, and conclusions found to be" in any of the following categories: arbitrary, capricious, abuse of discretion or otherwise unlawful in violation of the Constitution, in excess of jurisdiction or authority, in violation of procedural requirements, unsupported by substantial evidence (in the cases of adjudication and formal rulemaking), or so unwarranted by the facts that the matter is subject to a de novo trial in court.

Additional provisions of the APA dealt with agencies' obligations to make information about their operations public. Subsequent amendments have included the Freedom of Information Act (1966), the Privacy Act (1974), and the Government in the Sunshine Act (1976), all of which address administrative secrecy and disclosure.

The legislative history of the APA shows that Congress preferred even greater constraints on administrative rulemaking, stronger protection of individuals' rights, more easily obtained and comprehensive judicial review, and more uniformity in the administrative process. Provisions of this nature were incorporated in the Walter–Logan Act of 1940. The act would have made "administrative agencies the wards of the courts" (Rohr, 1986: 165). Not surprisingly, President Roosevelt vetoed it. He claimed, among other things, that the Attorney General would soon issue a report regarding comprehensive regulation of the administrative process. That *Report* (U.S. Senate Documents, 1941), issued in January 1941, was friendly to the executive branch, but nevertheless concerned with the protection of rights. The version of the APA enacted in 1946 diverged from the Attorney General's *Report* primarily in limiting agencies' powers and sanctions in the field of licensing and in placing hearing examiners within the civil service system.

The Employment Act (February 20, 1946)

The Employment Act ratified the New Deal and much of the administrative growth that accompanied it. In a single sentence, albeit a long one, the act rejected strict laissez-faire economics in favor of government intervention in the economy:

> The Congress hereby declares that it is the continuing policy and responsibility of the Federal Government to use all practicable means consistent with its needs and obligations and other essential considerations of national policy, with the assistance and cooperation of industry, agriculture, labor, and State and local governments, to coordinate and utilize all its plans, functions, and resources for the purpose of creating and maintaining, in a manner calculated to foster and promote free competitive enterprise and the general welfare, conditions under which there will be afforded useful employment opportunities, including self-

> employment, for those able, willing, and seeking to work, and to promote maximum employment, production, and purchasing power. (sec. 2)

Institutionally, the act established the Council of Economic Advisers, which among other requirements is charged with developing and recommending "to the President national economic policies to foster and promote free competitive enterprise, to avoid economic fluctuations or to diminish the effects thereof, and to maintain employment, production, and purchasing power. . . ." It also provided for a congressional Joint Committee on the Economic Report to make recommendations to the legislature regarding the council's annual report to the president. Practically speaking, the act formally made the federal budget a tool of fiscal policy.

The Employment Act was important to the administrative state because government spending, as needed for the purposes of promoting maximum employment, would be by or through federal agencies. It was hotly debated in Congress as a substantial departure from laissez-faire ideology. However, some critics correctly predicted that implementation of the act would be "honey combed with political expediency" (James Donnelly, August 30, 1945: 665). The act hardly invented pork barrel politics, but it offered a strong rationale and greater legitimacy for more federal spending on public works and other projects.

1946 In Retrospect

The legislation of 1946 has had an enduring impact on federal bureaucratic politics and administration. First, it confirmed a lasting shift in Congress's governmental role. Delegation and oversight took on greater importance. Much specific policymaking shifted from the legislature to administrative agencies. All of this was intentional and planned. What could not have been clearly foreseen, however, was the extent to which 1946 would provide the foundation of a new institutional politics. Morris Fiorina (1977, 46, 49) explains:

> [T]he growth of an activist federal government has stimulated a change in the mix of congressional activities. Specifically, a lesser proportion of congressional effort is now going into programmatic activities [that is, legislation and oversight] and a greater proportion into pork-barrel and casework [constituency service] activities. As a result, today's congressmen make relatively fewer enemies and relatively more friends among the people of their districts. . . .
>
> Congress does not just react to big government—it creates it. All of Washington prospers. More and more bureaucrats promulgate more and more regulations and dispense more and more money. Fewer and fewer congressmen suffer electoral defeat.

Pork barrel and casework can be considered legitimate representational functions. They can also be opposed and denounced as congressional "micromanagement" of administrative activities that interferes with universalistic administrative practices and values, such as economy and efficiency. Critics may well ask whether it was really necessary, from a defense standpoint, for "fewer than 75 of the 435 members of the House of Representatives . . . *not* [to] have a major defense plant or military installation in their district" in 1975 (Dye and Zeigler, 1975, 331).

If micromanagement affords Congress greater control over administration, it also provides the agencies with opportunities to manipulate the legislature. In a highly detailed study of administrative spending in three program areas, R. Douglas Arnold found that federal

> bureaucrats appear to allocate benefits strategically in an effort both to maintain and to expand their supporting coalitions. When it furthers their purposes, they broaden their program's geographic scope and increase the number of shares of benefits so that more

> congressmen can be brought into their supporting coalitions. When necessary, they allocate extra shares of benefits to leaders and to those who are crucial coalition members. (1979, 207)

In short, the relationship between Congress and administrative agencies is complex. Legislative–agency relationships are varied and messy. Although theoretically distinct entities of government, at times legislative (sub)committees and agencies blend together in terms of policy and electoral politics. At other times, a more traditional oversight role is maintained. In 1937, the Brownlow Committee asked Congress to empower and fund the administrative state and then to step aside and allow the president and his political appointees to run it. In 1946, Congress resoundingly said no, and it has remained very central to federal administration ever since.

The legislation of 1946 also protected individual rights against administrative agencies, provided for further judicialization of administrative processes, and fixed the terms of a continuing discussion of the appropriate scope of judicial review of administrative action. Developments in each of these areas have ultimately democratized American public administration to a greater extent.

DEMOCRATIZING PUBLIC ADMINISTRATION I: THE "ADMINISTRATIVE REVOLUTION"

Writing in the *Harvard Business Review* in 1964, Philip Slater and Warren Bennis claimed that "Democracy is Inevitable" in administrative organizations. In 1971, George Berkley authored an equally prescient work, *The Administrative Revolution*. In a broad sense, these authors noted the disjuncture between the American political and administrative cultures. The political culture valued individual rights, representativeness, democratic participation, and accountability through checks and balances. The administrative culture was still largely a legacy of Progressive top-down governance, staffed by specialists with appropriate credentials, imbued with Scientific Management, and insulated from the public and (ideally) politics. Slater, Bennis, and Berkley concluded that the received administrative format was out-of-date both technologically and culturally. They predicted that in the near future bureaucracies in the United States would become less hierarchical, more participatory, and more user friendly for human beings. Berkley's characterization of these developments as "revolutionary" may have been somewhat overstated, and their "inevitability" is a moot point, but the overall prognosis was essentially sound—even if the pace was far slower than anticipated.

Roughly speaking, the period from the 1950s to the early 1980s witnessed four democratizing trends in administrative law and public administration. These were (1) a vast expansion in the constitutional rights individuals could successfully claim in their encounters with public bureaucracies, (2) a strong movement toward making public administrative organizations more representative of the nation's social diversity, (3) a growing emphasis on employee and citizen participation in public administration, and (4) greater judicial review of administrative action.

The Revolution in Rights

Beginning with the Warren Supreme Court (1953–1969) and continuing under the Burger Court (1969–1986), the federal judiciary declared a host of "new" (or, never previously declared) constitutional protections for individuals in their interactions with public bureaucracies (Rosenbloom, 1983). These rights augmented those already protected by the APA and many state equivalents. There were several proximate causes, including the abuses of the McCarthy period and the political and constitutional unacceptability of legally enforced racial segregation. But the vast expansion of individuals' constitutional protections against public administrative encroachments on their rights was also part of a generalized judicial concern that earlier constitutional doctrines failed to protect a citizenry that had become increasingly dependent upon public bureaucracy for employment, welfare, housing, health, and other benefits. Justice William O. Douglas captured the basic apprehension, though in dissent, in *Spady v. Mount Vernon* (1974: 985): "Today's mounting bureaucracy, both at the state and federal levels, promises to be suffocating and repressive unless it is put into the harness of procedural due process." The revolution in rights consisted of three main steps.

First, the courts afforded individuals a host of new constitutional rights that could be asserted against public bureaucracies. Since the 1960s, clients of administrative agencies, such as welfare recipients and public school pupils, gained far greater substantive, equal protection, and procedural due process rights. Government benefits that were once defined as a privilege to which one had no constitutional right, were redefined as a "new property" (in Charles Reich's [1964] words) in which one does have constitutionally cognizable interests. The constitutional rights of public employees to freedom of speech and association, procedural due process, and equal protection have also been vastly expanded. Civil servants now even have a constitutional right to disobey unconstitutional directives and to engage in whistleblowing (*Harley v. Schuylkill County*, 1979; *Pickering v. Board of Education*, 1968). Individuals involuntarily confined to public mental health facilities have a new constitutional right to treatment and/or training (*Wyatt v. Stickney*, 1971; *Youngberg v. Romeo*, 1982), and some of their ordinary rights as members of the political community have been afforded greater protection. The Eighth Amendment and equal protection rights of prisoners have also been dramatically strengthened through radical departure from earlier constitutional doctrines (Rosenbloom, 1983: chapter 5). Additionally, greater constitutional protections have developed for individuals caught in "street-level" encounters with police (and, presumably, public administrators not engaged in law enforcement, as well) (*Kolender v. Lawson*, 1983; *Delaware v. Prouse*, 1979). In doctrinal terms, these changes were revolutionary. In practice, they augment the APA in providing a "bill of rights" for the individual in the administrative state. They place new and genuine constraints on public administrative activity in many areas of public policy.

Second, the courts developed—or at least accepted—a new form of suit, variously called "public law litigation," as Abram Chayes (1976) termed it, or "remedial law" (Wood and Vose, 1990). The public law litigation suit is typified by adjudication to desegregate an entire school system or to reform a state's prisons. The remedy sought for constitutional violations is a prospective regime of reform that requires continuing judicial supervision and deeply affects administrative practices and governmental budgets. Judges have taken over the management and design of school, prison, and public mental health systems in efforts to ensure that they operate constitutionally.

Third, in a remarkable development during the 1970s the Supreme Court reversed centuries of settled common law by allowing individuals to sue most public administrators whose official actions may have violated their constitutional rights. Whereas previously American governmental officials generally had an absolute immunity from civil suits seeking money damages, today, with some important exceptions, most can be held liable if they knew or reasonably should have known that their actions would violate someone's constitutional rights (see Rosenbloom and Carroll, 1990; chapter 2, for a discussion and several key cases). What better way of enforcing individuals' new rights against bureaucrats than to make the bureaucrats personally liable for breaches of them?

The net result of the revolution in rights is that American public administration has become infused with constitutional values, reasoning, and concerns. Even such mundane matters as the hiring, promotion, and firing of public employees have become constitutionalized, as have many aspects of social service, police, prison, public mental health, and public educational administration. Utilitarian-based public administration has been tempered by contractarian constitutionalism. The Rehnquist Court has been less enthusiastic about some aspects of the changes brought about by the Warren and Burger Courts, but, overall, there has been more fine tuning than rolling back the rights of individuals in the administrative state (Rosenbloom, 1992; *Missouri v. Jenkins*, 1990).

The Revolution in Representation

Between the 1960s and the present time, public personnel policy in the United States shifted dramatically in favor of establishing more representative public services. There are many political rationales and pressures for representative bureaucracy (Krislov and Rosenbloom, 1981). Overall, as Theodore Lowi argued (1969: 93–94),

> With each significant expansion of government in the past century there has been a crisis of public authority. . . . [E]ach such expansion of government and its ensuing crisis of authority has been accompanied by demands for equally significant expansion of representation. Our ambivalence toward power has thus brought about regular improvements in the mechanisms of representation.

In terms of public bureaucracy, legitimization and harmonizing with the political culture have been sought by increasing the social representatives of the civil service and by incorporating interest groups into administrative policymaking.

Social representativeness was traditionally opposed as antithetical to neutral administrative expertise. At the beginning of the 1970s, the U.S. Civil Service Commission flatly rejected the presumption that "the only manifestation of a successful equal employment program is immediate proportional representation of minorities at all grade levels, in every occupation, in all regions of the country" as "inconsistent . . . with the concept of the merit system itself" (Rosenbloom, 1977: 108). However, by 1978, the Civil Service Reform Act explicitly made it a national policy goal to establish a "Federal work force reflective of the Nation's diversity" that draws its personnel from "all segments of society." The act defines "underrepresentation" as "a situation in which the number of members of a minority group designation . . . within a category of civil service employment constitutes a lower percentage of the total number of employees within the employment category than the percentage that the minority constituted within the labor force of the United States." The Supreme Court also speaks in terms of minority and female "underrepresentation" (e.g., *Johnson v. Transportation Agency*, 1987).

The policy thrust toward more socially representative public bureaucracies has been moderately successful. Since 1969, each of the following groups has gained greater proportional representation in the federal bureaucracy: African-Americans, Hispanics, Asian-Americans, American Indians, and women. The average civil service grade level of each has also risen. State and local civil services have also become more socially diverse and representative of the nation's work force.

The extent to which a more socially representative civil service makes public bureaucracy more legitimate and politically representative of the citizenry is unknown. However, the "official" theory is that social representation promotes democratic legitimacy and reduces the likelihood that such bureaucracies will be dominated by elites inclined to thwart political responsiveness (Rosenbloom, 1977: 105–124). Just as the First Amendment values intellectual and social pluralism, the drive toward representative bureaucracy is premised, in part, on the assumption that the more socially diverse the civil service, the greater the likelihood that a variety of perspectives will be brought to bear on the formulation, implementation, and evaluation of public policies.

Representation through interest group involvement in administrative policymaking and implementation has also increased. The New Deal sought to temper administrative power and make its use effective by incorporating interest groups into the administrative process. The APA's rulemaking provisions are also predicated on the belief that interested parties should have their viewpoints weighed in the formulation of rules. The Federal Advisory Committee Act of 1972 sought, among other objectives, to ensure that the advice garnered by agencies from their advisory committees was representative of the interests involved. The act declares that "Congress finds that there are numerous committees, boards, commissions, councils and similar groups which have been established to advise officers and agencies in the executive branch . . . and that they are frequently a useful and beneficial means of furnishing expert advice, ideas, and diverse opinions. . . ." It "[requires] the membership of . . . advisory committee[s] to be fairly balanced in terms of the points of view represented and the functions to be performed . . ." (sec. 5B).

Lowi concluded that interest group representation in bureaucracy is a leading, if undesirable, characteristic of American government. He argued that

> The United States is far from 100 percent a corporate state; but each administration, beginning with the New Deal Revolution, has helped reduce the gap. And it is equally significant that few if any programs organized on the basis of direct interest representation or group self-administration have ever been eliminated. To the undoubted power of organized interests has now been added the belief in their virtue. There would always be delegation of sovereignty to interest groups in some proportion of the total body of governmental activities. The new context of justification simply means far more direct delegation than the realities of power, unsupported by legitimacy, would call for. (1969: 84–85)

The Revolution in Participation

Since the 1960s, a far greater emphasis on participation by public employees and citizens in public administrative decisionmaking has also developed. This aspect of the ongoing administrative revolution is also consonant with democratization. Political speech is a prerequisite for effective citizen participation in the nation's political life. In contrast, however, the administrative theory of an earlier age frowned upon such participation as an interference with the ability of experts in the public service to do their jobs objectively. Public opinion and participation were viewed as obstacles to efficient public administration by such outstanding theorists as Woodrow Wilson (1887) and Luther Gulick and L. Urwick (1937: 192–193). Employee participation through collective bargaining was held in court to be "incompatible with the spirit of democracy, [and] inconsistent with every principle upon which our government is founded" (*Railway Mail Association v. Murphy*, 1943, 607). Nevertheless, "participatory bureaucracy" is emerging, even as voter turnout and other manifestations of political participation do not seem very strong.

Public participation in bureaucratic policymaking is encouraged by a wide variety of statutes and practices. Contemporary administrative and environmental law encourage it. Hearings of one kind or another are routinely held at the grass roots level by public utility commissions, agencies such as the federal Departments of Housing and Urban Development and Agriculture, and environmental protection agencies, among many others. Today's administrative theory embraces participation and even "coproduction," or direct citizen involvement in the delivery of administrative services such as sanitation and police and fire protection. New York State's Department of Environmental Conservation employs full-time "citizen participation specialists," whose job is to encourage exactly what their title suggests.

Greater participation by public employees in agency decisionmaking has occurred through labor relations and changes in managerial doctrine. The federal government and the overwhelming number of states now have elaborate systems for public sector collective bargaining. Aside from the usual humdrum of personnel administration, the following have been negotiated in some governments: the number of police officers assigned to a squad car; conditions under which police may use deadly force; decentralization or consolidation of school systems; school discipline, calendars, and class size; and the observance of Martin Luther King, Jr. Day as a paid holiday. Outside the collective bargaining format, governmental surveys of federal employees report that majorities or near majorities believe they are involved and encouraged to participate in agency decisionmaking (U.S. Merit Systems Protection Board, 1990: 19). A book by Shan Martin documents successful public sector examples of *Managing Without Managers* (1983). The IRS has also experimented with replacing traditional management with work teams.

Expansion of Judicial Review

Judicial review of agency action promotes the U.S. version of constitutional democracy by adding an important check on administrative power. Within the executive branch, political executives can check career administrators, and agencies can be pitted against one another. But the potential for abuses and coverups is substantial. Congress, as noted previously, only haphazardly checks administrative agencies. It is more likely to respond to crises than to policy changes that do not offend the relevant members' constituencies and supporters (McCubbins and Schwartz, 1984). The courts, being more insulated from electoral politics but consequently less institutionally democratic than the other branches, have a checking role that has been difficult to exercise well. History has judged the courts too hostile to administrative power from the 1890s to the mid-1930s. Some would say they were too acquiescent in accepting administrative rules and orders, except where constitutional rights were involved, from the mid-1930s to the 1970s (Shapiro, 1968). Subsequently, they have been criticized for being too zealous, not probing enough, inconsistent, and inept in their approaches. Evaluation is sometimes in the eye of the beholder, but the following appear true.

First, although it may be that "generalizations about standing to sue are largely worthless as such," as Justice William Douglas remarked (*Association of Data Processing Service Organizations v. Camp*, 1970, 151), most would agree with Kenneth C. Davis's conclusion in the mid-1970s that

> Beginning in 1968 the Supreme Court has given the federal law of standing a new basic orientation. Many now have standing who were denied it before 1968. . . .
>
> The present law of standing differs no more than slightly, if it differs at all, from the simple proposition that one who is hurt by governmental action has standing to challenge it. (Davis, 1975, 72)

Second, by the 1970s, it was fair to conclude with federal circuit court Judge David Bazelon that

> For many years, courts have treated administrative policy decisions with great deference, confining judicial attention primarily to matters of procedure. On matters of substance, the courts regularly upheld agency action, with a nod in the direction of the "substantial evidence" test, and a bow to the mysteries of administrative expertise. Courts occasionally asserted, but less often exercised, the power to set aside agency action on the ground that an impermissible factor had entered into the decision, or a crucial factor had not been considered. Gradually however, that power has come into more frequent use, and with it, the

> requirement that administrators articulate the factors on which they base their decisions. (*Environmental Defense Fund v. Ruckleshaus*, 439 F.2d 584 [1971], 597)

This "hard look" approach came to characterize enough judicial behavior to lead many to agree with Donald Horowitz that judges have moved beyond protection of the rights of parties aggrieved by administrative action to participation in general problem solving and defense of more general public interests against agencies accused of indifference to the public interest (1977: 4–9).

The relative merits of agency and judicial analyses of substantive policy issues are a subject for virtually endless debate. There have been successes and failures on both sides. What agencies gain from expertise they sometimes sacrifice to self-interest and tunnel vision. Generalist courts openly admit difficulty with science and elementary statistical analysis (*Industrial Union Department, AFL-CIO v. American Petroleum Institute*, 1980; *Craig v. Boren*, 1976). Eventually the Supreme Court began to rein in the lower courts. In *Vermont Yankee Nuclear Power Corporation v. Natural Resources Defense Council* (NRDC) (1978), the Court unequivocally held that the judiciary should not require agencies to go beyond the minimum requirements of the APA in their rulemaking activities. In *Chevron v. NRDC* (1984), the Court held that an agency, in this case the Environmental Protection Agency, could legitimately adopt any plausible interpretation of a statute it was charged with enforcing, even if other interpretations were available. In *Heckler v. Cheney* (1985), it held that an agency's discretionary decision not to enforce a statute in a specific case was not reviewable by the courts. Where judicial review is appropriate, the courts may still employ the hard look approach, but these cases do much to protect agency discretion in choice of rulemaking procedures, statutory interpretation, and nonenforcement.

A Coherent Administrative Revolution?

The changes toward greater rights, representation, participation, and judicial review from the 1950s through the 1970s developed in separate arenas, without an overall vision. None of them has been without substantial criticism. The courts have been criticized for interfering in administrative matters and usurping legislative and executive powers (e.g., see McDowell, 1982). Efforts to promote social representation have sometimes been opposed as establishing "quota systems" in which race, ethnicity, and gender matter more than ability and in which recipients of affirmative action are stigmatized (e.g., see Justice Scalia's dissent in *Johnson v. Transportation Agency* [1987] and Carter, 1991). Participation is so imperfect that it may chiefly enhance the clout of public employee unions, civil servants, and the NIMBY (not-in-my-back-yard) syndrome. Yet, each of the changes also obviously enjoyed strong political and institutional support.

It would be surprising if evaluations of such dramatic change did not differ. However problematic each of the parts, it is difficult to argue that together they failed to move American public administration toward greater harmony with its democratic constitutionalism. The expansion of individuals' constitutional rights in their encounters with bureaucracy and the movement toward greater social representation have been of particular and lasting importance. For many civil servants, knowledge of the constitutional rights is now a necessary component of administrative competence. It is no longer plausible to contend, as did Woodrow Wilson (1887: 18), that "at most points [the field of administration] stands apart even from the debatable ground of constitutional study" (1887: 493–494). Protection of constitutional rights is now embedded in much standard administrative procedure. The U.S. Office of Personnel Management provides courses in "constitutional literacy." Indeed, nowadays it is hardly surprising when a member of the Supreme Court calls upon public employers to provide their employees with appropriate constitutional training, as did Justice Stevens in *Anderson v. Creighton* (1987).

Social and interest group representation are also well established. Although the Reagan and Bush administrations were opposed to affirmative action, federal equal opportunity programs are well entrenched, and federal service employment patterns during the 1980s did not reflect trends toward less social diversity (Kellough and Rosenbloom, 1992). Anecdotal information suggests that the impact of interest groups has also continued to grow.

Participation and enlarged judicial review have had more mixed results. Public employee collective bargaining is well established but not necessarily participatory, owing to the structure of unions and the limited scope of bargaining found in some jurisdictions, most notably the federal government. Citizen participation is accepted in theory by many agencies and jurisdictions, but in practice it may be less effective than anticipated. By contrast, judicial review may be less forceful in doctrine than in practice. The Vermont Yankee, Chevron, and Cheney cases indicate doctrinal shifts limiting judicial review. However, the courts are still deeply involved in reviewing public administrative action. For some agencies, such as the EPA, judicial review is a normal aspect of operations (O'Leary, 1993).

Thus the democratizing impact of the changes discussed seems undeniable, if also incomplete. During the 1980s, a movement toward even more democratization developed through direct responsiveness to the public. The "administrative revolution" was a substantial modification of the overhead democracy model into which Progressive public administration fit with difficulty. A more populistic vision of democracy underlies the current effort to transform public bureaucracy.

Democratizing Public Administration II: Toward Market Based Public Administration

"Bureaucracy bashing" has been common in American politics. However, beginning with the Carter administration, it became rampant and symptomatic of a deep movement for administrative change. Carter complained about governmental inefficiency and strongly backed the Civil Service Reform Act of 1978 as a vehicle for improving government (Ingraham and Rosenbloom, 1992). His lead was followed by President Reagan, who viewed government as part of the problem, rather than the solution to the nation's problems (Salamon and Lund, 1985). Among the initiatives emphasized by both presidents were deregulation, privatization, load shedding, devolution of functions to the state and local governments, and public choice. Underlying these, especially during the Reagan years, was a broad effort to make public administration responsive to citizen demands through marketlike mechanisms. President Bush maintained the same direction, and by the end of his administration many federal agencies were using the language of Total Quality Management (TQM) and "customer service."

Blaming bureaucracy and an "inside the beltway" mentality for America's many economic and social failings was good electoral politics—at least in the short-run. The public seemed to be fed up with the legacy of Progressive bureaucracy, even though it had been substantially modified and democratized. As Table 1.1 indicates, confidence in government declined from 1958 into the 1980s, when it appears to have hit bottom. Bureaucracy did not seem to be either sufficiently efficient or responsive to the citizenry. Fed by politicians and political entrepreneurs, in a series of tax revolts the public demanded the only change immediately available: that of less government. "Market-based" public administration was presented as a viable means of making government work again.

Table 1.1 The Public's Confidence in Government, 1958–1991

Statement	Percent of Public Agreement				
	1958	1970	1974	1980	1991
The government wastes a lot of money	43	69	74	78	75
Government is run for the benefit of a few big interests	24	50	66	70	70
You cannot trust government to do right most of the time	23	44	62	73	70
People like me don't have any say about what the goverment does	41	46	40	39	34**
Public officials don't care much what people like me think	25*	47	50	52	59

*In 1960.

**In 1989.

Sources: Seymour Martin Lipset and William Schneider, *The Confidence Gap Business, Labor, and Government in the Public Mind* (New York: Free Press, 1983), Figs., 1-1, 1-2; Dan Balz and Richard Morin, "A Tide of Pessimism and Political Powerlessness Rises,'' *Washington Post*, November 3, 1991; University of Akron Survey Research Center, May 5, 1989.

The logic of market-based public administration is well captured in the phenomenally popular book by David Osborne and Ted Gaebler, *Reinventing Government* (1992). They argue:

> We live in an era of breathtaking change. We live in a global marketplace, which puts enormous competitive pressure on our economic institutions. We live in an information society, in which people get access to information almost as fast as their leaders do. We live in a knowledge-based economy, in which educated workers bridle at commands and demand autonomy. We live in an age of niche markets, in which customers have become accustomed to high quality and extensive choice.
>
> In this environment, bureaucratic institutions developed during the industrial era—public and private—increasingly fail us.
>
> Today's environment demands institutions that deliver high-quality goods and services, squeezing ever more bang out of every buck. It demands institutions that are responsive to their customers, offering choices of nonstandardized services; that lead by persuasion and incentives rather than commands; that give their employees a sense of meaning and control, even ownership. It demands institutions that *empower* citizens rather than simply *serving* them. (Osborne and Gaebler, 1992: 15)

The main approaches to developing market-based public administration have well-explicated logics. The arguments for deregulation are that markets are more efficient and responsive to consumer choice than administrative regulators have proven to be. As Derthick and Quirk show in *The Politics of Deregulation* (1985), "ideas matter" and the proponents of deregulation of the airlines and other enterprises were convincing. Critics' counterarguments about the inability of markets to ensure equity were not persuasive in an environment where special interests seemed to have captured whole arenas of public policy. Even where capture was not an issue, equity was hard to define. The equity involved in regulatory policy that cross-subsidizes one group by another is often unclear.

Public choice initiatives have a similar logic. Empowering the citizen-consumer to choose the mixes and amounts of services he or she desires at a range of costs from government will make the public sector more responsive and efficient. Much discussed voucher systems for education at public expense are an example. The neighborhood school system severely limits parents' choices and contains cumbersome mechanisms for making schools highly responsive to their wishes. A family with two or more children with different educational needs is stuck in one neighborhood public school system, which may be perfect for one child but far less than optimal for the others. Vouchers would enable such a parent to come closer to selecting an appropriate school, whether public or private, for each child. Schools that were insufficiently responsive to parent demands would lose students and funding to those that provided better customer service. Other public choice approaches, such as encouraging many separate governments in metropolitan areas to compete with one another for residents and businesses, employ a similar market-based logic. Consolidation of metropolitan government, by contrast, limits citizen-consumer choice. Whatever may potentially be gained through economies of scale may well be lost by the inefficiencies in responding to citizen demands non-competitively.

Privatization seeks to use the market to enable government to procure the services it provides in the most cost-effective way. The theory behind privatization holds that when government agencies are the sole providers of public services, they act like monopolies generally. They set prices that are higher than would be the case if they faced competition, and they build in considerable organizational slack. They may also put their own organizational needs before those of their citizen-customers. Privatization can take advantage of market competition when several firms seek to win government contracts for the provision of services. In a hybrid form of privatization, public agencies may be allowed to compete with private firms in this context.

Devolution of administrative functions to lower levels of government appeals to both public choice and grass roots democracy. In theory, community-based government will be more responsive to residents than will national government in a very wide range of administrative activities. Cost savings may be gained by cutting layers of bureaucracy and the need for accountability that they entail. During the 1980s, the proportion of all state and local spending that came from the federal government declined in both absolute and proportional terms (Rosenbloom, 1993: 120).

Load shedding is similar to devolution except that whether the function involved is provided at all is not a matter of immediate governmental concern. It may be picked up by a private organization, often a not-for-profit social service agency, or thrust onto members of the public at large. Increasing homelessness is partly due to load shedding in public mental health care and public housing. It is market-based in the sense that government makes a decision that it is not cost-effective for it to supply the function. It also assumes that if there is sufficient demand for the function, private organizations will take steps to provide it.

The logic behind market-based public administration is clear, as is its populistic appeal. Osborne and Gaebler's chapter headings convey the latter well:

Catalytic Government: Steering Rather than Rowing
Community-Owned Government: Empowering Rather than Serving
Competitive Government: Injecting Competition into Service Delivery
Mission-Driven Government: Transforming Rule-Driven Organizations
Results-Oriented Government: Funding Outcomes, Not Inputs
Customer-Driven Government: Meeting the Needs of the Customer, Not the Bureaucracy
Enterprising Government: Earning Rather than Spending
Anticipatory Government: Prevention Rather than Cure
Decentralized Government: From Hierarchy to Participation and Teamwork
Market-Oriented Government: Leveraging Change Through the Market.

However, it is far too early to know whether such public administration will be successful over a substantial period of time.

The main theoretical critique of market-based public administration may be that like markets generally it will have antisocial externalities. Turning citizens into customers may harm community in the process of serving self-maximizing individuals. Using markets effectively involves different skills from those needed to be politically effective. As a consequence, political skills and even self-government may suffer. Managing privatization may prove difficult. Public choice may foster niche markets at the price of less social integration, greater stratification, and less mobility. As Martin and Susan Tolchin argued, such public administration may encourage the *Dismantling* [of] *America* (1983). Such concerns will no doubt prompt reevaluation and transformation of existing legal doctrine.

"Reinventing" State Action and Accountability

Market-based public administration poses immediate issues for traditional legal approaches to state action and accountability. Privatization and service delivery by public–private partnerships can potentially lead to circumvention of traditional constitutional protections and requirements. For instance, an employee of a private not-for-profit organization may not be entitled to constitutional due process in an adverse action, even though the organization is extensively funded and regulated by the government (*Wolotosky v. Huhn*, 1992). Along with privatization, public administrative entrepreneurship and decentralization pose challenges to effective maintenance of accountability.

State Action

By the late 1980s, the Supreme Court was sharply divided in the application of the very type of state action issue that is sure to arise frequently in the context of market-based public administration. In *National Collegiate Athletic Association v. Tarkanian* (1988: 461), the Court repeated the longstanding fundamental premise that

> Embedded in our Fourteenth Amendment jurisprudence is a dichotomy between state action, which is subject to strict scrutiny under the Amendment's Due Process Clause, and private conduct, against which the Amendment affords no shield, no matter how unfair that conduct may be.

Such a bright line may often be easily recognized. For instance, in *West v. Adkins* (1988), the Court was unanimous in finding that a private physician under contract with a state prison hospital to provide medical services on a part-time basis was engaged in state action. It noted that public employees, other than public defenders, are generally considered state actors and that the same premise should cover private individuals under employment contracts with the government.

However, in Tarkanian, the Court split 5-to-4 on whether the University of Nevada—Las Vegas (UNLV) had clothed the National Collegiate Athletic Association (NCAA), a private organization, with governmental authority. The majority opinion, written by Justice Stevens, did not find state action in the NCAA's investigation of UNLV's basketball coach, Jerry Tarkanian, despite the fact that the university subsequently suspended him on the basis of the NCAA's findings. In a dissent joined by Justices Brennan, Marshall, and O'Connor, Justice White reasoned that the university and the NCAA had acted jointly to such an extent that the private organization was engaged in state action. White reasoned that the NCAA and UNLV became commingled as the NCAA held the hearings upon which the university acted and the university enforced the NCAA's rules.

The facts in Tarkanian were complicated enough to divide the Court. However, the potential range for complexity in public–private partnerships is much greater than Tarkanian may suggest. The Supreme Court's action in *Wyatt v. Cole and Robbins* (1992) is indicative of problems inherent in applying traditional state action doctrine. Cole obtained attorney Robbin's help in filing a complaint in replevin against Wyatt, with whom he had "a soured cattle partnership" (509). The action was executed against Wyatt, who later brought suit in Federal District Court, successfully challenging the constitutionality of the Mississippi statute authorizing replevin. (The statute violated due process because it did not afford judges the discretion to deny writs of replevin.) The District Court held that the governmental officials involved and the private parties, Cole and Robbins, were entitled to qualified immunity under 42 USC § 1983.

The Supreme Court reversed the decision, finding that the private parties were not entitled to such an immunity. It divided as follows: The opinion of the Court was written by Justice O'Connor and joined by Justices White, Blackmun, Stevens, Scalia, and Kennedy; Justice Kennedy filed a concurring opinion joined by Scalia; the Chief Justice dissented in an opinion joined by Justices Souter and Thomas.

O'Connor offered a two-pronged test to determine whether private individuals have acted under color of state law within the meaning of 42 USC § 1983. "First, the 'deprivation must be caused by the exercise of some right or privilege created by the State or by a rule of conduct imposed by the State or by a person for whom the State is responsible.'" *And* "[s]econd, the private party must have 'acted together with or . . . [sic] obtained significant aid from the state officials' or engaged in conduct 'otherwise chargeable to the State'" (*Wyatt v. Cole and Robbins*, 1992: 511). There is no doubt that this test may prove difficult to apply. However, O'Connor's reasoning with regard to qualified immunity displayed even more clearly the intellectual difficulty of drawing clear distinctions between the actions of private individuals and government officials. She noted that the question was not an easy one, and set forth the following distinction between private and public defendants in such suits:

> Private parties hold no office requiring them to exercise discretion; nor are they principally concerned with enhancing the public good. . . . Moreover, unlike with government officials performing discretionary functions, the public interest will not be unduly impaired if private individuals are required to proceed to trial to resolve their legal disputes. (515)

However, in many public–private partnerships, private individuals do exercise discretion in the provision of a public function. They may also be principally concerned with enhancing the public good, and suits against them may harm the public interest. Indeed, some federal agencies have contracted out rulemaking functions; not-for-profits or other nongovernmental organizations have engaged in a host of social welfare and correction functions at the state and local levels.

Justice Kennedy's concurring opinion avoided reliance on distinctions between public officials and private individuals acting under color of state law. In his view, there were neither compelling legal nor policy reasons to extend the same qualified immunity enjoyed by public officials to private parties. The Chief Justice's dissent reached diametrically opposed conclusions. Rehnquist concluded that the private parties would be entitled to a good faith defense under common law and that, in practice, there was little useful distinction between such a defense and qualified immunity. His views with regard to public policy are more relevant to the issues presented by the intermixing of public and private action. He asked whether "reasons of public policy would warrant immunity for private parties as well" as public officials and answered:

> I believe there are such reasons. The normal presumption that attaches to any law is that society will be benefitted if private parties rely on that law to provide them with a remedy, rather than turning to some form of private, and perhaps lawless, relief. In denying

> immunity to those who reasonably rely on presumptively valid state law, and thereby discouraging such reliance, the Court expresses confidence that today's decision will not "unduly impai[r]" (sic) . . . the public interest. I do not share that confidence. I would have thought it beyond peradventure that there is strong public interest in encouraging private citizens to rely on valid state laws of which they have no reason to doubt the validity.
>
> [I]t is at least passing strange to conclude that private individuals are acting "under color of law" because they invoke a state garnishment statute and the aid of state officers, . . . but yet deny them the immunity to which those same state officers are entitled, simply because the private parties are not state employees. (522–523)

To say that the many issues posed by private action under color of state law will not be immediately resolved by the justices' reasoning in Wyatt is to state the obvious. Prior to the Court's decision, the Fifth, Eighth, and Eleventh Circuits had held that private defendants are entitled to qualified immunity, the First and Ninth Circuits had reached the opposite conclusion under some circumstances, while the Sixth Circuit had rejected qualified immunity but had gone its own way in establishing a good faith defense for private defendants! Although Wyatt establishes that qualified immunity is not now available to private individuals, it leaves ample room for the development of different views regarding the elements of a valid defense in such suits. Moreover, as O'Connor's majority opinion relies heavily on public policy assumptions, it may be successively narrowed as other contexts bring forth different policy conclusions.

Accountability

Some aspects of contemporary accountability law are also likely to come under increasing pressure for refinement in the near future. Modern *respondeat superior* doctrine seeks to protect public agencies against vicarious liability for the wayward actions of their employees. As the Supreme Court explained in *Pembaur v. City of Cincinnati* (1986: 479–480),

> [t]he conclusion that tortious conduct, to be the basis for municipal liability under [42 U.S. Code] 1983, must be pursuant to a municipality's "official policy" . . . was intended to distinguish acts of the *municipality* from acts of *employees* of the municipality, and thereby make clear that municipal liability is limited to actions for which the municipality is actually responsible.

But it is not always crystal clear when principals are responsible for their agents.

Contemporary case law seems to indicate that public agencies may be liable for negligent hiring (Walter, 1992) and failure to train their employees (*City of Canton v. Harris*, 1989). At the same time, however, they may not be accountable for their employees' failure to provide correct information and to follow prescribed procedure. For example, in *Schweiker v. Hansen* (1981), a Social Security Administration (SSA) field representative gave incorrect advice to a woman seeking mothers' insurance benefits. He also failed to advise her to file a written application in accordance with procedures contained in the agency's Claims Manual. The Supreme Court reasoned that

> the Claims Manual is not a regulation. It has no legal force, and it does not bind the SSA. Rather, it is a 13-volume handbook for internal use by thousands of SSA employees, including the hundreds of employees who receive untold numbers of oral inquiries . . . each year. If [the field representative's] minor breach of such a manual suffices to [prevent the agency from withholding benefits to which the individual was actually entitled], then the Government is put "at risk that every alleged failure by an agent to follow instructions to the last detail in one of a thousand cases will deprive it of the benefit of the written application requirement which experience has taught to be essential to the honest and effective administration of the Social Security Laws." (*Schweiker v. Hansen*, 1981: 789–790)

The same general principle holds true regarding individuals' inquiries to other administrative personnel in public contact positions, including Internal Revenue Service agents.

The policy rationale for not allowing lower-level agents to bind public agencies is clear enough and will be clearer still when the agent is not even an agency employee but rather someone employed by an organization holding a government contract to provide a public service. At the same time, however, the rationale is unclear for not providing relief to individuals victimized by following the advice of those employed to dispense it accurately. The Schweiker principle is a blunt legal instrument that is likely to be tested increasingly as private organizations engaged in governmental functions inevitably make mistakes in their treatment of individuals.

CONCLUSION: UNDERSTANDING ADMINISTRATIVE CHANGE

In recent years there have been calls to "rebuild," "refound," and "reinvent" the American public service (National Commission on the Public Service [Volcker Commission], 1989; Wamsley et al., 1990; Osborne and Gaebler, 1992). They have been part of a long tradition that includes the nineteenth-century civil service reformers, the Progressives, the New Dealers, as well as the Jeffersonians and Jacksonians before them. The need for administrative change is a theme that runs through American political development. The analysis and review of such change presented here offers several conclusions:

1. Change in administrative thought and practice—even vast change—has occurred and is possible. Such change goes beyond issues of the scope and size of public administration. Today's administrative thought, values, and practices are considerably different from those dominant under the orthodox or classical public administration of the 1920s and 1930s.

2. The law governing public administration, whether it be statutory, common, or constitutional, also changes. Legal change has sometimes followed administrative change, as in the case of New Deal and 1946, but it can also lead, as was clearly the case from the 1950s into the 1980s (Rosenbloom, 1983).

3. Administrative change has been the product of both ideas and politics. The ideas matter, but administrative theories appear to require the backing of political institutions to become dominant. Progressive public administration was very much part of the overall ideology of the Progressive movement. The movement toward market-based public administration today is strongly linked to broad populistic sentiment that may eventually come to dominate the political system. Change associated with the New Deal was largely driven by an effort to strengthen the presidency. The congressional response in 1946 looked toward establishing a more coherent role for the legislature in the administrative state. The changes in legal doctrines that formed part of the "administrative revolution" of recent decades immensely strengthened the judiciary's influence over public administration.

4. The constitutional separation of powers has been central to administrative development. The enlarged and strengthened New Deal executive eventually became increasingly micromanaged by Congress after the restructuring of 1946. The judiciary was unable to sustain its reliance on the common law to check administrative action, but by the mid-1970s it had refashioned constitutional law sufficiently to make "constitutional competence" a job requirement for public managers (Rosenbloom and Carroll, 1990). Like common law, however, "constitutional law is what the courts say it is," as Justice Powell put it in *Owen v. City of Independence* (1980: 669).

5. Since the 1930s, the overall direction of administrative change has been to harmonize public administration more fully with democratic constitutionalism. However, history does

not suggest that this direction is inevitable. Progressives like Woodrow Wilson were fully cognizant that the changes they advocated were not democratic.

6. Since administrative change and legal change have been so strongly connected, it behooves those calling for major administrative or legal reforms to show how each is related to the other. This is a dimension as sorely lacking in Osborne and Gaebler's *Reinventing Government* (1992) as in the Volcker Commission Report (1989) and in Woodrow Wilson's "The Study of Administration" (1887).

7. In the same vein, researchers, scholars, and pundits in the fields of public administration and administrative law should pay considerable attention to one another. For more than a century, law has been central to administrative development, and administrative development has been central to legal change in the United States. The relationship is likely to endure.

8. More generally, both administrative and legal doctrine have from time to time over the years been seriously out-of-touch with empirical reality. Both have dealt in abstractions without clear or strong factual referents. The politics–administration dichotomy that was so central to public administrative thought is an easy mark. But contemporary knowledge of "representative bureaucracy" remains very incomplete (Krislov and Rosenbloom, 1981), as does understanding of public participation in public administration (see R. Schwartz, *infra*). On the judicial side, remedial law has sometimes manifested a very incomplete understanding of administrative possibility (Horowitz, 1977; Rosenbloom, 1983).

9. Finally and more contentiously, it may be time to "refound" the study of public administration by turning Leonard White (1926) on his side: "The study of public administration should be fully grounded in an understanding of law, and is therefore as absorbed in the decisions of the courts as in the study of management."

NOTE

1. The term "market failure" is conventionally used to denote conditions that impede market functioning, such as information asymmetry and labor immobility, and the inability of markets to reflect total social and other costs, including, perhaps, those thrust upon future generations ("externalities"). However, in a more fundamental sense, markets may be socially defective, owing to their impact on culture (see Etzioni, 1988; Sternberg, 1993).

REFERENCES

Appleby, Paul (1949). *Policy and Administration*. University of Alabama Press, University, Ala.

Arnold, Peri (1986). *Making the Managerial Presidency*. Princeton University Press, Princeton, N.J.

Arnold, R. Douglas (1979). *Congress and the Bureaucracy*. Yale University Press, New Haven, Conn.

Beam, David (1978). Public Administration Is Alive and Well—and Living in the White House. *Public Administration Review, 38*: 72–77.

Berkley, George (1971). *The Administrative Revolution*. Prentice-Hall, Englewood Cliffs, N.J.

Black, C. (1979). *Black's Law Dictionary*, 5th ed. West, St. Paul, Minn.

Brownlow, Louis (1949). *The President and the Presidency*. Public Administration Service, Chicago, Ill.

Carter, Stephen (1991). *Reflections of an Affirmative Action Baby*. Basic Books, New York.

Chayes, Abram (1976). The Role of the Judge in Public Law Litigation. *Harvard Law Review, 89*: 1281–1316.

Dahl, Robert (1947). The Science of Public Administration: Three Problems. *Public Administration Review, 7*: 1–11.

Davis, Kenneth C. (1975). *Administrative Law and Government*, 2nd ed. West, St. Paul, Minn.

Derthick, Martha and Paul Quirk (1985). *The Politics of Deregulation*. Brookings, Washington, D.C.

Doig, Jameson (1984). "If I See a Murderous Fellow Sharpening a Knife Cleverly . . .": the Wilsonian Dichotomy and the Public Authority Tradition. In Jack Rabin and James Bowman, eds., *Politics and Administration*. pp. 175–199. Marcel Dekker, New York.

Donnelly, James (1945). Testimony Before Full Employment Subcommittee of the Committee on Banking and Currency. Senate Hearings 763, August 30, pp. 665-668. Washington, D.C.: U.S. Government Printing Office.
Dye, Thomas and L. Harmon Zeigler (1975). *The Irony of Democracy*, 3rd ed. Duxbury Press, North Scituate, Mass.
Eaton, Dorman (1880). *The Civil Service in Great Britain*. Harper & Bros., New York.
Etzioni, Amitai (1988). *The Moral Dimension*. Free Press, New York.
Fiorina, Morris (1977). *Congress: Keystone of the Washington Establishment*. Yale University Press, New Haven, Conn.
Friedman, Lawrence (1973). *A History of American Law*. Simon & Schuster, New York.
Goodnow, Frank (1900). *Politics and Administration*. Russell & Russell, New York.
Gulick, Luther (1937). Notes on the Theory of Organization. In Jay Shafritz and Albert Hyde, eds., *Classics of Public Administration*, pp. 38–47. Moore Publishing, Oak Park, Ill. [1978].
Gulick, Luther and Urwick, L., eds. (1937). *Papers on the Science of Administration*. Institute of Public Administration, New York.
Gunther, Gerald (1975). *Cases and Materials on Constitutional Law*, 10th ed. Foundation Press, Mineola, N.Y.
Heclo, Hugh (1977). *A Government of Strangers*. Brookings, Washington, D.C.
Hofstadter, Richard (1955). *The Age of Reform*. Alfred A. Knopf, New York.
Horowitz, Donald (1977). *The Courts and Social Policy*. Brookings, Washington, D.C.
Ingraham, Patricia and David H. Rosenbloom, eds. (1992). *The Promise and Paradox of Civil Service Reform*. University of Pittsburgh Press, Pittsburgh, Penna.
Jackson, Robert (1941). *The Struggle for Judicial Supremacy*. Knopf, New York.
Johnson, John (1981). *American Legal Culture, 1908–1941*. Greenwood Press, Westport, Conn.
Kellough, J. Edward and David H. Rosenbloom (1992). Representative Bureaucracy and the EEOC: Did Civil Service Reform Make a Difference? In Patricia Ingraham and David H. Rosenbloom, eds., *The Promise and Paradox of Civil Service Reform*. University of Pittsburgh Press, Pittsburgh.
Krislov, Samuel and David H. Rosenbloom (1981). *Representative Bureaucracy*. Praeger, New York.
La Follette, Robert, Jr. (1947). Congress Wins a Victory over Congress. *New York Times Magazine*, August 4, pp. 11, 45–46.
Lowi, Theodore J. (1969). *The End of Liberalism*. W. W. Norton, New York.
Martin, Shan (1983). *Managing Without Managers*. Sage, Beverly Hills, Cal.
McCarran, Walter (1946). *U.S. Congressional Record*, 79th Congress, 2nd Session, March 12.
McCubbins, Matthew and Thomas Schwartz (1984). Congressional Oversight Overlooked: Police Patrols Versus Fire Alarms. *American Journal Political Science, 28*: 165–179.
McDowell, Gary (1982). *Equity and the Constitution*. University of Chicago Press, 1982.
Mosher, Frederick (1976). *Basic Documents of American Public Administration, 1776–1950*. Holmes and Meier, New York.
National Commission on the Public Service (1989). *Leadership for America: Rebuilding the Public Service*. National Commission on the Public Service, Washington, D.C.
O'Leary, Rosemary (1993). *Environmental Change: The Federal Courts and EPA*. Temple University Press, Philadelphia, Penna.
Osborne, David and Ted Gaebler (1992). *Reinventing Government*. Addision-Wesley, Reading, Mass.
Pound, Roscoe (1914). Justice According to Law. *Columbia Law Review, 14*: 1.
Pritchett, C. Herman (1977). *The American Constitution*, 3rd ed. McGraw-Hill, New York.
Reich, Charles (1964). The New Property. *Yale Law Journal, 73*: 733–787.
Ripley, Randall and Grace Franklin (1976). *Congress, the Bureaucracy, and Public Policy*. The Dorsey Press, Homewood, Ill.
Rohr, John A. (1986). *To Run a Constitution*. University Press of Kansas, Lawrence, Kan.
Rosenbloom, David H. (1971). *Federal Service and the Constitution*. Cornell University Press, Ithaca, N.Y.
____ (1977). *Federal Equal Employment Opportunity*. Praeger, New York.
____ (1983). *Public Administration and Law*. Marcel Dekker, New York.

____ (1992). Public Administrative Liability for Constitutional Torts, the Rehnquist Court, and Public Administration. *Administration and Society, 24*: 115–131.

_____ (1993). *Public Administration: Understanding Management, Politics, and Law in the Public Sector*, 3rd ed. McGraw-Hill, New York.

Rosenbloom, David H., and James D. Carroll (1990). *Toward Constitutional Competence: A Casebook for Public Administrators*. Prentice-Hall, Englewood Cliffs, N.J.

Rosenbloom, David H. and Jay Shafritz (1985). *Essentials of Labor Relations*. Reston/Prentice-Hall, Reston, Va.

Salamon, Lester and Michael Lund, eds. (1985). *The Reagan Presidency and the Governing of America*. Urban Institute Press, Washington, D.C.

Schurz, Carl (1893). Editorial, *Harper's Weekly, 37*: 614.

____ (1913). *The Speeches, Correspondence, and Political Papers of Carl Schurz*, ed. by Frederick Bancroft, G. P. Putnam's Sons, New York.

Shapiro, Martin (1968). *The Supreme Court and Administrative Agencies*. Free Press, New York.

Short, Lloyd (1939). An Investigation of the Executive Agencies of the United States Government. *American Political Science Review 33*: 60–66.

Simon, Herbert (1947). *Administrative Behavior*. Free Press, New York.

Skowronek, Stephen (1982). *Building a New American State: The Expansion of Administrative Capacities, 1877–1920*. Cambridge University Press, New York.

Slater, Philip and Warren Bennis (1964). Democracy Is Inevitable. *Harvard Business Review, 42*: 51–59.

Sternberg, Ernest (1993). Justifying Public Intervention Without Market Externalities: Karl Polanyi's Theory of Planning in Capitalism. *Public Administration Review, 53*: 100–109.

Stewart, Richard (1975). The Reformation of American Administrative Law. *Harvard Law Review, 88*: 1669–1813.

Taylor, Frederick (1917). *The Principles of Scientific Management*. Harper & Bros., New York.

Tolchin, Martin and Susan Tolchin (1983). *Dismantling America*. Oxford University Press, New York.

U.S. Bureau of the Census and Social Science Research Council (1951). *Statistical History of the United States from Colonial Times to the Present*. Fairfield Publishers, Stamford, Conn.

U.S. Merit Systems Protection Board (1990). *Working for America: A Federal Employee Survey*. U.S. Merit Systems Protection Board, Washington, D.C.

U.S. Senate Documents (1941). *Report of the Attorney General*, 77th Congress, 1st session, Document No. 8. U.S. Government Printing Office, Washington, D.C.

Van Riper, Paul (1958). *History of the United States Civil Service*. Row, Peterson, Evanston.

Waldo, Dwight (1948). *The Administrative State*. Ronald Press, New York.

____ (1961). Organization Theory: An Elephantine Problem. *Public Administration Review, 21*: 210–225.

Walter, Robert (1992). Public employers' potential liability from negligence in employment decisions. *Public Administration Review, 52*: 491–496.

Wamsley, Gary, Robert Bacher, Charles Goodsell, Phillip Kronenberg, John Rohr, Camilla Stivers, Orion White, and James Wolf (1990). *Refounding Public Administration*. Sage Publications, Newberry Park, Cal.

White, Leonard (1926). *Introduction to the Study of Public Administration*. Macmillan, New York.

Wilson, James Q. (1986). The Rise of the Bureaucratic State. In Pietro Nivola and David Rosenbloom, eds., *Classic Readings in American Politics*, pp. 427–447. St. Martin's Press, New York.

Wilson, Woodrow (1887). The Study of Administration. *Political Science Quarterly, 56*: 481–506 (1941 republication).

Wood, Robert and Clement Vose (1990). *Remedial Law: When Courts Become Administrators*. University of Massachusetts Press, Amherst.

LEGAL CASES

Anderson v. Creighton (1987). 438 U.S. 635.

Association of Data Processing Service Organizations v. Camp (1970). 397 U.S. 150.

Carter v. Carter Coal Co. (1936). 298 U.S. 238.

Chevron v. Natural Resources Defense Council (1984). 467 U.S. 837.
Chicago, Milwaukee and St. Paul Railway Co. v. Minnesota (1890). 134 U.S. 418.
City of Canton v. Harris (1989). 489 U.S. 387.
Craig v. Boren (1976). 429 U.S. 190.
Dalehite v. U.S. (1953). 346 U.S. 15.
Delaware v. Prouse (1979). 440 U.S. 648.
Environmental Defense Fund v. Ruckleshaus (1971). 439 F.2d 584.
Harley v. Schuylkill County (1979). 476 F. Supp. 191.
Heckler v. Cheney (1985). 470 U.S. 821.
Interstate Commerce Commission v. Cincinnati, New Orleans and Texas Pacific Railroad Co. (1897). 167 U.S. 479.
Industrial Union Department, AFL-CIO v. American Petroleum Institute (1980). 448 U.S. 607.
Johnson v. Transportation Agency (1987). 480 U.S. 624.
Kolender v. Lawson (1983). 461 U.S. 352.
Lochner v. New York (1905). 198 U.S. 45.
Missouri v. Jenkins (1990). 110 S.CT. 1651.
Muller v. Oregon (1908). 208 U.S. 412.
National Collegiate Athletic Association v. Tarkanian (1988). 109 S.Ct. 454.
Owen v. City of Independence (1980). 445 U.S. 622.
Pembaur v. City of Cincinnati (1986). 475 U.S. 469.
Pickering v. Board of Education (1968). 391 U.S. 563.
Railway Mail Association v. Murphy (1943). 44 N.Y. 2d 601.
Schechter Poultry Co. v. U.S. (1935). 295 U.S. 495.
Schweiker v. Hansen (1981). 450 U.S. 785.
Spady v. Mt. Vernon (1974). 419 U.S. 983.
Texas and Pacific Railway Co. v. Abilene Cotton Oil Co. (1907). 204 U.S. 426.
U.S. v. Butler (1936). 297 U.S. 1.
Vermont Yankee Nuclear Power Corporation v. Natural Resources Defense Council (1978). 435 U.S. 519.
West v. Adkins (1988). 108 S.Ct. 2250.
Wickard v. Filburn (1942). 317 U.S. 111.
Wolotosky v. Huhn (1992). 1992 WL 44880 (6th Cir. Ohio).
Wyatt v. Cole and Robbins (1992). 118 L.Ed. 2d 504.
Wyatt v. Stickney (1971). 325 F. Supp. 781.
Youngberg v. Romeo (1982). 457 U.S. 307.

2

The New Separation and Delegation of Powers Doctrine

Samuel Krislov *University of Minnesota, Minneapolis, Minnesota*

The constitutional issues of separation of powers and delegation have not historically been as heated or controversial as those of federalism. Exclusive of issues of improper delegation to the judiciary (which antedate *Marbury v. Madison* and arise continually in any legal system), the sole decisions of constitutional invalidity based upon separation prior to *Chadha*[1] were concentrated in a handful of years in the New Deal era. The delegation issues in *Carter v. Carter Coal, Panama Refining v. Ryan*, and *U. S. v. Schechter Poultry*[2] have not drawn the same universal disdain from constitutional writers as the more central, though intertwined, commerce clause reasoning. The reason is that there is agreement that the National Industrial Recovery Act (NIRA) was poorly drafted, and its administration ineffably worse. Since Courts operate with an informal "suspect agency" principle (not limited to American administrative review), otherwise marginal legal arguments can be easily interposed when ineptitude is visibly present. And of course NIRA did represent delegation in its extreme form, with the Court's denunciation of "delegation run riot" only a bit hyperbolic. The Supreme Court also was confronted by a constitutional issue (which it sideswiped and has never faced directly), of delegation of actual power to "civilians" outside the legal order, and whether the formality and/or reality of signature approval by a high government official is sufficient to bring such matters within normal delegation standards.

Though the delegation issues in those famous cases were overshadowed by the commerce clause issues, and discounted for extraordinary circumstances, the prevailing verdict has been that the majority overstated and overreached in its claims and that Cardozo's concurrence in *Panama* and *Schechter* states standard delegation principles more accurately, summarizing them for both the century-and-a-half retrospectively, and the half-century or so of jurisprudence since. The loose articulation of standards permitted to Social Security in *Steward Machine v. Davis,*[3] where Cardozo wrote for a majority, reestablished the court tradition that so long as Congress made a stab at reasonable standards, so long as outrageous violence was not done to the formality of separation, legislation was almost certainly to be sustained.

The recent emergence of new hard-line "separation" and "delegation" doctrines, therefore, comes both as a sport and a surprise. Its major source—neoconservative economic and political theory—deviates from traditional conservative critiques in that it views with suspicion not excessive discretion given to the executive but, rather, monolithic control claimed by an allegedly micromanaging Congress. Traditionally American conservatives have been Whigs, not Tories, suspicious of populist "Tribunes of the People," and not their backers and advocates.

The transformation of American conservativism is not unique, but rather part of the historic cycle of ox-goring. Liberals once hailed the presidency as "steward" or "tribune" of the people, and looked down upon Congress as a system of rotten boroughs coordinated by the seniority system. Now an "imperial president" is seen as held in check by a benevolent, mainly progressive (if excessively interest-group beholden), Congress. The Senate is incongruously hailed as the truest bastion of democratic will. Thus the different sides have found equal and opposite "new" rationales for reversing their positions, and have largely accepted their opponents' former arguments.

The current conservative formulation suggests that the Founding Fathers had a puristic understanding of separation of power similar to the famous presumptions of the Constitution of the Commonwealth of Massachusetts. Functions are declared inherently executive, legislative, or judicial. Commingling is improper. In doubtful cases, the touchstone for identifying positions is to be found in the removal power, and the dismissing agent.

The conservative delegation theory is equally stark, in parallel with its separation dogma. What can be delegated by Congress to a nonlegislative employee must congruently be given either an "executive" or "judicial" function. Those are treated as identifiable and distinct species. The more standard "process" and "clearly-articulated-standards" approach most clearly associated with the *J. W. Hampton and Company* decision (discussed more fully below) is not yet directly challenged but given both a cold shoulder and short shrift. (Exercise of discretion is a sure sign of executive functions.[4]) However, both on and off the court, Justice Scalia, the principal ideologist of the new separatism, has made it clear that the *Humphrey* approach is neither in concordance with his view of original intent nor constitutionally permissible.[5] The political independence of an officer "in the executive branch" is not justifiable, and commingling of powers also creates constitutional dilemmas for the Justice. Since any agency not historically identifiable as judicial or legislative is seen *ipso facto* as "executive," it must be politically controlled from the White House.

While Scalia's puristic notions have not gained support in their broadest application, there have been of course important decisions based upon the separation of powers notions. *Chadha* and *Bowsher v. Synar*[6] thwarted key efforts by Congress to maintain legislative influence. The constitutional demise of the legislative veto (though in practice a demise still highly exaggerated,[7] ("still dying after all these years") and the elimination of the Controller General's role in reconciling budget discrepancies which help make Gramm–Rudman a grotesque remnant, has grievously limited legislative innovations. In essence, Scalia has been to pure separatism what Black was to "absolute" free speech—an outlier who constantly pulls the Court toward his vision.

It had been assumed that Chief Justice Rehnquist's visible disenchantment with the consequences of Scalia's razor had stopped the "pure separation" approach in its tracks. The use of the device of the independent prosecutor in *Morrison v. Olson* was sustained over Scalia's fervid objection to judicial involvement in her choice. The key to that case, however, is the surgical care with which the separation issue was pared, including admonitions to the supervisory Court of Appeals panel not to exercise supervision—presumably executive in nature—to avoid going over an ill-defined limit the majority found nonetheless to exist. The sentencing guidelines commission was easily upheld as well even though established within the judiciary.[8]

That the Scalian doctrine is still alive—merely sharply confined—is made clear in a little noticed decision in the 1990 term written by Justice Stevens, *Metropolitan Washington Airports Authority v. Citizens* (1991).[9] Congress magnanimously devolved control of Washington National Airport to a local airways authority. A congressional board of review nonetheless retained peremptory veto rights over major issues. A floor manager of the legislation authorizing this explained that in fact Congress would have more rather than less power under this arrangement. Stevens' opinion essentially applies "horizontal" or "separation" doctrine to a "vertical," essentially federal, delegation because the commission is in fact an arm of Congress.

Technically, the delegation is federal not functional, and no previous decision had ever held that the separation doctrine applies to such delegations from Congress to a district governmental agency. It is difficult to see on what constitutional basis federal separation doctrine could be applied to state and local governmental structure or delegations made within their structures. (Indeed Stevens, in dissent in *Minnesota v. Cloverleaf Creamery*[10] made precisely that argument—that it did not—which may have been why he was assigned this opinion, to allay fears of expansion.) Nonetheless, the Court, no doubt affronted by the almost cynical nature of the delegation, found the power of Congress over the district to be bound by its formal national limits, not its functional power which is equivalent to state action. This delegation affronted the new standards by allowing a congressional committee to exercise executive functions. Whether states would be so controlled is left to the future, though dissenters raise fears.

This decision puts a decisive gloss on *Morrison*. It represents an abatement, an easing, but not a quarantine of the separationist logic. That doctrine is still available for other areas, even those as novel as the venture into separationist federalism.

But *Metropolitan Washington Airports* is also symptomatic of continued concern over the issue of delegation and separation, well beyond that posed by delegation within the federal government. When states and localities act in consonance with federal programs, what are their limits and prerogatives? A key issue arises as to whether or, more properly, when there is exemption from federal antitrust legislation, since by its nature state regulation effects restriction of trade. There is slow recognition that we have virtually no clear thinking about when a state is empowered, and to what degree, by federal action. That is to say, there is no mirror image thinking comparable to preemption or supersedure. It is not especially harsh to say that any theory of federal empowerment of the states lags just about a half-century behind preemption logic.

There is another dimension of delegation separation that has resisted scholarly analysis—the question of delegation to "nongovernmental" governmental units. These range from the Post Office "corporation" model and the Federal Reserve Board to users or producers committees in agriculture, governmental-leveraged setting of product standards by "private groups" dominated by the major producers, and other aspects of what comparative government scholars call "corporatism" that are evident throughout our society. Chief Justice Harlan Stone insisted in later years that this was the gravamen of the invalidity of NIRA: that it delegated legislative power out of government in an improper way. No legal decisions accept that logic (and Stone and Cardozo's opinions in the NIRA cases barely hint at this), but it would be foolish to ignore the issue he raised. Given the Scalia–Meese challenge, it assumes even more moment.

Courts sidestep such issues by concentrating on the formal route by which such decisions become a law or regulation. A farmers' group sets production limits by making a recommendation to the Secretary of Agriculture, and that official's imprimatur is taken formally as the decisive event, even though in fact it is not. Electrical codes, for example, are drawn up by the industry and ancillary experts. Thus governmental units who would be put to time, expense, and invocation of expertise do not have to go that route. But it is the local council's action that makes it legally binding. To date, Courts generally accept the formal action as the real exercise of judgment, though in the latter case they will sometimes construe laws obviously promulgated by a clearly advantaged grouping, more narrowly; some state decisions have even referred to "vested interest codes" that should be approached gingerly. In his writings, Richard Posner raises questions about such pressure group use of government, much as Stone and Cardozo did. After much ado, he suggests stricter scrutiny.[11] Perhaps there is no need to go beyond official authorization, and a simple rule of "construction with a jaundiced eye." But the issue is on the table and has been given special attention by the raising of these neighboring questions. The answers that will emerge are clearly already seen as interrelated. Separation and delegation are now understood to be issues of tomorrow, not of yesteryear.

SEPARATION AT THE CREATION

Whether, in order to arrive at the primordial "understanding" of the Framers, one concentrates upon the text, the Convention notes, the ratifying conventions, or the ethos of the times, there is scant evidence of any rigid notion of separation of powers. This is not to deny that the Founders thought separation was a useful principle but, rather, that like checks and balances they thought of it primarily as an architectonic building block, more to guide constitution makers than judges, more as admonishment to each and all branches than as a legal device. Furthermore, checks and balances is paradoxically both supplementary to and antithetical toward separation.

The Founders' concern, as expressed in the ratifying conventions, was mainly to prevent concentration of power in one institution. This could be achieved in a number of appropriate ways. The debate on a Council of Revision (which would have encompassed roughly what are now known as the "executive powers of the Senate" plus the Presidential veto) centered on its awkwardness and the inappropriateness of judicial participation (threatening neutrality), rather than strict cabining of executive and legislative authority. Even on the participation of judges, there was less concern expressed than current readers might expect, and such compound institutions were operating in several states.

However, a draft provision was deleted that would have allowed the President "to execute such other powers not legislative nor judiciary in their nature as may from time to time be delegated." Madison records only Pinckney's comment that the provision was redundant and his own plea to retain the language as clarifying. If redundancy was the true reason for deletion—or even if it was not—it seems clear that the consequence is to leave delegation less channelized, rather than more. But it is equally clear from this small matter that the Founders clearly did believe there were functions inappropriate to the different branches, and that it was an operative concern.

If the Philadelphia debates give little solace to a tight constriction of separation and delegation—indeed the persistent discussions of the Council of Revision remain powerful evidence to the contrary—the constitutional text is on the whole even barer. There is no ringing Massachusetts assertion of water-tight compartments; assignment of power is highly generalized, and the principal reliance for channelization is clearly checks-and-balance, the institutionalization of functional rivalry and friction that such diverse thinkers as Brandeis and Publius (himself a diverse thinker) valued so much. A ringing declaration was drafted for the Bill of Rights, but it did not gain two-house approval and never went to the states.

The sole manifestations of separation are in the vesting clauses, which were clearly the contribution of the Committee on Style, and were presumably therefore not thought of as substantive, even though they subtly differentiate allocated authority ("all legislative powers herein granted" are vested in Congress, whereas "the executive power" is vested in a President and "the judicial power of the United States" is vested in one Supreme Court and others "as the Congress shall establish"). The vesting clauses indicate that functional distribution notions were present, but only Congress is by any stretch of the language given some functional monopoly. Assuming that the Committee on Style was accomplishing more than felicitous generalized introductions to the complexities of each article, it would appear they were making clear the assignment and distribution of power in the Constitution, rather than creating sharp-edged weapons for cutting down the authority of the other branches. Thus the fact that congressional powers are distributed throughout the document suggests the motivation for the assignment of "all legislative powers." The definition of presidential authority in Article II, through broad assignments rather than detailed powers ("Commander-in-Chief"; "take care that the laws be obeyed"), also suggests a less targeted purpose and appropriateness of the broader language in the vesting clause.

In broader terms, too, there is confirmation of the limited bite intended by the Framers. While speakers endorsed separation, they quite generally underscored that approval by quotations from both Montesquieu and Locke, as well as others such as Burlamaqui. Since these theorists differed as to the number of divisions of power, as well as substantively as to the correct units, it is hard to ascribe to them an intent to prescribe a hard-and-fast scheme. (Locke, for example, had differentiated the executive into two functions, the second a kingly remnant involving foreign policy and emergency powers. many theorists of separation did not include the judiciary as a major branch.) Much of the difference among the theorists flowed from their relative familiarity or lack of familiarity with the government of Great Britain, from which the separation notions were developed. Montesquieu particularly fell wide of the mark in this regard. Since Britain was, in any event, in the process of evolution from a Crown-dominated system to a cabinet-dominated system the theorists were in some perplexity, with the less prescient concentrating on the power of a waning monarchy. The fiction of Parliamentary Supremacy was the dominant delusion. All of the theorists, as well as the heavy preponderance of the Founders, missed the fact that the claims of Parliamentary sovereignty was a way-station for a growing reality of cabinet dominance, though Ville makes an argument that Morris showed considerable sophistication on this issue.[12]

Within the American colonies the emphasis on separation of powers had served as an ideological convenience in the attacks upon royal governors. Its popularity rose with the revolutionary struggle, but waned as the colonists experienced self-government. There was little correspondence between the rhetoric and practice of separation, and gradually the principle was largely supplanted by the principles of checks and balances. The early radical Pennsylvania Constitution of 1776, for example, makes no mention of separation but, on analysis, is suffused with it. Conversely, the celebrated separatist formula, Article XXX of the Bill of Rights of the Massachusetts Constitution of 1780, is a somewhat alien appendage to a document (largely written by John Adams), which reflects a quite different sharp, countervailing, contesting of power. And, regardless of the language of the state constitutions the Articles period was characterized by legislative imperialism and extensive encroachment on both judicial and executive functions. Corwin concluded the revolutionary and Articles period use of separation was "verbal merely." This is too sweeping, but hardly fanciful.

Though there are occasional dissents, modern historical research emphasizes an early radical tradition and a later Humean nationalist view of power. The first approach emphasized Republican virtue and a strict cabined separation of powers. The later Humeaians, more mistrustful of human nature, emphasized interbranch checks and balances as building ambition and passion as a subordinate check in these matters. Overlap of these views was considerable in practice.

The growing authority of the checks and balances philosophy was continuously disguised by an insistence on the total compatibility of separation and checks, an insistence that seems almost dialectical. By the time of the Philadelphia Convention, checks and balances were in fact seen as exemplifying (not contrasting with) the basic and essential element behind separation of powers—that authority never be concentrated in a single office holder. As Madison summarized it in Federalist 47, "The accumulation of all powers legislative, executive, and judiciary in the same hands, whether few or many, and whether self-appointed or elective, may justly be pronounced the very definition of tyranny." Of course, distribution of power can be accomplished in many ways, and how this supports absolute intrabranch control is not clear.

David Currie's comment in *The Supreme Court Review*[13] is typical of conventional defenses of the seminal nature of the separations principle, but its blandness is exceeded only by its lack of evidence. "Above all, the distribution of these powers serves as a powerful check against arbitrary action." Lamenting the fact that "today's government bears so little resemblance to the constitutional model," Currie seems oblivious to the fact that it is not only in its deviation from an alleged model of strict separation that government today is vastly different from 1789.

One looks in vain for the clear, unvarnished, dominant embodiment in the Constitution or debates—or elsewhere—of what Currie and others assert so confidently. Forrest McDonald, the iconoclastic, meticulous, and conservative historian seems much more to the mark with his sweeping conclusion that "the doctrine of separation of powers had clearly been abandoned in the framing of the Constitution."[14]

The Founders had no difficulty in rejecting both Crown prerogatives as irrelevant to the American experience and the weak, compound Articles of Confederation executive as proven inadequate to American needs. As Thatch has shown, their institutional model was largely the "strong governor" model of the State of New York, and Washington himself, their personification of an ideal president in front of their eyes as chair of the Philadelphia proceedings.[15]

But they continued to believe in a basic legislative supremacy as the emanation of public concern. The final document continues to speak of public offices as created by Congress, of legislation as that of Congress, even though the presidential signature (or the extraordinary overruling majority) is involved. That this legislative dominance was prescriptive as well as descriptive emerges from the reluctance to give the president any veto, as well as in the debate on the Council of Revision. The reasons that led them to doubt the desirability of vesting any veto power at all in a single individual, doubts which they reluctantly overcame, were those that also led them to deny to the executive the item veto, a power presidents have sought in vain ever since.

Far from being an indication of fixed notions of separation, the ebb and flow of proposals and debates indicates a desire to find mete and appropriate measures to ensure a balance of contradictory impulses, institutional vigor, and mutual interaction. Congressional choice of the president was rejected not on any notion of theory; interestingly, the British cabinet-in-Parliament system was not condemned as a violation by any of the political theorists who seem to have accepted anything they thought British as the embodiment of separation but, rather, rejected on the common sense and experiential argument that it would render the presidency subservient to Congress. The Council debate counterpoised the relative complexities and inconvenience of a cumbersome Senate or unilateral presidency versus a cumbersome body with multiple and divergent institutional loyalties. Ultimately, the Council was rejected in part as the price of resolving other bargains but, in major part as too jerry-built but, insofar as the record shows, not for conceptual reasons.

The Founders, in short, espoused separation, but that notion was defined mainly by the axiom that power should be dispersed, and that no one branch should be judge of its own cause. Intrusions of one branch on the other are, however, clearly built into the system: impeachment by Congress, presidential messages on the State of the Union, the Veto, congressional (actually legislative and executive) authority over Court jurisdiction, and eventually a Bill of Rights motivated by a desire "for the legal check it puts in the hands of the judiciary."

Not surprisingly, opponents of the Constitution argued precisely that it violated separationist elements. The minority report from the Pennsylvania ratifying convention criticizes the role of the Senate on treaties and ratification. But the "pure doctrine" of "separation" was seen by other Anti-Federalists as having failed in practice and they were not able to mount an effective answer to the "separation means checks" argument advanced by the Federalists.[16] To justify this at least paradoxical position, Madison, in *Federalist* 47 (Modern Library, pp. 314–315), reduced Montesquieu to "amount to no more than this, that where the *whole* power of one department is exercised by the same hands which possess the *whole* power of another department, the fundamental principles of a free constitution are subverted." Perhaps even more strikingly, he devotes the rest of the article to prove the thesis that "notwithstanding the emphatical, and in some instances the unqualified terms in which this axiom has been laid down, there is not a single instance in which the several departments have been kept absolutely separate and distinct in state constitutions" (p. 316). *Federalist 48* goes on to echo Madison's main thesis of separation in the Convention: Separation can be effective only if there is a proper blending, afforded in fact by the contrarian dimension of checks and balances.

Above all it is clear that the Founders did not wish to assign to the executive anything approaching Crown prerogatives.[17] The picture of a sovereign presidency in total control of the operative machinery is incompatible with the language of the document which has Congress as the nerve center of the system. An energetic and active executive was sought, but the other branches were to constrain the president even as they were to be constrained, in part by piercing any simple notion of appropriate boundaries. A core concept of each branch's power and limitations indubitably remains and has been one of the fonts of constitutional equilibria. But it is subtle and permeable, not solid and simple.

SEPARATION OF POWERS IN THE FIRST AND OTHER EARLY CONGRESSES

The early Congresses faced these issues in a number of contexts. The most salient contexts involved executive participation in legislative proceedings, the degree of control Congress would legislatively endow the president over subordinates (especially whether they should make dismissal dependent upon congressional approval), and the nature of executive accountability to the judicial branch.

These seminal discussions, the cream of which the "premature conservatives" Charles Hyneman and George Carey assembled in a well-conceived work brilliantly entitled *A Second Federalist*, confirm impressions derived from the Convention. The early congressional debates are suffused with the prudential guidance afforded by the separation of powers, but they surprisingly seldom suggest that such a principle is embodied even in the spirit of the Constitution, let alone legally enforceable limits. On the whole they exhibit confidence that the Constitution bestows legislative freedom to define a wide variety of patterns for the new government, an obligation to use institution-building judgment within some, but nonconstricting perimeters. If the Constitution rejected separation, the early Congress restored it, but not necessarily as a rigid wall, more for practical than theoretical reasons.

This is evident in the rejection of executive participation in Congress. The decision of the Senate not actually to confer with President Washington on treaties (and on appointments) is well known. But parallel decisions were made in the House: for example, not to permit cabinet members to address the full body. One of the major impetuses to the emergence of the committee system in Congress has in fact been an effort to contrive ways of securing executive input without executive influence. Perhaps the early Congresses appreciated better than the Philadelphia Convention the growing domination of the British Cabinet. Perhaps they were merely keener analysts of power; perhaps they themselves were merely hungry for their own authority, but their wisdom seems apparent. Only in multiparty systems do legislatures preserve power independent of a cabinet that is embodied within it. In any event, these strategies were never articulated as dictated by a constitutional necessity of separation.

Removal power was argued partly as a constitutional issue but largely within the political arena. The congressional debate on this issue echoed themes already heard in Philadelphia. The executive was seen as having a need to control subordinates. Energy and effectiveness in the presidency were consistently viewed in both bodies as more important an argument than any constitutional or theoretical reason adduced against such authority. And equation of energy and dispatch as the essence of executive power was fashionable among separationists of the time. Purist arguments were in any event directly confronted, for example, by such speakers as Jackson of Georgia.[18]

Indeed the most pregnant constitutional argument was advanced by an advocate of congressional power, who pointed out that the provision that the president "might require the opinion in writing of the principal officer in each of the Executive Departments upon any Subject relating to the Duties of their respective offices" (Art. 2, sec. 12) hardly implies presidential omnipotence. It suggests expectations of considerable independence of Cabinet officials, and to this day stands as a textual difficulty for the Meese–Scalia advocates of simple executive domination.

The questions of the right of different branches to require or withhold evidence in investigations, trials, or day-to-day affairs clearly did involve claims of separation and need for fundamental autonomy. In point of fact, though, after sparring along the lines of privilege or duty, the branches mutually agreed to accommodations. In *Marbury*, Madison was allowed to be constructively rather than actually involved in the litigations. Similarly, in the *Burr* case, Jefferson refused to appear in court but did provide written answers to Court inquiries. In parallel, Washington insisted that Congress had no right to demand information about the Indian campaigns but would provide evidence. Nonetheless, Raoul Berger's contention that "executive privilege" was a contemporary myth created by the Department of Justice on behalf of President Eisenhower is clearly exaggerated. But presidential assertions have become much bolder and cruder in the past half-century than in our first century-and-a-half. The ultimate accommodation among the branches has generally allowed the investigating branch—whichever it might be—to obtain adequate information, through means face-saving enough to permit both sides to claim legal and moral victory.

THE PRE-*MYERS* CASES: A MEAGER HISTORY

The early decades are not replete with Supreme Court decisions about bright-line delineation of the powers of coordinate branches. Major interpretation of presidential power was treated by the Court as cases of first impression—as to the appointing power in *Myers* (1926) and as to the scope of presidential emergency power in *Youngstown* (1952).[19] It must be realized that issues of structural constitutional law prior to the Civil War were concerned almost exclusively with the delineation of national authority—federalism or vertical division of authority—not separation of powers or horizontal allocation. Furthermore, it was congressional authority (or the limits of national legislative power) that was generally at issue.

Most of the early cases commingle two issues of great importance. They raise separation issues in the context of defining court power. Some cases are rejected because they interfere with separation of powers, but many more essentially reject judicial subordination to decision by other branches because the judges would be assistant administrators unable to do justice in an appropriate way. These concepts criss-cross in complex ways, whether in construing the original Fifth Amendment provision or in the historically more pregnant Fourteenth.

The absence of landmark constitutional precedents in this domain does not mean a total absence of cases. But it is difficult both conceptually and in the fact-situations of the decisions to find much to extrapolate in our more complex world. Thus Corwin characterized the *Youngstown* opinions, as basic as they were, as "bricks without straw."

Not too surprising, and not too helpful, are the firmer line of decisions relating to a separation between judicial and other duties. The courts have refused to assume assigned executive functions, basically because they reflect upon the independence of the judiciary. Resting on this much stronger ground of the need to preserve this essence, such decisions are not equally powerful in defining separation notions, though they are involved and invoked. The operative test for ultimately differentiating a judicial from administrative decision—the finality or autonomy of the judicial decision—so overwhelms any other consideration that the cases are not easily invoked in broader domains, though an occasional sentence will be quoted.

Removal power over the bureaucracy continued to be a constitutionally framed issue, but generally fought in the political arena, as when Congress censured Jackson over removal of the Secretary of the Treasury. Jackson angrily asserted his control over "purely executive officials" and that claim was echoed shortly thereafter by so passive a president as Millard Fillmore, and ultimately in Court language a century later.

An aggressive post–Civil War Congress began to curtail presidential removal, passing legislation requiring advice and consent of the Senate for removal of the comptroller of the currency prior to expiration of a five-year term. That requirement in an 1863 statute was generalized with the passage of the 1867 Tenure of Office Act, which remained in force even though Grant expressly urged repeal.[20]

The early cases were less sweeping. In the early case of *Ex parte Hennen* (1839),[21] the Court sustained legislation vesting removal power of a clerk in lower court judges. In 1854 the chief justice of the Minnesota territorial Supreme Court (not an Article III Court) was removed by the president, relying upon an opinion of the attorney general in *U.S. v. Guthrie.*[22] The majority disposed of the case by ruling the remedy sought—a suit for salary—improper, and the president's action therefore not reviewable. Justice McLean, dissenting, suggested that the presidential removal power over executive officers was now settled by usage (though hardly conclusive on its own terms) but saw no reason to extend the doctrine to any judges—even Article I judges.

The Court also dodged constitutional questions in a succession of cases, by requiring strict construction of any statute limiting presidential authority in *Parsons v. U.S.* (1897), *Shurtleff v. U.S.* (1901), and *Reagan v. U.S.* (1901). Illustrating its attitude of avoidance, the Court, in *Wallace v. U.S.* (1922), held that a dismissed quartermaster could not recover, since the Senate had already confirmed a replacement, implicitly giving its consent to removal, by approving the full complement of such officers.[23]

Only in the case of devolved appointment when Congress had exercised the textually clear power to vest appointment of an "inferior" officer did the Court unequivocally uphold congressional restrictions. In *Perkins v. U.S.* (1886), the Court held "it (Congress) may limit and restrict the power of removal as it deems best for the public interest," extrapolating the textual grant of power to delegate appointment to a congressional right also to limit removal.[24]

The pattern of weak cases and a strong commitment to avoidance of the issue explain the lack of a ruling on the Tenure of Office Act for half a century. Taft, in *Myers*, explicitly notes the Court's earnest desire to avoid a final settlement of the question until it should be inevitably presented, as it is here (*Myers* at 173). It is the essential background of *Myers*, a case that ushered in a modern era of litigation on removal and came in an era in which government employment was emerging as a major factor in the economy.

Delegation issues were also not really handled by the judiciary, especially since the interests of Congress and president proved more often congruent than at odds. As Louis Fisher points out, the first Congress had a discussion of whether the commissioners for the establishment of the District of Columbia could be made responsible to the Congress, and rejected such a policy, expressly delegating authority the following year to the President. The first major delegation case, *The Brig Aurora v. U.S.* 382 (1813), upheld a congressional authorization enabling the president to implement provisions of a bill, when he deemed it necessary to protect foreign trade. Congress could delegate contingency discretion without diminution of claims of legislative power. The principle was amplified a decade later in asserting that at times governance "must therefore in a complex world be a subject of inquiry and determination outside of the halls of legislation."[25] Subsequent decisions—most prominently the *Buttfield* and the even better known *J. W. Hampton* cases[26]—have embellished these notions but are basically in conformity with them. The fullest opinion, *Hampton*, outlines two justifications for the concept that executive decisionmaking is not legislative in nature: (1) Congress has established a process and machinery for the executive to follow; and (2) there are standards and contingencies that condition executive decisionmaking. It is not explicit that both contingencies are necessary nor even that they are sufficient, though the latter would seem to be the case, given the underlying logic of the case. These expansive, broadly understanding and permissive decisions laid the framework for subsequent efforts to lay down boundaries which, like those involving removal, are largely a twentieth-century development.

THE GROWTH OF SEPARATION JURISPRUDENCE

Myers came to the Court with a sitting Chief Justice who uniquely could speak from a previous acquaintance from the Oval Office. The majority opinion by Taft emphasizes the problems of chief executive in controlling the bureaucracy, and the exacerbation of problems of control already faced by a president. His opinion is thus fully in accordance with one line of reasoning, from the Convention on to the present age, emphasizing the need for dispatch and effectiveness—energy, the Founders would have said—within the executive branch.

The Holmes and Brandeis dissents echo objections raised from the earliest times of the Republic as well. The preeminence of the Congress in establishing a system of governance is seen as authorizing the legislative branch to create flexible adjustments, according to Brandeis, as it has historically with only occasional challenges. In general, Congress has been trustworthy and not excessive in achieving that balance, but if not, the executive could and would have to strike back with its weapons. Holmes concluded that Brandeis and Reynolds had demonstrated that Taft's opinion was based neither upon experience nor hard-headed realities but "mere spider's webs" of abstract theory.

The net effect of *Myers* was not theoretical. It was to further and make explicit a new line of constitutional doctrine: Presidential power to remove purely executive officers not only was present but could not be abridged. Presumably, only "inferior officers" were protectable by Congress, as in Civil Service and related measures, and presumably there was a "bright line" ascertainable difference. Taft ran roughshod over history; Reynolds and Brandeis both elaborated instance after instance of Congressional limitations. In a brilliant side-argument largely overlooked, Brandeis pointed out that no one challenges congressional authority to define qualifications and thus limit presidential nominations (expressly provided for by the Constitution). Parallelism suggests that removal (not mentioned) might be qualified as well.

Taft did wrestle with Story's suggestion that Congress had erred in permitting exclusive presidential removal, focusing on the doubts Story expressed as to the effect of historical usage. He ignored Story's suggestion (later echoed by Corwin) that "inferior officers" were the great bulk of office holders. In those cases, "which appellation probably includes 99 of a hundred of the lucrative offices in the government" (sec. 1544), there was no doubt in Story's mind that Congress could simply require "the consent of the Senate to removals," regardless of whether Congress had by inaction given up its other rights.

Taft stressed two things: (1) the original vote in the First Congress on removals (which was only in part based upon arguments that Congress had no authority to limit removal), and (2) that removal was inherently executive, and therefore untrammeled. Oddly, he did not make the argument that the impeachment power was lodged in Congress and that it was arguably anomalous for the Senate to be able to put office holders in some sort of double jeopardy. Understandably, Taft simply ignored the self-styled middle-ground of Solicitor General Beck, who suggested that Congress had the right to specify general terms and conditions of removal, but not to participate in any specific judgment of individual officeholders.

From a doctrinal standpoint, the most interesting part of Taft's sprawling opinion may well have been a half-hearted attempt to formulate a separationist "rule of construction" establishing some entrenchment of separation, an analogy with the Tenth Amendment.

> From this division on principle the reasonable construction of the Constitution must be that the branches should be kept separate in all cases in which they were not *expressly* blended, and the Constitution should be expounded to blend them no more than it affirmatively require.

This rule is attributed to Madison (Annals of Congress 497), and three cases are said to follow it. Perhaps the real reason other opinions have not referred to Taft's abortive "rule of construction" is not the blandness of the cited language in those cases but the rationale in *Merriwether v. Garrett* (102 U.S. 472 at 516), *Kilborn v. Thompson* (103 U.S. 168, 190), and *Mugler v. Kansas* (123 U.S. 623, 662), which actually favors the Court's limiting their claims and allowing other branches to exercise greater discretion.

The great constitutional historian Edward Corwin argued almost instantly (like the Solicitor General) that there must be a middle-ground, but based upon the nature of the bureaucratic position involved. He reasoned that there were degrees of "executiveness" rather than a simple dichotomy. Yet when Sutherland seemed to achieve such a result through attribution of "quasi-judicial" and "quasi-legislative" functions to certain positions but especially the independent regulatory commissionerships, Corwin waxed sarcastic at such patent legal fictions. The Court he said, saw such posts as resembling Mohammed's coffin "suspended between heaven and earth." Rather than scrap separation of powers and falsify the true nature of the agencies, the Court should simply accept some sharing of power over all but heads of departments, or employees of agencies crucial to presidential authority.[27]

Sutherland achieved this by slight of hand in the *Humphrey* case, striking a blow against President Roosevelt's New Deal in the process. Roosevelt had removed Humphrey from the FTC on policy grounds in spite of term restrictions and in reliance on the result in *Myers*. Sutherland ingenuously distinguished "quasi-legislative and quasi-judicial positions" as ones Congress might wish to insulate from presidential control. This functional desirability or independence could be the basis for a decision by the legislature to limit the removal power of officials who were not purely executive.

Purporting to follow *Humphrey*, the Court in *Weiner v. U.S.*[28] actually went far beyond its logic. The *Weiner* decision ruled that "quasis" could be removed only when Congress provided for removal. That is to say, the Constitution per se somehow established the distinction between "pure executives" and "quasis" and by its own terms exempted the nonexecutives from presidential removal, unless Congress chose to further permit removal. Congressional denial was no longer the basis for insulation from presidential power; zero-power of removal for such officials was a constitutional floor. Presidents were therefore dependent on Congress to secure only explicitly legislated removal power.[29] In these decisions the Court was clearly intensifying and reformulating the Sutherland test.

Paralleling *Humphrey's* resuscitation of removal power, the Hughes Court also found new life in the delegation doctrine, the better to strike yet another blow at the Roosevelt administration. To be sure, the delegations of the New Deal era were ambitious and extensive, providing easy targets. Nonetheless, the Court for the first time in history found excessive delegation to be a basis for invalidation, not exposition or constriction of a statute. In the hot oil case, *Panama Refining v. Ryan*,[30] the Court found an absence of the necessary constraints and guidelines: "The Congress did not declare in what circumstances that transportation should be forbidden; or require the President to make any determination as to facts or circumstances." The grant to the president was therefore legislative and, to permit it, was to give Congress *carte blanche* to vest such power to anyone or any body. In *Schechter*[31] the NIRA was labeled by Cardozo as delegation run riot—authorization to the executive that burst the bounds of the Constitution. The attributed authority to private groups to establish standards enforced by the federal government further compounded the delegation problem. Even Cardozo, who dissented in *Panama*, ended up by concurring in *Schechter*. The decision in *Carter v. Carter Coal*,[32] a year later, was even more explicit condemning "private" delegation as legislative delegation in its most obnoxious form.

Still, in *Steward Machine v. Davis*,[33] Cardozo effectively restored the traditional flexibility of standards and guidelines, simply by blandly deciding that case in traditional dimensions and permitting vaguely defined delegations. But the Court had nonetheless shown that the delegation doctrine had teeth and could be used to restrict and not merely ratify congressional acts.

The decisions in *Humphrey* and *Weiner* had immediate and much more far-reaching consequences. They legitimatized the growth (and later expansion) of independent regulatory institutions, a judicially approved alternative to the frowned-upon NIRA. Together with advances in commerce clause decisions, it laid the foundations for the "second New Deal," the Fair Deal, and the Welfare state generally. Kenneth Davis epitomized the situation in fulsome praise he later found embarrassing. In criticizing Marxist predictions of doom and gloom for capitalism, he suggested that Marx failed to anticipate the development of the Independent Regulatory Commission and that the commissions were bulwarks of the system.

Time has demonstrated that "independent" regulation can be a cesspool of iniquity that escapes public scrutiny and that regulation need not be "in the public interest." Nonetheless the major independent, or semi-independent structures like the Securities Exchange Commission (SEC) and the National Labor Relations Board (NLRB) are in fact bulwarks of the modern regulatory regime. The professionalism of these organizations varies over the lot. But at their best they can provide a politically moderately responsive and yet task-oriented direction that is impressive. It is of course precisely the lack of political subservience to the president that encourages Congress to entrust functions to the agencies, and also—but alas—to make their own political demands upon them. For those intent on either White House control or sharp, across-the-board deregulation generically, that independence has become an obvious target.

SEPARATION AND BALANCE SINCE WORLD WAR II

The growth of executive power throughout the world has been evident in this half-century of emergencies, crises, and growing international interdependence. Presidential power has been aggrandized, and innovations enhancing executive authority have flourished. Yet as Richard Pious pointed out, Congress has historically moved to recoup after each such growth of the executive.[34] In our time, Congress has asserted its claims by its own innovations, and by drastically expanding and upgrading its own staff, and by trying to "micromanage" through its own institutional imperialism and the flexing of its legal muscle.

We may contrast the alleged dangers attributed to presidential agreements with the Senate's quiet use of treaty reservations. Presidential agreements (though much less common than generally assumed) cover a wide range of international issues and in many ways have supplanted treaties as the preferred method of conducting foreign policy, avoiding the need for an extraordinary Senate majority. Only salient matters—peace treaties, the Panama Canal, and SALT—are dealt with by treaty. (In the latter case the failure of the Senate to ratify the Strategic Arms Limitations Treaty [SALT] was cured by de facto executive conformity with the treaty.)

The 1950s witnessed a savage debate over the possibility that the president could enter into, for example, an agreement with the Soviet Union forbidding newspaper criticism of the Communist regime. Since the courts treat presidential agreements as on a par with treaties, and therefore self-executing, such an agreement would be part of the Supreme Law of the land. Senator Bricker of Ohio moved for a Constitutional Amendment to control agreements, an effort blocked by President Eisenhower with adroit behind-the-scenes maneuvering.[35] The Supreme Court largely allayed such fears by deciding (in the face of unfortunate language by Holmes in *Missouri v. Holland*, 1920)[36] that neither a treaty nor an agreement could override a clear right granted in the Constitution, a position consistent with a host of Fifth Amendment-taking cases over decades by the courts. A political detente was achieved with legislation requiring that the Executive Agreements must be filed with Congress, which has the option of recording dissatisfaction with such proposals.

The Senate has found it useful from time to time to sneak a "rider" into treaties that enhance its power over the House or executive. For example, it introduced a provision in a treaty with Canada dealing with creation of hydroelectric power, a provision dealing with U.S. disposition of the power, enhancing its policies over the preferences of the House. A Court of Appeals decision invalidated this as the intrusion of a domestic issue into a treaty, and therefore improper, but to this day the Supreme Court has not ruled definitively on the matter. Similarly, a Court of Appeals found that presidential agreements may not transcend the limits of previous legislation, but the reasoning is not persuasive and the distinction between that case and many others treating executive agreements as on a par with legislation is not at all clear. The Supreme Court eventually decided the case on grounds quite independent of that issue. Obviously, it is no coincidence that these somewhat anomalous decisions were reached during the Bricker Amendment controversies and side-stepped by the Supreme Court on settlement of the large issues involved.[37]

Whether there are limits imposed on the treaty power (and by inference on executive agreements) by virtue of structural constraints as opposed to individual rights is much more the problem. Courts have interpreted Field's effusive endorsement of the treaty-making power as extending to any matter "properly the subject of negotiation with a foreign country"[38] as implying a limitation, which I suppose is correct enough. Yet this language is seldom invoked actually to limit any power.

What is interesting is the lack of concern over Senate intrusion, in contrast to major political controversy over presidential authority in similar circumstances. The fact that Congress operates in the open seems to allay fears, since there are many watchdogs in such a situation. Yet there is considerable potential for hidden mischief and less public scrutiny than we usually imagine. There is, in short, a disposition to see the presidency as the most "dangerous branch" in the modern constitutional order, and the history of most countries buttresses that fear.

Congress and the Executive have been consciously vying for power generally. The growth of the White House staff and the congressional staff give both institutions ample aides asserting maximal claims for their own masters (and their own aggrandizement as well). Caught in the crossfire are the agencies, generally loyal to most presidents but keenly aware of congressional authority over butter. Some of the mediating effect of the practical accommodations, the older gentler rules of the game, were lost when the White House staff began to centralize key decisionmaking, including control of choice of personnel. With the proliferation of congressional staffing, agencies now lie in a bipolar political world.[39]

Another conditioning factor has been the change in current attitudes toward judicial standing of agencies and participants. It is now standard, for example, for the Interstate Commerce Commission (ICC) and the Defense Department to be recognized as litigants on opposite sides. More importantly a house of Congress or even individual members may be accorded standing to pursue an issue not of policy substance but of institutional power. Thus Congressman Synar and others challenged Gramm–Rudman, successfully alleging that the challenged provision (though passed by both the full House and Senate) diminished the prerogatives of Congress. A rump was given standing to challenge the determination of the whole. In contrast, it was regarded as a great concession of the Court only decades earlier to permit congress to be represented as *amicus curiae* and allow Senator Pepper in *Myers* and Congressman Hatton Summers to make an oral argument in *U.S. v. Lovett* over a rider forbidding payment to named employees in the Executive.[40]

The modern growth of Court intervention in both interbranch and intraexecutive disputes has been accelerated by generous adaptation of rules of standing, an adaptation developed for a much broader range of issues.[41] The Court also accepted a more pragmatic and much more limited definition of the "political questions" doctrine and has gained confidence that it can handle the issues of interunit boundaries and powers from its familiarity with the issues. In many of those areas, the "big winner" is the judiciary, not Congress or the Executive.

As Louis Henkin has shown, the new attitude toward political questions has transformed rather than scuttled the doctrine at the national level and can be expected to produce the same ruling most of the time. What has changed is the Court's acceptance of responsibility for enunciating a balanced rationale for deference to other branches rather than a hidden black-box process, or a *deus ex machina* result. The justices basically continue to use the same tests of justiciability when the other branches of the national government are involved, though it would appear not against local government. Deference to states has continued to be urged, but as an argument about desirable outcomes, as a special role of the Courts to maintain a system balance. Nationally, though, on separation reasoning, the Supreme Court accepts the fact that there are inappropriate actions, foreclosed to judicial action on constitutionally based as well as prudential grounds. Whether invoking the rubric of "political questions" or not in a specific instance, the Court accepts such inherent limits.

The essence of the misleadingly named political questions doctrine has always been that some matters inherently must be decided outside the courts. Declarations of war, and recognition of foreign governments are often cited examples. The reasons lie in the lack of capacity of the courts, the overweening capabilities of the other branches, the participatory need for a single decision maker, or some combination of them.

A clear "textural demonstrable constitutional commitment" has been and continues to be the major reason for Court refusal to hear arguments, particularly when the court has neither policy competence nor an obvious means of enforcement. When as in, say, deployment of troops in battle a confusion of authority could be disastrous, or Court intervention could undermine a coordinate branch (e.g., congressional power to tax), the use of legal means becomes dicey.

For roughly a century-and-a-half the Court would announce a matter was or was not a "political question" usually with scant explanation. Today it is less inclined to foreclose whole areas of litigation, and more likely to look at the specific issues, which therefore requires a more detailed and concrete justification for nonjusticiability which is therefore both more circumscribed and more definitively attached to an analysis of the functional needs of the different branches.

When an individual's rights are at stake in challenging congressional and/or executive action, the Court will normally resort to "political question" reasoning only if the basic policy is at stake. It is easy enough to grant an exemption from the draft, but harder to invalidate a statute. A challenge to any compulsory military duties as "involuntary servitude" could be dismissed as historically inaccurate, or simply as an issue so broad as to be outside judicial competence. The Court has refused to rule on which of contesting state governments is really in charge, or when a constitutional amendment is adopted. The first decision was rooted in the presidential authority to provide troops on request of a governor, and the delegation of the national government to maintain a "republican form of government" presumably is firmly established. The lack of judicial authority over amendments is much more problematic; it is not clear whether a majority has ever explicitly so held.

While most decisions on general grounds will result in substantially the same end product in particularized cases, there remains the possibility some will not. The black-box process is a cruder one, and more sensitive evaluation allows Justices to decide ultimately that the consequences to separation are negligible and/or outweighed by others.

The most conspicuous example has dealt with congressional internal processes, allocated by section 5 clause to the individual House. The courts historically avoided entanglement except with respect to noncooperative witnesses of congressional investigations. In those instances, the judiciary had been entrusted by Congress with the duty of punishing contempt, since legislative contempt procedure was deemed cumbersome and unfair. Asking the judges to sanction such witnesses also forced judges to examine the rights of those they were to punish.

But in *Powell v. McCormack*[42] the Warren Court dealt with an issue that historically justices would have summarily dismissed. The decision invalidated House denial of a seat to Congressman Powell, taken by an overwhelming vote, exceeding two-thirds. But the action taken was an "exclusion" limited by the Constitution to qualification, while the House clearly was punishing him for misconduct particularly of a financial nature as a committee chair. Since there was a clear violation of the qualification clause, the justices could use "judicially manageable standards" and not infringe excessively on congressional prerogatives. Uncertain of their vote, the managers had sought to exclude (requiring only a majority) and had misused that power. The techniques and tone of *Powell* are quite convincing. (Stewart's solo dissent is based on the fact Powell's claim is moot, and therefore, the Court should not take on such an issue, not over the core argument.)

But no one draws the parallel between *Powell* and *Chadha* because of the obvious difference in ideology and the more important one of function. *Powell* was an intramural dispute, whereas *Chadha* is in the stream of modern heroic efforts to draw boundaries between executive and legislative power, of *Youngstown Sheet and Tube v. Sawyer* (1952).[43] The steel seizure case ended with a curiously inconclusive result with virtually every justice writing a separate opinion. Its major influence was not in Black's stark and simplistic formula (officially the opinion of the Court), but Jackson's more complex concurrence which both acknowledged presidential emergency power and suggested that Congress can curtail and channel emergency power, minimizing but not diminishing presidential discretion. Diffusive and complex, the decision influences much legal thought but controls few decisions.

But *Powell*, in contrast, affects both long-range thought and represents a very clear, and pregnant precedent. Even actions totally within a branch are subject to judicial analysis, albeit one that overwhelmingly should result in a judgment of no judicial control. This follows from both the dissolution of the "political questions" doctrine on the one hand, and the restoration of the "flexible separation of powers" doctrine on the other.

The most important byproduct of *Powell* involves the Senate's current abbreviated process for judicial impeachment. For decades Congress had chosen to ignore judicial misconduct in order to avoid having to devote days of proceedings to a full-fledged trial in the Senate.

Finally, Congress did take up authorization to use a simplified procedure, and proceeded to impeach and convict several judges. The procedure sets up a committee to hear the full case, and an abbreviated (two hours for each side) proceeding in the full Senate. Two removed judges turned to the courts on the claim that only the full Senate could hear the case. Judge Sporkin, who set aside the Senate's removal of Judge Hastings, also distinguished between his case—where Hastings had been found innocent of the charge by a jury—and others where there had been a conviction. Judge Sporkin thus distinguishes the Senate's reliance upon a committee from its reliance upon Court processes, which seems artificially generated.

Nonetheless, the Court gave an emphatic endorsement to the Senate's authority in *U.S. v. Nixon*[44], involving impeachment of a convicted Federal Judge. The majority opinion by Rehnquist, joined by O'Connor, Stevens, Scalia, Kennedy, and Thomas, held impeachments non-justiciable. Souter, White, and Blackmun concurred. White and Blackmun argued for reaching the merits but found the Senate process constitutionally acceptable. Souter agreed with the majority that in general the judiciary should keep hands off impeachments, but would have reserved some authority in extreme cases of denial of due process—as e.g. if the Senate resorted to a coin toss for the verdict.

That impeachment was heard by the full Senate in the early Republic is undeniable, and there is a lingering sense of disquiet over any curtailment of it reflected in Congress's reluctance to employ the simplified process long after it was available. Certainly all senators must ultimately vote, and they should (consistent with due process) understand what they are voting about.

Rehnquist's opinion marshals impressive arguments. The constitutional text mentions no other participants but actually assigns to the Senate "the sole power to try all impeachments." There is no hint from the text that "try" implicates current criminal court standards, and both British and American history suggest otherwise. (Rehnquist has published a work on Senate impeachments and could draw on that knowledge, but the facts are rather clear.) The presence of a clear contextual assignment—including the pregnant use of "sole power"—and the support of historical example is in consonance with other difficulties caused by judicial intervention. Impeachments could be thwarted by delays that could easily last longer than a presidential term, rendering the congressional power illusory. The absence of any discernible constitutional standards would leave the Senate in perplexity, and the courts would be engaged in elaborate rule-making of their own creation. It was, Rehnquist suggested, "counter intuitive" that the Framers would have disarmed this major weapon of the legislature and involved another branch of government without explicit discussion of that co-participation, while still describing the Senate's authority as "the sole power." So, textual analysis history and the inadequacy and, indeed, mischief of judicial intervention as well as respect for the separation of powers dictated a strict hands-off rule.

The consequence of adjudicating rather than merely announcing a "political question" is evident in the strange ratification process of the Twenty-seventh Amendment in 1992. The amendment originally was proposed in 1789 and deals with mid-term salary increases for senators and representatives, paralleling the prohibition on members taking federal office, "the emollients whereof shall have increased" during that term. Congress has long since realized the complexities caused by open-dated amendments and thus has set time limits for ratification so that an amendment has roughly the same meaning as originally involved. In the context of 1992, Congress was in an embarrassing situation over its finances and chose not to contest the question of whether ratification could occur after all this time. The fact that adjudication could occur and would keep the wounds open was probably not determinative in Speaker Foley's mind: The political discomfort level in 1992 was high enough that added pressure was not required. But it certainly added to the decision to capitulate and accept a basically harmless provision.

THE DRIVE TOWARD RADICAL SEPARATION

All of these factors, including the ideological push, have moved to result in a reevaluation of the package of separation and delegation issues in recent decades. The conservative agenda hastened the process, but the claims of all three branches (including the emergence of the Court as a more vigorous overseer of the separation of powers) made such reappraisal necessary—perhaps overdue.

The first sign of reappraisal came, in an unlikely and innocent enough place, the Court's decision in *Buckley v. Valeo*.[45] In that case the Court invalidated a federal election commission which would have consisted of two appointees each by the President, House, and Senate. The appointments clause was controlling in the eyes of the Court, which found no room for legislative appointments to operating agencies. Recognizing that total separation of powers was not contemplated, it nevertheless found the principle to be "the heart of the Constitution." This part of the decision, however, is like *Chadha*—explicitly grounded on a close reading of the text, not abstractions which are added as flourishes.

Chadha is an even more significant and far-reaching decision. In terms of its effects, the single decision doubled the number of acts of Congress ever declared unconstitutional. At stake was a growing pattern of congressional delegation to the executive of power subject to a right of recall of the authorization or reversal of a decision by a vote of one or both houses. Because the executive agency takes the first step and the house or houses may negate the initiative, the device has been known as the "legislative veto." Its invalidation has had conceptual as well as practical constitutional impact.

To Corwin, the executive seemed only to gain by the legislative veto because the initially proffered power was discretionary.[46] If the executive did not find the delegation by Congress to augment its power, no action would be forthcoming. A president could even gauge whether the gains would outweigh the potential loss in authority over subordinates now looking over both shoulders. Justice White, in dissent, argued valiantly in *Chadha* that the device created the "mirror image" of the enactment process, in that all the players—House–Senate–President—could prevent policies they constitutionally could have thwarted by the ordinary legislative route.

Yet, it is difficult not to agree with David Currie's verdict that *Chadha* was "not really a hard case."[47] The majority opinion leans heavily on the precise language of the Constitution, its reiteration of the requirement that legislation be presented to the president, and that both Houses legislate; it is almost as if the document's provisions had been presciently written to avert the legislative veto. Lurking behind the unusually explicit text was the "sorcerer's apprentice" problem of finding a basis for preventing further devolution (to a committee or even a committee chair's veto), should legislation authorize such steps. On both conceptual and pragmatic grounds it was difficult for the courts not to reject even so useful a device. The legislative veto is a victim of a constitutional order that cannot easily wink at anomalies at least in the face of clear words in a usually vague document.

The decision in *Synar v. Bowsher* is a more complex matter. To begin, with the Gramm–Rudman Bill was a Rube Goldberg contrivance, a desperate effort to force Congress to face up to fiscal realities. The ultimate weapon, actually designed to force internal discipline, was either delegation to a designated team of budget types or the "automatic" provisions that were in place in the event the preferred devolution should be (as in the event it was) declared unconstitutional. The contested but preferred method was that reconciliation of income and expenditure would be left to the head of OBM (under direct control of the President), and the head of the Congressional Budget Office (who serves at the pleasure of Congress), and the Comptroller General, who serves a nonrenewable 15-year term. Though the Comptroller's position has from its creation been regarded as the "watchdog of Congress," the long term of office and ineligibility for reappointment were based on the expectation that the officer would also be true decisionmaker exercising independent judgment.

The devolution provision of Gramm–Rudman was to culminate in a decision of unconstitutionality on the grounds that an executive function had been delegated to a legislative official. It was constitutionally irrelevant that the problem was congressional abandonment of its core legislative responsibility over the budget, and the case demonstrates the inherent bankruptcy of any pure concept of separation. It was to compensate for legislative failure that the Comptroller was called on to act, not to function in a presidential mode. (One is reminded of Powell's purposed resolution of *Chadha*; he would have found the action of the House improper because it was exercising a *judicial* function.)

Bowsher, the Comptroller, was deemed a congressional employee because authority to remove was retained by the legislature. Blackmun's suggestion that this never exercised removal power could be invalidated with less inconvenience—freeing the Comptroller from an alleged leash—was ignored by the majority, as was White's suggestion the Comptroller's connection with Congress remained constitutionally minimal.

Having been designated a legislative employee, Bowsher could not be asked to exercise an "executive function"—namely act as a substitute *legislature* in cutting a budget. As Robert Cushman pointed out long ago, the Court's reasoning is at best circular, if not contradictory, on these issues.[48] Since it operates on the principle that legislative power is nondelegatable, whatever is delegated is by definition "executive." In any event, the Court found Gramm–Rudman to be an unconstitutional mismatch.

The *Bowsher* decision was a highwater mark for the new separation amalgam. However, in short order three cases based upon its claims were decided negatively by the Court. Scalia's faith in a strong pure doctrine took on something of the tone of scolding, by a prophet rejected.

In *Young v. U.S. ex rel Vuitton* the central issue was the right of a federal court to appoint the attorneys for the plaintiffs in a case as special prosecutors when the defendants were perceived as having committed contempt of court by continuing to use the Vuitton label after reaching a court agreement to cease unauthorized use. Convicted of criminal contempt by a jury and sentenced to terms ranging from six months to five years, defendants appealed, arguing that courts had no right to hire any prosecutors, or alternatively, that it was improper to use as prosecutors nonneutral individuals with stakes beyond the issue of contempt.

The justices agreed that it was bad practice to use biased prosecutors even for limited purposes. All but White agreed that such practice was illegal, and White would have done so in the absence of a federal rule which he thought authorized the practice. Three justices (including the chief justice) approved the plurality decision, that such practice be banned prospectively, but thought the instant case should be remanded for "harmless error" analysis. The plurality emphasized that the very appearance of partiality made "harmless error" irrelevant.

The key to reversal was Scalia's fifth-vote concurrence which denied courts any power to hire prosecutors at all. The executive, he argued, must make those decisions. Accepting the defense's argument that a judge acting alone could punish only in-court contempt, he argued that just as *Anderson v. Dunn*[49] made Congress dependent on the judiciary, courts had to trust the executive to vindicate their authority in out-of-court cases. Criminal contempt was a crime, and prosecution of crime inherently executive. As Scalia seems to be aware, the argument is unhistorical, and could not have been the "original understanding" since the Founding period was one of transition from English "private prosecution" to the first public prosecution in the world; many forms of selection and control of prosecutors were being tried during the formative years of the republic.

Scalia's position was especially at odds with that of the other justices (including White's) in its overweening claims for the executive. Scalia would have invalidated many longstanding ad hoc arrangements including the practice whereby judges appoint temporary prosecutors, when the Department of Justice dallied over such a choice. Theory was endangering the most plebian accommodations easily cured by executive action at any time.

The "special prosecutor" case drove a deep wedge between Scalia and his colleagues. The Constitution authorizes Congress to delegate appointment of "inferior officers" to heads of departments and to the courts. Given the limited assignment of special prosecutors, such a delegation was upheld in *Morrison v. Olson,*[50] though the justices found the continued monitoring of functions involved not untroubling and admonished the panel to limit its intervention in those respects.

Mistretta v. U.S.[51] seemed to administer a coup de grace to the faltering purism. Mistretta appealed his conviction because his sentence followed guidelines set by the Federal Sentencing Commission. This violated separation in his view. Blackmun's opinion for the majority draws heavily and carefully from Federalist Forty-Seven and makes it clear that separation is a matter of practical concern, not ideology. Speaking for all the justices, he drives the point to its conclusion: "Consistent with the separation of powers, Congress may delegate to the judicial branch any adjudicatory functions that do not trench upon the prerogative of another branch and that are appropriate to the judiciary" (at 66). As to delegation standards, they were clearly more than sufficient.

Scalia had no difficulty with the delegation boundaries or standards. The real problem to Scalia was that the delegation was to a body steeped with constitutional illegitimacy. Since its purpose was to aid the judiciary, it can hardly be in the executive, and *Mistretta* is essentially a "*Humphrey* decision" for the judiciary. *Morrison*, he suggests, was a shock to the system, but *Mistretta* compounded the problem: "today's next step—recognition of an independent agency in the *judicial* branch—makes *Morrison* seem, by comparison, rigorously logical" (at 681). Virtually all commentators echoed Blackmun's suggestion that Madison, particularly in the *Federalist* and subsequent decisions, adopted a "flexible understanding of separation of powers" based upon invasion of core functions and checked power rather than "a hermetic division between the Branches" (at 659). Quietly Blackmun replied to Scalia by answering the plaintiff. "Petitioners' fears for the fundamental structural protections of the Constitution prove at least in this case, to be 'more smoke than fire.'

An even more farfetched challenge on separation grounds was also rejected.[52] Ordered to make restitution for criminal damages to victims, a defendant challenged the assessment as a "tax." If deemed a revenue bill, the original bill creating restitution should, under the Constitution, have originated in the House. The Court did not doubt that what was involved was neither a "tax" nor a "revenue," but in any event the ability of the House to act to protect its own prerogatives was obvious both to the majority and to Justice Scalia, who based his concurrence solely on that ground. Certainly in borderline cases, the Court indicated that the House was the first line of defense of, and was owed respect in interpreting, the origination clause. This concept of the Court's nonintervention to protect an agency not eager to defend itself seems to fit the spirit of Madison's "flexible separation" (i.e., "checks and balances").

But any conclusion that the new doctrine was quarantined and abandoned was quickly belied by an almost unnoticed case, *Washington Metropolitan Washington Airways v. Citizens* (1991).[53] Congress had "ceded" control over the Washington airports, but with characteristic self-solicitude gave a Congressional Board of Review veto over most matters. What was involved was a complex "federalism legislative veto," and the Court responded in an equally complex way. Although the delegation was obviously a "vertical" one—to a local entity—the Court applied "horizontal" standards of delegation to hold the congressional action improper. The "new separation" was held not merely viable, but Stevens's opinion in fact gave it added applicability.

Yet Stevens's decision seems to be more in accordance with conscious past-practice than other separationist assertions. The anomalous role thrust upon Congress by the Constitution to govern the District of Columbia and exercise "exclusive control" was construed historically to require executive enforcers in a strict constitutional sense. Congress must act in consonance with the dictates of being like a local government and a national delegator. It would be a naive individual who did not notice that congressional committees have managed nonetheless to retain congressional influence in matters as different as cab fare zones (which keep fares to the capital low) and protection of flights into the National Airport (minimizing the long, dull ride to Dulles). In this respect, blatant aggrandizement is a red flag. As one of the Congressman noted, "We are getting our cake and eating it too. The beauty of the deal is, that Congress retains its control without spending a dime."[54]

Although Stevens does note that *Mistretta* expressly finds that "separation of power analysis does not turn on the labeling of an activity," he finds it significant that eight of the nine members of the commission were selected from specified congressional committees and therefore removable from the board through reassignment. More importantly, the board, though nominally a local entity, was created at congressional insistence, and was logically an agency of Congress. In effect, he finds that Congress is delegating legislative power to an agglomeration of members of Congress. Quoting his own concurrence in *Bowsher*, Stevens concludes that "Congress may not delegate the power to legislate to its own agents or to its own members."

THE PRESIDENCY AND SEPARATION

The contraction of the political question doctrine, and the line of decisions suggesting limits on presidential emergency power has eased but not eliminated fears on the potential for an "imperial presidency." Congressional efforts to limit the executive through legislative means have also had mixed results, constitutionally and politically. The difficulty in constraining the president in foreign matters is evident in both spheres as a product of the urgency, primacy, and vagueness of the need for national security. The constitutional and legal dilemmas result from the rather general and indeterminate specification of presidential power in Article II. The Founders consciously delineated the functions of the office precisely because they did not believe one could list the powers in a changing world. They expected the legislative to be the aggrandizing institution and Congress to be amply endowed in limiting the president.

It was largely with respect to emergency power that the political questions doctrine was developed. All the classic justifications for nonjusticiability tend to coalesce in the domain of foreign and defense issues: constitutional assignment to a branch of the national government, need for a single decision, unlikelihood of effective judicial action. This enhances the executive and helps to create constitutionally, in parallel what Aaron Wildavsky has noted politically, the "two presidencies" in which the zone of executive operations in foreign affairs is largely unchecked.

Under both the old and new political questions doctrines, the essential authority of the presidency has prevailed in foreign policy and military matters, though reviewability creates both a potential for restraint, and a subtle reminder to the president of the possibility of both legal and political checks. Thus challenges to the Viet Nam War on such theories as violation of Nuremberg principles, or the stupidity of a decision to defend a bastion, get only slightly shorter shrift today than under the older formulae.

Congress's right to restrict the use of funds in specific circumstances has been established, with mixed practical results. Bombing of specified areas or use of troops in specified areas, especially after a cutoff date permitting orderly withdrawal, has become the method of choice in foreign incursions, and the presidency has largely gone through the motions of protesting unconstitutionally. As a legal matter it is hard to see how Congress is deprived of a right to make policy by a presidential need to act quickly. But if the legalities are clear, the practicalities are not. Presidential evasions abound as has been demonstrated by Iran-gate, which involved complex moving of funds from one enterprise (providing arms to Iran through nominally "private" persons) to supply funds to a forbidden recipient (the contras of Nicaragua). Governments, too, can launder money, even using friendly powers for this purpose. Executive departments can mask the providing of expertise and "consultants." Where Congress has sought to restrain the president—for example, requiring congressional assent for deployment of troops within sixty days after the action—presidents have simply found their actions not of the kind limited by the act, and Congress has found itself lacking in will to challenge that determination. In the case of Iraq, President Bush chose simply to go to Congress prior to action rather than comply with the War Powers Resolution; in the main, a president's calculations would seem to suggest the worst of all political situations in complying: having exclusive responsibility for such a move, with Congress evaluating it a few weeks later.

Presidential power over foreign agreements has also been substantially vindicated, with only slightly increased leverage accorded to Congress. Such agreements go on a congressional calendar and objections are filed, leading invariably to modifications. This is a sharing of executive power, analogizing agreements to treaties, and is seen as a modification of historical presidential practice, but one that could be rendered null and void if Congress passed legislation contrary to the agreement. Current arrangements thus simplify without short-circuiting any constitutional requirements. Indeed, such presidential agreements, though regarded from the earliest years as implied and necessary to implement foreign policy, are not constitutionally provided for and have been justified solely as an adjunct of presidential power to carry on foreign policy.

The mystery is how such agreements have been enshrined as part of domestic law, as opposed to their binding nature in international law. Unlike many countries, the United States recognizes treaties as part of domestic law without concomitant legislation. Treaties are "self-executing" because the supremacy clause recognizes them, legislation, and the Constitution as the "supreme law of the land." Having equated presidential agreements with treaties, the Court in the 1930s explicitly recognized domestic consequences from such agreements, though there is not mention of them in the supremacy clause. On any logic this would seem to be the single most far-reaching violation of "original intent" separation since the executive changes domestic law unilaterally.

This, as noted earlier, raised a storm of protest, and a proposed constitutional amendment (the Bricker Amendment) climaxing in the Eisenhower years. The drive for the amendment lost steam when the Supreme Court ruled that treaties as well as presidential agreements could not per se deprive anyone of rights, including property, guaranteed by the Constitution. For example, our treaty with Iran which in effect exchanged properties confiscated by that country for assets held here, was upheld only because it specifically allowed the owners of the assets to sue the United States for their property. The case that established that principle involved an agreement that American civilians accompanying troops stationed in Japan could be tried by U.S. military courts. The treaty, it was held, could not deprive civilians of the right to a jury trial. If treaties were limited, so too were presidential agreements (*Reid v. Covert,* 354 U.S. 1, 1957). This legal adjustment was paralleled by the political conciliation offered by tabling such agreements for Congress to act on.

The momentous issue of presidential emergency power has been given a bit more definition by *Youngstown.* The conclusion from the multiple-opinion morass is that Black's opinion is an oversimplification; both dissenters and concurrers agreed that an unpredictable emergency power inheres in the presidency. Some of the justices prefer to hide this conclusion behind a figleaf: the vesting clause's "executive power," the "take-care" clause, the "commander-in-chief" role. Admitting the obvious—that there are gaps in the Framers' scheme—strengthens presidential claims but allows a bit of realism to sink in too.

More importantly, the majority not only invalidated President Truman's seizure that was involved, but also laid the foundation for review of presidential domestic actions taken in the name of foreign affairs. Jackson's elegant statement of the theme that presidential power is at a maximum when conjoined with Congress but at a minimum when in opposition is echoed in most of the concurrences, and is solidly based upon important cases like the *Curtiss-Wright* decision, and provides the impetus for, among other developments, subsequent congressional efforts to limit the executive. Above all else, the decision establishes for the federal government the equivalent of *Sterling v. Constantine*[55] on the state level: Federal courts must decide whether executive invocation of emergency meets reasonable conditions. The executive may not bootstrap itself into total power by declaring an emergency and then taking decisive steps to deal with its self-proclaimed problem. This is not a lot, but it is something, and it may be the most important something any society needs or can afford.

The implied challenge by Jackson to Congress to achieve constitutional balance through its own actions has been heeded and has achieved quite a bit. Presidents have had their powers to pick out from existing expenditures, by congressional actions vesting rights in appropriations, by explicit language, minimizing presidential authority to impound funds and therefore make the final efficient decision as to real appropriations. To be sure, Congress was here curing a disease where it had itself been the carrier. By over-appropriating, yet maintaining expenditure and debt limits, Congress for years forced the presidency into the impoundment role and then seemed shocked at its use for political and ideological purposes. The courts have generally approved congressional fiscal power to so rein in the president, absent a clear invasion of individual rights or (as we have seen) clear executive prerogatives, especially in the face of congressional language.

Troubles between Congress and president produced two other landmark decisions although clouded by the specific circumstances. A president's right to confidentiality of advice were constitutionally conceded in *U.S. v. Nixon*[56] but circumscribed as a conditional privilege. The showing by Special Prosecutor Cox that specific tapes of conversations recorded by the president were crucial to determining the veracity of key witnesses, and the specificity of the intrusion outweighed the presidential claim. Similarly, Congress required President Nixon to leave behind tapes and documents that executives had normally been allowed to take with them. A case of presidential wrongdoing had been built up, but by Nixon's resignation and President Ford's extension of a pardon, resolution of the issue had been made unlikely. Since Congress allowed Nixon to seek financial recompense, the resigned president was not wronged by what some called a bill of attainder.[57] The unique legislation was a product of a singular (hopefully unique) situation.

IS THERE A DELEGATION DOCTRINE?

The contradictions in separation theory operate with a multiplier effect to engulf delegation theory. If one cannot identify what is being delegated, how can one limit its quantity or its propriety? Under such circumstances it is indeed tempting to move the issue from proper delegation, to finding the proper agent to whom to delegate.

Locke found the problem simple. As agents of the people, the legislature had no right to entrust that power to anyone, but personally and collectively had to exercise its responsibility. Thus any authorization of properly cabined authority to anyone was by definition executive (or more rarely judicial). The delegation of authority creates particularly vexatious problems as to the growth of administrative structures not provided for in the Constitution. This reaches the point where scholars suggest a crisis of legitimacy for a fourth, imperfectly justified branch of government.

Such theoretical crises are of rather more interest and concern to scholars in schools of public administration than to politicians or the public. And there is little evidence that even the bureaucrats lose any sleep over the absence of a specific clause in the Constitution to sanctify their posts.

Nineteenth-century European theory translated much the same legal-theoretical heritage into a simpler doctrine. All government was created by the people, and therefore, all structures of government (including the judiciary) derive their power from the legislative matrix of power.

In our system, delegation has been scrutinized but only twice invalidated and only infrequently reconstructed to fit the claims of constitutional propriety. Only in *Panama* and *Schechter* has legislation failed to meet the tests judges impose based on *Hampton and Co.* and its predecessors. Given Congress's record on unconstitutional legislation in other domains, this record is nothing but extraordinary. It is in fact necessary to explain why the presumption of constitutionality is so effective in what might at first sight appear to be a difficult and sensitive area replete with minefields.

Both logic and history provide the answer. It is the precariousness of the definitions that has caused the Court to tread ever so carefully, and the lack of definition that has historically caused the Court not to enter this thicket. But it has managed to create and maintain an aura of judicial review, and has been content with legislative forms of conformity and the leverage that statutory construction, including construction to avoid unconstitutionality, affords it.

The Court operates with a formula that is both plausible and formally irrelevant—the "intelligible principle" rule. Plausibly, the justices agree, Congress cannot set out totally ministerial instructions. The legislative task becomes one of providing an outline for day-to-day governance, constraining and guiding the executive task. The issue once known as adequacy of legislative standards has figured in cases since the early Republic. What has emerged is the formula that the executive function is to work within guidelines, and Congress is not delegating "legislative power" when executive power is sufficiently reined. The executive is seen as engaged on a fact-finding mission. When a predetermined fact arises, the executive fits the situation to a predetermined role, and as agent for Congress announces a result. Of course, the Court is fully aware that in a real and complex world agents have to adapt the prescribed system to cope with emergent circumstances, and thus they ask only that Congress create a reasonably ordered regime, not a determinate one. In recent decades the Court has summarized the approach with what was a casual phrase in *Hampton*—the "intelligible principle" concept—but the thinking behind it is coterminous with Court reasoning.

But it does not follow that each and every governmental set of constrained discretion is inherently "executive," and the Court must be aware that this is a way of avoiding a will-of-the-wisp definition of essences by adroit substitution of a judicial rule of thumb. This permits the justices to wrestle with the definition of each branch's essence in concrete situations and in specific historical contexts. The difficulty is rather that the delegation test is not really helpful in determining what can be delegated; this is cured by the Court's behavior in not taking it too seriously.

The "intelligible principle" could have been a sharper, more consistent test than that of setting standards. The original test, supposedly designed to deal with the occurrence of specific predetermined fact situations, had from its beginnings been blurred by being embedded in the vaguer context of loose standards of delegation and further diluted by the suggestion that a determinate process for fact-finding also helped distinguish proper delegation to the executive from improper delegation.

More recent cases do not confute the two and ignore process as a delegation. The reason is in part that *Hampton* is taken as having codified the true nature of delegation, so that it is not necessary to discuss in detail the general theory of delegation (where procedure is part of the proof of the constitutional legitimacy of delegation). It is sufficient to set forth the *Hampton* and subsequent standards, and test both the specific standards and process against those established ones. But it also seems to reflect a mindset that the primary test is based upon the content of discretion, that procedures that cannot cure excessive discretion but must meet independent tests—especially, of course, due process grounds.

Since an "intelligible principle" seems to be more precise than "standards" (which need not have coherence), and since procedures are seemingly no longer seen as an alternative by which a delegation is properly justified, it would appear that the post-*Hampton* era is one of tighter Court control, and that *Panama* and *Schechter* should be hailed as harbingers of the present, but of course, that is not the case.

The reason lies in the Court's subtle transformation of the shibbeleth into "any intelligible principle" or even "any plausibly intelligible principle." Unable to find a real handle, they have historically accepted Congress's guidelines as constitutionally defensible when these seem to have no bite at all. The justices themselves make this point in most decisions, citing as the best evidence the cases in which they have accepted "the public interest" as a sufficient "intelligible principle" for a congressional delegation. Few administrators or legislators claim to regulate for the public detriment.

In *Touby v. U.S.*[58] the Court seems to be citing with approval plaintiffs' argument that the main advantage of the intelligible principle test is that it permits judicial review of agency means–ends relations. But if so, there is little evidence that the justices believe in, let alone apply, such a rule.

In *Mistretta*, Justice Scalia summarized the situation in terms more flattering to both Congress and the Court, but essentially drawing the same picture. Delegation, he wrote,

> must be fixed according to common sense and the inherent necessities of . . . government coordination. Since Congress is no less endowed with common sense than we are and better equipped to inform itself of the "necessities" of government . . . it is small wonder that we have almost never felt qualified to second guess Congress regarding the permissible degree of policy judgment that can be left to those executing or applying the law.[59] (At 416)

Does this support that there then is no room for a delegation doctrine? More particularly, might it be sensible for the Court to coordinate its activities totally under the separation doctrine which overlaps and undergirds delegation theory anyway?

There are several discernible ways in which a delegation has been historically challenged or overridden: (1) by the subject matter delegated; (2) as to the governmental entities involved, by the nature of the delegator or the identity of delegatee; (3) by the manner and terms of the delegation; and (4) by the extent of the delegation.

The vaguest of these is the last and yet in some ways is the clearest. The charge in *Schechter* that had power even over Cardozo and Stone was the breadth of the allocation. In some sense it is clear Congress cannot constitutionally give away its total legislative power, though it is not clear whether that is ultimately a political or a legal question. The Constitution, for example, suggests that martial law is highly circumscribed, and it would appear that Congress could not create presidential rule by decree without bursting the bounds of the Constitution. Rational legal discussion would probably be to no avail under any circumstances where such an extreme event would occur, but one would hope in most instances the Court would go down fighting. Although it would rally around the Madisonian flexible concept of separation, objecting on delegation grounds would be logically helpful too. Such a doctrine seems mischievous under other less extreme circumstances. If NIRA had been successful and vital to economic recovery instead of an administrative catastrope, the Court's decision might have been both deleterious and divisive, and perhaps ultimately futile.

The other three bases are much more in the nature of live and cross-cutting issues. Delegations may be objectionable because they require judges to make decisions under conditions whereby they are subordinate to executive officers (thus objectionable essentially on the grounds of independence of the judiciary), or because, for example, the death penalty is delegated to an executive officer. To be sure, executive officers make decisions identical to those of members of the judiciary (compare, e.g., Art. I and Art. III judges), but some matters are "inherently"—that is, instinctively—judicial. Similarly, the seminal legislative taxing power cannot be delegated, since Congress may not delegate "legislative" authority, even though it can function with some flexibility internally.[60] Chief Justice Hughes suggested that the wording creating "one Supreme Court" made it impossible for adjudications to be made (as in most world appellate courts) by panels. It is easier to justify these holdings as violating *both* separation and delegation, and that may be adequate grounds for preserving a nettlesome and inadequate basis of decision.

This elementary breakdown suggests that separation theory would at the least have to be supplemented by the specific terms of the Constitution to produce some of the results the Court has found desirable in the past and would be wise to retain. There would be times when the Court would be hard pressed also to explain why functionally similar delegations to identical participants were objectionable on the grounds of the need to preserve separation since consent of the branches was involved. Delegation doctrine could easily be dispensed with and would in most instances simplify analysis. But it would also have the additional effect of weakening and limiting the doctrine of separation.

PRIVATE GROUPS AND DELEGATION

Lurking in the shadow of the current delegation reconsideration is the murky unresolved issue of delegation to nongovernmental groups. This issue was a focal one in the anti-NIRA cases and supposedly routed, yet in fact such delegations permeate our administrative system. For example, the Court has held constitutional many rights of choice devolved to farmers and agricultural producers including a veto right by organized farmers over price determinations made by the Secretary of Agriculture. These arrangements were upheld within three years of *Carter*.[61] These are choices superficially "legislative" (i.e., largely discretionary), but are labeled for constitutional purposes "executive" and "administrative" and operate within broad, even wide-open, contingencies. Many such arrangements have rather precise legislated or administratively established procedures, but virtually all have broad purposes, such as "controlling deleterious competition" or "maintaining the purchasing power of farmers." In those respects they nominally meet traditional standards and are arguably (not overwhelmingly convincingly) more channelized and cabined than the NIRA. Certainly that is true with regard to the total scope of any single agricultural regime under congressional legislation. But the cumulative effect is not necessarily that different from "delegation run riot." It is usually piecemeal but is surprisingly far-ranging in the aggregate. The fact remains that the delegation of authority is to private hands, a practice that was held in the New Deal cases (and never repudiated on that point by any opinion of the Court) to be a cardinal and ineluctable sin.

Such delegation is commonplace in our government and includes the role of banks in selecting the leadership of the Federal Reserve System, that of unions and management in the operations of the federal apprenticeship programs or of failed programs like OEO's old "CAP" neighborhood structures. If a tightened noose is to control delegation within the federal government, and limit federalized devolution of power, it must logically begin to have consequences for the least well legitimized delegation power of them all.

In the absence of judicial constraints, such governmental, quasi-public, and private partnerships are likely to be resorted to on a greater scale. The growth of bureaucracy to liberate the citizenry, known as the "welfare state," has universally proceeded to have a paradoxical (some would argue predictable) negative, consequence. While providing "safety nets" to empower the disadvantaged in society as to some minimum sustenance and opportunity, they make the costs of citizenship higher by creating a host of arenas—most of low salience—that make it difficult to understand and control the policies involved. One must become an expert on, for example, housing or health, pay close attention to a myriad of subagencies, discover the dates of hearings, and ensure that protests are filed by a specific deadline. Each arena is a separate and closed world.

Western democracies have evolved three general strategies to deal with the situation:

1. The British increased normal political supremacy, and Parliament devolved nonreviewable discretion on appropriate government officials. They in turn permit low-level

"friends-and-neighbors" decisions to be made under the umbrella of that broad discretion. When the system works, it is efficient and minimizes friction. But when there is a breakdown at any level, no one is truly accountable, except in the rare instance where it rises to a political issue normally in Parliament. This breakdown results in some spectacularly arbitrary miscarriages of justice. As a result, British courts, aided by the EEC, have taken timid steps toward the legal model favored by the United States.

2. The Scandinavian model is overtly and legally to coopt major groups into the process of formulating, adopting, and implementing programs. To some extent, this freezes political power and also makes changes in policy difficult. Some reviewability by the judiciary and less formal judicialization—the ombudsman is an example—have characterized these systems. The rejection of socialism in recent years has not jeopardized the basic order as yet, though more flexible adaptation is being sought. The system works fairly well because of the homogeneous nature of the society, and the relatively small cross-cutting of the major interests involved.

3. The United States and France rely on judicialization but in sharply different ways. The Gallic bureaucracy relies on official innovation and discretion, tempered by internal legalized review. The Conseil D'Etat is a spectacularly successful, highly independent channelizing instrument. Like its parent bureaucracy, the Conseil D'Etat remains elitist, even patronizing. Political controls gain impetus particularly when Socialist or other reformers come to power.

The United States has had a relatively weak, patronage-dominated bureaucracy with generally low élan. (Some eras and agencies are exceptions.) Presidential control over agencies has varied enormously but has grown in recent decades with the White House staff and new technology and management innovation. The freedom from the executive afforded by "independent" status has furnished the stage for congressional claims of authority, and in some instances "cozy triangles." These are explicit or implicit alliances between an agency, the supervising committee, subcommittee, and/or chair, and the regulated group. Such arrangements, often called "iron triangles," are both more vulnerable, especially when publicized, and less frequent, than in populist demonology of regulation. They are nonetheless realities.

The American model is held in reasonable check through judicial oversight. This tends to be sporadic and varies not only with variations in authorizing statutes and fact situations, but also with changing reputation of an agency. While some have extolled its virtues, especially its minimization of interest politics,[62] judicial oversight has been demonstrated to be expensive, time consuming, of unpredictable effectiveness, and often demoralizing to administrations.

Corporatist decisionmaking with all its unpredictability is, like voting and other forms of participation, a creative act for participants. It introduces nonelitist possibilities even with restricted access. It creates a base of support for administration. It is, in short, firmly based in social realities and is even a building block for many theoretical utopias.[63] With all of these advantages, it would be tragic if thwarted by artificial theories such as separation. But like posses channelized into juries by the legal order, the administrative structure would benefit from innovative ways of ensuring responsible—and controlled—involvement in decisionmaking. Indeed, left untamed, the potential for evil in participation rivals the potential for good. Like other governmental devices, "civilian" participation can be a source of abuse of the political order. Thus it was an omnipresent weapon for racial discrimination against tenant farmers (disproportionately black) in the South in the 1930s, by organizing and supporting the dominant landlords.

But such participation has grown in our society, and has been sanctioned largely in indirect ways by the courts. The most clear-cut development has been a growing exemption of such efforts and ensuing regimes from antitrust liability. The Supreme Court has done so, following the logic of *Parker v. Brown*[64] which sustained state-sponsored growers cartels aimed at restricting supply of agricultural products to the market. It was not reasonable to suppose that Congress intended to foster activities that would later be declared illegal and subject to damages under antitrust laws; and thus an implied exemption has been explicitly granted. This is in one sense a curious way to acknowledge devolution to private groups. But since it is a side effect of federalism, it is not surprising that the ultimate issue was only indirectly addressed.

The Court has also expanded exemption by following an alternative holding in *Parker*, namely that the antitrust statutes were in any event not intended to apply to state-sponsored regulatory schemes which as public measures, were not legislatively regarded as "conspiracies." It has even refused to adjudicate a "camel's nose" argument that a cable TV's granted monopoly within a city was in fact an enrichment of the company and public officials, and in no sense a regulatory measure.[65]

There is one area where the majority of the Court, drawn like the dissenters from all ideological wings, has enunciated a strong stand against delegation to private groups, and that is when pricing is essentially left in their hands. When price is developed in a fully controlled system, it is protected by the *Parker v. Brown* rationales. But if the state simply adopts prices or totally delegates prices, the Court labels this a "hybrid system" and, although admittedly a matter of statutory interpretation, will find a violation of antitrust.[66] Presumably the logic is that total control of price is protectionist and a denial of free flow of commerce so clearly prohibited that Congress would expressly have to create such an exemption. The absence of real state control makes it unlikely that Congress truly wished to allow the practice.

It does not follow that these off-hand acknowledgments of state regulations and acceptance of private groups in regulatory regimes will be ultimately deemed to have any connection with federal delegation standards. The courts are playing with statutory construction in somewhat fanciful ways, but they are still a long way from constitutional contradictions. The state actions, after all, must be justified under local constitutional standards as well as federal. It is not unheard of for the federal courts to accept cases with promises conditioned on state standards that would be precluded as direct action by the federal government (e.g., taxpayer suits).[67] The state courts can also wrestle with the tricky delegation issue under their own constitutional tradition. Still, such "two-tier" standards are not abundant and are usually often fragile. Certainly the courts would be expected to offer some exculpatory remarks explaining a difference.

If the federal doctrines became sharply limiting, state constitutional doctrine could easily become challengeable on due process grounds. The quietly friendly interpretation of federal legislation could also be at risk.

SIGNIFICANCE OF THE "NEO-CLASSICAL" SEPARATION THEORIES

There is an extensive literature in public administration as to the legitimacy or lack of it for the "fourth branch of government" in the Constitution. Whether there is sufficient rooting of administration in that document is perhaps a matter of philosophical taste. But clearly the Constitution provides a basis for our construction of modern institutions as well as the old.

The "legitimation" of the administration rests upon its ultimate enfranchisement by the "popular" branches of government and reflects the powers conferred by those agencies. This dependence and reflected power are concededly contemplated by the Constitution. It is the size and scope of administration and the degree of penetration of social interests that are out of line. In a sense, these antimonies reflect the debate on legitimacy. Like nineteenth-century parliamentary theory, which asserted simple command from people to legislature, and from legislator to administrator, such an approach omits any realistic view of the process and its difficulties. These anomalies existed in 1789 also, though two centuries were inevitably to exacerbate them.

As Justice Jackson argued in a narrower sense, the parameters of administrative activity present a minimum of difficulty when president and Congress are in concert, for the bureaucracy then essentially exhausts constitutional national power. But when president and Congress conflict, the questions quickly compound. Who's entitlement is the root of administrative authority? Who is to control? Who is the true avatar of the majority? Who sets the boundaries? What is the interest of society in expansive power over limited government of executive dynamism versus pockets of independence?

These issues become more significant at times of expansion or deflation of bureaucracies, as new structures are created and new limits are explored. Changes in idealogy generated conflict and litigation. Divided partisan authority between president and Congress will maximize the effect of those cleavages. In this best-and-worst of times that so neatly describes our (and almost every) era, reappraisal of separation and delegation doctrine was likely, and it is now a reality.

With division and conflict between the executive and legislative branch has come a breakdown of the rules of the game. Congress has attempted to circumvent the basic rule that it acts as a legislative body and does not delegate final authority to a subgroup. The executive accepted, albeit under protest delegation with the "legislative veto," then turned around to bite the string attached.

The courts have historically played a reluctant game in drawing such lines between their national powers, but when the two branches throw down gauntlets, courts are forced to pick up the gauntlet for one side or the other or, at a minimum, help define the rules for the ensuing duel. The arrival in the courts of idealogues interested in resolving those issues in ways highly delimiting the possibilities of any regulation at both national and local levels has accelerated the push definitively to answer questions left dangling for two centuries and perhaps best kept unresolved.

The Supreme Court had developed a practical though uninspiring *modus vivendi*. The distinction between "purely executive" offices and those with "quasi-legislative" and "quasi-judicial" responsibilities has been an easy target of pundits and precise thinkers. Corwin, who had all but called for some such test, derided it and was fond of quoting the young lawyer in an early post-*Humphrey* case who indicated that the regulatory commissions were not in the executive branch. Justice Sutherland somewhat sardonically inquired where, only to be told, "in the judiciary." "And where did you get that idea?" "From your opinion in *Humphrey*" was the reply that silenced Sutherland and elated Corwin.

The Humphrey-Weiner standard—which facilitated congressional-sensitive evaluation of degrees of independence necessary—was constructed of whole cloth itself, woven of "spiders' webs." But it accomplished the purpose of Corwin's original suggestion—balancing presidential and legislative concerns—with a constitutional fiction.

Validating either branch's extreme claims does not have the same flexibility and has no great constitutional warrant either. Leaving the executive to the tender mercies of Congress, making all power over subordinates subservient to the legislative power, has historically been rejected as improvident. Limiting all operative functions of the United States to White House control—eliminating professional independence, peer review, the substantive independence of Article I judges—for an abstraction that every schoolboy can demonstrate to be theoretically unsound, and historically never embraced, is equally unfortunate. It would leave Congress with only H-bomb solutions: abolition of positions or resort to political impeachment. The early Congresses, in little conflict with the president, created a latitudinarian system. It is strange to attempt an even more puristic system, deemed simplistic then, in a twentieth-century atmosphere.

The claim for executive control is neither inherently liberal nor conservative, whether viewed in classical theory or in the context of American politics. Historically executive dominance has usually been a Tory program, but not in American politics where social reform has tended to be the product of presidential reform.

The earliest claims against congressional involvement with agencies were probably put forth in vigorous form by Lloyd Cutler, who was a White House counselor under Jimmy Carter, in the heady days when deregulation was seen as a positive (and not merely a ground-clearing) stage of evolution. But Cutler's position on constitutional grounds was more hedged, and he embraced limits on executive power totally to control administration.[68] There can be no doubt, however, that the call for executive dominance is ultimately an antiregulatory agenda.

Of course, if one wishes to deconstitutionalize the modern welfare state, such a program makes some sense. Making all federal power directly subservient to the White House is a concentration of power that should frighten social theorists and reformers. The irony of accomplishing this in the name of "separation" is merely an additional oddity. Congressional willingness to consider programs and structures would of course decline with such an empowerment of an autocratic presidency.[69]

The separation–delegation pincer has been accompanied by a neoclassic revival of Justice Field's concept of "takings," in which governments have to reimburse property owners for regulatory costs and escalating costs, thereby limiting regulation at the state and local level. We could then have a neoclassic revival of the 1920s "twilight-zone" (when federal regulation was cramped by the commerce clause) Tenth Amendment jurisprudence of the time, and local regulation was constrained by the due process clause.

Judicial libertarians will welcome political paralysis and expansion of laissez-faire. The "takings" doctrine is old wine, with a new but appropriate label. It has a good history. But the paralysis at the federal level—a product of heightened conflict between Congress and the president and fear of an overweening executive—should not be understood as furthering separation of powers, but rather threatening a concentration. This program's reputed origin in an "original understanding" is to understate the case, doubtful on both theoretical and historical grounds.

The real need is to restructure "separation" on the basis suggested by Corwin, or to perpetuate the same sort of evasive formulae as the *Humphrey* doctrine. It wasn't actually broke, but it was cracking. Present efforts do not seem promising. Ultimately we shall be forced to fix it.

REFERENCES

1. *INS v. Chadha* 103 *S. Ct.* 2764 (1983).
2. *Carter* 298 U.S. 238 (1936). *Panama* 293 U.S. 388 (1935). *Schechter* 295 U.S. 495 (1935).
3. 301 U.S. 548 (1937).
4. 276 U.S. 394 (1928). It should be noted that in *Touby v. U.S.* 111 S.Ct. 1752 (1992), Scalia joined in upholding the "intelligible standard" in delegation.
5. *Humphrey v. U.S.* 295 U.S. 602 (1935), in an opinion by Justice Sutherland, sustained Congressional power to insulate "quasi-legislative" and "quasi-judicial power" from the long-and-immediate reach of presidential authority. That removal power of "purely executive" officials had to be vested in the president was the main holding of Taft's opinion in *Myers v. U.S.* 272 U.S. 52 (1926).

6. *Bowsher v. Synar* 478 U.S. 914 (1986).
7. Congress has adroitly responded actually to tighten control in many instances, by "legislative veto look-a-likes" that avoid the specific pitfalls cited in *Chadha*. See, e.g., Harold Koh, "Congressional Controls on Presidential Trade Policymaking After *INS v. Chadha*," *Journal of International Law and Politics 18*: 1191 (1986). Jessica Korn in a 1991 APSA paper entitled "The Political Effects of Separation of Powers Jurisprudence" has done a quantitative study of 183 vetoes doomed by *Chadha*. Congress left three quarters of these intact. Nineteen percent either expired or had severability clauses. While the remaining 56% are presumably now unrestricted delegations, she finds them relatively unimportant politically or even dead-letters. More importantly, the amended 25% divides roughly 2:1; the presidency gained (but not typically an absolute delegation) in 17%, but Congress actually tightened the strings in 8% of the cases.
8. 487 U.S. 677 (1988). See, in particular, footnote 29 criticizing Scalia's claims for presidential exclusivity. Scalia also makes an interesting argument (undiscussed by the other justices) that congressional legislation dealing with the other two branches has no presumption of constitutionality. The majority does distinguish between self-aggrandizing acts of Congress (e.g., legislative vetoes) and others, but as a factor in dealing with the legislation, nor as a rule of interpretation. See also *Mistretta v. U.S.* 109 *S. Ct.* 647 (1989), for the guidelines decision.
9. 111 *S. Ct.* 2298 (1991). Rehnquist (and Marshall) joined White's dissent which urges a narrower interpretation of *Chadha* and *Bowsher*.
10. *Minnesota v. Cloverleaf Creamery* 449 U.S. 456, 477 (1981).
11. Richard Posner, *Economics of the Law* (Boston: Little, Brown, 1972), Chapter 23.
12. See M.J. C. Ville, *Constitutionalism and the Separation of Powers* (Oxford: Clarendon Press, 1967), p. 155 on Morris; and Chapter 6 generally for the broad distinction. J. A. Pocock and Forrest MacDonald are among the more significant other writers on these themes.
13. David P. Currie, "The Distribution of Powers After Bowsher," 1986 *Supreme Court Review*, pp. 20–39. It should be noted in fairness that Currie does not set out to provide a detailed outcome but "a concise general view of the distribution of powers" (p. 21).
14. Forrest McDonald, *Novus Ordo Seclorum* (Lawrence: University of Kansas Press, 1985), p. 258. The volume generally pays close and impressive attention to concepts and history, and its step-by-step sensitivity to the flow of events limns a complex reality rather than a simple unanimity.
15. Charles Thatch, Jr., *The Creation of the Presidency, 1775–1789: A Study in Constitutional History*, Baltimore: Johns Hopkins University Press, 1923.
16. See Ville, *Constitutionalism and the Separation of Powers* (Oxford: Clarendon Press, 1967) esp. pp. 141–157.
17. W. W. Crosskey, *Politics and the Constitution*, Chicago: University of Chicago Press, 1953, argues that some provisions are specifically designed to grant or limit prerogatives, but that is a more complex argument.
18. *Annals*, June 19, 1789, 1st Cong., 1st Sess., pp. 553–554
19. *Meyers v. U.S.* 272 U.S. 52 (1926).
20. See on this and many other issues Louis Fisher's highly useful *Constitutional Conflicts Between Congress and the President* (3rd Edition, Lawrence: University of Kansas Press, 1991), especially pp. 58 ff.
21. 13 Pet 230 (1839).
22. 58 U.S. 17 (1854).
23. *Parsons* 167 U.S. 324 (1897); *Shurtleff* 182 U.S. 419 (1901), *Reagan* 189 U.S. 311 (1901); *Wallace* 257 U.S. 541 (1922).
24. *Perkins* 116 U.S. 483 (1886) at 485.
25. *Brig Aurora* 17 Cranch 382 (1813); (*Wayman v. Southard* 10 Wheat (1825).
26. *Buttfield v. Strahan* 192 U.S. 470 (1904); *J. W. Hampton and Co. v. U.S.* 276 U.S. 394 (1928).
27. See Joseph Story, *Constitutional Commentaries* esp. sec. 1544, though the preceding sections are lucid and helpful as well.
28. 357 U.S. 349 (1958).

29. See Corwin, *The Removal Power of the President* (New York: National Municipal League, 1927) and *The President Office and Powers* (New York: New York University Press, 1940) esp. pp. 103–104 and pp. 93, 378–379.
30. *Panama Refining Co. v. Ryan* 293 U.S. 388 (1934).
31. 295 U.S. 495 (1935).
32. 298 U.S. 238 (1936).
33. 301 U.S. 548 (1937).
34. *The American Presidency* (New York: Basic Books, 1979).
35. See Duane Tananbaum, *The Bricker Amendment Controversy: A Test of Eisenhower's Leadership* (Ithaca: Cornell University Press, 1988) and Williard Bunce Cowles's older and wise work, *Treaties and Constitutional Law* (Washington: American Council of Public Affairs, 1944).
36. 252 U.S. 416 (1920).
37. *Power Authority of New York v. FPC* 247 F.2d. 538 (1957); *U.S. v. Guy Kapps* 204 F.2d. 655 (1953).
38. *De Geoffrey v. Riggs* 133 U.S. 258 (1890).
39. A good sense of this is conveyed in Anthony King (ed.), *Both Ends of the Avenue* (Washington, D.C.: AEI, 1983).
40. 328 U.S. 303 (1946).
41. 424 U.S. 1 (1978).
42. 395 U.S. 486 (1969).
43. 343 U.S. 579 (1952).
44. No. 91–740 (January 11, 1993).
45. 424 U.S. 1 (1978).
46. For Corwin's endorsement of the legislative veto, see his *Office and Powers*, op. cit. (n. 29), pp. 124–126.
47. Currie, op. cit. (n. 13), at 30.
48. Cushman, *The Independent Regulatory Commission* (New York: Appleton Century, 1941), pp. 447–451.
49. *Anderson v. Dunn* 19 U.S. 204 (1821).
50. *Morrison v. Olson* 108 *S. Ct.* 2597 (1988).
51. 109 *S. Ct.* 647 (1989).
52. *U.S. v. Munoz-Flores* 110 *S. Ct.* 1946 (1992).
53. See above, p. 39, and footnote 9.
54. Rep. Smith 132, Cong. Rec. 32135 at 32141 quoted in 111 *S. Ct.* 2298, 2307 (1991).
55. 287 U.S. 378 (1932). This important case held a governor's establishment of martial law as justiciable.
56. 418 U.S. 683 (1974).
57. *Nixon v. Administrator of General Services* 433 U.S. 425 (1977). In 1992, Nixon's right to compensation was finally upheld in the light of the continuous practice of regarding presidential papers as the personal property of a department executive.
58. *Touby v. U.S.* 111 *S. Ct.* 1752 (1992).
59. *Mistretta v. U.S.* 488 U.S. 361 (1989).
60. But the judicial branch has power over existing taxes under highly special conditions. See *Missouri v. Jenkins* 110 *S. Ct.* 16571 (1990).
61. *Currin v. Wallace* 306 U.S. 1 (1939).
62. See, e.g., Richard Neely, *How Courts Govern America* (New Haven: Yale University Press, 1981).
63. The classic example is Mary Parker Follett, *The New State: Group Organization the Solution of Popular Government* (New York: Longmans, Green, 1918).
64. 317 U.S. 341 (1943).
65. *City of Columbia v. Omni Outdoor Advertising* 111 *S. Ct.* 7344 (1991).
66. See *California Retail Liquor Association v. MidCal Aluminum* 445 U.S. 97 (1980) and its progeny.

67. See for example, *Fuerson v. Board of Education* 330 U.S. 1 (1947) or *Wiemann v. Updegraf* 344 U.S. 429 (1952).
68. Compare his sweeping call for presidential dominance with his requirements for presidential notice in the *Federal Register*, etc. See extracts from Cutler, *Washington Post*, October 18, 1978 and coauthored *Yale Law Journal* articles, 1975, published in Stephen G. Breyer and Richard Stewart, ed., *Administrative Law and Regulatory Policy* (Boston: Little, Brown, 1979), pp. 149–153.
69. As these pages near publication, a dispute between the Postal Service, the Postal Rates Commission, the Department of Justice, and the White House seems about to require Supreme Court answers to some of the broader claims of White House control of important agencies, unless the Clinton administration eases the stands taken by the Bush White House.

II

TRENDS IN REGULATORY ADMINISTRATION

3

Trends in Social Regulation

Gary C. Bryner *Brigham Young University, Provo, Utah*

Social regulation comprises a broad range of statutes, agencies, and administrative programs that are aimed at controlling and restricting the behavior of individuals, organizations, and governments. There is no agreement over exactly how to define social regulation; some emphasize direct intervention in societal affairs, whereas others include any governmental action that indirectly shapes behavior. The purposes of social regulatory programs include environmental quality, occupational safety and health, consumer protection, and civil rights. Unlike traditional areas of economic regulation, social regulation cuts across industries and sectors of the economy. The heart of social regulation is comprised of health and safety programs aimed at protecting consumers. Environmental regulation is also a major element of social regulation, but is discussed in detail in another chapter. Although environmental regulation is not expressly discussed in this chapter, it has much in common with other areas of social regulation.

Statutes that are part of this broad category of social regulation are usually based on broad, expansive goals. These statutes delegate immense powers to regulatory agencies who, in turn, are expected to issue specific regulations that become as binding on regulated parties as the laws themselves. In reality, regulations may become even more important for the targets of regulation than the laws themselves, as regulations are written in great detail and govern the day-to-day functioning of businesses, state and local governments, and others who fall within the jurisdiction of the regulations. The statutes themselves often included detailed prescriptions in addition to the powers delegated to regulatory agencies, resulting in a rich array of restrictions on behavior.

Most of the regulatory functions of government have traditionally been exercised at the state levels. State law regulates property use, marriage and divorce, banking and credit, public health, construction standards, insurance, occupational and professional standards, and a host of other areas of life. Local governments have also enjoyed significant authority to regulate public services, public works, and regulatory powers. Social regulation was primarily a state function until the twentieth century. The Constitution empowered the federal government to "regulate Commerce with foreign Nations and among the several States" (Art. 1, sec. 8), but most regulation in the nineteenth century was a by-product of government attempts to develop natural resources, to provide for the basic elements of the economic system, and to promote industry. The failure of state regulation of railroads led to the creation of the first modern federal regulatory agency, the Interstate Commerce Commission, in 1887.

The history of social regulation in the United States is largely one of cycles of expansion and contraction in regulatory activity. Public outrage over social harms, fueled by political entrepreneurs, results in legislation. Victory is declared, interest is dissipated, and the public and policy entrepreneurs alike move on to other issues. Support for social regulation has been strongest during periods of economic expansion; with contraction, regulation becomes an intolerable burden, dragging the economy down. The first part of this chapter briefly traces the cyclical history of federal regulation; the second part discusses some of the issues that have been at the heart of the debate over social regulation.

THE RISE OF FEDERAL REGULATION

The progressive era triggered the first round of federal social regulatory legislation. Widely published exposés of practices in the food and drug industries led to the Food and Drug Act of 1906 which prohibited shipping across state lines food and drugs that were misbranded or adulterated. A number of regulatory agencies were created between 1915–1927 to regulate commercial and financial activities. The great depression and the New Deal engendered a whole generation of regulatory agencies aimed at stabilizing the economy and managing commercial enterprises. Social welfare programs and agencies were established for the first time at the national level.

Between 1969 and 1976, Congress produced the greatest burst of regulatory legislation in its history. More than 120 new regulatory programs were created by statute during this period, compared with the 40 programs enacted during the New Deal 1930s. Among the most important laws were the following:

Child Protection and Safety Act of 1969
National Environmental Policy Act of 1969
Clean Air Act Amendments of 1970
Egg Products Inspection Act of 1970
Fair Credit Reporting Act of 1970
Occupational Safety and Health Act of 1970
Poison Prevention Packaging Act of 1970
Securities Investor Protection Act of 1970
Federal Boat Safety Act of 1971
Lead-Based Paint Elimination Act of 1971
Wholesome Fish and Fisheries Act of 1971
Consumer Product Safety Act of 1972
Equal Employment Opportunity Act of 1972
Federal Election Campaign Act of 1972
Motor Vehicle Information and Cost Savings Act of 1972
Ports and Waterways Safety Act of 1972
Noise Control Act of 1972
Federal Water Pollution Control Act Amendments of 1972
Agricultural and Consumer Protection Act of 1973
Flood Disaster Protection Act of 1973

Commodity Futures Trading Act of 1974
Consumer Product Warranties/FTC Improvement Act of 1974
Council on Wage and Price Stability Act of 1974
Employee Retirement Income Security Act of 1974
Federal Energy Administration Act of 1974
Hazardous Materials Transportation Act of 1974
Housing and Community Development Act of 1974
Pension Reform Act of 1974
Privacy Act of 1974
Safe Drinking Water Act of 1974
Equal Credit Opportunity Act of 1975
Consumer Leasing Act of 1976
Toxic Substances Control Act of 1976
Medical Device Safety Act of 1976

These laws, and the regulatory programs they created, shared several important characteristics. They rested on broadly defined, expansive objectives; they extended well beyond specific industries, as was generally true of earlier regulatory programs, and they relied on broad delegations of authority to regulatory agencies. One of the most important characteristics of these laws was the elaborate procedural provisions included to constrain administrative discretion and ensure public participation in agency deliberations. Statutes mandated public hearings, advisory bodies, and committees, and increased opportunities for judicial review of regulatory agency action or inaction. The latter kind of review became particularly important to public interest groups that sought to reverse what they saw as excessive timidity on the part of regulatory agencies to pursue aggressively their statutory missions. Some statutes even provided public funds to help finance participation by public interest groups in agency hearings and meetings that would otherwise be unable to participate.

As a result of these statutes, the regulatory activities of federal agencies exploded. The number of pages of the *Federal Register*, the official publisher of all federal regulations, grew from about 20,000 pages in 1970 to 60,000 pages by 1975. Virtually every sector of the American economy became subject to a host of new regulatory requirements. Concerns over worker health and safety, consumer protection, the state of the environment, and food and drug quality were intertwined as Congress greatly expanded the regulatory reach of the federal government.

The expansion of federal regulatory power aimed at protecting the consumer occurred rapidly. Several conditions came together in the 1960s and 1970s that made it possible to challenge the privileged position of industry and create the vast array of regulatory powers and agencies. The U.S. economy was booming, and members of Congress and others believed that the nation could afford to address consumer and environmental concerns and problems. Industry officials had grown complacent in their ability to shape public policies to their advantage. Indeed, throughout the 1950s, it was largely industry representatives who wrote the occasional regulatory statutes that were enacted. Corporate executives gave little attention to government relations because there was little threat of harm. Scandals in industry eroded public confidence in big business. General Motors was embarrassed by revelations that it spent less than $1 million on safety-related research in 1964 despite corporate profits of $1.7 billion and major increases in traffic fatalities. Cigarette companies continued to aim their advertisements at young people despite growing evidence of the health effects of smoking.[1]

A second set of developments centered on the rise of policy entrepreneurs in Congress, a new class of liberal members who were willing to take on the established practices and power bases of the American political economy. Senate liberals like Estes Kefauver, Hubert Humphrey, Warren Magnuson, Edmund Muskie, George McGovern, Eugene McCarthy, Gaylord Nelson, William Proxmire, Henry Jackson, Edward Kennedy, Wayne Morse, Abraham Ribicoff, Jacob Javits, and Charles Percy were very effective advocates for major policy initiatives. Labor unions, relatively secure in traditional areas of interest, expanded their efforts to address civil rights and social welfare. Opposition to the war in Vietnam was directed to military power and authority but spilled over to challenge the power of large corporations. Academic scholars, the media, and other elites promoted the tremendous changes in American politics and society.[2]

The rise of policy entrepreneurs was a particularly critical element in the rise of consumer regulation in the 1970s. James Q. Wilson describes entrepreneurial politics as producing policies that confer benefits throughout society while imposing costs on a relatively small sector. Given this kind of distribution of costs and benefits, such policies would be rarely achieved, since the incentive is so strong for industry to organize against the initiatives, and so weak for the beneficiaries to take action. The number of opportunities in the American political system to defeat policy proposals would seem to render consumer-oriented regulation a real anomaly. Wilson argues that regulation can occur as a result of the actions of a skilled entrepreneur who can activate "latent public sentiment" by exposing or drawing attention to a scandal or major problem; putting industry on the defensive for causing the crisis; and then proposing a legislative solution that is consonant with "widely shared values" such as health and safety or protection of children and the elderly. The entrepreneur "serves as the vicarious representative of groups not directly part of the legislative process."[3]

The key element in entrepreneurial politics is the ability of the entrepreneur to tap into widespread public values and concerns and to channel public outrage. Entrepreneurs rely on an aggressive staff, advocacy, and investigative journalists who help draw public attention to the problems that are the subject of legislation, and nongovernmental actors who are also skilled at exposing industry blunders and carelessness. The tremendous growth of congressional staffs in the 1970s gave Congress the resources it needed to expand regulatory initiatives. Journalists played an independent role as well, sometimes working closely with policy entrepreneurs in drawing attention to problems and placing blame on companies, politicians, and others who were either at fault or who tried to block remedial efforts. Few threats to politicians were greater than the power of the media to label them as anticonsumer or antienvironment. The kind of mass political power that was the basis of the consumer protection movement did not involve the direct political mobilization of large numbers of people or groups; the key was its ability to channel widespread public outrage with unsafe automobiles and children being burned by inflammable pajamas into demands for legislative action that could not easily be ignored by members of Congress.

In addition to the importance of policy entrepreneurs and their staffs, a number of individuals played major parts in generating support for new consumer protection laws and regulations. No nongovernmental actor played a more critical role in the rise of consumer regulation in the 1960s and 1970s than Ralph Nader, a perpetual critic of business neglect of community responsibilities and government domination by special interests. Nader's considerable skills as a political strategist, articulator of public concerns, and motivator of other consumer advocates, and his dogged determination generated tremendous pressure for new statutes and regulatory programs to protect consumers. He associated himself with consumers' frustration and anger over the unresponsiveness of business in a way that made him a widely recognized spokesperson for millions of Americans. His unyielding criticism of the inadequacy of current regulatory efforts provided the impetus for much more aggressive statutes that included deadlines for actions, stringent provisions, or "hammers" that would go into effect unless agencies took action, and enhanced opportunities to sue agencies in federal courts for failure to take the actions mandated by law.[4]

While consumer champions used broad public sentiment and values to pressure politicians to support new legislative and administrative regulatory initiatives, organized consumer groups also played a significant role. Nader himself launched a flotilla of advocacy groups, from the Center for Science in the Public Interest to Public Interest Research Groups. These groups provided analyses of corporate practices and shortcomings of regulatory agencies that were essential in building the public case for new laws and programs. The Consumer Federation of America, led by the efforts of Carol Foreman, was a loose coalition of groups formed in 1968 that demonstrated the breadth of support for consumer protection issues. The Consumer's Union, long an organization that focused primarily on the testing of products and the dissemination of information about the safety and effectiveness of merchandise sold in the United States, took a more public stance and lobbied for more aggressive consumer regulation.

A third set of forces leading to the expansion of regulatory activity at the federal level was rooted in American liberal democracy and the welfare state. During this period of regulatory activism, welfare programs also greatly expanded. Social security benefits were significantly increased, and benefits were automatically tied to cost of living increases, Medicare and Medicaid programs were instituted, and food stamps were made a regular rather than an experimental part of the welfare program. Government became increasingly viewed as being responsible for socializing risk, for protecting individuals against more and more kinds of misfortunes. More and more conduct fell under the purview of government as a way to indemnify individuals against risk. Perhaps the clearest manifestation of this development occurred in the federal courts, where personal liability litigation literally exploded in the 1970s and 1980s (see below). But the idea of expanding public responsibility for private problems underlay the expansion of regulatory authority in the 1970s.[5]

While there was considerable activity and a number of notable legislative successes in enhancing the power of government to protect consumers, it is not at all clear what impact this activity had on consumer safety. The Consumer Product Safety Commission, for example, was given one of the broadest mandates of any regulatory agency, but was created and maintained as one of the smallest regulatory agencies. At its peak, it only had 900 employees and a budget of $44 million, and has never had sufficient resources to begin to accomplish its statutory mandate. Its political power was always tenuous at best; Congress authorized it only for three years, ensuring that the agency would come under regulatory review by its congressional overseers. It was continually under attack from industries seeking to escape regulation. The high expectations surrounding the agency when it was created have never been realized.[6] In any event, a commitment to expanding the scope of federal regulation was short-lived.

The courts have been the other focal point for increasing the protection given consumers. Lawsuits, for example, were the major impetus for encouraging U.S. automakers to offer air bags and shoulder belts for rear seat passengers, after years of efforts by consumer advocates to get federal legislation or regulation.[7] Lawsuits have also challenged food safety and the use of pesticides, airline safety, and a host of other areas in which advocates believe that regulatory efforts are insufficient. Corporate liability for injuries suffered by consumers has been a longstanding element of the American legal system, but case law has undergone a major transformation as courts have become increasingly willing to impose responsibility for consumer product health and safety, even when customers have been negligent or otherwise at fault. The size of awards has skyrocketed as juries have become increasingly sympathetic to the plight of victims and increasingly willing to tap deep corporate financial pockets to help compensate them.[8] Insurance and industry associations have lobbied hard for legislation to limit liability awards, but have been countered by lawyer and consumer groups. The future of restrictive federal legislation is uncertain, but some states have enacted limits on product liability litigation. Nevertheless, American newspapers regularly carry articles about the latest multimillion-dollar award in product liability suits.

THE RETREAT FROM REGULATION

The momentum for a strong federal government effort to protect consumers stalled by the late 1970s, for a number of reasons. The Carter administration, elected on a platform of anti-Washington sentiment, joined with Congress in promoting reform of federal regulatory efforts. Early reform, actually begun in the Ford administration, sought to enhance economic competitiveness and was actually supported by consumer activists. Deregulation of the securities market, banking, railroads, airlines, and trucking were to a significant extent championed as pro-consumer reforms, promising to reduce costs and improve service and quality through increased competition.[9] But the rhetoric of regulatory reform was captured by the Reagan presidential campaign in 1980, and the reform agenda was greatly expanded to include consumer, safety, and environmental protection.

The Reagan administration sought to restrain regulation in four primary ways. First, it singled out regulatory agencies for abolition, or at least major budget cuts. The Reagan transition team recommended the abolition of the Consumer Product Safety Commission, and although it survived, its budget was cut more than any other regulatory agency. Second, it established the Vice President's Task Force on Regulatory Relief, charged with the task of identifying regulations that were particularly burdensome to business and state governments. The task force identified hundreds of regulations, primarily in the area of civil rights, environmental quality, and consumer protection, and began working with agencies to amend or rescind the regulations. A third reform centered on requiring regulatory agencies to use cost–benefit analysis in formulating initiatives. Guidelines established by the administration for the analysis focused on the calculation of costs and gave little attention to the difficulties of estimating the often unquantifiable benefits of improved environmental quality or consumer protection. Finally, the administration created a mandatory review process for all major regulations, located in the powerful Office of Management and Budget, to ensure that proposed regulations passed the cost–benefit test and that regulatory options were the least burdensome possible. Noticeably absent in the Reagan administration's approach was statutory reform. Administrative changes were perceived to be much easier to achieve, and the president's statutory priorities were in the budget rather than in the regulatory arena.[10]

Congress largely acceded to the regulatory relief efforts of the Reagan administration. Regulatory agencies that were criticized as being too aggressive by business were reined in through oversight hearings, statutory changes, and the legislative veto. The legislative veto was a particularly visible tool of congressional control over zealous agencies. The veto itself was rarely exercised, but its threat was designed to reflect a clear sense of congressional intent that agencies could not easily ignore. In one of the most celebrated cases, the veto was used to overturn a very modest Federal Trade Commission regulation that would have simply required funeral homes to provide information to its customers on the cost of each service offered.[11] Even though the legislative veto was declared unconstitutional by the Supreme Court in 1983, Congress continued to employ variations of the veto, along with other oversight tools, to check regulatory agencies.[12] Legislative initiatives largely ceased, and even the reauthorization of existing consumer and environmental laws became tortured, drawn-out affairs. Congress failed to meet deadlines for reauthorizing the Consumer Product Safety Commission, and the

Federal Trade Commission was forced to forced to shut down for a short time because Congress could not decide how to respond to congressional and executive branch opposition to the agency. Other programs such as those provided for under the Clean Air Act, were forced to operate throughout the 1980s without formal reauthorization.

A number of factors led to the decline of congressional support for consumer protection throughout the 1980s. To some extent, the conditions that led to the rise of consumer protection in the late 1960s were now reversed. The most serious recession since the Great Depression of the 1930s occurred in 1981–2, fueling the belief that the country could no longer afford to impose new regulatory costs on industry. The Reagan administration was relentless in its efforts to blame American economic problems on excessive government regulation. Domestic spending, tax cuts, and regulatory relief were heralded as the president's electoral mandate, and few members of Congress challenged the president's popularity.[13]

The declining competitiveness of U.S. companies in global markets has became one of the most important issues on the nation's policy agenda. U.S. industries that dominated world markets two decades ago saw their share of global markets shrink dramatically during the past two decades. U.S. firms that developed the technology for video cassette recorders and color televisions now have less than 2 percent of the VCR and 10 percent of the TV markets. Japanese sales of semiconductor chips, another product developed by American scientists, have eclipsed sales by U.S. companies. Analysts warned that if current relative rates of growth continue, Japan will replace the United States as the leading manufacturer of electronics in the world by the mid-1990s.[14]

Other indicators of the competitive position of the U.S. economy in the world showed similar dramatic decline and fueled antiregulation concerns. The United States, long the world's major creditor nation, became the largest debtor nation, with a net indebtedness rapidly approaching $1 trillion. The balance of trade account position of the United States shifted from a longstanding position of a net exporter to one of major trade deficits. The merchandise trade balance deficit reached more than $150 billion by the mid-1980s. Imports increased at an average rate of 8 percent a year throughout the 1980s, well ahead of export activity.[15] The optimism of the 1950s, 1960s, and early 1970s and the confidence in America's technological and industrial preeminence was replaced with doubts about the role the United States will play in a global economy where U.S. firms have become overshadowed by Asian and European enterprises.[16]

The political rhetoric as well as the analytic underpinnings of the regulatory reform debate over how to increase competition that occurred in the mid-to-late 1970s was applied with renewed vigor in other areas of regulation. Antiregulatory sentiments were couched in the politically "neutral, objective" vocabulary of cost–benefit analysis and efficiency. The ability of regulatory advocates to tap into public outrage over human suffering caused by unsafe products and greedy business executives was dissipated as the debate over regulation was translated into quantifiable costs and benefits. Industry groups were quick to appreciate the arguments made by economists and policy analysts that "the relentless pursuit of private gain is the best way of serving the public interest."[17]

American industry executives also came to realize the importance of business–government relations, and began investing more seriously in electoral politics and a Washington lobbying presence. The tremendous growth in political action committee (PAC) contributions to congressional campaigns, increases in honoraria paid to members for meetings with corporate officials, and the swelling of the Washington lobby significantly strengthened the ability of business to protect itself against regulatory burdens. Business-related PAC spending on congressional races, for example, grew from about $8 million in 1972 to $63 million by 1980 to over $150 million by 1986.[18] The increased sophistication of industry lobbying, combined with an administration clearly attuned to doing whatever it could to facilitate business interests and promote economic growth, overwhelmed consumer-oriented advocates.

The decline of consumer protection activism at the national level of government in the United States slowed considerably with the election of George Bush in 1988. Presidential rhetoric called for more social legislation (a "kinder, gentler nation") since the nation could afford to consider once again the possibility of doing more to protect citizens from harm. Appointees to regulatory agencies were less hostile to the missions of the organization they were to direct. Speeches and press releases that were once vehicles to attack regulation now praised the benefits promised by new initiatives. While little attention was given by the Bush administration to consumer protection itself, the related area of environmental quality was the subject of a fairly high level of presidential interest, including a major administration push that resulted in the reauthorization of the Clean Air Act.

Two other developments gave support to renewed consumer regulation in the 1990s. First, the savings and loan debacle in the United States has been blamed, to a great extent, on deregulation of financial institutions. In a 1990 Cable News Network–*Time* magazine nationwide poll, 66 percent of the respondents agreed that the savings and loan crisis was one of the most serious financial scandals in the nation's history. Some 88 percent of the respondents in a Harris poll agreed that weak and lax federal regulation was to blame for the scandal.[19] Second, the federal budget deficit has made if difficult to launch new spending programs. Advocates for new policy initiatives will find regulation increasingly attractive, since the costs of compliance are not reflected in budget figures. The debate over national health insurance, for example, has moved from a discussion of federal funding of insurance to requiring that employers provide insurance for all full-time employees. While such a program, if developed, would still leave many without insurance, it would rely on federal regulation rather than spending to achieve the intended goal of expanding protection.

Nevertheless, concerns of economic growth and international competitiveness dominate. As part of his initiative to stimulate the economy, Bush announced in his 1992 State of the Union Address a three-month moratorium on new regulations that "could hinder growth" and ordered agencies to "carry out a top-to-bottom review of all regulations, old and new, to stop the ones that will hurt growth and speed up those that will help growth."[20] Absent was the commitment to making regulations more cost-effective or to balance the costs and benefits of regulations: Any effort by regulatory agencies that could not be directly translated into economic growth were to be sacrificed.

The void in consumer protection left by the Reagan and Bush administrations' commitment to regulatory relief has largely been filled by state governments and the courts. State legislatures have always been heavily involved in consumer protection legislation. Most of the federal initiatives of the 1960s and 1970s were based on state precedents, but consumer advocates were quick to take advantage of federal laws that provided protection across the country, rather than working with each state's legislature. As federal legislative action declined, progressive legislatures in states like California, Oregon, New Jersey, and Wisconsin once again became the focus of consumer protection activity. Consumer groups have been adept at working with state legislatures as well as using ballot initiatives to take direct action in creating new consumer protection regulatory programs. State laws have mandated strict standards for food safety, nutritional labeling on food packaging, health warnings for cigarette smoking, regulation of hazardous chemicals, disclosure of credit card and interest costs, and oil spills prevention and cleanup that go well beyond what is required by federal laws.

Industry groups have raised alarms at the growth in state regulation, arguing that interstate and international commerce are impossible if they have to meet 50 different sets of standards. Trade associations have prophesied of "distributional chaos and consumer confusion" if state laws continue to proliferate. Consumer advocates respond that the "fight against regulation has become a fight against the states." Industry has "tamed the federal regulatory beast" and has now set its sights on restraining state efforts. The fear of having to meet differing state requirements has generated increased support among industry groups for federal statutes that would preempt state regulations. Consumer advocates have found themselves in a quandary. The new-found industry interest in national legislation makes it possible for them to once again get Congress and the regulatory agencies to expand protection of consumer health and safety. But industry support comes with a high price: Federal laws must, as a condition of industry support, include provisions that prohibit states from imposing additional, more stringent regulations in areas covered by the federal law. Industry would "rather deal with one federal gorilla than 50 state monkeys." Public interest groups fear "Faustian bargains that produce federal legislation but at a cost of weakening the power of states to provide additional protection for their citizens.[21]

THE DEBATE OVER SOCIAL REGULATION

Two issues have been at the heart of the recent debate over social regulation. One set of disagreements center on whether there is too much or too little regulation. The second set focuses on whether or not regulation should be made more "efficient." The future of social regulation will likely rest on how these debates are played out.

Too Much or Too Little Regulation?

Much of the opposition to regulation is rooted in ideological commitments to a free market or minimal governmental intervention in business and individual decision-making. Throughout the 1980s and early 1990s, critics of regulation seemed to dominate the debate, and proponents of more regulation found they could do little more than keep the regulatory relief bandwagon from rolling back laws and regulations. There was little success in building the case for an expansion of regulatory authority or to a more aggressive implementation of existing regulations, despite investigations and reports of a lack of regulatory oversight of the savings and loan industry, agricultural inspection and food safety, pharmaceutical companies, medicare and medicaid providers, toxic waste dumpers, and a host of others.[22]

Critics of regulation argue that regulation must be curtailed in order to ensure that U.S. companies can compete in global markets. Other critics emphasize the costs of compliance on smaller businesses: Larger companies have the resources to monitor regulatory requirements and make required investments and may support regulations that will be more burdensome on competitors than on themselves. The political and economic stakes of this debate are enormous. As superpower tensions have decreased during the late 1980s and early 1990s, international relations have increasingly emphasized economic security. Domestic politics continues to give primary attention to the health of the economy in general and to levels of employment, wages, and economic growth. The threat to U.S. economic power from Japan and a united Europe has increased each year. Recent Congresses and administrations have engaged in a broad ranging debate over the general health of the economy and the prospects for the competitiveness of U.S. industries. The competitiveness of U.S. firms in global markets has major implications for the standard of living Americans will enjoy in the future. World economic leadership also has important symbolic importance to Americans and helps determine the influence the United States is able to exert in international affairs.[23]

Regulations have been widely criticized as being too stringent and unjustified when their expected costs are compared with the benefits they promise. These criticisms are rooted in analyses, initiated in the Ford administration, of the costs and benefits of regulation. They continued during the Carter presidency, but culminated in the Reagan administration in 1981 with the creation of the regulatory review process in the Office of Management and Budget and the Vice-President's Task Force on Regulatory Relief.[24] The Bush administration continued with these presidential initiatives, and created the Vice-President's Council on Competitiveness to oversee regulatory reform efforts. OMB officials have been relentless critics of regulatory agencies. Federal agencies and, by implication, Congress, have been criticized for failing to provide adequate justification for the need for regulation. In many cases statutes specify in detail what regulations are to be issued, so OMB officials have focused on areas where agencies have discretion. According to principles outlined in Executive Order 12291, issued in 1981, regulation is justified only if markets suffer from externalities (market transactions that impose costs or benefits on third parties), if there is inadequate information to inform choice, or if there is a natural monopoly. Regulation should not seek to alter market outcomes.[25]

Regulatory agencies have been regularly criticized for failing to separate assessments of the likely effects of behavior that might be regulated from assessments of available policy choices. Industry groups and others who have been critical of regulation argue that agencies have not been committed enough to ensuring a solid scientific basis for regulations; agencies should restrain themselves from taking regulatory actions unless sufficient scientific evidence is available to justify intervening. What this often means is that no regulatory action should be taken until scientific uncertainties are reduced and ambiguities are eliminated. The National Academy of Science, in a widely cited 1983 study, recommended that agencies carefully distinguish between "scientific findings and policy judgments embodied in risk assessments" and the "political, economic, and technical considerations that influence the design and choice of regulatory strategies."[26]

In a recent Regulatory Program of the U.S. Government, a compilation of regulatory actions proposed by agencies, OMB repeated a charge it has been making for several years: In regulatory agencies, "risk-assessment practices continue to rely on conservative models and assumptions that effectively intermingle important policy judgments within the scientific assessment of risk." As a result, senior agency officials are forced to make regulatory decisions "based on risk assessments in which scientific findings cannot be readily differentiated from embedded policy judgments." Not only does this "make it difficult to discern serious hazards from trivial ones, and distorts the ordering of the Government's regulatory priorities," but may even "increase health and safety risks" by regulating less serious problems and ignoring more serious ones.[27]

OMB has also charged that agencies employ unreasonably conservative or cautious assumptions in assessing risks; they adopt upper bounds of estimates rather than most likely projections, treat benign tumors as malignant, use the most sensitive species and sex in laboratory tests and in determining acceptable exposure levels, and apply the most cautious models in extrapolating from animals to humans and from low to high exposure levels. While such conservative approaches may not individually be particularly unreasonable, the cumulative effect is to produce assessments of risks that have "extremely conservative biases" and "do not provide decisionmakers with the information they need to formulate an efficient and cost-effective regulatory strategy.[28]

Once risk assessments have been prepared, they serve as the basis for calculating the costs and benefits of regulatory options. OMB has criticized the EPA and other agencies for failing to provide adequate analyses of the benefits and costs of regulations they want to impose.[29] Agencies have failed to rely on market-based measures such as the "willingness to pay" that are, for OMB, the only real means of "comparing alternative sources of value to individuals . . . and allocating goods and services to the highest-valued use."[30]

Cost–benefit analysis is generally understood to require the quantification of all costs and benefits and the calculation of their dollar values in a numerical ratio. These calculations are, of course, extremely controversial when one is addressing questions of the value of human life or the protection of ecosystems. Calculations of cost-effectiveness in these areas are a means of comparing alternative regulatory strategies or different regulations without requiring explicit calculations of the value of life. Agencies may select a regulatory option with the highest cost-effective ratio, and may compare the cost-effectiveness of different regulations in deciding whether to pursue them. Problems with this approach remain, and OMB officials have criticized the EPA (and other agencies) because regulations vary greatly in their cost-effectiveness.[31]

Many economists also lament the inefficiency of regulation. Traditional complaints about the burdens regulations impose on industry have been joined by other criticisms that regulation is simply too inefficient and expensive, that we cannot afford the inefficiency inherent in traditional regulatory schemes, and the way in which regulation often insulates some companies from competitive forces. National standards have been roundly rejected as inefficient and wasteful since problems are much more serious in some areas than others. The diversity of the American economy means that uniform standards will only perpetuate arbitrariness, inequity, and waste.[32]

Critics argue that Congress has passed, and agency officials have been unwilling to challenge, statutes that impose unreasonable expectations or unrealistic criteria for policymaking. They have failed to help inform and educate the public about the nature and inevitability of health hazards, the complexity of risk assessment, the costs of trying to eliminate risks, and the other tradeoffs that are an essential part of policymaking. They have failed to help structure debate over environmental quality so that it is more responsive to the public and more accountable to elected officials. They have been insensitive to the impact of the regulations it issues on state and local governments. They have been unable and unwilling to integrate environmental health problems with broader concerns of quality of life, such as crime and personal safety, that affect people directly and immediately.[33]

The Case for More Regulation

In contrast, a second set of criticisms conclude that government has not gone far enough during the past two decades in regulating social harms. Regulatory statutes have created expectations for regulatory activity that greatly exceed what federal agencies and states have actually accomplished. Regulators have generally been unwilling to impose regulations that would close down factories and cause major job losses. Environmental, health, and safety regulations have been of particular interest to OMB and White House reviewers, because of their large compliance costs and their political visibility. But it is not at all clear that there is too much government intervention in these areas and that, as was true for the EPA, the number of regulations should be dramatically reduced. A continual stream of health hazards and problems have been published in books, journals, newspapers, and broadcast on television.

Regulatory agencies have been constrained by recent administrations concerned about controlling inflation and increasing the competitiveness of American firms in international markets. The executive branch, particularly during the past eight years, has insisted that reducing risks be treated as only one of several competing social goals. The Reagan administration was particularly successful in restraining the growth of regulation, through appointments made to the agencies and OMB review of all proposed and final regulations.[34]

The regulatory review process, as participants in the process themselves have admitted, has clearly been oriented toward relief rather than reform, toward reducing costs more than improving the quality of regulations. The goal is a reduction in regulatory costs and burdens. This may be an important goal, although the architects of the review process have not been able to establish that the problem is too much regulation, and a better case may be made that there is not enough regulation. In any event, many statutes simply call for more regulation, and it is hard, from a constitutional perspective, to justify a process that seeks to avoid faithfully implementing laws. The review is not neutral. It is not oriented toward a balanced assessment of costs and benefits. It does not address the costs to society, of pollution and other problems, but only how to reduce the costs of compliance with responsibilities placed on industry by law. It provides a forum for industry interests to gain concessions that they were unable to get in public settings, in Congress and in agency hearings, comment periods, and negotiations. The form developed by OMB to monitor compliance with EO 12291, for example, included four categories of costs but no provision for calculating benefits.[35]

The agenda of many senior executive branch officials, when the process was instituted, was simply to reduce research, rulemaking, and enforcement rather than reforming and reshaping policy. Analysis was not a tool for improved policymaking, but a means of limiting agency action. Tolchin and Tolchin have described how the review process gave business interests an opportunity to block regulatory initiatives they disagreed with. The primary concern was to "alleviate the burdens of excessive regulation." The Reagan administration's regulatory "reform" efforts were an "exercise in national self-deception because of the singularity of its dominant goal: short-term relief for business."[36]

Defenders of presidential prerogatives in regulatory review often argue from the perspective of constitutional theory, that the Framers and everyone else who is sensible recognizes the importance of a unified executive. A unified executive branch must have a mechanism for setting priorities, eliminating or reducing conflicting policy efforts, coordinating overlapping undertakings, and so on. It is hard to argue with the need for those kinds of administrative initiatives; but they do not really explain what is happening in the regulatory review process. The regulatory review process is not a systematic approach to regulatory coordination and improvement. Critics of regulation argue that the process is weak and aimless, subject to haphazard intervention by White House staffers. Defenders of regulation see the real concern as trying to protect industry from the cost of complying with legislation passed by Congress.[37]

After a decade in place, there is still no evidence that it has made any real contribution to improving coordination among regulatory agencies, eliminating duplicative and contradictory programs, and increasing administrative efficiency through sharing information and analyses. The review process has clearly reduced the number and stringency of new regulations, and has heightened concern over the costs of compliance with regulatory programs. The secrecy surrounding OMB review of regulations has inhibited improvements in agency analysis. If the real purpose of regulatory review was to improve the analytic basis for regulations, then the review process would be formalized and open and the OMB–agency interactions widely publicized so that other agencies could learn from these experiences.

Is the Regulatory Process Inherently Inefficient?

Critics argue that regulation is simply too inefficient and expensive, that we simply cannot afford the inefficiency inherent in traditional regulatory schemes, and that the way in which regulation often insulates some companies from competitive forces. The diversity of the American economy precludes uniform standards that can only perpetuate arbitrariness, inequity, and waste.[38] There is great uncertainty surrounding the causes and consequences of many risks that are the targets of social regulation. Many problems are characterized by long lead times before the adverse health effects and other consequences are discovered. Policymaking must include learning from experience and making adjustments, particularly when problems take so long to manifest themselves.

There is little agreement over how much needs to be known about risks before taking regulatory action, what the balance between waiting for more research and policy interventions to prevent harm should be, and how much risk we should accept. A central issue is how risks should be calculated: Some argue that all persons should be protected, including the most susceptible to the harm, whereas others insist that the risk posed to members of the community in general or on average be the basis of regulation action. Once risks are estimated, a second round of questions grapple with how reducing risks should be balanced with other values such as individual freedom and corporate autonomy.

Cost–benefit analysis has been widely heralded as the way to balance social regulatory concerns and economic growth. But the determination of what costs and benefits are to be included in the calculations is rarely uncontroversial. There is usually little agreement about how far along the causal chain of costs resulting from regulation one should go in determining total expenses. Should costs be limited to direct expenditures to come into compliance with regulations, for example, or should they be extended to include the impact on individuals who lose their jobs when industries cannot afford to meet regulatory requirements? The benefits of lives saved or illnesses prevented are similarly difficult to measure. Disagreements also focus on how to assess the intergenerational distribution of costs and benefits and whether the monetary value of costs and benefits should be discounted in comparing their long-term value. Cost–benefit formulae provide little help in sorting out the distribution of advantages and disadvantages affecting different industries that are affected in different ways by regulation.

Because regulatory statutes delegate such enormous powers to regulatory agencies, they usually include a number of procedural requirements on agency decisionmaking. Administrative law represents an entire body of legal procedures that are designed to ensure that agency actions are consistent with legal and constitutional provisions and subject to supervision and review by federal courts. Public comment periods, hearings, provisions for petitions by citizens to request that particular regulations be issued, a formal record of agency decisions, and judicial review of final agency actions are all part of the attempt to constrain regulatory agencies. Discretion is limited in other ways. Statutes also impose decision rules on agencies: They may be required to compare the costs and benefits of regulatory options or include analyses of the impact of regulation on small businesses or inflation. Both Congress and the president have significant supervisory powers over agency decisionmaking, ranging from congressional scrutiny of appropriations and oversight hearings, to review of proposed regulations by the Office of Management and Budget located in the Executive Office of the President. As a result, the regulatory process is complicated and cumbersome.

From a constitutional perspective, policymaking in the American political system was designed to be inefficient, to check the power of policymakers, and to permit action only when there is widespread support among different sets of constituencies and their representative institutions. What was once defended as a virtue, however, is now regularly derided as a vice. Deliberative democracy has been replaced with deadlocked democratic processes. Institutional barriers to coherent, unified, and effective policymaking are believed by many to prevent the United States from responding to the challenges confronting the nation. Of particular concern is the fear that divided government—Congress and the White House being held by leaders of different political parties whose primary goal is the political defeat of the opposition—makes good, effective policymaking extremely difficult at best, and often impossible. Other institutional and structural characteristics of American government impede attempts to develop coherent, long-run strategies to resolve and prevent problems.[39]

The tension that is part of divided government and political competition, coupled with the separation of powers and competing institutional prerogatives, pose challenges for the kind of legislation enacted. Some scholars have long argued the importance of clear statutes that give implementing agencies unambiguous direction and preserve a commitment to the rule of law and limits on bureaucratic discretion. Others argue that the price of political compromise and policy complexity is statutes that blur distinctions and permit differing interpretations.[40] The tension between the two branches of government during the 1980s and into the 1990s has focused debate over how specific statutes ought to be: Should they minimize discretion, so that congressional will is more likely to prevail? Should they include deadlines for executive action and legislative "hammers" or provisions that take effect unless agencies promptly issue regulations? Or should laws give administrative officials the kind of discretion and freedom that will permit flexible and efficient administration?[41] While such a debate takes place throughout government, it has been particularly sharp in Congress for social regulatory legislation, given the great frustration many members had with the Reagan administration when the ranking agency officials defied their congressional overseers and rejected traditional interpretations of congressional intent surrounding regulatory statutes.

MAKING REGULATION MORE EFFICIENT

One way for government regulations to be effective is to increase the incentives for compliance that go beyond fear of penalties to include incentives that relate to their market status. Critics of regulatory agencies have championed reforms that rely on marketlike incentives. Economic incentives are widely heralded as the most efficient and effective mechanism for accomplishing social regulatory goals. Incentives are championed as being essential to "harnessing the 'base' motive of material self-interest to promote the common good."[42] It is simply not effective to condemn industries as being immoral or selfish; what is needed is clear incentives to encourage them to change their behavior, to ensure that they take actions that are consonant with the public good. Incentives are also preferable to more traditional regulatory interventions because they promote flexibility and freedom of choice and minimize the need for coercion. Regulatory policies that rely on economic incentives include:

Taxes levied on emissions of pollutants or on dangerous products
Tradable emission permits that can be traded, banked or saved for future use, or sold by polluting companies as long as limits on total emissions are not exceeded
Tax concessions or direct subsidies for health or safety investments
Deposits and refunds on products
Legal liability and associated fines for certain kinds of environmental, health, or safety risks.[43]

Using economic incentives to reduce risks may also represent middle ground that is important in public debate. Conservatives can champion an approach that tries to make markets work, that is consistent with a market economy, and that promotes choice and autonomy for business decisionmakers. Liberals who favor increased levels of protection can get more of that for the same levels of expenditures. Pollution taxes and emissions permit charges are a form of user fees that ensure that those who benefit from the use of a natural resource pay for those benefits.

Opposition to them is rooted in other philosophical and ideological concerns as well. Marketlike incentives may send the wrong signal that certain behavior is acceptable if companies are wealthy enough to pay for them. The efficiency promised by economic incentives is not a universal goal, but must compete with the promotion of other values such as equity, fairness, and unselfish concern for others. Placing these values in a market would ultimately result in their unequal distribution.[44]

THE FUTURE OF THE DEBATE OVER REGULATION

Environmental regulation takes place in an extremely complex political arena. In part, this is the result of the naturally competing interests of the governmental branches—in particular, the differing perspectives of the Congress and the executive branch.[45] Congress, the Office of Management and Budget, the courts, and public and private interest groups scrutinize regulatory agencies. Congressional oversight poses particular challenges to agency management. The agency is confronted by an extremely diverse and fragmented set of overseers: It is not clear how political accountability is enhanced by current oversight processes. The future of social research will depend, to some extent, on how the well Congress and the president come to grips with the questions of whether there is too much or too little regulation and whether regulations can or should be made more efficient. Those questions, in the short run, will likely be answered by a number of more specific ones, such as:

1. How can the competing claims of the White House and Congress for control and influence over regulatory rulemaking be sorted out? Can congressional and White House oversight efforts better take into account the nature of the tasks delegated to regulatory agencies and the ways in which agencies are caught between competing overseers?
2. What are the strengths and weaknesses of the executive branch's institutional and procedural innovations: the regulatory analysis under EO 12291, the regulatory program mandated by EO 12498, a replacement for the Council on Competitiveness? Are these efforts sufficient to redress the problems of rulemaking, or are other innovations such as the regulatory budget needed?
3. How can oversight be more coordinated and effective, so that duplicative and wasted efforts are reduced? Should the review process be shifted to the legislative branch in order to respond to concerns that White House politics is displacing authority delegated to regulatory agencies?
4. What are the consequences of different kinds of approaches taken in regulatory statutes, particularly those that promise to harness marketlike incentives to accomplish regulatory goals?
5. What kinds of provisions in statutes and rules are most likely to result in compliance? Should rules be more specific, detailed, and prescriptive, or should they give regulated parties more flexibility? Should they mandate goals and performance standards, or should they include design standards and other means by which the goals are to be achieved? How effective are the incentives and sanctions provided?
6. How do regulations fit together over time? To what extent do they form a coherent, consistent, long-run oriented regulatory agenda?

REFERENCES

1. For examples of contemporary studies of these developments, see Elizabeth Drew, "The Politics of Auto Safety," *Atlantic Monthly* (October 1965); Daniel Patrick Moynihan, "Next: A New Auto Insurance Policy," *New York Times Magazine* (August 27, 1967); and Edwin Epstein, *The Corporation in American Politics* (Englewood Cliffs, N.J.: Prentice-Hall, 1969).
2. Michael Pertschuk, *Revolt Against Regulation: The Rise and Pause of the Consumer Movement* (Berkeley, Cal.: University of California Press, 1982).

3. Wilson, *The Politics of Regulation* (New York: Basic Books, 1980), p. 370.
4. Pertschuk, *Revolt Against Regulation*, pp. 30–33.
5. Theodore J. Lowi, "Liberal and Conservative Theories of Regulation," in Gary C. Bryner and Dennis L. Thompson, *The Constitution and the Regulation of Society* (Ithaca, N.Y.: Brigham Young University/SUNY Press, 1988).
6. Congressional Quarterly, *Federal Regulatory Directory, 1981–82* (Washington, D.C.: Congressional Quarterly, 1981), pp. 101–02; Gary C. Bryner, *Bureaucratic Discretion* (New York: Pergammon Press, 1987), pp. 146–173.
7. Neal Templin, "Auto Shoulder Belts for Rear Seats Came Too Late for Many," *Wall Street Journal* (August 24, 1990); John Holusha, "Air Bags on the Way as Chrysler Gives In," *New York Times* (May 26, 1990).
8. For a critical look at liability law, see Peter W. Huber, *Liability: The Legal Revolution and Its Consequences* (New York: Basic Books, 1988).
9. See, generally, Stephen Breyer, *Regulation and Its Reform* (Cambridge, Mass.: Harvard University Press, 1981).
10. National Academy of Public Administration, *Presidential Management of Rulemaking in Regulatory Agencies* (Washington, D.C.: NAPA, 1987).
11. For a discussion of the legislative veto, see, generally, Harold H. Bruff and Ernest Gellhorn, "Congressional Control of Administrative Regulation: A Study of Legislative Vetoes," *Harvard Law Review* (Vol. 90, May 1977), pp. 1369–1440.
12. Louis Fisher, *The Politics of Shared Power* (Princeton, N.J.: Princeton University Press, 1988).
13. Susan J. Tolchin and Martin Tolchin, *Dismantling America: The Rush to Deregulate* (Boston: Houghton Mifflin, 1983).
14. U.S. Department of Commerce, *The Competitive Status of the U.S. Electronics Sector* (Washington, D.C.: U.S. Government Printing Office, April, 1990); Richard Gephardt, "Statement of Majority Leader Richard A. Gephardt Announcing the Action Agenda for High Technology" (June 20, 1990).
15. U.S. Congress, Office of Technology Assessment, *Paying the Bill: Manufacturing and America's Trade Deficit* (Washington, D.C.: U.S. Government Printing Office, June 1988), pp. 2–4; U.S. Congress, Office of Technology Assessment, *Making Things Better: Competing in Manufacturing* (Washington, D.C.: U.S. Government Printing Office, February 1990), pp. 3–4.
16. Robert Z. Lawrence, "Innovation and Trade: Meeting the Foreign Challenge," in Henry J. Aaron, ed., *Setting National Priorities: Policy for the Nineties* (Washington, D.C.: Brookings Institution, 1990), pp. 146–152.
17. Grant Gilmore, *The Ages of American Law* (New Haven: Yale University Press, 1977), p. 66.
18. Norman J. Ornstein, Thomas E. Mann, and Michael J. Malbin, *Vital Statistics on Congress, 1987–88* (Washington, D.C.: Congressional Quarterly, 1987) p. 105.
19. "Opinion Outlook," *National Journal* (September 22, 1990).
20. Text of President Bush's State of the Union Address, reprinted in *The New York Times*, January 29, 1992: A14.
21. John Moore, "Stopping the States," *National Journal* (July 21, 1990), 1758–1762.
22. See, generally, Kirk Victor, "Tale of the Red Tape," *National Journal* (March 21, 1992), pp. 684–87; Pamela Fessler, "Beyond the Campaign," *Congressional Quarterly Weekly Report* (September 26, 1993), pp. 2887–2914.
23. John A. Young, "Technology and Competitiveness: A Key to the Economic Future of the United States," *Science* (July 15, 1988), 314.
24. For a review of these efforts, see National Academy of Public Administration, *Presidential Management of Rulemaking in Regulatory Agencies* (Washington, D.C.: NAPA, 1987).
25. U.S. Office of Management and Budget, *Regulatory Program of the United States Government, April 1, 1990–March 30, 1991* (Washington, D.C.: U.S. Government Printing Office), pp. 33, 35.
26. National Academy of Sciences, *Risk Assessment in the Federal Government: Managing the Process* (Washington, D.C.: National Academy Press, 1983): pp. 151, 153.
27. OMB, *Regulatory Program,* 1990–1, p. 14.

28. OMB, *Regulatory Program* (1986): xxii–xxvi. According to OMB, a reliance on conservative or worst-case assumptions and analyses may overstate risks by orders of magnitude. Assessments usually include "margins of safety" factors and upper-bound estimates that really represent policy choices rather than scientific assessments. While it may make sense to take such approaches initially as screening devices to exclude risks that are shown to be insignificant even in the worst-case scenarios, OMB complains that agency officials continue to rely on these biased estimates to overstate greatly the benefits result that from regulatory interventions. Given the uncertainties surrounding animal bioassays, agency officials have considerable discretion in how results are used. Officials often rely on tests using the most sensitive animals available and expose animals to such high doses that some response is inevitable. Models used to extrapolate human risks from animal tests, according to OMB, are from 9 to 30 times more likely to produce false positives (where the test erroneously appears to demonstrate an effect) than false negatives (tests that mistakenly indicate no effect). Models used to extrapolate from high to low doses require use of the upper limit of a 95 percent confidence level (so that there is only a 5 percent chance that the real risk exceeds the estimate), rather than an unbiased estimate. OMB cites differences in modeling that produce estimates of the risk from dioxin, for example, that vary by as much as 5000.
29. OMB and agencies have differed over the calculation of both costs and benefits. Benefits are particularly difficult to determine, as they often rely on minimal information concerning the levels of exposure to the regulated substance and the nature of the exposure–response relationship. But the calculation of costs also requires choices that are not strictly technical. Costs may be limited to direct expenditures for compliance or may include allowances for the projected impact on prices and competitiveness and on unemployment, and allowances for other possible consequences of increased expenditures by the regulated industries. Basic assumptions and beliefs concerning the appropriateness and value of regulations cannot help but color the way in which actual dollar values are assigned in the cost–benefit analysis.
30. OMB, *Regulatory Program, 1990–1*, pp. 36–37.
31. OMB, *Regulatory Program* (1986): xxi.
32. Allen V. Kneese and Charles L. Schultze, *Pollution, Prices, and Public Policy* (Washington, D.C.: Brookings Institution, 1975).
33. Marc K. Landy, Marc J. Roberts, and Stephen R. Thomas, *The Environmental Protection Agency: Asking the Wrong Questions* (New York: Oxford University Press, 1990), pp. 279–281.
34. NAPA, *Presidential Management of Rulemaking.*
35. Harris and Milkis, *The Politics of Regulatory Change* (New York: Oxford, 1989), p. 257.
36. Tolchin and Tolchin, *Dismantling America*, pp. 58, 266.
37. Marianne Lavelle, "For Bush, a Subtler Approach," *National Law Journal* (May 20, 1991), 32.
38. Kneese and Schultze, *Pollution, Prices, and Public Policy.*
39. See, generally, Burke Marshall, ed., *A Workable Government? The Constitution After 200 Years* (New York: Norton, 1987); Donald L. Robinson, *Reforming American Government: The Bicentennial Papers of the Committee on the Constitutional System* (Boulder, Colo: Westview Press, 1985); Robert E. Hunter, Wayne L. Berman, and John F. Kennedy, *Making Government Work: From White House to Congress* (Boulder, Colo.: Westview Press, 1986); James MacGregor Burns, *The Power to Lead: The Crisis of the American Presidency* (New York: Simon and Schuster, 1984); and James L. Sundquist, *Constitutional Reform and Effective Government* (Washington D.C.: Brookings Institution, 1986).
40. For more on this debate see Theodore J. Lowi, *The End of Liberalism* (New York: W. W. Norton, 1979); Richard A. Harris and Sidney M. Milkis, *The Politics of Regulatory Change: A Tale of Two Agencies* (New York: Oxford, 1989); and Cass R. Sunstein, *After the Rights Revolution: Reconceiving the Regulatory State* (Cambridge: Harvard University Press, 1990); and Gary C. Bryner, *Bureaucratic Discretion: Law and Policy in Federal Regulatory Agencies* (New York: Pergammon Press, 1987).
41. See, generally, Lawrence Dodd and Richard Schott, *Congress and the Administrative State* (New York: Wiley, 1979); Energy and Environment Study Institute, "Statutory Deadlines in Environmental Legislation: Necessary But Need Improvement," (Washington, D.C.: EESI, 1985); National

Academy of Public Administration, *Congressional Oversight of Regulatory Agencies: The Need to Strike a Balance and Focus on Performance* (Washington, D.C.: NAPA, 1988).

42. Charles L. Schultze, *The Public Use of Private Interest* (Washington, D.C.: Brookings Institution, 1977), 18.
43. Timothy Wirtz and John Heinz, *Project '88* (U.S. Senate, 1988).
44. Steven Kelman, *What Price Incentives?* (Boston: Auburn House, 1981).
45. See, for example, U.S. Senate, Committee on Governmental Affairs, *Office of Management and Budget: Evolving Roles and Future Issues* (1986).

4

Economic Regulatory Policies: Regulation and Deregulation in Historical Context

Marc Allen Eisner *Wesleyan University, Middletown, Connecticut*

The term *regulation* encompasses a broad array of policies governing economic activity and its consequences. Economic regulations—the subject of this chapter—extend controls over the price and supply of goods, the number of participants, and the conditions of entry. They purposively restrict the behavior of economic actors, often imposing large costs on corporations and the consuming public. They shape economic development by influencing the determination of what is produced, where it is produced, and how it is produced. In recent decades, the dialogue surrounding regulation has been animated by discussions of efficiency, cost-effectiveness, and the need to balance costs and benefits. The "regulatory burden" and its effects on U.S. economic performance have been used to justify a series of deregulatory and regulatory reform measures. While the concern over the economic effects of regulatory policies is justified, it is largely a product of contemporary political debate. In earlier decades, the regulatory debates focused on other factors, such as the need to force corporate accountability, protect small businesses and local markets, and promote economic stability and growth. Depending on the period in question, regulatory initiatives were positively associated with one or more of these goals. Regulation was seen, in large part, as a legitimate governmental response to popular demands.

The major waves of regulatory change in the past century have found their origins in the political reactions to significant economic-structural changes. The emergence of a large-scale corporate economy around the turn of the century, the economic cataclysm of the Great Depression, and the economic stagflation of the 1970s posed threats to various economic and political groups that sought relief through public policy. It was quite natural that the broad goals of policy reflected the historical origins. Thus, the Progressive Era resulted in a host of new regulations justified in one fashion or another by the need to force corporate accountability and place constraints on certain forms of corporate behavior. The New Deal witnessed a host of new regulations designed to promote industrial stability and impose a politically defined distribution of income. During the 1970s and 1980s, Congress and a series of Presidents promoted regulatory reform and deregulation to reduce the burdens imposed on the economy in hopes of stimulating new investment and restraining prices. In each period, regulation was characterized by a somewhat different set of goals reflecting, in large part, the economic and political environment of the time.

This chapter provides a selective overview of economic regulation. After addressing the origins of economic regulation in the Progressive Era and New Deal, the chapter turns to a brief examination of several key regulatory subsystems. The regulatory policies governing trucking, airlines, agriculture, and finance were premised on the need to promote economic stability—a goal that was shared by most New Deal regulatory initiatives. The chapter then turns to a discussion of the critique of regulation that emerged in the postwar period. The theories of regulatory failure became highly salient in the 1970s, largely in response to stagnant growth and persistent inflation. The chapter then reviews the regulatory reform and deregulation initiatives of the 1970s and 1980s, when a number of economic regulations were revised and new review processes were instituted in hopes of promoting efficiency and reducing the economic impact of policy. The chapter concludes with a brief discussion of regulatory policy change.

THE POLITICAL ORIGINS OF ECONOMIC REGULATION

Most economic regulatory policies find their origins in the Progressive Era and the New Deal. The first major wave of regulation was a response to the massive economic changes that occurred during the last quarter of the nineteenth century. The emergence of the large corporation, the dissemination of mass production technologies, and advances in transportation and communications allowed for the integration of formerly local markets and forced core firms to adopt various forms of intercorporate relationships to manage competition. Railroad pools, corporate trusts, and holding companies were, in many ways, rational and necessary responses to the dilemmas of economic development. Coordination in investment and pricing was necessary to maintain profitability and prevent over-expansion.[1] However, actors in many sectors of the economy interpreted the rise of the corporate economy and the growing network of intercorporate relations as threats to their existence and prosperity. In some instances, they organized into economic associations in the hope of exerting some power over prices and supplies. These defensive strategies were seldom successful.[2]

In addition to organization, many economic groups turned to government in hopes of gaining the protection of policy. The demands for a policy response found an early expression at the state level, as populists, farmers, shippers, and merchants demanded and received railroad regulations and antitrust laws. Congress considered a number of legislative initiatives to regulate the railroads. However, the differences between the Senate bill that reflected railroad interests and the House bill that favored shippers created an impasse until the Supreme Court invalidated state railroad regulations in *Wabash v. Illinois,* 1886.[3] The next year, Congress passed the Interstate Commerce Act—a legislative compromise combining elements of the House and Senate bills—to create the Interstate Commerce Commission (ICC). Three years later, Congress passed the Sherman Antitrust Act of 1890, providing the foundation for a national competition policy. Although these early initiatives would be eclipsed by the explosion of regulation in the next half-century, they are illustrative of some of the problems encountered during the period.

Early regulatory initiatives were impaired by several factors. First, there were significant problems of regulatory design. The dramatic transformation of the economy mobilized multiple economic interests seeking relief. Even the industries for which regulation was being considered commonly sought policies to manage competition or lessen the vulnerability to a diverse set of state-level regulations. Faced with myriad unrelated and often contradictory demands, Congress could do one of two things. First, it could include key demands from various interests into a single piece of legislation. Thus, the Interstate Commerce Act combined provisions demanded by the railroads, agricultural organizations, independent oil producers, and a host of other shipping interests.[4] As an alternative, Congress could cast policy at a high level of abstraction, and fail to alienate any of the interested parties. Thus, the Sherman Act contained vague prohibitions of restraints of trade without specifying what forms of corporate conduct would constitute a violation. In either form, regulatory authority was extended without a clear statement of goals. Key decisions regarding the scope of regulation and the priority of competing policy goals were left to be determined by administrators and the courts.

Second, regulatory initiatives were commonly backed with insufficient administrative and financial resources. This was critical because, without careful regulatory design, important decisions were delegated to administrators. Thus, the Interstate Commerce Act failed to give the ICC clear rate-making powers. Although such powers were initially assumed by the commission, the Supreme Court rejected such a broad reading of the agency's legislative mandate, thus disabling the ICC's rate-making activities. The ICC could assess the "reasonableness" of a given rate but was powerless to establish new rates. Likewise, when Congress passed the Sherman Act, it failed to provide the new Justice Department with any resources for antitrust enforcement. Because attorneys worked on the fee system that provided compensation on the basis of successful prosecutions, there were few incentives to file antitrust suits.[5] The lack of administrative and financial resources reflected, in part, the lack of a strong regulatory tradition and the weak consensus that provided the basis for the new initiatives. However, vague legislation and insufficient resources, when taken together, limited the impact of the new regulations.

These problems were partially remedied over the course of the next few decades. Growing experience with national regulations, a reduction of partisan competition following the realignment of 1896, and Progressive Era's confidence in expert administration allowed for a period of experimentation and an expansion of administrative capacities. Thus, Congress passed a number of new acts, including the Hepburn Act of 1906, which provided the ICC with explicit rate-making powers and clarified and strengthened key portions of the ICC's mandate. Likewise, Congress passed the Federal Trade Commission (FTC) Act and the Clayton Act in 1914, creating a new independent regulatory commission and introducing far greater legislative specificity into the antitrust laws. Moreover, the period witnessed an expansion of regulation, as new initiatives addressed activities in a number of sectors. Thus, Congress and a series of Presidents created the Commerce Department's Bureau of Corporations (1906), the Federal Reserve (1913), the Federal Power Commission (1920), and the Commodity Exchange Authority (1922).

In addition to the poor regulatory design and inadequate resources, early efforts were frustrated by the courts. The courts proved highly protective of private property rights, limiting the success of many early regulatory initiatives at the state and national levels. They routinely dismissed regulatory actions by invoking conservative interpretations of the interstate commerce clause, employing highly questionable distinctions (e.g., interstate commerce versus manufacturing) and extending the 14th Amendment's protections against the deprivation of "life, liberty, and property without due process of law" to corporations subject to regulation.[6] Virtually all of the regulatory agencies came into conflict with the courts, in clashes that frequently resulted in reduction of agency authority. In some cases (e.g., the ICC, the FTC), court decisions removed so much of an agency's power that meaningful regulation became contingent on additional legislation. During the decade of the 1920s alone, the Supreme Court held unconstitutional more than 130 regulatory laws.[7] The policy response to the Great Depression, when combined with strategic judicial appointments during the Roosevelt administration, would force a significant reduction in the Court's hostility to regulation.

Progressive regulations were a reaction to the rise of a new national corporate-based economy; the legislation of the 1930s was a response to its collapse. During the Great Depression, a number of new regulatory agencies were created, including the Food and Drug Administration (1931), the Federal Home Loan Bank Board (1932), the Federal Deposit Insurance Corporation (1933), the National Recovery Administration (1933), the Agricultural Adjustment Administration (1933), the Federal Communications Commission (1934), the Securities and Exchange Commission (1934), the National Labor Relations Board (1935), the Federal Maritime Commission (1936), and the Civil Aeronautics Board (1938). While some of the New Deal initiatives revealed a strong continuity with the central strands of Progressivism, most were informed by a new public philosophy that reflected the associationalism and institutional economics of the 1920s. During the 1920s, Herbert Hoover and others promoted the creation of trade associations as a forum for the development of new standards and the coordination of various corporate activities.[8] Hoover envisioned a system of economic governance similar to what existed, albeit in a nascent form, under the War Industries Board of World War I. It was believed that economic associations could cooperate, with the assistance of the federal government, to expand production rationally, bring greater efficiency into the workplace, and extend the benefits of the new economic era to society as a whole.

This associational vision of industrial self-governance found its clearest expression during the New Deal, as Franklin Roosevelt sought to promote recovery and economic stability through an extension of regulation. The National Industrial Recovery Act (NRA) and the Agricultural Adjustment Act (AAA) are regularly discussed as components of a broader and ultimately unsuccessful economic recovery package. What is commonly overlooked, however, is their significance with respect to regulation. Roosevelt and his advisers sought to prevent further economic disruptions by creating a broad regulatory framework in which economic actors would promote price and wage stability on a sector-by-sector basis. While corporations and farmers would have to abide by certain standards to participate, they would be freed from competitive forces and gain access to politically defined rates of return. Although both programs ran afoul on the Supreme Court, they established certain expectations and provided a model for future economic regulatory initiatives.[9] As Ellis Hawley explains:

> The programs of the early New Deal . . . had generated a new organization consciousness among previously weak and relatively unorganized groups. For [those] that lacked market power in an economic world where price and production control had become increasingly characteristic, the NRA and AAA had been eye openers. Public power, they learned, could be used to reinforce private power and control markets; and the group that could develop sufficient political strength and a plausible ideological rationale could secure governmental intervention of this type.[10]

The model of industrial self-regulation established in the early New Deal found an expression in the regulation of industrial relations, agricultural production, corporate finance, communications, civil aeronautics, and motor transportation. In each case, authority was delegated to administrators who, in turn, provided distinct services to the regulated to protect them from competition and allow for greater financial stability. In each case, regulations were defined, in large part, through the close interplay of regulators and organized economic actors (e.g., trade associations, commodity groups, unions). Where producers were not organized into associations (e.g., over-the-counter securities dealers, certain agricultural commodity producers), regulators consciously stimulated organization.[11] While the new regulatory agencies were nominally created to promote the "public interest," policy was explicitly designed to enhance artificially the income of key groups of economic actors. Regulation became, in essence, a system of wealth redistribution that would promote stability.

REGULATION IN ACTION

By the end of the Roosevelt administration, the nation's core economic regulatory policies were largely in place. Controls over entry, exit, and/or prices existed in railroads, trucking, airlines, communications, commercial and investment banking, electricity generation, pharmaceutics, and agriculture. These sector-specific regulations were combined with regulations addressing industrial relations and corporate consolidation and conduct across the economy. Although many small businesses avoided regulations and the network of regulations was inundated with exemptions, much of the economy functioned under one or more set of regulations. It is useful, at this point, to examine briefly several key regulatory subsystems that were in place by the end of the New Deal to illustrate the means by which regulations promoted economic stability.

Regulating Surface Transportation

Motor carrier regulation was a state issue up to the 1930s. Demands for trucking regulation came from a number of sources, including the railroads that were having difficulties competing with the unregulated carriers. The trucking industry largely opposed regulation until its experience with the National Recovery Administration revealed that federal intervention could promote profitability and limit entry. Following the collapse of the NRA, Congress passed the Motor Carrier Act of 1935, vesting regulatory authority in the Interstate Commerce Commission. The act established a number of regulatory goals, including the promotion of industry stability, the encouragement of quality service by financially sound carriers, and the maintenance of reasonable rates. The ICC regulated entry and rates, much as it was doing in the area of rail transportation. By exercising these powers, the ICC could effectively prevent competition and allow for rates of return above what would have existed under market conditions.[12]

The ICC limited competition by making commission authorization (i.e., route authority) a prerequisite for operation. The Motor Carrier Act directed the ICC to provide operating authority to any carriers operating after June 1, 1935. Any new entrants would be given operating authority only if they could meet two criteria. First, they had to prove that they were "fit, willing, and able." Second, and more important, they had to show that the new service was in the public interest, could not be provided by existing carriers, and would not endanger or impair the existing carriers. Because existing carriers could file a protest in response to applications for operating authority, it was extraordinarily difficult for new competitors to enter the market. Thus, many markets remained under the dominance of the carriers grandfathered in under the provisions of the 1935 legislation.

The ICC sought to promote financial stability and limit ruinous competition by regulating rates. Initially, tariffs were filed by carriers and could be challenged by other carriers, including truckers, railroads, or regulated water carriers. Because motor carriers sought to avoid the lengthy delays associated with rate investigations, their proposed rates seldom challenged those charged by the railroads. Following the Reed-Bulwinkle Act of 1948, which granted carriers an exemption from the antitrust laws, motor carriers (often working through their associations) determined rates in rate bureaus prior to their submission for ICC approval. Although carriers could seek approval for lower rates than those determined in the bureau, such applications were often protested by other carriers, resulting in a lengthy investigation. The ICC essentially served to maintain a motor carriers' cartel by limiting entry and penalizing those that sought to undercut the agreed upon rates.

The effects of ICC regulation of motor carriers were quite predictable. First, regulation increased the costs of trucking. Shippers were charged some 25 percent above competitive rates, thus forcing consumers to absorb billions of dollars of additional expenses.[13] These added costs were realized in carrier profits: motor carrier rates of return were commonly between 15 and 23 percent, far greater than the returns realized by manufacturing firms. In addition to high shipping costs and supracompetitive profits, regulation resulted in a declining number of carriers as part of the policy of impeding entry. Thus, between 1940 and 1970, the number of ICC-regulated motor carriers fell by one-quarter, from 21,058 to 15,100. Given the lack of economies of scale in trucking, one could conclude that regulation bore the full responsibility for this change.[14]

Regulating Civil Aeronautics

The regulatory system created for airlines was similar to those covering surface transportation. Prior to the passage of the Civil Aeronautics Act of 1938, regulatory authority over civilian air transportation was divided among the Post Office, the Commerce Department, the ICC, and, for a short period of time, the Army. After a prolonged debate over who should bear primary responsibility for regulating air transportation, Congress passed the Civil Aeronautics Act of 1938, establishing a five-person independent agency, the Civil Aeronautics Authority, later renamed the Civil Aeronautics Board (CAB). The new agency was in many ways the equivalent of the ICC in terms of its responsibilities and authorities. Indeed, the Civil Aeronautics Act was modeled on the recently passed Motor Carrier Act. Like the ICC, CAB licensed air carriers by providing them with a certificate of necessity acknowledging that "the applicant is fit, willing, and able to perform such transportation properly, and to conform to the provisions of [the] Act" and "that such transportation is required by the public convenience and necessity." Beyond the power to approve routes, the Act echoed the earlier transportation regulation by giving CAB the responsibility over route abandonment and consolidations. CAB also exercised control over rates. The enabling legislation required that all air carriers file their rate schedules with CAB 30 days before they went into effect. Rates had to be "just and reasonable" and CAB had the authority to reject or adjust rates and rate changes if found unreasonable. The act also prohibited rebates and discrimination. CAB exercised rate-making authority in determining compensation for carrying U.S. Mail, an authority that provided a means of subsidizing the industry in its early days.[15]

As with the ICC's regulation of surface transportation, CAB interpreted its mandate as requiring it to promote safeguards against "uneconomic, destructive competition and wasteful duplication of services."[16] The congressional debates repeatedly expressed the fear that excessive competition would undermine the growth of the industry and force carriers to de-emphasize safety. CAB thus sought to manage competition while guaranteeing a rate of return sufficient to fund orderly expansion. This entailed the erection and maintenance of significant barriers to entry, primarily in the agency's control over certificates of convenience. During the first four decades of its existence, CAB refused to approve a single new trunk carrier to begin service on a major route despite tremendous increases in the amount of air traffic. Indeed, as a result of mergers within the industry, the number of carriers actually declined from the 16 that were grandfathered in under the provisions of the 1938 legislation to 11. Although barriers to entry were relaxed for charter and local service (i.e., feeder lines) there were continuing attempts to limit or prevent competition between local carriers that could provide service between two cities and trunk carriers that had already been authorized to carry passengers on that route.[17]

As noted above, early airline regulation focused on maintaining adequate subsidies for airmail service. The regulation of fares began in earnest in the 1940s. Although CAB initially approved increases with little concern for acceptable rates of return, it adopted a target return of 10.5 percent in the 1960s and 12 percent after 1974, focusing on costs and revenues for the industry as a whole rather than on a route-by-route basis. It is critical to note that CAB required airlines to submit rate changes 30 days in advance, thus allowing adequate time for other carriers to challenge the new rates. Since rate reductions could be overturned on a number of grounds (e.g., rate discrimination, unreasonableness) and the advance notice provided other carriers with the opportunity to increase their fares in tandem, the system carried a bias toward rate increases. Although there were modest rate reductions with the introduction of the jet aircraft, these reductions were much less than the reduced industry costs derived from the technological advances. Thus, in the 1960s, a 21 percent reduction in seat-mile costs was accompanied by a 7 percent reduction rates. As with the regulation of motor carriers, airline regulation resulted in a limited number of carriers realizing supracompetitive profits.[18]

Regulating Agriculture

Contemporary agricultural regulation finds its origins in the New Deal. Agricultural production accounted for some 30 percent of the workforce, making its economic status a key factor in the recovery effort. However, the farm economy was hit harder than manufacturing due to the inherent features of agricultural production. As a sector of the economy, agriculture is distinguished by the combination of demand inelasticity and phenomenal increases in farm productivity resulting, in large part, from government policies and technological advances dating back to the last half of the nineteenth century. The core problem in agriculture has been one of preventing excessive supplies of commodities that may depress prices and farm incomes.

The U.S. Department of Agriculture (USDA) has pursued the goal of maintaining high farm incomes through the use of a variety of policy tools established in New Deal legislation including the Agricultural Adjustment Acts of 1933 and 1938. Depending on the commodity, regulators use a combination of nonrecourse loans, deficiency payments, set-aside programs and marketing orders.[19] Through nonrecourse loans, the USDA lends money to farmers at a predetermined rate, using future crops as collateral. Loan rates provide a guaranteed price for a given commodity, since the farmer will only repay the loan if the commodity can be sold for a greater amount of money. Deficiency payments work in a similar fashion, albeit without the pretense of a loan. Congress establishes target prices for various commodities and then makes a commitment to disburse payments equal to the difference between the target and market prices. The USDA often requires farmers to participate in set-aside programs as a condition of receiving loans or deficiency payments. By removing acreage from cultivation, set-asides reduce the supply of commodities available on the market, thus increasing prices.

Marketing orders are agreements establishing regulatory authority over a given commodity group. Orders issued by the USDA follow the approval of two-thirds of the growers voting (or growers accounting for two-thirds of the commodity produced) and cover the production of a host of commodities, including fruits, vegetables, nuts, and milk. Commodity groups formulate marketing agreements that become effective once signed by farmers responsible for the production of at least 50 percent of the given commodity. Commodity agreements commonly specify various qualitative authorities (e.g., grade, size), the quantity produced, and the rate of flow to markets or processors. Compliance with marketing agreements is largely voluntary, although the benefits associated with participation can be great.[20]

The agricultural regulatory system established during the New Deal evolved into a relatively insulated system dominated by organized commodity producers, the USDA, and the relevant congressional committees. To facilitate the interaction of so many interests, the USDA organized its Agricultural Stabilization and Conservation Service, which administers price supports, and its Agricultural Marketing Service, which facilitates the formulation and implementation of marketing orders, on a commodity-specific basis. A similar level of disaggregation characterizes the organization of the agriculture subcommittees in Congress. The close relationship between actors in Congress, the USDA, and the commodity groups, combined with norms of voluntarism and a devolution of public authority to producers, created a relatively stable system of self-regulation that allowed farmers to increase prices and their share of national income. Within this system of self-regulation, the majority of the benefits have accrued to the large farms, at the expense of smaller farms and consumers. Indeed, three decades after the New Deal legislation was passed, the largest 19 percent of the nation's farms claimed over 62 percent of the benefits from the farm commodity programs, with 42 percent of the overall benefits going to the top 7 percent. In contrast, 50 percent of the farms—those that were the smallest units in terms of annual incomes—received approximately 9 percent of the subsidy benefits. The wealthiest farms in the nation claimed 42 percent of their incomes from the commodity programs, compared with 5 percent for the farms in the bottom half of the income distribution.[21]

Regulating Commercial Banking

Before the erosion of regulatory distinctions in the 1970s and 1980s, the regulation of commercial banking, like that of surface and air transportation, rested on the absence of effective competition.[22] The McFadden Act of 1927 allowed national banks and state members of the Federal Reserve System to engage in limited branching to the extent permitted by state regulators, but prohibited interstate branching. Because regulators hoped to maintain the financial stability of the industry, the Comptroller of the Currency issued new charters only after a consideration of the effects of entry on existing banks. Geographical limits on competition were combined with functional restrictions when Congress passed the Banking Act of 1933. The belief that financial conflicts of interest contributed to the financial collapse of 1929 led Congress to mandate the separation of commercial banking (deposit-taking and loan-making) and investment banking (securities underwriting and dealing) and restricted national banks and state members of the Federal Reserve system from dealing in anything other than U.S. Treasury securities and general obligation state and municipal bonds.[23] By prohibiting the payment of interest on demand deposits, the Banking Act of 1933 eliminated price competition for these funds while providing commercial banks with access to free funds. The Banking Act of 1933 and 1935 authorized regulators to impose interest rate ceilings for time and savings deposits, thus further extending the limitations on competition.

The elimination of competition, it was hoped, would reduce incentives to engage in various forms of behavior that would contribute to financial instability. The goal of promoting stability was furthered with the regulation of capitalization and reserves under the Federal Reserve Act of 1913 and required membership in the insurance offered by the Federal Deposit Insurance Corporation (FDIC). The FDIC insured deposits up to $2,500, a figure that was progressively increased until it reached $100,000 in the 1980s. The deposit insurance was established in hopes of averting future bank runs and restoring consumer confidence after the wave of bank failures in the early 1930s. Restrictions were placed on the loan-making activities of Federal Reserve members, and banks were subject to regular inspections to assess their financial performance and determine whether they were complying with applicable regulations.

While competition among commercial banks was limited by regulations governing interest rates, financial instruments, and branching, there remained limited competition among commercial banks, savings and loan institutions, savings banks, and credit unions. Although all of these financial institutions competed in one form or another, they were differentiated by limits on their market for deposits (e.g., credit unions serviced members with certain common attributes, such as place of employment), the composition of their loan portfolios (e.g., savings and loan institutions were required to work primarily in the long-term mortgage market), or the kinds of services they could offer (e.g., commercial banks had a monopoly on demand deposits). They were also distinguished by their regulators. Commercial finance was characterized by what was by far the most complicated and decentralized of any national regulatory subsystem. Thus, commercial banks were regulated by the Comptroller of the Currency, the Federal Reserve, and the FDIC. Savings and loan institutions were regulated by the Federal Home Loan Bank Board and its Federal Savings and Loan Insurance Corporation. Credit unions were regulated by the National Credit Union Administration. Because of the dual banking system (i.e., banks are awarded state or national charters), the national financial regulators were combined with a collection of regulatory agencies in the 50 states. Moreover, a host of additional national regulators like the Federal Trade Commission, the Justice Department, and the Securities and Exchange Commission exercised some control over depository institutions.[24]

For several decades the regulations governing commercial banking provided for financial stability. Bank failures were quite rare, with an annual failure rate of less than 0.001 percent up to the mid-1970s. With regulations restricting or prohibiting geographical, price, and product competition, banking was among the most profitable industries. However, the same restrictions that promoted stability and profitability became a liability in the 1970s, as the combination of growing inflation and interest rate ceilings threatened the capacity of all regulated institutions to attract funds. In an inflationary environment, portfolios laden with long-term, low-rate, fixed mortgages threatened profitability. A host of actors began competing with regulated institutions on the deposit-taking or loan-making side of banking. So called nonbank banks exploited loopholes in the existing regulations and offered new financial instruments and competitive interest rates. The growing competitive difficulties suffered by the regulated institutions and concerns over disintermediation set the stage for deregulation.[25]

As these examples suggest, regulations initiated during the Progressive Era and New Deal were designed to promote industrial stability and profitability. As reactions to the tumultuous changes that characterized the late nineteenth century and the Great Depression, these goals were understandable. Consumers, workers, corporations, and farmers sought public policies to counter the potential costs of economic–structural transformation. They sought a politically defined distribution of income when a market-based distribution became fraught with uncertainty. However, the same qualities that made an extension of regulatory authority politically expedient in the first half of the century made regulations vulnerable to political challenges in the postwar period.

REGULATION AS A CHALLENGE TO THE PUBLIC INTEREST

Economic regulation can be justified as a remedy to market failure. Working from a list of conditions that characterize perfect markets, one can identify various policies that compensate for the violation of one or more of these conditions. For example, perfect information is necessary for market actors to make rational consumption decisions. When information is lacking, regulations can prohibit the use of substances that have harmful effects and require corporations to provide labels listing ingredients. Likewise, for markets to function efficiently all actors must be price-takers. When various forms of collusion or the existence of a natural monopoly allow firms to administer prices, policy can prohibit the troublesome forms of intercorporate relationships or establish rate-making. Through regulation, in short, policymakers can compensate for market failure, thus contributing to economic efficiency and public welfare.

The public interest interpretation of regulation fell under fire during the postwar period as a number of scholars drawn from different disciplines and ideological camps began to frame related explanations of regulatory failure and business influence in the policy process. The most influential work on regulatory capture was Marver Bernstein's *Regulating Business by Independent Commission*. Bernstein hypothesized that all independent regulatory commissions pass through an organizational life cycle with distinct stages of gestation, youth, maturity, and old age. During its youth, a commission may vigorously fulfill its mandate. According to Bernstein, a decline in issue salience and public support often accompanies the passage into maturity. Without the benefit of a supportive political environment, "the commission becomes more concerned with the general health of the industry and tries to prevent changes which adversely affect it. Cut off from the mainstream of political life, the commission's standards of regulation are determined in light of the desires of the industry affected."[26] The commission subsequently enters a stage of old age when "the regulated interests become so fixed that the agency has no creative force left to mobilize against the regulated groups. Its primary mission is the maintenance of the status quo in the regulated industry and its own position as recognized protector of the industry."[27] In short, independent commissions tend quite naturally toward capture and organizational rigidity. As they enter maturity, the only support they can rely upon is that provided by the very interests that Congress has directed them to regulate.

A similar argument was presented by Samuel Huntington in his classic article on the Interstate Commerce Commission.[28] According to Huntington, the ICC was a vigorous regulator during the period separating the passage of the Hepburn Act of 1906 and the Transportation Act of 1920. During this period, railroad regulation received a great deal of political attention. The ICC's successful efforts to stabilize rates and eliminate the worst forms of discrimination received the strong support of Congress and shippers who demanded lower rates. In paradoxical fashion, the ICC's success was its own undoing: it limited the political salience of rail regulation and the active support of shippers. The ICC thus became an agency in search of a constituency. It was quite predictable, therefore, that it looked to the industry it was charged with regulating. Following the passage of the Transportation Act of 1920, the ICC consistently approved rate increases or maintained rate stability in the face of wholesale price reductions. The ICC became a railroad agency committed to promoting industry profitability, even at the cost of inhibiting the growth of more efficient forms of surface transportation.

Bernstein and Huntington presented regulatory capture as the product of pluralist politics in a changing political environment. Interest group pressures, more than any other factor, were critical in determining regulatory policy decisions. As the salience of an issue declines, the only powerful interests with the incentive to mobilize belong to the regulated industry.[29] Some of the capture theories presented in the 1960s departed from this pluralist interpretation. Gabriel Kolko, for example, argued that key regulatory initiatives of the Progressive Era were enacted at the behest of major corporations. They sought relief from both the chaos of competition that threatened corporate profitability and survival in many sectors and the radicalism of some state-level regulations that could place meaningful restraints on business conduct. Regulation thus constituted "the victory of big businesses in achieving the rationalization of the economy that only the federal government could provide."[30] Likewise, Murray Edelman argued that most regulatory initiatives were symbolic acts designed to stimulate popular support and meet, albeit superficially, the demand for a policy response. The broad declarations of purpose were only rarely met with anything approaching a commensurate allocation of resources.[31]

Many of the discussions of regulatory capture focused on the independent regulatory commissions, reflecting in part the poor performance and rigidity of many well-established agencies like the Federal Trade Commission, the Interstate Commerce Commission, and the Federal Communications Commission. However, the critique went beyond the question of organizational form to address the very nature of the policy process. Most influential, in this respect, was Theodore Lowi's *End of Liberalism.* Lowi described the system based on the delegation of authority as "interest group liberalism." He explained that the policy system promotes "a policy agenda that is accessible to all organized interests and makes no independent judgment of their claims . . . it defines the public interest as a result of the amalgamation of various claims."[32] According to Lowi, the interplay of delegation, the lack of precise statutory standards, and a public philosophy supportive of interest group access generates severe problems of coordination and policy evaluation. Most important is that majority rule in Congress is subverted by the rule of powerful interests at the agency level. The dominant public philosophy has "promoted concentration of democratic authority but deconcentration of democratic power . . . it has opposed privilege in policy formulation only to foster it quite systematically in the implementation of policy."[33] Delegation, for Lowi, was a serious matter precisely because it vitiated democratic norms and provided the structural basis for group capture of agencies and subversion of policies. Similar critiques of delegation were presented by Kenneth Culp Davis and Richard Stewart.[34]

By the end of the 1960s, the basic components of the capture thesis were in place. In each case, business interests were seen as playing the determinative role in the definition of policy. Most of the work on capture accepted the thesis that a reduction in the popular support for a regulatory agency resulted in industry dominance, facilitated by delegation. Regulators seeking to maintain political support thus turned to the regulated as a key constituency, with foreseeable effects on policy. During the 1970s, economists entered the debate on regulatory capture following the publication of George Stigler's article "The Theory of Economic Regulation."[35] While much of Stigler's article was a highly stylied presentation of what had been argued a decade earlier, its influence within the economics discipline is beyond question. Following Stigler, economists appeared less concerned with the question of whether regulatory agencies were captured than with the factors that determine which groups would effectively mobilize to shape policy.[36]

For Stigler, regulatory policies are designed and administered to provide benefits both to the regulators and to the industry in question. Regulators are self-interested actors who rationally exchange policies for votes and resources while forcing the general public to bear the burdens of industry support. Industry actors demand and receive four kinds of policies. First, they seek policies creating barriers to entry. Political officials award licenses, charters, frequencies, new routes, and a host of other resources that are essential for economic activity. The conditions imposed on potential entrants may be sufficient to insulate established actors from new competition. Second, industry may seek direct subsidies, although this is less beneficial than barriers to entry. Third, industrial actors may seek to impose regulatory burdens on firms producing potential substitutes. Finally, they may demand price controls administered by a regulatory agency, thus allowing for higher rates of return without price competition. These policies allow regulated firms to restrain competition and extract monopoly rents under the protective umbrella of regulatory policies. Regulators trade supportive policies for the political and financial resources that businesses can provide. Policy creates a de facto cartel; taxpayers and consumers absorb the costs of cartel maintenance. Regulation becomes a source of market failure rather than a remedy.

Outside of academic circles, the capture thesis caught the attention of many public interest groups and consumer advocates. A Nader report, for example, attributed regulatory failure to "influence peddling, incestuous job interchange with industry, [and] lack of appointment integrity."[37] Mark Green, director of Nader's Corporate Accountability Research Group, claimed that government regulations "undermined competition and entrenched monopoly." This was considered problematic because "competition is to the economy what political freedom is to our policy: both oppose unchecked power and both value diversity in the contest for solutions." The means of eliminating regulatory distortions were clear: "Where there would be a viably competitive market but for economic regulation, that industry should be freed from regulatory restraint."[38] The capture thesis facilitated the integration of deregulation in a larger reform agenda.

The capture thesis became prominent in a period of steady economic growth. It became politically salient in the 1970s as regulatory capture and mismanagement were linked with the dual problems of inflation and economic stagnation. The distortions and high prices that result from economic regulations were commonly cited as factors contributing to inflation. Officials and economic analysts in a number of agencies and members of key congressional committees began advocating deregulation. As the Council of Economic Advisers explained in its 1975 economic report, deregulation "could save billions of dollars by releasing resources for other uses, helping combat inflation, and making the economy more efficient and more productive in future years."[39] The costs of regulation became even more troublesome as new social regulations were appended to the existing regulatory system. In a widely cited study, Murray Weidenbaum attempted to assess the costs of regulation. He noted that the administrative costs had increased rapidly over the course of the 1970s, driven in part by the creation of new agencies. In 1974, the administrative costs were approximately $2.2 billion, growing to $4.8 billion by 1979. In some years, the annual rate of growth was 22 percent, more than double the inflation rate. Indeed, by 1979, there were approximately 215,000 federal employees working at the regulatory agencies. Of course, the administrative expenses were insignificant when compared with compliance costs and related economic distortions. Weidenbaum provided the example of the Occupational Safety and Health Administration. While the agency had an annual budget of some $150 million, it forced corporations to incur an estimated $3 billion per year in capital outlays. The aggregate effects of regulation were even more striking. When all factors were taken into account (e.g., capital expenses, deadweight efficiency losses, and impediments to the rapid diffusion of technological innovations), Weidenbaum calculated that the direct and indirect costs of regulation were $65 billion in 1976, increasing above the $100 billion mark by the end of the decade.[40]

While Weidenbaum's estimates were widely disputed, the central theme was rarely challenged. Since there was little doubt that regulations forced society to incur large costs, the key question became whether these costs were justified by the social benefits. The combination of economic stagflation, a failure of existing macroeconomic policy tools, and debates linking part of this record to regulatory failure provided sufficient justification for regulatory reform and deregulation. By the 1970s, deregulation had assumed a central position on the policy agenda.

A Challenge to the Public Interest?

Economic regulations may have run counter to the public interest in providing benefits to a narrowly defined set of industry actors and imposing higher costs on the public as a whole. However, for two reasons it is difficult to support the contention that regulatory capture was the norm. First, certain regulatory agencies are simply not subject to capture. The policies they administer either fail to focus on a single sector of the economy or fail to provide any real benefits to the regulated. We can take the example of the antitrust agencies. With broad economy-wide mandates and no licenses, routes, or frequencies to award, the agencies fail to create the kinds of incentives necessary to promote group mobilization. Indeed, when groups mobilize they focus on Congress, hoping to acquire antitrust exemptions. A similar point could be made with respect to the contemporary social regulatory agencies such as the Environmental Protection Agency (EPA) or Occupational Safety and Health Administration (OSHA), which regulate across sectors of the economy.

Second, some variants of the capture thesis begin with a faulty premise: that regulation was established to promote efficiency or address market failure. As an expression of a changing political environment or the self-interest of regulators, policies evolved to provide benefits to the regulated. However, few regulatory policies were initiated in the hopes of promoting efficiency. Indeed, one may search the legislative history of major regulatory statutes and find few references to efficiency as a policy goal. As suggested earlier, most agencies were created to promote the viability, stability, and profitability of firms operating in a specific industry. This was the explicit goal of the major regulatory initiatives of the Progressive Era and the New Deal. When seen in historical context, sectoral stability, limited competition, and profitability are not indicators of policy failure but of success. As a result, it may be unfair to assess the performance of an agency by examining its impact on economic efficiency unless one first asserts that the goals associated with regulation—and the evaluative criteria—have changed to reflect contemporary concerns.

The economic regulations established during the Progressive Era and New Deal reflected the economic and political context of the times. Dramatic structural changes and the subsequent collapse of the industrial economy stimulated demands for stability and guaranteed profitability and growth. These demands found an expression in regulatory policy. The regulatory politics of the 1970s and early 1980s were derivative of a specific economic and political context as well. Declining economic performance—the dual problems of economic stagnation and inflation—directed the debates toward the question of how the regulatory system could be redirected to promote efficiency and growth. We turn now to an examination of the two key thrusts of regulatory politics in this period: regulatory reform and deregulation.

REFORMING REGULATORY ADMINISTRATION

While the terms *regulatory reform* and *deregulation* are commonly used interchangeably, there are differences worth exploring. The regulatory reform initiatives of the 1970s and 1980s were attempts to enhance the internal management of the regulatory agencies by promoting the consideration of the economic costs and benefits of policy alternatives. Regulatory review and clearance were centralized in the Executive Office of the President and the Office of Management and Budget (OMB), in the hope of coordinating agency actions, avoiding contradictory policies, and imposing new criteria on agencies. By making executive review part of the regulatory process, agencies were compelled to enhance their own policy planning and evaluation staffs and to internalize the review process. Deregulation, in contrast, describes the elimination of regulations determined to be unnecessary or prohibitively expensive.[41] Regulatory reform and deregulation worked in tandem, commonly contributing one to the other. When agency analysts determined that policies imposed excessive costs on the economy, they became ripe for deregulation. As economic criteria were introduced into regulatory decision-making, regulators increasingly addressed incentive-based solutions to regulatory problems. Agencies seeking to reintroduce market mechanisms as part of a deregulatory initiative were able to rely on the economics staffs in the policy analysis and evaluation offices created in response to the reform efforts. Economic professionalization created a natural constituency for deregulation. Despite the obvious connections, it is useful to consider reform and deregulation separately.

Regulatory reform was a goal of each president from Nixon through Reagan. A review of the reform initiatives reveals continuity both in centralization and the application of economic analysis in policy evaluation. In 1971, the Nixon administration inaugurated an interagency Quality of Life review process, largely in response to Commerce Department and OMB apprehension over the recently created Environmental Protection Agency and the potential costs of environmental policy. The Quality of Life review process required agencies to submit significant rules for OMB review 30 days prior to the announcement of rule making in the *Federal Register.* The agencies also had to submit their analyses, including a discussion of principal goals, the costs and benefits of the proposed rule and the alternatives, and the justification for the final decision. These materials would then be open for examination by other agencies, whose written comments would be forwarded to the OMB and to the agencies responsible for the proposed rule. Prior to the publication of the final rule, agencies were required to submit the final draft and a summary of the public comments and new issues raised during rulemaking.[42]

Gerald Ford attempted to expand the executive review process with the creation of a Council on Wage and Price Stability (COWPS). COWPS was authorized to oversee events in the private sector that might affect price stability and review government programs and determine their inflationary impact.[43] Ford's Executive Order 11,821 created the Inflation Impact Statement as a means of standardizing the review of government activities. In essence, the order required that executive agencies certify that they had assessed the inflationary impact of major legislative proposals, regulations, and rules. COWPS and OMB shared responsibility for reviewing the statements, with Council economists playing the major role with respect to regulations. COWPS placed its formal economic analyses of proposed rules in the public record as part of the rulemaking process. The executive order also empowered the OMB to establish procedures for the evaluation the significant rules and regulations. To this end, the OMB recommended the use of a quantified comparison of costs and benefits whenever regulations resulted in costs in excess of $100 million and/or had a specified effect on productivity, employment levels, energy consumption, and the supplies of important inputs.[44]

The Carter administration's regulatory review initiatives were a continuation of earlier efforts, albeit within a new institutional context and with a new set of procedures. In January 1978, Carter established the Regulatory Analysis and Review Group (RARG), consisting of representatives of several executive agencies and headed by an executive committee that included a member of the CEA, a representative of the OMB, and two additional members of the group. Unlike COWPS, RARG was directed to review a limited number (between 10 and 20 per year) of select rules and regulations deemed to have a potentially significant impact on inflation (i.e., those with an annual cost to industry of $100 million). RARG could review but four rules per agency per year.[45]

Three months after the creation of RARG, Carter issued Executive Order 12,044. The order explained: "Regulations shall be as simple and clear as possible. They shall achieve legislative goals effectively and efficiently. They shall not impose unnecessary burdens on the economy, on individuals, on public or private organizations, or on state and local governments." Pursuant to these policy goals, the Executive Order required agencies to accompany major significant rules with a regulatory analysis containing a statement of the problem being addressed, a discussion of alternative responses, an analysis of the economic impact of each of the alternatives, and a detailed justification for the agency's decision. The executive order did not require cost–benefit analysis but required that options be compared on the basis of their cost-effectiveness. Once the policy goals were accepted, the objective became to determine the most efficient means to their realization. Agencies were also required to give the public early and meaningful opportunities to participate in the development of new regulations. This was to be facilitated through publishing advanced notice of proposed rulemaking, publicizing the event, holding open hearings, and providing at least 60 days for public comment.[46]

Following a review of RARG, Carter created the Regulatory Council in October, 1978. Unlike RARG, which represented executive branch agencies and was chaired by the head of the CEA, the Council was composed of representatives of regulatory agencies, both executive and independent. Overall, 35 agencies were represented. It was chaired by EPA Administrator Douglas Costle and funded out of the EPA's budget. As George Eads and Michael Fix suggest, it "was seen as a counterweight to RARG and a regulator's lobby," representing regulatory agencies rather than those within the administration who sought to limit the economic impact of regulatory policies.[47] The Council also had a different mandate than RARG: it was directed to prevent regulatory duplication by publishing semiannual regulatory calendars and providing a context in which regulators could consider the compatibility, flexibility, and cost-effectiveness of their regulations.[48]

The regulatory review processes established in the 1970s suffered from a common set of problems. First, because agencies were responsible for determining whether their regulations were "significant" and thus subject to review, participation was essentially voluntary. Second, when agencies submitted their regulations to review, the agency responsible for assessing their analyses lacked the authority to stop promulgation. Because compliance could not be forced, the OMB, COWPS, and RARG had to rely on the power of persuasion. Third, because analyses were conducted late in the policy process, they commonly did little more than justify decisions that had already been made. Economic analysis was not effectively integrated into the policy process at an early stage. Finally, regulatory review was embroiled in controversy from the beginning. Nixon's Quality of Life review process, for example, focused undue attention on the EPA, creating the appearance that the President was attempting to use the process to undermine environmental policy. During the Carter administration, a highly publicized dispute over OSHA's cotton dust standard was resolved only when the President (under pressure from Congress and the AFL-CIO) sided with the agency against RARG.[49]

Despite these problems, the review processes established in the 1970s provided an ever-greater role for economics in the regulatory process and established economic efficiency as an important factor to be considered during the regulatory process. Thus, Susan and Martin Tolchin referred to RARG as a "turning point in presidential management of regulation" characterized by "the ascendancy of economists over lawyers." They continued: "Shaped by their own discipline, White House economists did not even bother to conceal their disdain for what they considered rigid, legalistic approaches adopted by many of the agencies, especially when they encountered opposition."[50] The growing importance of economic analysts in assessing the justification for regulatory policies and the centralization of power in the Executive Office provided an important basis for the events of the Reagan administration when regulatory review came of age. Indeed, many of the central problems plaguing regulatory review were addressed during the Reagan presidency.

Ronald Reagan came to Washington with a firm commitment to regulatory reform and relief. On the campaign trail, he freely linked regulation to the economic decline of the past decade. On January 22, 1981, President Reagan created the Presidential Task Force on Regulatory Relief, chaired by Vice-President George Bush. The Task Force was charged with reviewing proposed rules and existing regulations, addressing the need for the regulation, and assessing the net social benefits of policy. The task force was to recommend changes and compile a list of those regulations that were most burdensome for business. From January, 1981, to August, 1983, when the Task Force was disbanded, it identified 119 regulations for review; 76 were revised or vacated.[51]

Less than a month after the creation of the task force, Reagan issued Executive Order 12,291, the centerpiece of the administration's regulatory reform effort. The order placed a freeze on pending executive branch regulations and called on the executive regulatory agencies to cease issuing final rules for the next 60 days as the task force examined their impact. It also established as the administration's policy that "regulatory action shall not be taken unless the potential benefits to society for the regulation outweigh the potential costs to society." Pursuant to this policy, all executive branch agencies were required to prepare a Regulatory Impact Analysis (RIA) to accompany major rules, defined much as they had been during the Carter administration. However, the OMB was authorized to identify any rule as a major rule subject to review. Unlike the Regulatory Analysis mandated under Carter's Executive Order 12,044, the RIAs were to require a cost–benefit analysis to determine "the potential net benefits of the rule, including an evaluation of effects that cannot be quantified in monetary terms." The RIA was to be presented, along with the proposed rulemaking package, to the OMB 60 days before the publication of the proposed notice. A final RIA was to be submitted to the OMB along with a draft of the final rule 30 days before its publication in the *Federal Register.*

Earlier review efforts were limited by a lack of enforcement powers. Executive Order 12,291 addressed this problem by giving the OMB the power to delay the rule-making process. Upon filing the initial RIA, agencies could be prohibited from publishing the notice of proposed rulemaking until the review and necessary consultation were completed. Moreover, agencies were ordered to refrain from publishing a final RIA or rule "until the agency has responded to the [OMB] Director's views, and incorporated those views and the agency's response in the rulemaking file." In essence, agencies could be prevented from proceeding until they had met the conditions established by the OMB. Any conflicts arising under the executive order would be referred to the Task Force on Regulatory Relief.

The requirement of conducting an RIA and the technical demands of cost–benefit analysis often strained agency resources. According to one estimate by Paul Portney, the costs paid to outside contractors could range from $100,000 to several million dollars, depending on the heterogeneity of the sector being regulated, the complexity of the regulation, and the kinds of primary research required to determine the magnitude of the benefits. Including the agency personnel required to conduct in-house analyses and monitor work done outside of the agency, the direct costs of conducting the regulatory review were within the range of $17 to $25 million per year.[52] These costs effectively stressed the resources of agencies that were already functioning under budget reductions. Between 1981 and 1984, there was a 14 percent reduction in agency budgets, once adjusted for inflation. This had a predictable affect on staffing: by 1984, the number of full-time positions in the major regulatory agencies had declined by 16 percent over 1980.[53] The need to devote funds to RIAs undoubtedly exacerbated existing resource constraints. The Reagan administration increased the analytical requirements for extending regulations at the same time it reduced the administrative resources available to the task.[54] Thus, the annual number of new rules declined by approximately one-fourth, using the Carter administration as a base. Moreover, as a result of the executive review process and the agenda of Reagan administration appointees, new rules tended to place a greater emphasis on compliance costs borne by business and the use of market mechanisms rather than the much-vilified command and control approaches to regulation.[55]

The executive review process quickly became embroiled in controversy. Executive Order 12,291 provided the OMB with a tremendous amount of discretion. It was given the power to classify any regulation as requiring an RIA, even if the regulation failed to have significant economic consequences. Likewise, it could waive the RIA requirement, as was commonly done in changes that weakened or eliminated existing regulations. Moreover, there were persistent concerns that the OMB had become a court of appeals for businesses.[56] By the end of Reagan's first term, the administration de-emphasized regulatory reform. Unified Democratic control of the Congress and a series of scandals (particularly those involving EPA's Ann Gourch and Rita Lavelle, and the Secretary of the Interior James Watt) increased the political costs of further efforts to limit regulation. However, additional movements toward reform took place during the Bush administration, with the creation of the President's Council on Competitiveness. The Council, a direct descendent of the Task Force on Regulatory Relief, actively sought to expand the use of cost–benefit analysis in agency decision-making, to identify and eliminate unnecessary regulations, and to reduce the burdens associated with compliance. The Council's achievements were limited by a lack of resources and the results of the elections of 1992.

DEREGULATION

The regulatory reforms described above entailed a progressive centralization of regulatory authority in the OMB. The executive review processes had an impact on staffing, administration, and the kinds of alternatives considered by regulators. Agencies subject to executive review were commonly forced to create, expand, and/or professionalize their analysis offices in order to comply with the review requirements and develop an independent data base that could be used to counter the challenges posed by other agencies, regulated interests, or public advocacy groups. This was certainly the case at the Environmental Protection Agency. Challenges posed by Nixon's Quality of Life Review Process forced Administrator Ruckelshaus to establish an Office of Policy and Evaluation. As Alfred Marcus explains, Ruckleshaus "needed EPA economists to gather information and run a regulatory review process that would internalize the debate taking place outside the agency. By trying to internalize this debate, Ruckelshaus hoped to recapture the autonomy the EPA was losing to the White House and the Commerce Department."[58]

Many regulatory agencies created or expanded policy planning and evaluation offices during the 1970s. The Justice Department's Antitrust Division created an Economic Policy Office in 1973, which grew in importance over the decade. By the 1980s, it exercised de facto veto power over case filings. The Federal Trade Commission professionalized and expanded its Bureau of Economics and created an Office of Policy Planning and Evaluation and a number of screening committees during the same period.[59] Under the direction of Chairman Charles Ferris, the Federal Communication Commission's Office of Plans and Policy was expanded in the late 1970s and placed under the control of an economist. By 1979, all professional positions in the office were occupied by economists.[60] The Civil Aeronautics Board's Office of Economic Analysis was created in 1977, under the direction of Alfred Kahn, and staffed with top flight economists. It was given a broad mandate to oversee and identify problems in CAB policies and processes.[61] At the same time, Daniel O'Neal, Chairman of the Interstate Commerce Commission, created an Office of Policy and Analysis, once again staffed by economists and given an expansive mandate.[62] Of course, the effects of the regulatory reform efforts on agency professionalization cannot be separated from the deregulatory debates of the period that suggested that sound regulations had to be justified in economic terms. Likewise, the courts increasingly addressed the economic rationale for regulatory decisions and considered economic evidence in hearing appeals. In the independent agencies, formally immune from executive orders, reform-minded executives were critical in creating the analytic capacities necessary to redirect the policy process.

The new reliance on professionalized planning and evaluation staffs promoted the application of economic analysis in the policy process. At times, this was a defensive measure designed to prevent court challenges or conflicts during regulatory review. On other occasions, reform-minded executives, concerned with the economic impact of agency decisions, looked to the economists as a natural constituency for deregulation. Finally, in some instances economists gradually assumed a greater role in the policy process as attorneys realized the importance of considering the economic costs of their actions and the potential benefits of using economic analysis as a guide to enforcement decisions. Economists working within the agencies, many of whom had been employed in response to the reform efforts discussed above, were familiar with the economic critique of regulation. Policies that prevented market competition and promoted high prices and inefficiency were antithetical to the norms of their profession. As economists gained a greater role within the agencies, these norms came into conflict with the policies they were charged with implementing.

The growing status of economic analysis and criteria in the regulatory process facilitated a host of deregulatory innovations. In some cases the reliance on economic analysis forced changes in agency priorities as regulations without economic merits were not enforced. This was certainly the case in antitrust. Over the course of the 1970s, the Antitrust Division's Economic Policy Office was expanded and staffed with economists recruited from the nation's best economics programs. Economists were assigned to each investigation to work with attorneys in determining whether there was a sufficient basis for prosecutions. The growing judicial concern with the economics of antitrust heightened attorneys' responsiveness to economic analysis and advice. Economists routinely refused to support cases that they considered lacking economic merits, even if they could be prosecuted under existing precedents. Reflecting the growing dominance of Chicago School economics, the caseload evolved to focus almost exclusively on horizontal restraints. Thus, enforcement of many of the antitrust prohibitions effectively ceased. These changes occurred without the explicit instruction of a series of Assistant Attorneys General who continued to stress the importance of a broad enforcement agenda. A similar sequence of events took place at the Federal Trade Commission.[63]

Economic theory was also applied to solve implementation problems and increase the efficiency and flexibility of regulation. The Securities and Exchange Commission (SEC), for example, progressively simplified and integrated its registration requirements in response to the academic debates concerning the economics of information. The simplification of regulatory requirements was justified on the basis of the efficient market hypothesis, which suggests that all relevant information about a corporation is reflected in the market prices of its existing securities. Market actors (especially large institutional investors) scrutinize all public information on a corporate issue and base their investment decisions accordingly. The disclosure requirements of the New Deal securities regulation were based on the desire to eliminate fraudulent securities issues and thus provide greater stability in investment finance. However, the economic arguments regarding market efficiency became ever more influential as Commission economists sought to improve policy performance. Similar considerations resulted in the elimination of fixed brokerage fees in the early 1970s and the introduction of competition in securities underwriting through self registration a decade later.[64]

The activities at the Antitrust Division and the SEC were shaped, in large part, by agency economists. In the case of the Antitrust Division, economic criteria were integrated into the policy process; the changing mix of professional norms had an influence on enforcement decisions. In the case of the SEC, bureaucrats appealed to contemporary economics debates when seeking to make regulations more effective and less burdensome. In each case, the staffs of highly professionalized agencies were engaged in broader debates that linked the agencies, congressional staff members, interest groups, and academic communities. They drew on these debates and their particular expertise to address key regulatory problems. Economic analysis was employed by regulatory staffs and reform-minded administrations to promote deregulation through administrative means. However, in the most striking cases of deregulation, administrative activities had to be combined with new statutory authority. Because the interplay between administrative and legislative actions was often quite subtle, it is useful to examine a few important cases of deregulation in somewhat greater detail.

Deregulating the Airlines

As noted earlier, the Civil Aeronautics Act of 1938 established a regulatory system largely analogous to that created for regulating surface transportation. Over time, CAB regulations maintained airline profitability by accepting rates that bore little relationship to the underlying costs of service. Moreover, CAB created and maintained significant barriers to entry: no new trunk airlines had been authorized during the first four decades of its existence despite dramatic increases in air travel. Working in a system that discouraged price competition, airlines commonly attempted to compete by offering more flights. This left air carriers with much excess capacity and increased costs, which, in turn, justified additional rate increases. The high rates, lack of competition, and inefficiency made airline transportation an area ripe for deregulation.[65]

In 1975, the Senate Judiciary Committee began investigations into the deregulation of air transportation. The high-profile hearings, orchestrated by Senator Edward Kennedy, publicized a significant amount of evidence against existing CAB regulations and revealed that deregulation had the support of a broad coalition, including some businesses and consumer groups and a number of government agencies. The attention attracted by airline regulations led President Ford to recommend deregulatory legislation, albeit with little impact. Likewise, Jimmy Carter advocated airline deregulation both in the presidential campaign and upon assuming office. While the Kennedy hearings facilitated the passage of major deregulatory legislation, the legislative process lagged behind the deregulatory efforts at CAB.[66]

In response to a 1975 self-study, CAB initiated its own deregulatory actions in 1976, lowering barriers to entry and opening the door to price competition. It relaxed regulations on charters, allowing them to offer lower prices than established carriers. Responding to concerns over the new competition, CAB authorized established carriers to provide discount fares under a limited set of restrictions in 1977. In the next year, CAB continued its administrative deregulation of the industry by granting requests to award markets to multiple carriers at fares far below those charged by the established carriers. With an introduction of price competition and a reduction (and proposed elimination) of barriers to entry, major strides had been made toward deregulating the industry.[67]

Much of the agency efforts toward deregulating the industry reflected the influence of Alfred Kahn, an academic economist and advocate of competitive deregulation appointed to be Carter's CAB chairman in 1977. Together with Elizabeth Baily, another economist and Carter appointee, Kahn reorganized the agency and created and staffed a new Office of Economic Analysis. This provided a base for CAB economists who had been strong supporters of deregulation under previous administrations while expanding the economics staff. Working with these economists and under a number of newly recruited bureau chiefs who shared training in economics and a commitment to deregulation, Kahn proceeded to eliminate or weaken most of the price and entry restrictions within a short period of time. Indeed, within 1 year of his arrival, nearly half of all coach-class passenger miles were being flown at discount rates. This had the immediate effect of increasing the number of passengers by 10 percent and almost doubling the profitability of the industry within a single year.[68]

With the passage of the Airline Deregulation Act of 1978, Congress authorized and extended the deregulatory actions initiated by CAB. The Act authorized airlines to enter one new route per year until 1981, when CAB would case to exercise control over entry. The act extended the flexible approach to fares adopted by CAB, eliminating fare regulations in 1982. Finally, the act eliminated CAB in 1984, transferring the remaining duties to the Department of Transportation. The Kennedy hearings and the intensive lobbying of Alfred Kahn popularized the critique of CAB regulations and promoted the formulation of a broad legislative coalition. However, one must recognize the importance of CAB's successful deregulatory efforts. They limited industry opposition and legislative uncertainly regarding the effects of deregulation and played a critical role in shaping the provisions of the legislation.[69]

Deregulating Trucking

The sequence of events at the Interstate Commerce Commission was even more striking than those at CAB.[70] As noted earlier, the ICC's regulation of rates and entry dramatically increased the profitability of trucking while forcing consumers to absorb billions of dollars of excess costs per year. Trucking regulation was difficult to justify. Given the structure of the industry (i.e., a lack of economics of scale and the large market), competition would promote prices that reflected costs.[71] While the costs and competitive effects forced many to question the wisdom of trucking regulation, deregulation was opposed by the industry and the Teamster's Union, making it politically untouchable.

Deregulation began in earnest in 1975, when the ICC issued a rule prohibiting rate bureaus from challenging the rate filings of its members. This decision permitted carriers to defect from the regulatory cartel that had played a critical role in undermining competition. Six months later, the ICC expanded the commercial zones around major cities, areas formally exempt from ICC rate regulations. This act completely deregulated a significant portion of previously regulated markets. Deregulation accelerated under the direction of Carter's ICC Chairman Daniel O'Neal and three subsequent Commission appointees. The ICC approved an increasing proportion of applications for operating authority and continued to promote competition by expanding the commercial zones exempt from regulation, thus allowing private carriers to engage in activities that had been regulated in the past. The ICC also deregulated all shipments being made under government contract. Finally, the ICC reduced barriers to entry by limiting the conditions under which carriers would have standing to protest new applications and shifting the burden of proof from the potential entrant to the established carrier. The effects of the ICC's deregulatory initiatives were immediate.[72]

Congress got involved in the movement toward motor carrier deregulation when Senator Kennedy's Antitrust and Monopoly Subcommittee held hearings in October, 1977. As with the case of airlines, the hearings on the ICC allowed for a public discussion of the negative impact of regulation. However, in this case Congress was forced to restrain the deregulatory actions of the regulators. In 1979, the Senate Commerce Committee and Senate Appropriations Committee instructed the ICC to restrain further deregulatory efforts until Congress provided new statutory authority. With the Motor Carriers Act of 1980, Congress authorized and extended many of the deregulatory initiatives of the ICC. It reduced barriers to entry by limiting possible objections to those carriers authorized to provide the service and forcing them to bear the burden of proof when protesting the authorization of new applicants. It also eliminated barriers to price competition, loosened territorial and operating restrictions, and limited the antitrust exemption for collective rate making. The Motor Carriers Act and earlier ICC decisions stimulated further deregulation by providing an impetus for action at the state level.[73]

Deregulating Finance

As noted earlier, the system of financial regulation in place by the end of the New Deal created a relatively stable system in which depository institutions functioned without engaging in active geographic, price, or product competition. This state of affairs changed dramatically in the 1970s, largely as a result of inflation. The growing difference between the interest rate ceilings established under the Federal Reserve's Regulation Q and the market rate created incentives for a host of financial innovations outside of the regulated institutions. Money market funds were one response. Beginning in the early 1970s, a host of unregulated firms began allowing small investors to pool funds and participate in a host of high-yield investment instruments (e.g., commercial paper, certificates of deposit, Treasury bills), an opportunity usually reserved for the largest institutional investors. The money mutual fund was refined in 1975 when Merrill Lynch began offering cash management accounts, which combined high returns with services like checking and cash advances. A wave of subsequent innovations allowed firms to offer these services to an ever growing set of investors, thus placing significant pressure on regulated institutions.[74]

There were also new threats tied to the services that banks could provide. Beginning in 1972, state savings banks in New England began offering negotiated order of withdrawal or NOW accounts. Because NOW accounts were interest-bearing savings accounts with check-writing privileges, they posed a competitive threat to regulated institutions that were not allowed to offer interest on demand deposits. Congress responded with legislation in 1973, 1975, and 1978 extending the authority to offer NOW accounts to national banks in the region. The Federal Reserve authorized national banks to provide analogous services by authorizing telephone and automatic transfer of funds from savings to checking accounts. In essence, money could be kept in interest-bearing accounts and then instantly transferred to non-interest-bearing checking accounts. The same competitive pressures led the National Credit Union Administration to authorize its members to provide share drafts on interest-bearing accounts in 1975. Savings and loans institutions entered the game as well when the National Home Loan Bank Board authorized the use of automatic teller machines.

As in the cases of trucking and airlines, a great deal of deregulation took place via administrative means. However, the case of finance differed for two reasons. First, competition between the regulated and unregulated institutions created pressures for deregulation. In contrast with the cases addressed above, the regulated were key proponents of deregulation. Second, as administrative initiatives lowered regulatory barriers, thrifts and commercial banks began competing with each other. As the agencies promoted greater competition, the relevant trade associations initiated court challenges in the hopes of shielding themselves from new competition. The Circuit Court of Appeals for the District of Columbia addressed the challenges simultaneously and gave Congress a deadline for providing explicit authorization for the deregulatory actions.[75] In response, Congress began to craft deregulatory legislation.

Congress passed the Depository Institutions Deregulation and Monetary Control Act of 1980 (DIDMCA). The legislation simplified reserve requirements and directed federal reserve banks to provide nonmember banks and thrifts certain important services including access to the discount window. Most important, DIDMCA allowed regulated financial intermediaries to compete for funds and provide new services. It did this by phasing out Regulation Q interest rate ceilings and authorizing all federally insured institutions to offer NOW accounts. Savings and loan institutions, placed at a disadvantage by existing regulations, were authorized to invest up to 20 percent of their assets in commercial paper, corporate debt instruments, and consumer loans, thus allowing thrifts to compete with commercial banks. Finally, DIDMCA increased the deposit insurance ceilings from $40,000 to $100,000.[76]

Two years later, Congress passed the Garn–St. Germain Depository Institutions Act of 1982. Garn–St. Germain further enhanced the freedom of depository institutions by authorizing money market deposit accounts with unregulated interest rates, protected by deposit insurance. Moreover, thrifts were given additional asset powers with respect to commercial and agricultural loans and investments in state government securities. Following the passage of these two pieces of legislation, the regulatory distinctions between various forms of depository institutions were largely stripped of significance. As a result, the advantages claimed by the so-called nonbank banks were minimized.

BEYOND DEREGULATION

By the early 1980s, all major deregulatory policies had been implemented. The low inflation rate and the return of economic growth following the recession of 1981 reduced the pressure for further deregulation. Of course, deregulation via administrative means continued to take place as regulators placed a greater emphasis on the economic effects of regulatory enforcement actions. An evaluation of the major deregulatory initiatives described above reveals mixed results. The clearest example of success is the case of trucking. The deregulatory stance of the ICC and the Motor Carriers Act of 1980 had an immediate impact on the industry. Within a year of the passage of the legislation, there were large increases in applications for interstate operating authority. Moreover, there were increases in independent actions in the rate bureaus, as truckers filed new rates. In the surveyed bureaus, some 95 percent of the new rates were reduced from those that existed under regulation. Rate reductions and increased entry had a negative effect on the income of the Teamsters Union and resulted in the bankruptcy of many marginal trucking firms. However, these negative effects were the predictable consequences of the elimination of monopoly power in an industry with few economic barriers to entry.[77]

In other cases, the effects of deregulation are either mixed or difficult to separate from other factors. In the case of airlines, deregulation has had no negative impact on safety. Indeed, the air fatality record actually declined following deregulation.[78] The effects of competition and fares are somewhat less positive. Following the passage of the Airline Deregulation Act, the industry witnessed an influx of new airlines that offered lower fares largely on the basis of labor savings. Effective antitrust enforcement might have contributed to the maintenance of a decentralized structure. However, after a wave of large mergers (e.g., Northwest–Republic, Texas Air–Eastern, TWA–Ozark) and bankruptcies during the 1980s, the airline industry was once again characterized by high levels of concentration. Prior to the passage of deregulatory legislation, the top four firms controlled 53.14 percent of the market. One decade later, the top four firms controlled 60.58 percent of the market. Most disturbing was that where mergers effectively eliminated competition between major carriers, rate increases were dramatic.[79] Whether competition in a deregulated environment will place long-term downward pressures on rates remains to be seen.

The record with respect to financial deregulation is also mixed, albeit with clear signs of policy failure. There is little question that the deregulatory legislation of the early 1980s allowed depository institutions greater freedom to compete on the basis of prices and services. However, rather than flourishing in the new regulatory environment, many depository institutions encountered growing difficulties. The high inflation rates of the late 1970s, the exposure to bad loans to less developed countries, and the recession of 1981–82 made many institutions highly unstable. While it is possible to attribute part of the troubling wave of bank and thrift failures to these factors, some blame rests with the deregulatory legislation.[80] The DIDMCA of 1980 increased deposit insurance coverage to $100,000, without imposing a system of risk-based premiums. Because the regulators were not in the practice of closing insolvent institutions in a timely fashion, policy created incentives for banks and thrifts to engage in risky investments. Of course, the high rates of return were necessary for savings and loans, burdened with portfolios of long-term, low-interest home mortgages.[81] With the costs of the financial collapse estimated to be in excess of $500 billion over the course of the next several decades, the financial deregulation of the early 1980s may be considered to be among the greatest policy failure in U.S. history.

The growing concentration in the airline industry and the instability in commercial finance have stimulated debates concerning the need for reregulation. As existing regulations and the effects of deregulation are subjected to critical scrutiny and efforts are initiated to adjust the regulatory system, one can expect the goals to change once again to reflect contemporary problems and concerns. Whether they represent the need to promote U.S. economic competitiveness in a rapidly changing international market or return, once again, to concerns over stability in the face of domestic economic restructuring remains unresolved. The history of economic regulation provides few indicators. It suggests only that the broad objectives of regulation will be formulated and reformulated to mirror contemporary problems. Thus, the economic decision rules that provided clear guidance to regulators may well decline in relevance once seen in light of the new goals. As the economic and political context changes, the broad purposes of regulation will once again come into question; new criteria will be imposed to assess policy performance.

REFERENCES

1. Thomas K. McCraw, Mercantilism and the market: Antecedents of American industrial policy. In *The Politics of Industrial Policy,* ed. by Claude E. Barfield and William A. Schambra. (Washington, D.C.: American Enterprise Institute, 1986).
2. See Samuel P. Hays, *The Response to Industrialism,* 1885–1914. (Chicago: University of Chicago Press, 1957), pp. 48–70. More generally, see Robert H. Wiebe, *The Search for Order, 1877–1920.* (New York: Hill and Wang, 1967).
3. *Wabash, St. Louis & Pacific Railway Co. v. Illinois,* 118 U.S. 557 (1886).
4. See the discussion in Stephen Skowronek, *Building a New American State: The Expansion of National Administrative Capacities, 1877–1920.* (Cambridge: Cambridge University Press, 1982).
5. See William Letwin, *Law and Economic Policy in America.* (New York: Random House, 1965).
6. See Archibald Cox, *The Court and the Constitution.* (Boston: Houghton Mifflin, 1987), pp. 117–44.
7. Lawrence Baum, *The Supreme Court,* 3rd ed. (Washington, D.C.: Congressional Quarterly Press, 1989), p. 21.
8. Ellis W. Hawley, Herbert Hoover, the Commerce Secretariat, and the vision of an associative state, 1921–1928. *Journal of American History* 61 (June 1974): 116–40.
9. *Schechter v. United States,* 295 U.S. 495 (1935); *United States v. Butler,* 297 U.S. 1 (1936).
10. Ellis W. Hawley, *The New Deal and the Problem of Monopoly: A Study in Economic Ambivalence.* (Princeton: Princeton University Press, 1966), p. 189.
11. See, for example, Thomas K. McCraw, With consent of the governed: SEC's formative years, *Journal of Policy Analysis and Management,* 1,3 (1982): 346–70.
12. This discussion draws on Michael Pustay, Deregulation and the US trucking industry. In *The Age of Regulatory Reform,* ed. Kenneth Button and Dennis Swann. (Oxford: Clarendon Press, 1989), pp. 236–56, and Thomas Gale Moore, Rail and trucking regulation. In *Regulatory Reform: What Actually Happened,* ed. Leonard W. Weiss and Michael W. Klass. (Boston: Little, Brown, 1986), pp. 14–39.

13. Moore, Rail and trucking regulation, p. 17.
14. Pustay, Deregulation and the US trucking industry, pp. 244, 243. See Stephen Breyer, *Regulation and Its Reform.* (Cambridge: Harvard University Press, 1982), pp. 222–39.
15. See the Civil Aeronautics Act of 1938, reprinted in *The Economic Regulation of Business and Industry,* ed. Bernard Schwartz. (New York: Chelsea House Publishers, 1973), Vol. IV: 2987-3061.
16. Civil Aernautics Authority, *Annual Report.* (Washington, D.C.: Government Printing Office, 1939), p. 2.
17. Daniel P. Kaplan, The changing airline industry. In *Regulatory Reform: What Actually Happened?* Ed. by Leonard W. Weiss and Michael K. Glass. (Boston: Little, Brown & Co., 1986), pp. 41–42.
18. Steven A. Morrison, US domestic aviation. In *The Age of Regulatory Reform,* ed. Kenneth Button and Dennis Swann. (Oxford: Clarendon Press, 1989), pp. 144–45.
19. This discussion draws on Kenneth J. Meier, *Regulation: Politics, Bureaucracy, and Economics.* (New York: St. Martin's Press, 1985), pp. 124–25.
20. See James E. Anderson, Agricultural marketing orders and the process and politics of self-regulation. *Policy Studies Review,* 2,1 (August 1982): 97–111.
21. Charles L. Schultze, *The Distribution of Farm Subsidies: Who Gets the Benefits?* (Washington, D.C.: The Brookings Instituion, 1971), p. 29.
22. This discussion draws on John E. Owens, The state regulation and deregulation of financial institutions and services in the United States. In *The State, Finance and Industry,* ed. Andrew Cox. (New York: St. Martin's Press, 1986), and Arthur F. Burns, The ongoing revolution in American banking. In *Capital, Technology, and Labor in the New Global Economy,* ed. James H. Cassing and Steven L. Husted. (Washington: American Enterprise Institute, 1988).
23. See Helen M. Burns, *The American Banking Community and New Deal Banking Reforms,* 1933-1935. (Westport, CT: Greenwood Press, 1974).
24. See the discussion of the regulatory subsystem in Meier, *Regulation,* pp. 41–45.
25. Roger W. Garrison, Eugene D. Short, and Gerald P. O'Driscoll, Jr., Financial stability and FDIC insurance. In *The Financial Services Revolution: Policy Directions for the Future,* ed. Catherine England and Thomas Huertas. (Washington, D.C.: CATO Institute, 1988), p. 196. See the discussion in Burns, The ongoing revolution in American banking, pp. 11–24.
26. Marver H. Bernstein, *Regulating Business by Independent Commission.* (Princeton: Princeton University Press, 1955), p. 87.
27. Ibid., p. 92.
28. See Samuel P. Huntington, The marasmus of the ICC. *Yale Law Journal,* 61 (April 1952): 467–509.
29. For an explanation of the cost-benefit combinations that promote mobilization of various groups, see James Q. Wilson, *Political Organizations.* (New York: Basic Books, 1973).
30. Gabriel Kolko, *The Triumph of Conservatism: A Reinterpretation of American History, 1900-1916.* (New York: Free Press, 1963), p. 284.
31. See Murray Edelman, *The Symbolic Uses of Politics.* (Champaign: University of Illinois Press, 1964), Grant McConnell, *Private Power and American Democracy.* (New York: Alfred A. Knopf, 1966), and Kim McQuaid, *Big Business and Presidential Power: From FDR to Reagan.* (New York: William Morrow and Company, 1982).
32. Theodore J. Lowi, *The End of Liberalism: The Second Republic of the United States,* 2nd ed. (New York: W.W. Norton & Co., 1979), p. 51.
33. Ibid., p. 297.
34. See Kenneth Culp Davis, *Discretionary Justice: A Preliminary Inquiry.* (Baton Rouge: Louisiana State University Press, 1969), and Richard B. Stewart, The reformation of American administrative law. *Harvard Law Review,* 88,8 (June 1975): 1667–1813.
35. George J. Stigler, The theory of economic regulation. *Bell Journal of Economics and Management Science,* 2,1 (Spring 1971): 3–21.
36. See Richard A. Posner, Theories of economic regulation. *Bell Journal of Economics and Management Science,* 5 (Autumn 1974): 337–52; Sam Peltzman, Toward a more general theory of

regulation. *Journal of Law and Economics,* 19 (August 1976): 211–40. See the critical discussion of Stigler's thesis and its extensions in Kenneth J. Meier, *The Political Economy of Regulation: The Case of Insurance.* (Albany: State University of New York Press, 1988), pp. 18–29.

37. Robert C. Fellmeth, ed., *The Interstate Commerce Omission: The Public Interest and the ICC.* (New York: Grossman, 1970), p. 37.
38. Mark J. Green, Uncle Sam the monopoly man. In *The Monopoly Makers: Ralph Nader's Study Group Report on Regulation and Competition,* ed. Mark J. Green. (New York: Grossman, 1973), pp. 4, 27.
39. *Economic Report of the President, February 1975.* (Washington, D.C.: U.S. Government Printing Office, 1975), p. 159.
40. Murray L. Weidenbaum, On estimating regulatory costs. *Regulation,* (May/June 1978), pp. 14–17.
41. The discussion of regulatory reform and deregulation draws on Marc Allen Eisner, *Regulatory Politics in Transition.* (Baltimore: Johns Hopkins University Press, 1993), Chapter 8.
42. George C. Eads and Michael Fix, *Relief or Reform? Reagan's Regulatory Dilemma.* (Washington, D.C.: The Urban Institute Press, 1984), p. 48.
43. This section draws on Howard Ball, *Controlling Regulatory Sprawl: Presidential Strategies from Nixon to Reagan.* (Westport, CT: Greenwood Press, 1984), pp. 51–54 and Eads and Fix, *Relief or Reform,* pp. 50–54.
44. Larry N. Gerston, Cynthia Fraleigh, and Robert Schwab, *The Deregulated Society.* (Pacific Grove, CA: Brooks/Cole, 1988), pp. 43–44; Thomas O. McGarity, *Reinventing Rationality: The Role of Regulatory Analysis in the Federal Bureaucracy.* (Cambridge: Cambridge University Press, 1991), pp. 18–19.
45. See the discussion of the Carter initiatives in Gerston, Fraleigh, and Schwab, *The Deregulated Society,* pp. 44–48.
46. McGarity, *Reinventing Rationality,* p. 19; Gerston, Fraleigh, and Schwab, *The Deregulated Society,* pp. 46–47.
47. Eads and Fix, *Relief or Reform,* p. 61.
48. Ibid., pp. 61–2.
49. James C. Miller III, Lessons of the economic impact statement program, *Regulation* (July/August 1977), p. 16–18; Ball, *Controlling Regulatory Sprawl,* pp. 58–60; Susan Tolchin, Presidential power and the politics of RARG. *Regulation,* (July/August 1979): 44–49.
50. Susan J. Tolchin and Martin Tolchin, *Dismantling America: The Rush to Deregulate.* (Boston: Houghton-Mifflin, 1983), p. 49.
51. Richard N. L. Andrews, Economics and environmental decisions, past and present. In *Environmental Policy Under Reagan's Executive Order: The Role of Benefit Cost Analysis,* ed. V. Kerry Smith. (Chapel Hill: University of North Carolina Press, 1984), pp. 73–74; Ball, *Controlling Regulatory Sprawl,* pp. 66–68; Timothy B. Clark, If Reagan wants to trump the regulators, here's OMB's target list for openers. *National Journal,* 13,3 (January 17, 1981): 94–98.
52. Paul R. Portney, The benefits and costs of regulatory analysis. In *Environmental Policy Under Reagan's Executive Order: The Role of Benefit-Cost Analysis,* ed. V. Kerry Smith. (Chapel Hill: University of North Carolina Press, 1984), pp. 229, 231.
53. Murray L. Weidenbaum, Regulatory reform under the Reagan administration. In *The Reagan Regulatory Strategy: An Assessment,* ed. George C. Eads and Michael Fix. (Washington, D.C.: The Urban Institute Press, 1984), pp. 32, 34–35.
54. See Lawrence Mosher, Will EPA's budget make it more efficient or less effective? *National Journal,* 13,33 (August 15, 1981): 1466–69.
55. William A. Niskanen, *Reaganomics: An Insider's Account of the Policies and the People.* (New York: Oxford University Press, 1988), p. 131.
56. Ball, *Controlling Regulatory Sprawl,* pp. 93–97.
57. Kirk Victor, Quayles' quiet coup. *National Journal,* 23, 27 (July 6, 1991): 1676–80; and Jonathan Rauch, The regulatory President. *National Journal,* 23 48 (November 30, 1991); 2902–06.
58. Alfred Marcus, Environmental Protection Agency. In *The Politics of Regulation,* ed. James Q. Wilson. (New York: Basic Books, 1980), p. 289. Also see Eads and Fix, *Reform or Relief,* pp. 49–50.

59. These events are detailed in Marc Allen Eisner, *Antitrust and the Triumph of Economics: Institutions, Expertise, and Policy Change.* (Chapel Hill: University of North Carolina Press, 1991).
60. Jeremy Tunstall, *Communications Deregulation: The Unleashing of America's Communications Industry.* (Oxford: Basil Blackwell, 1986), p. 248. Martha Derthick and Paul J. Quirk, *The Politics of Deregulation.* (Washington, D.C.: The Brookings Institute, 1985), pp. 79–81.
61. Thomas K. McCraw, *Prophets of Regulation.* (Cambridge: Harvard University Press, 1984), pp. 274–75.
62. Derthick and Quirk, *Politics of Deregulation,* p. 82.
63. See Marc Allen Eisner, Institutional history and policy change: Exploring the origins of the new antitrust. *Journal of Policy History,* 2,3 (1990): 262–89; Thomas E. Kauper, The role of economic analysis in the antitrust division before and after the establishment of the Economic Policy Office: A lawyer's view. *The Antitrust Bulletin,* 29,1 (Spring 1984): 111–32.
64. Joseph Auerbach and Samuel L. Hayes, III, *Investment Banking and Diligence: What Price Deregulation?* (Boston: Harvard Business School Press, 1986), pp. 108–19; Joel Seligman, *The SEC and the Future of Finance.* (New York: Praeger, 1985), pp. 195–280.
65. Daniel P. Kaplan, The changing airline industry. In *Regulatory Reform: What Actually Happened,* ed. Leonard W. Weiss and Michael W. Klass. (Boston: Little, Brown and Co., 1986), pp. 42–44.
66. Stephen Breyer, *Regulation and Its Reform.* (Cambridge: Harvard University Press, 1982), pp. 317–40.
67. Ibid., pp. 44–45; Derthick and Quirk, *Politics of Deregulation,* pp. 76–77.
68. McCraw, *Prophets of Regulation,* pp. 274–77.
69. Kaplan, The changing airline industry, p. 45.
70. This section draws on Thomas Gale Moore, Rail and trucking deregulation. In *Regulatory Reform: What Actually Happened,* ed. Leonard W. Weiss and Michael Klass. (Boston: Little, Brown and Co., 1986), pp. 14–39; and Derthick and Quirk, *The Politics of Deregulation.*
71. Breyer, *Regulation and Its Reform,* p. 224.
72. Moore, Rail and trucking deregulation, pp. 17–22.
73. Ibid., pp. 26–27; Derthick and Quirk, *Politics of Deregulation,* pp. 73–74, 97–98. See the detailed case study of trucking deregulation in Dorothy Robyn, *Braking the Special Interests: Trucking Deregulation and the Politics of Policy Reform.* (Chicago: University of Chicago Press, 1987).
74. This discussion draws on Meier, *Regulation,* pp. 57–71.
75. *American Bankers Association v. Connell,* 194 U.S. App. D.C. 80. (1980). The cases consolidated in this decision addressed the savings and loans use of automated teller machines, the credit union share drafts, and the commercial banks' automatic transfers.
76. See the discussion of the deregulatory legislation in Burns, The ongoing revolution in American banking, p. 55.
77. Pustay, Deregulation and the US trucking industry, pp. 247–51.
78. Richard B. McKenzie and William F. Shughart, Deregulation's impact on air safety: Separating fact from fiction. *Consumer's Research,* 71,1 (January 1988): 10–13.
79. See Fred Siegmund, Competition and performance in the airline industry. *Policy Studies Review,* 9:4 (Summer 1990): 649–63.
80. See Kenneth J. Meier and Jeff Worsham, Deregulation, competition, and economic changes: Assessing the responsibility for bank failure. *Policy Studies Journal,* 16,3 (Spring 1988): 427–39.
81. See Edward J. Kane, *The S&L Insurance Mess: How Did It Happen?* (Washington, D.C.: The Urban Institute, 1989).

5

The State of State Regulation

Paul Teske *State University of New York at Stony Brook, Stony Brook, New York*

INTRODUCTION AND DEFINITION

States have regulated important sectors of the American economy for over 200 years. Over much of the last 100 years, as interstate commerce expanded relative to intrastate commerce, the federal government became increasingly involved in regulatory activities and the central role of the states in regulation declined somewhat. Yet, state regulation remained important, if understudied, and a reduced role for federal regulation in the 1980s has led to an even more prominent role for the states in many regulatory arenas.

State regulation previously experienced cycles of activity related to federal regulation, especially near the growth periods of the 1880s, 1900s, 1930s, and 1960s. After the Civil War, states became involved in the regulation of banking and insurance (Williams, 1983), and states initiated railroad regulation (McCraw, 1984) and antitrust regulation (Kansas in 1889 predated the 1890 Sherman Antitrust Act) prior to federal regulation. Richard Nathan (1989) argues that federal/state relationships in the 1980s were analogous to those in the 1920s: "In the 20s, when America was keeping cool with Coolidge, it was the states that developed the programs that later became the elements of Roosevelt's New Deal." Workmen's compensation programs were passed first in the American states, 14 in 1911, with 11 more by 1918 and all states but Arkansas by the New Deal's peak of 1935 (Thompson, 1982). Several states had unemployment insurance programs before the federal government (Amenta et al., 1987).

In the 1980s, state regulation became more important still, particularly as many federal regulatory activities were reduced or eliminated, and it deserves study. For political scientists, comparing "comparative state regulation" studies can provide better answers to important research questions than can the limited number of federal regulatory agencies.

Such analysis must include a definition of regulatory activities, which can be so broad as to include nearly all forms of government intervention into private market activities. Reeves (1985) notes that states have long had jurisdiction over property and contract laws, taxation, commercial codes, incorporation and partnership laws, and unfair business practices. Regulation, in the most general sense, involves the authoritative bounding of behavior by government (Williams, 1983: 330). Other definitions include: "any attempt by the government to control the behavior of citizens, corporations, or subgovernments" (Meier, 1985) and "limitations on the discretion that may be exercised by individuals or organizations, which is supported by the threat of sanction" (Stone, 1982).

More specifically, regulation is often broken down into "economic" and "social" regulation. Economic regulation deals with service, pricing, and entry into markets, as practiced in telecommunications, electricity, transportation, financial markets, and antitrust monitoring generally. Social regulation deals with product and worker safety, environmental problems, and insurance against risk. Also included in a broader definition of regulation are government intervention into corporate decisions in either direct form or through consumer regulation, employment (e.g., affirmative action), as well as regulation of quasigovernmental organizations, such as hospitals, in which government establishes many operating rules, but in a marketlike setting.

The scope of U.S. state regulation in 1993 that I address focuses on areas that have been studied most by political scientists. It includes regulation left almost entirely up to the states, such as insurance, occupational regulation, and utility regulation by state commissions, such as intrastate telecommunications, electricity, water, sometimes transportation, and waste (including hazardous waste). It also includes regulation with shared jurisdiction. For example, financial firms are mainly regulated at the federal level, but they must also deal with a series of state level regulations. States also share consumer regulation with Washington, D.C., by mandating the provision of information about goods and services. When not pre-empted by the federal government on interstate commerce grounds, states regulate several aspects of corporate activity, including antitrust, mergers and acquisition rules, plant closings, and employee firing. In addition, some states implement federal policies, as with occupational safety and environmental protection; if they do not, the federal government regulates. In fact there are very few federal regulatory agencies that do not have a state counterpart or cooperative relationship with state agencies.

Despite the substantial amount of evidence gathered below, some areas have only been explored by a single study and others have been unexplored. Relatively unexamined at the state level, as far as I can tell, are the areas of intrastate trucking and railroad regulation, and the growing state antitrust activity.

WHY STUDYING STATE REGULATION IS IMPORTANT

There are several reasons why state regulation is an important area of study for political science. First, as noted above, recent trends make it far more important in the economy. One piece of evidence comes from those regulated: "We hear it all the time, companies moaning about needing to do more in the states," says Raymond L. Hoewing, president of the Public Affairs Council, a Washington-based association of government affairs professionals from 400 major U.S. corporations. "They say, 'While we've been watching the federal level, we're being pecked to death on the state scene'." (Watson, 1989). Several recent articles confirm that state regulatory activity is causing corporations increasing concern (Warner, 1990; Holusha, 1991).

Second, there are important "horizontal" elements to regulation across the 50 states. Businesses are mobile. While states are regulating firms they are also competing to attract them, creating an interesting dynamic tension that can help us to study tradeoffs that policymakers face across these two dimensions (see for example Rowland and Marz, 1982;

Skalaban, 1990). It is not necessarily true that regulation and economic development involve fundamentally opposite goals; sometimes the two arenas act in tandem, but their interrelationship can create a dilemma for policymakers.

Third, there are "vertical" dimensions relating to trends in federalism, national policy, and externality jurisdictional issues (Gray, 1983; Mashaw and Rose-Ackerman, 1984; Chubb, 1985). Many forms of state regulation involve extensive federal–state cooperative implementation, a form of federalism that is too little studied. On other regulatory issues the states and federal government are often in conflict.

The main research advantage of studying state regulation is that states give us a larger sample size (50), to test theories of policy formulation. Even using time series analysis, there may be too few federal cases and too many independent variables to do conclusive quantitative analysis. Looking across the 50 states also provides more variation in institutions, and in relationships between interests and institutions; therefore tests can be performed of interest group vs. institutional theories (see Moe, 1987a). In this sense, cross-state studies are really more truly comparative than most cross-national ones (which are very rare in regulation): institutions are more similar, the overall political and economic climates vary less, and data are collected in more uniform fashions. Weber (1989) notes: "The study of policymaking is probably the one area of research that has benefited the most from state and local politics studies during the past 25 years or so." Still, for the specific category of state regulation, Weber points to a relatively small number of studies and does not draw any conclusions from them. And, as Browne (1987: 47) laments: "[Because of] a lack of attention to institutional relationships . . . political scientists know very little about the relative influence of various state-level political participants on policy outcomes."

A MODEL OF REGULATORY POLITICS

To draw conclusions from the different studies of state regulation, we need to apply a common model of regulatory decision-making. I am most interested in understanding who has influence or control over state regulatory policy. Most of the studies examined here address that question, although some also ask about whether regulatory policies are effective and what impact they ultimately have on society (such as Gormley's [1991] study of the impact of state child care regulations on the supply of services).

Compared to the narrow interest group model of regulation that has emerged in economics (Stigler, 1971; Peltzman, 1976; Becker, 1983, 1985), political scientists have moved towards a broader model that includes contextual factors in the external environment, interest group pressure, and voter/consumer interests acting on governmental institutions. Political scientists have made substantial progress studying institutions and it has become clear that we must consider the interests, motivations, and resources of such actors as governors, state legislators, and bureaucrats at various levels (see Moe, 1987a; Meier, 1988), as well as the influence of judges through the courts (see Gormley, 1989a).

These governmental institutions do not exist in a vacuum but were created and shaped by political forces over time. Thus, they are influenced politically, but also are partially insulated and can develop a "life of their own" (Moe, 1989). Certainly, theories of the autonomy of the state, on a more macro-level, suggest the ability of state actors to maintain their own interests. For all institutional variables, there is always the concern that they are endogenous, and findings of their influence may ignore that fact. To some extent, this issue drove the debate about the relative importance of socioeconomic (exogenous) variables vs. political (endogenous) variables in the 1960s cross-state literature. This concern about the endogeneity of bureaucrats is legitimate (Moe, 1987a), but some models have tested for it (see, for example, Teske, 1990a), and found that there is still an independent bureaucratic influence. More testing of this type needs to be done.

While some (see Munger's [1989] review of Meier [1985; 1988] and Shepsle's [1982] review of Wilson [1980]) suggest that the kind of model described above is not a viable political or institutional *theory* because it is not parsimonious, it at least provides a common perspective from which to compare the various state-level studies. To summarize, external social, economic, and political factors shape interest group demands and needs, and those of voters/consumers, which then pressure political actors, including, governors, legislators, and bureaucrats. Bureaucrats carry out policies as directed and overseen by governors and legislators. Political scientists have also found direct links from earlier actors to later actors in the process, as well as feedback loops.

COMPARING THE STATE STUDIES

It quickly becomes apparent that different state studies result in different findings, which raises an important problem for a synthesis: Why do they differ? I suggest three explanations. First, it is certainly true that some studies are better than others. Some may be "wrong" in their conclusions compared to an unseen reality. Some state scholars have expressed concern about the use of cross-sectional methodology (Gray, 1976; Tucker, 1982), although the majority of these studies have employed exactly that. Still, I must assume that the methodology of most of these studies is sound and that the data are accurate. Since I analyze overall trends and do not draw conclusions based on any single study, this is only a major problem if reviewed and published social scientists are wrong more than they are right.

Second, no doubt there are real differences in the politics of regulation across sectors. How can these differences best be explained? One possibility is differences in the nature of the regulation, based on the economic market failures paradigm, which separates regulation involving natural monopoly, information asymmetry problems, and externalities. Political scientists have advanced other methods of analysis: Wilson (1980) argues that the concentration or dispersion of costs and benefits is critical; Gormley (1986) suggests that the complexity and saliency of the issue shape regulatory politics; McCubbins (1985) argues that conflict and uncertainty shape legislative and hence regulatory politics; while others focus on differences between regulatory rulemaking and enforcement (Ferejohn, 1987). Another possible difference is time; while most of these studies are quite recent and they mostly analyze the 1960s through 1980s, studies of different regulatory periods may yield different findings (see McCraw, 1984). I will return to the implications for these theories of regulatory politics after reviewing the findings of the studies.

Third, different theoretical and empirical approaches (particularly those normally employed by political scientists versus economists) lead to tests of different independent or predictor variables and different model specifications. Based on their theories and training, economists focus more on economic conditions, technological change, and interest group pressure. While political scientists mostly do not ignore these variables, they tend to focus more on institutional and political factors. If a study does not test for the influence of a variable, it is highly likely to appear unimportant. One other important methodological difference that can lead to different findings is the choice of dependent variables measuring "regulation." Where possible, I will try to tease out these differences.

Working "inside-out" from the general model of regulation sketched above, I will present the positive evidence of these studies for the influence over regulation of bureaucrats, legislators, governors, interest groups, and contextual conditions.

Bureaucrats

The studies yield overwhelming evidence of the importance of bureaucrats, both regulators themselves and their staffs, in influencing state regulatory outcomes. Only strict "economic" studies find no influence because they include no bureaucratic variables. Finding influence by bureaucrats, of course, does not mean that other factors are not influential; like Moe's (1985, 1987a) studies of national regulation, many studies find that bureaucrats are *one* important source of influence over policy, but only one.

Evidence of bureaucratic influence comes from many sources and seems unassailable. In state telecommunications regulation, using both quantitative and case study analysis, Teske (1990a) found that state regulatory budgets (resources) and "regulatory climate" (commission ideology) are important predictors of pricing and entry choices. Cohen (1988) also found bureaucratic influence, the extent of which, compared to the legislature, depends upon the type of policy; Cohen found that bureaucrats influence redistributive policies less than more technical ones. From an economic perspective, Smart (1990) found that regulatory commissions structured by elections act differently (they favor business interests more than consumers) than commissions appointed by state governors, which Teske's evidence also supported.

Staying in the public utility area, but focusing on energy regulation, Gormley (1983) found evidence of the primary importance of bureaucratic staff in policy. Berry (1979, 1984) found that bureaucratic professionalism and agency resources influence regulatory choices. Kemp (1981) found that a range of powers previously given to regulatory bureaucrats by state legislators influence the adoption and stringency of state power plant siting rules. Welborn and Brown (1980) focused on the importance of staff competence in utility regulation. Anderson (1981) used case studies that also showed the important role of regulators themselves, and argued that staffs have more influence in issues that require continual monitoring. Anderson suggested that the rise of entrepreneurial politics and the decline of political party strength have increased the independence and importance of bureaucrats in regulation.

In the regulation of the insurance industry, in which states have the primary role, Meier (1988) found that bureaucrats are important, and that budgets (resources) are influential. Using case studies and interviews, rather than regression analysis, Miles and Bhambri (1983) focused on bureaucratic "type" as being the crucial factor in insurance regulation. On the other hand, Williams (1983) argued that state bureaucrats do not have enough resources to regulate adequately insurance firms.

Moving to the arena of state "social" regulation, in hazardous waste, Williams and Matheny (1984) found that overall state fiscal capacity (resources of a different type) is important. Lester et al. (1983) also found that agency resources influence hazardous waste regulation. In the area of consumer regulation, Meier (1987) found that the powers given to the Attorney General of the state are important. Thompson (1982) found that the organizational structure—single administrator, commission, or court-administered—of state workmen's compensation programs, can influence the implementation of policy. Kiholm Smith (1982) found that states with full-time regulators administered liquor sales in more detail than states with part-time regulators.

In the area of Occupational Safety and Health Administration (OSHA) regulation, Scholz and Wei (1986) found influence by "street-level" inspectors. Thompson and Scicchitano (1985) argued that bureaucratic organizational search best explains OSHA enforcement vigor across the states, as regulators respond to real problems with worker safety and complaints about such problems. Wood (1989) found that both state and federal environmental bureaucracies, strengthened by mandates and established routines, resist much political control, and respond rationally to historical patterns and resource allocation efficiencies. In a sense then, these studies show that regulatory bureaucrats mostly "do what they are supposed to do" in their role as professionals. On the other hand, Hedge et al. (1990) found that "objective need" is *not* a driver of hazardous waste regulation.

In an area of local regulation that utilizes the police power of the state, Fleischmann and Pierannunzi (1990) found that appointed planning boards are highly influential in local rezoning decisions, more so than pressure from real estate developers.

Given strong evidence that bureaucrats are not simply captured and have substantial influence of their own, the next question is: What do bureaucrats do with their discretionary power? Although some studies show a Niskanen-like view that bureaucrats try to increase their role and budgets with little concern for policy (Kiholm Smith, 1982), most studies show that bureaucrats respond to needs with professional norms of behavior based on their training, that they take ideas and resources into account, and that higher-level regulators are influenced by their (lower-level) staff analysis.

Legislative Influence

Weingast and Moran (1983), Faith et al. (1982), McCubbins (1985), and others refocused attention on the role of Congress in federal regulation, collectively developing the perspective of "Congressional dominance." Even those who feel that this view has been taken too far (Moe, 1987b) agree that the legislative role must be explored. This is equally true at the state level, especially as legislatures become more professionalized and "capable" (e.g., Bowman and Kearney, 1988), and as they increase regulatory activity through legislative oversight, sunset laws, audit bureaus (Rosenthal, 1990), and administrative procedure acts (Renfrow et al., 1985; Clingermayer, 1989). On the other hand, however, Gormley (1986: 603) argues: "Because state regulation tends to be highly complex, state legislators are especially reluctant to immerse themselves in the substantive details of regulation." Do we find evidence of state legislative influence in state-level regulation?

It is fortunate that although more work needs to be done on this issue, there is already some available evidence to consider. In these studies, legislative influence is sometimes tested as simple legislative party control or as percentage party control (as with the Ranney Index), sometimes using measures of legislative professionalism, and sometimes by analyzing specific legislative rules and powers. So far, most of these studies have not been *fine-grained* enough to focus on the influence of state legislative committees, as have many of the federal studies. Mostly this is because of lack of resources for research; studying the detailed makeup of 50 legislative committees is very time-consuming.

In state telecommunications regulation, Teske (1990a) found that differences in party control of the legislatures are important, with the expected result that Republicans are more favorable to business interests and Democrats to consumers. Also in telecommunications, Cohen (1988) found that the powers held by different state legislatures can affect the influence they wield over regulatory policy. In his study of energy regulation, however, Gormley (1983) did not find consistent legislative party differences. Perry (1981) found that legislative professionalism is associated with state energy conservation policies. In a historical study of early state railroad regulation in the 1870s, Kanazawa and Noll (1990) found that the Illinois Constitution was an important institutional constraint used by legislators to "bind themselves" to regulation. In insurance regulation, Miles and Bhambri (1983) found that regulators cited state legislators as the most important influence on them, more than insurance firms, media, consumers, or other actors. Begun et al. (1981) found that the regulation of optometrists is more relaxed when legislative party competition is greater, when legislative turnover is low, and when states are more "innovative" in policy (Walker, 1969; Gray, 1973).

In consumer regulation, Sigelman and Smith (1980) found that greater legislative professionalism leads to tighter regulation. In regulatory enforcement, Wood (1989) found that the higher the percentage of Democrats in a state legislature, the more environmental enforcement by the state regulators. Ethridge (1981) found that use of the state legislative veto is related to more relaxed air pollution regulations. Scholz and Wei (1986) found that the partisanship of individual local legislators is important. On the other hand, in hazardous waste regulation, Williams and Matheny (1984) found that the "quality" of the state's law is *not* important.

In terms of legislative rules and procedures, for states as a whole across policy areas, Clingermayer (1989) found little evidence of McCubbins' (1985) theoretical notions of conflict and uncertainty shaping the degree of legislative delegation to bureaucrats, although the study relies heavily on legislative and other cross-state indices for most of the independent variables, rather than more direct measures.

In an attempt to link the several state studies that focus more on political culture and ideology Erikson and colleagues (1987) found that legislative party and preferences are intervening variables that often are not found to be influential because they really reflect general state ideology. This may help to explain why some studies have found state ideology or measures of "policy innovativeness" to be important (Walker, 1969; Gray, 1973; Lin and Scholz, 1986), and other studies have not found substantial state legislative influence over regulatory policy. It raises the question of what these innovativeness scores really measure: independent actions of the legislature or influence from the state population's ideology, or some combination.

Gubernatorial Influence

Moe (1982), Cohen (1986), Eisner and Meier (1990), and others have provided quantitative evidence of the impact of Presidents on regulatory policy, while others have provided ample anecdotal evidence of such influence, particularly during the Reagan years (Fix, 1984; Harris and Milkis, 1989). It is surprising, then, that there is not a large body of evidence supporting gubernatorial influence over state regulatory policy.

Several studies have tested for the influence of governors but have not found it. There are only a few exceptions. Thompson and Scicchitano (1985) found that Republican governors influence whether a state establishes its own OSHA regulatory enforcement mechanism, but that gubernatorial partisanship does not influence subsequent regulatory enforcement vigor. Wood (1989) found that state environmental agency enforcement is greater in states with Democratic governors. Contrary to expectations, Hedge et al. (1990) found that Democratic governors are associated with more lenient hazardous waste enforcement and they found no evidence of gubernatorial influence over surface mining regulation. These findings are all for social regulation, jointly shared with the federal government; none of the studies of state economic regulation showed significant gubernatorial influence.

Why are governors not more important in state regulation, particularly since they appoint many of the regulators and have several tools of potential influence over policy (see Rosenthal, 1990)? It may be that governors can only focus on a few important issues at a time (Browne, 1987; Sigelman and Smith, 1981; Weinberg, 1977). As Moe (1987a) notes about Presidents, governors may not care greatly about regulatory policy, but simply try to appease various interest groups in making appointments to regulatory bodies, while not exerting further active pressure. Sabato (1978) analyzes the key issues that governors raise in their "State of the State" addresses as well as the issues that defeat governors politically. Regulatory issues are not high on either of these lists, although energy, environmental, consumer, and hazardous waste issues do achieve salience in some states at some periods of time. Governors appoint more state regulators than several years ago (Gormley, 1989b), but perhaps these appointees really are very independent from them, as in the classic model of independent regulatory agencies (Bernstein, 1955; McCraw, 1984).

On a methodological basis, it may be true that it is difficult to measure gubernatorial ideology across states, and that simple party differences are insufficient. Beyle (1983) notes that gubernatorial powers differ substantially across states; perhaps there is influence in some states but not in others, with the result that influence does not show up in cross-sectional studies. It may be that sophisticated, interrupted time-series analyses are necessary at the state level to determine gubernatorial influence.

Interest Groups

The studies reviewed here definitely show that interest group pressure is important in shaping state regulation. It would be cause for some alarm and theoretical reorientation if they did not. Evidence suggests not only that industry interest groups are influential but also that they are saavy about choosing the best level of regulation for their activities (Noam, 1982; Anderson, 1980; Cohen, 1991), and that they can make superior choices about seeking legislative versus bureaucratic arenas in which to maximize their influence (Teske, 1991).

In addition to the main regulated firms or industry in a particular arena, however, there are many kinds of interest groups that have influence. I will consider the main regulated firms first because they have been most prominent in the literature and probably remain the single most important interest group in most state regulatory arenas.

The influence of main regulated firm or industry varies by area, but they seemingly are not dominant in most policy areas. The evidence does not generally support a narrow view of dominant influence like that of Stigler (1971), and in fact several political science studies have aimed explicitly to show empirically how insufficient Stigler's theory really is (see especially Meier, 1988). These industry interests generally are not found to have more influence over state regulatory policy than are bureaucrats. It may be true that interest group power in particular industries (Thomas and Hrebener, 1989) and interest group density generally (Lowery and Gray, 1990) varies by state, in which case aggregate cross-sectional data could find mixed results, when in fact influence varied state by state.

In telecommunications, Teske (1991) found strong influence by one firm that tried very hard to be influential, US West, but did not find overwhelming influence from other regulated firms. In energy regulation, Gormley (1983) found strong evidence of industry influence. In insurance regulation, Meier (1988) found some industry influence, but that the overall industry position is often split: some firms gain from regulation, while others lose. Williams' (1983) perspective is more that state insurance regulation approximates capture or client politics. Smith (1982) found that automobile dealers are able to use state franchise regulations to impose higher costs on consumers, although the immediate conflict appears to be between dealers and automobile manufacturers.

In social regulation, in the area of hazardous waste, Williams and Matheny (1984) found strong industry influence. However, Hedge et al. (1990) did not find large industry influence in the regulation of hazardous waste. Scholz and Wei (1986) found strong industry influence in the enforcement of OSHA regulations. Lowry (1988) found that industry influences state air pollution regulation but not water pollution regulation. On the opposite side of industry influence, with OSHA, Thompson and Sciccitano (1985) found influence from the strength of labor unions in a state, as did Scholz and Wei (1986).

The studies of occupational regulation may show the strongest consistent influence of the regulated parties, optometrists in the case of Begun et al. (1981) and generally in Young

(1987). On the other hand, Lynk (1981) showed that the presence of doctors on state Blue Shield boards does not lead to higher payments for physicians, and Lin and Scholz (1986), who seem to measure hospital interests well, did not find any measurable influence over regulations.

Thus, somewhat surprisingly, the regulated firms seem to show as much or more influence over regulation in areas of "social," or asymmetrical information and externality, regulation, than in more traditional "economic" regulation. This may be because of the time period, in the late 1970s and 1980s, economic regulation often featured "deregulation," a set of choices over which the dominant firms arguably would have less influence (Derthick and Quirk, 1985).

Other Industry Groups

The interest group environment in most regulatory arenas is much more rich than simply the regulated firms. Firms in related (substitute and complementary) industries have reasons to seek influence and organized large users of regulated services may also be important. Leone (1986) argued that these firms need to be cognizant of the impact of regulation on them, and Ackerman and Hassler (1981) and Noll and Owen (1983) illustrated how intraindustry differences can affect regulation.

At the state level, for example, scholars have long recognized that shipper groups were important in initiating railroad regulation in the 1880s (McCraw, 1984; Gilligan et al., 1989). Kanazawa and Noll (1989) found that even railroad shipping interests disagreed substantially, depending on whether they were already served and whether they were shipping their product long or short distances. In state trucking weight regulations, Stigler's (1971) original article on the "economic theory" found that agricultural shippers and competitor railroads have influence. In telecommunications, Teske (1990a) found that large business users were influential and Smart (1990) found very strong evidence of influence by businesses that rely on telecommunications services. In energy regulation, Anderson (1981) found that large electricity users played an important role in policy changes in the 1970s. In insurance regulation, Meier (1988) found that other firms related to the insurance industry were important.

Most of this evidence is in "economic regulation." In a social regulation area, Harris (1985) found that large and already complying coal mining firms opposed lenient state enforcement of regulations. In workmen's compensation, Thompson (1982) found that insurance and legal interests are able to influence policy, in addition to the influence of labor groups.

Dispersed Consumers Evidence

Olson (1965) has shown how difficult it is for dispersed consumers to organize and develop the political influence of concentrated producer interests. Wilson (1980), Gormley (1983), Berry (1984), and Derthick and Quirk (1985) have all shown different ways that consumers can be and have been represented in regulatory policy. Empirical studies do support their influence to some degree. Both Gormley (1983) and Berry (1984) found some influence in state energy regulation, as did Clingermayer (1986), who tested several different measures of consumer strength. Teske (1990a) found some influence for government-sponsored consumer groups in telecommunications. In the area of consumer protection legislation, where one might expect consumer influence, Meier (1987) found that the consumer values held by elected officials were influential but not Consumer Union membership per capita. Kiholm Smith (1982) found that Protestant groups are able to influence state laws regulating the sale of liquor. Williams and Matheny (1984) found some influence of environmental public interest groups in state hazardous waste regulation. On the other hand, Lowry (1988) found that Sierra Club members do *not* influence state air or water pollution regulation.

Precise measures of consumer strength are difficult to capture, particularly those in a specific area of regulation, but when scholars have developed adequate measures they seem to show some, although not overwhelming, evidence of influence. Anecdotal evidence related to consumer groups shifting their focus of activity from Washington, D.C., to the state capitals suggests that they have been influential there, at least in some (particularly progressive or innovative) states (see Holusha, 1991), such as California, New York, and Massachusetts.

Some scholars (Gormley, 1989a) suggest that public policy would be better served by having bureaucratic choices more subject to influence from below, which Gormley calls "catalytic controls" rather than "coercive controls" from above (especially from governors and legislators). Evidence suggests that this source of influence is active and may be growing in the states.

State Social, Demographic, and Economic Factors

Much debate in state policy studies in the 1960s and 1970s focused on the relative importance of socioeconomic factors versus political factors (Weber, 1989). Some scholars argued that external factors shape the demand for certain kinds of policies, which then get translated through the political system. On the other hand, others suggested that political institutional factors shape how interests get translated into policies and are thus more important.

There is evidence that external factors are influential. Although Teske (1990a) found little evidence in telecommunications, Smart (1990) found a great deal. Kemp (1981) found that middle class populations (defined by income) influence state power plant siting regulations. Regens (1980) and Perry (1981) found that state energy regulation is influenced significantly by state energy capacity factors. Several occupational regulation studies found that levels of state education, income, and urbanism are important.

Several studies of consumer protection regulation indicated that economic and demographic factors are important. Bernacchi (1976), Ford (1977), and Sigelman and Smith (1980) found the relative income level of the state to be important. Sigelman and Smith (1980) also found a significant influence for state political culture, which Smith and Young (1974) in no-fault insurance, Bernacchi (1976) in consumer protection, and Meier (1987) in consumer protection found degree of urbanism to be influential. In the area of worker safety, Thompson and Schicchitano (1985) found that wealthier states are more likely to pursue more vigorous OSHA enforcement.

In addition to these state-level factors, there are also vertical and horizontal (external) factors that can partially shape state regulatory policy. Federal actors are the most important vertical factor. The horizontal dimension comes into play when states compete for economic development in industries that are regulated at the state level. The next two sections consider the evidence available for these factors.

Federal Goals, Federalism, and State Regulation

Of course, we can never forget that state regulation takes place in the context of a federal system and that if federal goals become more important, some forms of state regulation can be pre-empted (see Gray [1983] for the Reagan administration's philosophical approach to this issue; see also Chubb [1985] and Fix [1984]). Recently, particularly with the development of pooled cross-sectional, time-series models, several scholars have analyzed regulations developed at the federal level but often implemented at the state level.

It is important to consider how autonomous the state role is versus the federal regulatory role. Dresang and Gosling (1989) suggest five categories: (1) sole state responsibility (e.g., insurance); (2) sole federal responsibility (stock market regulation); (3) federal pre-emption (interstate commerce); (4) partial pre-emption (environmental regulation); (5) state veto (nuclear waste siting). Redford (1965) suggests four categories: (1) those left to state by the Constitution (e.g., property rights); (2) those delegated by the federal government (insurance); (3) parallel activity (energy); (4) cooperative (OSHA). The politics of state regulation may differ across categories because the relevant actors and constraints will be different. The more autonomous the state role, the less we would expect influence from federal actors, and the more we might expect state-level interest groups to be influential. For example, Tucker (1984) illustrated how the long-term increasing convergence of state policies has slowed, particularly as differences between the south and the rest of the country remain.

Wood (1989) found that internal bureaucratic decisions, as a response to historical patterns and resource allocation efficiencies, are more influential than any level of political pressure in the implementation of clean air policy by the EPA and the states. Hedge et al. (1990) found that federal influences are as strong or stronger over state-implemented regulation than are state influences. Scicchitano and Hedge (1989) found that federal influence over state programs can be continued even after some devolution of responsibility. Lowry (1988) found a mix of influences from the federal and state levels, with the initial federal design of implementation, regarding means or ends forcing, crucial to influence. Cone and Dranove (1986) found that state hospital rate regulation occurs mostly in liberal states that suffered most financially from incentives and inefficiencies in the federal Medicaid program, rather than state-level interest groups. Marvel (1982) found that federal and state regulatory implementation of OSHA are different, and that state regulation is more subject to state and local influences. More recent studies by Scholz et al. (1991) found that the federal, state, and local political environments all influence OSHA enforcement of regulations. Thus, in programs with a significant shared regulatory enforcement element, we see patterns of influence from both the federal and state levels.

Economic Development and State Regulation

The linkages between state-level regulation and economic development suggest that regulated firms have even more power than sometimes ascribed to them because they can "vote with their feet." The need for states to attract and retain jobs and income may overcome their desire to regulate externalities such as pollution. Rowland and Marz (1982) developed this argument explicitly for state regulation, as a variant of Gresham's Law: "lax regulation drives out stringent regulation." Such economic development constraints on state regulatory choices can lead to a situation in which only prosperous states can afford to regulate severely. This "law" is worth testing, although it apparently does not always hold: by 1984, for example, 19 states had established more extensive regulatory programs for air pollutants than those of the EPA (Reagan, 1987).

It is important to consider how mobile are the regulated businesses. Public utilities have generally been given geographic franchises and are not mobile (although this is slowly changing), while chemical companies can locate nearly anywhere. Market location can be the critical factor for these firms. While examples of firms actually moving due only to state regulation are rare, there is little doubt that regulation can create such incentives. The degree of state regulatory intervention into private markets may affect choices to leave a state. Laws restricting plant closing or setting rules for the firing of employees are more intrusive than those that force companies to provide consumer information. Business organizations believe that the intrusiveness dimension is increasing at the state level, after decreasing on the federal level in the 1980s (Warner, 1990).

Feiock and Rowland (1990) found that chemical firms do in fact move to states that regulate their environmental activities more lightly than others. State financial regulation may also be heavily influenced by economic development concerns. Citicorp agreed to move some facilities and jobs to Hagerstown, MD, as an incentive for the state to allow interstate banking. Some of the savings and loan misregulation at the state level (especially in states like Texas and California) was driven by economic development concerns of regulators (as well as by capture and corruption). Skalaban (1990) found that interstate banking is more likely to be allowed in a state when it faces economic problems; interstate economic development competition predicted interstate banking patterns better than measures of state ideology or interest group power. Williams (1983) cited evidence of insurance firms leaving states like Texas and Wisconsin when these states tightened regulation. Kiholm Smith (1982) found that the more tourism is important to a state, the more lenient are liquor regulations. In an infrastructure industry that is important to the long-term economic development of several other industries, Teske (1990b) found that development issues are increasingly affecting the form of state telecommunications regulations. Thus, there is some evidence that economic development competition affects state regulatory choices, usually to the benefit of the regulated industry.

TESTING THEORIES OF REGULATORY POLITICS

Various approaches to the understanding of regulatory policy can be tested against this state information. Economists generally rely upon basic market failure concepts to categorize normative justifications for regulation, based on (1) natural monopoly or anticompetitive activity, which typically have led to forms of economic regulation in a particular industry; (2) asymmetric information (typical when producers know more about products than consumers), which justifies much food and product regulation; and (3) externality effects on third parties, which justify environmental regulation. Despite the fact that the politics of these areas should differ, since regulators often specialize in one or two industries in the case of (1), while the regulations can cross-cut many industries in (2) and (3), the evidence from the states does not clarify many patterns of politics using this framework. Nor does it provide much support for the "economic theory" of consistent industry (or even interest groups generally) dominance of regulation.

It may be possible to use the market failure distinctions to argue that much social regulation, since it was written into law with more explicit detail than economic regulation, should show more influence from the initial interest groups and legislators than later interest groups or politicians, and more bureaucratic influence over time (see Moe, 1989). Most of the state studies analyzed here do not allow for that type of test. Social regulation should also show more influence from dispersed consumers, since it arguably favors them. Economic regulation should likewise show more industry influence and less legislative control, since the statutes often are more vague. In general, the state-level evidence does not provide strong or consistent support for this hypothesis.

Joskow and Noll (1981) note that using the market failure paradigm as a positive theory can be called "normative analysis as a positive theory" (or NPT). That is, the NPT theory suggests that society *does* regulate certain industries because government *should* try to improve market failures. However, there are obviously areas of regulation in which this is not the case. Often, interest group or other political pressure is crucial to why we regulate, generally and at the state level (Williams, 1983).

Since this paradigm does not illuminate the politics of regulation, political scientists have found it useful to develop other categories to analyze and understand regulatory activity. Of course, Lowi (1964) classified policies into distributive, redistributive and regulatory. Since we are already focusing on regulatory politics this is not specific enough to be helpful. James Q. Wilson's (1980) framework of dispersed and narrow costs/benefits of regulatory policies provides more insight. Williams (1983) applied Wilson's framework specifically to state regulation to show how client politics (occupational regulation, insurance regulation, and utility regulation before 1973), interest group politics (workmen's compensation), and entrepeneurial politics (hazardous waste) can apply on the state level. Williams' application of Wilson's ideas provided a useful framework, but it does not allow us to go much further.

Although many state regulatory arenas are complex (Gormley, 1986: 603), there is enough variance in this state-level evidence to do a simple test of Gormley's twofold classification of regulatory politics. Gormley identified: (1) saliency: How important is the issue? and (2) complexity: How difficult is the issue for nonexperts to understand? Table 1 below, taken from Gormley (1986), identifies the areas of state regulation on the scale of salience and complexity, using Gormley's own placements, where available, and my own when not.

Gormley calls cell 1 "hearing room" politics, which is influenced by the activity of a wide array of actors, since politicians are attracted to high-salience, low-complexity issues. It can reflect Wilson's entrepreneurial politics, or interest group politics, or democratic politics. Gormley's view is that politicians make choices, and the bureaucracy and regulated interests are not free to do as they wish. The evidence in this paper shows that in zoning (a local power derived from the state) Fleischman and Pierannunzi (1990) found that citizen planning boards are important as well as developers and local politicians. In consumer protection regulation, studies found that legislative professionalism matters (Sigelman and Smith, 1980), as do the consumer values of legislators and the powers they give to Attorneys General (Meier, 1987), and many economic factors. In workmen's compensation, Thompson (1982) found that labor, business, insurance, and legal interests were influential as well as bureaucrats. The state evidence largely supports Gormley's theory in this category of high-salience, low-complexity politics.

Gormley characterizes high-salience and high-complexity regulation in cell 2 as part of "operating room" politics. Politicians are driven to procedural rather than substantive action. The regulated do not capture bureaucrats, and most decisions are ultimately made by professional, high-level bureaucrats. Expertise is important and often the courts play an important role. Evidence shows that in state telecommunications (more salient since 1984) and energy regulation, high-level bureaucrats are important, capture is not the dominant pattern, and politicians do undertake largely procedural action. In siting power plants (Kemp, 1981), bureau-

Table 1 Salience and Complexity

		Complexity	
		Low	*High*
Salience	*High*	1 Consumer protection Zoning Worker's compensation	2 Energy, Environment, Hazardous waste, OSHA Telecommunications
	Low	3 Occupational regulation Liquor licensing, Transportation	4 Antitrust, Insurance Finance, Hospitals

cratic powers are important. Evidence from hazardous waste showed that the specific law is not important, that state and agency resources are, and that industry is influential. Evidence from OSHA showed multiple influences, with expertise as one important influence on policy outcomes. Evidence in environmental protection (Wood, 1989) showed the importance of bureaucratic resources and routines. The state evidence for high-salience, high-complexity decision-making largely supports Gormley.

Gormley characterizes cell 3, with low salience and low complexity, as "street-level" politics. The standard operating procedures of lower-level bureaucrats are crucial, and capture by regulated interests or rigidity is each a possible outcome, on a case-by-case basis. Some evidence on occupational regulation (Begun et al., 1981) showed capture predominantly, although there is not enough evidence available. Schutz (1983) found little impact from citizen participation on licensing boards in California, which suggests capture. Kiholm Smith's (1982) liquor licensing study showed that bureaucratic structure matters. Recent evidence in state level trucking regulation (Teske et al., forthcoming) shows that capture remains the dominant pattern in most states, although shipper and agricultural interests also influence policy. The low-salience, low-complexity issues of state franchising of automobile dealers analyzed by Smith (1982) fits a pattern of seeming interest group politics really being capture by the regulated. In some ways, Gormley's description fits better the several recent studies of street-level implementation of OSHA and environmental protection, since implementation may be somewhat less salient and less complex than rule-making in Washington. Overall, the evidence from cell 3 is limited but tends to support Gormley.

Gormley notes that low-salience and high-complexity "board room" politics characterizes cell 4. A small business elite usually is most influential in decisions, although bureaucrats can play important roles, if business interests are divided. Sometimes capture takes place, but the elite are divided on many issues. In insurance, Williams (1983) found industry dominance, while Meier (1988) argued that if Stigler's (1971) theory were to hold anywhere it should be here, but he finds influence by several industry and bureaucratic players. Miles and Bhambri concluded that the insurance industry and regulators are important. In interstate banking, Skalaban (1990) found that interest groups are not important but savings and loan regulation suggests elite dominance. Before 1984, when state telecommunications regulation became more salient, regulated firms were fairly dominant (Teske, 1990a). On the other hand, a study of hospital regulation (Lin and Scholz, 1986) found that private interests were less influential than ideology, and Lynk (1981) found that doctors on reimbursement boards did not overpay (relatively) their colleagues. State antitrust, in which Attorneys General are crucial, fits here but there are no studies. Overall, while there are not enough studies, existing evidence of low-salience, high-complexity politics provides some confirmation and some challenges to Gormley's categories.

Overall, the categorization developed by Gormley seems to be more helpful than the others that have been developed, and available evidence in state regulation tends to support many of his conclusions. Cells 1 and 2 are largely supported, while cell 3 and cell 4 show some support. Not surprising is that social science research has focused more on high-salience policies, which is why there is less evidence for cells 3 and 4.

To provide more explanatory power, perhaps more elements of this theory must be added or specified; in particular, the simple high/low characterization for salience and complexity may be inadequate. Perhaps we can measure salience more directly using media coverage and/or public opinion data. Gormley argues that salience is a function of a necessity imperiled, aspects of the American dream threatened, affronts to community values, or key elements of employment conditions.

There may also be better ways to organize and classify complexity, which, according to Gormley, is higher when regulating monopolies, large firms, new technologies, and substances. The problem is that most of these concepts relating to both salience and complexity can be stretched to include most areas of regulation.

Furthermore, one can dispute some of Gormley's placements. For example, I would not be sure where to place state child-care regulations, which Gormley (1991) recently analyzed; there are analogies to nursing home inspections, which Gormley (1986) stated were low-salience but increasing. Inadequate child-care would seem to threaten the American dream, but it still seems a relatively back-burner issue in most states, except in the event of a scandal.

As a first cut toward developing more of a continuum, I suggest the following classification.

Most complex (full understanding of key issues requires technical training): nuclear energy, hazardous waste
Moderately complex (an intelligent layperson could understand the important issues, with some work): telecommunications, energy, insurance, banking
Least complex: occupational regulation, OSHA, consumer regulation

Similarly, we could expand the saliency dimension:

Most salient: nuclear energy, environment, hazardous waste
Moderately salient: telecommunications, energy, OSHA, hospitals
Least salient: occupational, insurance, finance, antitrust

Perhaps a distinction can be drawn between technological complexity, as with nuclear power or new chemicals, which few laypeople can understand fully, and financial/administrative complexity, as with insurance and banks, which can be understood by a larger set of actors. Most Americans pay mortgages and are covered by insurance policies, about which they must take active choices. On the other hand, while electricity comes when a consumer flips a switch, that consumer may not know or care about whether the power comes from nuclear or nonnuclear sources. This suggests that financial and insurance regulation may be closer to cell 3, adding more influence by lower-level bureaucrats (auditors, inspectors) to the influence of business elites.

Fusing some more deductively generated (but empirically untested) ideas from McCubbins (1985) might add to the Gormley typology. McCubbins focused on legislative delegation, which should influence the role of bureaucrats and other key players in policy choices, and used conflict and uncertainty to explain the political incentives of legislators. Conflict is related to salience but is not exactly the same; an issue could be widely salient but have relatively little conflict (such as the war in the Persian Gulf recently), or an issue could be both salient and highly conflictual, as with abortion. Politicians may be attracted to salience but they may also be repelled by the electoral threats inherent in conflictual situations (abortion is so highly salient that some state legislatures are passing abortion-related bills, but high conflict makes them extremely problematic for many legislators). Salience would seem to be more of a mass phenomenon, while conflict is either an interest group versus the masses or, more often, interest groups against each other. My placements are as follows: *most conflictual*: nuclear, telecommunications, insurance, finance, OSHA, zoning; *least conflictual*: occupational regulation, antitrust.

This discussion holds an important implication for the type of power that legislators delegate. Complexity leads to what can be called "expertise-oriented" legislation, but conflict focuses more on "hot potato passing" delegation, as when politicians do not want to handle these problems themselves but pass them on down the line, if possible. A legislature may not be shy about dealing with complex issues if salience is high (potential political payoffs) *and* if conflict is not too intense. Adding a dimension of conflict, then, in addition to salience, may help to clarify the situations in which Gormley noted the possibility of different kinds of politics within a single cell. Of course, it makes the development of a parsimonious framework of regulatory politics more complicated.

CONCLUSIONS

The extent and type of political influence over federal regulation have provided one the most important and controversial topics of social science research in the past decade. This line of research has not yet pushed hard enough to allow us to ask similar questions about state-level regulation, where, I believe, we can learn even more. Still, researchers have prepared many separate studies of different regulatory arenas in the past decade. By synthesizing the findings of these eclectic studies, I argue that we do have substantial empirical evidence from the states and that we can use this information to develop and test theories of regulatory politics and the role of bureaucrats, legislators, governors, interest groups, and consumers.

While state regulation provides a richer laboratory than federal regulation, it also has a growing importance in the American economy. The reduction in federal regulation in the 1980s may prove to be a temporary reversal of a longer-term trend toward more regulation, or it might prove to be a more permanent reversal in the role of the federal government in the private economy. More likely is that we will see cycles of increasing and decreasing federal attention to private market regulation. In any case, however, the development of state institutions with more resources and capacity to regulate will keep the state role prominent, whatever direction Washington, D.C. takes in the next decade and century. The relatively smooth and symbiotic relationship of American state and federal regulation is likely to provide a model for other nations, particularly for the growing economic unification of Western Europe and for the previously Soviet-dominated nations of Eastern Europe.

Certainly regulatory politics at the American state level became more complicated in the 1980s. As the stakes rose, more actors got involved and there is clear evidence that many of these actors have become influential. In fact, the political and interest group environment of state regulation has started to look more like a miniature version of federal regulation, where simple models of capture are insufficient, at least in the larger states. The studies reviewed here highlight the role of bureaucrats, the importance of state legislators, and the surprising lack of consistent gubernatorial influence.

The evidence analyzed here shows that the political factors wielding influence vary by type of regulatory policy. Thus, we need a theory of when different actors are more or less likely to be influential. We have a few contending theories to test with this accumulating evidence. My simple analysis here suggests that Gormley's concepts of salience and complexity provide a useful guide to regulatory politics. By operationalizing Gormley's parameters more clearly and by integrating additional elements, we may be able to get a better handle on the increasingly interesting and important venue of state regulation, and shed substantial light on federal regulation in the process.

REFERENCES

Ackerman, Bruce, and William Hassler. 1981. *Clean Coal/Dirty Air*. New Haven: Yale University Press.

Amenta, Edwin, Elisabeth Clemens, Jefren Olsen, Sunita Parikh, and Theda Skocpol. 1987. The political origins of unemployment insurance in five American states, pp. 137–82 in *Studies in American Political Development,* edited by Karen Orren and Stephen Skowroneck, New Haven: Yale University Press.

Anderson, Douglas. 1981. *Regulatory Politics and Electric Utilities: A Case Study in Political Economy,* New York: Auburn House.

Becker, Gary. 1983. A theory of competition among pressure groups for political influence. *Quarterly Journal of Economics* 98: 371–400.

Becker, Gary. 1985. Public policies, pressure groups, and dead weight costs. *Journal of Public Economics* 28: 329–47.

Begun, James, Edward Crowe, and Roger Feldman. 1981. Occupational regulation in the states: A causal model. *Journal of Health Politics and Law* 6 (2) (Summer): 229–254.

Bernacchi, Michael. 1976. A regional analysis of state consumer protection budgets. *Journal of Consumer Affairs* 10 (Winter): 239–44.

Bernstein, Marver. 1955. *Regulating Business by Independent Commission.* Princeton: Princeton University Press.

Berry, William. 1979. Utility regulation in the states: Policy effects of professionalism and salience to the consumers. *American Journal of Political Science* 23 (May): 263–77.

Berry, William. 1984. An alternative to the capture theory of regulation: The case of public utility commissions. *American Journal of Political Science* 28 (August): 524–558.

Beyle, Thad. 1983. Governors, in *Politics in the American States,* edited by Virginia Gray, Herbert Jacob, and Kenneth Vines, Boston: Little Brown.

Bowman, Ann and Richard Kearney. 1988. Dimensions of state capability. *Western Political Quarterly* 41: 340.

Browne, William. 1987. Policymaking in the American states: Examining institutional variables from a subsystem perspective. *American Politics Quarterly* 15 (1) (January): 47–84.

Chubb, John. 1985. The political economy of Federalism. *American Political Science Review* 79 (December): 994–1015.

Clingermayer, James. 1986. Government-sponsored consumer advocacy and the cost of capital: The case of electric utility rate regulation. Paper presented to the Southern Political Science Association Annual Meeting, Atlanta.

Clingermayer, James. 1989. Administrative innovations as instruments of state legislative control: An exploratory analysis. Paper presented to the Midwest Political Science Association Annual Meeting, Chicago.

Cohen, Jeffrey. 1986. The dynamics of the revolving door on the FCC. *American Journal of Political Science* 30 (November): 689–708.

Cohen, Jeffrey. 1988. Bureaucratic influence in redistributive versus technical policies. Paper presented to the Southern Political Science Association, Atlanta.

Cohen, Jeffrey. 1991. The telephone problem and the road to telephone regulation in the United States, 1876-1917. *Journal of Policy History* 3 (1).

Cone, Kenneth, and David Dranove. 1986. Why did states enact hospital rate-setting laws? *Journal of Law and Economics,* October.

Derthick, Martha, and Paul Quirk. 1985. *The Politics of Deregulation.* Washington, D.C.: Brookings Institution.

Dresang, Dennis, and James Gosling. 1989. *Politics, Policy, and Management in the American States.* New York: Longman.

Eisner, Marc, and Kenneth Meier. 1990. Presidential control versus bureaucratic power: Explaining the Reagan revolution in antitrust. *American Journal of Political Science* 34: 269–87.

Erikson, Robert, John McIver, and Gerald Wright. 1987. State political culture and public opinion. *American Political Science Review* 81 (3) (September): 797–813.

Ethridge, Marcus. 1981. Legislative-administrative interaction as 'intrusive access': An empirical analysis. *Journal of Politics* 43 (2) (May): 473–92.

Faith, Roger, et al. 1982. Antitrust pork barrel. *Journal of Law and Economics* 25 (2) (October): 329–342.

Feiock, Richard, and C. K. Rowland. 1990. Environmental regulation and economic development: The movement of chemical production among states. *Western Political Quarterly* 561–76.

Ferejohn, John. 1987. The structure of agency decision processes, in *Congress: Structure and Policy,* ed. Mathew McCubbins and Terry Sullivan, Cambridge: Cambridge University Press.

Fix, Michael. 1984. Transfering regulatory authority to the states, in *The Reagan Regulatory Strategy: An Assessment,* ed. George Eads and Michael Fix, Washington, D.C.: Urban Institute Press.

Fleischmann, Arnold, and Carol Pierannunzi. 1990. Citizens, development interests, and local land-use regulation. *Journal of Politics* 52 (3) (August): 838–53.

Ford, Gary. 1977. State characteristics affecting the passage of consumer legislation. *Journal of Consumer Affairs,* Summer.

Gilligan, Thomas, William Marshall, and Barry Weingast. 1989. Regulation and the theory of legislative choice: The Interstate Commerce Act of 1887. *Journal of Law and Economics* 32: 35–61.

Gormley, William. 1983. *The Politics of Public Utility Regulation,* Pittsburgh: University of Pittsburgh Press.

Gormley, William. 1986. Regulatory issue networks in a federal system, *Polity* 18 (Summer).

Gormley, William. 1989a. The bureaucracy and its masters: A comparative analysis. Paper presented to the APSA Annual Meeting, Atlanta.

Gormley, William. 1989b. *Taming the Bureaucracy: Muscles, Prayers, and Other Strategies.* Princeton: Princeton University Press.

Gormley, William. 1991. State regulations and the availability of child-care services. *Journal of Policy Analysis and Management* 10 (1) (January).

Gray, C. Boyden. 1983. Regulation and federalism. *Yale Journal on Regulation*: 93–110.

Gray, Virginia. 1973. Innovation in the states: A diffusion study. *American Political Science Review* 67 (December) 1174–85.

Gray, Virginia. 1976. Models of comparative state politics: A comparison of cross-sectional and time series analyses. *American Journal of Political Science,* May.

Harris, Richard. 1985. *Coal Firms Under the New Social Regulation,* Durham, NC: Duke University Press.

Harris, Richard, and Sidney Milkis. 1989. *The Politics of Regulatory Change,* New York: Oxford Press.

Hedge, David, Michael Scicchitano, and Charles Davis. 1990. The state and devolution: Implementing federal mandates. Paper presented to the APSA Annual Meeting, San Francisco.

Holusha, John. 1991. Some corporations plead for the firm hand of Uncle Sam. *New York Times* February 24, p. E6.

Joskow, Paul, and Roger Noll. 1981. Regulation in theory and practice: An overview, *Studies in Public Regulation,* edited by Gary Fromm, pp. 1–65, Cambridge: MIT Press.

Kanazawa, Mark, and Roger Noll. 1989. State-level regulation of railroads and grain elevators during the Granger era: The Illinois State Constitution of 1870. Paper presented to the Public Choice Society Annual Meeting, Orlando.

Kemp, Kathleen. 1981. Symbolic and strict regulation in the American states. *Social Science Quarterly* 62 (3): 516–526.

Leone, Robert. 1986. *Who Profits? Winners, Losers, and Government Regulation,* New York: Basic Books.

Lester, James, James Fronke, Anne Bowman, and Kenneth Kramer. 1983. Hazardous waste politics and public policy: A comparative state analysis. *Western Political Quarterly* 36 (June): 258–85.

Lin, Sherrie, and John Scholz. 1986. Public and private interests in hospital regulation. Unpublished manuscript.

Lowery, David, and Virginia Gray. 1990. The deep structure of state interest group systems I: Interest group system density. Paper presented to the APSA Annual Meetings, San Francisco, September.

Lowi, Theodore. 1964. American business, public policy, case studies, and political theory. *World Politics* 16: 677–715.

Lowry, William. 1988. Federalism and pollution policies. Paper presented to the APSA Annual Meetings, Washington.

Lynk, William. 1981. Regulatory control of the membership of corporate boards of directors: The Blue Shield case. *Journal of Law and Economics,* April.

Marvel, Mary. 1982. Implementation and safety regulation: Variations in federal and state administration under OSHA. *Administration and Society,* May.

Mashaw, Jerry, and Susan Rose-Ackerman. 1984. Federalism and Regulation, in *The Reagan Regulatory Strategy: An Assessment,* edited by George Eads and Michael Fix, Washington, D.C.: Urban Institute Press.

McCraw, Thomas. 1984. *Prophets of Regulation.* Cambridge: Harvard University Press.

McCubbins, Mathew. 1985. The legislative design of regulatory structure. *American Journal of Political Sciece* 29: 721–48.

Meier, Kenneth. 1985. *Regulation: Politics, Bureaucracy, and Economics.* New York: St. Martin's Press.

Meier, Kenneth. 1987. The political economy of consumer protection. *Western Political Quarterly,* 30 (June).

Meier, Kenneth. 1988. *The Political Economy of Regulation: The Case of Insurance,* Albany: SUNY Press.

Miles, Robert, and Arvind Bhambri. 1983. *The Regulatory Executives,* Sage.

Moe, Terry. 1982. Regulatory performance and presidential administration. *American Journal of Political Science* 26 (2) (May): 197–224.

Moe, Terry. 1985. Control and feedback in economic regulation: The case of the NLRB. *American Political Science Review* 79 (4) (December): 1094–1116.

Moe, Terry. 1987a. Interests, institutions, and positive theory: The politics of the NLRB, in *Studies in American Political Development,* edited by Karen Orren and Stephen Skowroneck, pp. 236–99, New Haven: Yale University Press.

Moe, Terry. 1987b. An assessment of the positive theory of 'congressional dominance.' *Legislative Studies Quarterly* 12 (4) (November): 475–520.

Moe, Terry. 1989. The politics of bureaucratic structure, in *Can the Government Govern?* edited by John Chubb and Paul Peterson, Washington, D.C.: Brookings Institution.

Munger, Michael. 1989. Book review of Ken Meier's *Regulation: Politics, Economics, and Bureaucracy* and *The Political Economy of Regulation. Public Choice* August.

Nathan, Richard. 1989. Federalism: The great 'composition,' in *The New American Political System,* edited by Anthony King, Washington: American Enterprise Institute.

Noam, Eli. 1982. The choice of government level in regulation. *Kyklos* 35.

Noll, Roger, and Bruce Owen. 1983. *The Political Economy of Deregulation.* Washington, D.C.: American Enterprise Institute.

Olson, Mancur. 1965. *The Logic of Collective Action.* Cambridge: Harvard University Press.

Oster, Sharon. 1980. An analysis of some causes of interstate differences in consumer regulations. *Economic Inquiry* 18: 39–54.

Peltzman, Sam. 1976. Toward a more general theory of regulation. *Journal of Law and Economics* 19 (August): 211–40.

Perry, Charles. 1981. Energy conservation policy in the American states: An attempt at explanation. *Social Science Quarterly* 62: 540–546.

Reagan, Michael. 1987. *Regulation: The Politics of Policy,* Boston: Little, Brown.

Redford, Emmette. 1965. *American Government and the Economy.* New York: MacMillan.

Reeves, Mavis. 1985. *The Question of State Government Capacity: A Commission Report.* Washington, D.C.: Advisory Commission on Intergovernmental Relations.

Regens, James. 1980. State policy responses to the energy issue: An analysis of innovation. *Social Science Quarterly* 61: 44–57.

Renfrow, Patty, et al. 1985. Rulemaking provisions in state administrative procedures acts. Paper presented to the Midwestern Political Science Association Annual Meeting, Chicago.

Rosenthal, Alan. 1990. *Governors & Legislatures: Contending Powers.* Washington, D.C.: CQ Press.

Rowland, C. K., and Roger Marz. 1982. Gresham's law: The regulatory analogy. *Policy Studies Review,* February.

Sabato, Larry. 1978. *Goodbye to Goodtime Charlie*. Lexington, MA: D.C. Heath.

Scholz, John, and Feng Heng Wei. 1986. Regulatory enforcement in a federalist system. *American Political Science Review* 80 (4) (December): 1249–1270.

Scholz, John, Jim Twombly, and Barbara Headrick. 1991. Street-level political controls over federal bureaucracy. *American Political Science Review* 85: 829–850.

Schutz, Howard. 1983. Effects of increased citizen membership on occupational licensing boards in California. *Policy Studies Journal* 2 (3) (March): 504–16.

Scicchitano, Michael, and David Hedge. 1989. Federal oversight and the states: The surface mining case. Paper presented to the Midwest Political Science Association Meetings, Chicago.

Shepsle, Ken. 1982. Book review of James Q. Wilson's *Politics of Regulation. Journal of Political Economy*: 216-221.

Sigelman, Lee, and Roland Smith. 1980. Consumer regulation in the American states. *Social Science Quarterly* 61 (June): 58–76.

Sigelman, Lee, and Roland Smith. 1981. Personal, office and state characteristics as predictors of gubernatorial performance. *Journal of Politics* 43: 169–180.

Skalaban, Andrew. 1990. Models of public policy and state strategies to deregulate interstate banking. Paper presented to the Midwest Political Science Association, Chicago.

Smart, Susan. 1990. The impact of divestiture on telephone pricing: State regulatory responses. Paper presented to the 18th Annual Telecommunications Policy Research Conference, Airlie, VA, October.

Smith, Roland, and Sidney Young. 1974. Correlates of policy output: The case of no-fault insurance. Paper presented to the annual meeting of the Southwestern Political Science Association.

Smith, Janet Kiholm. 1982. An analysis of state regulations governing liquor store licenses. *Journal of Law and Economics* 25 (October): 301-320.

Smith, Richard. 1982. Franchise regulation: An economic analysis of state restrictions on automobile distribution. *Journal of Law and Economics* 25 (April): 221–33.

Stigler, George. 1971. The theory of economic regulation. *Bell Journal of Economics and Management Science*: 3–21.

Stone, Alan. 1982. *Regulation and Its Alternatives*. Washington, D.C.: Congressional Quarterly Press.

Teske, Paul. 1990a. *After Divestiture: The Political Economy of State Telecommunications Regulation*. Albany: SUNY Prses.

Teske, Paul. 1990b. The policy role of actors beyond the PUCs. Paper prepared for Columbia University conference on State Regulation of Telecommunications, October.

Teske, Paul. 1991. Rent-seeking in the deregulatory environment: State telecommunications. *Public Choice* 68: 235–243.

Teske, Paul, Samuel Best, and Michael Mintrom. 1993. The economic theory of regulation and trucking deregulation: Shifting to the state level. *Public Choice*, (December).

Thomas, Clive, and Ronald Hrebenar. 1989. Interest group power in the American states: Some reconsiderations. Paper presented to the Midwestern Political Science Association Annual Meetings, Chicago.

Thompson, Joel. 1982. Implementing workmen's compensation programs in the states. *Administration and Society*, August.

Thompson, Frank, and Michael Sciccatano. 1985. State implementation effort and federal regulatory policy: The case of occupational safety and health. *Journal of Politics* 47: 687–763.

Tucker, Harvey. 1982. It's about time: The use of time in cross-sectional state policy research. *American Journal of Political Science*, February.

Tucker, Harvey. 1984. The nationalization of state policy revisited. *Western Political Quarterly*, Sept.

Walker, Jack. 1969. The diffusion of innovation among American states. *American Political Science Review* (September): 880–99.

Warner, David. 1990. Watch the states. *Nation's Business* November: 15–22.

Watson, Tom. 1989. Dale Florio: A lobbyists' middleman who helps business navigate state capitol halls. *Governance* February.

Weber, Ronald. 1989. The study of state and local politics: A preliminary exploration of its empirical contributions to political theory. Paper presented to Midwestern Political Science Association Annual Meetings, Chicago.

Weinberg, Martha. 1977. *Managing the State.* Cambridge: MIT Press.

Weingast, Barry, and Mark Moran. 1983. Bureaucratic discretion or congressional control? Regulatory policymaking by the Federal Trade Commission. *Journal of Political Economy* 91 (5): 765–800.

Wellborn, David, and Anthony Brown. 1980. *Regulatory Policy and Process: The Public Service Commission in Tennessee.* Knoxville, TN: University of Tennessee.

Williams, Bruce. 1983. Bounding behavior: Economic regulation the American states, pp. 329–72, in *Politics in the American States,* edited by Virginia Gray, Herbert Jacob, and Kenneth Vines. Boston: Little Brown.

Williams, Bruce, and Albert Matheny. 1984. Testing theories of social regulation: Hazardous waste regulation in the American states. *Journal of Politics* 46: 428–58.

Wilson, James. 1980. *The Politics of Regulation.* New York: Basic Books.

Wood, B. Dan. 1989. Centralized federalism and clean air implementation. Paper presented to the Midwest Political Science Association, Chicago.

Young. S. David. 1987. *The Rule of Experts: Occupational Licensing in America,* Washington, D.C.: Cato Institute.

6

What Every Administrator Should Know About Environmental Law

Rosemary O'Leary *Syracuse University, Syracuse, New York*

Environmental issues pervade every area of our society. There is scarcely a public organization today that has not confronted an environmental challenge. With these environmental problems often come personal and organizational liabilities. In recent months, for example, a public high school was found liable for the improper disposal of waste products from its chemistry department while another school was charged with allowing asbestos-laden insulation to go untreated. State vehicle maintenance workers have been told to change the way they dispose of used oil and other automobile wastes lest they be the subject of litigation. Universities have been charged with violating the Clean Air Act when stacks from their coal-burning power plants were found to be emitting excessive pollutants. An Army maintenance worker was found criminally liable for the way he disposed of his organization's hazardous wastes.

Environmental laws affect nearly all public administrators and hundreds of government functions. It is not just the stereotypic "environmental" administrator (such as a waste water treatment plant operator or an individual who works in a state environmental agency) who is affected by today's environmental laws. Examples of affected government functions include the purchase of land, the operation of schools, wastewater collection and treatment, refuse disposal, the operation of hospitals, land use planning, road maintenance, water supply and delivery, the operation of parks, and the operation of airports.

This chapter examines six areas of environmental law about which every administration should be knowledgeable. The six areas are the erosion of government immunity, hazardous waste liabilities, the criminal liability of lower- and middle-level government employees, increased reporting requirements, liability for regulatory takings, and the municipality as mini-water pollution control agency. This chapter concludes that these environmental law developments will prompt nothing less than a fundamental change in public administration as we know it today. Proactive steps are suggested as a means of addressing the challenges that environmental laws pose to public managers.

THE EROSION OF GOVERNMENT IMMUNITY

In instances when federal and state entities have been charged with violating laws, the typical defenses include sovereign immunity and Eleventh Amendment immunity. The basic principle behind sovereign immunity is that the United States may not be sued without its consent. The basic principle behind Eleventh Amendment immunity is that a citizen of one state may not sue another state in federal court without the state's consent. It also has been interpreted as preventing federal court suits by citizens of the state being sued. (It should be noted that the Eleventh Amendment does not prevent suits against state subdivisions, such as counties and municipalities.) In the environmental field, these defenses slowly are being eroded.

Both sovereign immunity and Eleventh Amendment immunity can be waived by consent. In the case of sovereign immunity, that consent may be granted by a federal statute. In the case of Eleventh Amendment immunity, a federal cause of action also may be created by a law passed by Congress pursuant to its power under either the Commerce Clause (see *Pennsylvania v. Union Gas,* 109 S.Ct. 2273 [1989] discussed below), or the section of the Fourteenth Amendment that authorizes Congress to enforce the amendment (*Fitzpatrick v. Bitzer,* 427 U.S. 445 [1976]). The rationale here is that by approving the Constitution and its amendments, the states consented to suits based on these powers.

All major federal antipollution laws waive government immunity in some way, although the specifics differ from statute to statute. The most significant waivers of sovereign immunity include provisions for citizen suits and judicial review. Of the seven major environmental statutes implemented by the U.S. Environmental Protection Agency (EPA), for example, six provide for citizen suits and all provide for judicial review of some sort.[1]

The Clean Air Act (CAA) contains provisions that waive such immunity, with the intention of treating public and private defendants equally. The citizen suit provision of the CAA, for example, states that a civil action may be commenced "against any person . . . including the United States and . . . any other governmental instrumentality or agency" who is alleged to be in violation of certain sections of the act (42 U.S.C. 7604[a]). The statute includes in its definition of "person" who may be sued not only federal agencies operating sources of air pollution, but states and local governments.

The Clean Water Act (CWA) also waives sovereign immunity. The citizen suit section of the CWA, for example, states that "any citizen may commence a civil action . . . [for violation of the statute] against any person . . . including . . . the United States and . . . any other governmental instrumentality or agency" (33 U.S.C. Section 1365[a]). The definition of a "person" who may be sued provided by the statute is "an individual, corporation, partnership, association, State, municipality, commission, or political subdivision of a State, or any interstate body" (33 U.S.C. Section 1362[5]).

The Comprehensive Environmental Response, Compensation, and Liability Act (CERCLA), commonly known as the Superfund Act, waives immunity for the United States by defining a "person" who shall be liable for violating the act as "an individual, firm, corporation, association, partnership, consortium, joint venture, commercial entity, United States Government, State, municipality, commission, political subdivision of a State or any interstate body" (42 U.S.C. Section 9601[D][21]). The Act further provides that federal agencies are subject to and must comply with the statute in the same manner and to the same extent as nongovernmental entities (42. U.S.C. Section 9620[a][1]). Similar language is provided in the Resource Conservation and Recovery Act (RCRA) which states that "each department, agency, and instrumentality of the executive, legislative and judicial branches of the Federal Government" . . . shall be subject to and shall comply with all federal, state, interstate and local laws concerning waste disposal (42 U.S.C. Section 6961). The Superfund Amendments and Reauthorization Act (SARA) waives state immunity from suit under the Eleventh Amendment of the Constitution.

There has been a conflict, however, among the federal circuit courts concerning whether RCRA and CWA allow states to sue federal agencies for civil penalties. The conflict arose in part because of the different language and definitions provided in RCRA in several sections (particularly 42 U.S.C. Sections 6961, 6972, and 6928) and in CWA (particularly 33 U.S.C. Sections 1323 and 1365). The issue is especially important to states that are suing federal facilities for noncompliance with environmental laws. [See e.g., *Colorado v. Idarado Mining Co.*, no. 83-C-2385 (1989); *State of Colorado v. United States Department of the Army*, No. 86-C-2524 (1989)]. Efforts to address the split among the appellate courts through congressional legislation succeeded in part last year, but only after the Supreme Court issued a controversial decision.

On April 21, 1992, the Supreme Court issued an opinion in the case of *United States Department of Energy v. Ohio* (112 S.Ct. 1627), in which the state of Ohio was seeking punitive fines from the Department of Energy (DOE) for violations of environmental laws at the DOE uranium-processing plant in Fernald, Ohio. The pivotal issue was whether Congress waived the federal government's immunity from liability for civil fines imposed by a state for past violations of CWA and RCRA. The Supreme Court held, in a 6 to 3 decision, that Congress had not done so in either instance. Examining the full text of both statutes, the Justices reasoned in part that the fact that the United States is mentioned in some sections of the laws but not others yielded the conclusion that a "clear and unequivocal waiver" of immunity from liability for civil fines imposed by a state could not be found.

Five and one-half months later, on October 6, 1992, President George Bush significantly increased the EPA's and the states' power in dealing with the DOE ad other federal organizations by signing into law the Federal Facilities Compliance Act (P.L. 102-386). The law expressly waives the sovereign immunity of federal facilities under RCRA, thus making it clear that the EPA and the states may assess fines and penalties against government entities such as the DOE for violations of that law.[3] The State of Washington lost little time implementing the law: On March 11, 1993, the Washington Department of Ecology assessed fines totaling $100,000 against the DOE for RCRA violations at its Hanford nuclear site (BNA Environment Reporter, March 19, 1993).

While government immunity under environmental laws is not totally dead, and still stands, in certain discrete circumstances, as a powerful defense, the major implications of the trend toward the erosion of government immunity under environmental laws is significant. Governments can no longer assume that the defense of sovereign immunity will be available in environmental lawsuits. Governments are increasingly being treated as private parties under environmental laws and in environmental enforcement proceedings. With increased environmental litigation, this trend will be especially challenging and resource intensive as public organizations and employees are forced to put forth greater efforts to defend themselves and their actions.

HAZARDOUS WASTE LIABILITIES

Government organizations are increasingly being held liable under federal laws for hazardous waste cleanup costs, primarily because of their roles as generators or transporters of hazardous waste or as owners/operators of facilities that receive hazardous wastes. Cleanup costs have reached well into the millions of dollars. Even if not a liable party to a cleanup, state and local governments may incur substantial legal and oversight expenses. Consider the following recent hazardous waste lawsuits involving governments.

In *United States v. Stringfellow* (no. 83-2501 JMI [C.D. Cal. 1989]), the state of California had taken an active role from 1950 through 1973 in locating, supervising, and regulating an industrial waste facility in the Jarupa Mountains near Glen Avon. In 1974, the state took control of the site to contain wastes that were migrating offsite, and the EPA and the state brought suit in 1983 against 31 defendants who generated or transported wastes dumped at the site. During the trial, it was determined that the generator-defendants could assert a counterclaim against California for part of the cleanup costs since the state acted as a "quasiprivate consultant" in the operation of the landfill. On June 2, 1989, a jury found the state guilty of negligence in its consultant role. Current estimates of the state's liability range from $450 to $750 million (Bingenheimer, 1989).

Six years ago, the city of Corvallis, OR, was notified by the EPA that the United Chrome Products plant south of town was Oregon's worst hazardous waste site. Soil and water around the plant had been contaminated with chromium during 28 years of chrome-plating operations. Because the city currently owns the land on which the former plant stood, the EPA held the city responsible for cleanup of the site. In 1989, the city filed a $19.7 million lawsuit against United Chrome Products to force the company to pay for the cleanup, which should be completed by the year 2000 (City of Corvallis, Oregon, 1989).

When the EPA began cleaning up four Superfund sites on the East Coast in the mid-1980s, 476 parties were sued as generator-defendants in an effort to recoup EPA expenses. The defendants included the town of Barnstable, MA, the Barnstable High School, the Barnstable Public School System, the Barnstable Water Company, and the Barnstable Dump. Total cleanup costs were estimated at $52 million. One-half of the defendants, including all the Barnstable defendants, were determined to fall under EPA's "de minimis" policy for small volume generators of hazardous waste. (The main concept behind de minimis settlements is to assess those who contributed a minimal amount of waste to a site for response work based on such factors as toxicity and amount of waste.) Together the de minimis parties settled with the EPA for $11 million (53 Fed. Reg. 28 [1988]).

GAF Corporation had dumped industrial wastes in the Colesville municipal landfill, operated by Broome County, NY, in 1973 and 1974. Thirteen years later, Broome County and GAF Corporation agreed, in a $6 million consent agreement, to share the cleanup costs. Once the cleanup is complete, New York state will reimburse the county for 75 percent of its cleanup costs as long as the county takes the lead in conducting the cleanup (*BNA Environment Reporter,* 1987).

Legal Liability of Governments

These are just a few of the many recent examples of hazardous waste cleanup suits involving governments and government organizations. A 1991 survey sponsored by the International City Management Association concluded that approximately 51 percent of U.S. municipalities and counties own their own landfills (Good et al., 1991). Of the approximately 1,200 Superfund sites on the EPA's National Priority List, 25 percent involve municipalities or municipal wastes. Of those, about one in five sites is a municipal landfill. The EPA expects the number to increase in the future. The current average cost of cleanup of a Superfund site is more than $21 million, and the EPA projects this amount to exceed $40 million.

A 1990 study by the Congressional Budget Office concluded that more than 2,300 facilities owned by federal agencies handle hazardous wastes or contain hazardous waste contamination. That same report found that more than 7,100 properties formerly owned by federal agencies may incur financial liabilities from contamination problems. The United States owns one-third of the nation's land, making it a major "potentially responsible party" or PRP under hazardous waste law. There are over 1,000 federal facilities on the EPA's Federal Agency Hazardous Waste Compliance Docket. Many of these sites are old mining and oil and gas sites owned by the U.S. Department of the Interior and the U.S. Department of Agriculture. Department of Defense installations also have been cited for hazardous waste contamination.

The potential liability facing governments for hazardous waste cleanup is great. They can be sued under a number of federal statutes, including CERCLA or Superfund, and RCRA. Under these statutes, they may be sued in a variety of capacities, most often as a generator of hazardous wastes, as an owner or operator of a waste-generating facility, as one who arranged for the disposal of the hazardous wastes, and/or as an owner or operator of a disposal facility.

CERCLA Liability

CERCLA was enacted in 1980, establishing a Superfund to enable the federal government to clean up hazardous waste disposal sites. CERCLA expanded the class of parties liable for the cleanup of such sites, specifically identifying site owners and operators, waste transporters and generators. The act also authorized the EPA to commence legal action to force the abatement of hazardous waste pollution at Superfund sites that pose an "imminent and substantial" threat to public health or the environment (*United States v. Conservation Chemical Co.,* 619 F. Supp. 162 [1985]; *United States v. Ottati & Goss,* 23 Env't. Rep. Cas. 1733 [1984]; *United States v. Reilly Tar,* 546 F. Supp. at 1109 [1982]; *United States v. NEPACCO,* 579 F. Supp. 846, n.28 [1984]; *United States v. Waste Ind.,* 734 F.2d 159 [1984]; *United States v. Seymour Recycling Corp.,* 618 F. Suppl. 1 [1984]; *United States v. Vertack Chemical Corp.,* 489 F. Supp. 870 [1980]; *United States v. Hardage,* 18 Env't Rep. Cas. 1685 [1982]. Contra: *Outboard Marine Corp. v. Thomas,* 773 F.2d 883 [1985]).

Courts have universally held that CERCLA imposes strict liability, meaning that a waste generator, such as a city or state, may be subject to liability even if it has not departed in any way from the standard of reasonable care and has not violated any environmental laws (42 U.S.C. 9601 [32]; *United States v. M/V Big Sam,* 681 F.2d 432 [1982]; *United States v. Lebeouf Bros. Towing Co.,* 621 F.2d 787 [1980], cert. denied, 452 U.S. 906 [1981]; *Steuart Transportation Co. v. Allied Towing Corp.,* 596 F.2d 906 [1979]; *Burgess v. M/V. Tamano,* 564 F.2d 964 [1977], cert. denied 435 U.S. 941 [1978]; *United States v. Bear Marine Services,* 509 F. Supp. 710 [1980], reversed on other grounds, 696 F.2d 1117 [1983]; *United States v. Tex Tow,* 598 F.2d 1310 [1978]; *United States v. Ward,* 618 F. Supp. 884 [1985]; *United States v. Mirabile,* slip op. at 4 [1985]; *United States v. Conservation Chemical Co.,* 619 F. Supp. 162 [1985]; *United States v. SCRDI,* 21 Env't. Rep. Cas. at 1756, n. 2 [1984]; *United States v. Price,* 577 F. Supp. 1103 [1983]; *United States v. NEPACCO,* 579 F. Supp. at 843 [1984]; *United States v. Chem-Dyne Corp.,* 572 F. Supp. 802 [1983]; *City of Philadelphia v. Stephan Chemical Co.,* 544 F. Supp. 1135 [1982]; *United States v. Argent Corp.,* 21 Env't Rep. Cas. 1354 [1984]; *United States v. Cauffman,* 21 Env't Rep. Cas. 2167 [1984]; *United States v. Dickerson et al.,* 640 F. Supp. 228 [1986]; *In Re T.P. Long Chemical, Inc.,* 45 B.R. 278 [1985]; *United States v. Ottati & Goss,* 23 Env't Rep. Cas. 1705 [1985]; *United States v. Miami Drum Services, Inc.,* 25 Env't Rep. Cas. 1469 [1986]; *Violet v. Picillo,* 25 Env't Rep. Cas. 1319 [1986]; *United States v. Tyson,* 25 Env't Rep. Cas. 1899 [1986]).

Where injury is indivisible (i.e., where it is not clear whose wastes caused what damage), liability is joint and several. Joint and several liability means that the federal government can proceed against any one or a group of potentially liable parties for the total costs of the cleanup, for which each is jointly or individually liable. If such liability is established, traditionally the only remedy for the defendants has been to seek contribution from other responsible parties, if they can be found, through legal action.[2] (For case law defining "indivisible," see *United States v. SCRDI,* 21 Env't. Rep. Cas. at 1759 [1984]; *United States v. Ottati & Goss,* 23 Env't Rep. Cas. 1705 [1985]; *United States v. A&F Materials, Inc.,* 578 F. Supp. 1249 [1984]; *United States v. NEPACCO,* 579 F. Supp. 845 [1984]; *United States v. Dickerson,* 649 F. Supp. 448 [1986]; *United States v. Northernaire Plating Co.,* No. G84-1113CA7 [1987]). For case law concerning joint and several liability, see *United States v. Mirable,* 14 Env't Law Rep. 20992 [1985]; *United States v. SCRDI,* 21 Env't Rep. Cas. 1759 [1984]; *United States V. Chem-Dyne,* 572 F. Supp. 811 [1983]; *United States v. Conservation Chemical Co.,* 619 F. Supp. 162 [1985]; 589 F. Supp. 62 [1984]; *United States v. A & F Materials, Inc.,* 578 F. Supp. 1249 [1984]; *United States v. NEPACCO,* 579 F. Supp. 845 [1984]; *United States v. Ottati and Goss,* 23 Env't Rep. Cas. 1733 [1985]; *New York v. Shore Realty,* 579 F.2d 1032 [1985]; *United States v. Ward,* 618 F. Supp. 884 [1985]; *United States v. Shell Oil Company,* 605 F. Supp. 1064 n.9 [1985]; *United States v. Miami Drum Services, Inc.,* 25 Env't Rep. Cas. 1474 [1986]).

Moreover, the federal government (or any other plantiff) need not prove that a defendant's actions were the cause of environmental threat or harm in question. Courts have held that CERCLA requires no more proof than showing that a generator sent out hazardous wastes for disposal, that the wastes ended up at a site at which a release or threatened release of any hazardous substance necessitated response action, and that wastes of the type the generator disposed of are present at the site (*United States v. Ottati and Goss,* 23 Env't Rep. Cas. 1734 [1985]; *United States v. A & F Materials, Inc.,* 578 F. Supp. 1249 [1984]; *United States v. South Carolina Recycling and Disposal, Inc.,* 20 Env't Rep. Cas. 1759 [1984]; *United States v. Wade,* 546 F. Supp. 792 [1983]; *United States v. NEPACCO,* 579 F. Supp. 834 [1984]; *United States v. Dickerson,* 640 F. Supp. 448 [1986]; *United States v. Northernaire Plating Co.,* No. G84-1113CA7 [1987]).

Although CERCLA initially defined a "person" subject to hazardous waste cleanup liability as including the "United States Government, [a] State, municipality, commission, political subdivision of a State or interstate body," this definition was further clarified in 1986. In SARA, Congress added a section clarifying that a state "shall be subject to the provisions of this Act in the same manner and the same extent" as any nongovernmental entity. The Supreme Court has noted that this amendment unmistakably withdraws any state immunity that may have been previously implied (*Pennsylvania v. Union Gas,* 109 S.Ct. 2463 [1989], discussed below). Local governments also are not immune from suit. (For representative cases concerning municipal landfills, see *South Macomb Disposal Authority v. United States Environmental Protection Agency,* 681 F. Supp. 1244 [1988]; *New Castle County v. Hartford Accident and Indemnity Company,* 685 F. Supp. 1321 [1988]; *The City of New York v. Exxon Corporation,* 697 F. Supp. 677 [1988]; *City of Stoughton, Wisconsin v. U.S. Environmental Protection Agency, and City of Elyria, Ohio v. U.S. Environmental Protection Agency,* 858 F.2d 747 [1988]; *Robert Ayers et al. v. Township of Jackson,* 525 A.2d 287 [1987]; and *City of Philadelphia v. Stephan Chemical Company et al.,* No. 81-0851, 83-5493 [1987]).

RCRA Liability

RCRA regulates hazardous wastes from their initial generation to their ultimate disposal, or from "cradle to grave." There are several major sections of RCRA that are of particular importance to governments. These sections concern on-site storage of hazardous waste (42. U.S.C. 6922-6925), a manifest system for tracking hazardous wastes from generator to transporter to disposal facility (42 U.S.C. 6922-6923), and minimum standards for hazardous waste disposal, enforced through a permit system for disposal facilities (43 U.S.C. 6924-6925).

Pursuant to RCRA, when presented with evidence that the past or present handling, storage, treatment, transportation or disposal of any waste may present an "imminent and substantial endangerment," the EPA may bring suit against any entity that has contributed to the situation. Possible defendants include past or present generators, transporters, and/or owners or operators of treatment, storage, or disposal facilities. In such a situation, the EPA may order a government entity to restrain from specific activities, may order the government to take specific actions as deemed necessary by the agency, or both. The EPA may also take appropriate administrative actions (42 U.S.C. 6973[a]). Any state or local government that violates a court order under such circumstances may be subject to fines of up to $5,000 for each day that the violation or noncompliance continues (42 U.S.C. 6973[b]).

If convicted of violating any other applicable requirements of RCRA, a state or local government may face civil penalties of up to $25,000 per day (42 U.S.C. 3008[g]). Criminal penalties can be as high as $50,000 a day (42 U.S.C. 3008[d][7][A]). Upon a second criminal conviction, the fine is doubled (42 U.S.C. 3008[d][7][A]). The Act also contains penalties for the offense of "knowing endangerment," for which an organization may be fined up to $1 million (42 U.S.C. 3008[e]).

Supreme Court Examines the Issue

The gravity of the potential liability for hazardous waste cleanup can be seen clearly in a case decided by the United States Supreme Court. The pivotal issue in *Pennsylvania v. Union Gas* (109 S.Ct. 2463 [1989]), was whether a state that contributed to a hazardous waste discharge can be sued by a private party in an effort to recoup a portion of the costs of cleaning up the site. Pennsylvania asked the Supreme Court to interpret the 1986 Superfund amendment when it appealed a lower court decision that a state can be sued by a private party for hazardous waste site cleanup costs.

The case began in 1980 when the Commonwealth of Pennsylvania, carrying out flood control measures, excavated at a site formerly owned by Union Gas Company, to which the state held an assessment. Workers struck a large deposit of coal tar that began to seep into a nearby creek. The EPA immediately ordered a cleanup, which Pennsylvania and the United States carried out jointly. The U.S. government spent an estimated $1.4 million on the cleanup, which included reimbursing Pennsylvania for its costs.

As is typical in such a case, the federal government then sued Union Gas in district court for recoupment of costs incurred in cleaning up the spill. Union Gas responded by denying liability and filing a complaint against Pennsylvania, alleging that the Commonwealth had "negligently caused, or contributed to, the discharge" and should therefore share a portion of the cleanup costs.

Pennsylvania defended itself by asserting that the Eleventh Amendment of the Constitution had been interpreted by courts as a grant of sovereign immunity to the states in federal court. The district court agreed, and dismissed that portion of the lawsuit. Later, the EPA and Union Gas settled the primary portion of the suit, and the district court also dismissed that action. Union Gas, however, appealed the district court's dismissal of Pennsylvania as a defendant in the case. In a divided opinion, the Court of Appeals for the Third Circuit affirmed the lower court. Reasoning that "Congress must express its intention to abrogate the Eleventh

Amendment in unmistakable language in the statute itself," the court found no such expression of intent in CERCLA.

On October 8, 1986, Union Gas appealed the decision to the U.S. Supreme Court. Nine days later, the President signed into law the Superfund amendments, previously discussed, which sought to clarify whether a state could be sued under CERCLA. The Supreme Court responded by remanding the case to the Appellate Court with orders to consider if the new changes in the law would affect the outcome of the case.

In its second examination of the case, the Third Circuit reversed itself and held that the Superfund amendments provided the clear language the court previously found lacking in CERCLA. Thus, Pennsylvania could be sued by private parties as well as by the federal government under CERCLA. Pennsylvania immediately appealed to the Supreme Court arguing, among other things, that the Court of Appeals erred since the Superfund amendments never explicitly referred to the Eleventh Amendment. Pennsylvania also argued that even if the lower court's interpretation of the statutory change was correct, the court erred by applying the law retroactively. When oral arguments were heard on November 31, 1988, Pennsylvania was joined by a coalition of 17 states that maintained that the decision placed an improper burden on state treasuries.

On June 15, 1989, the Supreme Court issued a decision affirming the Court of Appeals. Unpersuaded by Pennsylvania's arguments, the Court agreed with Union Gas that Congress had unmistakenly provided clear language rendering states liable for monetary damages for hazardous waste cleanup and that such action is within congressional powers. The five to four decision forced Pennsylvania later to defend itself against a Union Gas lawsuit seeking to recover cleanup costs. The decision opens the door to similar lawsuits against state governments.

In conclusion, there are important implications of the growing liability of governments for hazardous waste cleanup. As congressional pressures on the EPA to recoup Superfund monies and to clean up waste sites grow, so too will the pressures to file suit against governments. The issues of who will pay and how they will pay are significant. Liability for hazardous waste cleanup may severely curtail important governmental functions as programs are extinguished to provide funds for hazardous waste cleanup costs. Furthermore, local governments may be reluctant to provide traditional services, such as refuse control and landfill space, for fear of liability. Finally, such liability undoubtedly will be considered in bond ratings that evaluate solvency, affecting state and local governments' ability to borrow funds for projects and services.

CRIMINAL LIABILITY OF LOWER- AND MIDDLE-LEVEL GOVERNMENT EMPLOYEES

Before 1980, there were no felony penalties for criminal conduct under federal environmental statutes. Following the enactment of such provisions in the major federal environmental laws,[3] the primary targets of prosecutions were private sector employees and businesses who were "midnight dumpers," even though most federal environmental statutes make no distinction between public and private violations. Recently, however, government employees increasingly have become the target of criminal lawsuits for violations of environmental laws. Today several former public administrators are convicted felons because of violations of environmental laws. Penalties for such felony activity can reach as high as $1 million and 15 years' imprisonment.

The old saying that "ignorance of the law is no excuse" has been rigidly adhered to in environmental law cases. As mentioned above, under some statutes, such as the Superfund hazardous waste cleanup act, liability is "strict," meaning that a waste generator (such as a city or state) may be subject to liability even if it has not departed in any way from reasonable practices and has not violated environmental laws (see O'Leary, 1990). In most environmental statutues, criminal liability is judged by whether the public administrator acted "knowingly," a term that is interpreted by a judge on a case-by-case basis. In assessing liability under such provisions, courts have looked only at whether there was a "general intent" to take the action that prompted the violation in question. Knowledge of the law or intention to break the law has been considered irrelevant. Furthermore, failure of a public administrator to act may be considered an environmental crime.

Federal environmental statutes do not specify who within a public organization should be held liable for environmental crimes. Such designation varies from case to case and is usually dictated by the prosecutors, judges and juries. In private sector cases, low-level employees, middle-level managers, top-level corporate officers, and even corporations themselves have been found liable. This has not been the case, however, in criminal litigation involving violations of environmental laws by public administrators. Federal prosecutors, judges, and juries have shown a preference for targeting lower- and middle-level government employees in environmental law criminal cases. Government agencies and their top decision makers, with a few exceptions, have not been targeted in such suits.

There are several examples of lower- and middle-level public administrators who have found themselves criminally liable for violations of environmental laws:

Three civilian engineers employed by the Department of the Army to work on chemical warfare systems are now convicted felons. They each were found personally liable for illegally storing, treating, and disposing of Army hazardous wastes on Army property. Neither the Department of the Army nor the commanding officers at the Aberdeen Proving Ground in Maryland, however, were cited as defendants, despite the fact that such practices have been found to be widespread in the Defense Department, and the engineers were not acting on their own behalf (*United States v. Dee,* 912 F.2d 741 [1990]).

The former Director of Public Works for the city of Ocean Shores, WA, became a convicted felon when he was found guilty of aiding and abetting the illegal disposal of hazardous waste. The wastes included paint left over from road maintenance and grease sludge removed from the kitchen of the city's golf course. Both sets of wastes were buried by another employee, in response to an order of the Director, near the city sewage treatment plant. No one else in the city hierarchy was held liable for this violation (*United States v. Hoflin,* 880 F.2d 1033 [1989]).

A civilian maintenance employee at Fort Drum, an Army camp in upstate New York, is today a convicted felon. He was found guilty of failing to report the release of hazardous substances. The maintenance worker, who was supervised by Army officers, directed a work crew to dispose of waste cans of paint in an improper manner and failed to notify state or federal environmental authorities when the buried cans leaked. The public employee maintained in court that he was too low in the chain of command to be held liable since he was not "in charge" of the facility, as articulated in the statute. In keeping with the trend of wide discretion given to the judge, jury, and prosecutor to decide who is ultimately responsible for such environmental crimes, the judge gave the following instructions to the jury.

> The paint waste was released from a truck assigned to the workers by the Defendant. . . . The truck, individually and the area of the disposal constitute facilities within the meaning of . . . [the statute]. So long as the Defendant had supervisory control or was otherwise in charge of the truck or the area in question, he is responsible under this law. The Defendant is not, however, required to be the sole person in charge of the area or the vehicle.

> If you find that he had any authority over either the vehicle or the area, this is sufficient regardless of whether others also exercised control (880 F.2d at 1551).

A Court of Appeals confirmed that any person, such as the defendant, "in a position to detect, prevent, and abate a release of hazardous substances" could be considered "in charge," and so may be found liable for such an environmental crime (*United States v. Carr,* 880 F.2d 1550 [1989]).

The public administrative implications of the targeting of lower- and middle-level government workers in environmental crime prosecutions are several. First is the obvious issue of fairness. In many instances it may not be fair to prosecute a lower-level career bureaucrat when his or her supervisor knew or should have known of the actions that triggered the violation. Next, there is the possibility that if higher-level government executives are not held to the same standard as lower-level employees, they simply may not be concerned with such environmental issues. A clear message is being sent to higher-level managers that they do not need to be aware of the environmental issues facing their organizations. Last, there are implications for the attraction and retention of public managers. In this era of shrinking resources and growing demands, the threat of a felony conviction for violating environmental laws may be enough to push valuable career public servants out the door and to discourage others from entering.

INCREASED REPORTING REQUIREMENTS

Environmental statutes and regulations increasingly are demanding a greater amount of information from governments. "Manifest" forms, for example, must be filled out and filed with the EPA whenever hazardous waste is transported or disposed of. The Clean Water Act and the Clean Air Act both require self-monitoring and reporting by government entities. The Occupational Safety and Health Act (OSHA) has more than 100 recordkeeping and training requirements, many concerning environmental practices. Consider the following cases in which public administrators have been found guilty of violating the reporting requirements of environmental laws.

In Oklahoma, a former Superintendent of the Public Utilities Department of the city of Enid was found guilty of 18 felony violations and 2 misdemeanor violations of the Clean Water Act. The public employee was charged primarily with falsifying reports concerning the discharge of raw sewage into a stream. Each felony conviction carries with it a maximum penalty of 5 years in prison and a $10,000 fine, while each misdemeanor conviction carries with it a maximum penalty of 1 year in prison and a $25,000 fine (*United States v. Brittain,* NO. 89-283-P [1990]).

In Texas, the Superintendent of Utilities for the city of Big Spring was convicted for knowingly making false statements on wastewater treatment plant discharge reports he had filed on behalf of the city. He was sentenced to 1 month in prison for each of five counts of violating the Clean Water Act (*United States v. Windham,* Cr. 1-89-00001 [1989]).

In Pennsylvania, a former Superintendent of a local government sewage treatment plant was fined $1,000 and put on probation for 3 years. The public administrator had admitted that he had submitted false laboratory results to the State Department of Environmental Resources (*Pennsylvania v. Frey,* No. 904C1989 [1989]).

In Ohio, a former Commissioner of the Cleveland Hopkins International Airport was found guilty of failing to report the release of hazardous substances and making false statements to the EPA. The public administrator was ordered to perform 1,000 hours of community service while being sentenced to 180 days of home detention and 4 years of probation.

His conviction was part of a prosecution centering around the illegal burial of 148 barrels of hazardous wastes that were then crushed by a bulldozer, causing the barrels to leak (*United States v. Bogas,* No. 88-282 [1990]).

While each of these cases concerned atypical instances of lying or falsifying reports to other government entities, even the most scrupulously honest public administrator may be caught in the legal quagmire surrounding federal and state environmental reporting and recordkeeping requirements. Environmental laws are complex, difficult to understand, and expensive to comply with. It is not hard to imagine a busy public administrator with a general education failing to keep up with environmental requirements, not being aware of environmental laws, or not having the funds to comply adequately with environmental regulations. Yet such individuals may be imprisoned or fined heavily for their ignorance. As mentioned above, it also is not difficult to imagine a political appointee director of a public organization failing to allocate funds needed to support the necessary environmental programs, knowing that it is not he or she who is most likely to be prosecuted, but a lower-level employee. Reporting requirements under environmental laws are a growing challenge for all public administrators.

LIABILITY FOR REGULATORY TAKINGS

Another important issue in environmental law that affects many public functions is liability for regulatory takings. The idea of regulatory takings is not a new one. The Fifth Amendment of the Constitution clearly states that private property shall not be taken for public use without just compensation. In 1922, Justice Holmes wrote, "while property may be regulated to a certain extent, if regulation goes too far it will be recognized as a taking" (*Pennsylvania Coal Co. v. Mahon,* 260 U.S. 393, 415 [1922]). What is relatively new is the use of the concept of regulatory takings in actions where a government entity has been enforcing an environmental law.

In deciding whether there has been a regulatory taking without just compensation, the courts examine two aspects of a case. First, the courts look at whether the government regulation at issue fails to substantially advance a legitimate governmental interest. Second, the courts look at whether the implementation of the government regulation deprives the owner of all economically viable uses of the land. Consider the following cases.

In 1991, a federal court of appeals held that the mere passage of the Surface Mining Control and Reclamation Act of 1977 effected a regulatory taking without just compensation of property owned by the Whitney Benefits company. The passage of the Act, the Court reasoned, prevented the mining of hundreds of acres containing coal and thus deprived the mining company of all economic use of its property, even though no mining permit had been applied for by the company. The court ordered the U.S. Government to pay the company $60,296,000, plus prejudgment interest from August 3, 1977 (*Whitney Benefits v. United States,* 926 F.2d 1169 [1991]).

In a case decided the year before, a court found that the residential and commercial development of 12.5 acres on Long Beach Island, NJ, was prevented by the enactment of the New Jersey Wetlands Act and certain wetlands provisions of the federal Clean Water Act. Finding that such action was a regulatory taking without just compensation, the court ordered the U.S. Government to pay the developer $2,658,000 plus interest from the date of the taking, May 5, 1982 (*Loveladies Harbor, Inc. v. United States,* 21 Cl. Ct. 153 [1990]).

In a third case, a court found that the denial of a permit by the Corps of Engineers to Florida Rock Industries to mine 98 acres protected under the Clean Water Act constituted a regulatory taking without just compensation. The court reasoned that the denial of the permit deprived Florida Rock Industries of all economically viable uses of its land. The federal government was ordered to pay $1,029,000 plus interest from the date of the taking, October 2, 1980 (*Florida Rock Industries, Inc. v. United States,* 21 Cl. Ct. 16 1[1990]).

On June 29, 1992, the United States Supreme Court announced its decision in the case of *Lucas v. South Carolina Coastal Council* (1992 U.S. LEXIS 4537, 60 U.S.L.W. 4842 [1992]), in which the pivotal issue was whether the implementation of the South Carolina Beachfront Management Act (BMA) was a regulatory taking of property. The decision, while narrowly drafted, has implications for the future of public administration, especially in the areas of budgeting and finance.

In 1986, David H. Lucas, the petitioner, purchased two vacant oceanfront lots on the Isle of Palms in Charleston County, SC for $975,000, with the intention of building single-family residences. In 1988, the South Carolina Legislature enacted the BMA (S.C. Code Ann. Sections 48-39-10 *et seq.* [1989 Cum. Supp.]), which had the effect of prohibiting the construction of any permanent structure, including a dwelling, except for a small deck or walkway, on the Lucas property. Lucas filed suit in the Court of Common Pleas, asserting that the restrictions on the use of his lots amounted to a taking of his property without just compensation. The lower court agreed with Lucas, maintaining that the state act rendered the land "valueless," and awarded him the amount of $1,232,387.50 as just compensation for the regulatory taking. Upon appeal, the Supreme Court of South Carolina reversed the lower court's decision, maintaining that the regulation under attack prevented a use seriously harming the public, and so no regulatory taking occurred (*Lucas v. South Carolina Coastal Council,* 404 S.E.2d 895 [1991]).

The United States Supreme Court, however, in a six to three decision, reversed the holding of the highest court in South Carolina and remanded the case for further action. In its decision, the Court articulated several pivotal principles. First, the Court emphasized that regulations that deny a property owner of all "economically viable use of his land" will require compensation without inquiry into the public interest advanced in support of the restraint. Next, the Court said that the fact that a regulation addresses or prevents a "harmful or noxious use" cannot be used to negate the rule that total regulatory takings must be compensated by government entities.

Finally, the Court threw the issue of whether a taking occurred in this specific instance back to the South Carolina courts. The Court maintained that the lower courts must examine citizens' historic understandings regarding the content of the state's power over the "bundle of rights" they acquired when they took title to the property in question. The pivotal question, then, becomes whether the restrictions in a state regulation merely make explicit what already inheres in the property title, or whether the state regulations are subsequent decisions that eliminate all economically beneficial uses of the property. It is that question that the South Carolina courts have been struggling with snce the announcement of the *Lucas* decision.[4]

Of equal importance is what the Court did not discuss in its narrowly worded opinion. First, the Court did not say that David Lucas is entitled to compensation. Rather, it implied that the South Carolina Supreme Court was hasty in concluding that Lucas was not entitled to such compensation. Second, the Court did not address the issue of property that is merely diminished in value, a far more common occurrence. Instead the Court only addressed the issue of property that was totally rendered valueless. Finally, in pushing the regulatory takings issue back onto the state, the Court did not say that state laws may never change. "Changed circumstances or new knowledge may make what was previously permissible no longer so," the majority held. Hence the Court left the door open for some regulation of newly discovered environmental harms.

Over 200 takings cases currently are pending in the Court of Claims, and it is estimated that many of these concern environmental and natural resources regulations. Other statutes affected to date include the Clean Water Act, the Endangered Species Act, and the Wilderness Act. Despite the cautious Supreme Court opinion in the *Lucas* case, the surge of such cases in recent years has many speculating on the effects of such a trend. Environmental groups charge that the holdings of these cases may destroy years of hard-fought incremental progress in protecting the environment. Some government regulators agree, adding that the trend could devastate already ailing government budgets, especially if proposed federal legislation is enacted that would require the payment of such judgments directly out of the coffers of the federal agencies that promulgated the regulations in question. Affected land owners argue that this development is merely just compensation for years of losses triggered by environmental regulations and is no different than being reimbursed for the taking of property to be used for roads and parks.

The major public administration implications of liability for regulatory takings are twofold. First, because takings law is still developing and takings determinations are made on a case-by-case basis, it is difficult for public administrators to act proactively to minimize the chances of such suits. In most of these instances the government acted legitimately to preserve the general environment. It would have been difficult, and in some instances impossible, to predict the ensuing effects of the environmental laws on many specific properties as well as the reaction of the courts. Second, the fiscal implications of this trend obviously are quite grave. While the mere promulgation of a regulation is not enough to trigger regulatory takings liability (since the property must be shown to have been affected), the issue of who will pay for such takings is an important one that will not go away. The regulatory takings trend has the potential of changing public administration as we know it today.

THE MUNICIPALITY AS MINI-WATER POLLUTION CONTROL AGENCY

A final area of environmental law that affects thousands of public administrators concerns the growing responsibilities of municipalities as miniature water pollution control agencies. In the past, municipalities needed only to be concerned about their own water pollution. Today, these local government entities not only are responsible for their own wastes but also must control industrial discharges to all "publicly owned treatment works" (POTWs) and prohibit illegal discharges into separate municipal storm sewer systems.

Pursuant to the Clean Water Act, municipalities that discharge wastewater from POTWs must apply for and adhere to a National Pollutant Discharge Elimination System (NPDES) permit. In order to obtain such a permit, "large municipality" POTWs (those that treat more than 5 million gallons per day), must agree to accept and implement a number of new responsibilities, including identifying and educating industrial users concerning all pertinent regulations, inspecting industrial users and monitoring their actions, investigating industrial users, violations of pretreatment standards, and prosecuting any violations by industrial users (40 CFR sections 403.8[f] and 403.9[b] [1990]).

Under storm sewer laws, municipalities with "large" separate storm sewer systems (defined as a population of 250,000 or more) or "medium" separate storm sewer systems (defined as a population of 100,000 or more but less than 250,000) must, again, apply for and comply with an NPDES permit for stormwater discharges from the system. One condition of such a permit is the control of discharges into the storm sewer system. Other conditions include writing a storm water quality plan, identifying all potential industrial storm water dischargers, inspecting and monitoring all discharges into the storm sewer system, and prosecuting any violations (40 CFR section 122.26[d]).

Furthermore, Congress and the EPA have increased the likelihood that a municipality will be sued for noncompliance with such laws. First, the EPA, states, and citizens may all file suits against a municipality for noncompliance with the CWA. Hence, an action may come from several sources. Second, action can be brought against a municipality not only for not complying with the letter of the law but also for not enforcing the law as stringently as EPA or a state thinks it should be enforced. This subjective call may be made "after the fact," with little guidance given to the municipality that might prevent such problems.

If a municipality acting as a water pollution control agency is the subject of an enforcement action, sanctions range from a phone call for minor violations to 3 years in prison and fines of $50,000 per day for criminal violations (33 U.S.C. Section 1319). A municipality will typically agree to take certain actions to remedy the problems and to prevent them from recurring. Ordered actions may include the municipality filing suit against an industrial violator, meeting deadlines for the compliance of all who discharge into the POTW, or shutting down the violating industry.

The potential impacts on public administration of such liability provisions are great. First, performing the tasks of a water pollution control agency can be costly and resource-intensive, depending on the size of, and environmental challenges facing, the municipality. In many instances new ordinances must be passed giving the local government the necessary legal enforcement powers. Such efforts require legal expertise initially, and engineers, inspectors, and additional clerical staff later. Second, by imposing more and more demands upon municipalities, Congress and the EPA are reducing citizen discretion and managers' options. As local choices narrow and mandates grow, the chances of taking action that might prompt lawsuits increase. This creates a difficult environment in which to work, especially with local government managers being judged with "20/20 hindsight." Finally, should a municipality be found liable for violating the CWA, penalties may be more than city coffers may bear. Special taxes or fees may be needed to support such sanctions. Other local government programs may need to be terminated in order to pay the required penalties.

CONCLUSION: PROACTIVE STEPS CAN MINIMIZE LIABILITIES

This chapter has highlighted what every administrator should know about environmental law. Government immunity is being eroded in environmental statutory provisions that clearly leave public servants and public organizations vulnerable to lawsuits. Hazardous waste liabilities affect the operation of hundreds of government functions, from landfills to vehicle maintenance shops to the purchase of land. Lower- and middle-level government employees are being targeted in environmental lawsuits and are being held personally criminally liable for violations of environmental statutes. Reporting requirements are increasing not only in frequency but also in technical difficulty. Liability for regulatory takings is challenging even our most basic regulatory functions and yielding large financial liabilities for our governments. Responsibility for water pollution regulation, as well as the accompanying liabilities, is shifting to the municipal level, turning our cities into miniwater pollution control agencies. The implications and challenges of these trends for public administration are formidable.

These developments will prompt nothing less than a fundamental change in public administration as we know it today. Public decision making will become more difficult as public employees are forced to deal with the environmental law implications of their actions. With more variables to consider, decision making may become slower and potentially more costly. The issue of how we will pay for the staff and resources needed to meet these increased environmental responsibilities, as well as the potential monetary damages assessed by the courts, is a major challenge. In an era of shrinking resources and increased demands, old programs will have to be terminated: a difficult and potentially divisive dilemma for public administrators.

Attracting and retaining public employees may become more difficult. Doing more with less, in itself, is a stressful challenge for most government workers. Add to this challenge the need to understand new technical environmental information with the threat of a felony conviction and large liability judgments, and many quality workers may opt out of a career in the public sector. Maintaining a reasonable level of morale and a public service ethic in such an atmosphere will become an even tougher challenge for public managers.

Yet several proactive steps can be taken to address the growing challenges posed to administrators by environmental laws. Knowledge of environmental laws and liabilities must be incorporated into public administration courses. This knowledge should go beyond the requirements of a single statute, and should encompass an understanding of how major regulatory programs relate to each other. The National Association of Schools of Public Affairs and Administration (NASPAA) requires knowledge of law in all public administration and public affairs programs. This requirement should include knowledge of at least the basics of environmental law.

Public administrators currently in the field must "retool" to become aware of the responsibilities and liabilities facing them. Continuing education courses in the area of environmental law are essential. Managers also must make great efforts to educate their employees about environmental law challenges. Once public servants grasp the basics of environmental law, they must be helped to keep abreast of statutory changes and new case law that may affect the administration of government.

Environmental assessments should be made of all government organizations. An environmental assessment is a complete examination of an organization and its operations to pinpoint areas in need of environmental strengthening. For example, an environmental assessment can help a manager to identify and control hazardous substances at a government facility. Environmental assessments are important both for functioning operations and for facility closure and restoration.

Public managers can further minimize their liabilities by working in tandem with the EPA, state, and local environmental agencies to address environmental problems. Cooperation from the very beginning is not only wise, it is the law. Toll-free "800" numbers can link managers with several helpful EPA "hotlines." Peer consultation is available through many organizations such as the International City Management Association. Such advice from those who have been through similar environmental challenges can often be invaluable.

Public managers should document all actions taken to address and prevent environmental problems. Included in such a record should be actions taken, rationale, and individuals consulted. Efforts to train employees must be included in such documentation. Records must be exact and in compliance with appropriate requirements. Proper records can be invaluable in defending a government organization's or employee's actions in a subsequent lawsuit.

Perhaps the wisest thing a public manager can do is to use the budgetary process as a defensive mechanism. By requesting funds to addres environmental problems, the prudent public manager has gone on record as being aware of and concerned about environmental protection. In this way the manager may establish that he or she has taken appropriate steps to acquire thefunds needed to address environmental challenges.

Government liability under environmental laws *can* be managed through the education of public administrators, the education of the public, and the education of our elected officials. Government liabilities under environmental laws can be minimized by careful, cooperative implementation of environmental laws. Government liability under environmental laws will significantly affect the administration of our governments for years to come.

NOTES

1. The seven major EPA statutes are the Clean Air Act; the Clean Water Act; the Toxic Substances Control Act (TSCA); the Resource Conservation and Recovery Act; the Comprehensive Environmental Response, Compensation and Liability Act, or Superfund; the Federal Insecticide, Fungicide and Rodenticide Act (FIFRA); and the Safe Drinking Water Act. Of these seven statutes, only FIFRA does not contain a citizen suit provision.
2. Exceptions to this rule include the "innocent landowner" defense and the EPA's "de minimis" policy.
3. TSCA, FIFRA, the Clean Air Act, the Clean Water Act, CERCLA (Superfund), the Safe Drinking Water Act, and RCRA are examples of major environmental statutes that contain felony sanctions.
4. Upon remand, the South Carolina Supreme Court concluded that Lucas "has been only temporarily deprived of the use of his land" since he still may apply for a special permit to build seaward of the baseline established by the BMA. The court then sent the case back down to the trial court to determine the actual damages of Lucas sustained, to be calculated from the date of passage of the Act. In doing so, the court emphasized that its action would not preclude further litigation by Lucas should he apply for, and be denied, a special permit [*Lucas v. South Carolina Coastal Council*, 424 S.E. 2d 484 (1992)].

REFERENCES

Bingenheimer, Ken. (1989). Jury rules California liable for cleanup. *Waste Tech News* 1.

BNA Environment Reporter. (1987).

City of Corvallis, OR. (1989). *The City: Special Report—United Chrome.*

Federal Register. (1988). *53*: 28.

Congressional Budget Office. (1990). *Federal Liabilities Under Hazardous Waste Laws.*

Good, David, John Kissel, Dan Mullins, and Rosemary O'Leary. (1991). *The Solid Waste Crisis.* Washington, D.C.: The International City Management Association.

O'Leary, R. (1990). Will hazardous waste cleanup costs cripple our state and local governments? *State and Local Government Review* 22: 84.

CASES

Burgess v. M/V. Tamano (1977). 564 F.2d 964; cert. denied (1978) 435 U.S. 941.

City of Elyria, Ohio v. U.S. Environmental Protection Agency (1988). 858 F.2d 747.

The City of New York v. Exxon Corporation (1988). 697 F. Supp. 677.

City of Stoughton, Wisconsin v. U.S. Environmental Protection Agency, and City of Philadelphia v. Stephan Chemical Co. (1982). 544 F. Supp. 1135.

Colorado v. Idarado Mining Co. (1989). No. 83-C-2385.

Esposito v. South Carolina Coastal Council (1991). U.S. Sup. Ct. No. 91-941.

Fitzpatrick v. Bitzer (1976). 427 U.S. 445.

Florida Rock Industries, Inc. v. United States (1990). 21 Cl. Ct. 161.

In Re T.P. Long Chemical, Inc. (1985). 45 B.R. 278.

Loveladies Harbor, Inc. v. United States (1990). 21 Cl. Ct. 153.

Lucas v. South Carolina Coastal Council (1991). 404 S.E.2d 895.

Lucas v. South Carolina Coastal Council (1992). U.S. LEXIS 4537, 60 U.S.L.W. 4842.

Lucas v. South Carolina Costal Council (1992), 424 S.E. 2d 484.

New Castle County v. Hartford Accident and Indemnity Company (1988). 685 F. Supp. 1321.

New York v. Shore Realty (1985). 759 F.2d 1032.

Outboard Marine Corp. v. Thomas (1985). 773 F.2d 883.

Pennsylvania v. Frey (1989). No. 904C1989.

Pennsylvania v. Union Gas (1989). 109 S.Ct. 2463.

Pennsylvani Coal Co. v. Mahon (1922). 260 U.S. 393.
Robert Ayers et al. v. Township of Jackson (1987). 525 A.2d 287.
South Macomb Disposal Authority v. United States Environmental Protection Agency (1988). 681 F. Supp. 1244.
State of Colorado v. United States Department of the Army (1989). No. 86-C-2524.
Steuart Transportation Co. v. Allied Towing Corp. (1979). 596 F.2d 906.
United States v. A & F Materials, Inc. (1984). 578 F. Supp. 1249.
United States v. Argent Corp. (1984). 21 Env't Rep. Cas. 1354.
United States v. Bear Marine Services (1980). 509 F. Supp. 710; reversed on other grounds, (1983) 6967 F.2d 1117.
United States v. Bogas (1990). No. 88-282.
United States v. Brittain (1990). No. 89-283-P.
United States v. Carr (1989). 880 F.2d 1550.
United States v. Cauffman (1984). 21 Env't Rep. Cas. 2167.
United States v. Chem-Dyne Corp. (1983). 572 F. Supp. 802.
United States v. Conservation Chemical Co. (1985). 619 F. Supp. 162.
United States v. Dee (1990). 912 F.2d 741.
United States v. Dickerson et al. (1986). 640 F. Supp. 228.
United States v. Hardage (1982). 18 Env't Rep. Cas. 1685.
United States v. Hoflin (1989). 880 F.2d 1033.
United States v. Lebeouf Bros. Towing Co. (1980). 621 F.2d 787; cert. denied, (1981) 452 U.S. 906.
United States v. Miami Drum Services Inc. (1986). 25 Env't Rep. Cas. 1469.
United States v. M/V Big Sam (1982). 681 F.2d 432.
United States v. Mirable (1985). 14 Env't Law Rep. 20992.
United States v. NEPACCO (1984). 579 F. Supp. at 843.
United States v. Northernaire Plating Co. (1987). No. G84-1113CA7
United States v. Ottati & Goss (1984). 23 Env't Rep. Cas. 1733.
United States v. Price (1983). 577 F. Supp. 1103.
United States v. Reilly Tar (1982). 546 F. Supp. 1109.
United States v. SCRDI (1984). 21 Env't Rep. Cas. 1756.
United States v. Seymour Recycling Corp. (1984). 618 F. Supp. 1.
United States v. Shell Oil Company (1985). 605 F. Supp. 1064.
United States v. South Carolina Recycling and Disposal, Inc. (1984). 20 Env't Rep. Cas. 1759.
United States v. Stringfellow (1989). No. 83-2501 JMI.
United States v. Tex Tow (1978). 598 F.2d 1310.
United States v. Tyson (1986). 25 Env't Rep. Cas. 1899.
United States v. Union Gas (1987). 26 Env't Rep. Cas. 1769.
United States v. Vertack Chemical Corp. (1980). 489 F. Supp. 870.
United States v. Wade (1983). 546 F. Supp. 792.
United States v. Ward (1985). 618 F. Supp. 884.
United States v. Waste Ind. (1984). 734 F.2d 159.
United States v. Windham (1989). Cr. 1-89-00001.
Violet v. Picillo (1986). 25 Env't Rep. Cas. 1319.
Whitney Benefits v. United States (1991). 926 F.2d 1169.

7

Regulatory Takings

Charles R. Wise *Indiana University, Bloomington, Indiana*

The "taking issue" grows out of the Fifth Amendment of the Constitution: "nor shall private property be taken for public use without just compensation." Thus, if a governmental decision, by whatever means, has the effect of taking private property for public use, the owner of the property has to be compensated. This principle applies even if the government has not secured title to the property. Regulation that so restricts or substantially impairs the use of property by a property owner can render the property "taken." In that event, compensation must be paid or the regulatory act is unconstitutional. Most of the cases in this area arise in the context of land-use regulation, but the principles apply to the regulation of any type of property and cases have arisen in contexts other than land use (see *Andrus v. Allard* 444 U.S. 51 [1979]).

INTRODUCTION

Although the main principle has been present in federal law for a considerable amount of time, there had been relatively few losses by government agencies in actual cases due to the application of the principle by the courts. This has now changed. In the late 1980s, the Supreme Court interpreted a series of cases to indicate that public officials may violate the Fifth Amendment's requirement that a persons may not be deprived of their property without just compensation when those officials apply a regulation, even temporarily. When this violation occurs the public regulators must pay compensation to the property owners, even if the regulators repeal the offending regulation. Until these recent decisions were handed down, the Supreme Court had largely left the application of the just compensation clause to regulation to the state courts. As such, the clause had been effectively closed to those who would use it to challenge regulatory actions in federal courts.

By 1987, however, the Supreme Court's reluctance had clearly changed, as signified by the Supreme Court decisions in *Nollan v. California Coastal Commission* (483 U.S. 825 [1987] and *First English Evangelical Lutheran Church of Glendale v. County of Los Angeles*

(482 U.S. 304 [1987]). Henceforth, government regulations as applied to private property may increasingly be judged by the courts to have deprived the owner of the property of such substantial use of it that they violate the Fifth Amendment and compensation must be paid. Repeal of the offending regulation is an insufficient remedy, since the Supreme Court has now held that the government must also compensate the owner for the time during which the regulation deprived him or her of the property's use (*First English* 482 U.S. 304 [1987]). The Supreme Court has made it clear that the application of this rule under the Just Compensation clause of the Constitution is a self-executing remedial provision, and thus applies to Federal as well as state and local government regulatory actions (*First English* 482 U.S. 304, 316 n.9 [1987]).

Thus, one consequential result of the new regulatory takings decisions is that the courts are now participating in a more direct way in administrative regulatory decisions affecting property rights, especially land use. As two legal commentators put it, First English and Nollan "represented a dramatic break with the deferential approach which the Court had used in testing zoning and other land-use legislation for more than 50 years" (March and Rosenthal, 1978: 3).

The Supreme Court set the stage for a less deferential approach on behalf of the Supreme Court in regulation affecting property by Justice Brennan in his dissent in *San Diego Gas and Electric v. City of San Diego,* when he stated " . . . after all, if a policeman must know the Constitution, then why not a planner" (450 U.S. 621 [1980]). Of course, "knowing the Constitution" is not a simple matter. The primary issue is how can public administrators come to know it better as it applies to regulatory takings.

THE EVOLUTION OF REGULATORY TAKINGS LAW

The jurisprudence requiring compensation by governments in the United States for interfering with individual's property rights is grounded in the Fifth Amendment to the Constitution. The Fifth Amendment states in relevant part:

> No person shall . . . be deprived of life, liberty, or property, without due process of law; nor shall private property be taken for public use, without just compensation

The regulatory taking theory involves an attack on regulation, which asserts that the Fifth Amendment has been violated because a regulatory action constitutes a de facto "taking" of property for the public good. Federal regulatory action is implicated directly by the Fifth Amendment, and state and local action is implicated by incorporation by virtue of the Fourteenth.

The Early Period

The interpretation that a regulation could cause a taking was introduced 67 years ago by the Suprême Court in *Pennsylvania Coal v. Mahon* (260 U.S. 393 [1922]). Justice Holmes' famous majority opinion stated, "[t]he general rule at least is, that while property may be regulated to a certain extent, if regulation goes too far it will be recognized as a taking" (260 U.S. 415 [1922]). However, the Court did not lay down any rules for regulatory takings at the time. The issues the courts have been wrestling with ever since are what is "too far," and what compensation is due once "too far" has been crossed. The U.S. Supreme Court had, for the most part over several decades, been willing to leave this matter of interpretation to the state courts based upon the regulation of land use approved shortly after *Pennsylvania Coal* in *Village of Euclid v. Amber Realty* (272 U.S. 365 [1926]). Fifty-two years later, however, the Supreme Court attempted to set some guidelines for helping courts determine what would constitute "too far" in *Penn Central Transportation v. New York City* (438 U.S. 104 [1978]). In that case, the regulation at issue was New York City's Landmark Preservation Law, under which an administrative commission had designated Grand Central Terminal as a historical landmark. The owners had planned to build a high-rise office building in the air space above the terminal, but were denied permission under the Preservation Law. The Supreme Court denied the owners' petition, but stated the following criteria for making a finding that no taking had occurred:

> In engaging in these essentially ad hoc, factual inquiries, the Court's decisions have identified several factors that have particular significance. The economic impact of the regulation on the claimant and, particularly the extent to which the regulation has interfered with distinct investment backed expectations are, of course, relevant considerations. So, too, is the character of the governmental action. A "taking" may more readily be found when the interference with property can be characterized as a physical invasion by government, than when interference arises from some public program adjusting the benefits and burdens of economic life to promote the common good (438 U.S. 124 [1978]).

Thus, the Court said that the three factors of "economic impact," "investment backed expectations," and "character of the governmental action" must be weighed and balanced with the public purpose underlying the regulation. A year later in *Kaiser Aetna v. United States* (444 U.S. 164 [1979]), Justice Stevens expressed the Court's methodology in applying the factors "by engaging in essentially ad hoc, factual inquiries" (444 U.S. 175 [1979]). The Court summarized the approach and emphasized its factors in a 1986 case:

> There is no tidy formula for determining when a regulation or its application denies an owner economically viable use of its land and thereby results in a taking. Rather, the Supreme Court has characterized the analytic process as one relying instead on ad hoc, factual inquiries into the circumstances of each particular case. . . . To aid in this determination, however, we have identified three factors which have "particular significance" (1) "the economic impact of the regulation on the claimant," (2) "the extent to which the regulation has interfered with distinct investment-backed expectations", and (3) "the character of the government action." (*Connolly v. Pension Benefit Guarantee Corp.* 475 U.S. 211, 224–225 [1986]).

Confirmation of the Court's determination to stay with its methodology was provided in 1988 in Justice Rhenquist's six to two majority opinion in *Pennel v. City of San Jose,* which once again cited the " 'essentially ad hoc factual inquiry' involved in takings analysis" (108 S.Ct. 849, 856 [1988]).

Up to this point, the courts have employed no clear standard in weighing the factors. In *Ruckelshaus v. Monsanto* (467 U.S. 986 [1984]), the Supreme Court indicated that the relative significance of the three factors will vary from case to case. The Court did state in *Agins v. City of Tiburon* (447 U.S. 255 [1980]) that a taking may be found to occur if an "ordinance does not substantially advance legitimate state interests . . . or denies an owner economically viable use of his land" (447 U.S. 260 [1980]). The "substantially advance legitimate state interests" language, however, was used once again in *Agins* to approve an open space zoning regulation as a proper exercise of "the city's police power to protect the residents of Tiburon from the ill effects of urbanization" (447 U.S. 261 [1980]).

Therefore, while the Court in the 1970s and early 1980s was identifying factors that should be used in judging the occurrence of a regulatory taking, and also affirming an ad hoc judicial method for weighing the factors, it was, for the most part, deciding cases in land-use regulation on behalf of governments. This was to change with a trilogy of cases decided by the Supreme Court in 1978.

THE 1987 TRILOGY OF REGULATORY TAKING CASES

The first case in the trilogy of land-use regulation cases announced in March, 1987, was *Keystone Bituminous Coal Association v. DeBenedictus* (480 U.S. 470 [1987]), which seemed to continue the trend of government land-use regulation victories. The plaintiffs asserted that their takings claim required no more than a straightforward application of the Supreme Court's decision in *Pennsylvania Coal* decided 55 years earlier. In the 1922 case, Pennsylvania's Kohler Act prohibited mining that caused subsidence under certain structures. In *Keystone,* Pennsylvania's Bituminous Mine Subsidence and Land Conservation Act was challenged. Pennsylvania's Department of Environmental Resources had employed a formula that generally required 50% of the coal beneath protected structures to be left in place as a means of providing surface support. Plaintiff coal companies argued that since the regulation prohibited them from mining this coal, the regulation constituted a taking. The Court's majority opinion distinguished the Subsidence Act from the earlier Kohler Act using its factors (where the land-use regulation "deprives the owner of economically viable use of his land"—the majority decided it did not and if it fails to "substantially advance legitimate state interests," the majority decided it did not so fail (480 U.S. 486 [1987]).

However, in a footnote, the majority reaffirmed Pennsylvania Coal's instructions to courts "to examine the operative provisions of a statute, not just its stated purposes, in assessing its true nature" (480 U.S. 487 n.16 [1987]). Thus, the Court explicitly directed courts to examine how agencies operationalized regulatory statutes to judge substantial advancement of "legitimate state interests." This was a sword that could clearly cut both ways in a future case. The dissenters in *Keystone*—Rehnquist, Powell, O'Connor, and Scalia—also valued the economic issues in a way quite different than did the majority.

The decision in *Nollan v. California Coastal Commission* (483 U.S. 825 [1987]) bears most directly on the issue of when a regulatory taking will be found to have occurred by the courts. The genesis of *Nollan* was that the California Coastal Commission, which is authorized by state law to issue building permits along the coast, conditioned the granting of a permit to the Nollans to build a larger house in place of a small beach cottage on the deeding of an access easement laterally between two public beaches, one on either side of the Nollan's property. The Coastal Commission had defended its action by claiming that the larger house would impede visual and psychological public access to the beach from the road. In examining the fit between the purported problem caused by the larger house and the permit condition, the Court could not find a logical connection. The access impaired was perpendicular from the road, and the easement was lateral along the beach.

Justice Scalia's majority opinion, joined by the other three *Keystone* dissenters plus Justice White, delineated the character of the governmental action factor; "We have long recognized that land use regulation does not effect a taking if it 'substantially advance[s] legitimate state interests' and does not 'den[y] an owner economically viable use of his land' " (483 U.S. 834 [1987]). However, the majority opinion pinpointed the gap that Nollan would partially fill: "Our cases have not elaborated on the standards for determining what constitutes a 'legitimate state interest' or what type of connection between the regulation and the state interest satisfies the requirement that the former 'substantially advance' the latter" (483 U.S. 834 [1987]). While recognizing a broad range of purposes was possible, the Court found ". . . the lack of nexus between the condition and the original purpose of the building restriction . . ." (483

U.S. 837 [1987]). The Court is looking for the "essential nexus" between the "end advanced" and the "condition" imposed by the land use regulation. The Court found that in the absence of such a nexus, the regulation "is not a valid regulation of land use but 'an out-and-out plan of extortion' " (483 U.S. 837 [1987]).

Thus, the Supreme Court has directed lower courts to judge if the "essential nexus" between the application of a regulation and its purpose exists in order to decide if it "substantially advances a legitimate state interest." This raises the issue of how to know when the "essential nexus" is absent. The *Nollan* court does not define that, except to say, in the instance of the Coastal Commission's conditioning the granting of the building permit on the ceding of a lateral easement, "[W]hatever may be the outer limits of 'legitimate state interests' in the takings and land use context, this is not one of them" (483. U.S. 837 [1987]).

Since the 'outer limits" are not precisely defined, further delineation will come through subsequent litigation. Consequently, one of the principal sources of uncertainty for regulators is how closely the courts choose to scrutinize regulations under attack as takings (Peterson, 1988:357). The *Nollan* court did explicitly reaffirm that "a broad range of governmental purposes and regulations" would be considered as "legitimate state purposes" (483. U.S. 835 [1987]). In *Nollan,* the Court took pains to point out that while previous decisions had not set standards for "legitimate state interests" or what satisfies the requirement that a regulation "substantially advance" them; "They have made clear, however, that a broad range of governmental purposes and regulations satisfy these requirements" (483. U.S. 834,835 [1987]). The majority went on to review several regulatory requirements the Coastal Commission could have levied on the Nollans to preserve visual access to the beach as a condition of granting the permit that would not be judged a taking, including a height limitation, a width restriction, a ban on fences, the provision of a viewing spot on the property, or even forbidding construction of the house altogether (483 U.S. 836 [1987]). Thus, the Court both imposed a more exacting standard of review and recognized a broad range of governmental purposes as legitimate. There have been some lower court decisions that have followed the reasoning in *Nollan* (*Batch v. Town of Chapel Hill,* 376 S.E. 2d 22 [1989]; *Weingarten v. Town of Lewisboro,* 542 N.Y. 2d 1012 [1989]; *Holmdel Builders Association v. Township of Holmdel,* 556 A 2d 1236 [1989]), and so regulators should expect enhanced judicial scrutiny of the issue of whether the required nexus exists.

The Court's decision in *First English Evangelical Lutheran Church of Glendale v. County of Los Angeles* (482 U.S. 304 [1987]) focused on the appropriate remedy for temporary regulatory takings. Specifically, the question was whether governments would be liable to pay compensation for the time the regulation was in effect or whether invalidation of the regulatory action would be the only available remedy for landowner plaintiffs.

While the U.S. Supreme Court had not spoken on this issue, the California Supreme Court had, in its own decision in *Agins v. City of Tiburon* (24 Cal. 3d 266 [1979]). In that state case, the court held that invalidation, not money damages, was the appropriate remedy for a regulatory taking. Various U.S. Supreme Court majorities in four federal cases in the early 1980s did not reach the issue, because of perceived procedural inadequacies (*Agins v. City of Tiburon,* 447 U.S. 255 [1980]; *Williamson Planning Commission v. Hamilton Bank,* 473 U.S. 172 [1985]; *Mcdonald, Sommer, and Frates v. Yolo County,* 1477 U.S. 340 [1986]). However, in at least three of these cases, various justices who joined in dissenting opinions—Rehnquist, White, Powell, Marshall and Brennan—had all rejected California's *Agins* rule of no money damages for a temporary regulatory taking, although not in the same case (White and Barkhordari, 1988:157–158). Justice Brennan's dissenting opinion in *San Diego Gas and Electric* foretold the *First English* decision, where he argued that limiting a property owner to having the regulation invalidated was constitutionally inadequate, because it did not compensate the owner for the loss of use of his property during the time the regulation was in effect and before a court could overturn it (450 U.S. 651–661 [1980]).

The *First English* case was brought against Los Angeles County for its temporary flood plain ordinance, which prohibited "the construction, reconstruction, placement, or enlargement of any building or structure within any portion of the interim flood protection area delineated within Mill Creek, vicinity of Hidden Springs" (Los Angeles County Ordinate 11,855 [Jan. 11, 1959]). This ordinance prohibited the Church from rebuilding its camp buildings and recreational facilities that had been destroyed in a flash flood in 1978. The Church charged that the ordinance "denied all use" of its property.

It is important to note that the Supreme Court did not address whether the County's action in fact resulted in a taking of the Church's property. The County had successfully argued in lower courts that the *Agins* rule prevented the Church from recovering money damages at all for an alleged regulatory taking, and both the trial court and the California Court of Appeals had agreed with the county without even considering the Church's allegation that the application of the ordinance worked a "taking." Thus, the U.S. Supreme Court only addressed the remedy issue of whether money damages were appropriate if a regulatory taking were found to have occurred.

The Supreme Court stated that the issue of whether the ordinance had actually worked a taking would have to be resolved by the lower court on remand (482 U.S. 313 [1987]). (On remand, the California Court of Appeal denied that the ordinance in question worked a taking on the church property: *First English Evangelical Lutheran Church v. County of Los Angeles,* 1989 Cal. App. Lexis [636].) Thus, the Supreme Court assumed that the ordinance had worked a taking in order to answer the compensation question. The six to theee majority overturned the California Court's *Agins* rule and held, "[w]here the government's activities have already worked a taking of all use of property, no subsequent action by the government can relieve it of the duty to provide compensation for the period during which the taking was effective" (482 U.S. 321 [1987]). The Court made it clear that the liability of government to provide compensation applies to temporary regulatory takings just the same as permanent ones; " '[t]emporary' takings which, as here, deny a landowner all use of his property, are not different in kind from permanent takings, for which the Constitution clearly requires compensation" (482 U.S. 318 [1987]). The Court also made it clear that application of this rule under the Just Compensation clause of the constitution is a self-executing remedial provision, and thus applies to federal as well as state and local government regulatory actions (482 U.S. 316 n.9 [1987]).

The *First English* majority almost took pains to make it clear that the Court was not seeking to prohibit the regulation of private property. The majority focused attention on the language of the Fifth Amendment itself and opined, "this provision does not prohibit the taking of private property, but instead places a condition on the exercise of that power" (482 U.S. 314 [1987]). The majority went on to interpret, "[t]his basic understanding of the Amendment makes clear that it is designed not to limit the governmental interference with property rights per se, but rather to secure compensation in the event of otherwise proper interference amounting to a taking" (482 U.S. 314 [1987]). The "otherwise proper interference" language refers to other constraints on governmental actions imposed by the due process provision of the Fifth and the equal protection clause of the Fourteenth Amendments. Nonetheless, even when a taking is found, governmental action is not precluded, as the Court went on to make clear; "Once a court determines that a taking has occurred, the government retains the whole range of options already available—amendment of the regulation, withdrawal of the invalidated regulation, or exercise of eminent domain" (482 U.S. 321 [1987]).

As a consequence, the Court is not saying that regulation, even regulation that deprives someone of their property, is unconstitutional or impermissible, only that when it does, under certain circumstances the government must pay.

The argument, in and of itself, that a public or regulatory purpose will be harmed as a result of a requirement to pay compensation is unlikely to meet with much success in the courts. The majority in *First English* spoke to that issue:

> We realized that even our present holding will undoubtedly lessen to some extent the freedom and flexibility of land-use planners and governing bodies of municipal corporations when enacting land-use regulations. But such consequences necessarily flow from any decision upholding a claim of constitutional right; many of the provisions of the Constitution are designed to limit the flexibility and freedom of governmental authorities and the Just Compensation Clause of the Fifth Amendment is one of them. (482 U.S. 321 [1987])

In short, the Court finds that beyond a certain limit, a governmental regulatory action requires the public to compensate the landowner, even if governmental officials choose to shrink from regulatory actions in contemplation of such costs.

The standard for how long a regulation must be in effect before it will be found to have taken the property even temporarily is not clear. This uncertainty is evidenced by the First English majority opinion, "[w]e limit our holdings to the facts presented, and of course do not deal with the different questions that would arise in the case of normal delays in obtaining building permits, changes in zoning ordinances, variances, and the like which are not before us" (482 U.S. 321 [1987]). What constitutes "normal delays" and how the Court will treat the "different questions" remain to be answered.

DETERMINING WHEN A REGULATION WILL BE SUBJECTED TO TRIAL IN FEDERAL COURT

It should be understood that even after the recent Supreme Court cases in favor of property owners, the federal courts are not necessarily going to hold a full trial on the merits of an allegation of a taking brought against an agency for a regulation. The decisions in the 1987 cases do not invalidate the previous rulings that delineate when allegations of a regulatory taking are ripe for federal judicial review. Thus, all claims asserting that a regulation has effected a taking of property are not automatically reviewable in federal court.

Automatic review aside, the likelihood of court intervention at various stages of the regulation process is very much an issue, that is, at what point will the courts step in?

Facial Challenges

Plaintiffs sometimes have asked the courts hold a trial at the point that a newly issued regulation is promulgated. In certain circumstances the federal courts will allow a plaintiff landowner to attempt to such a facial challenge: prove a claim that a given regulation amounts to a taking of its face (*Martino v. Santa Clara Valley Water District,* 703 F 2d. 1141 [9th Cir. 1983]; *Lake Nacimiento Ranch Co. v. San Luis Obispo County,* 841 F. 2d 872, 876–877 [1988]). However, facial challenges have not been the Supreme Court's preferred method of proceeding in the past. In 1988, the Supreme Court emphasized its disdain for facial challenges and preference that courts judge the occurrence of a taking on an "as applied" basis; "we have found it particularly important in takings cases to adhere to our admonition that 'the constitutionality of statutes ought not to be decided except in an actual factual setting that makes such a decision necessary' " (*Pennel v. City of San Jose,* 485 U.S. 10 [1987] [citations omitted]). However, there have been some significant departures from this rule. A 1989 New York Court of Appeals case, which the Supreme Court declined to review, involved a successful facial challenge to New York City's ordinance establishing a 5 year moratorium on conversion, alteration, and demolition of single-room occupancy housing (*Seawall Associates v. City of New York,* 542 N.E. 2d 1059 [1989]). A decision by the Court of Appeals for the Federal Circuit found that a taking of the plaintiff's property occurred at the "moment the Surface Mining Control Act (SMCRA) was enacted" (*Whitney Benefits, Inc. v. U.S.,* 926 F.2d 1169, 1172 [Fed Cir 1991]). In that case, the Court noted its awareness of previous cases favoring administrative action prior to judicial action, but stated that the case fell within a category of cases "in which the Supreme Court has found no need to exhaust administrative remedies" (926 F.2d 1169, 1172 [Fed Cir 1991, citing *Weinberg v. Weisenfeld,* 420 U.S. 636, 641 [1975]: no need to exhaust because statute "on its face precludes granting benefits to men"], *McKart v. United States,* 395 U.S. 185 [1969]: no need where facts clearly fit statutory definition).

Ripeness: The Point at Which the Challenged Regulation Goes to Court

Even if one assumes that courts resist most facial challenges, the latitude regulators have in terms of both time and the stages of administrative processing the property owner must go through in the application of regulations before court intervention is not unbounded. The federal courts use ripeness doctrine as applied to the implementation of a regulation to decide when the administrative proceeding has progressed far enough to justify the finding that the property is due a day in court.

The Supreme Court's ripeness doctrine has historically constitute a shield behind which regulators utilized their discretion in administering land use regulations to avoid takings, and, where appropriate, provided compensation to landowners. There is an inherent relationship between the land use takings question and the ripeness issue. Knowing the allowable use of regulated private land is important to a court's determination of whether a taking has occurred, and courts have ordinarily looked to regulatory agencies and their actions to determine the allowable use remaining in the property with any degree of certainty. Without a final determination by regulators, it is difficult for courts to determine the severity of the regulatory impact and thus cannot make the determinations required to adjudge the occurrence of a taking. However, regulators cannot assume that the courts will continue to use ripeness to defer to their discretion at the same rate as in the past. The courts are refining the ripeness doctrine in the regulatory takings area and are assessing the effect of administrative procedures in more detail than previously.

The courts examine several factors to determine if the taking allegation is ripe. The inquiry starts with two requirements the Supreme Court established in *Williamson County Regional Planning Commission v. Hamilton Bank* (473 U.S. 172 [1985]). First, a final decision must have been reached with respect to the permitted uses of the land and, second, the landowner claiming compensation must have sought compensation through available procedures.

There is considerable development by the courts underway concerning the determination of when a final decision has been reached. The Supreme Court in a 1986 case refused to reach the merits of a claim that a rejection of a subdivision proposal had worked a taking, until the plaintiff made a meaningful application for less intense development (*Mcdonald, Sommer & Frates v. Yolo County,* 477 U.S. 340, 352 [1986]). Citing both *Williamson* and *Mcdonald,* the Tenth Circuit declared in a 1988 case

> A "final decision" requires not only an initial rejection of a particular development proposal, but a definitive action by local authorities, indicating with some specificity what level of development will be permitted on the property in question (874 F.2d 717 [1988]).

However, the Ninth Circuit has warned in another decision in which it rejected the ripeness of the plaintiff's claim

> [t]his decision should not be misinterpreted as requiring plaintiff to exhaust every possible administrative avenue of relief. . . . Instead, to determine the administrative finality of a zoning regulation to a given parcel of land, plaintiff must make "at least one meaningful application" for a reasonable development project (citations omitted) (*Stephans v. Tahoe Regional Planning Agency,* 697 F.Supp. 1149 [D.Nev. 1988]).

The Ninth Circuit also has developed a "futility" exception to the final decision requirement providing that the requirement of the submission of development plans subsequent to at least one meaningful application is excused if such applications would be a "idle and futile" act. The Ninth Circuit held that excessive delay may make compliance with local ordinances futile, as can "unfair procedures" (*Kinzli v. City of Santa Cruz,* 818 F.2d. 1449, 1455 amended, 830 F.2d. 968 [9th Cir. 1987]). However, some Federal Courts have criticized this "futility" exception (*Landmark Land Co. v. Buchanan,* 874 F.2d. 717 [1988] and *Zilber v. City of Moraga,* 692 F.Supp. 1195, 1199 n.3 [1988]). In a related fashion, the U.S. Court of Claims ruled in a case involving the refusal of a permit by the Corps of Engineers for filling in some wetlands acreage that a developer did not have to submit "less ambitious proposals, since the Corps has taken a final definitive position that any development on the wetlands is unacceptable" (*Loveladies Harbor, Inc. v. United States,* 15 Cl. Ct. 381 [1988]).

The second ripeness requirement under *Williamson* in state land use cases is use of state compensatory procedures, so called "state remedies ripeness." A plaintiff must first be denied compensation by the state before the Fifth Amendment action will be considered by the federal courts. However, these state remedies must exist at the time of the alleged taking (473 U.S. 194 [1985]). If a plaintiff fails to use the state procedures, the federal claim will be dismissed as premature (see *Beachy v. Bd. of Aviation Comm'rs of Kokomo, In.,* 699 F.Supp. 742, 746 [S.D.Ind. 1988]). However, the federal court does not have to impose the "state remedies ripeness" requirement if the state "inverse condemnation procedure is unavailable or inadequate" (473 U.S. 196–197 [1985]). It is unclear what makes a state procedure unavailable or inadequate, so that plaintiffs wishing to get their claim into federal court have every incentive to challenge state procedures. The Ninth Circuit has held that delay in the California judicial system and alleged hostility of the California courts toward taking claims are insufficient to invoke this exception (*Sinaloa Lake Owners Ass'n v. City of Simi Valley,* 864 F.2d 1475, 1479–80 [9th Cir. 1989]).

It should be noted that state courts are also required by *First English* to allow compensation for a temporary taking, so they will make at least the initial determination of ripeness in cases involving state actions.

The Effect of a Regulation on Property: How Much is Too Much?

What has to be the effect on property caused by a regulation before a court will declare that it has been taken? Recently the Supreme Court has acknowledged the

> [d]ifficult problem of how to define "too far," that is, how to distinguish the point at which regulation becomes so onerous that it has the same effect as an appropriation of the property through eminent domain or physical possession (473 U.S. 199 [1985]).

Legitimate State Interests

As discussed above, one prong of the Agin "standard" is that the regulation "substantially advance legitimate state interests," *Nollan* further defined this as requiring an "essential nexus," meaning that there must be a reasonable relationship between the regulation imposed on the property owner and the public purpose imbedded in the regulation as the reason for imposing it. If there is no rational nexus, this is sufficient for a court to find that a taking has occurred.

The court's inquiry does not stop with the finding that there is some public purpose. As Justice Holmes noted in 1922, "a strong public desire to improve the public condition is not enough to warrant achieving this desire by a shorter cut than the constitutional way of paying for the change" (260 U.S. 416 [1922]). The court will weigh the intended public benefit with the burden on the property owner. In doing this, the court may make a distinction between public purposes, weighing more heavily in the regulator's favor when the regulation is intended to prevent a public harm and more heavily in the property owner's favor when the regulation is intended to maintain a public benefit. In one case the Federal Circuit court found that a decision to deny a mining permit was intended to fulfill the public purpose of ensuring the continued existence of a wetland and that, weighed against the burden on the property owner, found the balance in favor of the property owner (*Florida Rock v. United States,* 791 F.2d 893 904 [Fed. Cir 1986]). This type of balancing is predicated on the Supreme Court's exhortation that the "determination that a governmental action constitutes a taking, is, in essence, a determination that the public at large, rather than a single owner, must bear the burden of an exercise of state power in the public interest" (*Agins v. City of Tiburon,* 447 U.S. at 260–61 [1980]).

The balance tips the other way if the public purpose falls under the nuisance exception. The nuisance exception originated in the British common law and has a long history in American law. It is rooted in the principle, long recognized by the courts, that an individual may not make a "noxious use of their property, to inflict injury upon the community" (*Mugler v. State of Kansas,* 123 U.S. 623, 669 [1987]). It asserts that the state has the power to abate a nuisance that threatens the health or safety of the community and that no individual should be able to stop the state from exercising its police power to protect the public.

As the Supreme Court recently explained the status of this exception, it may be understood by "the simple theory that since no individual has a right to use his property so as to create a nuisance or otherwise harm others, the State has not 'taken' anything when it asserts its power to enjoin the nuisance-like activity" (*Keystone Bituminous Coal Ass'n. v. DeBenedictus,* 480 U.S. 511 [1987]). The Supreme Court has operationalized this principle so that a taking has not been found when a regulation has been found to prevent serious public harm (*Mugler v. Kansas,* 123 U.S. 623 [1887], *Hadacheck v. Sebastian,* 239 U.S. 394 [1915], *Goldblatt v. Hempstead,* 369 U.S. 590 [1962]). This nuisance exception can apply even when significant diminution in property value results from state action, indeed total destruction of property value (*Miller v. Schoene,* 276 U.S. 272 [1928]).

The Supreme Court has recently made it clear that the nuisance exception "is not coterminous with the police power itself" (*Keystone,* 480 U.S. 491 n.20 [1987]). If this were not the case, the just compensation clause would become a nullity, always subordinate to the police power (*Lucas v. South Carolina,* 112 S.Ct. 2886, 2889 [1992]). In addition, the doctrine requires the court to find an actual relationship of the regulation to a real potential public harm, not merely to accept a general assertion in statute or regulation that the purpose of the regulation is to "protect the public safety." Thus, in order for the nuisance exception to be successfully invoked, "a statute purporting to have been enacted to protect the public health, the public morals, or the public safety" must have a "real and substantial relation" to those objectives (*Mugler v. Kansas,* 183 U.S. 661 [1887]). However, even a noxious-use justification for a statute cannot be used to avoid compensation for a regulation being used for taking the total value of a property (*Lucas v. South Carolina,* 112 S.Ct. 2886, 2889 [1992]).

Economically Viable Use

The other prong, as reiterated in *Keystone,* is "or denies an owner economically viable use of his land." There is no precise definition given for how economic viability is to be measured. As stated above, the Court has enunciated three factors for use in ad hoc analysis of regulations: (1) "character of the governmental action," (2) "economic impact of the regulation," and (3) "interference with distinct investment backed expectations." There are no exact criteria for these, nor is there a precise formula for weighing them. The net situation was summed up by the Ninth Circuit, also in 1987: "the precise meaning of 'economically viable use' of land is elusive and has not been clarified by the Supreme Court" (*Lake Nacimiento Ranch v. San Luis Obispo County,* 841 F.2d 877 [1988]).

With respect to the character of the government action, the courts look to determine the degree to which the regulation as applied to the property in question actually interferes with the owners use of his or her property. As the Supreme Court has opined, "determination that governmental action constitutes a taking, is in essence, a determination that the public at large, rather than a single owner, must bear the burden of an exercise of state power in the public interest" (*Agins v. Tiburon,* 447 U.S. 255, 260–61 [1980]).

Mere impact on the use of the property, however, is not enough to constitute a taking. The Supreme Court uses the "bundle of rights" concept, which defines property ownership as a bundle, the sticks of which representing such property interests as air space, minerals, surface use, development, profit, and attendant aspects such as the right to exclude others (see Michelman, 1967, 1988).

The courts must determine on what the regulation impacts, and how much, to determine if the regulation has "gone too far." As the Supreme Court reiterated in *Keystone* "Because our test for regulatory taking requires us to compare the value that has been taken from property with the value that remains in the property, one of the critical questions is determining how to define the unit of property whose value is to furnish the denominator of the fraction" (480 U.S. 470 citations omitted [1987]). Supreme Court majorities have not necessarily been consistent in their approach to the use of the bundle of rights concept to make this determination. Some have defined the denominator in terms of the size of the bundle remaining and others have used the stick taken as the denominator. The *Keystone* majority quoted the *Penn Central* opinion and emphasized that the appropriate focus is "on the nature of the interference with rights in the parcel as a whole" (480 U.S. 470 [1987]). The majority also repeated that "where an owner possesses a full 'bundle' of property rights, the destruction of one 'strand' of the bundle is not a taking because the aggregate must be viewed in its entirety" (480 U.S. 470 [1987] quoting *Andrus v. Allard,* 444 U.S. 51, 65–66 [1979]).

The *Nollan* majority placed emphasis on the part taken (an easement across a beach) in declaring that the state had taken an "essential stick" in the bundle of rights (483 U.S. 831 [1987]). Similar language was used by another Court majority in another 1987 case, which stated that "the right to pass on property" along with "the right to exclude others" are among "the most essential sticks in the bundle of rights that are commonly characterized as property" (*Hodel v. Irving,* 481 U.S. 704, 716 [1987]). If the whole-bundle approach is used, a regulation is less likely to restrict all the rights in the bundle, and consequently a taking requiring compensation is harder to prove. Thus, while the regulation may prevent even a substantial use of the property, this may very likely be insufficient to secure compensation because the owner's other rights to possess, dispose, and exclude others remain intact (*Loveladies Harbor Inc. v. United States,* 15 Cl. Ct. 381, 391 [1988]). If the essential-stick approach is used, a taking is more likely to be determined. In that event, the focus is on the nature of the governmental interferences with that essential property right.

A finding of a taking is more likely if the character of the action is equivalent to the physical invasion, occupation, or destruction of the property. The occupation does not necessarily have to preclude other uses to be judged a taking, and even if it is done pursuant to a legitimate public purpose, compensation may still be required by the court. In *Loretto v. Teleprompter Manhattan CATV Corp.,* a New York law required landlords to permit cable television companies to install cable facilities on their rental property. The court found the law to be a valid exercise of the police power. Despite this and even though the landlords could still rent out the apartments as before, the Supreme Court found a taking, since there was a physical occupation of the landowner's property (458 U.S. 419 [1982]). In a related fashion, the U.S. Court of Appeals for the Federal Circuit overruled a U.S. Claims Court ruling concerning an Environmental Protection Agency administrative order. The order authorized the installation of monitoring wells and equipment on a property owner's land in order to monitor possible discharges from a hazardous waste site not on the owner's land. The trial court had ruled that more evidence was needed to establish "whether the devices are truly permanently affixed to plaintiff's property" (*Hendler v. United States,* 11 Cl. Ct. 91, 97 [1986]). The Appeals Court asserted that this conclusion misperceived the thrust of Fifth Amendment protection and stated, " 'permanent' does not mean forever, or anything like it. A taking can be for a limited term" (*Hendler v. United States,* 1991 U.S. App. Lexis 30233, 31 [1991]). Furthermore, the Court held, "the concept of permanent physical occupation does not require that in every instance the occupation be exclusive, or continuous and uninterrupted" (*Hendler v. United States,* 1991 U.S. App. Lexis 30233, 37 [1991]). The court quoted the essential-stick language in *Nollan,* reaffirming that the right to exclude others is "one of the most essential sticks in the bundle of rights that are commonly characterized as property" (*Hendler v. United States,* 1991 U.S. App. Lexis 30233, 39 [1991]).

The second factor—determination of the economic impact of the regulation—and the third—interference with investment-backed expectations—are really intertwined and are often treated that way in judicial analysis. They require the court to determine the economic value of the land before the impact of the regulation and compare that with the economic value after the regulation is imposed.

The first step in the inquiry is to establish what exactly constitutes the property in question. If a regulation denies the use of part of a parcel of property, but the remaining property is unaffected, compensation is unlikely to be awarded. As the Court has reiterated in *Keystone,*

> [b]ecause our test for regulating taking requires us to compare the value that has been taken from property with the value that remains in the property, one of the critical questions is determining how to define the unit of property "whose value is to furnish the denominator of the fraction" (480 U.S. 497 [1987]).

The *Penn Central* rule that the appropriate inquiry focuses on the "parcel as a whole" means the land the landowner held at the time of the alleged taking. However, the court must still determine what that is, and such a determination can have a significant impact on the case outcome. As the United States Claims Court explained:

> Factors such as the degree of contiguity, the dates of acquisition, the extent to which the parcel has been treated as a single unit, the extent to which the protected lands enhance the value of remaining lands, and no doubt many others would enter the calculus. The

> effect of a taking can obviously be disguised if the property at issue is too broadly defined. Conversely, a taking can appear to emerge if the property is viewed too narrowly. The effort should be to identify the parcel as realistically and fairly as possible, given the entire factual and regulatory environment (*Ciampitti v. U.S.,* 22 Cl. Ct. 310, 319 [1991]).

Following the determination of the property in question, the court then compares the value before the regulation with the value remaining. The Supreme Court has repeatedly found that the "mere diminution" of property values is not enough. The Court in *Williamson* revisited Justice Holmes opinion in *Pennsylvania Coal,* which had observed that government had to be able to use its police power to diminish property to some extent without paying, or "government could hardly go on." However, the Court added emphasis to the following part of Holmes earlier statement

> One fact for consideration in determining such limits is the extent of the diminution. When it reaches a certain magnitude, in most if not all cases there must be an exercise of eminent domain and compensation to sustain the act. (473 U.S. 199 [1985])

Nonetheless, the Supreme Court has not given clear direction as to how to determine when this "certain magnitude" has been reached. The property owner cannot prevail simply because he shows an excess of costs over benefits derived from the regulation. There is not a constitutional presumption that it all must balance out. As the majority said in *Keystone*

> [t]he Takings Clause has never been read to require the States or the courts to calculate whether a specific individual has suffered burdens under this generic rule in excess of the benefits received. Not every individual gets a full dollar return in benefits for the taxes he or she pays; yet, no one suggests that an individual has a right to compensation for the difference between taxes paid and the dollar value of benefits received (480 U.S. 491 [1987]).

Some commentators apparently hoped after *First English* that the magnitude of diminution that must be demonstrated is 100%. This was based on the Court's reference to the alleged taking as being the taking of "all use." It seems more likely that the Court was not endorsing "all use" as a standard, but was merely proceeding on the assumption of the allegation, so that it could get on to the compensation question (Berger, 1988:770; see also Frank and Merrit, 1978:131).

Some lower courts have looked to much earlier Supreme Court cases to examine the certain magnitude issue (see Berger, 1988:762). In these earlier cases the Supreme Court rejected pleas that a taking had occurred where the remaining value was only 13 to 25 per cent of the unregulated value (*Village of Euclid v. Ambler Realty Co.,* 272 U.S. 365 [1926]; *Hadacheck v. Sebastion,* 329 U.S. 394 [1915]). However, this was over 50 years before the Court had used the term "economically viable use" and in none of the cases did the courts examine the facts to see if the remaining value in the property after regulation left it economically viable. The Court has said where the government has deprived a landowner of all economically beneficial uses, that is a total taking, then compensation must be paid (*Lucas v. South Carolina,* 112 S.Ct. 2886, 1895 [1992]).

In any event, the term "economically viable use" is not limited to immediate uses but can include future uses (*Florida Rock,* 791 F.2d 893 [1986]). This does not mean the regulator can merely plead hypothetical alternative uses and escape liability. As the U.S. Claims Court explained

> the court sitting as a finder of fact must discount proposed uses that do not meet a showing of reasonable probability that the land is both physically adaptable for such use *and* that there is a demand for such use in the reasonable near future (21 Cl. Ct. 153, 158 [1990]).

As to the factor of interference with investment-backed expectations, the courts seem to be trying to define the implications of this factor further. One of the difficulties they are apparently having is how to deal with the issue of profits. In 1979 the Court had said

> At any rate, loss of future profits—unaccompanied by any physical property restriction—provides a slender reed upon which to rest a takings claim. Prediction of profitability is essentially a matter of reasoned speculation that courts are not especially competent to perform (*Andrus v. Allard,* 444 U.S. 66 [1979]).

Also, in *Williamson,* the Court added profit to the investment factor making it "investment-backed profit expectations" (473 U.S. 200 [1985]). This really adds confusion to the issue of economic viability. Some lower-court decisions have held that frustration of the "highest and best" use by government (i.e., most profitable use), is not what is meant by investment-backed expectations, but that profit may figure into the court's valuation of the property. In a Federal Circuit case, the court held that "The fifth amendment, as backed by the safety net of the Tucker Act, does not find a taking in the mere denial of the 'highest and best use,' ie., most profitable use, that would be available in the absence of regulation" (*Florida Rock Industries v. U.S.,* 791 F.2d 901 [1986] [Fed. Cir. cert. denied 479 U.S. 1053] [1987]).

The Court went on to say, however, that relevant consideration for determining whether dimunition in market value from government regulation has resulted in a taking requiring compensation involves a consideration of "[t]he owner's basis or investment and the fair market before the alleged taking, compared to the fair market value after the alleged taking" (791 F.2d 905 [1986]). This should include, according to the court, consideration of testimony of those who might be willing to speculate regarding the potential market value of the land (791 F.2d 903 [1986]).

In another case, the Court of Appeals of New York focused on the role of expected profits in determining investment-backed expectations. In invalidating a city regulation, the court pointed to the owner's profit expectations as a result of developing the property to a different use

> Unquestionably, the effect of the law is to strip owners of SRO buildings who may have purchased their properties solely to turn them into profitable investments by tearing down and replacing the existing structures with new ones (as plaintiffs claim they have)—of the very right to use their properties for any such purpose (*Seawall Associates v. City of New York,* 542 N.E. 2d 1066 [N.Y. 1989]).

Whereas the *Florida Rock* Court denied the owner's expectation of immediate profit-making use as a criterion in determining investment backed expectations, it did, like the *Seawall* court, state that profits from future possible development under the regulation should be a criterion. The *Seawall* court asserted, "[t]here can be no question that the development rights which have been totally abrogated by the local law are, standing alone, valuable components of the 'bundle of rights' making up their fee interests" (542 N.E. 2d 1067 [N.Y. 1989]). Both courts are implicitly acknowledging the role of the market in determining the impact of profits and remaining value to be derived from future development of the property under regulation.

This emphasis on profit expectations is a marked departure from the Supreme Court's reasoning in *Andrus v. Allard,* in which the court refused to consider lost profits from sales as a criterion. That case seemed to mark the high point of the Court's reluctance to consider the role of investors' intentions in investment decisions, and thus property values. However, if the courts seek to define this area further, they will necessarily have to develop a fuller economic theory of investment. A key to this will be to clarify the role of profit expectations are to play in defining current value, how they are to be determined, and what other factors the courts should use along with them.

Providing standards would require, at a minimum, a clarification of the courts' conceptions of the nature of property ownership. This is unlikely to be fully delineated in the near future.

CONCLUSION

The courts are unlikely to provide clear and certain standards regarding regulations to guide regulators. The reason is that the preferred method is ad hoc analysis in particular contexts. Attacks on regulatory legislation as adopted (facial challenges) are not the preferred method for challenging regulations from the standpoint of the federal courts, but there have been some successful facial challenges in which it has been successfully demonstrated that the challenge legislation affords the administrators no discretion but to so restrict use of the property that it is effectively taken. The federal courts have developed and are developing criteria (ripeness doctrine) to assist in the determination of when administration of the regulation has proceeded to the point that a definite enough decision has been made regarding the application of the regulation to the property that its impact can be fairly assessed. In general, a final regulatory decision is required as long as undue delay is not experienced and further processing would not be futile.

While the courts have not worked out a clear doctrine of the relationship between property ownership and regulation, they have developed some factors to be employed in assessing the impacts of regulations applied to particular pieces of property.

The courts require, as a threshold issue, that the regulation "substantially advance legitimate state interests." While a broad range of interests will be found legitimate, it is important for regulators to have them stated explicitly and to demonstrate, as well, how the application of the regulation specifically serves to achieve particular public purposes. In short, regulators must be prepared to demonstrate an "essential nexus" between the specific public purpose and the action demanded by application of the regulation.

The courts move on to the determination of whether the regulation denies the owner "economically viable use" of the property. In making the determination, the courts weigh and balance three factors: (1) the character of the governmental action, (2) the economic impact of the regulation, and (3) interference with distinct investment-backed expectations. The balancing is done according to no set formula or principles and doctrine is evolving with respect to each of these factors and how they are to be combined to make the determination. It may take some time before these relationships are clarified to enable regulators to know when the courts are likely to find excessive impact on economic viability. There can be less doubt that courts will be looking for the essential nexus between an announced public purpose and a particular regulatory decision. Regulatory purposes should be clearly stated and the actions taken to fulfill them clearly related to the stated purposes.

It is unlikely that the courts will revert to a deferential posture toward regulators. Regulators are advised to establish a record of a direct linkage between a clear public purpose and the regulatory action, and to be prepared to establish that full due process protections were followed.

Whether the ultimate impacts on public regulation are as direct as some feared, remains to be seen. In recent years public officials facing continuing fiscal stringency have turned to regulation to achieve social goals they once might have sought by means of direct public programs. The courts have served notice that this avenue is not an unlimited one, and that property owners have basic constitutional rights that will be defended. The boundaries of these rights, however, are anything but certain.

REFERENCES

Berger, Michael (1988) Happy birthday constitution: The Supreme Court establishes new ground rules for land-use planning. *Urban Layer* 20: 735–800.

Frank, Richard, and Merrit, Robert (1987) Damages as a remedy for temporary 'regulatory takings' of property: The impact of First Lutheran. *California Real Property Law Reporter* 10: 125–148.

March, Robert, and Rosenthal, Stephan (1987) At long last, the Supreme Court speaks out on the taking issue. *California Real Property Journal* 5: 1–3.

Michelman, Frank (1967) Property, utility, and fairness: Comments on the ethical foundations of 'just compensation' law. *Harvard Law Review* 80: 1165–1258.

Michelman, Frank (1988) Takings, 1987. *Columbia Law Review* 88: 1618–1629.

White, Jack, and Barkhordari, Farzad (1988) The First English Evangelical Church case. *UCLA Journal of Environmental Law and Policy* 7: 155–172.

CASES CITED

Agins v. City of Tiburon 24 Cal. 3d 266 (1979)
Agins v. City of Tiburon 477 U.S. 255 (1980)
Andrus v. Allard 444 U.S. 51 (1979)
Batch v. Town of Chapel Hill 376 S.E. 2d 22 (1989)
Campitti v. U.S. 21 Cl. Ct. 310 (1991)
Connolly v. Penston Benefit Guarantee Corp. 475 U.S. 211 (1986).
First English Evangelical Lutheran Church of Glendale v. County of Los Angeles 482 U.S. 304 (1987)
First English Evangelical Lutheran Church of Glendale v. County of Los Angeles 1989 Cal. App. Lexis 639 (1989)
Florida Rock Industries v. U.S. 791 F.2d. 893 (1986) (Fed. Cir. cert denied 479 U.S. 1053 [1987])
Goldblatt v. Hempstedt 369 U.S. 590 (1962)
Hadacheck v. Sebastion 239 U.S. 394 (1915)
Hendler v. United States 11 Cl. Ct. 91 (1986)
Hendler v. United States 1991 U.S. App. Lexis 30233 (1991)
Hodel v. Irving (1987) 481 U.S. 704, citing *Kaiser Aetna v. United States,* 444 U.S. 164, 176 (1979)
Holmdel Builders Association v. Township of Holmdel 556 A 2d 1236 (1989)
Kaiser Aetna v. United States 444 U.S. 164 (1979)
Keyston Bituminous Coal Association v. DeBenedictus 480 U.S. 470 (1987)
Kinzli v. City of Santa Cruz, 818 F.2d 1449 amended, 830 F.2d. 968 [9th Cir. 1987])
Lake Nacimiento Ranch Co. v. San Luis Obispo County 841 F.2d 872 (1988).
Landmark Land Co. v. Buchanan, 874 F.2d. 717 (1988)
Loretto v. Teleprompter Manhattan CATV Corp. 458 U.S. 419 (1982)
Loveladies Harbor, Inc. v. United States, 15 Cl. Ct. 381 (1988)
Martino v. Santa Clara Valley Water District 703 F.2d 1141 (9th Cir. 1983)
McKart v. United States 395 U.S. 185 (1969)
Mcdonald, Sommer, and Frates v. Yolo County 477 U.S. 340 (1986)
Miller v. Schoene 276 U.S. 272 (1928)
Mugler v. State of Kansas 123 U.S. 623 (1887)
Nollan v. California Coastal Commission 483 U.S. 825 (1987)
Pennel v. City of San Jose 485 U.S. 850 (1988)
Penn Central Transportation v. New York City 438 U.S. 104 (1978)
Pennsylvania Coal v. Mahon 260 U.S. 393 (1922).
Robinson v. California 370 U.S. 660 (1962)
Ruckelshaus v. Monsanto 467 U.S. 986 (1984)
San Diego Gas and Electric v. City of San Diego 450 U.S. 621 (1980).
Seawall Associates v. City of New York, (1989) 542 N.E.2d 1059 (N.Y.) cert. denied, 110 S.Ct. 500 (1989)

Sinaloa Lake Owners Ass'n v. City of Simi Valley, 864 F.2d 1475 (9th Cir. 1989)
Stephens v. Tahoe Regional Planning Agency 697 F.Supp. 1149 (D.Nev. 1988)
Village of Euclid v. Amber Realty 272 U.S. 365 (1926)
Weinberger v. Weisenfeld 420 U.S. 636 (1975)
Weingarten v. Town of Lewisboro 542 N.Y. 2d 1012 (1989)
Whitney Benefits, Inc. v. U.S. 926 F.2d 1169 (1991)
Williamson Planning Commission v. Hamilton Bank 473 U.S. 172 (1985).
Zilber v. City of Moraga 692 F.Supp. 1195 (1988).

8

Deregulation and Reregulation: Policy, Politics, and Economics

Paul Stephen Dempsey *University of Denver, Denver, Colorado*

INTRODUCTION

1992 was a watershed year. For the first time in more than a decade, a Democratic Congress overrode a presidential veto, remarkably enough, to pass a cable television *reregulation* act. For the first time in history, the subject of aviation was addressed in a presidential debate. In the presidential elections, a majority of Americans rejected the failed economic policies of the past decade.

That is not to say that the American people fully comprehend or understand how or why previous administrations have mismanaged the economy. However, public polls reveal that their level of concern is quite high—high enough, in fact, to reject a known quantity (George Bush), for a somewhat unknown one (Bill Clinton).

One comprehensive anecdotal review of the nation's economic decline and its causes did find its way into the paperback shelves at grocery stores and into the hands of millions of Americans: *America: What Went Wrong,* by Donald Bartlett and James Steele (1992), reporters for the *Philadelphia Inquirer.* Ahead of its time, it chronicled a series of naive congressional and presidential steps down the path of economic decline, assaulted the conventional wisdom, and, therefore, was denied the Pulitzer Prize it deserved. The marshy hills and forests inside the Washington, D.C., beltway remain the crumbling citadel of laissez faire theology, where lavish praise continues to be given the emperor's new clothes.

America: What Went Wrong devoted a full chapter to the subject discussed here: deregulation. Contrary to popular perceptions, deregulation did not begin with Ronald Reagan and George Bush. It was advanced, first unsuccessfully, by Gerald Ford, then embraced passionately and implemented comprehensively by Jimmy Carter.

Beginning in the Carter administration, and perfected to an art form in the Reagan administration, federal oversight of industries as diverse as airlines, buses, railroads, trucking, telephones, cable television, radio and television broadcasting, savings and loan institutions, and oil and gas was largely eradicated. The substantive tentacles of deregulation transcended the infrastructure to reach more generic areas affecting the entire economy: safety, health, and the environment, for example.

The means applied to transform and radically shrink government proceeded along two planes. Congress caught the virus of laissez faire and passed major legislation mandating various forms of deregulation between about 1978 and 1986, while successive presidents appointed free market ideologues to the regulatory agencies with the implicit understand they would essentially ignore their oaths of office and defy the statutory mission they thereby promised to implement.

Appointing libertarian and free market ideologues to high government office is the equivalent of appointing atheists to the Vatican high council. The degeneration of government led a generation of loyal and dedicated public servants to leave government in disappointment. The civil service corps has been devastated of its talent and its mission: to serve the public interest. It will take years to rebuild.

President Clinton has promised to focus like a laser beam on the economy. However, he comes to Washington with its core gutted of competent civil servants dedicated to protecting the public interest.

INFRASTRUCTURE DEREGULATION AND DETERIORATION

Airlines were among the first of the major infrastructure industries to go, with the promulgation of the Airline Deregulation Act of 1978, which took the unprecedented step of sunsetting a major regulatory agency: the four-decade-old Civil Aeronautics Board (CAB). That was followed, in transportation, with the promulgation of the Staggers Rail Act of 1980, the Motor Carrier Act of 1980, the Bus Regulatory Reform Act of 1982, and the Freight Forwarder Deregulation Act of 1986 (Dempsey, 1989: 2).

Public infrastructure investment took a back seat to military spending in the 1980s. Potholes widened, bridges crumbled, and the airport trust fund accumulated unspent billions of dollars to counterbalance a growing and frightening $3 trillion deficit, in breach of the fiduciary responsibility owed the public who paid the airport taxes. Private infrastructure investment also dwindled as deregulation produced anemic profitability and unparalleled bankruptcies, thereby chilling the capital markets. Today, Americans fly the oldest fleet of aircraft in the developed world.

ECONOMIC THEORY OF DEREGULATION

Free market economists, like Cornell Professor Alfred Kahn, provided the intellectual justification for deregulation. To concerns that deregulation would result in increased concentration or destructive competition, he insisted that the airline industry possessed relatively few economies of scale and was impeded by few barriers to entry. In theory, large airlines had no advantages over small airlines. Aircraft were uniquely mobile resources that could be deployed to new markets at will. Public utility regulation was appropriate, if at all, for radically different kinds of industries, where, for example, an electric company made tremendous fixed and immobile investments in nuclear power production.

The free market economists saw nearly textbook levels of perfect competition and allocative efficiency everywhere they looked. If only we amputated the dead hand of regulation and sewed on Adam Smith's invisible hand, they insisted, we would prosper in the land of laissez faire.

The theoretical justification for airline deregulation embraced a third essential premise: not only were there ostensibly no economies of scale or barriers to entry, but also in the unlikely event that some carriers might exert market power to earn supracompetitive profits, new entrants would be attracted like sharks to the smell of blood. This was the theory of contestable markets, which posited that hit and run entry by airlines would adequately discipline pricing. No economies of scale, no barriers to entry, and contestability—the three legs of the theoretical stool.

RESULTS OF DEREGULATION

Deregulation theory is simple and seductive. Deregulation reality is profoundly different. The half-trillion dollar savings and loan catastrophe is one manifestation of that reality.

The author's work has been largely in the field of transportation, although empirical parallels exist in the other infrastructure industries: communications and energy. Let us take a closer look at the impact of deregulation on airlines, the first infrastructure industry to be deregulated:

Under deregulation, the airline industry lost all of the money it made since the Wright Brothers' inaugural flight at Kitty Hawk in 1903, plus $2 billion more.

Although the escalation in fuel costs in 1990, precipitated by the Persian Gulf crisis, has been deemed the culprit, real aviation fuel costs were less in 1990 than in the early 1980s.

After more than 150 bankruptcies and 50 mergers, Americans now fly the oldest and most repainted fleet of aircraft in the developed world. In 1991, we lost three major airlines: Eastern, Pan Am, and Midway.

By 1992, nearly 20 percent of the nation's fleet capacity was in bankruptcy. Of the 176 airlines to which deregulation gave birth, only one remains (America West) and, sadly, it too is in bankruptcy.

American, United, Delta, and Northwest now control two-thirds of the market (up from 42 percent in 1985), a rate of concentration unprecedented in American business history.

Deregulation has produced the highest level of national and regional concentration in history.

While most passengers now fly on a discounted ticket, the full fare has risen sharply under deregulation (156 percent in deregulation's first decade: more than double the rate of inflation). Discounts from the "Y" full coach fare are off a price twice as high as it should be. Moreover, the discounts have been encumbered with onerous prepurchase, nonrefundability, and Saturday-night-stayover restrictions. They are therefore an inferior product to the flexibility offered under regulation.

Despite allegations to the contrary, average real fuel-adjusted ticket prices are higher than they would have been had the prederegulation trend continued. Pricing has not only increased above prederegulation trend levels, it has also grown monstrously discriminatory.

Operating costs increased sharply under deregulation (96 percent in deregulation's first half-dozen years), while the long-term trend in productivity improvements fell flat. Industry profits fell 74 percent during deregulation's first decade.

Hubbing-and-spoking, the dominant megatrend on the deregulation landscape, has caused air travel in some markets to regress back to the DC-3 era, robbing aviation of its inherent advantage and our most precious commodity: time.

Business travelers lose billions of dollars in productivity imprisoned in cannisters of aluminum and steel or stranded in airports as a result of circuitous and time-consumptive hub-and-spoke operations.

Under deregulation, service has declined, while consumer fraud has increased.

Although fatality statistics do not reflect it, the margin of safety has also declined.

Labor–management relations have deteriorated. In 1991, more than 40,000 airline employees lost their jobs.

Americans now rate airlines as the industry in which they have least confidence (Dempsey and Goetz, 1992: xiv).

DEREGULATION THEOLOGY

Neither economic nor equity goals have been advanced by deregulation. The assumptions upon which it was based that (1) there were few scale economies in transportation, (2) there were no barriers to entry of consequences; and (3) "contestability" of markets (the purported ease of potential entry) would discipline pricing (the three legs of the theoretical stool) have proven false. Despite the disintegration of the intellectual foundation of deregulation, its proponents swear that it works.

During the past decade, the U.S. Department of Transportation published study after study praising the emperor's new clothes (U.S. DOT, 1990). Platoons of nineteenth century free markets economists in Washington-based laissez faire think tanks lavishly financed by Fortune 500 companies produced reams of data and statistically significant correlations proving conclusively and irrefutably that deregulation is the best thing to happen to the transportation industry since the invention of the wheel. Even the Brookings Institution joined the stampede of lemmings declaring deregulation a success (P. Dempsey and Goetz, 1992: preface).

Studies produced by free market economists suffer from a serious methodological flaw. They tend to focus narrowly on one single slice of the truth: the impact of deregulation (or indeed, any political/economic program) on the prices consumers pay. They tend to ignore the economic impact of policy on investors, creditors, or workers.

This methodological flaw infects the literature supporting free trade. Under David Ricardo's theory of comparative advantage, free trade lowers the price of products consumers buy, thereby enhancing consumer welfare. It seems to occur to no one that we have to have jobs to earn money to buy those cheap imported products, and that not everyone can cook hamburgers at MacDonald's. As Professor Martin Bradley of McGill University once pointed out to this author, "Free trade means you can keep your job, so long as you're willing to live in a mud hut and eat rice."

The Japanese government seems to have embraced a different approach, one of close cooperation with industry in the promotion of domestic industrial production: a national industrial policy. For the Japanese, free trade is fine as an *export* policy. The Japanese approach brings the focus to the *producer* side of the equation rather than the *consumer* side. The result is cutting-edge, state-of-the-art manufacturing facilities producing the world's most sophisticated and highest value consumer products, supplying its citizens with nearly full employment and a prospect for growth in their standard of living. In contrast, the United States suffers from aging factories, deindustrialization, a move of the work force from the manufacturing to generally lower-paid service sector jobs, and a prospect for a declining standard of living.

Moreover, the U.S. "eat the seed corn" movement seems to focus on immediate consumption rather than the need to position the nation to take advantage of long-term opportunities. Congress did nothing while the leveraged buy-out artists looted major American corporations. It is difficult to name a single major corporation that has been subjected to a leveraged buyout that is today stronger, has produced a new product, or is better able to compete in a global environment.

The implicit thesis of the theology of laissez faire is that unconstrained human greed will produce a better society. Deregulation and leveraged buy-outs are both products of the Jeffrey Dahmer school of economics.

Deregulation is a peculiar phenomenon. Its most fervent proponents embrace it, not merely as an abstract economic theory, but with political, almost theological, devotion. Much as religion requires a theological leap of faith to prove the existence of heaven or hell, free market economics requires nearly a theological leap of faith to prove the existence of the nirvana of a perfectly competitive market. Irresponsibility becomes justifiable in a quest to achieve that greater truth found in textbook economics and achievable somewhere over the horizon, if only government would get out of the way. The shakeouts, bankruptcies, and displacements suffered are a small price to pay on the path to paradise.

No matter what evidence is adduced of widespread failure (and there is plenty), laissez faire economists tenaciously insist that such evidence can be reinterpreted as success. The free market, laissez faire movement has earned a special place in history. Not since the Bolshevik Revolution has the discipline of economics embraced an ideology with such passion.

Remarkable too is that laissez faire has become more than the conventional wisdom. It has become "economically correct" to spout free market theory, and wrong to challenge it. Somehow, with no one watching, the left asserted control of what is "politically correct," in an Orwellian fashion, while the right grabbed control of what is "economically correct," with self-righteous indignation, moral superiority, and contempt for those with an obviously wrong view and the audacity to express it. Both attempt to silence their opponents by challenging their motives or intelligence.

Nineteenth century market economics has been resurrected and embraced as truth. Part of the explanation for its domination rests in the aging of the New Deal era economists; part in the decision of corporate America to finance Washington-based laissez faire think tanks as effective propaganda ministries; part in the control of government ministries and their enormous resources to produce an endless stream of studies proving the irrefutable wisdom of laissez faire; and part in the lack of intellectual rigor that seems to characterize the generation that grew up on television.

ADDITIONAL DEREGULATION AS A CURE

The People Expresses, Air Floridas, and Midway Airlines disappear in droves. Nonetheless, the free marketers insist that there is still plenty of competition. Never mind that the major carriers tend to price in lock-step and that their number is rapidly dwindling. The crucial question is: To how few will the number of surviving airlines dwindle before these free market ideologues admit that deregulation was a failure? Four? Three? Two? No doubt, some would still insist that one airline would still provide plenty of competition, for we could always drive or walk to our destination, or call, fax, or write our business associates in distant cities.

Some free market ideologues claim that the only problem with deregulation is that we did not deregulate enough. Privatize the airports and let the foreign airlines in, and we will at last achieve textbook levels of perfect competition, and prosper in the land of laissez faire. Never mind that they have been promising us that for nearly 20 years.

One is reminded of the cover of a grocery store tabloid on which the slim and trim young blonde proclaims "I lost 85 pounds on an exclusive diet of hot fudge sundaes." Now I understand. The reason we do not lose weight is that we do not eat enough hot fudge sundaes. The cure for the problems caused by deregulation is more deregulation.

ANTITRUST AS A CURE

Other insist that deregulation would have worked if only we had enforced the antitrust laws. Antitrust is of limited utility under contemporary law, and a clumsy regulatory tool. But one thing is certain: had the antitrust laws been enforced to prohibit the airline mergers of the

1980s, the catastrophic economic condition of the airline industry would have been even worse. Allowing the carriers to merge postponed the day of reckoning and the economic catastrophe that hit the industry in the early 1990s.

Moreover, contemporary antitrust law fails to address several important competitive issues that regulation has and can: discrimination (Robinson Patman deals only with discrimination in the sale of goods, leaving services untouched), and predation (gutted by the U.S. Supreme Court decision in *Matsushita*), for example. Furthermore, antitrust litigation is a long and costly mechanism (vis-á-vis regulation). Although a treble damage reward lies at the end of the rainbow for a plaintiff with the tenaciousness and resources to pursue an antitrust remedy, few cases are pursued (private actions have a better chance if brought on the coat tails of a Justice Department civil or criminal action, in which Department of Justice has assembled the evidentiary record). Moreover, even in the rare instance in which private antitrust actions are filed, pursued, and won, the award of damages puts dollars in the pockets of the victorious plaintiffs, but fails to vindicate the interest of consumers in restoring the competition that was lost. For example, Sir Freddie Laker brought an antitrust action against several airlines and aircraft manufacturers for driving his company, Skytrain, out of business. The settlement put a few million dollars in Sir Freddie's wallet; but Skytrain never again flew the unfriendly skies of deregulation.

In contrast, regulatory remedies are usually imposed prospectively, before competitors are driven from the market in a predatory fashion, thereby protecting the interests of the competitors and consumers before injury occurs. On a challenge to predatory or discriminatory rates, for example, the tariffs containing them may be suspended before they go into effect. Thus, the prophylactic effects of regulation appears superior to antitrust.

Regulation has shown its proficiency in dealing with problems like discrimination and predation. Moreover, regulation, if done right, is far less consumptive of resources than is antitrust litigation in dealing with identical problems.

Antitrust also suffers from schizophrenia: each federal trial or appellate court has its own view of the proper geographic and product market, and what constitutes an attempt to monopolize, for example. After years and years of differing and conflicting views, the U.S. Supreme Court may occasionally sort it out. In the meantime, confusion abounds. In contrast, a regulatory agency, by being the premiere forum for the resolution of such questions, can lend a greater level of consistency to these questions.

Moreover still, regulation can tailor the antitrust and public interest issues in a way appropriate to the industry being regulated, taking into account that dry cleaners have different economic and social characteristics, and public policy dimensions, from airlines, for example. In contrast, antitrust law developed for mergers of shoe companies is deemed generically appropriate for any industry, irrespective of its differing economic, social, and public policy dimensions.

DIAGNOSING THE ILLNESS: AIRLINES

To use a medical analogy, one way of assessing deregulation is to diagnose the symptoms, identify the causes, and prescribe a cure. We will perform this succinctly for two major transportation industries: airlines, and motor carriers (the trucking and bus industries).

Illness: Economic Anemia

The airline industry has lost all the profit it earned since the Wright Brothers' flight at Kitty Hawk in 1903, plus $2 billion more. Debt to equity ratios are highly unsatisfactory, and the industry lacks sufficient resources to re-equip.

Cause: Destructive Competition. Some have falsely put the blame on the spike in fuel costs associated with Operation Desert Storm. Fuel prices in 1990–1991 were set at levels lower than in the early 1980s. The real cause appears to be pricing below costs, attributable to Chapter 11 carriers being shielded from their creditors (and thus able to price unrealistically), predatory motives by the megacarriers to drive weaker carriers into liquidation, and the fact that most costs for scheduled flights are fixed or semifixed, and the product is instantly perishable if not sold. Moreover, hub-and-spoke systems are cost-intensive, resulting in lower equipment and labor utilization and higher fuel burn than linear route systems. For example, only Southwest, which operates a linear system, is profitable these days. Furthermore, corporate raiders were allowed to load TWA, Eastern, Continental, and Northwest with debt.

Cure. The DOT could use its "fitness" jurisdiction to revoke or suspend the certificates of carriers in bankruptcy, and to disapprove further leveraged buy-outs. But this would further reduce the number of competitors. Another alternative would be to amend the Federal Aviation Act to regulate prices to eliminate pricing discrimination and raise the level of revenue above costs. Eliminating most pricing discrimination may diminish the incentive to continue inefficient hubbing.

Illness: Aging Aircraft and Erosion of the Safety Margin

The United States now flies the oldest and most repainted fleet of aircraft in the developed world. Weaker carriers may lack the resources to maintain aging aircraft properly.

Cause: Destructive Competition. This is described above.

Cure. Congress has mandated the elimination of stage two aircraft by the end of this decade. But that will not provide the capital to buy new planes, or retrofit old ones. Improving the economic health of the industry may require pricing regulation. Congress could pass tax incentives for new aircraft purchases. In the interim, the Federal Aviation Administration (FAA) must be vigilant in enforcing its safety regulations, and rehire Professional Air Traffic Controllers Organization's (PATCO) controllers to provide adequate personnel.

Illness: Concentration

The airline industry is now more highly concentrated than at any time in its history. Three major airlines (i.e., Continental, TWA, and America West) were in bankruptcy in early 1993.

Cause. There are several causes, including destructive competition, which have driven 150 airlines into bankruptcy and chilled the financial markets, as well as the rash of mergers approved by DOT in the mid-1980s. Other reasons are the inability of smaller carriers and new entrants to penetrate fortress hubs and slot-constrained airports, as well as the significant advantages large carriers have in terms of computerized reservations systems (CRS) and frequent flyer programs.

Cure. The DOT should never have promulgated the "buy-sell" airport slot rule, allowing the megacarriers to buy up the landing slots at our nation's busiest airports (i.e., Chicago's O'Hare, Washington's National, and New York's LaGuardia and Kennedy). These rules should be repealed. The DOT needs to issue meaningful rules to eliminate bias in the CRS and the onerous revenue transfers from weaker carriers to the megacarriers. Merger requirements should be tightened, as should the transfer of international routes. Statutory amendments to allow eminent domain seizure (at just compensation) of airport gates and slots would also open up the doors of entry. The FAA should spend the $15 billion airport trust fund on infrastructure expansion.

Illness: Pricing Discrimination

In most markets, pricing reflects market power, not costs. For example, passengers who begin or end their trips at fortress hubs, slot-constrained airports, or small communities pay much higher prices to cross-subsidize the competitive battles being waged for market dominance in the larger markets. Large businesses negotiate contract rates at levels significantly below those of small businesses, placing them at a disadvantage, despite the fact that the latter create 90 percent of America's jobs.

Cause. All regulation of domestic pricing was terminated in 1983.

Cure. A statutory amendment to the Federal Aviation Act to circumscribe pricing discrimination.

Illness: Foreign Ownership

This jeopardizes international competition, the integrity of negotiations with foreign governments, and national security, in terms of the loyalty of the Civil Reserve Air Fleet (CRAF) during war.

Cause. The DOT's lax application of the statutory provision prohibiting foreign control of U.S. airlines, and their weakened financial posture.

Cure. Responsible application of the foreign control prohibitions in the Federal Aviation Act.

Illness: False and Misleading Competitive Practices

These include misleading code-sharing, advertising, and scheduling.

Cause. The DOT's abdication of its responsibility under the Federal Aviation Act to prohibit "unfair or deceptive practices" or "unfair methods of competition."

Cure. The DOT should enforce the law to protect consumers.

Illness: Labor Inequity

This includes lost jobs and no retraining or relocation allowance.

Cause. The failure of the DOT to find workers entitled to the training and relocation allowances provided under the Airline Deregulation Act, and the failure of Congress to fund it. Also, the failure of DOT to include labor protective provisions in mergers and acquisitions agreements.

Cure. A more responsible DOT.

Another way of assessing deregulation is to ask what would have been different had the CAB not been sunset. One might argue that with deregulation we have replaced the five-member CAB with the four or five top commercial airline executives.

1. Would prices have fallen? Adjusted for inflation, prices were falling steadily every decade preceding deregulation. As technological advances increased productivity, cost savings were passed through to consumers. Although prices fell dramatically in the 1977–1979 period, adjusted for fuel costs and inflation, they fell at a 30 percent slower rate in the decade following deregulation than in the decade preceding it (Dempsey, 1990: 27–30).

Hubbing, the dominant megatrend on the deregulation landscape, caused a shift away from larger aircraft with their lower seat mile costs. Hubbing also increases fuel and labor consumption, while reducing equipment utilization. (It is telling that only Southwest Airlines, which operates a prederegulation linear route system, shows a profit.) Hubbing likely would not have occurred under regulation. Neither would the industry have been denied the resources to reequip with new aircraft. Productivity improvements likely would have driven prices downward.

2. Would the CAB have allowed the largest three airlines to dominate the three busiest airports in the nation (i.e., Chicago, Dallas, and Atlanta)? Never.

3. Would the CAB have given the largest airlines the lion's share of the scarce landing slots at the four slot constrained airports? No. Certainly, small airlines would have a significant presence under the CAB's tutelage.

4. Would the CAB have awarded the most important international routes to the three or four largest airlines? Absolutely not.

5. Would the industry be in such dire financial condition had the CAB been in business? Profits were hardly robust under the CAB's tutelage, but they turned sharply south after deregulation, falling 74 percent in deregulation's first decade to a paltry margin of 0.6 percent. To his credit, Alfred Kahn (1988: 248) admitted that "There is no denying that the profit record of the industry since 1978 has been dismal, that deregulation bears substantial responsibility, and that the proponents of deregulation did not anticipate such financial distress—either so intense or so long-continued." These words were written by Kahn in 1988, 4 years before the airline industry lost all the profit it had accumulated in its entire history.

Had deregulation not been embraced, the CAB would likely have used a variety of regulatory mechanisms to restore profitability, including outlawing corporate raids, conferring lucrative market opportunities upon weaker carriers, and prohibiting predatory practices. The only solution the DOT has identified as a means of shoring up the financial condition of the disintegrating airlines is foreign ownership. Since most foreign airlines are governmentally owned or subsidized, this effectively means a government bail-out, with the novel twist that we are going to use the tax dollars of foreign citizens to rectify the mistakes of U.S. government policy, without ever having to admit that deregulation was a mistake. It is paradoxical that foreign socialism has become the preferred means of rectifying free market failure.

6. Would the CAB have allowed the corporate raiding of the 1980s to saddle the industry with enormous debt? The CAB would likely have scrutinized the leveraged buy-outs (LBOs) of Frank Lorenzo at Continental and Eastern, Carl Icahn at TWA, and Alfred Checchi at Northwest carefully and concluded that they failed to satisfy the public interest and fitness standards of section 408 of the Federal Aviation Act.

Like deregulation, LBOs are a product of the excesses of the 1980s, both masterminded under the theology of laissez faire, the implicit thesis of which is that unconstrained human greed will produce a better society. Both converged on the airline industry to strip it of assets and resources. I challenge you to name a single company that is today stronger, has produced a new product, or is better able to compete in a global environment as a result of an LBO.

Another way to view the public interest in a market system is to defer to the system of private ownership by stockholders. These widely diversified companies are, after all, controlled by the public in the form of stockholders, are they not?

If stockholders controlled UAL, would it have paid its chief executive officer $18 million in a year when it was losing three times as much? Would it have turned down a bid for $260 a share (in 1993, it was selling for less than half that)? If stockholders controlled American, would it have failed to pay dividends since 1982? If stockholders controlled Continental, would it have proposed to wipe out all the value of their stock in reorganization? Not.

With the collapse of Marxism in Eastern Europe, no responsible advocate of improved public policy argues that government should apply command economy-type restrictions over price and supply. But some believe that the appropriate level of government oversight for this critical infrastructure industry lies somewhere between the regulatory regimen established for airlines in 1938 and the conventional wisdom of the laissez faire.

Tragically, Alfred Kahn was true to his promise. The eggs have been so scrambled that they can never be put together again. We can neither resurrect the proud airlines that have been lost nor rectify the emotional and economic damage needlessly inflicted upon hundreds of thousands of loyal employees who have lost their jobs, or investors and creditors who have been stiffed. Unless Congress acts quickly and meaningfully, it will forgo its last opportunity to preserve competition.

This is not to suggest that the CAB should be resurrected in its 1938 clothes to fit what went wrong. Regulatory reform in the mid-1970s was a prudent dose of course correction that the CAB clearly needed.

DIAGNOSING THE ILLNESS: MOTOR CARRIERS

Illness: Economic Anemia

Industry profitability, whether measured by return on equity or operating ratio, has suffered terribly since deregulation, with rates much worse than in manufacturing sectors, and causing more than 1,000 motor carrier bankruptcies each and every year since 1983. This is a failure rate unprecedented in American business history. Despite the argument that smaller and less efficient carriers have exited the market, the profit margin for the survivors remains inadequate.

Cause. Excessive capacity, caused by the Interstate Commerce Commission's (ICC's) liberal reading of the entry provisions of the Motor Carrier Act of 1980, as well as the oligopsony power of larger shippers to dictate noncompensatory rates, have caused destructive competition in the industry. Productivity has declined because of excess capacity.

Cure. A more responsible interpretation by the ICC of the entry and pricing discrimination provisions of the Interstate Commerce Act.

Illness: Pricing Discrimination

Because of their oligopsony market power, large shippers exact significant discounts off the full rate. Small shippers pay undiscounted prices, which have risen significantly under deregulation. This discrimination gives larger firms a unfair competitive advantage over smaller firms in the broader market for the sale of goods. Because small businesses create 90 percent of America's jobs, any economic policy that favors job creation must look unfavorably on pricing discrimination. Small communities are also disadvantaged.

Cure. A more responsible interpretation of the pricing discrimination prohibitions of the Interstate Commerce Act by the ICC. Also, the Rate Bureaus should be enlisted to assist the ICC in policing pricing discrimination.

Illness: Billions of Dollars in Freight Undercharges

Motor carrier bankruptcies have been robust under deregulation, and trustees in bankruptcy have sought to recover the difference between the filed (lawful) rate and the discounted rate actually charged to shippers.

Cause. The ICC's failure to require carriers to file their tariffs, despite the statutory mandate that they must.

Cure. A more responsible ICC dedicated to enforcing the filed rate and nondiscrimination provisions of the Interstate Commerce Act.

Illness: Declining Safety

Many studies have found a declining margin of safety under deregulation. This appears attributable to the fact that profitability in most companies turned south under deregulation. Wages have been cut, forcing drivers to drive more hours to earn the same pay. Maintenance has been cut at many firms, despite aging fleets.

Cause. Destructive competition, which produces inadequate profits, forcing carriers to cut costs ruthlessly.

Cure. Congress has passed several laws increasing safety enforcement, which attack the symptoms rather than the illness. The ICC must restrain pricing discrimination and tighten entry. Also, a statute might be passed making shippers liable for accidents in circumstances in which they knew or should have known that the rates were inadequate for the carrier to maintain its equipment properly.

Illness: Concentration

The high failure rate is resulting in an industry increasingly dominated by large firms.

Cause. Destructive competition, described above, coupled with economies of scale, particularly in the less-than-truckload (LTL) general freight sector.

Cure. A more responsible ICC, dedicated to enforcing the entry and rate provisions of the Interstate Commerce Act.

Illness: A Highly Politicized Interstate Commerce Commission

Cause. Past presidential appointments of laissez faire ideologues to the Commission, as well as Reorganization Plan No. 1 of 1969, which gave the president the power to designate which commissioner shall be chairman.

Cure. Appointment of more moderate and responsible commissioners, and repeal of Reorganization Plan No. 1, which would strengthen the ICC's political autonomy.

TOWARD A NEW THEORY OF ECONOMIC REGULATION

A nation's government is inextricably intertwined with its economy. Neither trade nor, indeed, civilization can proceed without government. In modern Western nations, government guarantees property rights, provides standards of fair trade, a forum for peaceful resolution of disputes, and currency as a medium of exchange. These are essential if commerce is to flow freely. Prospects for economic growth are dim in a state of chaos and anarchy. Order and predictability are required: sheriffs and marshalls are necessary to enforce legal rights and responsibilities. Even private consensual ordering via contract and property transactions requires government and its law as a means of dispute resolution. Thus, government's participation in the economy is inevitable.

In modern nations, the fundamental question is not whether government will participate, but to what extent it will participate. Hence, governmental participation is a matter of degree. How shall a nation allocate decisional responsibility between private entrepreneurs and government over such matters as the price, quantity, and quality of goods produced, and the relationship between producers, on the one hand, and consumers, employees and the general public, on the other?

In socialist economies, the government itself owns the means of production and allocates resources by dictating the level of production, which goods will be produced, and at what price. This is an extremely difficult task, and several European communist nations appear to be abandoning it as costly, inefficient, and wasteful. In capitalist nations, most of these decisions are made by private entrepreneurs, driven by a profit motive to invest their own capital into privately owned and operated enterprises.

Profit is a two-edged sword. On the one hand, it serves as an effective stimulant for efficiency, productivity, and responsiveness to consumers, who cast votes of approval in the form of currency in favor of those entrepreneurs who best satisfy their desires. The lure of profit encourages producers to trim costs and satisfy consumers' tastes and preferences. In a fully competitive environment, consumers receive the goods and services they want at the lowest cost to society for their production: something economists describe as "allocative efficiency."

On the other hand, profit also inspires greed, producing the classic Scrooge, the miser who will do anything to maximize his personal wealth: pay workers slave wages and subject them to dangerous working conditions, pollute the air and the water with carcinogens, ruthlessly subvert competitors and competition, satisfy the public's hedonistic desire for sex and drugs, or take candy from a baby's mouth, for example—all for the lust of wealth.

Many of these results are deemed undesirable by modern societies. So in capitalist nations, government is employed in a somewhat schizophrenic capacity: as a means of facilitating the attributes of freedom in a market, while circumscribing those noxious results of too free a market. Government intrudes both to facilitate the cornucopia of goods and services private ownership can bring and to protect the public against harm.

Again, drawing the line becomes a problem. Which things ought to be encouraged in a market, and which discouraged? In democratic nations, these decisions are left to elected representatives, who draw lines, generally reflecting the will of the people, in laws that define the metes and bounds of acceptable behavior.

Free market economists argue that the lines should be drawn in a way that attempts to create perfect competition, which will achieve "allocative efficiency." While perfect competition exists in economic models, it rarely exists in the real world. As economist Dabney Waring (1984) notes:

> According to theory, the market is self-correcting—demand adjusting the amount of supply to produce equilibrium. This, however, is a theory which can be demonstrated only in the laboratory. If there is any impurity in the real arena, the formulae break down. Unfortunately, impurities are not merely a possibility, they are a certainty. The free market extremists fail to perceive the noneconomic forces which abound: political forces, social

forces, as well as the impossibility of manifesting an industry with the requisite characteristics of perfect competition.

Even in textbooks of economics, the theory of perfect competition requires some rather strict assumptions—for example, that pre-existing or resulting distributions of wealth are irrelevant, that consumers have perfect information, that they and producers behavior rationally, and that no single producer has "market power" (the ability to increase profits by unilaterally constricting production or raising price) (Dempsey, 1989: 11). Since these things often do not exist, government becomes involved to correct for "market failure," trying to encourage fair competition. Antitrust laws are an example of governmental intervention designed to punish efforts to diminish competition.

But even if perfect competition could be achieved, economic goals are not the only goals of a nation. A nation is a political body, and sometimes it chooses to achieve social goals that may even diminish efficiency in the distribution of its resources. For example, it may decide to transfer wealth to the elderly or the poor, even though they are unproductive.

The choice among economic and social goals is a difficult one, and is further complicated by the wide variety of means available to achieve such goals once identified. Government can attempt to (1) completely ban the enterprise (illicit drugs and prostitution, for example); (2) own and operate the industry (public education and the postal system, for example); (3) regulate levels of pricing and service (electricity and telephones, for example); (4) regulate industry standards and qualifications (the legal and medical professions, or cigarette advertising, for example); (5) sanction undesirable behavior through the judiciary (antitrust and punitive damages for product liability, for example); (6) tax and spend (high taxes on alcohol, and subsidies for low-income housing, for example).

What is this thing, regulation, which had become such a monster that its eradication was pursued with such triumphant zeal? Regulation involves government oversight. In effect, and in a general sense, the government looks over the shoulder of the private entrepreneur and says "You have an obligation to serve the public interest. You shall neither exploit nor harm your consumers, your workers, or others. You are entitled to make a fair profit, and no more. But you must also serve the public interest."

And what is the public interest? It is the interest of all who are affected by the industry—consumers, shippers, consignees, stockholders, passengers, highway motorists, managers and employers, large and small, urban and rural—to enjoy safe, adequate and dependable service at a reasonable price . . . to be treated fairly. It is also the national interest in such things as ubiquitous service and national defense.

Regulation is as old as the republic. Early on, the nation imposed tariffs on foreign imports and set standards of weights and measurements. The modern age of regulation is commonly thought to have begun in 1887 with the creation of the Interstate Commerce Commission (the nation's first independent regulatory agency) to regulate the most important infrastructure industry of the era: the railroads. Antitrust law (in effect, a regulatory enterprise employing different means) followed shortly thereafter, with the promulgation of the Sherman Act of 1890 and the Clayton Act of 1914.

A major growth of regulation occurred during the 1930s, in response to the economic collapse created by what then was perceived to be too free a market. During the New Deal, a number of additional regulatory agencies were created to regulate industries and enterprises important to the nation's economy, including the Federal Communications Commission, the Securities and Exchange Commission, the Federal Power Commission, the National Labor

Relations Board, and the Civil Aeronautics Board. The U.S. Supreme Court (1934) expressed the tenor of the times:

> [There] has been a growing appreciation of public needs and of the necessity of finding ground for a rational compromise between individual rights and public welfare. The settlement and consequent contraction of the public domain, the pressure of a constantly increasing density of population, the interrelation of the activities of our people and the complexity of our economic interests, have inevitably led to an increased use of the organization of society in order to protect the very bases of individual opportunity. Where, in earlier days, it was thought that only the concerns of individuals or of classes were involved, and that those of the State itself were touched only remotely, it has later been found that the fundamental interests of the State are directly affected; and that the question is no longer merely that of one party to a contract as against another, but of the use of reasonable means to safeguard the economic structure upon with the good of all depends.

The next major wave of regulation occurred during the 1960s and it took a different form, focusing on such problems as the environment, safety, health, and consumer protection.

These instances of growing government reflect an evolution in the national psychology: communitarian values came to supplant a traditional individualistic or more libertarian ideology. As noted above, it came to be recognized that in a crowded, interrelated society, the actions of individuals affect us all. It was the public interest that regulation was created to satisfy.

As noted above, government as a participant in economic decision-making has come in for a rhetorical savaging during the past decade, in a political movement that saw most restraints on economic freedom as a nuisance at best, and wasteful and unnecessary at worst. The political creed of "deregulation" became the ideological centerpiece of an economic policy that had laissez faire as its foundation.

In the 1970s, inflation drove many to complain about the aggregate drag on the economy provided by comprehensive governmental oversight. American business objected to the Kafkaesque metamorphosis of government into a grotesque creature it did not understand. Presidents Ford, Carter, Reagan, and Bush pursued an aggressive policy to eradicate regulation. In one instance, Congress abolished a regulatory agency (the Civil Aeronautics Board), and sowed the ground with salt.

In part, the new wave of individualism is a response to regulatory failure: the perceived inefficiency and waste engendered by an unresponsive and lethargic government bureaucracy. But it also reflects a more deep-seated ideological notion of individual freedom, which is at the root of the American experiment in liberty.

The trouble is, we cannot do without government. Someone must pave the roads, deliver the mail, and protect the borders. Collectively, we can do things we cannot do individually, like maintain parks in cities, and educate all our children. So again, it is not a question of whether we will have a government, but one of how much government we shall have, and what it shall do.

In a homogeneous society, such as many of the nations of Europe, communitarian values find less resistance. There is a collective public consciousness and responsibility in these nations by those who have to assist those who do not, for they are alike in race, religion, and culture. But in a heterogeneous society, such as the Untied States, those in need are not like those who are not; hence, there is perhaps more resistance to communitarian values here than abroad.

The pendulum on things political, legal, and economic tends to swing as popular opinion evolves. Just as regulatory failure brought cries for deregulation, market failure will inevitably bring demands for reregulation (Dempsey, 1989: 10–14). The excesses of one generation becomes the catalysts for reform of the next.

Indeed, that trend already appears to be emerging. Fresh with indigestion due to a myriad of problems, Congress has recently considered bills proposing reregulation of various aspects of the cable television, railroad, airline, telephone, savings and loan, and broadcasting industries. Many politicians have expunged "deregulation" from their campaign speeches as the dreaded "D" word.

Thus, among the most important issues facing our government is what shall be the proper relationship between government and our economy, and how can government achieve desirable social and economic goals most efficiently and at least cost. How can we tailor the governmental solution to our economic and social problems without making things, on balance, worse than they were before government intervened? It is the position of the author that neither extreme of rigid governmental supervision nor laissez faire is realistic or responsible. With that as a starting point, let us examine the origins of economic regulation of the motor carrier industry.

Problems of destructive competition in the motor carrier and airline industries, seemingly endless bankruptcies, and the deterioration of wages, working conditions, and safety they created gave birth to economic regulation in the 1930s. As this author has noted elsewhere:

> During the Great Depression, the motor carrier industry was plagued with an oversupply of transportation facilities. Intensive competition among truckers suppressed freight rates excessively and caused hundreds of bankruptcies. Entry into the industry was easy. The ranks of the unemployed provided an endless pool of drivers; with a drivers' license and a used truck they could haul goods for hire. Not knowing what their costs were, or victimized by shippers with greater market power, they frequently took traffic at below-cost rates. They drove for gas money, or to cover their monthly payments on the truck, and kept rolling until needed repairs brought the trucks to a halt. Soon they were bankrupt, while their truck was patched up and sold to yet another entrant and the cycle repeated itself. All the while, efficient and productive trucking companies and railroads were also hemorrhaging dollars (Dempsey, 1989: 16–17).

Even before the Great Depression, as early as 1926, the U.S. Department of Agriculture issued a report concluding that entry and rate stabilization of highway transport would be beneficial to prevent overexpansion (Jackman, 1935: 847). Beginning that year, Congress in each session considered bills for economic regulation of the motor carrier industry.

Several economists of the day also advocated the need for economic regulation. In 1928, at a meeting of the American Economic Association, William M. Duffus declared, "Most students of transportation will agree, I think . . . that there must be some sort of central planning looking toward the coordination of our various transportation agencies on a sound economic and financial basis"; Henry R. Trumbower argued that rail and motor carriage "should be regarded as a regulated monopoly" (Anderson and Felton, 1989: 7).

Other economists agreed. Shan Szto condemned excessive competition as of "no benefit to anyone," making the industry "unattractive to reasonable business people" (Anderson and Felton, 1989: 7). Harold G. Moulton and his Brookings Institution associates criticized the waste and instability created by excessive competition and urged comprehensive coordination of transportation (Anderson and Felton, 1989: 8). D. Philip Lockin summarized the inherent characteristics that warranted economic regulation:

> The ruinous type of competition does develop; discrimination in rates does appear; the condition of overcapacity does not correct itself automatically; and the struggle for survival

> in the face of inadequate revenues leads to deterioration of safety standards, evasion of safety regulations, financial irresponsibility and generally unsatisfactory service (Anderson and Felton, 1989: 8).

Professor Paul Kauper noted that

> The present demoralization of interstate motor transportation, due to unsound competitive practices, and the menace of much unrestrained competition to the detriment of the integrity of the national transportation system as a whole, creates problems that call imperatively for federal legislation (Kauper, 1933: 1111).

The Great Depression exacerbated the problems that had surfaced in transportation. In 1933, the Interstate Commerce Commission concluded that the ease of entry and the inadequate knowledge by unsophisticated entrepreneurs of their costs "condemned the industry to chronic instability and excessive competition" (Anderson and Felton, 1989: 5). Specifically, the ICC found that rate instability resulted in "widespread and unjust discrimination between shippers . . . the loss of much capital invested . . . a tendency to break down wages and conditions of employment . . . [and an] [i]ncrease in the hazard of use of the highways" (Anderson and Felton, 1989: 5). Two years later, the federal coordinator of transportation, Joseph B. Eastman, expressed even greater concern over the economic chaos plaguing the industry caused by unlimited entry and exacerbated by the Great Depression (Anderson and Felton, 1989: 5). Note the striking similarity between these economic conditions that preceded deregulation and the empirical results of deregulation, summarized above.

In promulgating the Motor Carrier Act of 1935, which gave the Interstate Commerce Commission entry and rate regulatory jurisdiction over trucking and bus companies, the 74th Congress concluded:

> Motor carriers . . . are engaged in intensive competition with each other and with railroads and water carriers. This competition has been carried to an extreme which tends to undermine the financial stability of the carriers and jeopardizes the maintenance of transportation facilities and service appropriate to the needs of commerce and required in the public interest. The present chaotic transportation conditions are not satisfactory to investors, labor, shippers, or the carriers themselves. . . .
>
> The ultimate objective of [the Motor Carrier Act of 1935] is a system of coordinated transportation for the Nation which will supply the most efficient means of transport and furnish service as cheaply as is consistent with fair treatment of labor and with earnings which will support adequate credit and the ability to expand as need develops and to take advantage of all improvements in the art. All parts of such a system of transportation should be in the hands of reliable and responsible operators whose charges for service will be known, dependable, and reasonable and free from unjust discrimination (U.S. Senate, 1935).

In the eyes of the early advocates of regulation, transportation was particularly prone to alternating periods of destructive competition and monopoly or oligopoly. Because of the tremendous economies of scale along many different dimensions exhibited by much of the transport sector, the out-of-pocket or marginal cost of providing service tends to lie far below its full or average cost. Moreover, transportation firms sell what is, in essence, in the nature of an instantly perishable commodity. Once the truck leaves its terminal or the aircraft pulls back from its gate, any unused space is lost forever. It cannot be warehoused and sold another day as could, say, canned beans.

Alfred Kahn once remarked that he could see no difference between transportation firms and grocery stores. Imagine a grocer who was selling commodities that had the spoilage properties of open jars of unrefrigerated mayonnaise. He would be forced to have a "fire sale" every afternoon in order to rid himself of unsold inventory, since it could not be warehoused and sold another day.

So it is with transportation capacity. Unlimited entry creates excessive capacity, which, in turn, creates destructive competition and economic anemia. Hence, unconstrained competition in these circumstances tends to drive the price down towards marginal cost, causing profits to disappear. Bankruptcies and mergers ensue as excess capacity is weeded out, and a profitable monopoly or oligopoly inexorably emerges. The restoration of market power may well be accomplished by a blatantly discriminatory rate structure with price differences between markets reflecting not relative costs but the differing degree of competition.

In the view of the early advocates of regulation these two phenomena—destructive competition and powerful monopolies—were simply two sides of the same coin. The purpose of regulation, under these circumstances, was to eliminate this Hobson's choice for consumers: preventing the potential threats to safety, service, and investment posed by destructive competition on the one hand, and the price-gouging and price discrimination associated with market power in a consolidated industry, on the other (Dempsey, 1990: 4). A healthy competitive environment was envisioned, with government protecting the public interest by establishing the perimeters of lawful behavior.

In addition to the discriminatory pricing that deregulation has unleashed, declining productivity engendered by excessive capacity appears also to have caused destructive competition between the motor and air carriers themselves (Murray, 1982). And it is worse for motor carriers than it is for the other modes of transport.

Railroads and airlines have significant advantages that motor carriers do not. True, all sell an instantly perishable product, and the short-term marginal costs of production are nil (adding an extra passenger to a scheduled flight costs the airline only a few additional drops of fuel and another cardboard meal). Yet (like telephone, electricity, and gas distribution companies) railroads and airlines can control a bottleneck (monopoly rail lines or airport infrastructure, respectively) and therefore exert market power to raise prices or reduce service levels to maximize profit. Thus, air fares for passengers who begin or end their trips at a concentrated hub airport are 27 percent more expensive than for passengers who do not. Electric utilities claim that their rail rates for coal from monopoly railroads are exorbitant.

In contrast, while a motor carrier can build a terminal facility that it operates exclusively, a competitor can builds its terminal facility across the street. Thus, until the trucking industry becomes very highly concentrated, there will be relatively and significantly less opportunity to enjoy market power compared with the other modes, for truckers control no equivalent bottleneck.

Second, airlines can, by lowering prices, tap the elasticities of demand to stimulate new business. Lower prices can lure the discretionary traveler to fill a seat that might otherwise go empty. A $99 fare will fill planes with throngs of passengers off to Disney World who might not otherwise make the trip. In contrast, trucking companies cannot, by lowering prices, appreciably increase the volume of freight shipped, since transportation rates are too small a percentage of the total cost of most products to stimulate additional demand. Certainly trucking companies can steal freight away from competing motor carriers, or from railroads, by lowering prices. But the aggregate volume of freight shipped will not grow appreciably.

Third, motor carriers are subservient to the whims of large shippers who, by threatening to withhold their vast volumes of freight, can unilaterally dictate rates far below the carriers' average costs. In order to survive, the carrier must cover its fixed costs by charging discriminatory prices: significantly higher rates charged to smaller and rural shippers.

Motor carriers have only a couple of shields from the ravages of destructive competition. First, an overwhelming number of states have rejected the federal experiment in motor carrier deregulation, and continue to regulate intrastate trucking. Second, the antitrust immunity accorded to rate bureaus allows some rationality in the rate structure. But, incredibly, the U.S. Department of Transportation would like to do away with both.

Other industries sell services that are in the nature of instantly perishable commodities, that have de minimus short-term marginal costs: hotels, movie theaters, bowling alleys, to name a few. Most can avoid destructive competition by making up fixed costs on auxiliary products and services. For example, popcorn and soft drink concessions are the real profit centers for the oligopoly theaters (they lose money or break even on admissions), and these are monopoly concessions for moviegoers in the theater. Hotels earn significant income from restaurants, room service, and leased space for shops in the lobby, and can differentiate their products based on location and class of service. Transportation firms have only two major variables with which to differentiate their product—speed and price—and have no auxiliary monopoly opportunities with which to make up fixed costs.

Moreover, transportation is even more prone to instant perishability than are hotel rooms or bowling alleys. Empty hotel rooms and unused bowling alleys can be sold 10 minutes or several hours later. In contrast, once the truck leaves its terminal, the aircraft pulls away from its gate, or the train pulls its cars away from its siding, any empty space is lost forever.

Moreover, and more importantly, we do not care whether movie theaters become an oligopoly charging exorbitant or highly discriminatory prices, since we can stay home and watch television, or rent a movie for our VCR, or read a good book, or do a thousand different things with our leisure time. The numerous alternatives of leisure keep pricing in check.

But transportation is a *necessity*. It is the circulatory system of the nation—the veins and arteries through which commerce flows—and an important facilitator of communications. We *must* get our goods to market, and too often, we *must* travel to business meetings (teleconferencing has made only a small dent in this market). Although discretionary airline travel is sometimes attractively priced (reflecting the varied alternatives to vacation time, including driving the station wagon to Lake Wobegon with the kids), business travel is not, and both are often restricted in onerous ways. If these markets are distorted by highly imperfect competition, we suffer distortions in other markets that depend upon them. Other businesses are adversely affected, and the ripple effect of distortion is pernicious.

Various sectors of the economy and various regions of the nation can be adversely affected by the aggregate impact of pricing and service discrimination. We depend upon the transportation network to allow us to exchange goods between all regions. This advances several economic and social goals, like promoting a geographic dispersal of population, avoiding the ills of overcrowding, allowing economic and social diversity and pluralism, expanding the production and consumption market, as well as promoting a geographic distribution of wealth.

Like telephone services, gas, and electricity, access to the transportation infrastructure is a necessity for the public and, hence, in the nature of a public utility. None of the transportation firms individually are public utilities, but the national transportation *system* is at least a quasipublic utility. The system is the fabric that binds the nation together, and regulation is the glue that holds the system together. Prudently administered economic regulation ensures that the national transportation system does not disintegrate into its antagonistic parts, and that individual firms cooperate to provide service that, from the perspective of the individual user, works effortlessly. (Conversely, deregulation has deleterious systemic effects in rating a flock of transportation firms competing to the death rather than cooperating to ensure that operations flow smoothly).

Service must be ubiquitously available at an adequate level and a fair price or the public will suffer. The process of production is not complete until goods are in the hands of consumers. Just as a clogged artery can halt the flow of blood and seriously damage a body organ, a constipated transportation (or energy or communications) system will cause industrial organization to collapse. The infrastructure industries affect consumers and the economy in a way that bowling alleys do not.

While economists insist that only natural monopolies should be regulated, they ignore the necessity feature of the infrastructure industries. Moreover, all the infrastructure industries, including transportation firms, do tend toward concentration in reaction to destructive competition.

Furthermore, we can regulate transportation firms with clear conscience because they consume a public resource. Airports and airways and highways belong to the public. Our tax dollars built them, paved them, and maintain them. Even the early railroads were given public land on which to build, and even those that were not have used the government power of eminent domain to obtain their rights of way. Our taxes built the public infrastructure, and therefore, we have a right to exact a quid pro quo from the private firms that use them: that these public resources be used in the *public* interest. If we had laid the wood for bowling alleys, perhaps we could justify their regulation (although again, we need not: they are not a necessity, other sectors of the economy do not depend upon them, and alternatives keep pricing in check).

We can legitimately insist that transportation firms satisfy the public need for ubiquitous service at a fair price, that the service not endanger public safety (we have a right not to be killed by the trucks with which we share the highways), and that they will serve the needs of national defense.

Prudently administered economic regulation can accomplish both economic and social goals deemed to be in the highest public interest. Among the economic goals are the prevention of distortions created by imperfect competition. Regulation can avoid the regressive wealth transfers created by market power, including the monopsony power of large shippers unilaterally to dictate rates that are noncompensatory. Regulation can also ameliorate the market power of large carriers, preventing them from charging excessively high rates to small shippers and undercutting their competing carriers.

Regulation can also avoid the problem of externalities, which manifests itself in the impact of inadequate profits upon highway safety, and the discriminatory pricing and service provided to small communities. Shippers have a strong incentive to keep their private fleets of trucks repaired and driven by well-trained drivers, since the tort system will hold them accountable for any innocent third parties injured or killed because of their negligence. In contrast, shippers can use unsafe common carriers with virtual impunity. They therefore have an economic incentive to shave the common carriers' profit margin to the bone, since their is no piercing of the corporate veil to hold shippers accountable for their ruthless greed, so to speak. Because the common carrier or its insurer pays for injury to innocent automobile drivers, the shipper can externalize the cost of unsafe transportation.

Of course, some injured parties find the carrier in bankruptcy, or without insurance, and are never compensated. And however well money can ease pain, it often fails to restore health, and almost never restores life. Thus, exerting monopsony power to shave the common carrier's rate below compensatory levels can be economically rational for the shipper, while causing an undesirable externalized costs on society in terms of deteriorating safety and loss of human life.

Regulation can not only ameliorate the problem of externalities it can also accomplish a number of important social goals. It can engender a regime of cross-subsidization that provides for equality of access to all shippers and to all communities, large and small. Regulation can create a geographic distribution of opportunity for economic growth spread over a larger and more diverse group of participants, thereby enhancing pluralism. It can ensure that small and remote users enjoy the same access to the broader market for the sale of goods as do large firms, thereby enhancing competition in that broader market for the sale of goods (Dempsey, 1989).

Dabney Waring, Jr. (1984: 242) eloquently summarized the appropriate role of government in the market with respect to motor carrier transportation:

> Government has responsibilities, principal among which is maintaining the infrastructure of essential services necessary for the commerce and amenities of a civilized nation. Certainly the government would be a poor manager of the motor carrier industry or of any business. But is not management of the motor carriers which is at issue. It is the metes and bounds, parameters, if you will, of performance. It is requiring that carriers fulfill their common carrier obligation; of seeing that service is not abandoned when there is not a viable alternative; of monitoring service offerings to see that capacity is not so far in excess of demand that gross waste results; of opening entry selectively to assure adequate numbers of carriers; of preventing any semblance of predatory pricing; of forbidding exploitation of market dominance situations be they in the area of geography, commodity, size of a shipment, or whatever. Such regulation, however, should leave a significant latitude for managerial discretion in pricing, service options, and operational decisions.

LEGISLATIVE REMEDIES

Congress has several bills before it to deal with such problems as computer reservations systems and slot-constrained airports. The patient is flat on his back hemorrhaging unmercifully, and Congress is offering a couple of aspirin and a glass of water. The disease is deregulation, and the patient desperately needs to be moved to the operating room.

If Congress does nothing, we will likely see an airline industry more highly concentrated than it now is. Because airline managers are rational wealth maximizers, prices will rise and grow even more obscenely discriminatory.

Transportation, like many public utilities, is a necessity. Distortions in its service and the extraction of monopoly rents cannot long be tolerated. Air transport is too critical to the productivity of the economy and the well-being of our citizens to abandon it to a handful of airline chief executive officers sitting around a Monopoly board. Eventually, Congress could be faced with the prospect of introducing public utility regulation to the few surviving firms or, failing that, nationalizing the industry. Regulated competition is preferable to regulated monopoly; regulated monopoly is preferable to nationalization; nationalization is preferable to unregulated monopoly.

Neither of the extremes of nationalization nor the contemporary environment of economic anarchy and market Darwinism are desirable. Public policy in this essential infrastructure industry would best be enhanced by preserving the level of competition that now exists and imposing light-handed regulation upon it, while there is still competition to preserve. How might that be accomplished?

Let us first review the goals that should be promoted by government in aviation.

The most pressing priority is to preserve the level of competition that now exists: to create a more profitable, stable economic environment to avoid additional bankruptcies, and eventually to encourage new entrants to emerge and survive. No more LBOs should be allowed; and those airlines that have suffered from them should be forcibly weaned from debt.

The industry's financial health must improve if airlines are to have the capital to re-equip with new aircraft.

Passengers should be shielded from monopoly exploitation. Equity demands some rationalization of pricing.

The high cost hub-and-spoke phenomenon, with its concomitant higher fuel and labor costs, congestion, and drag on travel time should be re-evaluated.

Consumer abuses must be controlled.

Safety must be vigorously guarded.

Let us examine what new legislation might contain to accomplish these objectives.

Indirect Subsidies

Recognizing the importance of transportation to commerce, communications, and national defense, Congress in earlier periods of American history appropriated direct federal subsidies to bail out transportation firms such as Conrail, Chrysler, Lockheed, and Amtrak. But the contemporary realities of a $3 trillion federal debt preclude direct subsidies to ameliorate the contemporary crisis in the transportation industry.

Nonetheless, weaker carriers, new entrants, and carriers that can best enhance the competitive environment ought to be favored as the government distributes the tremendously valuable public resources in the form of postal subsidies, international routes, and landing slots. However, these franchises ought not be allowed to be sold for profit, since they generally end up in the hands of the megacarriers when sold. They are public resources and should be used for the public good. They should be issued on a limited-term basis, and awarded to whichever carrier fulfills public needs best at their expiration or upon their surrender.

Nonstop Route Certificate

Hubbing-and-spoking, the dominant megatrend on the deregulation landscape, is choking the air transport system, causing flight schedules to regress to the piston and propeller era, and burning fuel unmercifully. New nonstop service overflying hubs might be inaugurated if airlines could be given an exclusive franchise to serve the market for, say, 3 to five years. A franchise to serve any city-pair not now receiving nonstop service ought to be available to an airline promising to provide at least one round-trip a day. If necessary, designated carriers would receive access to congested airport gates and slots, perhaps through use of federal eminent domain power, to condemn the necessary property at fair market value and sell it to the franchisee. Preference would again be given to weak airlines, new entrants, and carriers best able to enhance competition. To protect consumers, average yields in the market could be no higher than industry average yields for similar stage lengths.

Pricing Discrimination; Ceilings and Floors

As a general rule, the government should stay out of the business of setting fares where sufficient competition exists to discipline airlines. It could designate some appropriate measure of competition at airports or in city-pair markets (say, some appropriate point on the Herfindahl-Hirshman index), and in those markets that are sufficiently competitive, let airlines price as they will.

Carriers should be prohibited from extracting monopoly or oligopoly rents in markets where they enjoy market power. They should also be stopped from driving smaller carriers out by predatory pricing and other predatory behavior. Average fares per mile in any noncompetitive market should not exceed, say, 15 percent of industry average fares for similar stage lengths, unless the airline can show good cause why they should, usually in the form of extraordinary costs attributable to serving the market in question, or low demand. As to predatory conduct, a smaller aggrieved airline should be able to object to a larger competitor's price or service war poised to drive it out.

Pricing discrimination is another significant problem. The discounts offered to large corporations should probably be eliminated, since they distort pricing for small businesses. Since small businesses create 90 percent of America's jobs, they should not be burdened with excessively high air fares that jeopardize their ability to get their sales forces out to market their products.

Airline Agreements

Much could be done to alleviate congestion and excessive capacity problems by allowing airlines to sit down and discuss solutions. Cooperation between airlines can sometimes reduce industry costs while providing better service to the public. The government should, of course, monitor such discussions to protect consumers and other airlines from anticompetitive behavior. Antitrust immunity should be conferred for those arrangements that serve the public interest by better rationalizing the air transport system. This could help to alleviate wasted capacity, ease airport congestion and delays, reduce fuel consumption, and improve the economic health of airlines.

Airline Mergers and Acquisitions

Anticompetitive mergers and undercapitalized acquisitions should be prohibited.

Consumer Protection

Something must be done about the myriad of abusive practices such "bait and switch" advertising, unrealistic scheduling, deliberate overbooking, nonrefundable tickets, misleading code-sharing and change-of-gauge, and demand-based flight cancellations. Congress should adopt a code of fair competitive practices defining what is not permitted and providing penalties for violations. As an alternative, Congress could eliminate federal pre-emption over such questions, letting the state Attorneys-General loose.

Airport Regulation

Airports are public resources. Federal pre-emption of noise and other environmental issues might well enable the needed additional infrastructure development. Higher peak period landing feeds could flatten congestion. The government should also have eminent domain power to seize gates or slots at congested airports, for just compensation, and sell them to airlines best able to enhance competition goals.

Financial Fitness

The DOT had ample jurisdiction to prevent the airlines from being loaded with onerous debt or stripped or assets in leveraged buy-outs. It chose to do nothing while our airline industry was crippled. Congress should pass legislation prohibiting any future LBO of an airline, force existing owners to wean them of debt over a period of time, and prohibit public assets (such as international routes, landing slots and gates) from being sold off to enhance the personal wealth of corporate raiders. Fitness security should be exerted against any airline entering bankruptcy, or with an excessively aging or inadequately maintained fleet.

Foreign Alliances

Foreign ownership tends to reduce competition in international markets and endangers national security. As Operation Desert Storm revealed, we need a loyal Civil Reserve Aviation Fleet to ferry U.S. soldiers and their supplies to distant battlefields during times of crisis. Stricter limitations should be placed on foreign equity ownership of U.S. airlines. Also, again for national security reasons, cabotage restrictions should be retained.

U.S. Transportation Commission (or Court)

During the past decade, the DOT has shown little enthusiasm for protecting the public interest or performing its statutory obligations in a responsible way. That is because the DOT is an executive branch agency, with policy dictated by the White House. Yet Article I, section 8 of the U.S. Constitution vests in *Congress* the power to regulate interstate and foreign commerce. Hence, regulatory power over transportation should be extricated from the executive branch and vested in an independent agency.

Three alternatives come to mind. One is to split off the Federal Aviation Administration from DOT, making it an independent agency and enhancing its jurisdiction over economic matters. Another is to strip the economic regulation functions from DOT and consolidate them with the jurisdiction now held by the Interstate Commerce Commission and the Federal Maritime Commission into a new U.S. Transportation Commission, with broad jurisdiction over all modes of transport (after all, transportation is increasingly multimodal). The advantage of this approach is that we would eliminate a couple of existing agencies, allowing the survivor to coordinate intermodal transportation in a rational way. The third alternative would be to create a U.S. Transportation Court with appellate jurisdiction over the existing agencies and, it is hoped, power to promulgate substantive rules.

Under any of these alternatives, the agency (or court) should be headed by a collegial body of, say, seven or nine commissioners (or judges) having long but nonrewardable terms of office and appointed in a manner similar to the governing members of the Federal Reserve Board, an agency that performs major economic policy functions with relatively less political degeneration than most other federal agencies. Nonrenewability is important so that these individual do not have to look to the White House for a job at the end of their terms. They should also be prohibited from taking employment with any industry they regulated after leaving the commission (or court). Autonomy, responsibility, and fair-mindedness are essential to good government.

The American taxpayer owns the airports, runways, gates, radar, and communications facilities that make up our air transport system. The replacement value of that publicly owned system has conservatively been estimated to be worth $1 trillion. All the major airlines could be purchased on Wall Street for less than $15 billion, or about 1.5 percent of the value of the public investment. Yet under deregulation, that 1.5 percent drives the 85%. Under deregulation, we have turned over publicly owned bottleneck facilities in an essential infrastructure industry to a handful of chief airline officers sitting around a Monopoly board, playing their own game with the nation's mobility. Regulation may be the only means of enhancing competition.

The cyclical view of history posits that events repeat themselves. In the nineteenth century, a few railroad robber barons so dominated American transportation that Congress was compelled to regulate the industry to protect the public interest. In 1938, Colonel Edgar S. Gorrell, president of the Air Transport Association, successfully urged Congress to regulate the airline industry, saying:

> Since air transport was launched into meteroic growth, approximately $120,000,000 of private capital has been devoted to it, but, of that sum, there remains today scarcely 50 percent. Since the beginning of air transport, a hundred scheduled lines have traversed the airways in a struggle to build this newest avenue of the sky. But today scarcely more than a score of those companies remain. The industry has been reduced to the very rock bottom of its financial resources. . . .
>
> There are only two ways whereby the necessary capital can be provided to this industry. One is the way toward which the governments of foreign lands increasingly tend—the way of mounting governmental subsidies, whereby public funds are poured without stint into air transport. The other way is the traditional American way, a way which invites the confidence of the investing public by providing a basic economic charter that promises the hope of stability and security, and orderly and intelligent growth under watchful governmental supervision (U.S. Senate Hearings, 1938: 30–31).

As George Santayana once said, a nation that fails to learn from its history is doomed to repeat it. Economic disintegration and widespread pricing discrimination—the catalysts for regulation—have reappeared under deregulation. Eventually, Congress will reregulate the airline industry, since deregulation has been a catastrophic failure, for creditors, stockholders, labor, and yes, consumers.

CONCLUSIONS

A word about history is in order. In the 1930s, the United States enjoyed the finest passenger railroad system in the world. By the 1970s, the United States had seen its passenger railroad system decline to the worst in the developed world (where it remains today). But by the 1970s, the United States enjoyed the finest and most developed airline and highway systems in the world. Today, our airline system is, by many measures, the world's worst, while our highway infrastructure is crumbling. The result is a combination of market failure and governmental abdication of the public interest.

Recently, the Consumer Federation of America (1988) issued a report revealing consumer perceptions of the impact of deregulation. It found that (1) a plurality, perhaps a majority, of people support enhanced regulation; (2) with respect to neither transportation nor communications does a majority believe that deregulation has been in the best interest of individuals or the nation; and (3) a plurality believes that deregulation has hurt consumers. According to the study, support for transportation and telecommunications regulation reached a low point in the early 1980s, but has since climbed back to the higher levels of the 1970s (Dempsey, 1989a). Support for economic regulation has followed the reverse trend. In a *Business Week* poll conducted in 1987, 49 percent of respondents said "no" when asked whether the results of deregulation of airlines, trucking, and telecommunications has been positive; 46 percent said "yes." It is clear that as Americans become better acquainted with deregulation, they become less enamored with it.

But not the Reagan/Bush Department of Transportation. Despite growing evidence of widespread failure, DOT continued tenaciously to insist that "moves to deregulation were almost universally needed and well-founded" (U.S. DOT, 1990: 69). It is incredible that DOT believed that even more deregulation would be better. This is the same DOT that issued a long-awaited National Transportation Policy that argued that the states should pay for the deteriorating infrastructure of highways, but that they should be pre-empted from regulated intrastate motor carriage, thereby forcing them to follow the course of deregulation.

Transportation is a part of the broader infrastructure that is the foundation for economic growth. In most nations that infrastructure (communications, energy, and transportation) is owned, subsidized, or regulated by government. Only in North America have we entered the brave new world of deregulation and the imperfect economic environment it creates. Most nations view the infrastructure as an essential foundation for economic growth and, therefore, distortions in it cannot be tolerated. For that reason these industries are treated differently from other sectors of the economy. There is also a strong public interest in transportation because these firms are users of a public resource—highways, waterways, and airports—that are owned and were built and developed by taxpayers. If carriers are to use these scarce public resources, they have traditionally been required to do so in a way that achieves broader social goals. Moreover, the vital importance of transportation infrastructure as the very veins and arteries of commerce make it imperative that the public interest attributes of it be vigilantly guarded by responsible government oversight.

The net impact of deregulation is that the social objectives for which regulation has traditionally been a catalyst have been abandoned. We have left the industry and the public it serves to a highly imperfect market that has created gross distortions between large and small firms. The net effect of deregulation is that the larger users of the system (the large shippers and corporations) in the short run, and the larger providers of the service (the large carriers) in the longer run, are its principal beneficiaries. Small shippers, small communities, and small transportation firms are clearly disadvantaged in an unregulated environment. Professor Rakowski (1988: 21) succinctly summarized the results of motor carrier deregulation:

> The results of deregulation is the LTL [less than truckload] sector have been the opposite of what was predicted by the deregulators. Instead of more competition . . . [we have] increased concentration of both revenues and profits. Instead of more competitors, there are fewer firms in this segment of the industry now than prior to deregulation and open entry. Bankruptcies and voluntary departures (often because of impending doom) have thinned the ranks of competitors and there has been essentially no new entry.

The same problems that exist today in a deregulated transportation environment are those which existed in the 1930s before motor carrier and airline regulation (or in the 1880s before rail regulation) and differ only in their magnitude. A nation that does not learn from its history is doomed to repeat it. The United States has an extremely short memory, and is prone to reliving its past. The time has come to roll back deregulation.

REFERENCES

D. Anderson & R. Felton, *Regulation and deregulation of the motor carrier industry,* 7, 1989.

Donald L. Bartlett & James B. Steele, *America: What Went Wrong* (Andrews and McMeel, Kansas City, 1992).

Consumer Federation of America 1988. *Public Opinion About Regulation and Deregulation in the Transportation and Communications Industries* (May 1988).

Paul S. Dempsey, Market failure and regulatory failure as catalysts for political change: The choice between imperfect regulation and imperfect competition, *Washington & Lee Law Review* 46:1–40 (1989).

Paul S. Dempsey, Adam Smith assaults Ma Bell with his invisible hands: Divestiture, deregulation and the need for a new telecommunications policy, Hastings Communications & Entertainment Law Journal 11:527 (1989).

Paul S. Dempsey, *The Social and Economic Consequences of Deregulation* (Quorum Books, Westport, CT, 1989).

Paul S. Dempsey, *Flying Blind: The Failure of Airline Deregulation* (Economic Policy Institute, Washington, D.C., 1990).

Paul S. Dempsey & A. Goetz, *Airline Deregulation & Laissez-Faire Mythology* (Quorum Books, Westport, CT, 1992).

William Jackman, *Economic Principles of Transportation* (1935).

Alfred E. Kahn, Airline deregulation—a mixed bag, but a clear success nevertheless, Transportation Law Journal 16:229, 248 (1988).

Kauper, State regulation of interstate carriers, *Michigan Law Review* 31:1097 (1933).

Kauper, Federal regulation of motor carriers, *Michigan Law Review* 33: 239 (1934).

Murray, Turmoil in trucking, *Dun's Business Review* (May 1982).

James Rakowski, Marketing economies and the results of trucking deregulation in the less-than-truckload sector, *Transportation Journal* 11 (Spring 1988).

U.S. Department of Transportation, Moving America: New Directions, New Opportunities (1990).

U.S. Senate 1935. Report of the Committee on Interstate Commerce, Motor Carrier Act, 1935, 74th Cong., 1st Sess. 2-3 (1935).

U.S. Senate Hearings 1938. Civil and Air Transport Hearings on S. 3659 Before a Senate Subcomm. on Interstate Commerce, 75th Cong. 3rd Sess. (1938).

U.S. Supreme Court 1934. *Home Building & Loan Association v. Blaisdell,* 290 U.S. 398.

Dabney Waring, Motor carrier regulation—by state or by market? *ICC Practitioners Journal* 51: 240–241 (1984).

BIBLIOGRAPHY

Addus, Abdussalam A. Subsidizing air service to small communities. *Transportation Quarterly* 39 (1985); 537–49.

Ahmed, Samir. Air transportation to small communities: Passenger characteristics and perceptions of service attributes. *Transportation Quarterly* 38 (1984): 15–21.

Areeda, Phillip. Antitrust laws and public utility regulation. *Bell Journal of Economics and Management Science* 3 (Spring 1972): 42–57.

Areeda, Phillip, and Donald F. Turner. Predatory pricing and related prices under section 2 of the Sherman Act. *Harvard Law Review* 88 (1975); 697–733.

Bailey, Elizabeth E. *Economic Theory of Regulatory Constraint.* Lexington, MA: Lexington Books, 1973.

Bailey, Elizabeth E., and John Panzar. The contestability of airline markets during the transition to deregulation. *Law and Contemporary Problems* 44 (1981): 125.

Bailey, Elizabeth E., David R. Graham, and Daniel P. Kaplan. *Deregulating the Airlines.* Cambridge, MA: MIT Press, 1985.

Baker, David H. Section 214 of the Staggers Rail Act: Is it working as Congress intended? *Transportation Law Journal* 14:205.

Basedow, Jurgen. Common carriers—continuity and disintegration in United States transportation law—part one. *Transportation Law Journal* 13:1.

Basedow, Jurgen. Common carriers—continuity and disintegration in United States transportation law—part two. *Transportation Law Journal* 13:159.

Baumol, William J. Some subtle issues in railroad regulation. *International Journal of Transport Economics 10* (April/August 1983): 341–55.

Baumol, William J. Use of antitrust to subvert competition. *Journal of Law and Economics* 28 (May 1985): 247–65.

Beilock, Richard. Is regulation needed for value of service pricing? *Rand Journal of Economics* 16 (Spring 1985): 93–102.

Beilock, Richard, and James Freeman. Deregulated motor carrier service to small communities. *Transportation Journal* (Summer 1984): 71–82.

Berger, Robert G., and Stephanie J. Mitchell. Predatory pricing in the airline industry: A case study—the policies and practices of the CAB. *Transportation Law Journal* 13:287.

Boberg, Kevin B., and Dennis M. Gawlik. The evolution and implications of the market dominance concept in railroad ratemaking. *Transportation Law Journal* 13:259.

Bock, Edwin A. *Government Regulation of Business* Englewood Cliffs, NJ: Prentice-Hall, 1962, 1963.

Bowersox, Donald J., Pat J. Calabro, and George D. Wagenheim. *Introduction to Transportation.* New York: Macmillan, 1981.

Boyd, Alan S., Stanford G. Ross, and Richard L. Teberg. New dimensions in transportation law. *Transportation Law Journal* 1:1.

Braeutigam, Ronald R., and Roger G. Noll. The regulation of surface freight transportation: The welfare effects revisited. *Review of Economics and Statistics* 66 (February 1984): 80–87.

Breen, Denis A. Antitrust and price competition in the trucking industry. *Antitrust Bulletin* 28 (Spring 1983); 201–25.

Brenner, Melvin A. Airline deregulation—a case study in public policy failure. *Transportation Law Journal* 16 (1988): 179–227.

Brenner, Melvin A., James O. Leet, and Elihu Schott, *Airline Deregulation.* Westport, CT: Eno Foundation for Transportation, 1985.

Bruning, Edward and Edward A. Morash. Deregulation and the cost of equity capital. *Transportation Journal* (Winter 1983): 72–81.

Bruning, Edward, and Peter M. Lynagh. Carrier evaluation in physical distribution management. *Journal of Business Logistics* 5, no. 2 (1984): 30–47.

Carlton, D., W. Landes, and R. Posner. Benefits and costs of airline mergers: A case study. *Bell Journal of Economics* 11 (1980P 65.

Caves, Douglas W., Laurits R. Christensen, and Michael W. Tretheway. Airline productivity under deregulation. *Regulation* (November/December 1982): 25.

Caves, Douglas W. Productivity performance of U.S. trunk and local service airlines in the era of deregulation. *Economic Inquiry* (July 1983): 312.

Caves, Richard. *Air Transport and Its Regulators: An Industry Study.* Cambridge, MA: Harvard University Press, 1962.

Chow, Garland, and Richard D. Gritta. Motor carrier bankruptcy: An industry assessment of financial condition. *Transportation Research Forum Proceedings* 26, no. 1 (1985): 434–40.

Chow, Garland, and Richard D. Gritta. Motor carrier bankruptcy in an uncertain environment. *Transportation Law Journal* 14:39.

Civil Aeronautics board. *Report of the CAB Special Staff on Regulatory Reform.* 1975.

Civil Aeronautics Board. *Report of the CAB Special Staff on Regulatory Reform.* 1975.

Civil Aeronautics Board. *Implementation of the Provisions of the Airline Deregulation Act of 1978.* Civil Aeronautics Board Report to the Congress, January 31, 1984.

Civil Aeronautics Board. A staff study: Report on airline service, fares, traffic, load factors, and market shares. Service Status as of June 1, 1984, Issue No. 31. Washington, D.C.: 1984.

Cox, Ernest G. One third century of motor carrier safety regulation. *Transportation Law Journal* 2:173.

Crew, E. C., and Lester M. Bridgeman. Do antitrust laws provide a feasible alternative to regulation? *ICC Practitioners Journal* 47 (September/October 1980): 673–97.

Davis, Grant M. Transportation regulation: Another dimension. *ICC Practitioners Journal* 42 (January/February 1975): 164–74.

Davis, Grant M., and Linda J. Combs. Some observations regarding value of service pricing in transportation. *Transportation Journal* 14 (Spring 1975): 49–58.

Davis, Grant M. *Transportation Regulation: A Pragmatic Assessment.* Danville, IL: Interstate, 1976.

Davis, Grant M., and John E. Dillard, Jr. Collective ratemaking—does it have a future in the motor carrier industry? *ICC Practitioners Journal* 49 (September/October 1982): 1112–29.

Dempsey, Paul S. Transportation deregulation—on a collision course? *Transportation Law Journal* 13:329.

Dempsey, Paul S. The contemporary evolution of intermodal and international transport regulation under the Interstate Commerce Act: Land, sea, and air coordination of foreign commerce movements. *Vanderbilt Journal of Transportation Law* 10 (Fall 1977), 505.

Dempsey, Paul S. Entry control under the Interstate Commerce Act: A comparative analysis of the statutory criteria governing entry in transportation. *Wake Forest Law Review* 13 (Winger 1977), 729.

Dempsey, Paul S. Turbulence in the "open skies." The deregulation of international air transport. *Transportation Law Journal* 15:305.

Dempsey, Paul S. The international rate and route revolution in North Atlantic passenger transportation. *Columbia Journal of Transnational Law* 17, no. 3 (1978).

Dempsey, Paul S. The rise and fall of the Civil Aeronautics Board—opening wide the floodgates of entry. *Transportation Law Journal* 11 (1979): 91, 123–27.

Dempsey, Paul S. Congressional intent and agency discretion—Never the twain shall meet: The Motor Carrier Act of 1980. *Chicago Kent Law Review* 58, no. 1 (1981).

Dempsey, Paul S. Rate regulation and antitrust immunity in transportation: The genesis and evolution of this endangered species. *American University Law Review* 32 (1983): 335, 345–49.

Dempsey, Paul S. The Interstate Commerce Commission—disintegration of an American legal institution. *American University Law Review* 34 (Fall 1984), 1.

Dempsey, Paul S. The dark side of deregulation: Its impact on small communities. *Administrative Law Review* 39 (1987): 445–65.

Dempsey, Paul S. The role of the International Civil Aviation Organization on deregulation, discrimination, and dispute resolution. *Journal of Air Law and Commerce* 52 (1987).

Dempsey, Paul S. Aerial dogfights over Europe: The liberalization of EEC air transport. *Journal of Air Law and Commerce* 53 (1988).

Dempsey, Paul S. *Law and Foreign Policy in International Aviation.* New York, NY: Transnational Publishers, 1987.

Dempsey, Paul S. and William E. Thoms. *Law and Economic Regulation in Transportation.* Westport, CT: Quorum Books, 1986.

De Vany, Arthur. The effect of price and entry regulation on airline output, capacity, and efficiency. *Bell Journal of Economics* 5 (1975): 327.

De Vany, Arthur. Product quality, uncertainty, and regulation: The trucking industry. *American Economic Review* 67 (September 1977): 583–94.

De Vany, A. S., and T. R. Saving. Competition and value of service pricing in the trucking industry: Reply. *American Economic Review* 70 (March 1980): 181–85.

Dewey, Donald. Welfare and collusion: Reply. *American Economic Review* 72 (March 1982): 267–81.

Dively, Dwight. Applications of regulatory theory to the trucking industry. *Research in Law and Economics* 6 (1984): 211–26.

Douglas, George, and James Miller, III. The CAB's domestic passenger fare investigation. *Bell Journal of Economics* 5 (1974); 205.

Douglas, George, and James Miller, III. *Economic Regulation of Domestic Air Transport.* Washington, D.C.: Brookings Institution, 1974.

Dupre, Steven C. A thinking person's guide to entry/exit deregulation in the airline industry. *Transportation Law Journal* 9:273.

Ellison, Anthony. The structural change of the airline industry following deregulation. *Transportation Journal* 21 (1982): 58–69.

Enis, Charles, and Edward A. Morash. The economic losses from the devaluation of motor carrier operating rights. *ICC Practitioner's Journal* 50 (July-August 1983): 542–55.

Enis, Charles, and Edward A. Morash. Market protection, deregulation, and the question of industry losses. *Transportation Law Journal* 15:89.

Erenberg, Michael, and Bruce M. Kasson. Railroad—motor carrier intermodal ownership. *Transportation Law Journal* 12:75.

Fair, Marvin L., and John Guandolo. *Transportation Regulation.* Dubuque, IA: Wm. C. Brown Co., 1979.

Farris, M. T. Discrimination in transportation and antitrust laws. *ICC Practitioners Journal* 46 (May/June 1979): 509–25.

Felton, John Richard. The impact of rate regulation upon ICC-regulated truck back hauls. *Journal of Transport Economics and Policy* 15 (September 1981): 253–67.

Folse, Parker C. Antitrust and regulated industries: A critique and proposal for reform of the implied immunity doctrine. *Texas Law Review* 57 (May 1979): 751–828.

Freeman, James. The ties that bind: Railroads, coal, utilities, the ICC, and the public interest. *Transportation Law Journal* 14:1.

Freeman, James W., and Robert W. Gerson. Motor carrier operating rights proceedings—how do I lose thee? *Transportation Law Journal* 11:13.

Frew, James R. The existence of monopoly profits in the motor carrier industry. *Journal of Law and Economics* 24 (October 1981); 289–315.

Friedlaender, Ann F. *The Dilemma of Freight Transport Regulation.* Washington, D.C.: Brookings Institution, 1969.

Friedlaender, Ann F., and Richard Spady. *Freight Transport Regulation: Equity, Efficiency and Competition in the Rail and Trucking Industries.* Cambridge, MA: MIT Press, 1981.

Friedman, Jesse J. Collective ratemaking by motor common carriers: Economic and public policy considerations. *Transportation Law Journal* 9 (October 1978): 33–53.

Friedman, Jesse J. What's wrong with the case against collective ratemaking: Rejoinder to James C. Miller III. *Transportation Law Journal* 11 (December 1980): 301–22.

Gardiner, Paul S. Rate bureau functions without antitrust immunity: A suggested strategy for motor freight carriers. *ICC Practitioners Journal* 46 (July/August 1979): 651–68.

Gaskins, Darius W. and James M. Voytko. Managing the transition to deregulation. *Law and Contemporary Problems* 44 (Winter 1981): 9–32.

Gawlik, Dennis M., and Kevin B. Boberg. The evolution and implications of the market dominance concept in railroad ratemaking. *Transportation Law Journal* 13:259.

Glaskowsky, Nicholas A. *Effects of Deregulation on Motor Carriers.* Westport, CT: Eno Foundation, 1986.

Goetz, Andrew R. The effect of airline deregulation on air service to small and medium-sized communities: Case studies in northeastern Ohio. Ph.D. Dissertation, Ohio State University, 1987.

Goetz, Andrew R., and Paul S. Dempsey. Airline deregulation: Ten years later. Working paper, 1989.

Graham, David, and Daniel Kaplan. Airline deregulation is working. *Regulation* (May/June 1982): 26.

Gritta, Richard D. Profitability and risk in air transport: A case for deregulation. *Transportation Law Journal* 7:197.

Gritta, Richard D., and Garland Chow. Motor carrier bankruptcy in an uncertain environment. *Transportation Law Journal* 14:39.

Guandolo, John. Intermodal acquisition under the Interstate Commerce Act. *Transportation Law Journal* 2:11.

Guandolo, John. *Transportation Law.* Dubuque, IA: Wm. C. Brown Co., 1965, 1973.

Hardaway, Robert. Transportation deregulation (1978–1984): Turning the tide. *Transportation Law Journal* (1985): 101.

Harmatuck, Donald J. Effect of economic conditions on motor carrier tonnage and regulation. *Transportation Journal* 24 (Winter 1984): 31–39.

Harper, Donald V. Consequences of reform of federal economic regulation of the motor trucking industry. *Transportation Journal* 21 (Summer 1982): 35–58.

Harper, Donald V. Entry control and the federal Motor Carrier Act of 1980. *Transportation Law Journal* 12:51.

Harper, Donald V. The marketing revolution in the motor trucking industry. *Journal of Business Logistics* 4, no. 1 (1983): 35–50.

Havens, Arnold I., and David A. Heymsfeld. Small community air service under the Airline Deregulation Act of 1978. *Journal of Air Law and Commerce* 46 (1981): 641–86.

Hoover, Harwood, Jr. Pricing behavior of deregulated motor carriers. *Transportation Journal* 25 (Winter 1985): 55–61.

Illinois Commerce Commission. *Illinois Bus Service Since the Bus Act: A Diminishing Intercity Network.* Springfield: 1984.

Jacobs, Leslie W. Regulated motor carriers and the antitrust laws. *Cornell Law Review* 58 (November 1972): 90–135.

Janis, Russell A. A law and economics study of rail freight regulation: Traditional standards, Ramsey prices and a case of neither. *Transportation Law Journal* 15:31.

Jaskiewicz, Leonard A., and Edward J. Kiley. *Free Wheeling? A Reference for Economic Deregulation of the Motor Carrier Industry.* Alexandria, VA: Interstate Carriers Conference, 1987.

Jemiolo, Jerzy, and Clinton V. Oster, Jr. Regional changes in airline service since deregulation. *Transportation Quarterly* 41 (1987): 569–86.

Johnson, James C. Going, going, gone!—the ICC's regulation on trucking mergers. *ICC Practitioners' Journal* 51, no. 4 (1984).

Jordan, William. *Airline Regulation in America: Effects and Imperfections.* Baltimore: John Hopkins University Press, 1970.

Kahn, Alfred. The airline industry: Is it time to regulate? William A. Patterson Transportation Lecture, National Economic Research Associates, Inc. (April 28, 1982).

Kahn, Alfred. *The Economics of Regulation: Principles and Institutions.* Boston: MIT Press, 1971.

Kahn, Fritz. Abolition of the trucking exemption: Pros and cons. *ICC Practitioners Journal* 47 (January/February 1980): 154–61.

Kahn, Jeremy. The Bus Regulatory Reform Act of 1982 and federal preemption of intrastate regulation of the intercity bus industry: Where has it come from? Where will it lead? *Transportation Law Journal* 14 (1986): 179.

Kalish, Steven J. Antitrust considerations for shippers in a changing environment. *Transportation Practitioners Journal* 52 (Winter 1985): 185–97.

Kasson, Bruce M., and Michael Erenberg. Railroad-motor carrier ownership. *Transportation Law Journal* 12:75.

Keeler, Theodore E. Airline regulation and market performance. *Bell Journal of Economics* 3 (1972): 399–424.

Kenworthy, William E. Antitrust considerations in motor carrier ratemaking: Rate bureau operations and alternatives. *Transportation Law Journal* 11 (1979): 65–89.

Keyes, Lucille. *Federal Control of Entry and Exit into Air Transportation.* Cambridge, MA: Harvard University Press, 1951.

Kihl, Mary. The impacts of deregulation on passenger transportation in small towns. *Transportation Quarterly* 42 (1988): 243–68.

Kim, Moshe. The beneficiaries of trucking regulation, revisited. *Journal of Law and Economics* 27 (April 1984): 227–41.

Levin, Richard C. Railroad rates, profitability, and welfare under deregulation. *Bell Journal of Economics and Management Science* 12 (Spring 1981): 1–26.

Levin, Richard C. Railroad regulation, deregulation, and workable competition. *American Economic Review* 71 (May 1981): 394–398.

Levine, Michael. Is regulation necessary: California air transportation and national regulatory policy. *Yale Law Journal* 75 (1965): 1416–47.

Levine, Michael. Revisionism revisited? Airline deregulation and the public interest. *Law and Contemporary Problems* 44 (1981): 179.

Levine, Michael. Airline competition in deregulated markets: Theory, firm strategy, and public policy. *Yale Journal on Regulation* 4 (1987): 393–494.

Lowenfeld, Andreas. *Aviation Law.* New York: Matthew Bender, 1972.

Mabley, Robert E., and Walter D. Strack. Deregulation—a green light for trucking efficiency. *Regulation* (July/August 1982): 36–56.

MacAvoy, Paul, and John Snow, eds. *Regulation of Passenger Fares and Competition Among the Airlines,* 1977.

Meyer, James S. Section 419 of the Airline Deregulation Act: What has been the effect on air service to small communities? *Journal of Air Law and Commerce* 47 (1981): 151–85.

Meyer, James S. *Deregulation and the Future of Intercity Passenger Travel.* Cambridge, MA: MIT Press, 1987.

Meyer, John R., and Clinton V. Oster, Jr., eds. *Airline Deregulation: The Early Experience*. Boston: Auburn House, 1981.

Meyer, John R., and Clinton V. Oster, Jr., eds. *Deregulation and the New Airline Entrepreneurs*. Cambridge, MA: MIT Press, 1984.

Meyer, John R., and William B. Tye. The regulatory transition. *American Economic Review* 75 (May 1985): 50.

Miller, James C., III. An economic analysis of airline fare deregulation: The Civil Aeronautics Board's proposal. *Transportation Law Journal* 10:15.

Molloy, James F., Jr. *The U.S. Commuter Airline Industry*. Lexington Books, 1985.

Moore, Thomas Gale. The beneficiaries of trucking regulation. *Journal of Law and Economics* 21 (October 1978): 327–43.

Moore, Thomas Gale. U.S. airline deregulation: Its effects on passengers, capital, and labor. *Journal of Law and Economics* 29 (April 1986): 1–28.

Morash, Edward A. Entry controls on regulated households goods carriers: The question of benefits. *Transportation Law Journal* 13:227.

Morash, Edward A., and Charles R. Enis. Motor carriers mergers, mobility barriers, and regulatory reform. *Transportation Journal* (Fall 1985): 38–50.

Morrison, Steven A., and Clifford Winston. *The Economic Effects of Airline Deregulation*. Washington, D.C.: Brookings Institution, 1986.

Muller, E. K. Regional urbanization and the selective growth of towns in North American regions. *Journal of Historical Geography* 3 (1977): 21–39.

Murray, Richard. Turmoil in trucking. *Dun's Business Month*, May 1982.

National Academy of Sciences. *Motor Carrier Economics Regulation*. Washington, D.C.: NAS, 1982.

Nelson, James C. The emerging effects of deregulation of surface freight transport in the United States. *International Journal of Transport Economics* 10 (April/August 1983): 219–36.

Noll, Roger O. *Reforming Regulation*. Washington, D.C.: Brookings Institution, 1971.

Noll, Roger O., and Bruce M. Owen. *The Political Economy of Deregulation: Interest Groups in the Regulatory Process*. Washington, D.C.: American Enterprise Institute for Public Policy Research, 1983.

Nupp, Byron. National transportation policy in the United States—an analysis of the concept. *Transportation Law Journal* 2:143.

Olson, C., and J. Trapani. Who has benefited from regulation of the airline industry? *Journal of Law and Economics* 24 (1981): 75.

O'Neal, A. Daniel. Price competition and the role of rate bureau in the motor carrier industry. *Transportation Law Journal* 10: 309.

Oster, Clinton V., Jr. Deregulation and commuter airline safety. *Journal of Air Law and Commerce* 49 (1984): 315–16.

Oster, Clinton V., Jr., and C. Kurt Zorn. Airline deregulation, commuter safety, and regional air transportation. *Growth and Change* 14 (1983): 3, 7–8.

Owen, Wilfred. *Distance and Development: Transport and Communications in India*. Washington, D.C.: Brookings Institution, 1968.

Peterson, Rodney. An economic analysis of statutory changes in rail carrier entry and exit. *Transportation Law Journal* 13 (1984): 189, 210–13.

Popper, Andrew F. Collective ratemaking: A case analysis of the eastern central region and an hypothesis for analyzing competitive structure. *Transportation Law Journal* 10:365.

Popper, Andrew F. The antitrust system: An impediment to the development of negotiation models. *American University Law Review* 32 (Winter 1983): 283–334.

Popper, Andrew F., and Michael W. Pustay. Regulatory reform of motor freight carriage in the United States. *International Journal of Transport Economics* 10 (April/August 1983); 259–80.

Popper, Andrew F. Reform of entry into motor carrier markets: Was the Motor Carrier Act of 1980 necessary? *Transportation Journal* 16 (Summer 1977): 36–45.

Rakowski, James. Motor carrier size and profitability. *Transportation Journal* 16 (Summer 1977): 36–45.

Rose, Jonathan C. Surface transportation and the antitrust laws: Let's give competition a chance. *Transportation Law Journal* 8:1.

Rose, Nancy L. The incidence of regulatory rents in the motor carrier industry. *Rand Journal of Economics* 16 (August 1985): 299–318.

Sloss, James. Regulation of motor freight transportation: A quantitative evaluation of policy. *Bell Journal of Economics and Management Sciece* 1 (August 1970): 327–59.

Stafford, George M. The Interstate Commerce Commission and the consumer. *Transportation Law Journal* 4:1.

Sugrue, Paul K., Manfred H. Ledford, and Nicholas A. Glaskowsky. Operating economies of scale in the U.S. long-haul common carrier, motor freight industry. *Transportation Journal* (Fall 1982): 27–41.

Sweeney, Daniel J., Charles J. McCarthy, Steven J. Kalish, and John M. Cutler, Jr. *Transportation Deregulation: What's Deregulated and What Isn't.* Washington, D.C.: National Association of Small Shippers Traffic Council (NASSTRAC), 1986.

Taneja, Nawal K. *The International Airline Industry: Trends, Issues, Challenges.* Lexington, MA: Lexington Books, 1988.

Thayer, Frederic. *Air Transport Policy and National Security.* Chapel Hill, NC: University of North Carolina Press, 1965.

Thoms, William E. Amtrack revisited. *Transportation Law Journal* 5:141.

Thoms, William E. Clear track for deregulation—American railroads, 1970–1980. *Transportation Law Journal* 12:183.

Thoms, William E. Rollin' on . . . to a free market: Motor carrier regulation 1935–1980. *Transportation Law Journal* 13:43.

Tolchin, Susan, and Martin Tolchin. *Dismantling America: The Rush to Deregulate.* Boston: Houghton Mifflin, 1983.

Tye, William B. Scenarios of the motor carrier industry without collective ratemaking. *Transportation Practitioners Journal* 52 (Summer 1985): 493–511.

Tye, William B. *Encouraging Cooperation among Competitors: The Case of Motor Carrier Deregulation and Collective Ratemaking.* Westport, CT: Greenwood, 1987.

U.S. General Accounting Office. *Deregulation: Increased Competition is Making Airlines More Efficient and Responsive to Consumers.* Washington, D.C.: GAO, 1985.

U.S. General Accounting Office. *Effects of Regulatory Reform on Unemployment in the Trucking Industry.* Gaithersille, MD: GAO, 1982.

Webb, Charles A. Legislative and regulatory history of entry controls on motor carriers of passengers. *Transportation Law Journal* 8:91.

Wheatcroft, Stephen, and Geoffrey Lipman. *Air Transport in a Competitive Market.* London: Economist Intelligence Unit, 1986.

Williams, Ernest W., Jr. *The Future of American Transportation.* Englewood Cliffs, NJ: Prentice-Hall, 1971.

Williamson, Kenneth C., Marc G. Singer, and David J. Blomberg. Impact of regulatory reform on U.S. for-hire freight transportation: Carriers, perspective. *Transportation Journal* (Summer 1985): 28–51.

Wilner, Frank. Creating a linkage between rate and costs: A survival tactic for small carriers under deregulation. *ICC Practitioners Journal* 48 (November/Decemger 1980): 65–81.

9

Some Crucial Issues in Administrative Law

Bernard Schwartz *The University of Tulsa College of Law, Tulsa, Oklahoma*

According to Judge Friendly, "There seems to be a kind of spontaneous generation about the federal Constitution; the more questions about it are answered, the more there are to be answered."[1] The same is true about administrative law. Indeed, our administrative law is notable not only because of its importance but also because of its rapidly changing character. In 1943, the Supreme Court referred to a particular area of administrative regulation as one "the dominant characteristic of which was the rapid pace of its unfolding."[2] The same statement could be made about the entire field of administrative law. The paramount characteristic of the administrative law that has developed since the turn of the century has been what we may term its Heraclitean nature: the subject is one that has been in a continuing state of flux. To one working in administrative law, it may be truly said: "The world's a scene of changes, and to be Constant, in [such a field] were inconstant."[3]

CRUCIAL ISSUES HALF A CENTURY AGO

The extent of change in administrative law can be demonstrated by considering the different issues that have been crucial in the field over the years. We can start our discussion by going back to March, 1940, when Dean James M. Landis delivered a noted public lecture on "Crucial Issues in Administrative Law."[4] In it, he dealt with what he considered the principal problems in the field of administrative law, and more particularly with those posed by the highly controversial Walter-Logan bill, then pending before Congress. Although it is half a century since the Landis lecture was published, in terms of the development of administrative law it seems longer ago than that. The controversy aroused by the Walter-Logan bill was part of the era of extremism in administrative law fostered by the then recent New Deal expansion of agency authority and the almost fanatic efforts of those who resisted the new governmental devices. More recently we have come to see that neither the thrill of the New Dealers nor the chill of their opponents[5] adequately reflected the reality of the administrative process. The irrational hopes and fears of the 1930s have given way to more reasoned attempts to restrain administrative excesses while, at the same time, recognizing and desiring to retain the essentially good features of administration. Such attempts have sought largely to channel the exercise of agency authority within proper procedural bounds and culminated, as is well known, in the Administrative Procedure Act (APA) of 1946.[6]

What were the crucial issues noted by Landis 50 years ago, and to what extent have they been resolved since then? The Landis lecture emphasized two primary problems: (1) whether the federal agencies should be subject to a general administrative procedure statute, and (2) the proper scope of judicial review.

The first of these questions has, of course, been answered affirmatively by passage of the APA. With that law the controversy aroused by the question of whether uniform standards of fair administrative procedure should be formulated in statutory form has all but died down. When the Congress in 1946, with what Justice Frankfurter termed unquestioning unanimity,[7] enacted the APA, the first issue posed by Dean Landis was resolved. Since then, the basic principles behind the act have gained well-nigh universal acceptance, even from those who had formerly opposed such legislation.

The second crucial issue dealt with by Landis—the scope of judicial review—has not, to be sure, been settled in anything like the same way as the question of whether there should be an administrative procedure statute. Yet it cannot be denied that, on this issue, too, the situation is not at all what it was half a century ago. At that time the question of the proper scope of review was one of the most hotly contested ones in our administrative law. Today, as Professor Davis has pointed out, the controversy has become mostly a matter of history: "The long debate about de novo review vs. restricted review is about ended; the *Ben Avon* and *Crowell* cases[8] are of little interest except as history; extremists have moved from both ends toward the middle; and the substantial-evidence rule now dominates nearly all judicial review of administrative action in the federal courts."[9]

The problem of scope of review was resolved by a tendency to assimilate review of administrative agencies to appellate review in the judicial process itself. From this point of view, the substantial evidence rule, which governs judicial review of administrative agencies, has become analogous to the "clearly erroneous" rule that governs appeals under the Federal Rules of Civil Procedure.[10]

"A finding is 'clearly erroneous' when although there is evidence to support it, the reviewing court on the entire evidence is left with the definite and firm conviction that a mistake has been committed."[11] But the same can be said of the substantial-evidence test, when interpreted as it was in the now-celebrated *Universal Camera* case.[12] Can a finding be other than "clearly erroneous" when the reviewing court cannot conscientiously find that the evidence supporting that finding is substantial, when viewed in the light that the record in its entirety furnishes?[13] On the other hand, if a challenged finding is determined by the court to be supported by evidence deemed substantial, even when considered together with the body of evidence opposed to the finding,[14] how can the court be "left with the definite and firm conviction that a mistake has been committed"?

CRUCIAL ISSUES A QUARTER CENTURY LATER

In 1966, a quarter century after the Landis lecture, I attempted to bring his discussion up to date by writing about the crucial areas in administrative law at that time.[15] I noted two crucial questions that had come to the fore.

Administrative Search and Seizure Power

The first had to do with administrative powers of search and seizure, which had been brought into prominence by then-recent Supreme Court decisions. In the first place there was administrative arrest power, which had been confirmed in the *Abel* case.[16] I stressed the need for safeguards over such an anomalous administrative power, but the law has remained much as it was laid down in *Abel.* The only redeeming feature there has been that the power has remained confined to immigration law. The fear expressed by me that the *Abel* reasoning might be applied to agencies other than the Immigration and Naturalization Service (INS) has, it is fortunate, proven groundless.

Administrative Inspection Power

More important as a practical matter, because it applies generally to agencies, was my discussion of administrative inspection power. *Frank v. Maryland*[17] had recently held that that power was not a "search" subject to the Fourth Amendment. Hence, the power to inspect without a warrant existed as an adjunct to administrative regulation of both dwellings and business premises. My article pointed out the dangers posed by unrestricted administrative inspection power. But the law seemed settled on the matter by the *Frank* decision.

In the past quarter century, however, the Court has overruled *Frank* and worked out the rules governing agency inspection power. Those rules were summarized in the 1987 *Burger* case[18] involving administrative inspection of an automobile junkyard. The *Camera* and *See* cases[19] held that, despite *Frank,* administrative inspections were subject to the Fourth Amendment's warrant requirement. Later cases, however, developed an exception for "closely regulated" businesses.[20] "Because the owner or operator of commercial premises in a 'closely regulated' industry has a reduced expectation of privacy, the warrant and probable-cause requirements . . . have lessened application."[21] In the case of such a business, including the *Burger* junkyard, a warrantless inspection is valid if it meets three criteria: (1) there must be a "substantial" governmental interest in the regulatory scheme; (2) the warrantless inspections must be necessary to further the regulatory scheme; and (3) the inspection program, through the certainty and regularity of its application, must provide a constitutionally adequate substitute for a warrant.

Where a regulatory scheme satisfies these three criteria, it is valid notwithstanding the Fourth Amendment's general warrant requirement. This appears a satisfactory resolution of the administrative inspection issue. Private property is protected by the constitutional guaranty, but its requirements are more flexible where closely regulated businesses are concerned; with regard to them, rigid insistence upon the warrant requirement could make effective regulation virtually impossible.

Privileges vs. Rights

The most crucial issue discussed in my 1966 article was that of the legal position of the individual dependent upon government largess. At the time, such an individual was not protected by the requirements of administrative procedure developed by the courts and the APA. The prevailing rule was that no person had any "right" to the largess dispensed by government. On the contrary, such largess was, in the law, considered a mere "privilege" provided by the state. As such, it could be withheld, granted, or revoked at the pleasure of the donor. This was true regardless of the nature of the governmental largess dispensed in the particular case, whether a job,[22] a pension,[23] welfare aid,[24] veterans' disability benefits,[25] a government contract,[26] or any other benefit to which the individual had no pre-existing "right." In consequence, an ever-larger area of administrative power was being insulated from the safeguards of due process. The joyless reaches of the welfare state were littered with dependents outside the pale of procedural protection.

Under the law then, with government largess a mere "privilege" to which the individual concerned had no legal "right," the individual dependent upon public largess was placed in a legal status subordinate to that of others in the community. Under the prevailing law, such "privileges" could be withheld or revoked without adherence to the procedural safeguards that would otherwise be required by the due process clause before administrative action adversely affecting a particular person may be taken.[27]

My article sharply criticized the law on the matter and urged repudiation of the right—privilege distinction as the criterion upon which administrative procedure depends.[28] Four years later that call was heeded by *Goldberg v. Kelly.*[29] That case does not rank with the landmarks of Supreme Court jurisprudence; it remains largely unknown except to specialists. Yet, in its own field, it ranks as a leading case that Justice Brennan, who wrote the opinion, has said was "the opening shot in [the] modern 'due process revolution' "[30] that has transformed our administrative law.[31]

As more recently summarized by Justice Brennan, *Goldberg* held that, under due process, "a hearing was required before a welfare recipient's benefits could be terminated."[32] In his opinion, Brennan enunciated a rationale rejecting the privilege concept that had previously barred welfare recipients from procedural protection. Brennan stated that the recipient's claim could not be answered by the argument that "public assistance benefits are 'a privilege' and not a 'right.' " The opinion characterized welfare benefits as a "matter of statutory entitlement" and added in a note that it "may be realistic today to regard welfare entitlements as more like 'property' than a 'gratuity.' "[33]

The traditional approach denying procedural protection to "privileges" such as welfare benefits was repudiated by *Goldberg,* which did away with "the wooden distinction between 'rights' and 'privileges.' "[34] *Goldberg* introduced the concept of "entitlement," which is "more like 'property' than a 'gratuity' "[35] and is, as such, fully protected by procedural due process.

CRUCIAL ISSUES TODAY

What are the crucial administrative issues today? They stem directly from the resolution of the two most important issues already discussed: (1) the extension of procedural protection to recipients of government largess; and (2) the resolution of the proper scope of review by the extension of "the substantial-evidence rule [so that it] now dominates nearly all judicial review of administrative action."[36]

Resolution of these issues has only exemplified the already quoted Friendly truism;[37] the more administrative law questions are resolved, the more they give rise to others still to be answered. Two crucial administrative law issues today, flowing directly from the two issues referred to in the prior paragraph are: (1) does extension of procedural protection to what before *Goldberg* were considered only "privileges" mean that administrative action involving them must be preceded by the full evidentiary hearings traditionally required by due process? and (2) should the substantial evidence rule be extended to cover all aspects of the scope of review?

Cost–Benefit and Procedure

The *Goldberg v. Kelly* "revolution" extended due process procedural requirements to almost all the "privilege" cases that had previously been beyond the procedural pale particularly those involving government largess such as the welfare decisions in *Goldberg* itself. The problem is that in these newer areas of administrative procedure the traditional due process approach requiring full evidentiary hearings in all cases may do more harm than good. However fair in theory the procedure modeled upon the courtroom may be, fully judicialized procedure may frustrate effective administration in a field such as welfare. Undue judicialization there may defeat effective administration in the interest of those intended as the law's beneficiaries. This is true not only because of the nature of the cases involved but also because of their number. When we move from regulatory agencies such as the Interstate Commerce Commission to those administering social welfare programs, we move into mass administrative justice, where cases are measured not in the thousands but in the millions.

Fully judicialized procedure may be ill adapted to the needs of mass administrative justice. What is needed, as the Supreme Court has stated, is procedure that not only is fair but also works.[38] Procedure that is unduly cumbersome will only serve to frustrate effective administration. In the Court's words, "To impose in each case even truncated trial-type procedures might well overwhelm administrative facilities. . . . Moreover, further formalizing the . . . process and escalating its formality and adversary nature may not only make it too costly as a regular disciplinary tool but also destroy its effectiveness."[39] Somehow a procedure must be found that can cope with a great volume of cases and is suited to the relatively small sums of money involved in most of them. In a great many cases the sum at stake may be less than the cost of the record alone. At the same time it must be remembered that the few dollars in issue on a claim may be a vital matter to the individual who is completely dependent on the government grant. Somehow a middle way must be found.

The Court attempted to find such a middle way in *Mathews v. Eldridge*.[40] The decision there ruled that due process did not require a pretermination hearing before disability payments were ended. The opinion enunciated a three-pronged test to determine whether due process has been satisfied. As summarized more recently, the test requires balancing of "the nature of the private interest, the efficacy of additional procedures, and governmental interests,"[41] especially the costs that additional procedures would involve.[42]

The *Mathews* test is essentially a cost-benefit test[43] that "requires a comparison of the costs and benefits of giving the plaintiff a more elaborate procedure than he actually received."[44] The procedure should be required if it costs are less than the benefits likely to be produced. Under this approach, due process requirements should depend upon a balancing of the competing interests at stake,[45] with emphasis on the costs and benefits involved in each additional procedure required. In cases with the most serious consequences, such as welfare termination, "a fairly extensive evidentiary hearing may be constitutionally required."[46] In other cases, due process may demand less. Since there are alternatives less burdensome than fully judicialized hearings, the law should choose the less burdensome alternatives in which the benefits from the more burdensome procedure would be outweighed by the marginal costs (e.g., in time and expense).[47] In other words, as the Supreme Court has affirmed, "we have emphasized that the marginal gains from affording an additional procedure safeguard often may be outweighed by the societal cost of providing such a safeguard."[48]

It is, however, one thing to use a cost-benefit approach to the question of how judicialized a hearing required by due process should be. It is quite another to use it to determine whether any hearing at all is required by due process. Yet that is the way the Supreme Court has begun to apply the *Mathews v. Eldridge* test. In *Connecticut v. Doehr*,[49] a state statute authorized a judge to allow the prejudgment attachment of real estate without prior notice or hearing upon the plaintiff's verification that there was probable cause to sustain the validity of his claim. The Court ruled that the statute did not satisfy due process requirements. The Court determined the statute's validity by applying the *Mathews* test; all the Justices agreed that it failed the test: (1) the interests affected were significant; (2) the risk of erroneous deprivation that the state permitted was substantial; and (3) the interests in favor of an ex parte attachment were too minimal to justify the burdening of Doehr's ownership rights without a hearing to determine the likelihood of recovery.

As indicated, *Doehr* uses the *Mathews* test to determine whether a hearing is required by due process. That is, however, a misuse of the test. *Mathews* "established a cost–benefit test for determining whether the Due Process Clause requires a particular type of notice and hearing."[50] Once it is determined that there is a due process right to be heard, *Mathews* tells us what process is due, that is, the specific procedures that should be required. The *Mathews* balancing test should not be used to permit summary agency action. The Due Process Clause has already tilted the balance in favor of *some* procedure; *Mathews* only tells us the degree of formality demanded in the given case.

The course have, nevertheless, not stopped with misuse of the cost–benefit approach to determine whether there is a due process right to be heard in the given case. They have also used cost–benefit analysis (CBA) to determine whether other procedural rights exist in a given case. The leading case is *Immigration and Naturalization Service v. Lopez-Mendoza,*[51] in which the Court used CBA to hold that proper application of the exclusionary rule is not a due process requirement in an administrative hearing. *Lopez-Mendoza* arose out of a deportation proceeding in which the alien had objected to evidence introduced at the deportation hearing, contending that it should have been suppressed as the fruit of an unlawful arrest. In holding that the evidence was validly introduced, the Court followed a CBA approach that weighted the benefits secured from the exclusionary rule in the deportation case against the costs of applying the rule in such a case.

Justice O'Connor, who wrote the *Lopez-Mendoza* opinion, found the benefit to be significantly reduced in a deportation case. O'Connor noted that several factors significantly reduce the likely deterrence value of the rule: that deportation is still possible when there is other sufficient evidence not related to the arrest, and that as a practical matter every INS agent knows that it is highly unlikely that a particular arrested person will challenge proceedings. She added that any deterrence value is undermined by the availability of alternative remedies for institutional practices by the INS that might violate Fourth Amendment rights. On the other side of the scale, O'Connor called the social costs of the rule both unusual and significant. An application of the exclusionary rule would require the courts to close their eyes to violations of the immigration laws and to bureaucratize the hearing process further.

Under *Lopez-Mendoza,* it is not enough to ask the question normally asked in cases involving alleged violations of constitutional rights: Has a right guaranteed by the Constitution been violated in the given case? An affirmative answer is not enough to lead to a decision in favor of the individual. Instead, CBA must be applied to determine whether the right itself is guaranteed in the particular proceeding. If the CBA balance tilts against the right in the given case, the government will be upheld even though it has violated the right concerned.

Lopez-Mendoza has been followed by both federal and state courts.[52] Whether its CBA approach should be applied generally to procedural rights is one of the current crucial issues for our administrative law and, indeed, for our public law as a whole.[53] There are dangers in using CBA as a due process lodestar. CBA has about it a delusive aura of scientific objectivity that may be justified in the field of economics, in which it began and in which it has been used increasingly. As a public law tool, however, it is as subjective as the Benthamite "felicific calculus"[54] that was its primitive progenitor. Just as each utilitarian would apply the "greatest happiness of the greatest number"[55] principle according to his or her own subjective judgment of the pains and pleasures involved, so each judge employing CBA will use his or her own individual calculus in weighing the procedural rights at issue.

CBA in the law reduces our basic rights to the level of the counting house. It "invites members of the Bar to dust off their calculators and dress their arguments in quantitative clothing. The resulting spectacle will perhaps be entertaining."[56] But it will not really affect the inevitable result, by which CBA becomes the measuring rod for the protection of constitutional rights. When we deal with a constitutional right such as that protected by the exclusionary rule, it is much easier to quantify costs than benefits. It is, indeed, all but impossible to measure most constitutional rights in monetary terms, although it is not difficult to do so as far as the costs of protecting those rights in given cases are concerned. How much is freedom from illegally seized evidence worth?

In cases such as *Lopez-Mendoza,* it is much easier to measure the costs than the benefits. Since a constitutional right cannot really be quantified in monetary terms, the cost–benefit approach will always tend toward a weighing of the balance on the cost side of the scale. The result in a *Lopez-Mendoza*-type case is that the law is "drawn into a curious world where the 'costs' of excluding illegally obtained evidence loom to exaggerated heights and where the 'benefits' of such exclusion are made to disappear with a mere wave of the hand."[57] A system that values basic rights in more than dollars and cents terms should hesitate before following an approach under which *priceless* may too often mean *worthless.*

Chevron Doctrine

Legal rules, unlike those in the physical sciences, do not have fixed areas of strains and stress. Instead, legal rules are too often pushed to the breaking point permitted by expendiency. A crucial issue for administrative law today is whether that will happen to the *Chevron* doctrine[58] which Justice Scalia has proclaimed the most important administrative law doctrine in recent years.[59]

Chevron itself was a direct result of the resolution of the scope-of-review issue noted by Dean Landis half a century ago. As seen above, that issue was resolved by the predominance of the substantial evidence rule in judicial review of administrative action. The substantial evidence rule was interpreted in the *Universal Camera* case[60] as one that tests the rationality of agency findings of fact; it permits the courts to determine the *reasonableness,* not the *rightness,* of such findings.[61]

The scope of review in administrative law has been based upon the law–fact distinction, with application of the substantial evidence rule limited to agency findings of fact. The distinction between "law" and "fact" is, however, by no means clear-cut. It is not always easy to detect the line between legal and factual issues in an administrative proceeding.[62] More specifically, is an administrative finding that involves statutory interpretation one of law or one of fact for purposes of scope of review? That question, as Judge Friendly points out, is an old one.[63] Traditionally, the answer was that it was a question of law. *Chevron,* on the other hand, answers that it is to be treated like a finding of fact.

The *Chevron* opinion begins with the hornbook principle that interpretation of a federal statute depends upon congressional intent: "If the intent of Congress is clear that is the end of the matter."[64] That is as true when a court reviews an agency's construction of a statute as in other cases involving statutory interpretation. What happens, however, when Congress has not indicated any intent on the matter?

The lower court had held that, in such a case, the reviewing court might impose its own construction, just as it would do in the absence of any administrative interpretation. The Supreme Court reversed this. When a court determines that Congress has not directly addressed the precise question at issue, a court may not simply impose its own construction on the statute, as would be the case in the absence of an administrative interpretation. "Rather, if the statute is silent or ambiguous with respect to the specific issue, the question for the court is whether the agency's answer is based on a permissible construction of the statute."[65] In other words, the principle of deference is fully applicable where Congress did not have any intent on the precise question at issue. Once the court of appeals determined that Congress did not actually have an intent regarding the applicability of the bubble concept at issue in *Chevron,*[66] the question before it was not whether in its view the concept was "inappropriate," but whether the agency's view that it was appropriate was a reasonable one. Because the agency's use of the concept was a reasonable policy choice, its choice had to be upheld upon review.

As more recently explained by Justice Scalia, *Chevron* holds "that courts must give effect to a reasonable agency interpretation of a statute unless that interpretation is inconsistent with a clearly expressed congressional intent."[67] The "courts should determine whether an agency's interpretation of a statute is *permissible,* not *correct."*[68]

The agency in *Chevron* was engaged in rule-making. Hence, strictly speaking, *Chevron* lays down a principle that governs review of administrative regulations. However, the cases since *Chevron* indicate that *Chevron* cannot be limited to review of regulations alone. Instead, the *Chevron* doctrine applies to review of all statutory interpretation by agencies, whether in rules or adjudicatory decisions.[69]

According to an important opinion by Judge Bork, when adjudicative authority has been delegated to an agency, it is even clearer that the *Chevron* approach should be followed. Although in *Chevron* the delegation of power to the agency was implicit, here, "by contrast, the delegation of adjudicative authority to an agency that is empowered to hear disputes, receive settlement proposals, and enter binding orders is explicit—it closely resembles a direct congressional authorization to implement the provisions of a statute through regulations." The conclusion is that "this explicit delegation of power to an agency compels a court to give deference to the agency's conclusions even on 'pure' questions of law within that domain."[70]

Judge Bork supports his view that *Chevron* applies to review of " 'pure' questions of law" by the assertion that such a question was really involved in *Chevron* itself. "*Chevron* considered the proper standard for judicial review of an agency's statutory interpretation, and the construction of a statute has always been considered a 'pure' question of law."[71]

The Bork view in this respect is supported by Justice Scalia, who has also said that "in *Chevron* the Court deferred to the Environmental Protection Agency's abstract interpretation of the phrase 'stationary source.' "[72] Scalia's statement was called forth by the implication in *NLRB v. Cardoza-Fonseca*[73] that *Chevron* deference does not apply to "a pure question of statutory construction," which is "for the courts to decide."[74] More recently, however, the Court confirmed that *Chevron* did apply to "a pure question of statutory construction," in which the agency must be "accorded . . . deference . . . as long as its interpretation is rational and consistent with the statute."[75] This means that *Chevron* deference must be applied to "a pure question of statutory construction," as well as to "the application of a 'standar[d] . . . to a particular set of facts.' "[76]

Chevron and Jurisdiction

Extension of *Chevron* to all interpretations, both in rules and adjudicatory decisions, and even to those involving "pure" questions of law, upsets the balance in our administrative law. It blurs the distinction between law and fact upon which the scope of review has been grounded. It drastically limits review, not only of agency findings of "fact" in the narrow, literal sense,[77] but also of agency constructions of statutory law. The latter, under the traditional theory of Anglo-American judicial review, are matters more legal than factual in nature and hence are open for determination by the courts upon review.

One can even say, as Professor Sunstein recently has, that "the notion that administrators may interpret statutes they administer is inconsistent with separation-of-powers principles." The "basic principle" in our system is that "Institutions limited by a legal restriction are not to be permitted to determine the nature of the limitation, or to decide on its scope. The relation of the Constitution to Congress parallels the relation of regulatory statutes to agencies. In both contexts, an independent arbiter should determine the nature of the limitation."[78]

The *Chevron* doctrine presents the danger of undue deference to self-expansion of an agency's jurisdiction. This is particularly true when agency power to act may be dependent on findings involving statutory interpretation. If the agency misapplies the statute upon which its power rests, it may be acting beyond its authority. Misapplication of a statutory term may thus enable the agency to act in excess of its jurisdiction. If a workers' compensation agency is vested with authority to make awards to injured "employees," the agency's very power to act depends upon its finding that the given claimant is an "employee."[79] The same is true if the agency makes a finding that the injury "arose out of and in the course of employment," or a finding that there had been an "injury" at all, or any finding that makes the statutory scheme apply to the given fact pattern.[80] By misinterpreting the statute, the agency may legitimize action that might otherwise be *ultra vires.*

That this is not a mere hypothetical possibility is shown by *Dole v. United Steelworkers.*[81] At issue was a Department of Labor Hazard Communications Standard, which imposed disclosure requirements on employers aimed at ensuring that their employees were informed of the potential hazards posed by chemicals in the workplace. The department submitted the Standard to OMB for approval before it collected the information. OMB disapproved three of the Standard's provisions on the ground that their requirements were not necessary to protect employees. The department withdrew those provisions. Respondents challenged OMB's disapproval. They argued that *Chevron* should not apply in this case because OMB's regulations determined the scope of its jurisdiction under the act. The Court opinion did not deal with this argument, but Justice White stated in his dissent that the Court had never accepted it and "there are good reasons not to accept it." According to White, under *Chevron,* the cases "have deferred to agencies' determinations of matters that affect their own jurisdiction. . . . The application of *Chevron* principles cannot be avoided on this basis."[82]

Justice Scalia has also asserted the application of *Chevron* deference to an agency's interpretation of its own statutory authority or jurisdiction. To Scalia, such application

> is both necessary and appropriate. It is *necessary* because there is no discernible line between an agency's exceeding its authority and an agency's exceeding authorized application of its authority. To exceed authorized application is to exceed authority. Virtually any administrative action can be characterized as either the one or the other, depending upon how generally one wishes to describe the 'authority.'"[83]

Such an argument, however, is two-edged. If exceeding authority can be involved in every *Chevron* deference, it militates against *Chevron* itself in a system that had its origin in the jurisdictional basis of judicial review.[84]

Justice Scalia also asserts that "deference is *appropriate* because it is consistent with the general rationale for deference: Congress would naturally expect that the agency would be responsible, within broad limits, for resolving ambiguities in its statutory authority or jurisdiction."[85] One may, however, doubt that Congress did have the intention stated by Scalia. Statutory provisions confining an agency's authority manifest an unwillingness to give the agency freedom to define the scope of its own power. A "cardinal" administrative law principle, Professor Sunstein tells us, "is that those who are limited by law should not be empowered to decide on the meaning of the limitation: foxes should not guard henhouses. The *Chevron* rule disregards this principle by permitting agencies to interpret laws that limit and control their authority."[86] To give effect to the confining intent behind statutory limitations, the final word on jurisdiction should be with the courts, not the agencies.

Chevron Ad Absurdum?

Rust v. Sullivan,[87] the most controversial decision of the Supreme Court's 1990 term, illustrates how *Chevron* may skew the result in what would have once been a simple administrative law case. At issue in *Rust* were Department of Health and Human Services (HHS) regulations that prohibited federally funded Title X projects from engaging in counseling concerning, referrals for, and activities advocating abortion as a method of family planning. The statute specifies that none of the federal funds appropriated under the Act's Title X for family planning services "shall be used in programs where abortion is a method of family planning." Doctors challenging the regulations argued that this provision did not authorize the secretary to interfere with their First Amendment right to counsel their patients by prohibiting them from giving information and advice about abortion.

The controversy over *Rust* has been concerned with the Court's holding that the regulations did not violate plaintiff's First Amendment rights. But it was the Court's application of *Chevron* that was the foundation of the *Rust* decision. The opinion of the Chief Justice starts by finding the statutory language to be "ambiguous." In such a case, under *Chevron,* "substantial deference is accorded to the interpretation of the authorizing statute by the agency authorized with administering it." As interpreted by the Court, this means, "The Secretary's construction of Title X may not be disturbed as an abuse of discretion if it reflects a plausible construction of the plain language of the statute and does not otherwise conflict with Congress' expressed intent." Here, the secretary's construction comes within this test; hence, "we must defer to the Secretary's permissible construction of the statute."[88]

Several things should be noted about the *Rust* application of *Chevron.* The Rehnquist opinion states that *Chevron* deference requires the agency interpretation to be upheld "if it reflects a *plausible* construction of . . . the statute."[89] Until *Rust,* it had been assumed that "the *Chevron* yardstick [was one of] 'reasonableness.' "[90] In Justice Scalia's already quoted words, *Chevron* requires the courts to "give effect to a *reasonable* agency interpretation of a statute."[91] Now *Rust* transforms the reasonableness requirement to one of plausibility—a test met by an interpretation that has only an appearance or show of truth[92]—that is, it is only superficially fair or reasonable.[93] In this respect, *Rust* makes for a dilution in scope of review even beyond that made by *Chevron* itself.

Rust also makes for a change in *Chevron* in cases involving inconsistent agency interpretations. Petitioners had argued that the agency's interpretation "is not entitled to deference because it represents a sharp break with prior interpretations" of the statute in question. The Court declined to accept the argument, stating that it had been rejected by *Chevron* itself. *Chevron,* however, only said that inconsistent agency interpretations should not lead to *no* deference for the interpretation at issue;[94] it did not state that full *Chevron* deference should be accorded. Both logic and law indicate that the scope of review should be stricter in such a case. Where the administrative experts themselves are so unsure of their ground that they have taken different positions in different cases, the courts should feel something less than the confidence in agency expertise that called forth the rule of limited review. In such a case, the reviewing court may well declare that the agency decisions themselves hardly have the consistency to which it should yield its judgment.[95] Hence, as the Court put it not long ago, "An agency interpretation of a relevant provision which conflicts with the agency's earlier interpretation is 'entitled to considerably less deference' than a consistently held agency view."[96]

Most important is the question of whether *Chevron* carried to its *Rust* extreme does not leave to the agency questions of fundamental policy that in our representative system should be determined by the legislature. In an important case, the New York court struck down regulations prohibiting smoking in most public places on the ground "that the . . . line between administrative rule-making and legislative policy-making has been transgressed." It was for the legislature to decide whether it was the policy of the state to prohibit smoking.

> Striking the proper balance among health concerns, cost and privacy interest . . . is a uniquely legislative function. . . . Thus, to the extent that the agency has built a regulatory scheme on its own conclusions about the appropriate balance of trade-offs between health and cost to particular industries in the private sector, it was 'acting solely on [its] own ideas of sound public policy' and was therefore operating outside of its proper sphere of authority.[97]

In *Rust,* too, the agency imposed its own views on a basic question of policy. It should be as much for the legislature to determine whether abortion counseling should be prohibited as it is whether smoking should be prohibited. In fact, the abortion-counseling-prohibition decision is one that should more plainly be made by legislators, not unelected bureaucrats, because of its impact on constitutional rights and upon women seeking such counseling. Statutory ambiguity should not be taken as equivalent to delegation of law-making power in which a question of fundamental policy is resolved.[98] In such a case, "An agency cannot by its regulations effect its vision of societal policy choices [prohibiting] that which was never contemplated or delegated by the Legislature."[99]

CONCLUSION

Administrative law is also a magic mirror in which we see reflected the principal developments in the society which it helps to regulate.[100] The crucial administrative law issues noted by Landis half a century ago were a direct result of the mushrooming administrative process during the New Deal years. Critics of the agencies, particularly in the legal profession, claimed that the new administrative justice was a revival of the prerogative justice of Stuart days and that agency procedure smacked of star chamber jurisprudence. Even as restrained a body as the Attorney General's Committee on Administrative Procedure noted deficiencies in agency procedures in its 1941 report.[101] Three members of the committee went further and condemned the "substantial defects in adjudicatory practices"—particularly their "haphazard" and "formless" character.[102]

The solution to the procedure problem was seen to be a legislative code of standards of fair administrative procedure.[103] Such a law was strongly opposed by the agencies and many of their defenders. Hence, the key crucial issue of the day was whether agencies should be subjected to a general administrative procedure law.

Those disturbed by the growth of administrative power were also concerned about what they considered the ineffectiveness of judicial review. With the Attorney General's Committee minority, they believed that Congress should prescribe the scope of review rather than leave it to the courts to do so "without needed statutory direction."[104] A general feeling that judicial review was too narrow led to Congressional passage of the Walter-Logan bill, vetoed by President Roosevelt, which would have substantially broadened the scope of review. Because of the conflicting views on scope of review, Landis could note the proper scope of review as a second crucial issue.

The crucial issues stated by Landis were, we saw, resolved in the years following his lecture. As significant as the resolution of the Landis crucial issues was the change in the administrative law climate that occurred. The years after Landis spoke were critical ones in the development of American administrative law. They saw the publication of the report and studies of the Attorney General's Committee, which for the first time provided a detailed factual picture of the working of the federal administrative process; the enactment of the Administrative Procedure Act, based upon the report of the Attorney General's Committee: the first significant legislative intervention in the field of administrative law; and the continuing expansion in administrative authority, which led people on both sides of the political boundary to realize the need for safeguards.

When Landis spoke, only those on the so-called "right" (accused by their opponents of being concerned only with property rights and really aiming their shafts at the substance, rather than the administrative machinery, of the New Deal legislation) were articulate in their demands for controls over agency authority. More recently, proposals for safeguards have evoked a bipartisan response all but inconceivable 50 years ago. "Unless we make the requirements for administrative strict and demanding," a member of the Supreme Court noted for anything but hostility toward the administrative process asserted, "*expertise,* the strength of modern government, can become a monster that rules with no practical limits on its discretion. Absolute discretion, like corruption, marks the beginning of the end of liberty."[105] A decade or two earlier, it would have been almost unthinkable for one of Justice Douglas's political convictions to direct such a "sanguinary simile"[106] against administrative expertness. But it is not that the views of those involved were swayed by shifts in the political wind. Rather, developments in administrative law themselves led to the changing climate. Extremists on both sides moved toward the middle, and, that being the case, most of the controversy engendered by extremism tended to abate.

During the quarter century in question, another development occurred, pregnant with consequences for administrative law: the rise of the welfare state. By midcentury, the welfare state was an established fact in both the polity and the law. Administrative law was its primary instrument. This meant an expansion of administrative power into areas of social welfare. The trend, which began with the Social Security Act of 1935, intensified over the years. Disability, welfare, aid to dependent children, health care, and a growing list of other services (education, medical care, housing, slum clearance, urban development) all came under the fostering guardianship of the administrative process. The traditional area of administrative regulation was dwarfed by the growing field of social welfare.

The changing administrative law focus, reflecting the burgeoning of the welfare state, gave rise to the key crucial issue of the third quarter of the century: subjecting the new growing point of administrative law—social welfare administration—to the fundamentals of fair play that had been developed to control more traditional regulatory administration. That issue was resolved by *Goldberg v. Kelly,*[107] which held that there were "entitlements" in government largess that were protected by due process. The administrative apparatus of the welfare state was now as much subject to the requirements developed in our administrative law as the older regulatory apparatus.

The years after *Goldberg v. Kelly* saw an end to the unlimited economic expansion that had fueled the growth of the welfare state. In what came increasingly to be seen as a postaffluent society, attention was paid to the fear expressed in a *Goldberg* dissent "that new layers of procedural protection may become an intolerable drain on the very funds earmarked for food, clothing, and other living essentials."[108] Extending the full panoply of due process to social welfare would not only press these newer areas into an inappropriate judicialized mold; it would also channel scarce resources into procedure from the funds available to aid the poor.

The Supreme Court attempted to deal with this problem by its cost-benefit approach (CBA) in *Mathews v. Eldridge.*[109] However, the Court did not stop with the *Mathews* test in its utilization of CBA. It has, we have seen, been moving toward a general use of CBA to determine whether particular procedural rights are applicable in agency proceedings. CBA as *the* criterion in administrative procedure cases may lead to a major dilution in individual rights, since the CBA balance always tilts in favor of costs where rights that cannot be measured in mere monetary terms are at issue.

Application of CBA to administrative procedure gives increasing weight to agency autonomy in fashioning its own procedures. Agency autonomy is also favored by narrowing the scope of review, as is done by the *Chevron* doctrine that has come to dominate judicial review during the past decade. The end result of both CBA and *Chevron* is a renewed deference toward agencies that bears comparison with the comparable trend half a century ago.

The current trend coincides with the emergence of what a federal judge terms "a new school of thought"[110]—that of the New Right in jurisprudence. Its members have brought about a new tilt toward the executive in our administrative law. Under it, the lion's share of the interpretation, as in the carrying out of laws, has come once again to rest with administration, with the "hard look" approach to judicial review[111] giving way to renewed deference toward the administrative expert. The judges appointed by Presidents Reagan and Bush used their positions to begin to translate the New Right legal agenda into positive law.[112]

We should, however, remember that administrative law, like the law itself in the Cardozo aphorism, has its epochs of ebbs and flow.[113] The past decade has seen a flow toward deference and away from the distrust of the expert that had previously prevailed in the courts. Yet, if this chapter has shown anything, it is that the administrative law flow is never constant in one direction. With a Democratic administration in power, the Reagan-Bush judges may be more reluctant to apply the deference doctrine. The result may be a reversal in the tendency to defer unduly and a new period of judicial skepticism toward the administrative expert.

The opposite scenario is also possible: an increase in regulatory activity accompanied by a new zealousness in applying *Chevron* to support the activities of a reinvigorated administrative state. At any rate, by that time the current crucial administrative law issues may have been resolved, but we can be sure that new ones will have arisen to take their place.

NOTES

1. H. J. Friendly, The gap in lawmaking—judges who can't and legislators who won't, 63 *Col. L. Rev.* 787, 788 (1963).
2. *NBC v. United States,* 319 U.S. 190, 219 (1943).
3. Crowley, Inconstancy.
4. J. M. Landis, Crucial issues in administrative law, 53 *Harv. L. Rev.* 1077 (1940).
5. See L. Jaffe, The effective limits of the administrative process: A reevaluation, 67 *Harv. L. Rev.* 1105, 1107 (1954).
6. 60 Stat. 237 (1946), 5 U.S.C. §1001 (1964).
7. *Universal Camera Corp. v. NLRB,* 340 U.S. 474, 482 (1951).
8. *Crowell v. Benson,* 285 U.S. 22 (1932); *Ohio Valley Water Co. v. Ben Avon Borough,* 253 U.S. 287 (1920).
9. K. C. Davis, *Administrative Law* 868–69 (West Publishing Co., St. Paul, 1951).
10. Fed. R. Civ. P. 52(a).
11. *United States v. United States Gypsum Co.,* 333 U.S. 364, 395 (1948).
12. *Universal Camera Corp. v. NLRB,* 340 U.S. 474 (1951).

13. Idem, 488.
14. Ibid.
15. B. Schwartz, Crucial issues in administrative law, 34 *G.W.L. Rev.* 401 (1966).
16. *Abel v. United States,* 362 U.S. 217 (1960).
17. 359 U.S. 360 (1959).
18. *New York v. Burger,* 482 U.S. 691 (1987).
19. *Camara v. Municipal Court,* 387 U.S. 523 (1967); *See v. Seattle,* 387 U.S. 541 (1967).
20. For a summary, see B. Schwartz, *Administrative Law* 119–120 (Little Brown, Boston, 3d ed. 1991).
21. *New York v. Burger,* 482 U.S. at 702.
22. See *Bailey v. Richardson,* 182 F.2d 46 (D.C. Cir. 1950), aff'd per curiam, 341 U.S. 918 (1951) (4–4 decision); *McAuliffe v. Mayor of New Bedford,* 155 Mass. 216, 29 N.E. 517 (1982).
23. See *Lynch v. United States,* 292 U.S. 571, 577 (1934).
24. See *Wilkie v. O'Connor,* 261 App. Div. 373, 25 N.Y.S. 2d 617 (1941).
25. See *Slocumb v. Gray,* 179 F.2d 31, 34 (D.C. Cir. 1949).
26. See *Perkins v. Lukens Steel Co.,* 319 U.S. 113, 117 (1940).
27. See, for example, *Cafeteria Workers Union v. McElroy,* 367 U.S. 886, 896 (1961).
28. See similarly Reich, The new property, 73 *Yale L.J.* 733 (1964).
29. 397 U.S. 254 (1970).
30. W. J. Brennan, Reason, passion, and "the progress of the law," 10 *Cardozo L. Rev.* 3, 19 (1988).
31. See Schwartz, *Administrative Law* §5.16.
32. W. J. Brennan, loc. cit. supra, note. 30.
33. 397 U.S. at 262.
34. *Barry v. Barchi,* 433 U.S. 55, 71 (1979).
35. *Goldberg v. Kelly,* 397 U.S. at 263.
36. Supra note 9.
37. Supra note 1.
38. *Richardson v. Perales,* 402 U.S. 389, 399 (1971).
39. *Goss v. Lopez,* 419 U.S. 565, 583 (1975).
40. 424 U.S. 319 (1976).
41. *Zinermon v. Burch,* 110 S.Ct. 975, 995 (1990).
42. See *United States v. Raddatz,* 447 U.S. 667, 677 (1980).
43. *Propert v. District of Columbia,* 741 F.Supp. 961, 962 (D.D.C. 1990).
44. *Parrett v. Connersville,* 737 F.2d 690, 696 (7th Cir. 1984).
45. *Cleveland Bd. of Education v. Loudermill,* 470 U.S. 532, 542 (1985).
46. *Brock v. Roadway Express,* 481 U.S. 252, 261 (1978).
47. Idem at 263.
48. *Walters v. National Assn. of Radiation Survivors,* 473 U.S. 305, 320–321 (1985).
49. 111 S.Ct. 2105 (1991).
50. *Propert v. District of Columbia,* 741 F.Supp. 961, 962 (D.D.C. 1990).
51. 468 U.S. 1032 (1984).
52. See Schwartz, *Administrative Law* §7.12.
53. See *United States v. Leon,* 468 U.S. 897 (1984).
54. *3 Encyclopedia Brittanica* 486 (1969 ed.).
55. *10 The Works of Jeremy Bentham* 142 (Russell and Russell, New York, Bowring ed., 1962).
56. *American Hospital Supply Corp. v. Hospital Products,* 780 F.2d 589, 610 (7th Cir. 1985).
57. *United States v. Leon,* 468 U.S. 897, 929 (1984).
58. *Chevron v. Natural Resources Defense Council,* 467 U.S. 837 (1984).
59. A Scalia, Judicial deference to administrative interpretations of law, 1989 *Duke L.J.* 511, 512.
60. Supra note 12.
61. Schwartz, *Administrative Law* §10.8.

62. *Hi-Craft Clothing Co. v. NLRB,* 660 F.2d 910, 914 (3d Cir. 1981).
63. *NLRB v. Marcus Trucking Co.,* 286 F.2d 583, 590 (2d Cir. 1961).
64. *Chevron v. Natural Resources Defense Council,* 467 U.S. 837, 842 (1984).
65. Idem at 843.
66. The EPA regulations allowed all the pollution-emitting devices within the same industrial group ing to be treated as though they were encased within a single "bubble."
67. *INS v. Cardoza-Fonseca,* 480 U.S. 421, 454 (1987).
68. Scalia, loc. cit. supra note 59.
69. For an important case, see *National Fuel Gas Supply Corp. v. FERC,* 811 F.2d 1563 (D.D. Cir. 1987).
70. Idem at 1569–1570.
71. Idem at 1569.
72. *INS v. Cardoza-Fonseca,* 480 U.S. 421, 455 (1987).
73. 480 U.S. 421 (1987).
74. Idem at 446.
75. *NLRB v. United Food Workers Union,* 484 U.S. 112, 123 (1987).
76. Scalia, idem at 134.
77. *SEC v. Central Ill. Sec. Corp.,* 338 U.S. 96, 126 (1949).
78. C. Sunstein, *After the Rights Revolution* 143 (Harvard University Press, Cambridge, Mass., 1990).
79. *Crowell v. Benson,* 285 U.S. 22 (1932).
80. See Schwartz, *Administrative Law* §10.28.
81. 110 S.Ct. 929 (1990)
82. Idem at 944.
83. *Mississippi Power Co. v. Mississippi,* 487 U.S. 354, 381 (1988).
84. See H. W. R. Wade, *Administrative Law* 41 (Clarendon Press, Oxford, U.K., 6th ed. 1988).
85. *Mississippi Power Co. v. Mississippi,* 487 U.S. 354, 381–382 (1988).
86. Sunstein, op.cit. supra note 78, at 224.
87. 111 S.Ct. 1759 (1991).
88. Idem at 1767–1769.
89. Idem at 1767 (italics added).
90. *Continental Air Lines v. Dept. of Transportation,* 843 F.2d 1444, 1449 (D.C. Cir. 1988). See similarly *National Assn. for Better Broadcasting v. FCC,* 849 F.2d 665, 669 (D.C. Cir. 1988).
91. Supra note 67.
92. 2 *The Compact Edition of the Oxford English Dictionary* 2202 (1971).
93. *Webster's New International Dictionary of the English Language* 1886 (2d ed. 1951).
94. 467 U.S. at 863.
95. J. Learned Hand, in *Fishgold v. Sullivan Drydock & Repair Corp.,* 154 F.2d 785, 789 (2d Cir. 1946), aff'd, 328 U.S. 275 (1946).
96. *INS v. Cardoza-Fonseca,* 480 U.S. 421, 446 (1987). See similarly *NLRB v. United Food & Commercial Workers Union,* 484 U.S. 112, 124 (1987); *Seldovia Native Assn. v. Lujan,* 904 F.2d 1335, 1345 (9th Cir. 1990); *Board of Trustees v. Sullivan,* 763 F. Supp. 178, 184 (S.D. Miss. 1991).
97. *Boreali v. Axelrod,* 71 N.Y. 2d 1, 11–12 (1987).
98. Compare Sunstein, op.cit. supra note 78, at 143.
99. *Campagna v. Schaffer,* 73 N.Y. 2d 237, 242 (1989).
100. Compare O.W. Holmes, *Collected Legal Papers* 26 (Harcourt, Brace, and Howe, New York, 1920).
101. *Report of the Attorney General's Committee on Administrative Procedure* Chapters 4–5 (Government Printing Office, Washington, D.C., 1941).
102. Idem at 213.
103. Idem at 217.

104. Idem at 209.
105. *New York v. United States,* 342 U.S. 882, 884 (1951).
106. *Jones v. SEC,* 298 U.S. 1, 33 (1936).
107. Supra note 29.
108. 397 U.S. at 284.
109. Supra note 40.
110. A. Kozinski, in *Economic Liberties and the Judiciary* xi (George Mason University Press, Fairfax, Va., Dorne and Manne, eds. 1987).
111. *Greater Boston Television Corp. v. FCC,* 444 F.2d 841, 850–853 (D.C. Cir. 1970).
112. This theme is developed in B. Schwartz, *The New Right and the Constitution: Turning Back the Legal Clock* (Northeastern University Press, Boston 1990).
113. B. N. Cardozo, A ministry of justice, 35 *Harv. L. Rev.* 113, 126 (1921).

III

ADJUDICATION

10

Adjudication

Kenneth F. Warren *Saint Louis University, St. Louis, Missouri*

AGENCY ADJUDICATION: AN OVERVIEW

Public administration agencies today have the legal authority to make "laws" or the public policies that govern socioeconomic and political activities in the United States. In fact, scholars estimate that well over 90 percent of the laws that regulate our lives, whether at work or at play, are now made by our public administrators, not by our legislators or our traditional law-makers. These administrators promulgate public laws or policies through either rule-making or order-making (adjudication), although frequently a combination of the processes is employed to make and fine tune agency policies. Agency policies may target the whole society (e.g., general environmental regulations), an entire industry (e.g., passive safety restraints for all automobiles), particular companies or a single company (e.g., safety regulations directed at a specific nuclear power plant), or even an individual (e.g., a termination hearing decision involving a public employee).

Agency policy decisions may grant or deny benefits (e.g., permit an industry to operate or not operate under certain conditions; grant or deny a license to a business or an individual; grant or deny a welfare recipient, farmer, or veteran a benefit). Whether benefits are given or taken away, agency actions are ideally supposed to be guided by due process considerations. In agency rule-making, due process may mean allowing all interested parties ample opportunity to respond to a proposed rule, while in an agency adjudication it may mean allowing a person in a termination hearing sufficient time to examine and respond to allegations of misconduct.

The indisputable fact is that public agencies today, and for several decades now, have been delegated enormous law-making powers. A brief look back in American history helps to explain why agencies inherited so much public policy-making power. We know that the American colonists fought against what they considered an abuse of power by British governors in the American colonies. As a result, the founding fathers made sure after the Revolutionary War that the powers granted to the executive branch were limited and controllable.

This pattern was also established in the states. In some cases, state governors were not given enough power to govern properly, a fact of political life that still plagues some governors today.[1] Despite the fact that most state governors and even city mayors are still relatively weak, most governmental administrators today enjoy tremendous power that would almost certainly make the constitutional writers gasp with alarm. What has happened between then and now? Should Americans fear the trend toward more and more powerful administrators who cannot be checked through the ballot box?

The demand for more and more public services since the beginning of the republic in 1789 caused government to increase, especially since President Franklin D. Roosevelt was elected and given a mandate by the people to employ administrative machinery to end the suffering caused by the Great Depression. As government expanded its operations and agency tasks became more specialized, legislators lost the ability and enthusiasm to scrutinize administrative activities as closely at they had done when governmental bureaucracy was smaller and simpler. To permit the president to lead and public administrators the power and flexibility to administer their programs expeditiously, U.S. legislators increasingly began to delegate their law-making powers to the administrative branch. Even more germane to this chapter is that legislators even delegated limited judicial powers to administrators as well. But could such powers be delegated legitimately? Did this transfer of power from one branch to another violate the separation of powers doctrine, which seemed to be such a cherished constitutional principle?

Delegating Policy-Making Powers

Scrutiny of the Constitution from a literalist's perspective seems to indicate that the constitutional framers did not intend for the legislative branch to weaken itself by giving away its policy-making powers. The framers clearly made the legislative branch the strongest of the three branches, at least rhetorically.[2] Article 1, Section 1 of the U.S. Constitution states clearly that "all legislative powers herein granted shall be vested in a Congress of the United States, which shall consist of a Senate and House of Representatives." Section 8 of the same article also makes clear that "the Congress shall have power . . . to make all laws which shall be necessary and proper for carrying into execution" all the enumerated powers listed in the section.

Article 1, Section 8, specifically grants to Congress the powers to "collect taxes," "borrow money," "regulate commerce," "coin money," "establish post office and post roads," "declare war," "raise and support armies," "provide and maintain a navy," and so on. Could these specific powers be legally delegated to an administrative branch, thus encouraging the growth of vast bureaucratic power? Why did the constitutional framers spell out what powers the Congress should have if they did not really care who, for example, regulated commerce or maintained a navy? These questions are tough to answer confidently, especially since what was said in the Constitution and what was practiced by the constitutional framers clashed so sharply in the early years of the republic, when many who developed the Constitution served as congressmen. Despite what was written in the Constitution, as soon as the framers became congressmen, they enacted legislation that had the effect of giving away some of their legislative powers. For example, they allowed the courts to make all the rules necessary for carrying out the business of the courts as long as their rules were not offensive or inconsistent with United States law. They authorized the president to regulate the provision of military pensions and establish pay scales for injured or disabled soldiers as he saw fit. The first Congress also delegated to the secretary of the treasury the power to handle fines and forfeitures under certain circumstances, and it permitted superintendents to license at their will persons deemed carry out commerce with the Indians.[3]

Until the mid-1930s court opinions, especially in legal dicta, condemned in principle the broad delegations of policy-making powers to administrators, whether the policies were to be promulgated through rule-making or adjudicative processes. The prevalent and governing argument through a long list of cases, rooted in the separation of powers dogma, was essentially that only Congress should have the authority to make basic or fundamental public policy decisions, not administrators, because only legislators have the constitutional sanctioning to do so. Administrators should only have the power to "fill up the details" (*Wayman v. Southard,* 23 U.S. [10 Wheat], 1, 15–16) or make minor, practical adjustments to the laws when implementing policy (*Cincinnati, W. and Z. P. Co. v. Commissioner,* 1 Ohio St. 77, 88 [1852]; *Field v. Clark,* 143 U.S. 649 [1892]; *United States v. Shreveport Grain and Elevator Co.,* 287 U.S. 77 [1932]; *Panama Refining Co. v. Ryan,* 293 U.S. 388 [1935]; and *Schechter Poultry Corp. v. United States,* 295 U.S. 495 [1935]).

However, the Supreme Court in *United States v. Curtiss-Wright Export Co.,* 299 U.S. 304 (1936) began to reverse dramatically the directions of legal thinking on the nondelegation doctrine. Addressing the political realities that legislators no longer had the time, will, or expertise to make basic decisions in the increasingly complex and expanding public policy area, the Court reasoned that legislators could delegate away their basic law-making powers as long as they attached meaningful standards to guide agency administrators in their public policy-making decisions. Since *Curtiss-Wright,* the Supreme Court and lower courts have upheld increasingly broader delegations of basic policy-making authority to administrators, even in the absence of the attachment of any meaningful standards to guide agency policy makers (*Sunshine Anthracitic Coal Co. v. Adkins,* 310 U.S. 381 [1940]; *SEC v. Chenery Corp.,* 332 U.S. 194 [1947]; *United States v. Southwestern Cable Co.,* 392 U.S. 157 [1968]; *Amalgamated Meat Cutters v. Connolly,* 337 F. Supp. 737, D.D.C. [1971]; *National Cable Ass'n v. United States,* 415 U.S. 336 [1974]; *Algonquin SNG, Inc. v. Federal Energy Administration,* 518 F. 2d 1051 [1975]). Today, although a few state courts have recently overruled broad delegations of legislative powers to administrators (*Bio-Medical Laboratories, Inc. v. Trainer,* 370 F. 2d 223 [1977]; *Lousiana v. Broom,* 439 So. 2d 357 [L.a. 1983]), the federal courts, for all practical purposes, have endorsed broad delegations of basic policy-making powers to our public administrators.

Delegation of Judicial Powers

Most delegation court cases have historically dealt with the specific issue of whether legislative bodies can delegate legislative power to administrative agencies, but agency power has no doubt increased through legislative delegations of adjudicative powers as well. Public policies are generated through the order-making process as well as by rule-making procedures. In fact, some public agencies, such as the National Labor Relations Board, rely primarily upon adjudication to promulgate regulatory policies. It is worth noting that often scholars point out that agency hearing decisions have a more costly or punitive impact on individuals or companies that many court rulings (e.g., revoking a person's parole; taking away a doctor's "right" to practice medicine in a state; refusing to grant a company an operator's license; denying a veteran or welfare "claimant" a vital benefit). For the purposes of this chapter, it is important to understand why legislators, in addition to giving public administrators vast legislative powers, also felt compelled to delegate away significant judicial powers—a power that some scholars maintain legislators never had to delegate away.

Article 3, Section 1, of the Constitution clearly states that "the judicial power of the United States shall be vested in one Supreme Court and in such inferior Courts as the Congress shall from time to time ordain." In this light, can Congress legally bestow judicial powers on nonjudicial bodies or specifically on administrative agencies? The answer is obviously yes, but why? The delegation of judicial powers to administrative agencies has never caused the same serious concern as when legislative powers have been delegated, despite the similar encroachment upon the separation of powers doctrine. This is probably because, very generally speaking, legislative acts, whether by legislative assemblies or administrative agencies, have normally and traditionally had a greater impact on society than judicial acts. It is true that although certain court rulings have had profound social consequences (e.g., in the area of education, housing, criminal procedure, civil rights, reproductive rights), agency-adjudicated decisions in general have had comparatively minor impact. This is not to contradict what was said previously because certainly some agency adjudications have obviously affected some parties very significantly. Nonetheless, as a method for promulgating public policies, the legislative function, whether performed by a legislative or administrative body, would likely have a broader social impact because it tends to have a more macro focus, while judicial policy making tends to be more micro-oriented.

It is also true that agency rules are normally less reviewable than agency orders. This makes the delegation of judicial power to administrative agencies seem both reasonable and necessary. In judging the constitutionality of delegated judicial power to public agencies, the Court held that

> Congress did not attempt to define questions of law, and the generality of the description leaves no doubt of the intention to reserve to the Federal court full authority to pass upon all matters which this Court has held to fall within that category. There is thus no attempt to interface with, but rather provision is made to facilitate, the exercise by the court of its jurisdiction to deny effect to any administrative finding which is without evidence, or 'contrary to the indisputable character of the evidence,' or where the hearing is 'inadequate,' or 'unfair,' or arbitrary in any respect (at 49–50).

In *City of Waukegan v. Pollution Control Board,* 57 Ill.2d 170 (1974), Justice Ward argued that the U.S. Supreme Court has never found it appropriate to rule that judicial power had been vested improperly in a public agency. In addition, he contended, citing several administrative law experts, any delegation of authority, whether legislative or judicial, does not violate the separation of powers doctrine as long as effective legislative or judicial checks exist. He maintained "it may be irrelevant if an agency has legislative or judicial characteristics so long as the legislature or the judiciary can effectively correct errors of the agency"[4] (at 175).

However, in *Northern Pipeline Construction Co. v. Marathon Pipe Line Col.* 458 U.S. 5 (1982), the Supreme Court handed down a decision that created some confusion and controversy regarding the delegation of adjudicative powers to administrative agencies. In *Northern Pipeline* the Court's plurality applied vaguely the old public rights/private rights test to agency adjudicative authority, apparently arguing that questions of public rights can be heard in agency adjudications, but those involving private rights must be heard before a regular court established under Article III of the Constitution. Administrative law critic Professor Bernard Schwartz severely criticized this decision, arguing that the employment of the public rights/private rights test to determine adjudicative authority was rejected nearly a century ago.

> It is too late in the development of our administrative law for there to be any question of the legislative power to delegate adjudicatory power to agencies. Adjudications of both public and private rights may be committed to administrative agencies, as long as their decisions are subject to judicial review. To indicate otherwise, as *Northern Pipeline* did, is to go back almost a century in administrative law development.

Since *Northern Pipeline,* the high Court has evidently backed away from the use of the public rights/private rights test, but the Court's position on the issue remains unstable and uncertain. In 1985, in *Thomas v. Union Carbide Agriculture Products Co.,* 473 U.S. 568 (1985), the Supreme Court apparently rejected the public rights/private rights test and seemed to reaffirm the long-established judicial position that the legislature has the authority to delegate adjudicative powers to administrative agencies, regardless of whether public or private rights are involved, as long as agency adjudicative decisions are subject to judicial review. But in *Granfinanciera, S.A. v. Nordberg,* 109 S.Ct. 2782 (1989), the Court again employed the public rights/private rights test to judge the validity of delegations of adjudicative authority to administrative agencies. In *Granfinanciera, S.A.* the Court contended that Congress may statutorily restrict certain causes of action (disputes) to resolution by administrative agencies, but its power to do so depends upon whether they involve private or public rights (e.g., workplace safety regulations). If private rights are involved, Congress cannot prohibit individuals from bringing their disputes to the Article III courts. "Unless a legal cause of action involves 'public rights,' Congress may not deprive parties litigating over that right of the seventh Amendment's guarantee to a jury trial" (at 2796).

In 1990, however, the Supreme Court in *Local No. 391 v. Terry,* 110 S.Ct. 1339, ignored the public rights/private rights test in deciding whether union workers, governed by the National Labor Relations Act, Section 9(a), as amended, 29 U.S.C.A. Section 159(a), had a right to be heard by an Article III court (specifically, the right to a jury trial).

Despite the Supreme Court's mood swings on the public rights/private rights distinction, most federal and state courts do not employ the public rights/private rights test to determine whether delegations of adjudicatory authority to administrative agencies are constitutional. Most recently, they seem to be following the commonsense guidelines advocated by a California Court in *McHugh v. Santa Monica Rent Control Board,* 777 p. 2d91, 106 (Cal. 1989):

> An administrative agency may constitutionally hold hearings, determine facts, apply the law to those facts, and order relief so long as (i) such activities are authorized by statute or legislation and are reasonably necessary to effectuate the administrative agency's primary, legitimate regulatory purposes, and (ii) the "essential" judicial power (i.e., the powers to make enforceable, binding judgments) remains ultimately in the courts, through review of agency determinations.

To Bernard Schwartz, agency adjudications would not offend the judicial powers clause of the Constitution when such guidelines are followed, even if the cases involve private rights.[6] These guidelines, it should be stressed, are also basically in agreement with the Supreme Court's opinion in *Crowell v. Benson.*[7]

On the other hand, Professor Richard Fallon, Jr., maintains that judicial powers should not be recklessly delegated to administrative agencies because Article III courts possess a judicial independence that frankly administrative tribunals do not have. Article III judges have life tenure, protections against salary reductions, and a long tradition of independence, while administrative law judges or hearing examiners do not. Fallon advances an appellate review theory that permits and justifies agencies engaging in initial adjudications, but court review must normally be permitted to safeguard constitutional guarantees.[8]

FUNDAMENTALS OF THE ADJUDICATIVE PROCESS

As noted, our public administrators make public policies through agency rule-making and agency adjudications (order-making). Formally, or according to the language of the Administrative Procedure Act (APA), P.L. 404, 60 Stat. 237, Sec. 551 (1946), as amended, "rulemaking means agency process for formulating, amending, or appealing a rule," while "adjudication means agency process for the formulation of an order." While rule-making is a quasilegislative process, adjudication is a quasijudicial process. In technical terms, when a public agency engages in rule-making, the result is a rule. When the agency employs adjudication (order-making), the product is an order. According to the specific language of the APA, a

> rule means the whole or part of an agency statement of general or particular applicability and future effect designed to implement, interpret, or prescribe law or policy or describing the organization, procedure or practice requirements of an agency and includes the approval or prescription for the future of rates, wages, corporate or financial structures or reorganizations thereof, prices, facilities, appliances, servies or allowances therefor or valuations, costs, or accounting, or practices bearing on any of the foregoing.

In contrast, the APA states that an "order means the whole or a part of a final disposition, whether affirmative, negative, injunctive, or declaratory in form, of an agency in a matter other than rule making but including licensing."

When a public agency adjudicates (judges), the agency issues an order that represents a judgment in favor of one party or the other in a dispute. Just as Supreme Court decisions establish policies to be followed (e.g., court-ordered school desegregation), agency orders also set policies and establish precedents that commonly have the impact of laws. The need for agency adjudication arises normally when a dispute touches on a policy area within the regulatory jurisdiction of a particular public agency. The dispute may be between the agency and a private party (e.g., the Federal Communications Commission and a television station), between private outside parties (e.g., two television networks) seeking new policies or policy clarifications affecting operations in their industry, or between an intervenor or "party of interest" in a hearing involving an agency and a regulated company (e.g., an environmental group such as Union of Concerned Scientists intervening in a licensing hearing involving the Nuclear Regulatory Commission and a utility company).

Adjudications are mostly retrospective in focus. That is, agency adjudicative actions are aimed at trying to settle unresolved past conflicts between specific parties. Because participation is limited only to those parties involved in the agency's adjudicative proceedings, order-making is not supposed to lead to the development of broad public policies for the future. However, despite widespread criticism, some regulatory agencies have preferred to employ order-making to make prospective agency orders of general applicability. When orders play this role, they are made to function more like rules than orders. Critics claim that orders should be restricted in their application so that they are not used simultaneously as retrospective orders and broad prospective rules. That is, critics feel that administrators should not try to use the order-making process to kill two birds with one stone. Order-making is designed to deliberate adjudicative facts, not legislative facts. When an agency is considering *adjudicative* facts during adjudicative proceedings, either informal or formal, it is concerned with determining who did what to whom and for what reasons in order to settle a dispute between specific parties. Under normal conditions it would be inappropriate during adjudication to entertain *legislative* facts, which relate only to general public policy considerations but are irrelevant to the specific dispute. (An example of legislative facts is public attitudes toward subsidized housing. An example of a specific dispute about legislative facts is a determination of a housing agency illegally denying subsidy payments to a claimant.) The extent of the inappropriateness was made vivid by an insightful Federal Trade Commission comment published many years ago in the *Federal Register*:

> If the tribunal in an adjudicative proceeding is too intent upon fashioning rules for future guidance, the task of rendering a fair result on the record before it may be slighted. Since the task of assessing individual liability on the basis of past practices and the task of fashioning rules of general application for future guidance are different, it has been argued that

> a tribunal which seeks to lay down broad rules in deciding individual cases may frequently fail to do complete justice to the parties before it.[9]

In sum, since administrative orders are supposed to be directed toward particular parties involved in a controversy, participation excludes the general public, and only adjudicative facts should be seriously entertained. The vast majority of administrative law experts, among them Kenneth C. Davis, Henry J. Friendly, David Shapiro, J. Skelly Wright, and Richard K. Berg, believe that it is foolish under most circumstances to promulgate general public policies through the order-making process.[10]

DIFFERENTIATING ORDER-MAKING FROM RULE-MAKING

Definitive guidelines to determine when issues appear appropriate for the adjudicative process simply do not exist. However, a few very rough guidelines that administrative agencies and courts have, generally, endorsed may be helpful. In general, the order-making process (frequently referred to as the case-by-case approach to formulating regulatory policies) is used in lieu of the rule-making process when (1) the issue in question involves specific parties in a dispute; (2) the matter concerns past behavior and is not future-oriented (although orders do set precedents); (3) the issues or problems could not have been reasonably anticipated by the agency; (4) the agency wants to reach only a tentative decision because its administrators lack sufficient knowledge, experience, and confidence at the time in the specific area; and (5) the matter is simply too esoteric, complex, and varied to be resolved by the formulation of a general rule.

It is not always easy to differentiate between order-making and rule-making, nor is it easy to judge when order-making or rule-making should be employed to promulgate regulatory policies. The truth is that the legislative rule-making and judicial order-making functions in administrative agencies are frequently juxtaposed in practice. Adding to the confusion, asserts Edwin J. Madaj, ". . . is the anomaly that formal rulemaking is in many ways more procedurally like an adjudication than an informal adjudication."[11] Trying to differentiate between the two processes often turns out to be a futile academic exercise. For example, when the Federal Trade Commission (FTC) reviews the advertising practices of a certain company, concludes that the practices are deceptive, and orders the company to retract its earlier contentions publicly, is the agency functioning in a purely judicial capacity? The fact is that FTC decisions or orders (such as forcing a company to carry out corrective advertising) almost always shape FTC policy toward certain business practices. In many instances FTC hearing decisions establish rules that businesses dare not overlook. For example, Ford Motor Company would be foolish to ignore an FTC ruling against Chrysler, an industry competitor. To avoid future and costly complications, the normal procedure is to bring company policies in line with current FTC thinking regarding questionable business practices.

In 1908, in *Prentis v. Atlantic Coast Line Company,* 211 U.S. 210, the Supreme Court tried to make a practical distinction between rule-making activities and order-making activities. The Court said that "the establishment of a rate is the making of a rule for the future, and therfore is an act legislative, not judicial in kind" (at 226). But only a year later the New York Court of Appeals in *People ex rel. Central Park, N. and E.R.R. Company v. Willcox,* 194 N.Y. 383 (1909), complicated the definitional problem by contradicting the Supreme Court's interpretation of rule-making. The appeals court contended respectfully that the Supreme Court's definition ran contrary to established judicial authority in New York and added that it was not "convinced that the function of prescribing a rate is necessarily nonjudicial solely because it enforces a rule of conduct for the future" (at 386). Thus, because of the definitional problems, the courts have made a common practice of deciding administrative law cases, especially if the functions are hazy, without ever attempting to differentiate between judicial and legislative activities.

The failure to draw a distinction presents legal problems and causes some confusion because the APA specifies the procedural obligations of administrative agencies under sections of the act labeled "Rule-making" and "Adjudications." It may be difficult to establish an authoritative position and reach a respected decision based on certain procedural requirements or points of law in the APA if the courts cannot decide which sections of the act to apply, because they are uncertain as to which agency processes are in question.

Two simple tests have been used to try to determine whether agency decisions should have followed rule-making or order-making processes. Both tests fail as reliable measures, although they should not be discarded as useless since most agencies probably try to comply with the test requirements in general when promulgating policies. The first is the *past–future test,* which poses the question: Is the agency policy concerned with regulating past or future practices? If the regulatory policy is aimed at controlling future conduct, the policy should have been promulgated through rule-making procedures. However, if the policy is directed primarily at resolving a dispute involving past behavior, the policy position should have been the consequence of adjudication. The second test, called the *specific–general test,* seeks essentially to discover whether the promulgated agency policy is directed toward a specific or a general audience. If agency policy is aimed at regulating the activities of no specific parties, but parties in general, the policy should have been generated through rule-making. If the policy decision is directed toward specific parties (frequently even named parties in a controversy) the policy should have been developed through adjudication.

Unfortunately, however, agency policies almost never tend to be wholly past-specific or future-general in content or application. What compounds this problem further is that agencies have the legal, discretionary authority to decide whether they should employ the rule-making or order-making approach when making agency policies. Agency discretion is especially well respected by reviewing courts if agency officials take care to rationalize their approach selection as necessary to achieve a particular agency goal. About the only time courts would find an abuse of agency discretion in this matter would be in a situation in which an agency promulgated a policy through adjudication and then applied the new policy in such a way that serious adverse consequences resulted or the retroactive application obviously caused more harm than good (*SEC v. Chenery Corp.,* 332 U.S. 194; 1947; *NLRB v. Bell Aerospace Co.,* 416 U.S. 267; 1947; *First Bancorporation v. Board of Governors,* 728 F.2d 434, 10th Cir.; 1984; *District Lodge 64 v. NLRB,* 949 F.2d 441 [D.C. Cir. 1991]).

For all practical purposes, such agency discretionary power has allowed agencies to ignore the general–specific and past–future tests when making policies, although most agencies do take these tests into account because of external pressures to conform to what is expected. Nevertheless, agency leaders frequently decide to choose either rule-making or order-making procedures to promulgate agency policies, not because one procedure may be more appropriate, but because one process may be perceived as more convenient by the agency officials. For instance, some agency administrators believe they can control the development of their regulatory policies better if they use the more flexible case-by-case approach, since the courts have generally allowed agencies to change policy directions with each case. On the other hand, the courts have been much more insistent that policies resulting from rule-making be honored by agencies for the purpose of keeping these policies consistent over time (*Vitarelli v. Seaton,* 359 U.S. 535; 1959; *Motor Vehicle Mfrs. Ass'n v. State Farm Mutual,* 463 U.S. 29; 1983; *South Cent. Terminal Co. v. U.S. Dept. of Energy,* 728 F.Supp. 1083, 1096 [D. Del. 1990]).

PROS AND CONS OF ORDER-MAKING AND RULE-MAKING IN AGENCY POLICY-MAKING

It is very important to comprehend the character of order-making and rule-making if one is to develop conceptually strong insights into the agency policy-making process. After all, formal agency policies, which essentially represent the regulatory role played by an agency, are made either through the rule-making or order-making processes. Consequently, a great deal can be learned about agency behavior and its relationship to its external environment if these basic processes are contrasted. This section compares the more important features of order-making and rule-making, with an eye to their relative merits in generating sound regulatory policies rooted in democratic procedures fundamental to the maintenance and promotion of administrative due process. Special attention is devoted to how the public, regulated industries, and agency administrators perceive the comparative advantages and disadvantages of rule-making and order-making. Justifications are then presented to explain why a large number of administrative law critics prefer rule-making to order-making for the promulgation of most regulatory policies, and why they frequently become irritated at regulators who keep insisting on promulgating policies through adjudication.[12]

Procedural Differences

There are several basic procedural differences between rule-making and order-making. Although some of these differences have been made apparent in previous discussions, a brief review is helpful. The basic procedural difference between the two is that the rule-making process is legislative in character, and order-making is judicial in nature. Of course, this basic procedural difference makes these two approaches to administrative policy formation fundamentally distinct. While rule-making typically involves the notice and comment approach, order-making procedure is supposed to be trial-like, meaningfully reflecting procedures followed in regular court trials. Thus, unlike rules, hearing orders impose penalties and rewards directed at particular parties involved in the hearing proceedings. Hearing decisions (orders) must be based wholly on the hearing record. Specifically, this means that administrative law judges who preside over agency hearings must root their orders in evidence presented at the hearings. The bulk of hearing evidence results from written and oral testimony and cross-examinations involving specific questions pertaining to a particular dispute.

Final rules do not have to be based on the varied information and arguments submitetd to the rule-makers as a response to publication of a proposed rule in the *Federal Register.* Rule-makers have only the legal obligation to accept comments. They do not actually have to be influenced by these comments and data in drafting rules, although the courts, especially since *Overton Park,* have been insisting that rule-makers avoid "arbitrary and capricious" rule-making by rooting their decisions in substantial evidence based "on the record," especially after holding public hearings. The Court's position has probably forced many agency decision makers to pay more attention to submitted comments, but still discretion remains a powerful instrument on the side of administrators because it takes very little in practice for rule-makers to defend their rules against charges that they were arbitrarily and capriciously drafted.

Differences in Uniformity and Consistency

Because rule-making procedures are designed to facilitate the making of generally applicable rules that help to shape an overall regulatory game plan, attempts have been made to promote uniformity and consistency in agency policies. As a result of agency attempts to develop policies that can be applied in a uniform and consistent manner to those who will come under their regulatory umbrella, little effort is made to address unique objections and problems some of those to be regulated might have. Thus, rule-making procedures are designed primarily to produce broad, sweeping regulatory policies that are not particularly sensitive to individual cases or problems. In contrast, order-making, which utilizes the case-by-case approach, has the advantage of developing policies incrementally over time by addressing individual cases. Therefore, the real strength in the order-making approach lies in its emphasis on tailoring decisions (policy outputs) to special circumstances. In this sense, order-making is more compassionate than rule-making, at least for the individual parties involved. In fact, adjudicative procedures are much more elaborate than rule-making procedures simply because sincere efforts have been made to promote administrative due process during adjudication so that the rights of individuals are protected. The obvious disadvantage, however, is that this case-by-case approach may cause agency policies to fluctuate in an unpredictable manner over time, preventing the development of a stable and uniform policy climate for the regulated, who naturally prefer agency reliability to agency unreliability.

One serious problem with making policies through the order-making process is that resulting agency decisions come without warning, sometimes creating great hardships for those who must comply with the orders even though they were not parties in the dispute and who therefore did not have the opportunity to present data and arguments. Rules, on the other hand, are proposed in the *Federal Register* before they become law (a final rule). Despite the fact that some rule-makers give little attention to comments by outsiders on proposed rules, all interested parties are at least afforded the opportunity to provide input, which can lead to the alteration of the proposed rule before it becomes final and binding. In any event, concerned parties are at least given advance notice of agency intentions in a specific policy area.

In addition, because agencies are compelled under Section 553(b) of the APA to publish their proposed agency rules in the *Federal Register,* agencies are obligated to spell out their policy intentions rather clearly for all to scrutinize. This has the obvious advantage of forcing agencies not only to clarify their policy positions but also to justify them in anticipation of challenges to their position. Many people think this prevents rule-makers from hiding the ball from interested parties, helping to ensure democratically accountable agency actions.[13] Such an open policy-making process, as contrasted to adjudication, allows judicial review of proposed agency policy before it is too late, as long as the petitioning party can show the court that it would suffer unfairly if the proposed action were carried out. The order-making process clearly fails to provide these advantages to affected parties.[14]

Policy Planning

Intelligent administrative policy-planning for the future demands that agency regulators develop a comprehensive game plan so that rational actions can be taken by the regulatory agency for the purpose of reaching desired goals. Agencies can rely on either rule-making or order-making approaches to achieve their regulatory ambitions. When facts and arguments are considered, rule-making appears to be preferable to order-making for policy planning by an administrative agency. The most persuasive reason, noted previously, is that in general rule-making tends to be general-future oriented, while order-making is mostly specific-past in focus. Planning through rule-making allows agency planners to obtain varied feedback from a diverse environment every time the agency proposes a rule. This ability to build a comprehensive data base to aid future planning decisions is one of the key advantages of rule-making over adjudication in the area of policy planning.[15] Rule-making procedures, scholars contend, facilitate the collection of a broad range of valuable information that is necessary for insightful regulatory decision-making.[16]

In contrast, the adjudicative process in administrative agencies is poorly designed for wise agency planning, not only because the process has a past-specific orientation but because the focal policy areas are left too much to chance selection. That is, some agencies (for example, the NLRB) cannot adjudicate unless outside parties raise the issue in a dispute. This causes agency planning, Shapiro once wrote, to "depend on the accident of litigation than on conscious planning."[17] In fact, this largely causes agency planning to be left somewhat randomly to outsiders who are in no way concerned about an agency's efforts to develop sensible, long-range regulatory policies. It is true, however, as noted previously, that some agencies, like the FTC and the Environmental Protection Agency (EPA), do possess the power to initiate cases for the purposes of settling disputes and/or making and clarifying policies. This is considered overall to be a haphazard, inefficient, and ineffective way to approach agency policy-making, especially in view of the fact that the typical regulatory agency must confront massive regulatory problems with its very limited resources. In this regard, Shapiro concluded, "the fact remains, however, that when an agency like the FTC has concentrated on adjudication, it has been justifiably criticized for prosecuting violations, large, small, or utterly insignificant, when it finds them rather than attempting a more rational allocation of its limited resources."[18] In "Policy Oscillation at the Labor Board: A Plea for Rulemaking," Samuel Estreicher expresses agreement with Shapiro's position, arguing that the adjudicative approach to policy-making by the National Labor Relations Board has turned labor law into a "nightmare." He concludes by noting that the NLRB should "take its policymaking responsibility more seriously" by relying on the rule-making approach. Its use "should improve the quality of the Board's decision, its success rate in the courts, and, ultimately, its institutional standing."[19]

Rule-Making or Order-Making? Perspectives from the Regulated, the General Public, and Agency Officials

It is accurate to say that the perceived advantages and disadvantages of rule-making or order-making as policy-making approaches depend largely on how particular parties believe specific rule-making or order-making practices will benefit or harm their interests. Three broadly defined groups have a stake in agency policy-making procedures, and each perceives the pros and cons of rule-making and order-making procedures quite differently. This should be expected since the regulated, the general public, and the agencies themselves have radically different selfish interests to protect and promote.

The Regulated. Of course, the regulated seek to secure their position in society by attempting to influence administrative policy-makers to see things their way. Big, wealthy, and powerful interest groups have been successful in persuading rule-makers to see it their way. For this reason, the regulated industries generally prefer rule-making to order-making. Rule-making provides the regulated with advance notice and a chance to submit viewpoints for the purpose of altering a proposed rule more to the industry's liking. Since rule-makers do not want to promulgate policies that might meet with forceful resistance, including lawsuits, agencies frequently respond to the so called "suggestions" of the regulated.

The regulated also favor rule-making over adjudication because the process generally leads to quickly promulgated rules, uniformly applied in the industry. This has the advantages of minimizing unnecessary delays in the implementation of policies deemed necessary by a regulated industry and reducing business uncertainties and promoting fair competition among industry competitors. In sharp contrast, adjudication is generally perceived by the regulated as a closed, expensive, time-consuming process leading to uncertain and sudden policy stands. In the view of the regulated, the incremental order-making process excludes the general industry from agency policy decisions, leads to unnecessary litigations, and tends to promote instability and industry-wide inequities. However, at times particular industry competitors may prefer adjudication to serve their special interests. For example, companies with vast financial resources may want to delay the implementation of agency policies they believe to be unfavorable, particularly those they feel will prove costly or give their competitors a better relative position in the marketplace. Individual corporations, or groups of them, have been known to delay agency implementation efforts for many years, sometimes a decade or more. There was, for example, a controversy over the definition of peanut butter involving peanut butter manufacturers and the Food and Drug Administration (FDA) that continued for a decade or so during the 1950s and 1960s.

The General Public. The general public, who frequently regard the regulated as their nemesis and perceive the regulators as captives of those that they are entrusted with regulating, also favor administrative rule-making to administrative adjudication. In the first place, if policy-making through adjudication is perceived as expensive, unpredictable, and impractical by the regulated, one can imagine how the general public would react. The public, probably best represented by underfunded and understaffed consumer groups such as Common Cause and Nader's Raiders, do not commonly look with favor on fighting for their interests via the agency order-making process. Agency adjudicative processes are simply too complex, costly, and time-consuming; and the resulting orders frequently have limited applicability or social impact.

The resources of consumer or citizen action groups are generally so scarce that these organizations have learned that they can usually be more cost-effective in shaping agency policy development if they concentrate their efforts on influencing agency rule-making. The rule-making process ideally permits any interested party to present information and arguments for or against a proposed agency rule. Compared with agency adjudicative procedures, rule-making steps are simple and easily understood. For example, after reading the proposed rule in the *Federal Register,* all a party has to do is write or call the contact person at the agency cited along with the proposed rule. The example from the *Federal Register* shown here displays the apparent simplicity and openness of rule-making, naturally making it appealing to the general public, especially since access appears as open to the little person as to corporate giants.

> **Federal Register/Vol.** 57, No. 109/Friday, June 5, 1992/Proposed Rules
>
> **SECURITIES AND EXCHANGE COMMISSION**
>
> **17 CFR PART 270**
>
> **Exclusion From the Definition of Investment Company for Certain Structured Financings**
>
> **AGENCY:** Securities and Exchange Commission.
>
> **ACTION:** Proposed rule and request for comment.
>
> **SUMMARY:** The Commission is proposing a new rule under the Investment Company Act of 1940 (the "Act") to exclude certain issuers that pool income-producing assets and issue securities backed by those assets ("structured financings") from the definition of "investment company." The proposal would permit structured financings that meet the conditions of the rule to publicly offer their securities in the United States without registering under the Act and complying with the Act's substantive provisions. The proposed rule is

intended to remove an unnecessary and unintended barrier to the use of structured financings in all sectors of the economy, including the small business sector.

DATES: Comments must be received on or before August 4, 1992.

ADDRESSES: Comments should be submitted in triplicate to Jonathan G. Katz, Secretary, Securities and Exchange Commission, 450 Fifth Street, N.W., Washington, D.C. 20549. All comment letters should refer to File No. S7-12-92. All comments received will be available for public inspection and copying in the Commission's Public Reference Room, 450 Fifth Street, N.W., Washington, D.C. 20549.

FOR FURTHER INFORMATION CONTACT: Rochelle G. Kaufman, Senior Counsel, (202) 272-2038, Elizabeth R. Krentzman, Attorney, (202) 272-5416, or Karen L. Skidmore, Assistant Director, (202) 272-2048, Office of Regulatory Policy, Division of Investment Management, 450 Fifth Street, N.W., Washington, D.C. 20549.

Big money or a high-priced lawyer does not appear to be necessary to influence agency rule-making decisions. This public perspective is true as long as agency decision-makers do not play favorites when weighing submitted comments. It should be noted, however, that in reality the average person is very unlikely to read the *Federal Register* or even to be aware of its existence, a fact that works to the advantage of special interests, which pay much more attention to proposed rules published in the *Federal Register,* thus placing themselves in a better position to react to proposed agency rules they oppose.

Nevertheless, on its face, the rule-making process, as contrasted with order-making, seems to embrace the democratic principles of fair play more than agency adjudication. Rule-making is comprehensible, relatively quick, and democratically accountable, especially in the sense that decision-making is kept above board and equal access is provided to all. As Professor Estreicher asserted while making his plea for the use of the rule-making process at the NLRB: "Rulemaking ensures a level of public participation in the policymaking process not currently available. The opportunity for public participation is automatic with each notice of rule-making, and open to all concerned."[20] Pluralist interests are fairly represented also. Despite political interest group realities that suggest otherwise, the general public is probably correct in assuming that public policies are more fairly promulgated through rule-making than order-making and that their interests will probably be best represented by agency rule-making.

Agency Officials. It is difficult to state generally whether most agencies prefer rule-making or order-making for formulating agency policies. From the perspective of agency officials, there are obvious advantages and disadvantages of each approach. Rule-making allows agencies to propose and implement rules rather quickly; yet only under ideal circumstances is the process free from headaches for agency rule-makers. If the proposed rules are significant or controversial, agency administrators can expect vehement commentary protests from interests in their environment, some of which are very powerful and influential. Despite the total discretionary power of agency officials to consider or ignore submitted comments, agency leaders are always fearful of powerful protests to proposed agency actions that might jeopardize the stability and welfare of their agency.

Agency officials also see the difficulty of promulgating general policies through rule-making that will be fair to all affected parties. One chief advantage to rule-making, as contrasted with agency adjudication, is that it is quite cost-effective in the sense that it allows an agency to make efficient use of its limited resources, since blanket rules are made that can be applied, for example, industry-wide to resolve many questions all at once. This point was made very clear by the District of Columbia Circuit Court in *National Petroleum Refiners Assn. v. FTC,* 482 F.2d 672 (1973), by the Ninth Circuit Court in *Ford Motor Co. v. FTC,*

673 F.2d 1008 (1981) (cert. denied, 459 U.S. 999; 1982), and by the Tenth Circuit in *First Bancorporation v. Board of Governors,* 728 F.2d 434 (1984). In *Ford Motor Co.* the court was very clear in overruling an FTC order.

> The precise issue . . . is whether this adjudication changes existing law, and has widespread applicability. It does, and the matter should be addressed by rulemaking. . . . Ultimately, we are persuaded to set aside this order because the rule of the case made below will have general application. It will not apply just to Francis Ford. Credit practices similar to those of Francis Ford are widespread in the car dealership industry, and the U.C.C. section the F.T.C. wishes us to interpret exists in 49 states (at 1009–10).

To reiterate, rule-makers with a conscience realize that the application of a general rule benefits and harms some interests much more than others. For example, in 1979 the Office of Higher Education of U.S. Department of Health, Education, and Welfare (now the Department of Education), put into effect a controversial and well-publicized rule that apparently required all colleges and universities to spend equal dollar amounts on male and female athletics programs. The rule constituted technically a policy interpretation of Title IX, Section 901(a), of the Education Amendments of 1972, Intercollegiate Athletics, and was published on December 11, 1979, in the *Federal Register,* pp. 71413–23. Although rooted in noble equal opportunity principles, the rigorous application of this rule would have devastated certain college and university athletics programs, especially those of schools that spend millions on revenue-producing male football programs. Although small colleges would have felt the impact of this rule, such universities as Alabama and Ohio State, which use football revenues to subsidize other existing university programs, would likely have suffered great financial losses. Early in the first Reagan administration, the rule was changed to reduce the hardships it had created for some colleges and universities.

Thus, because of the inequities inevitably involved in the promulgation and implementation of general policies, some agencies have preferred to use adjudication or the case-by-case approach. On the whole, this approach provides agency administrators with more flexibility and thus the potential to avoid unnecessary and disruptive regulatory battles. The adjudicative process allows agency officials to assess the entire regulatory picture and to focus on specific problems they perceive as most troublesome. This is especially true if agencies possess the statutory authority to initiate cases. Agency administrators may also prefer the adjudicative approach because it allows them greater flexibility in reversing previous policy directions quickly, without having to advertise and defend their new policy decisions before all interested parties. As mentioned earlier, the courts are more tolerant of agencies reversing previous orders than they are of sudden agency rule reversals.

Agency administrators may also prefer the order-making approach over rule-making because they might be undecided on just what course of regulatory action to take. By proceeding by the case-by-case approach, agency decision makers have the flexibility of cautiously building regulatory policies at a time when insufficient data and technical knowledge should rightfully preclude risky, comprehensive policy stands. The Nuclear Regulatory Commission, for example, has been severely criticized for failing to prevent unnecessary and dangerous accidents in nuclear power plants because the commission irresponsibly promulgated rules not based on a thorough collection and evaluation of crucial scientific facts and questions concerning the safety of nuclear power plant operations, including the disposal of nuclear waste.

In reality, because circumstances differ significantly from one agency to another, the reasons for one agency preferring rule-making over order-making vary greatly. But systems theory does suggest that agency administrators would not only evaluate their choice of policy-making tools on the basis of perceived short- and long-range consequences but also consider which approach appears to be politically best. Since systems theorists maintain that agency survival needs must be considered first, the chances are good that agency officials will normally prefer the policy-making method that can best help them reach their statutory obligations without jeopardizing agency stability or causing any unnecessary headaches.

Why Davis Regards Agency Order-Making as Undesirable for Public Policy-Making

Probably no administrative law scholar has taken a stronger stand against agencies using order-making as an approach for making general regulatory policies for broad application in society than Kenneth C. Davis. Although Davis espoused these arguments in the 1970s, they are well reasoned and, consequently, still supported by the vast majority of administrative law scholars in the 1990s. Therefore, it seems appropriate to conclude a discussion of the pros and cons of rule-making and order-making by summarizing Davis's arguments regarding why he feels agency adjudicative procedures are far inferior to rule-making processes for promulgating public policies aimed either directly or indirectly at large numbers of persons or groups in American society. Davis presents basic democratic arguments in favor of rule-making, acknowledging that many more could be added. It should be understood that these arguments favoring rule-making over order-making in policy-making only apply when agency administrators promulgate orders to be broadly applied to affect many. Reflecting the opinion of many administrative law experts, Davis does not object to agency administrators who employ adjudication to make agency regulatory policies as long as they are intended to only affect a few.

Davis's funadmental contention is that rule-making provides for the systematic notification of all who may be affected by agency rules since all proposed rules must be published in the *Federal Register* so that they can be scrutinized by interested parties. This allows any party a chance to contact the appropriate agency to voice an opinion on a proposed rule before the rule becomes final. In contrast, during adjudication proceedings, agency officials normally listen to only those arguments made by the specific parties in the dispute, thus preventing outside interested parties from participating, even though they may be affected dramatically by the new agency order (policy).[21] To Davis, as to most observers, this appears patently unfair and undemocratic, especially when one considers that affected parties are left unrepresented in the policy-making process.

Davis is also convinced that agency policies that result from rule-making are likely to be more sound since they are products of a more sensible and efficient decision-making process. He holds that agency policies made through rule-making are likely to reflect a more comprehensive survey of relevant data and opinion than policies that are a consequence of agency adjudication. In Davis's words:

> An administrator who is formulating a set of rules is free to consult informally anyone in a position to help, such as the business executive, the trade association representative, the labor leader. An administrator who determines policy in an adjudication is usually inhibited from going outside the record for informal consultation with people who have interests that may be affected. In policymaking through adjudication, either the quest for understanding is likely to be impaired or the tribunal's judicial image is likely to be damaged.[22]

An important related point is suggested here. Although agency decisions reached through adjudications may be well supported on the basis of the record, it is also true that the data in the official record are normally quiet limited in scope. Since a hearing record usually includes only the information and arguments submitted by the particular parties in a specific dispute, only feeble documentation exists to justify broad policy decisions.

Another argument that Davis makes against order-making, when employed by agencies to promulgate general regulatory policies, is founded on the strong distaste he has for the retroactive character of agency adjudication. He asserts that retroactive policy-making constitutes an unfair and undemocratic practice in a nation that supposedly honors cherished constitutional principles and tries to operationalize in the political system its maxims of fundamental fairness and due process of law. To Davis, the making and implementation of prospective rules (rather than orders) make much more sense in the United States because such agency activity is considerably more supportive of administrative due process norms. Davis concludes prescriptively:

> Even when retroactive lawmaking through adjudication is not so unfair as to be a denial of due process, the retroactive feature may still be sufficiently unfair that good administrators ought to try to avoid it. Much lawmaking that is now retroactive can and should be avoided. For this reason alone, prospective rules often should be preferred to retroactive lawmaking through adjudication.[23]

Also, Davis holds that Congress cannot function properly in its vital watchdog role if agencies use adjudicative methods to draft general agency policies. He reasons that congressional investigatory committees, despite their spotty and unsystematic efforts to oversee administrative activity, nevertheless still play a valuable supervisory role simply because congressional watchdog committees at least have the potential to watch and check agency administrators as they proceed to make rules. If objections to proposed agency rules are in conflict with the desires of legislators, Congress can employ various tactics to block proposed agency action. For example, in the fall of 1979 the Senate Commerce Committee, besieged by influential industry lobbyists who complained that the Congress had gone too far in strengthening the FTC's regulatory role in some 1974 legislation, approved a bill designed to curtail the kinds of television advertising that could be aimed at children. To Davis, this action appears to be within the administrative process and therefore completely legitimate. That is, if Congress wants to change agency policy directions, he would hold that this is acceptable since Congress is really the most democratically representative body. However, Congress is prevented from influencing the adjudicative process in any effective manner since trial-like proceedings are insulated from outside forces in the policy. Even Congress is prohibited from tampering with order-making proceedings. This is an admirable restrictive overall, but not when administrators use adjudication to preclude democratically legitimate intervention in agency policy-making.

Finally, Davis believes that agency adjudication has its place in agency policy-making, but he feels that this procedure is relied upon too heavily by many public agencies. Some agencies, he demostrates, clearly abuse the order-making function, using it to reach virtually every regulatory decision, regardless of how many people or concerns can be affected by an order. In this context, Davis poses a crucial question:

> Assuming that the fundamental purpose of an agency is and should be to carry out *effectively* and *fairly* the policies chosen by Congress in the legislation the agency administers, do you think that purpose is better accomplished (a) singling out particular mergers for prosecution and adjudication after the mergers have occurred, or (b) making an industry-wide investigation, conducting a rule-making proceeding, and systematically stating the enforcement policy that will be applied to the industry, with possible later action in individual cases?[24] For Davis, the answer to this question is obviously (b)!

Davis's arguments for agency rule-making have evidently been persuasive. Not only have many administrative law scholars adopted his viewpoint, but the Council of the Administrative Law Section of the American Bar Association's (ABA) House of Delegates has also. In 1985 this ABA Council adopted the following resolution.

RESOLVED, That the American Bar Association approves the following principles respecting the choice between rulemaking and adjudication in administrative agency proceedings:

1. An agency is generally free to announce new policy through an adjudicative proceeding.
2. When rulemaking is feasible and practicable, an agency which has been granted broad rulemaking authority ordinarily should use rulemaking rather than adjudication for large-scale changes, such as proscribing established industry-wide practices not previously thought to be unlawful.
3. An agency should not be empowered to treat its adjudicatory decisions precisely as if they were rules. In particular, it is inappropriate to empower an agency or court to treat third-party departures from holdings in agency adjudications as, *ipso facto,* violations of law. Where the precedent of a prior adjudication is sought to be applied in a subsequent adjudication, a party should have a meaningful opportunity to persuade the agency that the principle involved should be modified or held inapplicable to his situation.

SERVING DUE PROCESS IN AGENCY HEARINGS

Earlier comments in this chapter on the difficulty of differentiating rule-making from order-making should not be interpreted to mean that it is never obvious which function is being performed by an administrative agency. When an agency is required by statute to hold a full hearing under specified conditions, the APA outlines how the hearing should be conducted. Section 554 of the act, "Adjudications," simply sets forth steps and features to be included in formal order-making (that is, in a fair hearing). It is estimated that fewer than 10 percent of agency adjudications are formal, while more than 90 percent are more or less informal.[25] The agency hearing is not expected to be a copy of a formal court trial, but hearings should reflect basic court procedures. One fundamental reason for this is that the courts have found that it is easier to review legal points and procedures if the agency hearing process closely resembles actual court proceedings.

Hearings should be conducted in such a way that due process is served. Because administrative agencies decide questions that may place heavy financial or personal hardships on persons who might lose, agency hearings are expected to uphold constitutional principles of fair play by not denying anyone freedoms, rights, or property without due process of law. Although due process is mentioned in the Constitution, it is not defined. But over the years the term has been given some meaning by legislatures and courts, although no clear meaning has been reached. In *Snyder v. Commonwealth of Massachusetts,* 54 S.Ct. 330 (1934), the Court held that due process should meet standards of "fundamental fairness"; in *Rochin v. California,* 342 U.S. 165 (1952), the Court argued that any governmental activity that is "shocking to the conscience" contradicts due process, or, as Edwin W. Tucker noted, "The constraints of due process are generally shaped by the contemporary collective intuitive sense of what is right and what is wrong."[26,27] More recently, the Supreme Court in *Cleveland Board of Education v. Loudermill,* 105 S.Ct. 1487, 1493 (1985), stated: "The point is straightforward: the Due Process Clause provides that certain substantive rights—life, liberty, and property—cannot be deprived except pursuant to constitutionally adequate procedures. The categories of substance and procedure are distinct. Were the rule otherwise, the Clause would be reduced to a mere tautology." The *Loudermill* decision makes clear that once "certain substantive rights" are granted by the legislature, they become "property interests" that cannot be taken away unless minimum due process procedures are employed. Consequently, since Congress and state legislatures have been granting persons more and more legal entitlements or property interests under law, we can expect to see in the future the granting of more hearings to persons, extending to them at least the minimum due process protections.[27] On the other hand the Supreme Court has held emphathetically that *only* administrative or procedural due process (a step down from more elaborate constitutional due process protections) need to be provided when property rights are not at stake. In *Board of Curators v. Horowitz,* 435 U.S. 78 (1978) and *Pension Benefit Guar. Corp. v. L.T.V. Corp.,* 110 S.Ct. 2668 (1990), the Court ruled that due process in the form of formal adjudications was not required because property interests were not involved. Thus, in administrative law the meaning of due process shifts with the kinds of interests at stake. Administrative agencies must be certain about the interests at stake so that they can extend to persons the appropriate due process procedures.

In an attempt to achieve due process in agency hearings, the major provisions of the APA require agencies to: (1) provide appropriate persons proper notice as to the "time, place, and nature of the hearing," "the legal authority and jurisdiction under which the hearing is to be held," and "the matters of fact and law asserted"; (2) take into consideration "the convenience and necessity of the parties or their representatives" when scheduling the time and place of the hearing; (3) afford all concerned parties (normally limited to litigants in the dispute) the opportunity to submit and consider all relevant facts, arguments, and proposed settlements or adjustments as time and public interest may permit; and (4) forbid agency employees who have acted as investigators or prosecutors in a case to participate in a hearing decision, except as counsel or a witness in the public proceeding. In addition to these provisions, sections subsequent to 554 strengthen the effort to achieve a fair hearing by legally obligating agencies to: (1) allow persons in hearings to be represented by counsel; (2) conclude hearing business "within a reasonable time"; (3) promptly inform interested parties as to the action taken or intended and, in the case of denied requests, the reason why the request was denied; (4) arrive at decisions, rules, or orders in light of the "whole record" or part of the record which is based on "substantial evidence"; (5) provide unbiased and quasi-independent administrative law judges (formerly known as hearing examiners), who can reach decisions fairly and impartially; (6) permit persons to dispute and challenge agency evidence and opinions by providing adequate time and opportunity for persons to present conflicting data, conduct cross-examination, and so on, "as may be required for a full and true disclosure of the facts"; (7) keep a complete transcript of the hearing proceedings to constitute the "exclusive record," or reviewable basis for decision; (8) state and substantiate in the record all findings and conclusions; (9) provide for within-agency appeal; and (10) permit and prepare for judicial review of agency actions.

A few relevant cases put contextual meaning and life into the statutory prescriptions of how public agencies ought to perform and dramatize the importance of administrative due process in the making of public policies through order-making. *Morgan v. United States,* 304 U.S. 1 (1938), in a classic administrative law case that focuses on some fundamental requisites that should be included in any fair hearing process. The judicial wisdom displayed in the case was influential in shaping the 1946 APA. The appellant, Morgan, a stockyard operator, argued in this case that the secretary of agriculture had set the maximum rate he could charge in his business without due process of law. The Packers and Stockyards Act of 1921 extended to the secretary of agriculture the power to "determine and prescribe" maximum and reasonable rate charges, but only after a "full hearing." Because Congress realized that it was granting the secretary vast discretionary powers, which could be abused by irresponsible secretaries, the Congress emphasized its intention that rates should never be imposed on stockyard operators without the benefit of a fair hearing. Morgan charged that: (1) the secretary's decision was made behind closed doors; (2) Mogan was not given proper notice; (3) specific charges were not made against him; (4) he was not given reasonable time to respond to the general charges made against him; (5) he was never able to see and examine agency evidence to be used against him; (6) he was not allowed to see and make a rebuttal to the department's findings and conclusions; and (7) he was denied an appeal or rehearing within the agency. Originally, Morgan appealed the secretary's order to the district court, which refused to hear the complaint. Morgan then appealed to the Supreme Court. Chief Justice Charles Evans Hughes, speaking for the majority, reversed the district court's decree and declared invalid the secretary's order, arguing that his decision could not stand "as the hearing was fatally defective" on several grounds (at 22).

In the first place, the Court held that administrative agencies must respect and uphold specific directions and intentions of Congress when executing congressional policies if liberty is to be retained:

> The vast expansion of this field of administrative regulation in response to the pressure of social needs is made possible under our system by adherence to the basic principles that the Legislature shall appropriately determine the standards of administrative action and that in administrative proceedings of a quasijudicial character the liberty and property of the citizen shall be protected by the rudimentary requirements of fair play. These demand 'a fair and open hearing,' essentially alike to the legal validity of the administrative regulation and to the maintenance of public confidence in the value and soundness of this important governmental process. Such a hearing has been described as an "inexorable safeguard" (at 15).

The Court elaborated further on the nature of a fair hearing:

> The right to a hearing embraces not only the right to present evidence, but also a reasonable opportunity to know the claims of the opposing party and to meet them. The right to submit argument implies that opportunity; otherwise the right may be but a barren one. Those who are brought into contest with the Government in a quasijudicial proceeding aimed at the control of their activities are entitled to be fairly advised of what the government proposes and to be heard upon its proposals before it issues its final command (at 18).

The Court was particularly disturbed by the secretary's choice to accept and make "as his own the findings which have been prepared by the active prosecutors for the Government, after an ex parte discussion with them and without according any reasonable opportunity to the respondents in the proceeding to know the claims thus presented and to contest them. That is more than an irregularity in practice; it is a vital defect" (at 22).

In *Cinderella Career and Finishing Schools, Inc. v. Federal Trade Commission,* 425 F.2d 583 (D.C. Cir., 1970), the United States Courts of Appeals for the District of Columbia focused on the vital importance of maintaining impartiality in the hearing process if hearings are to be fair or consistent with the principles of due process. In this case the FTC ordered a finishing school to "cease and desist" from its then-current advertising practices, which the commission concluded were "unfair and deceptive." But the Cinderella school protested the commission's decision, arguing that Chairman Paul Dixon had made biased public speeches and comments against the finishing school before the hearing took place, thus demonstrating that he had already prejudged the case. This action, the finishing school maintained, precluded the possibility of a fair and impartial hearing. The court agreed, acknowledigng that "there is in fact and law authority in the Commission, acting in the public interest, to alert the public to suspected violations of the law by factual press releases whenever the Commission shall have reason to believe that a respondent is engaged in activities made unlawful by the Act." But, the decision says,

> this does not give individual Commissioners license to prejudge cases or to make speeches which give the appearance that the case has been prejudged. Conduct such as this may

> have the effect of entrenching a Commissioner in a position which he has publicly stated, making it difficult, if not impossible, for him to reach a different conclusion

in light of the facts and arguments in the record (at 590). Noting the flagrant disregard Chairman Dixon had for the record and any litigant's right to a hearing by an impartial tribunal, the Court asserted that "it is appalling to witness such insensitivity to the requirements of due process" (at 591). According to the court, Dixon was legally obligated to disqualify himself from the case. By not having done so, he prevented due process from being carried out. Consequently, the court ordered the FTC to review the decision in light of the evidence on record and without Dixon.

However, in recent years courts have evidently forgotten about the *Cinderella* court's claim that such prejudgment violates due process standards in agency hearings. In this more conservative era courts have commonly applied the "closed mind" rule, which means that due process in agency hearings is not violated even if hearing examiners sitting on administrative tribunals have made prejudicial remarks as long as they do not have ". . . an unalterably closed mind on matters critical to the disposition of the proceeding" (*Housing Study Groups v. Kemp,* 736 F.Supp. 321, 332 [D.D.C., 1990]).

In sum, although in America the meaning of due process has remained relatively stable over time, unquestionably what constitutes precisely due process in, say, agency hearings at a given point in our history depends upon a lot of things. In posing the question, "what process is due," Supreme Court Justices, Souter, White, O'Connor, and Rehnquist, dissenting in *Burns v. U.S.,* 111 S.Ct. 2182, 2192 (1991), quoted cases to make this point. "Due Process unlike some legal rules, is not a technical conception with a fixed content unrelated to time, place, and circumstances, . . . but is 'flexible (calling for such procedural protections as the particular situation demands.' " In a sociopolitical context, the meaning of due process in general, but in agency adjudications specifically, changes with our political moods as we shift back and forth from relative conservativism to relative liberalism.[28] Of course, it is challenging to legal scholars and practitioners to follow these shifts to keep current. It is a major purpose of this chapter to note these shifts as they apply to due process procedures in agency hearings.

ADMINISTRATIVE HEARINGS VS. COURT TRIALS

Overview

As compared with rule-making, agency adjudicative procedures are typically much more elaborate. However, the agency hearing process is usually less elaborate or formal than typical court trials. Since parties may suffer substantial losses if they come out on the short end of agency hearings, adjudicative procedures must be elaborate enough to protect persons from blatant or gross denials of due process. However, since only administrative law matters are the subject of agency hearings (for example, license renewals, compliance with agency rules disputes, rate adjustments), it has been commonly argued that agency adjudicative procedures need not approach the rigorous and complex procedures demanded in court trials, in which the litigants may have much to lose. Of course, in criminal cases defendants sometimes literally have their lives at stake. Due process procedures in such cases, especially in a nation that cherishes human rights doctrines, are expected to be quite elaborate.

In fact, some observers have argued that many agency disputes involve privileges, not rights, and that the adjudicative procedures should therefore be informal, if granted at all. These critics think it is highly questionable whether hearings should be granted by agencies at all, since persons are not legally entitled to something if only privilege is in question. They feel that an agency is only being generous when it grants a hearing to a party who has a dispute involving a privilege.

However, because agencies could avoid confrontations with parties by regarding the matter in question as a privilege instead of a right, thus escaping the obligation of holding an inconvenient and time-consuming hearing, the courts in the past few decades have been placing an increasing number of areas of controversy in the rights category to protect persons against possible agency abuses. In *Goldberg v. Kelly,* 397 U.S. 254 (1970), the Supreme Court flatly rejected the value of the rights–privileges distinction, arguing essentially that the right to a hearing should not depend so much on whether the claim is considered a right or a privilege, but on the extent to which a person might be expected to suffer a "grievous loss."

However, not much seems certain in the development of administrative law. Just when it appeared that the "old" rights—privileges debate was administrative law history, the Ninth Circuit Court stunned many legal scholars in *Freeman v. Hittle,* 747 F.2d 1299 (1984), by rooting its decision in the argument that a liquor license could be taken away without a hearing because a liquor license is not a constitutionally protected right. Shocked by the ruling, Professor Bernard Schwartz exclaimed:

> Such a decision by a respected federal appellate court makes one gasp. All the post-Goldberg federal cases (none of which are [sic] in Freeman) have repudiated the notion of the liquor license as a mere 'privilege.' It is as though the court had never heard of the 'due process revolution' that has so transformed our law of administrative procedure. Or perhaps the Ninth Circuit is trying to outdo Attorney General Meese in the effort to undo much of the century's administrative law development.[29]

However, Schwartz should not be so concerned because the *Freeman* decision has been ignored, particularly by the Supreme Court.

Hearings can be more or less formal, but most agency adjudications are quite informal, frequently amounting to nothing more than discussions involving the concerned parties, which lead to a mutually acceptable settlement. However, to protect those involved, Congress has required minimum due process procedures. Specifically, the Administrative Procedure Act, the most rudimentary law governing administrative procedure, has set forth basic uniform standards that must be followed by agency administrators when conducting hearings. Not only has Congress, through various statutes, compelled agency administrators to honor certain procedural safeguards in adjudications, but pressures to comply with the principles of due process have also come from constitutional provisions, especially the Fifth and Fourteenth Amendments, as well as from the public, the media, the regulated, the courts, and even the agencies themselves. Some of the strictest rules to ensure fundamental fairness in agency adjudications stem from agency rules and regulations governing procedure.

Even so, many agencies have not done a very good job in ensuring that parties in disuptes are accorded fair treatment in agency hearings. Some agencies, according to the courts, have been content to allow adjudicative procedures that, even in the light of the existence of APA requirements, "are shocking to the conscience" (*Rochin v. California,* 342 U.S. 165 [1952]). As a result, the courts in recent decades have tried to ensure reasonable fairness in agency adjudications by imposing their collective will on agency administrators. In *John R. Gagnon v. Gerald H. Scarpelli,* 411 U.S. 778 (1973), a precedential case, the Supreme Court outlined what is believed should constitute *minimum* due process standards, especially in cases in which severe penalties may be attached to a decision (for example, a revocation of probation resulting in return to prison). In the *Goldberg* case the Supreme Court tried to place into perspective the weights that should be assigned to the obligation of the agency to extend procedural due process to "clients" vs. agency needs to reduce the demands on its limited resources. Although it appears that the Supreme Court would apply the principle more broadly, at least in the context of welfare claimants, the Court held: "Thus, the interest of the eligible recipient in uninterrupted receipt of public assistance, coupled with the State's interest that his payments not be erroneously terminated, clearly outweighs the State's competing concern to prevent any increase in its fiscal and administrative burdens" (at 266). But 3 years later, in *Gagnon,* the Court felt that some procedural protections (for example, the agency having to provide counsel to a party) go beyond minimum due process entitlements and tend to place a heavy burden on the limited resources of a public agency and that such procedural safeguards therefore need not always be granted. The Court remarked: "Certainly, the decision making process will be prolonged, and the financial cost to the State—for appointed counsel, counsel for the State, a longer record, and the possibility of judicial review—will not be substantial" (at 788).

In 1976 in *Mathews v. Eldridge,* 424 U.S. 319, the Supreme Court created a three-point analysis test that it felt should be used to determine what due process procedures should be extended to parties under various circumstances.

> First, the private interest that will be affected by the official action; second, the risk of an erroneous deprivation of such interest through the procedures used, and the probable value, if any, of additional or substitute procedural safeguards; and finally, the Government's interest, including the function involved and the fiscal and administrative burdens that the additional or substitute procedural requirement would entail (at 335).

This three-pronged test demands that agency administrators take a practical approach to agency hearings, realizing that providing certain due process procedures may cost way more than they are really worth.

This cost-conscious approach to due process in agency hearings has survived into the 1990s.[30] In *Cleveland Board of Education v. Loudermill,* 105 S.Ct. 1487 (1985), the Court argued that once a property right is granted, the state has the legal obligation to protect it by extending "some kind of hearing" (i.e., at least minimum due process procedures that need not be very elaborate or expensive). In this particular situation the Court held that allowing the employee at least the opportunity to respond to charges against him in a pretermination hearing ". . . would improve neither a significant administrative burden nor intolerable delays" (at 1495). In 1991 in *Burns v. U.S.,* 111 S.Ct. 2182, it was noted that the *Mathews* approach to the application of due process is still applied—and very broadly: "Although *Mathews* itself concerned the adequacy of administrative fact finding procedures, we have not confined the *Mathews* approach to administrative contexts. . . . The *Mathews* analysis has thus been used as a general approach for determining the procedures required by due process whenever erroneous governmental action would infringe [on] an individual's protected interest. . . ." (at 2192–2193).

The cost-conscious standards espoused by the Court in *Mathews* have unquestionably caused agency administrators to avoid having to provide elaborate hearing procedures or trial-like procedures where they felt they could get away with it. However, over the past two decades or so, as noted, legislative bodies and the courts at the national and state levels have conferred upon persons certain due process rights that they once did not have. This extension of rights, frequently making statutory entitlements property rights, has legally obligated administrators to resolve conflicts involving such rights through elaborate due process hearings. Even applying the cost-reduction analysis recommended in *Mathews,* it cannot be ignored that the Court in *Mathews,* in two of its three points in its three-point analysis test, stressed that the interest at stake must be considered along with the procedural impact upon that interest. Since the interests at stake are now frequently property interests, elaborate trial-like procedures are often granted by administrators to protect them.

Also, judges have often urged administrators to make many hearings more trial-like for selfish reasons. Judges have contended that sensible judicial review of administrative hearings cannot occur if agency hearing procedures fail even to resemble court trials. Judges have maintained that it is next to impossible to determine whether proper due process procedures have been extended in a hearing if no reasonable procedural structure is followed.

The bottom line is that judges do have a reason to be concerned with the uneven way due process is incorporated into agency hearings. Due to many factors (e.g., skeletal and vague legislation guiding hearing processes, inconsistent standards or hearing procedures adopted by courts, perceived uniqueness by administrators of their cases), hearing practices vary enormously from agency to agency. This has created two basic problems. First, procedural due process takes on various meanings in different agencies, thus contributing to the uneven application of administrative justice to parties in agency hearings. Second, uneven extension of due process in agency hearings has made intelligent judicial review of agency adjudications extremely difficult, especially in agencies in which hearing procedures are so flawed that judges are left stupefied.

Should Agency Hearings be More Trial-Like?

There is strong reason to suspect that despite the problems associated with the varied interpretations and applications of due process in agency adjudications, it probably would be wise not to formalize the agency hearing process too much. In many respects, the argument that agency adjudicative procedures should become more formalized or more trial like makes only limited sense. If agency hearing procedures were made more trial-like, judicial review of hearing actions would be facilitated simply because all procedures leading to agency rulings would be clearly spelled out for the reviewing judges to see. However, the costs of achieving due process in this kind of agency adjudication may be too high, especially when there is no significant evidence to suggest that very many parties participating in administrative hearings are denied fair treatment.

In the precedential case, *Mathews v. Eldridge,* 424 U.S. 319 (1976), the Court reflected on the practical costs of extending hearing rights, especially in making hearing procedures trial-like. The Court noted:

> Financial cost alone is not a controlling weight in determining whether due process requires a particular procedural safeguard prior to some administrative decision. But the Government's interest, and hence that of the public, in conserving scarce fiscal and administrative resources is a factor that must be weighed. At some point the benefit of an additional safeguard to the individual affected by the administrative action and to society in terms of increased assurance that the action is just, may be outweighed by the cost. . . . The ultimate balance involves a determination as to when, under our constitutional system, judicial-type procedures must be imposed upon administrative action to assure fairness. . . . The judicial model of an evidentiary hearing is neither a required, nor even the most effective, method of decisionmaking in all circumstances. The essence of due process is the requirement that "a person in jeopardy of serious loss (be given) notice of the case against him and opportunity to meet it." (at 348)[31]

Professor Todd Rakoff contends that essentially three models have been used to determine what sort of due process is due in agency hearings.[31] The first model or approach basically requires that administrators provide "some kind of hearing" procedures that minimally satisfy due process requirements as mandated by legislation. That is, administrators employ the minimum due hearing rights and then ask: "What's wrong with this? Do we need to provide anything else or are these procedures O.K.?" The second model starts from the opposite position and assumes that due process can only be obtained in trial-type hearings which employ the adversary approach. This model poses the question: "Is there justification for departing from a trial-type hearing in deciding the matter?" The third model, adopted by the Supreme Court in *Brock v. Roadway Express, Inc.*, 107 S.Ct. 1740 (1987), applies an unacceptable risk standard, which asks: "Are the procedures used so out of line that due process will be subjected to unacceptable risks," or in Court's language ". . . contain an unacceptable risk of erroneous decisions?" (at 1749)[32]

This unacceptable risk standard is the new applicable standard and, when applied, would rarely require that administrators must provide trial-like hearing procedures even when property or liberty interests are at risk. At this point in the 1990s, the Court's position is that trial-type hearings should normally not be granted, balancing the interests of the state against property interests, unless they are absolutely sanctioned by specific statutory provisions. Ultimately, due process is protected by making agency hearing procedures subject to judicial review.[33]

Some have argued that the Supreme Court since *Goldberg* has gone too far to reduce the procedural protections in agency hearings. Certainly, the high Court's decisions starting with *Mathews* have made it much easier for agency administrators to avoid having to provide elaborate trial-type hearings. But is this necessarily the wrong course to take? The plain truth is that administrative hearings should not be expected to provide formal, courtlike procedural protections to litigious parties because administrative agencies are not supposed to act like courts. The sole function of courts is to hear and decide controversies. This is their only constitutional obligation. On the other hand, the primary role of an administrative agency is to see to it that legislative statutes are faithfully executed. Agencies are not courts of law, and to expect that they should function like courts is to expect too much from the administrative system. It should be understood that lawmakers decided in the 1940s to require agencies to provide hearings so that affected parties could question the procedural soundness and fairness of agency actions. Such a legislative measure was taken to help ensure administrative accountability, but clearly legislators never intended to turn administrative agencies into trial courts.

Whether one looks at administrative hearings or court proceedings, employment of due process safeguards vary dramatically with the perceived importance of a case, especially in terms of agency or court time devoted to protecting specific due process requirements. For instance, both court judges and hearing officials may tolerate long presentations of evidence if they believe the issue in question is important, but they would unlikely be as patient with time-consuming evidence presentations if they felt the issue was not very consequential. The point is that in both court trials and administrative hearings, disputes are informally ordered as to rank, according to their perceived importance, thus making the kind of justice rendered dependent upon the informal rank-ordering process. In this light, given the relative importance of cases heard before administrative agencies and courts, especially to the parties involved, it would be most difficult to argue that justice is more evident in court trials than agency hearings.

As a practical consideration, of course, because agency officials have to handle so many disputes each day, they may frequently be tempted to skip even minimal adjudicative procedures in reaching decisions, believing that few parties would bother to appeal decisions that even the parties perceive as unrelated to their vital interests. Consequently, what might be called little injustices are probably quite common as the result of very informal agency adjudications. In fact, some scholars believe that it is in this area where most injustices occur.[34] But in all likelihood, serious injustices would be brought to light and rectified through the agency appeal process. If injustices are still not remedied after all appeals with the agency have been exhausted, the grieving party can still seek judicial review of agency hearing procedures.

Agency vs. Court Compassion

Despite the less elaborate due process standards of typical administrative adjudication compared with court trials, some critics believe that persons stand a better chance of receiving farier, more compassionate treatment from administrative agencies than from courts. According to Victor A. Thompson, this is so because administrative agencies have the luxury of being able to make more "particularistic," as contrasted to "universalistic," decisions than the courts. Therefore, Thompson concludes, administrative agencies tend on the whole to be more compassionate toward individual parties than the courts. In explanation, Thompson notes:

> A belief persists that an individual can get personalized, compassionate treatment in the courts if it is denied to him by the bureaucracy. Although the belief seems plausible because of the large amount of time and money spent by courts on individual cases, it is not well-founded. In the first place, court treatment is so expensive and time-consuming that most people forego it. Bad as it is, an administrative appeal, or a letter to a congressman, and especially the latter, gives the average individual a better chance of success.[35]

Thompson argues that judges, unlike public administrators, feel compelled to make universalistic decisions or decisions that largely ignore or sacrifice the individual for the sake of upholding the law:

> More important is the fact courts are institutionalized to seek the general principle in the individual case. Justice is blind. The individual is unimportant; only the principle counts. One of the hardest lessons for a young law student to learn is that he must give up his natural, compassionate interest in the outcome and dispositions for the actual persons involved in the cases he studies and that he must concentrate solely on the principle of the law involved.[36]

Therefore, Thompson reasons, "Since courts are staffed with law students grown older and professionally successful, courts are among our least compassionate institutions. They rule by deduction from general principles. . . . Decision by deduction from rules is the least compassionate kind there is."[37] Thompson does not deny that administrative agencies also make impersonal, insensitive, universalistic decisions that are patently unfair to individuals, but he does suggest that due process, when measured in terms of compassion instead of the degree of procedural formality alone, is less likely to be experienced in the courts. Although Thompson's argument is controversial, he certainly provides an interesting perspective worth serious reflection.

Professors Ernest Gellhorn and Ronald M. Levin argue an opposing view. In sharp contrast, they contend that court decisions are "essentially personal." They hold that agency decisions are bureaucratized because they are "institutional decisions" made by technical experts or bureaucrats way down in the hierarchy where power has been "subdelegated" to them. They maintain that the impersonal adjudicative decision tends to serve the bureaucracy more than the individual because ". . . it is the product of a bureaucracy rather than of a single person or a group of identifiable people."[38]

In summary, court trial procedures are more elaborate than those normally employed in agency hearings, but one should not necessarily conclude from this that court trials are more apt to reflect the principles of fundamental fairness than agency hearings. As Lewis Mainzer asserts, "Just, effective regulation need not always be grandly formal. In most administrative adjudication the hearing examiner does not exist or never enters, the courts are not approached."[39] Nevertheless, Mainzer maintains, "Most of the time it [agency adjudication] probably achieves practical justice."[40] But the most important point to reiterate it that administrative agencies are not supposed to function like courts. The chief task of an agency is to administer public policies. Also, agencies are required by statute to handle and resolve many disputes daily. Also, unlike courts, they do not have the luxury of being able to reject cases. As a result, agencies must routinely resolve disputes while attending to their administrative tasks. Thus, agency administrators are frequently forced to forgo elaborate hearings for the sake of administrative expediency. Given the limited human and financial resources characteristic of virtually all governmental agencies in the 1990s, as well as the much publicized failure of our federal government to curb the runaway budget deficit successfully, it is reasonable to assume that Congress does not realistically expect anything else. These realities should be kept in mind in the next few sections, which focus on specific features that characterize administrative adjudications, especially formal hearings.

BIAS, DUE PROCESS, AND REGULATORY EFFECTIVENESS

Administrative Law Judges: The Independence Issue

There are critics who are concerned over the apparent lack of independence of administrative law judges (ALJs) from agency control and political influence, yet others play down the independence problems as not serious. These defenders of the present regulatory system stress the importance of maintaining an agency adjudicative system that provides for fair hearings, yet simultaneously does not seriously undermine the effectiveness of the regulatory process. Norman Abrams, for example, voices conern about agency influences that might unfairly bias an administrative law judge's judgment, but nonetheless he understands why an agency would not want to see hearings conducted by adjudicators who are oblivious and insensitive to agency policies, "goals, special regulatory problems, and political considerations." He asks: "Is this inconsistent with the notion of an independent hearing officer?"[41] Also sympathetic to the real problems that agencies face in their efforts to regulate fairly and effectively, Kenneth C. Davis argues especially that the independence of administrative law judges helps to serve the promotion of objectivity and fairness in agency adjudications, but independence should not be so extreme that it frustrates the policymaking efforts of agency administrators."[42]

It should be understood that administrative agencies, boards, and commissions are not politically neutral institutions. Their leaders are political appointees and they serve, to a greater or lesser extent, political causes. Eleanor M. Fox acknowledges the political nature of agency adjudications in her study of two very different political personalities who chaired the Federal Trade Commission: Michael Pertschuk and James C. Miller, III. Chairman Pertschuk, President Carter's appointee and a liberal who tended to side with the underdog and believed that government should do its best to protect individuals from abuse, especially from big business, reached decisions in agency adjudications that reflected clearly his philosophical perspective. Chairman Miller, on the other hand, was President Reagan's appointee and a conservative who sided with the successful, believed that government tended to be the enemy of big business, and felt that governmental intrusion in the private sector only tends to protect the inefficient and weaken society. Chairman Miller's decisions also reflected his predispositions. "At every turn, Mr. Miller drew the inference against the intervention and Mr. Pertuschuk drew the inference for it."[43] Regardless of the facts, Fox concluded, ". . . one sees what one is predisposed to see."[44] Commenting on the value of her own research, she noted: "An understanding of the political nature of the FTC chairmanship helps the student of judicial decisionmaking to pierce the myth of the neutral judge applying economic principles dispassionately."[45] It is important to stress that Fox's study serves to acknowledge the political realities of agency decisionmakers, even those serving in a quasijudicial capacity. She, in actuality, did not condemn the fact that these men let their political philosophies guide them in their jurisprudential role.[46] Possibly Bernard Schwartz summarizes the bias of prejudgment situation best: "If freedom from bias is taken in the broad dictionary sense of absence of preconceptions, no one can ever have a fair trial. The judicial mind is no blank piece of paper; the judge or administrative adjudication starts with inevitable preconceptions. In this sense there is a prejudgment in every case."[47]

Obviously, then, the practical legal question is: How independent should hearing officers be from agency politics, philosophical orientations, outside political pressures, and any other potentially prejudicial influences, if agencies are to provide hearings that are "fair enough"? Predispositions should not bias hearing decisions to such an extent that a mockery is made of due process. To Norman Abrams, for an agency to conduct a reasonably fair hearing, only sufficient impartiality and fairmindedness should prevail, but not so much that administrative law judges must separate themselves from agency policy positions or their political ideas.[48] This viewpoint is upheld in a famous bias case, *American Cyanamid v. F.T.C.,* 363 F.2d 757 (1966), in which the court ruled that hearing officers should not be disqualified simply because they express strong attachment to agency policies. In *Rombough v. F.A.A.,* 594 F.2d 893 (2d Cir; 1979), the court held that it is not inappropriate for agency officials to make hearing decisions that are simply consistent with stated agency policy positions. In a more recent case, *Alma v. United States,* 744 F.Supp. 1546 (S.D. G.A.; 1990), the court argued that a hearing official should not normally be disqualified from hearing a case even though the official publicly stated his or her position on the issues.[49]

Closed Mind Rule

The courts have generally been guided by the "closed mind" rule in bias or prejudgment cases. To prevail before the court the petitioner must prove through "clear and convincing evidence" that the adjudicator has ". . . an irrevocably closed mind on matters critical to the disposition of the proceedings" (*Housing Study Group v. Kemp,* 736 F.Supp. 321, 332 [D.D.C.; 1990]). For example, in *Northwestern Bell Telephone v. Stofferahn,* 461 N.W.2d 129, 131 (1990), the South Dakota Supreme Court held that a Public Utility Commissioner should have recused himself because "clear and convincing evidence" showed that he had an "unalterably closed mind." This commission had previously been ". . . a zealous and active opponent of the deregulation legislation . . ." under question and South Dakota law provides that "[N]o commissioner shall participate in any hearing or proceeding in which he has any conflict of interest. . . ." (S.D.C.L., Sec. 49-1-9; 1983).

Prejudgment of Legislative vs. Adjudicative Facts

In deciding bias or prejudgment cases, courts often make a distinction between prejudgment of *legislative facts* and prejudgment of *adjudicative facts.* Legislative facts are general facts pertaining to law or public policy that help officials at the hearing understand the content of the policy or law. Legislative facts have a general and future orientation since disputes involving legislative facts often focus on the likely impact of certain policies. Normally, courts will not rule that hearing examiners or ALJs should have to disqualify or recuse themselves simply because they have taken or prejudged a prior position on laws, policies, or legislative facts unless, as mentioned, the prejudgment is so severe that it is certain that the adjudicator has an "irrevocably closed mind." Thus, the standard for disqualifying hearing officers who have prejudged legislative facts is not tough because it is assumed that virtually all adjudicators, as public officials, have expressed opinions on public policies.

One of the most famous cases involving prejudgment of legislative facts is *Federal Trade Commission v. Cement Institute,* 333 U.S. 683 (1948). In this case the Supreme Court did not feel that the Commissioners on the FTC had to have disqualified themselves simply because they had clearly expressed grave doubts about the legality of the Cement Institute's pricing scheme prior to a hearing before the FTC. The Court opined that due process was not violated because the Cement Institute was afforded the opportunity to defend its pricing system before the FTC's commissioners, who did not necessarily have an "irrevocably closed mind" on the pricing method (at 701). In *Stofferahn,* involving prejudgment of legislative facts, the Court upheld standards for determining bias as established in *Cement Institute,* but clear and convincing evidence showed that this particular commissioner has "an unalterably closed mind."

In cases involving alleged prejudgment of adjudicative facts, however, courts have generally applied a much tougher standard to ensure due process. Adjudicative facts, in contrast to legislative facts, do not pertain to general policy-oriented facts, but to the more specific facts in a particular dispute relating to the "who, what, where, and how" questions. Adjudicative facts are the kind of particular and immediate facts that judges and jurors decide (e.g., Did television station KZZZ-TV violate FCC Rule XX by broadcasting such and such a program on such and such a date?). Of course, prejudgment of adjudicative facts in administrative hearings would virtually guarantee that due process would not be served. As a consequence, courts have usually ruled that hearing officials must be disqualified if they have prejudged adjudicative facts.

Possibly the most frequently cited case involving the prejudgment of adjudicative facts is *Cinderella Career and Finishing School, Inc. v. FTC,* cited earlier. In this case the D.C. Circuit Court argued that Chairman Dixon prejudged not only legislative facts in his public speeches about the finishing school prior to the school's hearing before the FTC but also specific adjudicative facts, precluding any semblance of fair hearing.

In a highly publicized case former baseball star Pete Rose, who was accused of gambling on baseball games including his own team, argued successfully that baseball Commissioner Bart Giamatti had prejudged adjudicative facts by deciding that Rose's involvement in betting on baseball games had occurred. Giamatti had written a favorable letter to a judge for a convicted felon who was to act as an informer against Rose. In the letter Giamatti said he believed that what the informer said about Rose's gambling on games was true. In light of such prejudgment of accusations against Rose (adjudicative facts), the Ohio court ruled that a hearing conducted by Giamatti would deny Rose his procedural due process rights to a fair, unbiased tribunal free from "improper prejudice" (*Giamatti v. Rose,* 1989 W.L. 111386, 111447 [Ohio Misc., 1989]).

Personal Bias

Prejudice or personal bias for or against a person by an ALJ or hearing examiner also normally constitutes grounds for disqualification of the adjudicator(s). Personal bias (also called actual bias) is directed toward the person, not the issue. Personal bias can be established by showing that an adjudicator or adjudicators, possibly the whole administrative tribunal, have expressed a strong personal bias either for or against a party that would make a fair and impartial hearing virtually impossible. For example, personal bias was charged in a Colorado case because a hearing examiner had in the past called the plaintiff's lawyer a "nasty little fellow" and a "smart ass" (*Neopolan U.S.A. Corp v. Industrial Claims Appeals Office,* 778 P.2d

312 [Colo. Ct. App; 1989]). Such bias need not be enough to disqualify an adjudicator, however, if a reviewing court believes that otherwise the hearing officer allowed "thoughtful and discriminating evaluation of the facts" (*NLRB v. Pittsburgh S.S. Co.,* 337 U.S. 656, 660; 1949). Personal prejudice may also be demonstrated if it can be shown that an adjudicator consistently rules against one side (*NLRB v. Miami Coca-Cola Bottling Co.,* 222 F.2d 341 [5th Cir.; 1977]).

Conflict of Interest

Courts have held that hearing proceedings may be biased and violate procedural due process standards when conflicts of interest, ex parte contacts, or an appearance of unfairness can be shown. The most blatant conflict of interest can be seen when a hearing official stands to gain or lose something of value personally from the hearing decision. In New Jersey the superior court ruled that a public utility commissioner should have disqualified himself because he had entered into a clear conflict of interest when he had inquired about possible employment with a utility company involved in a hearing in which he was an adjudicator (*In re Bergen Co. Util. Auth.,* 553 A.2d 849, 853 [N.J. Super.; 1989]).

Ex Parte Contacts

Bias or prejudice may also compromise fair hearings as a reuslt of ex parte contacts or communications. Ex parte contacts tend to undermine procedural due process in agency hearings because they allow a particular party or party's representatives to communicate with hearing officials about adjudicative or legislative facts in the absence of the other parties in the dispute, thus giving the party making the contact an unfair opportunity to influence the adjudicator(s). Such ex parte contacts are normally prohibited whether court judges or agency administrators are involved, although ex parte contacts are not necessarily prejudicial if matters related to the case were not discussed (*Romey v. Landers,* 392 N.W. 2d 415, 421 [S.D.; 1986]). Nonetheless, ex parte contacts are normally frowned upon because such contacts give the appearance of impropriety. (Much more attention is given later to ex parte contacts in discussion of the exculsive record requirement.)

Appearance of Fairness Doctrine

An old doctrine known as the appearance of fairness doctrine is rooted in common law. Although this standard was at first applied to court trials, the Supreme Court of Washington applied the appearance of fairness doctrine to administrative hearings as far back as 1898 in *State ex rel. Barnard v. Board of Educ.,* 52 P 317 (Wash; 1898). The appearance of fairness doctrine is made quite clear in *Mordhorst v. Egert,* 223 N.W.2d 501, 505 (S.D.; 1974) where the court, quoting a prior case, wrote:

> A fair and impartial tribunal requires at least that the trier of fact be disinterested . . . and that he also be free from any form of bias or predisposition regarding the outcome of the case. . . . Not only must the procedures be fair, "the very appearance of complete fairness" must also be present. These principles apply not only to trials, but equally, if not more so, to administrative proceedings.

But the truth is that courts are very reluctant to require hearing officers to disqualify themselves because of any appearance of bias alone. Plenty of lip service is paid to violations of the appearance of fairness doctrine, but courts are much more likely to enforce this standard when it is coupled with findings of concrete bias.[50]

However, in *1616 Second Ave. Rest v. Liquor Auth.,* 550 N.E.2d 910 (N.Y.; 1990) the New York court of appeals held that the Chairman of the state Liquor Authority violated Second Avenue Restaurant's due process rights by failing to disqualify himself after making public statements against the restaurant, thus giving the "appearance of impropriety" that any "disinterested observer" (a popular standard applied by the court) could readily see. Judge Wachtler wrote

> But whether or not he had actually prejudged the matter, his statements nonetheless gave the impression that he had, and that impression lent an impermissible air of unfairness to the proceeding. More importantly, those statements and the message they conveyed to a "distinterested observer" established the Chairman's public position on the issue (at 913).[51]

Despite the fact that Judge Wachtler wrote for the majority in this case, Judges Simons, Alexander, and Hancock, writing in dissent, probably reflect better the opinion of most courts today when they held that simply an appearance of impropriety due to alleged bias is not sufficient to justify disqualification; existing law requires, quoting from *Matter of Warder v. Board of Regents,* 53 N.Y.2d 186 (1981), a "factual demonstration to support the allegation of bias and proof that the outcome flowed from it" (at 914).

Combination of Functions

One other major source of possible bias is from hearing officials who perform a combination of functions. A combination of functions occurs when an administrative agency allows a hearing official or body to perform not only the adjudicatory function but also the investigatory and possibly even the prosecutory function.[52] According to Stephen R. Miller and Larry T. Richardson, "[T]his practice compromises the objectivity of the administrative inquiry, favoring the interests of the agency."[53] They contend further that the "combination of functions is the most obvious source of bias in administrative hearings."[54] Critics, as well as many courts, have argued that combining the investigatory, prosecutory, and adjudicatory functions in the same hearing official or body presents a blatant conflict of interest, violating the appearance of fairness principle, and, of course, procedural due process. Realizing the procedural due process problems presented by the combination of functions problem, many agencies have in good faith tried to separate the investigatory, prosecutory, and adjudicatory roles within their agencies, but some observers charge that this still is not enough to save due process in agency hearings. The reality is, these critics assert, that all these functions are being performed by the same agency's personnel, leading the public to believe that agency officials are working together in a biased manner. Miller and Richardson comment: "Regardless of how the agency staff thinks or acts, the public perception will always be that the hearing officers are biased toward their agency is a chilling factor which discourages potential claimants and casts doubt on even those decisions that are correctly decided in favor of the agency."[55]

Technically, the federal Administrative Procedure Act, Section 554(d), as well as many state APAs, prohibit agency hearing officials (decision makers) from also serving in a prosecutory and investigatory role. However, Section 554(d), as well as the section's counterpart in most state APAs, applies only to certain formal hearings, thus allowing the combination of functions to be practiced when formal hearing procedures do not have to be observed, which, of course, accounts for most agency hearings. In 1981 the Administrative Conference of the United States rejected its Committee on Agency Decisional Processes's proposal essentially to limit the use of combination of functions in agency hearings by closing some loopholes in the APA.[56]

Today, although combination of functions practices are apparently condemned by most legal scholars and practitioners, the courts have generally not ruled against the use of combination of functions in agency hearings for mostly practical reasons. Courts have normally been sympathetic to agency administrators who have argued that separating functions is costly because it (1) prevents hearing officers from consulting with those who are the most knowledgeable about the case (i.e., those who participated in the investigation); (2) forces the use of more staff to handle cases; (3) causes confusion over what communications among staff are permissible; (4) delays hearing officials from hearing and disposing of cases rapidly; and (5) defies overall practical considerations of administrative efficiency and effectiveness.

In reviewing *In re Deming,* 108 Wash.2d 82 (1987), Stephen Hobbs concluded that one of the reasons that the Washington supreme court applied the "weaker" appearance of fairness doctrine to rule that due process was not violated by the state's Judicial Qualifications Commission when it combined investigatory, prosecutory, and adjudicatory powers was because practical administrative factors had to be weighed. Specifically, a ruling against the Commission would require a basic and costly restructuring of the Commission. "Such a restructioning," Hobbs held, "would not only have been exceedingly difficult to accomplish, it also would have been contrary to the will of the legislature and the people."[57]

A petitioner must overcome not only concerns of administrative practicality to prevail in a combination of functions charge, but also the presumption of honesty and integrity. In other words, the petitioner must overcome the presumption that professional and honest administrators cannot serve due process even if they combine functions.

Rule of Necessity

A controversial doctrine related directly to bias or prejudice cases is the *rule of necessity.* The rule of necessity, based in common law, is controversial because the doctrine appears blatantly to defy common sense. It precludes the disqualification of a hearing examiner, even though the adjudicator may in fact be biased, because no one else is eligible to hear the case. The rule of necessity applies to a single hearing official or an entire administrative tribunal. To many critics, denying due process to a party in an agency hearing this way is wrong and it certainly points to a problem within the administrative law system. Does it make sense to say "Allowing such bias is clearly unfair and will very likely deny the party procedural due process, but let's do it anyway"? To some courts, the rule does make sense and they have not hesitated to apply it. In *Brinkley v. Hassig,* 83 F.2d 351 (10th Cir.; 1936) the court reasoned that when disqualification means that no tribunal will be eligible to hear the case, the public interest must be upheld, even though the individual's rights may be compromised somewhat, by employing the rule of necessity. "From the very necessity of the case has grown the rule that disqualification will not be permitted to destroy the only tribunal with powers in the premises" (at 357).

It is true that the courts do not like to use the rule of necessity, but certain situations apparently give them little choice. Take, for example, the Federal Trade Commission's situation. Joseph E. Edwards contends that the full FTC would probably never be disqualified, despite prevailing prejudice, because no provision in the Federal Trade Commission Act provides for a change in venue.[58] This means that some commissions could be disqualified because of bias (as was Chairman Dixon in the *Cinderella* case), but never the entire FTC. In fact, in *Marquette Cement Mfg. Co. v. Federal Trade Commission,* 147 F.2d 589 (1945) and *FTC v. Cement Institute,* 333 U.S. 683 (1948), the courts said exactly this. In *Cement Institute,* for example, the Court, applying the rule of necessity, concluded: "Had the entire membership of the Commission [been] disqualified in the proceedings against the respondents, this complaint could not have been acted on by the Commission or any other government agencies" (at 701). It appears, then, that possibly the best way to do away with having to use the rule of necessity, which clearly undermines attempts to achieve due process in agency adjudications, is to make legislators provide sensible hearing alternatives when bias becomes an issue.

CONSIDERING EVIDENCE IN AGENCY HEARINGS

Overview: Common Body of Rules of Evidence Apparently Needed

The issues and questions surrounding the case of evidence in reaching decisions in agency haerings are often very technical and contradictory and thus quite confusing, even to legal experts. A major reason for this is that an accepted body of rules of evidence, which would govern all formal administrative hearings, has not made its debut into administrative law just yet. In contrast, in 1975 federal rules of evidence (FRE) were enacted to govern the handling of evidence by federal courts. The FRE provided common rules of evidence that helped to restructure and order the submission and use of evidence. Michael H. Graham, who believes that modified FRE should be used to guide the handling of evidence in agency hearings, contends that FRE have greatly benefitted federal courts and could also benefit agency adjudications. "The enhancement provided by the FRE of predictability and consistency in rulings on admissibility, along with explicit recognition of considerations of waste of time, fosters preparation and orderly conduct of trials."[59] Graham points out that hearings in our federal agencies are somewhat chaotic because they "are governed by more than 280 different sets of regulations controlling the admissibility of evidence."[60] Lack of a common body of rules of evidence also plagues hearings in state agencies. Graham admits that some critics have opposed applying FRE to agency adjudications because they feel that agency proceedings are significantly different from court trials, but he disagrees. "However, the fact is that the FRE apply in federal civil non-jury trials where the need to develop and control an evidentiary record is functionally indistinguishable from the analogous need in administrative adjudications." Elaborating, Graham notes that

> ALJs hear arguments and consider evidence, including live testimony; they apply relevant statutory precedents, and agency regulations in essentially the same manner as do federal or state trial judges sitting without juries. . . . Indeed, the United States Supreme Court has explicitly recognized that the duties of ALJs in formal adjudications are not functionally comparable to those of trial judges.[61]

Numerous cases have made it clear that a common body of rules of evidence does not apply to administrative hearings at the federal or state level, for example, *Goodridge v. Director,* 337 N.E.2d 927 (Mass., 1978); *Manhattan Scene v. SLA,* 397 N.Y.S.2d 495, 4th Dept.; 1977; *Murphy v. Department of Public Welfare,* 480 A.2d 382 (Pa. Commw Ct., 1984); *IHC Hospitals v. Board of Comm'rs,* 108 Idaho 136; 1985; and *Walter N. Yoder and Sons v. NLRB,* 754 F.2d 531 (4th Cir., 1985). Agreeing with Graham, Richard J. Pierce maintains that the fact that over 1100 federal ALJs apply 280 different evidentiary rules of evidence has made a mess out of the adjudicatory system. He claims that the ". . . evidentiary procedure now used in agency adjudications vary substantially along a spectrum from no reference to evidentiary rules at all, to horatory reference to the FRE as a source of guidance, to mandatory incorporation of the FRE."[62] As does Graham, Pierce concludes that steps should be taken to incorporate uniform codes of evidence into agency hearings, but he urges that newly developed standards should not be so rigid that they would prevent ajudicators from employing their discretion to exclude "unreliable evidence."[63] Unreliable evidence pertains mostly to questions involving the reliability of hearsay evidence. But critics claim that the best way to deal with hearsay in agency hearings is to adapt the hearsay rule, as applied in federal court, to unique administrative adjudications "by expanding the exceptions and exemptions, as well as by modifying self-authentication rules in various way to recognize and effectuate the fundamental values and goals of the administrative process."[64] These reforms hold that these measures would promote order and administrative justice in agency hearing without causing unwanted delays. Issues surrounding hearsay are discussed more fully later in the chapter.

Some of the key aspects of evidence that relate especially to due process and public policy considerations are covered in the following sections. For public administration, probably the central point regarding evidence is that in a free and open society, evidence employed to justify conclusions in trials or hearings should be gathered, presented, and evaluated in a manner that does not undermine the principles of fair procedure. Focus in the following sections is on how fairly evidence is presented and judged. To provide meaningful insights, once again some comparisons are made between procedures employed in administrative adjudications and court trials.

Introduction to Procedural Due Process Issues Concerning Evidence

Both administrative hearings and court trials have as an ideal reaching decisions that are both rational and fair. But how can one determine whether adjudicative findings (findings are decisions rooted in adjudicative facts) are rational and fair? Surely there are no foolproof tests, but common sense can play a significant role in assessing whether adjudicative decisions are based upon reasonable review and use of the facts and whether procedural due process has been accorded to the disputing parties. In *Bean v. Unemployment Ins. Comm'n,* 485 A.2d 630 (Me., 1984), the court stated that agency findings do not have to be very detailed or technical, but they must be elaborate enough to explain the basis for the decision. Therefore, it is not enough to summarize findings in a single sentence (*Ship Creek Hydraulic Syndicate v. Department of Transportation,* 685 P.2d 715 [Alaska, 1984]) or in statutory language in the absence of relevant facts (*Gibson v. Municipal Retirement System,* 683 S.W.2d 882 [Tex. Ct. App., 1985]) or cause a court to inquire into the thinking of agency adjudicators because they based their finding on a record ". . . so bare as to frustrate effective judicial review" (*Community for Creative Non-Violence v. Lujan,* 908 F.2d 992, 998 [D.C. Cir.; 1990]).

It would be a mistake even to lose sight of the immediate and chief purpose of agency adjudications: to resolve disputes. However, it must also be remembered that in agency hearings where "final decisions" resolve disputes, important public policy decisions are often developed as well. This dual purpose in administrative adjudications undoubtedly causes some ALJs to pay more attention to creating public policies they consider worthwhile than to resolving disputes in the most fair manner. ALJs are cognizant of the reality that agency chiefs can overrule their adjudicative decisions if their decisions run blatantly contrary to agency policies and goals.

Fairness and rationality in adjudicative proceedings depend not only on the factual quality of the evidence entered into the record but also on how the evidence is actually submitted, employed, and evaluated. Thus, the procedural steps used in employing evidence frequently become the main focal point of critics. Most experts agree that it is not the presentation of evidence by each party per se that is most crucial in allowing any tribunal to reach a fair and rational decision; rather it is providing parties in a dispute with the opportunity to scrutinize and challenge the reliability of the evidence the opposing party presents. Kenneth C. Davis, for example, holds that "the central feature of a trial is not affirmative presentation of evidence by each side; it is the opportunity for each side to attack the evidence presented by the other side."[65] Parties can use various tactics in an attempt to diminish the probative worth of the other disputant's evidence, including (1) written and oral arguments; (2) rebuttals; (3) explanatory statements; and (4) cross-examinations. These due process protections apply to agency hearings as much as to court trials.

Proper Notice

A hearing notice is equivalent to a complaint issued in a civil suit. The importance of providing proper notice when a procedural due process calls for a full evidentiary hearing or formal hearing ". . . with live witnesses and cross-examination and all the rest of the procedural hoopla . . ."[66] cannot be underestimated. In fact, as Bernard Schwartz exclaims, "[T]he first requirement of such 'procedural hoopla' is that of notice."[67] This is because the quality of evidence presented in one's defense would clearly suffer if proper notice is not given. Put simply, proper notice provides the party with essential and specific information about the complaint and sufficient time to prepare a defense. Under the federal APA, Section 554(b) "Persons entitled to notice of an agency hearing shall be timely informed of (1) the time, place, and nature of the hearing; (2) the legal authority and jurisdiction under which the hearing is to be held; and (3) the matters of fact and law asserted."

Courts have long noted that a part of the right to be heard includes proper notice. In *Goldberg v. Kelly,* 397 U.S. 254 (1970) the Supreme Court regarded notice, specifically "timely and adequate notice detailing the reasons for a proposed (action), as a fundamental requisite of due process." Two decades later a New York court held that "Fundamental due process requires reasonable notice sufficient to allow a party to adequately prepare and present a defense to charges that will be the subject of a hearing" (*Diamond Terminal Corp. v. New York State Dept. of Taxation and Fin.,* 158 A.D.2d 38, 41; 1990).

In a 1978 administrative law case the Supreme Court placed the role of notice in clear perspective when it said that the "purpose of notice under the Due Process Clause is to apprise the affected individual of, and permit adequate preparation for, an impending 'hearing' " (*Memphis Light, Gas, and Water Division v. Craft,* 436 U.S. 1, 14. 1978). This ruling was in reference to termination of utility service to a customer. The Court argued that the municipal utility company violated due process requirements when it failed to inform the customer of the availablity of procedures designed to protect against a termination of utility service. In other situations, due process does not necessarily obligate a public agency to tell parties how to complain. That is, due process does not always require an administrative agency to tell someone specifically how to use the protest procedures, as long as they are available. However, in this case the Court felt that because of the importance of utility termination and the varied educational levels of utility customers in general, due process should have entailed a rather specific explanation to the customer on how to complain (for example, where and when to complain, and to whom specifically).

Proper notice also means that actual fundamental fairness must be accorded, not just the appearance of fairness. In other words, the form of the notice, even though technically correct, may not constitute proper notice in actuality if common sense dictates that the notice did not convey in meaningful terms what should have been conveyed in the notice. That is, procedural due process regarding notice means ideally that the notice should actually or meaningfully notify and not deceive. Of course, courts differ considerably on what constitutes proper or actual notice. Nothing in administrative law seems very certain, even something as apparently so simple as notice. For instance, normally the courts hold that formal, written notice is appropriate, yet some judges have ruled that if it can be shown that parties actually were notified by other means so that they understood the essential facts, "the requirement of notification purposed to inform may be satisfied by actual knowledge, especially when it is acted upon" (*McLay v. Maryland Assemblies, Inc.*, 269 M.D. 465, 477; 1973). In *Landover Books, Inc. v. Prince George's County,* 566 A.2d 792 (1989) the Court ruled that an adult book store owner had received proper notice because he ". . . appeared and participated in the hearing on the appeal, thus indicating that it (Landover Books) knew the contents of the notice. . . . Under the circumstances presented, we hold that service was in compliance with the substantive requirements of the ordinance despite the technical irregularity since Landover had actual knowledge of the violation. . . ." (at 798). A Connecticut court upheld that proper notice had been served through a reprimand because the requirement was based on charges identical to the ones violated previously, of which he had received proper notice (*Lillis v. Department of Health Services,* 564 S.2d 646 [Conn. Super.; 1989]).

The truth is that courts will usually uphold the adequacy of notice if they believe that the record of the hearing clearly indicates that the party knew enough about the charges against him or her and had sufficient time to prepare an adequate defense. Nevertheless, courts have on occasion, possibly too often, upheld notices as proper when they have fallen far short of what a reasonable person would consider proper due process standards. Possibly this is so because proper notice in administrative hearings does not have to be as elaborate or detailed as in a criminal complaint, although proper notice for administrative hearings still must be fair enough to allow a party a *sufficient opportunity* to protect his or her rights. Sufficient opportunity is stressed because parties are not guaranteed a right to an adequate defense, but only an opportunity through proper notice to prepare an adequate defense. In *Diamond Terminal v. Dept. of Taxation,* 557 N.Y.S.2d 962 (A.D. 3 Dept.; 1990), a person went unprepared at his hearing because he contended that he did not have time to prepare, even though the record showed that the hearing officer had offered to give him a 30 day adjournment to prepare. The Court felt that the fact the petitioner was given the opportunity to prepare for his defense, even though he did not take advantage of it, "supports a finding that the notice given was sufficient under those circumstances" (at 963).

Burden of Proof

In criminal proceedings the burden of proof is always on the state. That is, criminal defendants are presumed innocent until the state proves them guilty beyond any reasonable doubt. However, in administrative adjudications the burden of proof does not always rest on the agency, although it often does. The federal Administrative Procedure Act incorporates the traditional common law practice that places the burden of proof on the party bringing the action (for example, a person applying for a government benefit must prove that he or she is eligible or an agency charging a company with a rule violation must prove the violation). In short, the mover under the APA normally has the burden of persuading the administrative tribunal that the evidence supports his or her position. The APA, Section 556(d) states: "Except as otherwise provided by statute, the proponent of a rule or order has the burden of proof."

Common sense should suggest that, as a practical matter, it makes a significant difference which side has the burden of proof at a hearing. It is frequently considerably more difficult to prove a charge than to defend against one. Thus, as Barnard Schwartz asserts: "All too often, determining where the burden of proof lies determines who prevails in the case."[68] When the APA does not apply and/or statutes are not clear as to which party has the burden of proof, courts have usually held that agency adjudication should follow customary common law, which assigns the burden to the initiator. However, often court rulings have required agencies to assign burden of proof in such a way that vital liberty and property interests are protected.

A few judicial opinions help to explain in context how the burden of proof standard is applied. In *Esposito v. INS,* 936 F.2d 911 (7th Cir., 1991) the court maintained that Esposito, an alien who had entered the United States through fraudulent and willful misrepresentation, had the burden of proof before the Board of Immigration appeals to show why the Board should exclude from consideration in its hearing a murder conviction by an Italian court. "The burden of course, is on him to point to exceptional procedural infirmities in the proceedings leading to his convictions, and he has failed to do so" (at 915). In *Tyra v. Secretary of Health and Human Services,* 896 F.2d 1024 (6th Cir.; 1990) the court acknowledged how the burden of proof can shift from the claimant to the agency. Parenthetically, under some circumstances the burden of proof may shift back and forth several times before a resolution is reached. In *Tyra* the court pointed out that under the Social Security Act, Section 223(d), as amended, 42 U.S.C.A., section 423(d), the "claimant has the ultimate burden to establish an entitlement to benefits by proving the existence of a disability" (at 1028). In this case Tyra had the burden of proving that he had a severe impairment that prevented him from returning to his previous work. The ALJ ruled that Tyra was impaired enough that he could not return to his past job. However, with this finding the Court noted that the burden of proof shifts to the agency to show what kind of work, if any, the claimant can perform. "At this step in the analysis it becomes the secretary's burden to establish the claimant's ability to work. The secretary must prove that . . . the claimant retains the capacity to perform a different kind of job" (at 1028–1029).

Hearsay Evidence and Its Controversial Status

Hearsay ("heard saying")[69] is discussed by many, but my experience has been that few really understand the meaning and uses of hearsay. What is hearsay or hearsay evidence? Hearsay evidence is second-hand evidence, either oral or written, because it does not come directly from those who made the original statement, but from those on the witness stand who claim that they heard another person say it (*Stockton v. Williams,* 1 Doug., Mich. 546, 570; 1845). Under the New Jersey Rules of Evidence, Rule 63(1)–63(33), which is very similar to Rule 801(c) of the Federal Rules of Evidence, hearsay evidence is defined as "[E]vidence of a statement offered to prove the truth of the matter stated, which is made other than by a witness while testifying at the hearing. . . ."

Hearsay evidence carries weaker probative force (i.e., weight in tending to prove something as true) than nonhearsay because it stands either wholly or partly on the credibility and competency of people other than the witnesses (*State v. Kluttz,* 206 N.C. 726, 804; 1927). Such evidence is not subject to cross-examination because the people who originally made the statements are not present at the hearing. An example of evidence considered hearsay is helpful in clarifying the suspicious nature of such evidence. Imagine that there are three people involved, Green, Black, and White. Green, who is on the witness stand, tells the tribunal that he was told by Black that she saw White, who is on trial for murdering her boyfriend, kill her boyfriend while engaged in a violent argument. Green's statement must be considered hearsay because it is indirect evidence coming from Black who is not present to offer direct testimony. In such a criminal case, the hearsay rule would be applied, thus excluding Green's statement. However, under special circumstances such inferior hearsay evidence has been allowed. In our case, for example, let us say that the court could not subpoena Black to testify because she had died prior to the trial; yet her dying words to Green were that she saw White kill White's boyfriend. Dying declarations have been allowed a hearsay exception by some courts in the past. Beyond the dying declaration exception, 39 other hearsay exceptions have been noted for criminal law alone (e.g., recorded recollections; entry in public record; assertion of pedigree).[70] Nonetheless, hearsay evidence is seldom admitted into evidence in criminal trials because of its obvious inferiority (*State v. Ah Lee,* 23 P.2 424 [Or. 1890]; *State v. Shaw*, 847 S.W.2d. 768 [Mo. banc 1993]).

Despite the fact that hearsay evidence is rarely allowed to enter the record in court trials, such evidence is accepted in agency hearings. For those of us who want hearing decisions to be based on sound and conclusive evidence, permitting hearsay evidence to be included in the official record, which is used ultimately to substantiate the hearing decision, may seem like kangaroo court nonsense. Hearsay evidence can be reliable and steer tribunals to accurate and just decisions, especially if a preponderance of hearsay all seems to support the same conclusion. However, hearsay evidence can also be completely inaccurate. The worst thing about hearsay, as implied earlier, is that it is evidence that cannot be tested for its reliability through cross-examination (*Wulfkuhle v. State Dep't of Revenue,* 234 Kan. 241; 1983; and *Pacific Gas & Electric Co v. FERC,* 746 F.2d 1383 [9th Cir., 1984]). Since cross-examination appears to most legal scholars to be the single best instrument for bringing the truth to light in disputes, hearsay evidence must be considered far inferior to presented facts that have survived the grueling test of cross-examination unshaken.

Nevertheless, despite the weak probative content of hearsay evidence, the Administrative Procedure Act and the courts have allowed hearsay to be presented and used as evidence in administrative hearings (*Flex v. Department of Labor,* 125 Ill. App.3d 1021; 1984); and *Kobilansky v. Liffrig,* 358 N.W.2d 781 [N.D. 1984]). In *Tyra v. Secretary of Health and Human Services,* 896 F.2d 1024, 1030 (6th Cir., 1990), the court said "relevant evidence not admissible in court, including hearsay, is admissible at an administrative hearing." Section 556 of the APA fails to exclude the use of hearsay evidence by stating that "any oral or documentary evidence may be received." However, although Section 556 allows hearsay evidence to be accepted at the discretion of the hearing examiners, it does obligate the agency to exclude as a "matter of policy" all "irrelevant, immaterial, or unduly repetitious evidence," thus discouraging the use of hearsay. Another provision in the same section also discourages hearing examiners from relying too much on hearsay evidence in reaching decisions: "A sanction may not be imposed or rule or order issued except on consideration of the whole record or those parts thereof cited by a party and supported by and in accordance with reliable, probative, and substantial evidence." Since hearsay evidence is rarely considered reliable or probative in content, this section in a sense contradicts its other provision that "Any oral or documentary evidence may be received." Is this section suggesting that hearsay evidence can be received but not used to support hearing decisions?

The controversy surrounding hearsay evidence focuses on two basic questions. Should hearsay be admissible? If it is admissible, what weight should the hearsay evidence be given by agency adjudicators. In criminal law the focus is more on the first question, while in administrative law the focus is more on the second question. That is, because administrative hearings are less formal than court trials, many critics believe that attention should not focus so much on whether the hearsay should be admitted into the hearing record, but on how much weight the hearsay evidence should be given by hearing examiners or ALJs when using it to reach decisions. Courts tend to agree. In *Requero v. Teacher Standards and Practices,* 789 P.2d 11, 14 (Or. App.; 1990), the court noted that "[T]he hearsay nature of evidence . . . may affect the weight that a fact finder chooses to give it, but does not in itself make it inadmissible. Similarly, the nonexistence of corroborating or independent evidence that tends to prove the same fact as the hearsay evidence is not a prerequisite to admissibility of the hearsay, but bears instead on the weight or sufficiency of the evidence offered."

In the first analysis common sense must be emphasized to answer both questions. Since hearsay is automatically somewhat suspect or questionably reliable, common sense should dictate whether it should be admitted into the record or not. Without question, the quality of hearsay differs substantially. Some hearsay may amount to wild and false rumor spread by an unreliable person, while other hearsay may be "the kind of evidence on which responsible persons are accustomed to rely in serious affairs" (*NLRB v. Remington Rand, Inc.*, 94 F.2d 862, 873 [2d Cir.; 1938]). Courts have normally upheld the admissibility of hearsay "in administrative proceedings, so long as the admission of evidence meets the tests of fundamental fairness and probity" (*Bustos-Torres v. INS,* 898 F.2d 1053 [5th Cir.; 1990]).

Ernest Gellhorn and Ronald M. Levin present five basic common sense questions that they feel ALJs should pose when deciding whether the particular hearsay evidence is reliable enough to help support hearing decisions (findings of fact). The first question is: "Are there circumstantial guarantees that the evidence is trustworthy?"[71] The circumstances surrounding some hearsay evidence would suggest that the hearsay is very reliable (e.g., public records, medical reports, and factual news releases by the media technically constitute hearsay evidence, but the circumstances dictate that the information is reasonably reliable). In contrast, the circumstances of other hearsay suggest that the information should not be trusted at all (e.g., hearsay three or four persons removed or a summary account of what another person may have said).

The second question is: Is better evidence available? Common sense dictates that stronger evidence should be used in place of weaker evidence even in administrative hearings, especially if it is not too inconvenient and costly to obtain the evidence. Remember, in more informal agency hearings, as compared to court trials, convenience and cost are factors to be considered. Therefore, ALJs may want to reject hearsay if more reliable and probative nonhearsay evidence can be obtained easily.

The third question is: Would the cost of acquiring better evidence be justified in relation to the importance of the subject matter? The question here focuses directly on the nature of the case. Again, common sense suggests that if the case involves very important property or liberty interests (e.g., revocation of parole, termination of employment), the ALJ should not give very much weight to the hearsay evidence.

On the contrary, if the matter does not involve an important property or liberty interest (e.g., a routine request for a benefit in which thousands of claims are processed), it may be more appropriate to give greater weight to the hearsay. Any serious abuse of discretion in handling the use of hearsay evidence by agency adjudicators could cause injustices to occur. Only a heavy dose of common sense and good faith professional conduct can increase the probability that justice is served.

The fourth question is: How precise must the agency's fact finding be? Hearsay evidence need not be perfect to be used to help substantiate a conclusion, but it should be "good enough." For example, the hearsay evidence may be incomplete as long as it is otherwise accurate or representative of a situation. That is, an administrative tribual may support its finding on the basis of a limited number or sample of complaints against an agency, not a complete sample.

Gellhorn and Levin's final question is: What is the policy behind the statute being enforced? At times the policy may be to handle cases in the most expedient and practical manner possible. If so, we would expect to see hearsay evidence used in a manner consistent with this policy. In contrast, policy may call for a very careful weighing of the evidence, especeially if wrong decisions would put society at grave risk (e.g., Nuclear Regulatory Commission hearing decisions involving plant safety).

In sum, it makes practical sense to use hearsay evidence in agency hearings even though the use of such evidence presents certain problems. However, the problems with hearsay evidence can be drastically minimized if agency adjudicators act professionally and in good faith to see to it that all evidence, including hearsay, is introduced and weighed in a responsible manner so that due process is honored. It should be stressed that administrative hearings are, by design, more informal than court trials, but it should be remembered that justice is served better by good intentions and professional conduct than by formality itself.[72]

Making Sense of Hearsay in Light of the Residuum Rule, the *Perales* Rule, and the Substantial Evidence Test

The residuum rule requires that a finding cannot stand unless it is supported by evidence that would be acceptable in a jury trial. When the residuum rule is applied to hearing decisions, it means that hearsay evidence can be used in helping to reach a decision, but the decision itself must not be supported by hearsay evidence alone but by substantial, nonhearsay evidence. Thomas R. Mulroy, Jr., and Douglas G. McClure provide a frank descriptive definition of the residuum rule: "In other words, hearing officers cannot base their findings on hearsay unless they could have legitimately reached the same result without the hearsay evidence."[73] In *Carroll v. Knickerbocker Ice. Co.,* 113 N.E. 507, 509 (1916), the district court, in rejecting a death benefit claim, noted: "Still in the end, there must be a residuum of evidence of legal (i.e., nonhearsay) evidence to support the claim before an award can be made." In *Requero v. Teacher Standards and Practices,* 789 P.2d 11, 14 (Or. App. 1990) the court, quoting Kenneth C. Davis, made clear that

> "[T]he residuum rule requires a reviewing court to set aside an administrative finding unless the finding is supported by evidence which would be admissible in a jury trial . . . no matter how reliable the evidence may appear to the agency and to the reviewing court, no matter what the circumstantial setting may be, no matter what may be the evidence or lack of evidence on the other side, and no matter what may be the consequences of refusing to rely upon evidence."

The residuum rule has always frustrated and angered many agency adjudicators from the very beginning because it prevents them from reaching decisions based solely upon hearsay evidence, which can be difficult for hearing officials with hefty caseloads who want to reach quick decisions on the basis of what they believe are reliable documents pertaining to the cases in their files (such documents technically constitute only hearsay evidence).[74]

Beyond the practical reasons for rejecting the residuum rule, opponents offer other criticisms. Most of their criticism focuses on the perceived illogical nature of the residuum rule. Critics argue that the residuum rule illogically classifies all hearsay evidence as incompetent regardless of the quality of the hearsay. In legal terms, the residuum rule makes even the highest quality hearsay technically incompetent and this contradicts reliability standards associated with the admission of evidence. That is, it is argued that properly admitted hearsay (hearsay allowed because any reasonable person would accept it as reliable) must still be considered incompetent or nonsubstantial evidence incapable of supporting a hearing finding. Kenneth C. Davis claims that the most illogical problem with the residuum rule "is the lack of correlation between reliability of evidence and the exclusionary rules of evidence. The exclusionary rules were designed for guiding admission or exclusion of evidence, not for weighing its reliability, and were designed for juries, not for administrators."[75]

However, the attacks on the worth of the residuum rule come mostly from those who believe that its application simply causes unnecessary and costly administrative inconveniences and delays. The residuum rule is not just another stupid rule that makes no sense. In the spirit of justice, it makes a lot of sense. It simply requires that at least some evidence used to reach a hearing decision should be based upon more than just hearsay, upon at least a residuum of substantial evidence (i.e., nonhearsay evidence). Is that too much to ask to help guarantee fair hearing decisions? Obviously, it is to those staunch critics of the residuum rule. However, it appears that residuum rule opponents are not really saying that the residuum rule will not serve administrative justice in agency hearings better. They contend, at least implicitly, that our administrative system cannot afford the luxury of using the residuum rule because its use will increase administrative costs even more in an age when supporting even vital governmental services has become increasingly difficult. Thus, some see limiting the application of the residuum rule as a cost-cutting measure.

The 1971 Supreme Court decision that stands apparently as the most outspoken word against the value of the residuum, *Richardson v. Perales,* 402 U.S. 389, encapsulates the prevalent sentiment of critics that the residuum rule is too impracticable to apply during a time when the administrative burden is so heavy. The *Perales* Court reasoned in rejecting strict reliance upon the residuum rule that

> There is an additional and pragmatic factor which, although not controlling, deserves mention. This is what Chief Judge Brown has described as "the sheer magnitude of the administrative burden," and the resulting necessity for written reports without "elaboration through the traditional facility or oral testimony." With over 20,000 disability claim hearings annually, the cost of providing live medical testimony at those hearings . . . would be a substantial drain . . . (at 406).

Ever since the *Perales* decision was handed down in 1971 there has been a lively debate over whether the residuum rule is still applicable law. The controversy is very much alive today because some legal scholars and court justices insist that the residuum rule is dead, while other scholars and justices argue that it is still governing law. For example, in 1990 in *Requero,* the Oregon court rejected the use of the residuum rule by arguing essentially that hearsay evidence can be "sufficiently trustworthy" and constitute "substantial evidence" (at 15). Many other state and federal courts have also rejected the residuum rule for the same or similar reasons. On the other hand, many other courts have held that the residuum rule has merit and must still be applied. In *Trujillo v. Employment Sec. Comm'n,* 610 P.2d 747, 748 (1980) the court stated emphatically that "[I]n many circumstances hearsay is reliable and probative, and at times it may be the only evidence available. Nevertheless, we believe that the residuum rule should be retained in those administrative proceedings where a substantial right, such as one's ability to earn a livelihood, is at stake. In those instances . . . hearing decisions . . . must be based upon . . . substantial evidence." In *Foust v. Leijan,* 942 F.2d 712, 719 (10th Cir.; 1991) the court held that Department of Interior hearing decisions involving land rights must be supported by "substantial evidence."

As noted, legal scholars also disagree over the survival of the residuum rule. Thomas R. Mulroy, Jr., and Douglas G. McClure assert that "[m]ost federal courts, and many state courts, no longer follow the residuum rule, a trend lauded by commentators. Illinois courts should follow this trend and abolish the residuum rule as well."[76] In the 1980s Kenneth C. Davis in his famous *Administrative Law Treatise,* reflecting the views of other scholars, pronounced the residuum rule near death by stating that it ". . . was once largely the law, but it is now largely abolished."[77] However, Bernard Schwartz, representing the opinion of others, argues that Davis's ". . . statement is inaccurate. Over thirty states follow the residuum rule; only a handful of states have expressly rejected it."[78] And, of course, federal courts, as seen in cases such as *Foust* have been reluctant to apply *Perales* in a way that flatly rejects the residuum rule, holding that hearing decisions must normally be based upon substantial evidence.

Confusion about applicability of the residuum rule has prevailed since the *Perales* decision over two decades ago because the *Perales* holding conveyed mixed messages about the legal status of the residuum rule. Many legal scholars felt that the *Perales* Court rejected the residuum rule because it upheld a Social Security hearing examiner's decision that was totally rooted in hearsay evidence, not "substantial evidence." The key to understanding the court's decision, however, is in understanding how the Court justified its decision. It then becomes clear that the Court did not in fact reject the residuum rule, but only added some flexibility in its use.

In many respects the circumstances in the *Perales* case are unique and these help explain why the *Perales* Court reached the decision it did. Pedro Perales, a 34-year-old truck driver, claimed that he had become permanently disabled by lifting an object while working. He applied for disability benefits under the Social Security Act. On the whole, his medical records indicated that the was not disabled and could resume work in a matter of months, although one doctor concluded otherwise. In fact, one doctor, Dr. Langston, who had great credibility before the hearing examiner and eventually the *Perales* court, concluded that Perales was clearly not disabled and was faking in order to collect undue disability payments. In fact, Dr. Langston recommended that he should see a psychiatrist. Later, Dr. Bailey, a psychiatrist, and Dr. Mattson and Dr. Leavitt all agreed with Dr. Langston's diagnosis. Beyond this, several other doctors' reports supported Dr. Langston's diagnosis. Only Dr. Morales, a former fellow employee of *Perales* perceived as biased by the hearing examiner and eventually the *Perales* court, reached an opposite conclusion.

Given these facts, it is clear from a careful reading of the *Perales* decision that the Court's majority was predisposed to rule against Perales. But the Court also felt that Perales was really treated very fairly by the hearing examiner. What became important to the Court was the fact that Perales, represented by counsel, was given an opportunity to subpoena the doctors so that they could be cross-examined, but that Perales declined the opportunity to do so. The Court noted: "Notice was given to claimant Perales. The physicians' reports were on file and available for inspection by the claimant and his counsel. And the authors of these reports were known and were subject to subpoena and to the very cross-examination that the claimant asserts he has not enjoyed" (at 407).

Given these hearing conditions, then, the *Perales* Court had to decide when and how the residuum rule should be applied and what should really constitute substantial evidence. The Court made a practical decision. It reasoned that it makes sense to suspend the strict application of the residuum rule when the opportunity is given to subpoena documents and witnesses so that the hearsay evidence can be cross-examined. If Perales took advantage of this opportunity, the hearsay evidence would have been transformed into substantial evidence. In effect, the spirit of the residuum rule was not really undermined by the *Perales* Court because Perales was given the opportunity to subpoena and cross-examine the "hearsay evidence." To the *Perales* Court this failure to take advantage of this opportunity made the hearsay evidence tantamount to substantial evidence.

It is also important to acknowledge that in *Perales* the Court noted that "[C]ourts have recognized the reliability and probative worth of written medical reports even in formal trials and, while acknowledging their hearsay character, have admitted them as an exception to the hearsay rule" (at 405). Is the Court not saying, then, that such medical records really constitute substantial evidence, consistent with the residuum rule, since such evidence, because of its reliability and probative value, is accepted in court trials under a hearsay exception? If so, this is just one more reason to doubt whether the *Perales* Court ever meant to reject the residuum rule.

As mentioned earlier, some scholars contend that the residuum rule was rejected by the *Perales* Court for practical administrative reasons. Although the *Perales* Court said that such pragmatic concerns deserve mentioning, the court noted that these practical factors are "not controlling" (at 406). This statement cannot be ignored because many scholars base their whole argument on the contention that the *Perales* Court abolished the residuum rule for administrative efficiency reasons. The *Perales* Court did no such thing. Yes, administrative efficiency is a factor, the Court held, but due process must be upheld.

In sum, the Supreme Court in *Perales* probably did not intend to abolish the residuum rule, but it evidently did intend to develop a new flexible standard for applying it. This new standard has become known as the "*Perales* rule." Under the new *Perales* rule, the residuum rule still largely applies, which means that hearing officials can use hearsay evidence to substantiate their rulings, but the decision must still be supported by some substantial evidence. This sounds identical to the residuum rule requirements but the different twist is that the substantial evidence test under the new *Perales* standard can be more easily satisfied. Reviewing courts must now look at the unique circumstances that surround the use of the hearsay evidence. For instance, hearsay can become very high-quality evidence, in fact, qualifying as substantial evidence, when certain reliable records are used that would be admitted in court trials under hearsay exception rules. Also, when the opportunity to subpoena and cross-examine witnesses and their documents is declined, the hearsay evidence takes on an understandably higher quality and can be accepted as substantial evidence consistent with what the residuum rule has always, at least in spirit, required (i.e., evidence that a reasonably prudent person would rely upon in conducting his or her serious affairs). In a nut shell, it seems that too much time has been spent in the literature debating whether the residuum rule was abolished by *Perales* because it is obvious that the *Perales* Court did not flatly reject the residuum rule, but probably strengthened it by making a more flexible and applicable rule out of one that was too rigid and difficult to apply in many situations.[79]

The Exclusionary Rule's Applicability in Administrative Hearings

From approximately the beginning of President Ronald Reagan's administration until the present the exclusionary rule, as applied to criminal law, has come under constant and vehement attack mostly by conservatives. They believe that the rule has been used too often to prevent otherwise good evidence from being admitted into evidence just because the evidence was seized illegally by police, thus allowing many criminals to get off on mere "procedural technicalities." Simply stated, the exclusionary rule has been used in criminal trials to exclude illegally seized evidence, which has given rise to the "fruit of the poisonous tree" doctrine. In criminal law the doctrine, although it may apply in administrative law, has had the practical effort of making all evidence and all secondary obtained evidence stemming from it) inadmissible ". . . because procedural steps in obtaining the evidence violated constitutional due process" (*Wong Sun v. United States,* 371 U.S 471 [1983]). Opposition to the exclusionary rule has evidently influenced the courts because recent decisions have tended to weaken the clout of the exclusionary rule.

The status of the exclusionary rule in administrative hearings is not clear.[80] Some courts have upheld the relevance of the exclusionary rule in agency adjudications, while other courts have not. For example, in a New York case in 1979 the court argued that the exclusionary rule should apply to administrative hearings as well as to criminal trials (*Piccarillo v. Board of Parole,* 48 N.Y. 2d76, 81). Some federal courts have agreed (e.g., *Knoll Assoc. v. FTC,*

397 F.2d 530 [7th Cir.; 1968] and *Navia-Duran v. INS,* 568 F.2d 803 [1st Cir.; 1977]). Supporters of the exclusionary rule often maintain that the Fourth Amendment's privacy protections, as well as the Fifth Amendment's protection against self-incrimination, would be upheld whether the government is prosecuting a person for burglary or deciding whether to revoke someone's medical license. Bernard Schwartz asserts: "It is anomalous to enforce opposite rules in administrative and criminal proceedings concerning evidence blighted by the same pollution; an unlawful search violates the identical privacy, whether its fruits are used to convict in a criminal case or to forfeit a personal right in an agency proceeding."[81]

Nevertheless, as in criminal cases, the courts have been increasingly very reluctant to compel agency adjudicators to honor the exclusionary rule. Of course, agency hearings are normally much less formal than court trials, thus making the admission of evidence more flexible. In fact, the federal APA, Section 556(d) says "Any oral or documentary evidence may be received" and it is well established in administrative law that virtually all admitted evidence, no matter how irrelevant or incompetent, cannot cause "reversible error" or fatally flaw the decision as long as the decision is otherwise supported by substantial evidence.

Exclusion of Privileged Evidence

This does not mean, however, that agency adjudicators can normally go so far as to require that privileged evidence be admitted. As the Revised Model State Administrative Procedure Act, Section 10 states: "Agencies shall give effect to the rules of privilege recognized by law." Privileged evidence is protected either by the Constitution or by statute or, sometimes, by common law. Privileged evidence, for example, consists of attorney–client, husband–wife privilege and other recognized constitutional and statutory testimonial privileges, as well as specifically the privilege against self-incrimination and the use of illegally obtained evidence. As expected, then, in *Southern Cal. Gas Co. v. Public Utils. Comm'n,* 784 P.2d 1373 (1990) the California court upheld the attorney–client privilege in a public utility commission hearing.

It may seem contradictory and confusing to note that illegally seized evidence is considered privileged evidence, yet at the same time point out that the trend, as noted, has been against compelling public agencies to honor the exclusionary rule, thus making them exclude from hearing proceedings illegally obtained evidence that should be considered privileged. The truth is that the situation is contradictory and confusing, but this is not unique to law, especially administrative law. Due to conservative political pressures and other factors, the vast majority of decisions since the early 1980s, although the trend against the exclusionary rule started earlier, have rejected the application of the exclusionary rule under most circumstances. In 1984 the U.S. Supreme Court in *INS v. Lopez-Mendoza,* 468 U.S. 1032 held that the exclusionary rule did not apply to civil deportation hearings, even though, it should be added, losing parties normally suffer a grievous loss. In *Lopez-Mendoza,* employing the most popular reason for throwing out the exclusionary rule, the Court opined that enforcing the use of the exclusionary rule would only minimally deter officials from conducting illegal searches. In *Finkelstein v. State Personnel Board,* 267 Col. Rptr. 133 (Cal. App. 3 Dist.; 1990) a California Court assumed for the sake of argument that the briefcase search in question was illegal under both federal and California constitutions, yet nevertheless rejected the application of the exculsionary rule, allowing the illegally seized evidence to be used to terminate a government employee's employment. Comparing *Finkelstein* to a prior ruling by the same court in which the court upheld the exclusionary rule, the court concluded that ". . . in this case there was no search for evidence of crime and no motive to use such evidence for disciplinary purposes. Because of this factual difference, the deterrent effect of the exclusionary rule . . . is lacking here" (at 138).

What is clear from *Finkelstein* and other cases is that courts are very unlikely to apply the exclusionary rule if they feel that the officials who illegally seized evidence did not know how it would be used later. The logic employed by the courts is that excluding illegally obtained evidence from, for example, an employee termination hearing, is not going to deter police officers from conducting illegal searchers where they had no idea that such evidence may be used later in a noncriminal termination proceeding. Do you accept this rationale? This rationale appears more like an excuse to toss out the exclusionary rule than a sensible reason to reject its use. It seems that the best way to discourage any governmental official from conducting illegal searches is to make certain that any illegally seized evidence is excluded from criminal trials or administrative hearings. This makes even more sense when one considers the other chief reason for using the exclusionary rule: the government should not benefit in a criminal trial or an agency adjudication from its own unlawful acts that produced the illegal evidence. Schwartz argues that in agency hearings

> the tainted evidence is the fruit of a governmental, not private, crime. The law should not allow a public agency to be the known beneficiary of stolen goods . . . An administrative agency, just as any other public organ, is obligated to conduct its activities in conformity with the demands of the Constitution. When its agents exceed those limits, it should not be permitted to avail itself of the fruits of such unlawful activity.[82]

Right to Counsel in Agency Hearings

Courts have insisted that a fair hearing should offer several procedural due procses protections, but does the call for fairness require agencies to permit persons in hearings to be represented by counsel, even appointed counsel (paid for by the government)? In 1963 in the now famous *Gideon v. Wainwright* case, 372 U.S. 335, the Supreme Court ruled that in criminal cases defendants have the right to appointed counsel if they cannot afford to pay a lawyer. Later, in 1972, the Court held that the *Gideon* decision applies even to misdemeanor trials from which a possible jail sentence could result (*Argersinger v. Hamlin,* 407 U.S. 25).

The right to counsel issue has been settled comfortably in criminal cases, but the right to counsel in agency hearings leaves many questions unanswered. During the 1970s a significant number of courts and legal scholars argued that unless legal counsel is actually provided to indigents across the board, blatant inequities in applying administrative justice in agency hearings will inevitably occur. In a sense, it would be simpler and fairer to apply the *Gideon* rule to all administrative hearings than to try to choose the hearings to which it would apply. On the other hand, given the millions of minor hearing cases heard each year by administrators, it became just as clear that it would be very impractical to apply the *Gideon* solution to agency adjudications. The cost to taxpayers would be prohibitive, not only because of the added costs for lawyers but also because these lawyers would unquestionably provide legal defenses that would delay case settlements and place extra financial and staff burdens on agency efforts to prepare, present, and defend their positions. A look at a few relevant cases conveys how the right to counsel issue has developed.

In *Goldberg v. Kelly,* 397 U.S. 254 (1970), the most influential right to counsel case during the 1970s, the Supreme Court stressed the crucial significance of the right to counsel by reiterating an earlier position that "the right to be heard would be, in many cases, of little avail if it did not comprehend the right to be heard by counsel."[83] However, although some applauded the decision as a giant step forward in extending the right to counsel to indigent parties in agency hearings, in fact, the *Goldberg* holding only confirmed a right that the federal Administrative Procedure Act has already granted to federal employees unless specific provisions in federal statutes placed restrictions on the right. Section 555(b) of the APA read:

"A person compelled to appear in person before an agency or representative thereof is entitled to be accompanied, represented, and advised by counsel or, if permitted by the agency, by other qualified representative." But it was also made clear in *Goldberg* that the welfare claimant did not have the right to government-appointed *free* counsel. Many legal scholars and social scientists became irritated by the obvious Catch-22 situation posed by the *Goldberg* decision. That is, what good is it to be allowed to obtain counsel if you can't afford to pay for such representation? As one prominent scholar recognized: "Those protected by *Goldberg v. Kelly* are, in the main, usually unable to afford counsel. Despite this, the right to appointed counsel, which has been extended to virtually all indigent criminal defendants, has not been recognized in administrative proceedings."[84]

Three years after *Goldberg,* in *John R. Gagnon v. Gerald H. Scarpelli,* 411 U.S. 778 (1973), in which the right to counsel question was discussed in the context of a revocation of parole hearing, the Court methodically reviewed what should be considered the minimum due process rights in administrative law hearings. Drawing from the precedential case, *Morrissey v. Brewer,* 408 U.S. 471 (1972), the Court acknowledged that even the right to counsel, let alone paid counsel, had not been established in a de facto sense as a minimum right. Nonetheless, the Court suggested that the right to government-provided counsel may be advisable under very rare circumstances and when deemed appropriate by the hearing officials.[85] However, Edwin W. Tucker points out that the Court required here that when "a request for counsel at a preliminary or final hearing is refused, the grounds for refusal should be stated succinctly in the record."[86] The court did provide guidelines to help hearing officers decide when counsel should be provided, considering, for example, "whether the probationer appears capable of speaking effectively for himself."[87] With great reservation, the Supreme Court in *Gagnon* opened the door just slightly to allow for appointed counsel in cases where very serious consequences (for example, return to prison, loss of life-sustaining welfare benefits, deportation) would occur to financially and/or educationally deficient persons if adverse rulings were reached.

At the same time, however, the Supreme Court presented in *Gagnon* a strong case for why counsel should not be provided in virtually all administrative hearings, contending that to do so would place a tremendous and unjustifiable burden on administrative tribunals: "Certainly, the decision making process will be prolonged, and the financial cost to the State—for appointed counsel, counsel for the State, a longer record, and the possibility of judicial review—will not be insubstantial" (at 788). In placing the right to counsel in the context of balancing due process entitlements with agency responsibilities, the Court reasoned that "due process is not so rigid as to require that the significant interests in informality, flexibility, and economy must always be sacrificed" (at 788). Thus, the Court held that there is "no justification for a new inflexible constitutional rule with respect to the requirement of counsel. We think, rather, that the decision as to the need for counsel must be made on a case-by-case basis in the exercise of a sound discretion by the state authority" (at 790).

Despite efforts by the Court to review systematically questions pertaining to the right to counsel, particularly the right to state-supported counsel, the *Gagnon* case left many questions unanswered by creating a vague circumstances test to be applied at the discretion of the hearing officials. Since it is understandable that such hearing officials probably identify somewhat with agency interests, how fair does it seem for the Court to leave the decision on whether persons in hearings should be provided with paid counsel to the very people who will be hearing the case? Would it not take exceptionally fair-minded hearing examiners to grant the request for appointed counsel to parties, knowing the extra time, expense, and headaches it will undoubtedly bring?

A related point is also noteworthy. The APA generally requires agency adjudicators to respect a person's right to obtain legal counsel. However, a loophole in section 555(b) does not obligate agencies to advertise that this right exists. As a consequence, some agencies have, as a matter of official policy, actively discouraged parties from being represented by counsel. At least one state court has spoken out against the administrative practice of not notifying parties that they not only have the right to counsel, but the possible availability of free or low-cost counsel (provided by various publicly and privately supported legal service units). For example, the Tennessee Supreme Court in *Simmons v. Troughber,* 791 S.W. 2d 21, 24 (Tenn. 1990) ruled that the Tennessee Department of Employment Security's failure to inform an employee of the possible availability of free or low-cost legal representation violated her statutory right to a fair hearing. In fact, the court ordered a new hearing because the court contended that the Department's failure to advise her of the possible availability of free or low-cost counsel and the fact that she had no legal representation at the hearing caused the hearing to be prejudiced against her. The Court reasoned: "Inadequate notice of the right to counsel creates a significant risk that a claimant will be unwittingly deprived of unemployment benefits. Advising claimants of the possible availability of free or low cost legal representation would help reduce the risk of an erroneous deprivation. . ." (at 25).

Beyond agencies simply keeping silent about the right to counsel, the most popular step to discourage representation by counsel is to place a fee limit on what attorneys can charge. For example, the Social Security Administration long ago adopted a rule that placed an absurdly low $10.00 fee limit on how much an attorney could earn while representing Social Security claimants in disability claims. In 1854 Congress set a $10.00 fee limit on the amount an attorney could receive for representing a veteran in a death or disability claim.[88]

Sympathetic to veterans' inability to secure counsel under this fee limitation rule, a district court in 1984 held this fee to violate due process protections (*National Ass'n. of Radiation Survivors v. Walters,* 589 F.Supp. 1302 [N.D. Cal.]). However, the Supreme Court reversed the decision, arguing that due process or "fundamental fairness" had not been violated by the $10 fee limitation (*Walters v. National Ass'n. of Radiation Survivors,* 106 S.Ct. 3180 [1985]). Speaking for the High Court, Justice Rehnquist asserted that the costs and benefits of extending certain "extra" procedural safeguards must be given serious consideration. Employing the balance test devloped in *Mathews v. Eldridge,* 424 U.S. 319 (1976), which basically calls for weighing the costs and benefits of applying the present governmental procedures to the government against the costs and benefits of applying the existing or alternative procedures to the government against the costs and benefits of applying the existing or alternative procedures to the private party, Rehnquist wrote: "We have emphasized that the marginal gains from affording an additional procedural safeguard often may be outweighed by the societal cost of providing such a safeguard" (at 3189). Rehnquist based the Court's decision not to override the fee ceiling on the argument that the costs to government and society would be too high, defeating the intent of Congress to keep the VA proceedings "as informal and nonadversarial as possible" (at 3191). The Court explained further that to do away with the fee limitation would "undoubtedly engender greater administrative costs, with the end result being that less government money reaches its intended beneficiaries" (at 3192).

The Supreme Court upheld the *Walters* decision in 1990 in *U.S. Dept. of Labor v. Triplett,* 110 S.Ct. 1428, by holding that even though fee limitations may make attorneys unavailable to claimants, this in itself does not deny claimants due process since they still have the right to counsel. Thus, in reviewing the state court's ruling, the Supreme Court concluded that ". . . the evidence . . . did not remotely establish *either* that black lung claimants are unable to retain qualified counsel *or* that the cause of such inability is the attorney's fee system administered by the Department. The Court therefore had no basis for concluding that the system deprives claimants of property without due process of law" (at 1435).

Agencies have also tried to prevent parties from employing counsel by arguing that the use of counsel impairs agency business, especially its investigations. However, this argument has been rejected by most courts since Section 555(b), even acknowledging the section's loopholes, only allows agencies to forbid the employment of counsel under exceptional circumstances. For example, in *Professional Reactor Operator Soc. v. U.S. NRC,* 939 F.2d 1047, 1051–1052 (D.C. Cir. 1991) the Court held that the NRC's exclusion of subpoenaed witnesses' counsel during NRC's investigations violates the APA's more weighty right to counsel provision. The Court contended that the NRC provided no "reasonable basis" to substantiate its claim that the presence of counsel would obstruct and impair NRC's investigations.

As Professor Bernard Schwartz acknowledged, citing Lord Denning in *Regina v. Preston Appeal Tribunal, ex parte Moore,* 1 W.L.R. 624, 631 (1975), Congress did not establish governmental agencies to make them "the happy hunting ground of lawyers."[89] Nevertheless, Schwartz maintains, one may seriously question whether it is wise and fair to use such a blanket approach (i.e., the $10 fee limitation) to keep lawyers from providing representation to veterans, especially when legal counsel would seem appropriate in certain complex cases in which VA decisions could lead to the denial of essential benefits. Even though Schwartz is sympathetic to the need to avoid the overjudicialization of the VA administrative process, he nonetheless feels that the broadside prohibition of counsel is far too extreme. He recommends a more moderate and fair approach (i.e., strict administrative and judicial oversight of attorneys' fees) to address the potential abuses of the VA administrative system. "Strict discipline for fee abuses could eliminate most of the problems without barring the minority from obtaining needed representation in complex cases."[90]

The right to counsel controversy in administrative law cases has been brewing for many years. Scholars seem to be divided on whether this "extra" procedural safeguard would prove too burdensome to the hearing process in our public agencies. Knowing the adversary character of lawyers, no doubt the pressure of legal counsel at administrative hearings would certainly slow things down—in the name of proper legal representation, of course! Several years ago, after examining the right to counsel debate, Judge Henry J. Friendly presented a fascinating and provocative idea to resolve the problem. Judge Friendly agrees that administrative hearings, handling routine questions pertaining to welfare benefits, school suspensions, and so on should not be turned into elaborate criminal adversary proceedings. In a now-famous administrative law article entitled, "Some Kind of Hearing," he argues that the adversary hearing approach should be abandoned in many administrative law areas that he categorizes as "mass justice" areas

> These problems concerning counsel and confrontation inevitably bring up the question whether we would not do better to abandon the adversary system in certain areas of mass justice, notably in the many ramifications of the welfare system, in favor of one in which an examiner—or administrative law judge if you will—with no connection with the agency would have the responsibility for developing all the pertinent facts and making a just decision.[91]

In so arguing, Judge Friendly attacks the basic need for counsel on the grounds that the provision of counsel in many administrative law areas cannot be justified in a cost-benefit sense: "The appearance of counsel for the citizen is likely to lead the government to provide one—or at least to cause the government's representative to act like one. The result may be to turn what might have been a short conference leading to an amicable result into a protracted controversy."[92]

Judge Friendly largely rests his call for experimentation in administrative mass justice (that is, doing away with the adversary process in many administrative law areas) on the legal argument that there exists "no constitutional mandate requiring use of the adversary process in administrative hearings unless the Court chooses to construct one out of the vague contours of the due process clause."[93] His nonadversary, investigative model would have the advantage of settling disputes informally and quickly in a conferencelike environment. Although Judge Friendly acknowledges that the experiment would represent "a sharp break with our tradition of adversary process," he claims that "that tradition . . . was not formulated for a situation in which many thousands of hearings must be provided each month."[94]

The whole question of whether claimants actually benefit from having counsel at administrative hearings, the resolution of which would be quite helpful in aiding our decision on whether the Friendly experiment should be tried, was addressed in "Effect of Representation on a Claimant's Success Rate: Three Study Designs," published several years ago in the *Administrative Law Review.*[95] Although only a few studies are cited, the preliminary data tend to cast great doubt on whether claimants in administrative hearings win more favorable decisions at a greater rate because they are represented by counsel. For example, one empirical study cited revealed that welfare claimants in Wisconsin won at " 'about the same' rate without counsel as claimants represented by counsel."[96] This should inspire one to ask: Should we encourage the growth of representation by counsel in certain administrative law areas if convincing evidence starts to emerge suggesting that individuals are not really helped by counsel? It appears that we would stand to benefit by encouraging further research in this area, as well as devoting our attention to who actually may be aided by appointed counsel.

In sum, the status of the right to counsel in agency hearings is much clearer in the 1990s than it was in the 1970s. Federal and state courts have made it fairly clear in the past two decades that parties generally have a right to legal counsel, but not guaranteed government-supported counsel. However, the possibility of free or low-cost legal representation is available on a limited basis to indigents through various legal services operations. Courts have normally insisted that proper notice includes informing parties that they have the right to be represented by legal counsel at agency hearings, but courts have been reluctant to push the advertising of legal representation too far, especially requiring agencies to inform parties about the possible availability of free or low-cost counsel. In a few instances the courts have ruled that certain circumstances, usually practical situations upholding a state interest (e.g., an excessive administrative burden), necessitate public agencies to not permit parties to be represented by counsel, particularly if the disputed issue is considered minor. For example, in *Williams v. Prina County,* 791 P.2d 1053 (1989) an Arizona court held that the due process rights under the Fourteenth Amendment are not violated just because a public employee was denied the use of legal counsel at a pretermination interview. The court reasoned that pretermination interviews are informal and the use of counsel would unnecessarily intrude on the employer's rights to deal with unsatisfactory employees.

DECISION-MAKING IN AGENCY ADJUDICATIONS

It has been made quite apparent by now that agency hearings are normally much more informal than court trials at every stage in the proceedings. Evidence is not only accepted and used in a more informal manner in agency adjudications than in court trials, but the process employed in reaching decisions is also considerably more informal in agency hearings. In fact, hearing proceedings are often so informal that evidence may be presented to and evaluated by the hearing officials and a decision reached in a matter of 10 to 20 minutes. However, as noted, some hearings have been very formal and elaborate and have continued for several years. A previous point should be reiterated: Only about 1 percent of all hearings are formal, while about 99 percent are informal. Although court trials can also be short, it is unusual, except in matters involving small claims, for decisions to be reached so quickly because of the more formal requirements associated with handling evidence and reaching decisions in light of the evidence. In this last section principles, doctrines, and rules associated with hearing decision-making are reviewed. And, it must be stressed, as it was in *Vollstedt v. City of Stockton,* 269 Ca.Rptr. 404, 408 (Ca. App. 3 Dist.; 1990), that ". . . the question of whether the trial was 'fair' encompasses posthearing actions of the agency as well" (i.e., the posthearing decision-making process).

Applying Standards of Proof in Decision-Making

There is a qualitative difference between decision-making in court trials and agency adjudications. As contrasted with agency hearings, judges or jurors in court trials should root their decisions in more weighty evidence than ALJs in agency hearings. Simply stated, the standard of proof should be higher for court decisions than agency hearing decisions. In criminal cases decisions must be based upon the highest possible standard or the *beyond a reasonable doubt* standard. In an ideal situation, judges or juries cannot convict a person of a crime if a reasonable doubt exists as to whether the person is guilty of the crime. This high standard has posed some problems because some guilty parties have either not been prosecuted or the prosecutors have failed to win their case under this lofty standard, thus allowing guilty parties to go free. On the other hand, many legal scholars contend that this is a small price to pay for a justice system that honors freedom and individual rights. These scholars reason that it is better to have a criminal justice system that allows some guilty parties to escape punishment than to punish wrongly those who are innocent.

There are those who hold that while the criminal justice system is "too fair," permitting many "guilty" parties to escape prosecution or conviction because of "due process technicalities," the administrative justice system is "too unfair," denying parties procedural due process rights while agency administrators rush to dispose of huge case loads as quickly as possible. Critics point out that the failure to honor reasonable due process protections in agency hearings can sometimes cause parties, guilty of no crime, to suffer more harm (e.g., loss of a professional license or business, revocation of parole, deportation) than they would have if convicted of certain criminal acts. This reality motivated Justice Brandeis to conclude many decades ago that deportation decisions, for example, may prove more harmful to persons in deportation hearings than verdicts in criminal trials because adverse deportation rulings may "result . . . in loss of both property and life; or all that makes life worth living" (*Ng Fung Ho v. White,* 259 U.S. 276, 284; 1922).

Most agency hearing officials have the unenviable task of having to resolve an enormous volume of cases, thus justifying to a certain extent why agencies must restrict procedural due process protections. It is understandable, then, that the standard of proof for reaching hearing decisions falls short of the higher standard of proof required in criminal trials. When reaching decisions in agency hearings, the burden of persuasion is satisified if the *preponderance of the evidence* supports the decision.

In *Steadman v. SEC,* 450 U.S. 91 (1981), the leading case in this area, the Supreme Court clearly established the application of the preponderance of the evidence standard for administrative hearings governed by the APA. A brief review of this case helps to clarify how the preponderance of the evidence standard became law, especially since the APA does not use the specific rhetoric "preponderance of the evidence." In 1971 the Securities and Exchange Commission (SEC) began disciplinary action against Steadman, charging that he had violated many federal securities laws. After a lengthy on-the-record (evidentiary) hearing before an ALJ and after review by the SEC, which employed a preponderance of evidence test to assess the weight of the evidence, the Commission concluded that Steadman was guilty of violating several antifraud, conflict of interest, proxy, and reporting provisions of federal security statutes. As a result, it ordered that Steadman be banned permanently from affiliating with any investment companies or associating with any investment companies or associating with any investment advisors, thus prohibiting him from practicing his profession. The SEC also suspended him from associating with any securities brokers of dealers for 1 year, thus causing him to incur substantial investment losses. Steadman sought judicial review, arguing that because of the potentially severe penalties, the SEC should not have used the preponderance of the evidence standard, but should have employed the stricter *clear and convincing evidence* standard to weigh the evidence to substantiate the very serious intent to defraud charges.

However, both the appeals court and the Supreme Court disagreed. The High Court reasoned that the substantial evidence requirement in the APA requires that a decision must be supported by a certain "quantity of evidence." The Court was not persuaded by Steadman's argument that the substantial evidence requirement pertains to the "quality" of evidence only. The Court argued that legislative intent was clear from the ". . . House Report, which expressly adopted a preponderance of the evidence standard: Nor is there any suggestion in the legislative history that a standard of proof higher than a preponderance of the evidence was ever contemplated, much less intended" (at 101–102). The Court went on to say that "Congress was primarily concerned with the elimination of agency decision making premised on evidence which was of poor quality—irrelevant, immaterial, unreliable and nonprobative—and of insufficient quantity—less than a preponderance" (at 102). Consequently, the Court concluded that through APA provisions Congress has "expressed its intent that adjudicatory proceedings subject to the APA satisfy the statute where determinations are made according to the preponderance of the evidence" (at 104).

Although the APA preponderance of the evidence standard normally governs agency adjudicators when reaching hearing decisions, specific statutory provisions may override the APA requirement calling for a higher standard of proof. For example, in deportation cases today, as long as the alien had entered the country legally, decisions are governed by the higher clear and convincing evidence standard. In *Bustos-Torres v. INS,* 898 F.2d 1053, 1057 (5th Cir.; 1990) the petitioner contended that evidence used against him ". . . is not the clear and convincing evidence necessary for deportation." The court acknowledged that "[A]lthough the government has the ultimate burden of providing deportability by clear and convincing evidence, in a Section 1251(a)(2) case charging deportability of an alien who entered the country without inspection, the government need only show alienage."[97]

There are many critics of the preponderance of the evidence standard. The most prevalent criticism is that the weak standard is applied when common sense should suggest that ALJs should employ stricter or higher due process standards when serious deprivations may result. Justices Lewis Powell and Potter Stewart, the dissenters in *Steadman,* present this criticism well. They argue that when potential penalties are equivalent to or greater than criminal penalties our common law tradition should supresede the APA, especialy since the APA does not specifically state that the preponderance of the evidence standard must be applied. In the *Steadman* case, for example, they maintained that the SEC, given the severity of the penalties involved, should have rejected the minimal APA requirement and applied more elaborate due process protections such as the clear and convincing evidence standard to substantiate charges of fraud. Writing the dissent, Powell wrote:

> In the absence of any specific demonstration of Congress' purpose, we should not assume that Congress intends the SEC to apply a lower standard of proof than the prevailing common law standard for similar allegations. With all respect, it seems to me that the Court's decision today lacks the sensitivity that traditionally has marked our review of the Government's imposition upon citizens of severe penalties and permanent stigma (at 100).

Another criticism is simply that these standards of proof are confusing because they are not clearly distinct. These different standards are used in agency hearings and in court trials to support decisions. But how useful or practical are these tests? Can these standards be applied meaningfully in different situations? Are you convinced that a person of reasonable intelligence could tell you the difference between, say, substantial evidence, preponderance of the evidence, clear and convincing evidence, and evidence that leaves no reasonable doubt. These standards all apply to the *weight* of the evidence, but do you think clear and meaningful distinctions and applications of these standards can be made? When it comes to weighing any evidence, whether in an agency hearing or court trial, the weighing process and the accompanying decision process are quite subjective. What is clear and convincing evidence to one person is not clear and convincing evidence to another. Nonetheless, the preponderance of the evidence standard is the basic standard of proof test used in agency hearings, whatever this standard really means in practice.[98]

Making Decisions on the Basis of the Whole Record

The APA, Section 556(d), requires ALJs to make hearing decisions leading to the issuing of any order only after "... consideration of the *whole record* or those parts thereof cited by a party and supported by and in accordance with the reliable, probative, and substantial evidence" (my emphasis). Requiring agency adjudicators to base their decisions on the whole record and not just part of the record seems like a very reasonable and patently fair requirement, yet before the APA was passed in 1946 hearing adjuciators were allowed to substantiate their decisions only part of the record. Of course, this permitted hearing decision-makers to ignore parts of the hearing record that may have contradicted the evidence they used to substantiate their decision. In fact, it clearly gave unscrupulous adjudicators the opportunity to reach outrageously unfair decisions by totally ignoring facts in the record that would cause any reasonable person to reach an opposite decision. Nevertheless, this practice of only having to look at part of the record to satisfy the "one-sided substantial evidence" test was upheld by the courts before the passage of the APA. In *Marzacco v. Lowe,* 58 F.Supp. 900, 903 (D.N.J., 1945) the court remarked: "Under the present prevailing system of administrative law, all evidence to the contrary ... is a closed book into which this court dare not peek, at least not effectively."

Louis J. Jaffe, among many others, found this narrow and absurd application of the substantial evidence rule horrifying. Rightfully, Jaffe insisted that it is very hard to believe that any truly reasonable and responsible person could, in good conscience, reach rational conclusions by looking at only part of the record: "Obviously responsible men would not exercise their judgement on only that part of the evidence that looked in one direction."[99] The court reached the same conclusion in *Holo-Krome Co. v. NLRB,* 947 F.2d 588 (2nd Cir.; 1991) when the court scolded the NLRB for ignoring important parts of the record (e.g., an ALJ's finding) to justify an unreasonable decision not substantiated by the whole record. The court noted that the whole record must be used in searching a decision, including weighing "... evidence opposed to the board's view" (quoting from *Local One, Amalgamated Lithographers v. NLRB,* 729 F.2d 172, 175 [2d Cir.; 1984]) (at 593). In fact, the court concluded that the NLRB's refusal to consider a critical part of the whole record made "... the evidence supporting the Board's decision . . . less than substantial" (at 592). Consequently, the court ruled that "(T)he Board's decision regarding this evidence was in no way justified by the record before it" (at 595). In so holding, this federal court relied heavily upon the arguments set forth in the classic case on the whole record requirement, *Universal Camera Corp. v. NLRB,* 340 U.S. 474 (1951), in which the Supreme Court stressed that hearing decision-makers must base their decisions on the whole record, including conflicting evidence. "The substantiality of evidence must take into account whatever in the record fairly detracts from its weight. This is clearly the significance of the (APA) requirement . . ." (at 488).

The question of what constitutes the whole record has also been disputed. The dispute is based generally on problems pertaining to definitions of formal and informal evidence and questions over which evidence needs to be included in the "whole" record. Of course, agencies have been charged with keeping incomplete records, failing to note ex parte communications that may influence adjudicators and should therefore be part of the record, and failing to admit certain kinds of evidence (e.g., hearsay, documents and testimony that are "too costly" or "too inconvenient" to obtain). Nevertheless, the whole record requirement is generally honored by responsible ALJs and does not present a significant problem in administrative law. The whole record rule has unquestionably greatly improved the quality of decision-making in agency hearings. Probably the best description of the whole record requirement in the context of the substantial evidence rule that agency adjudicators should follow is found in *300 Gramatan v. Human Rights Division,* 45 N.Y. 2d 176, 181 (1978): "In the final analysis, substantial evidence consists of proof within the whole record of such quality and quantity as to generate conviction in and persuade a fair and detached fact finder that, from that proof as a premise, a conclusion or ultimate fact may be extracted reasonably—probatively and logically."

Hearing Decisions Must be Based Upon the Exclusive Record

One of the most fundamental principles in administrative law is the "exclusiveness of the record" principle. It is a simple and easy to understand rule, but these simple principles normally carry the most practical weight in law because they are easy to comprehend, follow, and enforce. The exclusiveness of the record principle means that hearing examiners must base their decisions *only* on the evidence produced during the hearing proceeding that constitutes the exclusive record. There are only a few exceptions to this principle. The exclusiveness of the record principle is stated clearly in the federal APA, Section 556(e): "The transcript of testimony and exhibits, together with all papers and requests filed in the proceeding, constitutes the exclusive record for decision. . . ."

As noted, the exclusive record principle is and should be a basic maxim that must be followed in a judicial proceeding, whether an agency hearing or a court trial. How absurd it would be if parties in an agency adjudication presented and responded to evidence on the record and then the adjudicators later reached a decision based on evidence not entered as evidence during the hearing when parties had an opportunity to rebut it. The Court in *Mazza v. Cavicchia,* 105 A.2d 545, 554 (N.J.; 1954) noted how ridiculous and unfair such adjudicative behavior would be: "Unless the principle is observed, the right to a hearing itself becomes meaningless. Of what real worth is the right to present evidence and to argue its significance at a formal hearing, if the one who decides the case may stray at will from the record in reaching his decision." Bernard Schwartz acquiesces, contending that ". . . the exclusiveness of the record is at the core of the right to a fair hearing. Without that principle the hearing itself can be but a sham. The agency may go through the motions and receive mountains of evidence, testimonial and documentary; yet the elephantine record is but a facade if the agency may rely upon material not presented at the hearing."[100]

Of course, problems develop when agency adjudicators in fact do rely upon information to reach decisions that is not a part of the exculsive record. Ex parte contacts or communications may unduly prejudice hearing decisions because such contacts may provide hearing decision-makers with information not noted on the record. Ex parte communications are patently unfair and tend to undermine due process in hearing decision-making because the information tends to be one-sided, almost always favoring one party at the expense of the other. And since the ex parte information is not included as part of the record, a rebuttal to it could not be given by the other party in the dispute. Besides, since ex parte evidence is not part of the exclusive record, reviewing courts could never judge the weight adjudicators gave to it when making the decision.

Ex parte communications, contacts, or pressures can easily bias or severely contaminate a hearing decision, thus courts have found ex parte influence peddling generating ex parte evidence to be flatly illegal under most conditions. In a leading case, *Sangamon Valley Television Corp. v. U.S.,* 269 F.2d 221 (D.C. Cir.; 1959) the court overturned a decision by the FCC allowing a television station to relocate in St. Louis because of improper ex parte influence peddling. The court noted that such ex parte contacts struck at the core of the Commission's quasijudicial powers, corrupting the process. Fundamental fairness, the court argued, requires that the proceeding be conducted in the open with all the evidence becoming part of the exclusive record. In *First Savings and Loan Assn. v. Vandygriff,* 605 S.W. 2d 740, 742 (Tex. Civ. App.; 1980) the court stressed the point that ex parte evidence cannot be used to substantiate a hearing order: "Recognition of this fundamental rule means that ex parte (evidence) may not be a basis for such order." In *English v. Long Beach,* 217 P.2d 22 (Col.; 1950) the court held that the exclusiveness of the record rule prohibits talking to a doctor about the extent of injury off the record and outside of the hearing, while in *Cowart v. Schweiker,* 662 P.2d 731 (11th Cir.; 1981) the court concluded that the exclusiveness of the record principle had been violated because hearing examiners considered medical reports by doctors submitted after the close of the hearing.

The exclusiveness of the record principle is also violated by the gathering and use of "secret evidence" by hearing officials to help aid their decision. In an old state case, *Carstens v. Pillsbury,* 158 P. 218, 220 (Col.; 1916), the court held that to gather secret evidence ". . . and to consider it without even giving the parties an opportunity to . . . meet it in any reasonable way, is contrary to all principles of justice and fairness. It cannot be entertained for a moment." Ex parte "views or inspections also violate the exclusiveness of the record rule by allowing the viewer (agency adjudicator) to view something (e.g., accident site) outside of the record, preventing the "view" from being cross-examined. Of course, the ex parte view could cause injustices in hearing decisions, especially if the view happened to be a mistaken or incorrect one. In *Feinson v. Conservation Comm.,* 429 A.2d 910 (Conn.; 1981) an ex parte view was found to undermine the exclusiveness of the record because it was not noted on the record and no opportunity was given to rebut the view. But in *Zuniga v. San Mateo Dept. of Health Serv.,* 267 Cal. Rprt. 755, 761 (Cal. App. 1 Dist.; 1990) the court upheld the ex parte view because no prejudice from the viewing was identified and the other party was given sufficient opportunity to respond to the ex parte viewed evidence.

The *Zuniga* decision is rooted in a controversial application of the exclusiveness of the record principle regarding the use of ex parte evidence. Ex parte evidence is sometimes allowed by courts, especially if it can be shown that no prejudice resulted and an opportunity was given to rebut it. In *Market Street Ry v. Railroad Commission,* 324 U.S. 548 (1945) the

Supreme Court argued that in addition to showing that ex parte evidence was received, prejudice must be demonstrated to show that due process violations occurred. The Court noted the exclusiveness of the record principle should be honored to uphold due process standards in agency hearings, but that the substantive character of due process should "... not be trivialized by formal objections ... in the absence of any error or prejudice" (at 562).

Of course, the *Market Street* opinion was handed down a year before the passage of the federal APA. Because the exclusiveness of the record principle is considered so basic, any effort to compromise its application has attracted harsh criticism. The basic criticism of the *Market Street* ruling is that it tends to require opposing parties to prove that ex parte evidence or any extra-record evidence has somehow prejudiced the hearing decision. Since demonstrating prejudice is frequently very difficult to do, critics contend that such a requirement would really take the thunder out of the exclusiveness of record rule. Consequently, many courts have totally rejected the controversial ruling on the exclusiveness of the record principle espoused in *Market Street,* which is not that difficult since the *Market Street* Court spoke before the federal APA became law. Probably most courts follow the approach adopted in *First Savings and Loan Assn. v. Vandygriff,* "It is not the burden of the complaining party to demonstrate harm by showing the extent, if any, to which the official was persuaded by the secret information" (at 742).

Use of Official Notice in Reaching Decisions

Closely linked to the principle of exclusiveness of the record is the doctrine of *official notice.* In fact, official notice constitutes the most significant exception to the exclusiveness of the record requirement because officially noticed facts (i.e., "very obvious" facts) are permitted to be used by adjudicators to help substantiate their hearing decisions as "extra-record" evience after the hearing is over. Let us put the use of official notice into perspective.

In reflecting on the appropriateness of evidence employed to justify judicial decisions, Justice Louis Brandeis concluded: "Nothing can be treated as evidence which is not introduced as such." "If taken literally, and it never has been, Brandeis's holding would preclude the use of *judicially noticed facts* in court trials and *officially noticed facts* in administrative hearings. To avoid confusion at the outset, it should be made clear that judicial or official notice is not the same as "notice" "provided" to a party. Judicial and official notice refer simply to when a tribunal accepts a fact as obvious and notorious without further proof. When a court notices (recognizes) a fact as indisputably true, the court is judicially noticing the fact. Official notice is the administrative tribunal's counterpart to judicial notice. Therefore, when hearing officers accept facts as unquestionably true, these officials are giving official notice to these facts. Officially noticed facts are normally supposed to be so indisputable or obvious that reasonable people would accept them as common knowledge (for example, Christmas falls on December 25). Officially noticed facts, if they cannot be acknowledged as true on the spot, should at least be easily verified by consulting, say, a telephone book or public records. Because of the nature of such facts, officially noticed facts are normally not entered into the record; yet they do form part of the extra-record used by hearing examiners to reach their decisions (*Citizens of the State of Florida v. Florida Public Serv. Comm'n.,* 440 So.2d 371 [Fla. Appl., 1983]; and *Dionne v. Heckler,* 585 F.Supp. 1055 [D.Me., 1984]).

It is easy to justify the use of official notice; for Brandeis's standard to be applied literally would create unnecessary and counterproductive hardships for all tribunals. In administrative agencies, it would slow down to a crawl the disposition of cases. Surely it would be silly to not recognize and use facts that are obvious and helpful to those hearing officials wanting to make fair, reasonable, and practical decisions. It would be a serious mistake for independent regulatory commissioners, for example, to ignore practical and obvious facts when deciding public policy questions that, when implemented in the real world, will have significant social impact. Thus, it would be negligent of the Nuclear Regulatory Commission to consider in a hearing all those relevant scientific facts regarding the safety of a proposed nuclear power plant while ignoring the practical reality, not entered into the official record, that the proposed site is in downtown Manhattan, a densely populated area.

It would be just as absurd to permit unreasonable and time-consuming challenges to indisputable facts employed responsibly by hearing officials to reach decisions. Although there has been some scholarly and judicial debate over how flexibly official notice should be applied by administrative tribunals, in general, reviewing courts have allowed hearing examiners to officially notice facts that are not obvious to the general public, yet are readily accepted as common knowledge to agency experts who have acquired considerable expertise in specialized areas.[101] In a 1978 case, the Supreme Court acknowledged that hearing decisions cannot always be totally supported by the evidence in the record; nor is such support required. Therefore, decisions must ultimately rest in part on facts that are officially noticed by agency experts.[102] In an Oregon case, Justice Rossman provided some credible insights into the reasons that administrative agencies should be granted broader latitude in applying official notice:

> Administrative law is predicated upon a belief that no man is appointed to an office, such as public utilities commissioner, unless he possesses special fitness, and that through the daily performance of his duties he acquires a fund of practical knowledge concerning the problems which he daily faces. His fund of knowledge is properly employed by him in passing upon controverted matters.[103]

But expertise should not be irresponsibly used by agencies to notice facts which cannot be given such status legitimately. This would constitute an abuse of the function of official notice, thus causing the appropriate employment of official notice to "become lost in the haze of so-called expertise."[104]

Although there is no evidence to indicate that official notice has been misused to any significant extent in agency hearings, problems could arise to undermine the extension of fair adjudications if hearing officials acted irresponsibly. Most notably, they could use official notice to recognize facts that are not obviously true, even to the experts. When highly complex, technical questions are involved, giving official notice to facts is less convincing and inappropriate. Even worse, hearing examiners could use facts that are only officially noticed after the hearing proceedings have ended to help substantiate their findings. This practice has bothered reviewing courts because it unfairly prevents any challenges to the validity and use of the officially noticed facts. In *Heckler v. Campbell,* 103 S.Ct. 1952, 1953 (1983), the Supreme Court said that it is a basic administrative law principle "that when an agency takes official or administrative notice of facts, a litigant must be given an adequate opportunity to respond." In *Volstedt,* a California court held that any extra-record evidence, implicitly acknowledging the use of officially noticed facts, tends to undermine due process in agency hearings unless parties ". . . have an opportunity to refute, test, and explain it . . ." (at 410).

Also, the agency that initiates the action normally has the burden of proof. If hearing officers place significant weight on officially noticed facts to substantiate their decisions, even if they allow parties the opportunity to challenge these facts, in effect, the agency is illegitimately shifting the burden of proof from itself to the parties before it. This is so because now the facts are assumed to be accurate unless the parties before an agency show the facts to be untrue. With this in mind, Bernard Schwartz concluded:

> That is why it is so important that (1) official notice be limited to facts which are obvious and notorious to the expert and to facts established in documents such as a company's own

> reports, which cannot readily be questioned by it, and (2) that a full opportunity to show the contrary be given. Otherwise official notice can be a device to short-circuit the essence of the fair hearing requirement itself.[105]

In sum, few seem to have any serious reservations about the use of official notice, as long as its use does not jeopardize procedural due process protections in agency hearings. For fair procedures to be honored, most experts believe that official notice must be kept limited in its application. According to scholars, responsible employment of official notice would involve: (1) making certain that all officially noticed facts are actually obvious and well known to the average person; (2) noticing technical facts not considered common knowledge to the average person only if the facts are recognized as indisputable knowledge by experts in the field (for example, that recklessly disposing radioactive waste poses a serious health hazard); (3) informing all relevant parties in regard to the officially noticed facts considered to help reach the decision; (4) providing sources to officially noticed facts (for example, agency files); (5) exclusion of *litigation facts* (facts that have emerged in the pending dispute since such facts are presently in question); (6) prohibiting the use of officially noticed facts for establishing principle evidence on which the decision rests; (7) likewise, the preclusion of any officially noticed facts from becoming part of the substantial evidence; and (8) sufficient opportunity to contest all officially noticed facts that could be reasonably challenged (for example, facts in agency files cited but not brought forth). This last limitation seems to be the most vital in preserving fair use of official notice.

Concluding the Hearing Business

The final actions taken by ALJs to conclude hearing business involves the issuance of the written decision. Before the hearing officials write or issue a "recommended, initial, or tentative decision" ("final" decision of the ALJ, but tentative since it can be rejected by the agency head), Section 557(c) of the APA requires that all parties be given "reasonable opportunity to submit . . . (1) proposed findings and conclusions; (2) exceptions to the decisions or recommended decisions. . . ; and (3) supporting reasons for the exceptions or proposed findings or conclusions." Such is normally submitted in the form of legal briefs to the ALJ.110.

Section 557(c) also specifically requires that the record should ". . . show the ruling on each finding, conclusion, or exception presented." The Section also requires that "all decisions including initial, recommended, and tentative decisions" are part of the formal written record and ". . . include a statement of (A) findings and conclusions, and the reasons or basis therefore, on all the material issues of fact, law, or discretion presented on the record; and (B) the appropriate rule, order, sanction, relief, or denial thereof."

Regarding formal adjudicative decisions, the APA provisions are quite specific and demanding, but evidently the intent of Congress was to force adjudicators to act responsibly in making hearing decisions. Specifically, by compelling ALJs to justify in detail the factual and legal reasons for their findings, Congress in effect is forcing hearings officials to think seriously about its hearing decisions. Of course, this also tends to promote responsible and democratically accountable hearing decisions, as well as a justification for agency orders (public policies) that will make it easier for all affected parties to follow and understand. Possibly most important from a legal standpoint is that detailed justifications for findings and conclusions make judicial review considerably easier and much more effective. As discussed previously, judicial review is frustrated if hearing decisions are not justified in a complete and accurate record.

Despite the specific requirement regarding the documentation of hearing decisions, hearing records too often are woefully inadequate, resulting in poorly documented decisions. Many judges still complain that they cannot conduct competent judicial review of agency adjudications because of inadequate hearing records, despite repeated attempts by the courts over the years to make agency adjudicators keep adequate hearing records by complying with APA record-keeping requirements. Observers have maintained that adjudicators still keep poor hearing records because agencies conduct too many hearings and the actual drafting of the decisions has been delegated to lower-level bureaucrats ("opinion writers"). Such opinion writers end up justifying decisions in vague, generic legal reasons, failing to justify in specific legal terms the particular case. Consequently, "the opinion becomes more of a rationalization for the decision than an explanation."[106]

It must be stressed that ALJs do not make final decisions for the agency. Agency heads have the authority to make "institutional decisions" for their particular agency or bureaucracy by overruling the decision reached by an ALJ. This is a legally sanctioned agency right and it is considered legitimate because agency heads, almost always political appointees, have the obligation of promoting policies that are consistent with the administration's views (i.e., the presidential administration on the federal level and the governor's administration on the state level). As a consequence, an ALJ's decision technically constitutes only a tentative decision or an advisory opinion subject to being overruled by the agency chief. As a practical matter, most hearing decisions are quite routine and "apolitical" and, therefore, become the agency's final decision. However, hearing decisions that are politically sensitive may be reversed by the agency head to make agency policy consistent with the administration's policy. Courts urge that reasonable justifications be given to justify reversing an ALJ's decision, but reasonable justifications are not always given since political reasons do not always seem reasonable in light of the specific facts and law pertaining to a particular case (*Central Transport Inc. v. National Labor Relations Board*, 997 F.2d 1180 [1993]).

The current practice of permitting agency heads inevitably to decide a hearing decision bothers some practitioners and scholars because the practice rejects an old, commonsensical legal principle established in *Morgan v. U.S.,* 298 U.S. 468, 481 (1936) that "[T]he one who hears must decide." In this case Chief Justice Hughes argued that responsible and fair decision-making ". . . cannot be performed by one who has not considered evidence or argument" (at 481). However, increasing hearing caseloads forced a more practical, flexible approach, so in a follow-up case, *Morgan v. U.S.,* 304 U.S. 1, 18 (1938), known as *Morgan II,* the Supreme Court held that the decision-maker need not be present at the hearing, as long as he ". . . dipped into (the record) from time to time to get its drift." *Morgan II* had the effect of allowing subordinates to hear and decide cases. Today, and for many decades now, agency heads only casually review the tentative decisions reached by ALJs, rejecting those decisions that staffers recommend should be changed to suit administrative policy. As noted, even the ALJs assign out the writing of the decisions to their assistants or "opinion writers," bureaucratizing and impersonalizing the whole process, which at times causes due process to be undermined.

ACKNOWLEDGMENTS

I wish to thank Joe Miller and Homer Teng for their research assistance, as well as Cindy Hartson and Mike Hawkins for their technical assistance.

NOTES

1. Thad L. Beyle and Lynn L. Muchmore, Eds. *Being Governor: The View from the Office* (Durham, NC: Duke Press Policy Studies, 1983).

2. For a critique of theories behind the relationship between the intent of the Founders of the Constitution and modern public administration, see Michael W. Spicer and Larry D. Terry, Legitimacy, history, and logic: Public administration and the Constitution, *Public Administration Review,* 53 (May/June, 1993), pp. 239–245. Also see Jeremy Rabkin, *Judicial Compulsions: How the Law Distorts Public Policy* (New York: Basic Books, Inc. 1989), pp. 243–270.
3. Kenneth C. Davis, *Administrative Law: Cases-Test-Problem,* 6th ed. (St. Paul, MN: West Publishing Company, 1977), p. 43.
4. For a good analysis of *Waukegan* in the perspective of other cases, see Davis, *Administrative Law,* pp. 28–32.
5. Bernard Schwartz, Administrative law cases during 1984, *Administrative Law Review,* Vol. 37 (Spring, 1985), p. 134.
6. Bernard Schwartz, Administrative law cases during 1990, *Administrative Law Review,* Vol. 43, No. (Summer, 1991), pp. 475–476.
7. For a scholarly justification of the Congress's delegation of judicial powers to non-article III administrators' tribunals, which is rooted in "appellate review theory", see Richard H. Fallon, Jr., Of legislative courts, administrative agencies, and Article III, *Harvard Law Review,* Vol. 101 (March, 1988), pp. 916–992.
8. *Ibid.*
9. 29 *Federal Register* 8324, 8367 (1964).
10. See Kenneth C. Davis, *Discretionary Justice: A Preliminary Inquiry* (Chicago: University of Illinois Press, 1969), chap. 3; Henry J. Friendly, *The Federal Administrative Agencies: The Need for Better Definition of Standards* (Cambridge, MA: Harvard University Press, 1962), chap. 1; David L. Shapiro, The choice of rulemaking or adjudication in the development of administrative policy, *Harvard Law Review* 78 (March, 1965): 921–72; J. Skelly Wright, Rulemaking and judicial review, *Administrative Law Review* 30 (Summer, 1987): 461–66; and Richard K. Berg, Re-examining policy procedures: The choice between rulemaking and adjudication, *Administrative Law Review* 38 (Spring, 1986): 149–80.
11. Edwin J. Madaj, Agency investigations: Adjudication or rulemaking?—The ITC's material inquiry determinations under the antidumping and countervailing duty laws, *N.C.J. Int'l L. and Com. Reg.,* V. 15 (1990), p. 445.
12. For one critic's analysis, see William Funk, Rationality review of state administrative rulemaking, *Administrative Law Review,* Vol. 43 (Spring, 1991). Funk does a good job comparing the use of the rule-making approach for making public policies at the state and federal level.
13. Shapiro, Choice of rulemaking or adjudication in the development of administrative policy, pp. 940–41.
14. Bernard Schwartz, *Administrative Law,* 2d ed. (Boston: Little, Brown, 1984), pp. 145–49, 191–96; also Berg, Re-examining policy procedures, pp. 160–76.
15. It should be acknowledged that agency decisions, which have great impact on the shaping of regulatory policies, are so informal that they cannot be discussed in the context of the more formalized rule-making and order-making procedures. Nevertheless, basic agency policies are normally made through one or the other, order-making or rule-making. Informal discretionary decisions made outside rule-making and order-making only tend to refine and define basic agency policies.
16. Samuel Estreicher, Policy oscillating at the Labor Board: A plea for rulemaking, *Administrative Law Review* 37 (Spring, 1985): 170–81.
17. Shapiro, Choice of rulemaking on adjudication in the development of administrative policy, p. 932.
18. *Ibid.,* p. 933.
19. Estreicher, Policy oscillation at the Labor Board, p. 181.
20. *Ibid.,* p. 177.
21. Kenneth C. Davis, *Administrative Law and Government* (St. Paul, MN: West Publishing Company, 1975), p. 124.
22. *Ibid.*
23. *Ibid.,* p. 125.
24. *Ibid.,* pp. 114–115.

25. Kenneth C. Davis, *Administrative Law Treatise,* 2nd ed., Vol. 2 (San Diego: K.C. Davis Pub. Co., 1979), pp. 157-160.
26. Edwin W. Tucker, *Administrative Law, Regulation of Enterprise, and Individual Liberties* (St. Paul, MN: West Publishing Company, 1975), p. 108.
27. See *Reeve Aleutian Airways, Inc. v. U.S.*, 982 F.2d 594, 598 (1992).
28. Recent works have noted such shifts, see Jeremy Rabkin, *Judicial Compulsions: How Public Law Distorts Public Policy* (New York: Basic Books, 1989) and Christopher F. Edley, Jr., *Administrative Law: Rethinking Judicial Control of Bureaucracy* (New Haven: Yale University Press, 1990).
29. Bernard Schwartz, Administrative law cases during 1985, *Administrative Law Review* 38 (Summer, 1986): 298.
30. The obsession with the cost-conscious approach is epitomized by cost–benefit analysis, which became very "popular" during the Reagan presidency. See Christopher M. Heiman *et al.,* Project: The impact of cost-benefit analysis on federal administrative law, *Administrative Law Review,* Vol. 42 (Fall, 1990), pp. 545-654.
31. Todd D. Rakoff, *Brock v. Roadway Express,* and the new law of regulatory due process, *The Supreme Court Review,* Vol. 4 (1987), pp. 157–200.
32. Rakoff, *Brock v. Roadway Express,* and the new law of regulatory due process, pp. 157–200.
33. For an analysis of risk standards in administrative law, see Frank B. Cross, Daniel M. Byrd III, and Lester B. Lave, Discernible risk—a proposed standard for significant risk in carcinogen regulation, *Administrative Law Review,* Vol. 43 (Winter, 1991), pp. 61–88.
34. Kenneth C. Davis, *Administrative Law Treatise,* 2nd ed., Vol. 2 (San Diego: K.C. Davis Pub. Co., 1979), pp. 157-160.
35. Victor A. Thompson, *Bureaucracy and the Modern World* (Morristown, NJ: General Learning Press, 1976), p. 114.
36. *Ibid.*
37. *Ibid.,* pp. 114–15.
38. Ernest Gellhorn and Ronald M. Levin, *Administrative Law and Process in A Nutshell,* 3rd Edition (St. Paul, MN: West, 1990), p. 270.
39. Lewis Mainzer, *Political Bureaucracy* (Glenview, IL: Scott Foresman, 1973), pp. 45–46.
40. *Ibid.,* p. 46.
41. Norman Abrams, Administrative law judge systems: The California view, *Administrative Law Review* 2 (Fall, 1977): pp. 490–92.
42. Kenneth C. Davis, *Administrative Law Treatise,* 2d ed. (St. Paul, MN: West Publishing Company, 1980), 3: 325–27.
43. Eleanor M. Fox, Chairman Miller, the Federal Trade Commission, economics, and *Rashomon, Law and Contemporary Problems,* Vol. 50 (Autumn, 1987), p. 35.
44. *Ibid.*
45. *Ibid.,* pp. 34.
46. *Ibid., pp. 34–35.*
47. Bernard Schwartz, *Administrative Law: A Casebook* (Boston: Little, Brown and Company, 1988), p. 510.
48. Abrams, Administrative law judge systems, p. 491.
49. For a very comprehensive survey of when non-ALJs are used in federal adjudications, see John H. Frye III, Survey of non-ALJ hearing programs in the federal government, *Administrative Law Review,* Vol. 44 (Spring, 1992), pp. 261–353.
50. For a solid discussion the appearance of fairness doctrine, see Van Noy, The appearance of fairness doctrine: A conflict in values, *Washington Law Review,* Vol. 61 (1986). Also see Meierhenry, op. cit., pp. 565-567.
51. For a thorough analysis of this case, see Edward McGonagle, Administrative law, *Syracuse Law Review,* Volume 42 (1991).
52. Stephen Hobbs, Judicial discipline and due process in Washington state, *Washington Law Review,* Volume 63 (1988), pp. 732-737.
53. Stephen R. Miller and Larry T. Richardson, A central panel system for Mississippi's adminis-

trative law judges: Promoting the due process of law in administrative hearings, *Mississippi College Law Review,* Volume 6 (Spring, 1986), p. 133.
54. *Ibid.*
55. *Ibid.,* p. 134.
56. In the Chairman's Message of the Administrative Conference of the United States, Chairman Antonin Scalia in 1981 critiques the problems with the loopholes section 554(d). He notes that not only does the section not apply to all formal adjudications since "initial licensing and adjudications involving rates, facilities, or practices of public utilities and carriers are specifically exempted," but it does apply automatically to adjudications that are not absolutely *required* by statutory terms. See Chairman's message, separation of functions: Obscurity preserved, *Administrative Law Review,* Volume 34 (1982), pp. v–x.
57. Hobbs, op. cit., p. 737.
58. Joseph E. Edwards, Disqualification of Federal Trade Commission or members thereof, *American Law Reports,* Vol. 8 (1991).
59. Michael H. Graham, The case for model rules of evidence in administrative adjudications, *Federal Bar News and Journal,* Volume 38 (May, 1991), p. 189.
60. *Ibid.*
61. *Ibid.,* pp. 189–90.
62. Richard J. Pierce, Jr., Use of the federal rules of evidence in federal agency adjudications, *Administrative Law Review,* Volume 39 (Winter, 1987), pp. 2–3.
63. *Ibid.*
64. Graham, op. cit., p. 190.
65. Davis, *Administrative Law and Government,* p. 192.
66. *Altenheim German Home v. Turnock,* 902 F. 2d 582, 584 (7th Cir.; 1990).
67. Bernard Schwartz, Administrative law cases during 1990, *Administrative Law Review,* Vol. 43 (Summer, 1991), p. 481.
68. Bernard Schwartz, *Administrative Law: A Casebook* (Boston: Little Brown and Company, 1988), p. 553.
69. Hearsay represents the modern grammatical construction of the eleventh century Old English expression, "saying-heard" and the twelfth century's version, "heard saying." "Hear-saying" was noted by the year 1340 and by the sixteenth century the term "hearsay" first came into use in the practice of law. By the close of the seventeenth century rules governing hearsay had become firmly established in English law. See Dennis Murphy, Hearsay: The least understood exclusionary rule, *Journal of Criminal Justice,* Volume 17 (1989).
70. Murphy, op cit., p. 269. Because of all the exceptions to the hearsay rule and the controversy pertaining to its use, Eleanor Swift in Abolishing the hearsay rule, *California Law Review,* Vol. 75 (1987) discusses the consequences of abolishing the hearsay rule. She concludes that we should consider further many assumptions and values on the hearsay rule before thinking of abandoning it.
71. Ernest Gellhorn and Ronald M. Levin, *Administrative Law and Process,* op. cit., pp. 267–270. I quote their five questions without repeated citations.
72. For other articles focusing on the use of hearsay evidence, see Michael H. Graham, The case for model rules of evidence in administrative adjudications, *Federal Bar News and Journal,* Volume 38 (May, 1991); Steven P. Grossman and Stephen J. Shapiro, Challenging public investigative reports: How to fight the hearsay exception, *Trial* (February, 1991); Roger Park, A subject matter approach to hearsay reform, *Michigan Law Review,* Vol. 86 (October, 1987); Roger Park, I didn't tell them anything about you: Implied assertions as hearsay under the federal rules of evidence, *Minnesota Law Review,* Vol. 74 (1990); Allan A. Toubman, The ABCs of hearsay in administrative proceedings, *Maine Bar Journal* (November, 1990); Marita C. Sullivan and Margaret A. Marcouiller, Administrative Law, *Loyola University Law Journal,* Vol. 21 (1990); and Eleanor Swift, A foundation fact approach to hearsay, Vol. 75 (1987).
73. Thomas R. Mulroy, Jr., and Douglas G. McClure, The case for allowing hearsay in Illinois administrative proceedings, *Illinois Bar Journal* (June, 1989), p. 556.
74. It is not uncommon for courts to maintain that reliable documents such as medical reports are

only technically hearsay, but for all practical purposes, should be considered substantial evidence because of their high quality and probative value. For example, the Supreme Court in *Richardson v. Perales,* 402 U.S. 406, 407–408 (1971) noted that "[A]lthough the reports are hearsay in the technical sense, because their content is not produced live before the hearing examiner, we feel. . . ." that such evidence can constitute "substantial evidence" because of its "reliability and probative value."

75. Kenneth C. Davis, *Administrative Law Treatise,* Vol. 3, p. 242.
76. Mulroy, Jr., and McClure, op cit., p. 556.
77. Kenneth C. Davis, *Administrative Law Treatise,* 2nd ed., Vol. 3 (San Diego: K.C. Davis Pub. Co., 1980), p. 239.
78. Schwartz, Administrative law cases during 1990, p. 483.
79. Gellhorn and Levin (op. cit., p. 94) make the point that the old "legal residuum rule" was overly technical, which sometimes caused injustices to occur in hearings ". . . when hearsay is the only, or best, available evidence." Of course, under the new or revised residuum rule such injustices would be less likely to occur since reliable hearsay, which could pass the substantial test, would be used to substantiate hearing decisions.
80. For a lengthy discussion of the exclusionary rule in administrative law, see Scott Meacham, Evidence: The exclusionary rule in civil administrative hearings: *Turner v. City of Lawton, Oklahoma Law Review,* Vol. 40 (1987), pp. 321-337.
81. Bernard Schwartz, *Administrative Law,* 2nd edition (Boston: Little, Brown and Company, 1984), p. 365.
82. Bernard Schwartz, Administrative law cases during 1984, *Administrative Law Review,* Volume 37 (Spring, 1985), p. 141.
83. *Powell v. Alabama,* 287 U.S. 45, 68–69 (1982).
84. Schwartz, *Administrative Law,* p. 297.
85. A parole revocation seems to many people to be a criminal law matter, not an administrative one, but it is administrative because it involves the question of what to do administratively about a person's prison sentence after that individual has been convicted in a criminal court. Questions concerning the granting or revoking of parole are handled by an administrative tribunal, usually called a parole board.
86. Tucker, *Administrative Law, Regulation of Enterprise, and Individual Liberties,* p. 127.
87. *Ibid.*
88. For a review of legal representation at the SSA, see William Justin DeLoenardis, Representing your client at the Social Security disability hearing, *Washington State Bar News* (October, 1987), pp. 21–23; Prentice Cox, Social Security netting regulations: Balancing administrative convenience with the rights of beneficiaries, *Minnesota Law Review,* Vol. 73 (1989), pp. 1143–1174.
89. Bernard Schwartz, Administrative law cases during 1985, *Administrative Law Review* 38 (Summer 1986): 300.
90. *Ibid.,* p. 301. Also see Richard Gans, The Supreme Court's interpretation of section 1988 and awards of attorney's fees for work performed in administrative proceedings: A proposal for a result-oriented approach, *Washington Law Review,* Vol. 62 (1987), pp. 889–907; INS transfer policy: Interference with detained aliens due process right to retain counsel, *Harvard Law Review,* Vol. 100 (June, 1987), pp. 2001–2017.
91. Henry J. Friendly, Some kind of hearing, *University of Pennsylvania Law Review* 123 (June 1975): 1289.
92. *Ibid.,* p. 1288.
93. *Ibid.,* pp. 1290–91.
94. *Ibid.,* p. 1290.
95. William D. Popkin, Effect of representation on a claimant's success rate—three study designs, *Administrative Law Review* 31 (Fall, 1979): 449–61.
96. *Ibid.,* p. 451.
97. Despite exceptions to the preponderance of the evidence standard, the courts are very reluctant to require a higher standard of proof than the federal APA or state APAs minimally require. In *SEC v. Savoy Industries,* 587 F. 2d 1149 (D.C. Cir.; 1978), (issuing an injunction); *Walters v.*

Lucas, 497 F. 2d 1230 (9th Cir.; 1979) (revocation of pilot's license); and *In re Revocation of License of Polk,* 449 A2d7 (N.J.; 1982) (medical disciplinary hearing) the preponderance of the evidence standard was found to be sufficient.

98. In *Woodby v. INS,* 385 U.S. 276 (1966) the Supreme Court reviewed standards of proof, but did not discuss how the standards actually differed.
99. Louis J. Jaffe, Administrative procedure re-examined: The Benjamin report, *Harvard Law Review,* Vol. 56 (March, 1943), p. 732.
100. Schwartz, *Administrative Law,* op. cit., p. 368.
101. For a review of this debate see, Stephen G. Breyer and Richard B. Stewart, *Administrative Law and Regulatory Policy,* 2d ed. (Boston: Little, Brown, 1985), pp. 625–33.
102. *FCC v. Nat'l. Citizens Commission,* 98 S.Ct. 2096.
103. *Pierce Auto Freight Lines v. Flagg,* 159 P.2d 162, 177 (Ore., 1945).
104. *Baltimore & O.R. Co. v. Aberdeen & R.R. Co.,* 393 U.S. 87, 91–92 (1986); and *Carson v. Department of Employment Security,* 376 A.2d 355 (Vt., 1977).
105. Schwartz, *Administrative Law,* p. 297.
106. For an in-depth review of the politicalization of medicare adjudications, see Eleanor D. Kinney, In search of bureaucratic justice—adjudicating medicare home health benefits in the 1980s, *Administrative Law Review,* Vol. 42 (Spring, 1990).

11

Management of Federal Agency Adjudication

Jeffrey S. Lubbers *Administrative Conference of the United States, Washington, D.C.*

It is well known that during both the regulatory decade of the 1970s and the deregulatory 1980s, federal agencies generally relied on rulemaking as the procedure of choice for making policy. By all indications, the growth in agency proposed and final rules was strong and persistent. A key indication of rulemaking's centrality was the succession of presidential executive orders issued to bring this type of agency activity under firmer White House control.[1] In short, Professor Davis's oft-quoted 1970 proclamation that notice-and-comment rule-making is "one of the greatest inventions of modern government"[2] seemed to be not only prescient but justifiable.

Little noticed amidst this *illumina* of rules was the fact that agency adjudication—the seemingly forgotten half of the Administrative Procedure Act's procedural framework (and by far the most disputed part in the debate surrounding its passage[3])—was still there for the using. When a series of developments began "to take the bloom off the rulemaking rose,"[4] agency administrators were able to turn to the shelf and discover that adjudicating individual cases might be a promising alternative—a way to get things done without Office of Management and Budget (OMB) review and with less intrusive judicial review. If rulemaking was the hare, adjudication had become the tortoise.

Not that agency adjudication had not also undergone some changes since 1946. The government's agency caseload had grown in a fashion parallel to its rulemaking load: it had shot up in the 1960s and 1970s and had leveled off in the 1980s. The number of federal administrative law judges (ALJs) grew rapidly from 196 in 1947 to 278 (1954), 494 (1962), 792 (1974), 1070 (1979), 1119 (1981), and the number has remained about the same since

Prepared for presentation at "Managing Regulation," a Symposium on the Organization and Administration of Major Regulation Functions in Government Agencies, sponsored by The American University, School of Public Affairs, Washington, D.C., May 16, 1991. Updated February 1, 1993. Except where indicated, the views expressed herein are solely those of the author, and do not necessarily represent the views of the Administrative Conference.

then.[5] More important was that the character of agency adjudications had changed, with more fact-based benefit, labor, and enforcement cases and proportionately fewer policy-laden economic regulatory and rate cases.[6] Just as commentators were decrying the encumbrances on the once simple notice-and-comment rulemaking process, critics were pointing out that the agency adjudication process (once thought to be an expeditious alternative to court litigation) had itself taken on trappings of trial-type, adversarial formality.[7] The reaction to this recognition was an increasing reliance on "informal adjudication," "non-APA" adjudication, and "alternative dispute resolution."

This pattern of federal agency adjudication has become increasingly variegated. The many available options and strategies obviously pose challenges for legislators, agency administrators, and managers. This chapter describes existing patterns of agency adjudication and focuses on management initiatives that have attempted to come to grips with these options and strategies.

OVERVIEW OF AN AGENCY CASE

We will postpone for the moment a prolonged discussion of the "continuum" of agency adjudication, which ranges from the most informal decision (e.g., a determination to disclose an agency "record" requested under the Freedom of Information Act [FOIA]) to the most formal trial-type proceeding held under the Administrative Procedure Act hearing requirements (5 U.S.C. §§554, 556–57). At the outset, it is useful to describe in some detail the major stages of a typical case on the formal end of the spectrum. A familiarity with these stages is necessary for anyone seeking to practice case management. These stages can be classified into three: prehearing, hearing, and posthearing. A fourth, follow-on stage (judicial review), needs also to be kept in mind.

Prehearing Stage

A case may begin in several different ways, depending on the type of case and the particular agency's case initiation procedures. Some cases are triggered by an application, a private complaint, a petition, or a preliminary determination of violation made at an inspection. This initial step may lead to a denial of the petition or application, or to a citation or notice of violation based upon the private complaint or preliminary investigation. Further procedural steps may take place before referral of the case to an administrative law judge (ALJ) for hearing. These steps might include a formal order of investigation, a formal complaint, a staff recommendation of hearing, completion of an environmental impact statement, and issuance of a formal order or notice of hearing. Of course, not all cases go through the same prehearing stages. Moreover, as the Administrative Conference learned in its statistical study of agency adjudication,[8] it is often difficult for an agency to pin down the exact date that a case originates, especially if the first action in the case occurs in a field office. This presented a data-gathering problem since the prehearing stage often appears misleadingly short.

Hearing Stage

The hearing stage encompasses the period during which the ALJ has control of the case. This stage often begins when the case is referred to the chief ALJ's office. The case is then assigned to the ALJ who is to preside over it. Other key dates in this stage include the prehearing conference, the first day of hearing, the last interlocutory order (if any), the last day of hearing, the completion of the record/filing of final briefs, and date of the ALJ's decision or order. At some agencies, in simpler cases, ALJs issue an oral decision from the bench (read into the transcript).[9]

Presiding ALJs are given broad powers by the Administrative Procedure Act to control the hearings,[10] although they lack contempt powers. Hearings are "on the record" and are transcribed verbatim. Under the APA, "A party is entitled to present his case or defense by oral or documentary evidence, to submit rebuttal evidence, and to conduct such cross-examination as may be required for a full and true disclosure of the facts."[11] However, in certain types of cases oral hearings may be omitted or truncated: "In . . . determining claims for money or benefits or applications for initial licenses an agency may, when a party will not be prejudiced thereby, adopt procedures for the submission of all or part of the evidence in written form."[12] This flexibility inherent in the APA's provisions concerning cross-examination and in the special provisions for benefits and initial licensing cases are often forgotten by those who criticize the APA's "formalism."[13]

For case tracking purposes, the hearing stage dates (from referral to the chief ALJ to issuance of ALJs decision) are relatively certain and reliably retrievable. Thus statistics collected for this stage (for similar case type categories) should prove useful to managers and analysts alike.

Posthearing Stage

The posthearing stage begins when the ALJ's decision or order is released. The case then may or may not be reviewed by the agency head (i.e., a full board or commission, a panel thereof, or an individual administrator) or a delegate of the agency head (e.g., a judicial officer or review board). Review procedures vary almost as widely as prehearing procedures.[14] In some agencies, review by the agency head is within the discretion of the agency and is infrequent. In others, appeal may be had by right and review is frequent. Under some agencies' statutes, review is mandatory. Thus a series of posthearing events may take place in an agency adjudication: the filling of an appeal (sometimes called "exceptions"), the filing of briefs by the petitioners (and, thereafter, the respondents), oral argument to the reviewing body, and final agency action. Some agencies utilize an intermediate review board for some or all the cases, before consideration by the agency head.

The APA does allow initial decisions by ALJs to "become . . . the decision of the agency without further proceedings unless there is an appeal to, or review on motion of, the agency within time provided by rule."[15] Other statutes, however, may require review. The APA also gives agency heads great leeway in the scope of their review of ALJ decisions: "On appeal from or review of the initial decision, the agency has all the powers which it would have in making the initial decision except as it may limit the issues on notice or by rule."[16] In practice, however, this free hand has been somewhat circumscribed by reviewing courts.

From the standpoint of case tracking, this stage is relatively coherent in each agency although cross-agency comparisons are difficult due to the variety of review structures. Moreover, even within an agency, because the review structure is normally separate from the ALJ office, the logistics of following cases through both stages are problematic. Different docket personnel are often involved at each stage and the ALJ office usually loses track of cases after initial decisions are issued.

Judicial Review

Although the vagaries of judicial review of agency decisions are beyond the scope of this paper, agency case managers must keep in mind the impact of judicial oversight. Formal agency adjudications are normally reviewed on the basis of the record assembled by the agency. Reviewing courts' factual review is based on the substantial evidence test: if the court finds substantial evidence to support the agency's decision (even if there may also be substantial evidence to support another outcome), the decision is to be sustained.[17] However, to obtain an affirmance, the basis for the final agency decision must be adequately spelled out. Sometimes, of course, the agency simply relies on the reasoning of the ALJ's initial decision or that of its intermediate decisionmaker, which is then reviewed by the court. However, if the agency head reverses or modifies the underlying decision, the reviewing court will look for adequate justification for such departure in the agency's final decision.

Court challenges to agency orders can also be based on broader legal or constitutional bases, which if sustained by the courts, can lead to major impacts on the agency's adjudication process. Remands and reopenings not only play havoc with case-tracking statistics, and disrupt case assignments and scheduling, but also have ripple effects throughout an agency's adjudicative system.[18] Some mechanism has to be developed to translate judicial doctrine into agency policy transmitted down into the adjudicative system. This has been an especially big problem when agency policymakers have resorted to selective "nonacquiesence" in judicial review decisions, by refusing to apply the court's holding to any cases but the one actually reversed.[19]

ROLE OF THE ADMINISTRATIVE LAW JUDGE

As may be inferred from the foregoing description, the administrative law judge is the key actor in agency adjudication. ALJs preside over all agency adjudications (and those rule-makings) that are required by statute to be determined on the record after opportunity for an agency hearing.[20] In those "APA hearings" (often used as interchangeable with "formal hearings") only an ALJ or the agency head (single administrators, board or commission or members thereof) may preside, and it is exceedingly rare for the agency head to do the presiding.[21]

To protect ALJs from undue agency pressure, the APA gave them independence in matters of appointment, pay, and tenure. Agencies can appoint them only after applicants have passed a competitive "merit selection" examination administered by the Office of Personnel Management (OPM), which may not delegate this responsibility to the appointing agency.[22] ALJ pay, until recent amendments to the pay laws, was to be prescribed by OPM independently of agency recommendations or ratings.[23] The APA provides that ALJs are to be assigned to cases "in rotation so far as practicable,"[24] "may not perform duties inconsistent with their [ALJ] duties and responsibilities,"[25] and may not "be responsible to or subject to the supervision or direction of" agency prosecutors or investigators.[26] They are exempt from agency performance appraisals[27] and are subject to discipline and removed only for "good cause" as determined by the independent Merit Systems Protection Board (after an APA hearing).[28]

The Supreme Court has recognized that the ALJ's role is "functionally comparable" to that of a trial judge conducting civil proceedings without a jury.[29] A Senate committee has gone so far as to declare: "In essence individuals appointed as [ALJs] hold a position with tenure very similar to that provided for federal judges under the Constitution."[30]

This is not to say that ALJs are completely independent agents. They are agency employees who are bound to apply the published rules of the agency. And as pointed out above, the agency head may rather freely reverse the ALJ's initial decisions. They also remain subject to the general administrative direction of the employing agency. As the OPM Bulletin on ALJs points out, ALJs are subject to agency administrative directions in such non-adjudicatory matters as hours of duty, travel, parking space, office space, office procedures, staff assistance and organizational structure. Of course, administrative direction in such matters may not be used as a means of affecting, controlling, or sanctioning Administrative Law Judges' decisions in "formal" proceedings.[31]

Demographics

As of May 1, 1992, there were 1185 ALJs employed by 32 federal departments and agencies (see Table 1). Another dozen or so agencies borrow ALJs under the "loan" program administered by OPM. Approximately 73 percent of these ALJs are employed by the Social Security Administration and another 14 percent are employed by the U.S. Department of Labor and the National Labor Relations Board. The other 29 agencies employ the remaining 13 percent. Only about 200 of the 1185 ALJs are based in the Washington, D.C., area with the others located across the country.

Applicants for ALJ positions must meet a series of minimum qualifications requirements.[32] They must be attorneys with a minimum of 7 years of experience involving the preparation, presenting, hearing, and/or review of formal cases before either an administrative agency or a court. Minimally qualified applicants are then rated by OPM on a numerical scale. They are asked to submit a "supplemental qualifications statement" that describes their experience in rules of evidence and trial procedures, analytical ability, decision ability, oral communications ability and judicial temperament, and writing ability. Those scoring high enough on this statement are then given a written demonstration, a panel interview, and a reference check. The maximum composite score for any applicant based on this examination is 100, but federal law also requires that "veterans preference points" (5 for veterans, 10 for disabled veterans) be added to the score.

Applicants who score above 80 points are then placed on a roster of eligibles (highest scores at the top) and they are referred to employing agencies to fill vacant positions as they occur in various geographical areas of the applicants' choice. Veterans preference also obtains in the agency selection from the register: an agency may not select a nonveteran over a veteran with an equal or higher score.

OPM's Office of ALJs has been very diligent in refining its process for examining and qualifying ALJ applicants, although the office has not reopened its application process since 1987. The ALJ selection program was designed to be a true merit selection system, far more rigorous than the ad hoc selection process for most state and federal judges. However, recruitment of women and minorities has lagged considerably. More than 90 percent of all ALJs are white men. Of the 1,024 ALJs in 1989, 38 (3.71 percent) were women, 26 (2.54 percent) were black, and 25 (2.44 percent) were Hispanic.[33] Almost as troubling is the fact that many ALJs apparently see the position as one to retire from: the mean age of ALJs is approximately 58.[34].

It is a shame that the ALJ corps is not able to attract a wider pool of younger and more diverse judges. The Administrative Conference of the United States (ACUS) has recommended that the ALJ selection process be opened up significantly so that agencies could choose from a larger number of OPM-qualified applicants, without application of the veterans preference to these positions.[35]

ALJ's Role Under the APA

Under the Administrative Procedure Act, ALJs are (subject to the agency's published rules and to the powers granted to the agency by statute) authorized to:

Table 1 Total ALJs According to Grade and Agency (May 1, 1992)

Agency/department	AL-3 A	AL-3 B	AL-3 C	AL-3 D	AL-3 E	AL-3 F	AL-2	AL-1	Total
Agriculture				1	2	1	1		5
Commerce						1			1
Commodity Futures Trading Commission						3			3
Education				2	1				3
Environmental Protection Agency					4	2	1		7
Federal Communications Commission				1	4	3	1		9
Federal Energy Regulatory Commission	1			1	1	18		1	22
Federal Labor Relations Authority				1	2	5	1		9
Federal Maritime Commission						3			3
Federal Mine Safety & Health Review Commission			1	3	1	5	1		11
Federal Trade Commission						2			2
HHS/Departmental Appeals Board			1	2					3
HHS/Food and Drug Administration						1			1
HHS/Social Security Administration	92	190	70	415	80	8	11		866
Housing and Urban Development		1		3			1		5
Interior				8	2	2			12
International Trade Commission				1	1		1		3
Interstate Commerce Commission						2			2
Justice/Drug Enforcement Administration					1	1			2
Justice/Executive Office of Immigration Review					3	1			4
Labor			4	20	43	7	9	1	84
Merit Systems Protection Board						1			1
National Labor Relations Board					36	39	5	1	81
National Transportation Safety Board				2	1	3			6
Nuclear Regulatory Commission						1		1	
Occupational Safety and Health Review Commission				3	4	8	1	16	
Office of Thrift Supervision						2			2
Postal Service					1	1			2
Small Business Administration					1			1	
Securities and Exchange Commission						3	1		4
Transportation/Coast Guard				8		2			10
Transportation/Office of the Secretary					2	1	1		4
Total	93	191	76	471	190	126	35	3	1,185

Source: U.S. Office of Personnel Management, Office of Administrative Law Judges.

1. Administer oaths and affirmations
2. Issue subpoenas authorized by law
3. Rule on offers of proof and receive relevant evidence
4. Make depositions or have depositions taken when the ends of justice would be served
5. Regulate the course of the hearing
6. Hold conferences for the settlement or simplification of the case by the consent of the parties
7. Inform the parties as to the availability of one or more alternative means of dispute resolution, and encourage use of such methods
8. Require the attendance at any conference held pursuant to number 6 (above) of at least one representative of each party who can negotiate over the resolution of the dispute
9. Dispose of procedural requests or similar matters
10. Make or recommend decisions in accordance with 5 U.S.C. §577
11. Take other action authorized by agency rule consistent with the procedural provisions of the Administrative Procedure Act, 5 U.S.C. §551–559[36]

Several of these powers have led to questions.

Subpoenas. The authority of ALJs to issue subpoenas on behalf of the agency seems relatively clear. However, in practice there remains some reluctance on the part of a few agencies to allow the ALJ to issue them without some sort of agency head approval or signature. This problem led the Administrative Conference in 1974 to urge (so far unsuccessfully) that the APA be clarified to provide the presiding officers in all APA adjudications be authorized to sign and issue subpoenas.[37] More recently, the Conference focused on the need to encourage Social Security ALJs to use the subpoena power they possess. ACUS Recommendation 90-4 urged ALJs to issue subpoenas on their own motion "where necessary to ensure that medical evidence is complete, and to obtain other evidence not otherwise available."[38] It further recommended that subpoenas requested by claimants should be issued except where the ALJ finds good cause not to, and proposed that SSA develop "form subpoenas" for use by disability claimants along with instructions.

Rules of Evidence. The authority to "receive relevant evidence," when coupled with the APA provision in section 556(d), has led to questions about whether more guidance is needed to either make these evidentiary rulings easier or to give ALJs more encouragement to clamp down on irrelevant and case-lengthening submissions. Section 556(d) states:

> Any oral or documentary evidence may be received, but the agency as a matter of policy shall provide for the exclusion of irrelevant, immaterial, or unduly repetitious evidence. A sanction may not be imposed or rule or order issued except on consideration of the whole record or those parts thereof cited by a party and supported by and in accordance with the reliable, probative, and substantial evidence.

Bearing in mind that administrative adjudication does not involve juries, and that therefore many of the technical evidentiary rules concerning the admission of prejudicial evidence need not apply, the drafters of the APA sought to avoid the use of these technical rules of evidence. However, over the years, concerns grew that ALJs were too often lax in excluding the irrelevant, immaterial or unduly repetitious evidence, feeling that the only risk of reversal was in excluding admissible evidence. Thus the tendency became "letting the evidence in for whatever it's worth."[39] The Federal Rules of Evidence (FRE) were enacted in 1975, applicable to federal court adjudication (jury and nonjury alike).[40] In 1986, the Administrative Conference urged agencies to give greater authority and encouragement to ALJ exclusion of unreliable or repetitious evidence by reference to FRE rule 403, which allows for exclusion of evidence when its probative value is substantially outweighed by other factors, including its potential for undue consumption of time. The Conference, however, did not wish for Congress simply to require agencies to use the FRE in its totality.[41] More recently, however, as the FRE has become increasingly familiar to the bench and bar, there has been more movement toward adoption of at least a modified FRE by federal agencies. The Department of Labor has done so[42] and the American Bar Association and Federal Bar Association have nudged agencies to consider use of the FRE.[43] This may result in wider use of the FRE and, perhaps, better managed adjudications.

Controlling Hearings. The authority to "regulate the course of the hearing" has also led to questions about the ALJ's authority to take immediate action against disruptive actions by participants in the hearing.

Because most agencies have or claim statutory authority to regulate the conduct of attorneys through exclusion from particular proceedings or disbarment from future proceedings, the ALJ's power to exclude attorneys is derivative. ALJ exclusion of disruptive counsel has been sustained on occasion, but these decisions have treated the exclusions not as disciplinary measures but as flowing from the common-law right of an adjudicator to protect the integrity of the adjudicatory process.[44] ALJ actions in this regard must be grounded in agency statutory authority and in regulations implementing that authority. Moreover, such action would normally be reviewable by the agency head and subject to judicial review. Future debarment actions normally require separate formal hearings.[45]

Insulation

Some of the APA provisions designed to protect the ALJ's independence from agency coercion also have the effect of insulating the presiding ALJ from the agency policymakers. Some critics have asserted that, at least in nonaccusatory proceedings, this wall of separation has become too restrictive.[46]

In addition to the prohibition (discussed earlier) against having ALJs be responsible to or supervised by agency investigators or prosecutors, two other "separation of functions" provisions in the APA serve to insulate them. Section 554(d)(1) provides that an ALJ may not "consult a person or party on a fact in issue, unless on notice and opportunity for all parties to participate." As Professor Asimow has stated, this "'hearing officer nonconsultation rule' has always been shrouded in mystery."[47] If read literally, it would bar conversations between judge and law clerk on disputed facts. Although many have argued that it should only be applied to consultations with outsiders, the Supreme Court has not followed that view.[48]

This provision must be read with the even broader separation of functions provision in section 554(d).

> An employee or agent engaged in the performance of investigative or prosecuting functions for an agency in a case may not, in that or a factually related case, participate or advise in the decision, recommended decision, or agency review pursuant to section 557 of this title, except as witness or counsel in public proceedings.

This means that a certain class of employees, investigators, or prosecutors in the particular case being adjudicated or one that is factually related may not furnish off-the-record advice to any decisionmaker. Thus ALJs are clearly barred from being advised by internal staff investigators or prosecutors, even if the "nonconsultation" rule were to be applied only to outsiders.

From a management point of view, what issues are raised by these provisions? It is easy to see that ALJs should be insulated from adversary staff in accustory processings such as civil penalty proceedings or license revocation cases. What about nonaccusatory adjudication such as ratemaking, initial licensing, merger approvals, and similar economic regulatory cases? The APA specifically exempts these types of cases from the separation of functions requirements, yet according to Asimow, most agencies adhere to them anyway, thus preventing ALJs from seeking the assistance of uninvolved staff experts, supervisors or colleagues of involved staff adversaries, and other staff members who might help the judge come to a faster, better informed decision.[49]

As Asimow has commented,

> While these costs [of strict separation of the adjudicator from uninvolved experts] may be acceptable in accusatory adjudications, they must be minimized in economically significant, nonaccusatory disputes that by law or custom are settled by formal adversarial adjudications. In such disputes, the economic and environmental impact of the decision is frequently far-reaching and often unpredictable, and the costs of error are very high. Moreover, such matters are procedurally cumbersome and already take an unbearably long time to conclude. Agencies must engage in prophecy and resolve abstruse economic, technological, or scientific questions that are seldom quantifiable and that trigger intense professional controversy. The claims of diverse economic, social, and political interests conflict irreconcilably, and the agency must select from an almost limitless number of policy options and solutions. Consequently, the decisionmakers urgently need as much technical, legal and political advice as can be provided.[50]

A final separation of functions issue also has management implications. Once the ALJ has issued his or her initial or recommended decision and it is before the agency head for review, nothing in the APA would prevent the agency head from asking the ALJ for advice or clarification about the decision. Yet this is apparently rarely, if ever, done and an Administrative Conference recommendation proposing this practice in appropriate circumstances was tabled after ALJ opposition.[51]

Can ALJs be Managed?

The short answer to this question is yes and no. Although it is true that ALJs are by statute exempt from employee performance appraisals, they are not necessarily immune from performance *evaluations*. Courts have reasoned that because an ALJ may be removed for poor performance, it follows that an agency may gather data and form an opinion of an ALJ's performance.

Much of the law concerning the limits of ALJ independence derives from MSPB and court decisions construing the "for good cause" standard for ALJ discipline and removal actions found in 5 U.S.C. §7521. In his exhaustive study of the "good cause" provision for the Administrative Conference, Professor Victor Rosenblum examined the history and application of the provision.[52] He wrote in 1984, in the context of a surge of disciplinary actions against ALJs, including, for the first time, removal actions based on allegations of low productivity rather than acts of misconduct.[53] Most of these proceedings resulted from a long-lasting dispute between the Social Security Administration and its ALJs over elements of the agency's case management program.[54]

Taking its cue from a congressional directive expressing concern about the high rate at which ALJs were reversing initial disability claim determinations made at the state level and the variance in these rates among ALJs, the Social Security Administration (SSA) embarked on a series of measures to scrutinize individual ALJ decisional activity. Based on a review of

ALJ allowance rates, individual ALJs with the highest allowance rates were targeted for full review of all their decisions by the SSA Appeals Counsel. Individual "counseling" sessions for ALJs were also proposed by SSA, although never implemented. Furthermore SSA, in memoranda to its ALJs, focused heavily on allowance rate "goals."[55] The SSA ALJ Association sought injunctive relief against these practices in 1984, and although the court denied injunctive relief because the practices complained about had been changed, it severely criticized the agency's "unremitting focus on allowance rates in the individual ALJ portion of the [review program] [which] created an untenable atmosphere of tension and unfairness which violated the spirit of the APA, if no specific provision thereof."[56]

In another challenge to SSA procedures brought by an individual ALJ, the agency fared somewhat better. The Second Circuit affirmed the district court's dismissal of the ALJ's claim that his decisional independence had been infringed by the SSA's "peer review program," even though the court had found that some of the components of the program may have been "questionable."[57] The Second Circuit was equally supportive:[58]

> Regarding the Secretary's policy of settling a minimum number of dispositions an ALJ must decide in a month, we agree with the district court that reasonable efforts to increase the production levels of ALJs are not an infringement of decisional independence.
>
> The settling of reasonable production goals as opposed to fixed quotas is not in itself a violation of the APA.

The court went on to uphold the Secretary's setting of "monthly production goals."

In the administrative arena, SSA also sought to remove several ALJs on grounds of low productivity. Again, the results were mixed. In the lead case, *SSA v. Goodman,*[59] the agency charged that the judge's productivity was "unacceptably low" because his average monthly disposition rate was only half the agency-wide average of about 31 cases per month. It was also shown that the judge's annual average "pending" caseload was 64 compared with 178 for all SSA judges. The MSPB ALJ recommended dismissal of Goodman, but the full Board unanimously reversed. In what can only be described as a compromise verdict, the Board established the principle that "there is no generic prohibition to" filing charges based on low productivity. It also characterized Goodman's manner of handling his cases as "unreasonably methodical." Nevertheless the Board ruled that the agency's showing that Goodman's disposition rate was half the national average was not adequate proof of the charge. The Board cited the agency's acknowledgment that its cases "did vary in difficulty" and "are not fungible" and ruled that if the agency's case relied totally on comparative statistics, then more proof of their validity was needed. Several subsequent SSA actions against ALJs for low productivity also failed on these grounds, and several judges (including Goodman) were awarded attorneys fees for their trouble.[60]

In the end, although the MSPB established the principle that agencies could base removal actions on grounds of low productivity, the amount of statistical proof required (especially given the dearth of government statistics on agency adjudication) may make such cases nearly impossible to win. Still, the threat of such an action, and the possibility of having to mount an expensive defense to it, may itself serve as a spur to agency productivity efforts.

A better approach for everyone would be a consensus-based approach to setting productivity standards. As Professor Rosenblum has concluded:

> Failure quantitatively to meet a minimum or to stay within a maximum average disposition rate could, arguably, provide a rebuttable presumption of good cause, if the rates have been determined for each agency through consultations with and recommendations by representative experts from the bench, bar and academia concerned with that agency's admin-

> istrative adjudication, and if the agency has made reasonable effort to accommodate to particular judges' perceived and expressed needs for assistance.[61]

In its Recommendation 86-7, the Administrative Conference has also recognized the need for appropriately derived productivity norms:

> 1. *Personnel management devices.* Use of internal agency guidelines for timely case processing and measurements of the quality of work products can maintain high levels of productivity and responsibility. If appropriately fashioned, they can do so without compromising independence of judgment. Agencies possess and should exercise the authority, consistent with the ALJ's or other presiding officer's decisional independence, to formulate written criteria for measuring case handling efficiency, prescribe procedures, and develop techniques for the expeditious and accurate disposition of cases. The experiences and opinions of presiding officers should play a large part in shaping these criteria and procedures. The criteria should take into account differences in categories of cases assigned to judges and in types of disposition (e.g., dismissals, dispositions with and without hearing). Where feasible, regular, computerized case status reports and supervision by higher level personnel should be used in furthering the systematic application of the criteria once they have been formulated.[62]

Role of the Chief ALJ. OPM has authorized the creation of about 15 chief ALJ positions with higher grade levels than the other ALJs at the agency.[63] The establishment of such positions is based on certifications from the agency that their chiefs devote a significant portion of their time to administrative and management duties. There are, however, no government-wide norms as to what those duties should entail. The General Accounting Office urged that the chief judges at each agency play a lead role in establishing performance standards for the quality and quantity of the ALJs' work and that they also "review the procedures by which cases are formally adjudicated to determine if simplified procedures can be used."[64]

A congressional study focusing on delay in the regulatory process also urged agency chief judges to take more responsibility for reviewing the work of their judges, for both quality and quantity.[65] The Administrative Conference, building on this earlier work, has recommended that a new system be established for the evaluation and discipline of ALJs and for receiving complaints: both about ALJ performance and by ALJs about agency actions infringing upon their independence.[66] Under the Conference's proposal, the chief ALJs at each agency would be responsible for implementing this system.

ALJs and IGs. Another potential player in the debate over management of the adjudicative process is the agency inspector general (IG). IGs are in place in virtually all the agencies employing ALJs and are charged with, among other things, promoting economy, effectiveness, and efficiency in the administration of agency programs.[67] The IG's independence and authority to investigate certainly carries with it the potential to encroach upon the ALJ's decisional independence.

The tension has been tested in a related administrative judicial context in which judges of the U.S. Navy–Marine Corps Court of Military Review (a legislatively created tribunal for resolving military classification and discharge disputes) sought an injunction to prevent the Department of Defense IG from requiring its judges to appear before the IG to answer questions regarding improper influence allegedly exerted against judges in their review of a court-martial conviction. The U.S. Court of Military Appeals granted the petition and appointed a special master from one of its member judges to investigate the underlying allegations.[68]

The appeals court did not dispute the IG's authority to investigate certain improprieties such as "an allegation that an appellate military judge has submitted a false voucher or has made a false claim for reimbursement of travel expenses incurred in performing his duties as a judge."[69] On the other hand, the court concluded that "investigation of a court's deliberative processes . . . is limited by a judicial privilege protecting the confidentiality of judicial communications."[70]

One such dispute has so far surfaced in the ALJ arena. At the Nuclear Regulatory Commission (NRC), pursuant to a congressional request, the agency IG conducted an inquiry into the mechanics of the issuance of an initial decision authorizing a full power license for the Seabrook power plant.[71] The congressional request was based on the suggestion that some time between the rendering of the initial decision by the Atomic Safety and Licensing Board, the NRC's adjudicatory tribunal, and the release of the decision to the parties and the public four days later, it was "corruptly" changed. The Office of the IG conducted an investigation of the panel staff, although the Office conspicuously refrained from interviewing the board members themselves. In this case the NRC IG was properly sensitive to the concern that the judges' decisional independence not be infringed.

ALJ Corps Proposals

Whether or not there is a problem of insufficient actual or perceived independence of federal ALJs or inefficiencies due to the decentralized nature of the administrative judiciary, one solution that has persistently been proposed has been the "ALJ corps bill."[72] This legislation would separate the ALJs from the employing agencies and put them in the employ of a new agency known as the Administrative Law Judge Corps. The corps would be headed by a chief ALJ and organized into eight subject-matter divisions, each headed by a division chief ALJ. The chief and division chiefs (all appointed by the president with the advice and consent of the Senate) would form a Council to administer the corps. It would assign judges to divisions, appoint new ALJs (from an OPM register), prescribe rules of practice and procedure for cases heard by the corps, and manage the corps' operations. The bill also includes new provisions for the discipline and removal of ALJs. The bill acknowledges the potential for change in the dynamics of agency review of ALJ decisions by mandating a study of this subject.

This concept (which has been enacted in over a dozen states[73]) has consistently received the support of the major ALJ organizations as well as the American Bar Association, but it has been opposed by the executive branch (as well as by some ALJs)[74] and has fallen short of passage. (In the 101st Congress, the proposal was reported favorably on a vote of 9–5 by the Senate Judiciary Committee.[75] It never reached the floor. In the 102d Congress both the House and Senate bills were reported to the floor, but no floor votes were held.)

Support for the concept is based on two separate arguments: efficiency and fairness (or at least perceptions of fairness). Opposition to the idea is based on a generalized feeling both that the current system is not "broke" and that changes to it would lessen expertise in the administrative judiciary and create a new "bureaucracy" of judges independent of agency policy input. Indeed, despite the passage of a decade, the basic arguments pro and con remain little different from the ones I summarized in a 1981 article for *Judicature*:[76]

> Proponents of the corps concept point to the following benefits:
>
> - Operational efficiency would be enhanced by a corps made up of interchangeable judges, who could be assigned to agency cases as the need arises. Since agency caseloads are not always predictable or within the agency's control, the number of ALJs employed under the present system by agencies may be too high or too low.
> - Centralized housekeeping and accounting would save money. Present redundancies in law libraries, docket clerks, case-tracking systems, administrative assistants, travel arrangements and the reservation of hearing facilities would be eliminated. And unification

would promote uniformity in the quality of office space, law clerks and secretarial assistance.

- Public confidence in the impartiality and independence of ALJs would be enhanced by a divorce from agency administration. Since many ALJs were also formerly lawyers for their agency, since some perquisites of the job (e.g., office space, parking privileges and travel to seminars) remain in agency control, and since long-term association with one agency's policies and personnel may subtly influence behavior, ALJs may be susceptible to a pro-agency bias that would be lessened if they were centralized in a separate corps.
- If the judges were not attached to agencies, they would require agencies to articulate their regulations in clearer language, much as federal judges often do.
- Individual ALJs would acquire a diversified experience and not become stale from repeatedly hearing similar cases. This, apparently, has been a salutary by-product of the existing, but limited loan program in which OPM allows understaffed agencies to temporarily borrow the services of willing ALJs from other agencies. This diversity of caseload might also stimulate the recruitment of new ALJs.
- Operation of a corps might facilitate performance evaluation of ALJs, both quantitatively and qualitatively. This is obviously a controversial issue since evaluation of judicial performance bears such a close relationship to independent values. But since the agencies would have a less direct interest in the evaluation of any particular judge, it could probably be done more objectively.
- Operation of a corps might permit a return to a multi-level grade system whereby more routine cases could be handled by lower-level, less experienced ALJs. Professor [now Justice] Antonin Scalia has argued that a multi-level system would be more efficient and would also inject needed performance incentives into the corps.

Opponents think the problems and drawbacks would outweigh any of the advantages, however:

- A unified corps would reduce efficiency, since it would dilute the expertise that staff ALJs bring to their agency. Agency statutes, regulations and precedent can be difficult to master in a short time, and practitioners would be forced to educate—and reeducate—ALJs unfamiliar with the particular field of regulation.
- A new bureaucracy would have to be created to train and rotate over 1,100 judges to 30 agencies for over 200,000 hearings all over the country. If evaluation or promotional responsibilities were also given to the new office, the director's independence and "clout" would become a critical concern. The wrong mix could lead to greater politicalization than critics find in the current program.
- An equitable system for allocating ALJs to agencies for hearings would have to be devised. Since judges are not "free goods," perhaps some sort of "user's fee" would have to be charged agencies. Otherwise, agencies might draw too liberally upon ALJs for non-judicial functions or reduce their own efforts to settle cases prior to the hearing stage.
- The agency's reviewing function might be altered in unforeseen ways. Some proponents argue that establishment of a corps should be linked to a restriction of the agency's ability to review initial decisions of ALJs. The wisdom in this is debatable, but without such a change agencies likely would feel the need to review more initial decisions more intensively (in light of their reduced rapport or familiarity with the judges), leading to an overall lengthening of the decisional process.

All of these arguments still apply today, although the dominance of three agencies (SSA, NLRB, and the Labor Department) in the ALJ cadre tends to make the case for the corps somewhat more difficult to make. The efficiency argument retains force with respect to the other 29 agencies with a few ALJs, and I continue to believe that an experiment with a pooling of judges among some of those agencies would be a good idea.[77] Another change that may take some of the steam out of the corps proposal is the recent pay raise for all ALJs, with a proportionally larger raise going to lower-graded Social Security ALJs who have been among the strongest proponents of the corps legislation.[78]

MANAGEMENT INITIATIVES

Other than managing the ALJs themselves, what types of initiatives can agencies pursue to introduce more efficiency and expedition into their adjudication process? The Administrative Conference studied one of the more efficient adjudicative operations in the federal government, the Department of Health and Human Services (HHS) Departmental Appeals Board,[79] which adjudicates disputes arising out of the department's many grant programs. The Conference distilled a series of recommendations for case management.[80]

Several general recommendations were made, covering the proceeding as a whole:

> 2. *Step-by-step time goals.* Case management by presiding officers and their supervisors should be combined with procedures designed to move cases promptly through each step in the proceeding. These include (a) a program of step-by-step time goals for the main stages of a proceeding, (b) a monitoring system that pinpoints problem cases, and (c) a management committed to expeditious processing. Time guidelines should be fixed in all cases for all decisional levels within the agency, largely with the input of presiding officers and others affected. While the guidelines should be flexible enough to accommodate exceptional cases and should maintain their non-obligatory nature, they should be sufficiently fixed to keep routine items moving and ensure that any delays are justified. Agencies should encourage a management commitment by including specific goals or duties of timely case processing in pertinent job descriptions.
>
> 3. *Expedited options.* Agencies should develop, and in some instances require parties to use, special expedited procedures. Different rules may need to be developed for handling small cases as well as for larger ones that do not raise complex legal or factual issues.
>
> 4. *Case file system.*
>
> (a) Agencies should develop procedures to ensure early compilation of relevant documents in a case file. This will help the presiding officer delineate the legal and factual issues, the parties' positions and the basis for the action as promptly as possible. The presiding officer may then structure the process suitably and issue preliminary management directives.
>
> (b) Disputes preceded by party interactions or investigations which create a substantial factual record, as in most contract and grant disputes, are especially amenable to this approach. Cases involving strong fact conflicts or in which data are peculiarly within the possession of one party who has motivations to suppress them may be less suitable for a case file system.
>
> 5. *Two stage resolution approaches.* In proceedings where the case file system is less appropriate, as where factual conflicts render discovery important, agencies should consider using a two-phase procedure.
>
> (a) Phase one might be an abbreviated discovery phase directed by a responsible official, with the product of that discovery forming the "appeal file" for the next phase. Alternatively, parties could be channeled into a private dispute resolution mode, such as mediation, negotiation or arbitration, which, even if unsuccessful, can serve to define major issues and to advance development of the record. Before employing this alternative, agencies would have to determine whether the confidentiality rule that normally attaches to arbitration, mediation and negotiation is so critical that it cannot be abandoned for the sake of a more efficient second stage.
>
> (b) A second stage, if necessary, should proceed under active case management, as recommended.

The step-by-step time guideline suggestion in paragraph 2 was bolstered by a detailed examination of the experience of three other agencies (Civil Aeronautics Board, NLRB, and Federal Trade Commission [FTC]), which also developed successful case processing systems incorporating such guidelines.[81]

The "private dispute resolution mode" suggestion in Paragraph 5 was the Administrative Conference's first tentative reference to what would become a major theme in ensuing years: alternative dispute resolution. Even more important was that Recommendation 86-7 was specifically incorporated into the President Bush's civil justice reform executive order.[82]

Prehearing Stage

The recommendation concerning compilation of a case file has special significance for the prehearing stage. A consistent theme of Administrative Conference recommendations over the years is that agency presiding officers should make better use of prehearing conferences. As early as 1970, ACUS asserted that presiding officers should normally hold at least one prehearing conference in complex or potentially lengthy cases and that evidentiary witness lists be exchanged by the parties at that time.[83] Twenty years later, ACUS reiterated the usefulness of such conferences, this time in the context of cases at the other end of the complexity spectrum: Social Security cases. ACUS urged SSA to encourage its ALJs to use prehearing conferences "to frame the issues involved in ALJ hearings, identify matters not in dispute, and decide appropriate cases favorably without hearings.''[84] Telephone prehearing conferences were also contemplated, but a caution was given that when claimants were not represented by counsel (a dwindling number of SSA cases), prehearing conferences were rarely appropriate.[85]

The importance of the prehearing conferences was also recognized in the recently enacted Administrative Dispute Resolution Act, which amended the APA's list of presiding officer's powers by adding the explicit power of requiring the attendance at prehearing conferences of at least one representative of each party who has authority to negotiate over settlement of the case.[86]

This legislation will go a long way in helping to implement another key element of recommendation 86-7, much of which derived from the successful mediation activity performed by the Departmental Appeals Board in HHS:[87]

> 6. *Seeking party concessions and offering mediation.* Presiding officers should promote party agreement and concessions on procedural and substantive issues, as well as on matters involving facts and documents, to reduce hearing time and sometimes avoid hearings altogether. Agencies should also (a) encourage decisional officers to resolve cases (or parts thereof) informally, (b) provide their officers training in mediation and other ADR methods, and (c) routinely offer parties the services of trained mediators.

The prehearing phase is also often the best time to consider using the settlement judge technique for resolving cases.[126]

Hearing Stage

Recommendation 86-7 also prescribes several other nuts-and-bolts techniques for presiding officers to use in managing the hearings:

> 7. *Questioning techniques.*
>
> (a) Requests for clarification or development of record. If a party makes a statement in a notice of appeal, brief, or other submission which a presiding officer does not understand, doubts, or wishes clarified, the officer should consider requiring the party to expand upon its position. The ambiguity may relate to a factual matter, or an interpretation of a

legal precedent or a document. Similarly, by preliminary study of the case file, the presiding officer could identify missing information and require the party with access to such information to remedy the deficiency. The officer could also issue "invitations to brief" difficult questions of statutory interpretation or the like.

(b) Written questions for conference or hearing. The presiding officer should manage cases so as to limit issues, proof, and argument to core matters. Having ascertained the factual and legal ambiguities in each side's case by careful study of the briefs and documentation submitted, the presiding officer should structure a prehearing conference or hearing as a forum for addressing these ambiguities by seeking responses to carefully formulated questions and providing appropriate opportunity for rebuttal. In this way, and by otherwise seeking to identify the specific questions in dispute early on, the presiding officer would focus parties attention on key issues and deflect unproductive procedural maneuvers.

8. *Time extension practices.* Time extensions should be granted only upon strong, documented justification. While procedural fairness mandates that deadlines may be extended for good cause, presiding officers should be aware that casual, customary extensions have serious negative effects on an adjudicatory system, its participants, and those wishing access thereto. Stern warnings accompanying justified extensions have had good success in curtailing lawyers' requests for additional time.

9. *Joint consideration of cases with common issues.* Whenever practicable and fair, cases involving common questions of law or fact should be consolidated and heard jointly. Consolidation could include unification of schedules, briefs, case files and hearings.

10. *Use of telephone conferences and hearings.* Presiding officers should take full advantage of telephone conferences as a means to hear motions, to hold prehearing conferences, and even to hear the merits of administrative proceedings where appropriate. While telephone conferences may be either employed regularly for handling selected matters or limited to a case-by-case basis at the suggestion of the presiding officer or counsel, experience suggests that maximum benefits are derived when telephone conferences are made presumptive for certain matters.

All of these suggestions are more or less applicable to most types of agency adjudications, although one must always remember the difference in presiding officers' responsibilities in different types of cases. For example, while an SSA ALJ may not have to worry about settlement negotiations, multiparty proceedings, or extensive procedural maneuvering, he or she must be especially diligent in making sure the claimant's evidence is complete. This "apples and oranges" problem is the reason that there may never be a truly uniform "code" of administrative adjudicative procedures. Nevertheless, on a "macro" scale, there are some initiatives promoting greater uniformity that are worth mentioning.

The Administrative Conference's *Manual for Administrative Law Judges* is one longstanding effort to bring more uniformity to agency adjudications.[88] The aforementioned study of the applicability of a modified set of the Federal Rules of Evidence to agency adjudications is another. Perhaps the most ambitious is a continuing Administrative Conference effort to draft a set of "model" rules of practice and procedure for agency ALJ proceedings. The Conference's effort is based on successful agency efforts to develop consolidated rules of practice for all of the adjudications heard by ALJs in that agency. For example the Department of Labor's (DOL) consolidated rules of practice cover more than 60 different types of hearings ranging from benefit cases (black lung compensation) to civil money penalty and other enforcement cases.[89] The Department of Agriculture has a similar set of unified agency rules of practice.[90] Most recently Congress required the five federal banking regulatory agencies to develop a uniform set of rules of procedure for their adjudications.[91] The Conference's working group hopes to develop model rules (with commentary) that can be used as a reference point for other such efforts.

Posthearing Stage

Delays in the agency review stage have bedeviled administrative adjudicators for a long time. A major problem that was addressed by the Administrative Conference in one of its earlier recommendations was the commonplace statutory or regulatory requirement that the agency head review all of the decisions issued by the agency's ALJs. This problem was exacerbated in some multimember boards or commissions where the entire body did the reviewing. The Conference first urged agency heads to use intermediate appellate boards to screen the appeals.[92] Needless to say, this is a time-saver only if the intermediate board screens enough cases. The model has been used sparingly, most notably at the NRC and Federal Communications Commission (FCC) with mixed success.[93] Second (and more significantly), the Conference urged that agency reviewing officials use (and be authorized to use) a system of discretionary review of initial decisions.[94] In other words, the agency should announce that it will deny petitions for review or summarily affirm initial decisions unless petitioners make a reasonable showing of an erroneous material finding of fact or legal conclusion or that the decision has a policy importance that warrants review. With some important exceptions,[95] most agencies now utilize the discretionary review model.

Use of these screening techniques should bring down the average posthearing elapsed time for all cases, but delay problems persist in those cases accepted for review by agencies. For example an internal Securities and Exchange Commission (SEC) study of adjudications in the 8-3/4 years since January, 1982, found that the average elapsed time for the ALJ phase of the case was 13 months, while the Commission took 17 additional months to render its decision.[96] Rough statistics developed by the Administrative Conference, collated by the Senate Governmental Affairs Committee in 1977, showed that the agency review phase exceeded the hearing phase in both licensing and ratemaking cases and was a significant period in enforcement cases as well.[97]

Reduction in these delays requires a combination of internal management initiatives and outside oversight. If pressures are brought to bear on agency administrators and chairs, steps can be taken to raise the priority of completing action on appealed cases. Time limits can be promulgated and honored (at least by enforced explanation as to why the time limit has been missed). More frequent board and commission meetings can be devoted to decisional activity. More resources can be devoted to opinion-writing staffs. Of course, a willingness to decide politically difficult cases without undue procrastination is also necessary.

Little is likely to happen without outside monitoring of each agency's record in this area. Congressional oversight in this area does take place occasionally when problems with delay emerge from the mist. The problem is that there is too much mist, and it can only be dispelled by a concerted effort to collect and evaluate agency statistics on administrative adjudication.

Need for Statistics on Administrative Proceedings

There is no dearth of data concerning activity of the federal courts. Extensive statistics have been systematically collected and disseminated since 1940 in the annual reports of the Director of the Administrative Office of the U.S. Courts. Moreover, in 1968 the Federal Judicial Center was created to serve as the research arm of the courts, and it has relied heavily on the statistics gathered by the Administrative Office.

In the administrative arena, a small unit in the Department of Justice compiled statistics on formal proceedings conducted by hearing examiners from 1957 to 1959. This effort was continued by the Temporary Administrative Conference in 1961 to 1962 and by a Senate Judiciary Subcommittee in 1963 to 1965. These disjointed efforts led to a mass of unusable data.

In 1973, ACUS began another effort to compile statistics on agency cases (called the Uniform Caseload Accounting System), which led to two volumes of data arranged by agency and case type for the years 1975 to 1978.[98] In 1977, the Senate Governmental Affairs Committee made extensive use of these statistics and concluded that the ACUS "effort is a step in the right direction, but needs refinement, enforcement capability, permanence, and adequate funding."[99] The Committee went on to recommend formally that:

> • An appropriate committee of the House and Senate should oversee management efforts comprehensively, including the setting and meeting of deadlines, at Federal regulatory agencies. Each agency should be required to submit periodically to Congress a report describing deadlines imposed on agency proceedings, the agency's degree of success in adhering to the deadlines, and the reasons for any delays.
>
> • The Administrative Conference should have the permanent tasks of insuring that statistics are generated by the various agencies, and that the statistics are brought together and comprehensively explored. The information compiled should include the deadlines established for proceedings, the rates of success at meeting these deadlines, and the reasons for failure to meet them.[100]

Despite these words of encouragement, the Administrative Conference had to discontinue its limited statistical efforts in 1979 for budgetary and staffing reasons and has not been able to garner the resources for this important effort in the ensuing decade. (In comparison, the Conference's total budget grew from $250,000 in 1969 to almost $2 million in 1990, while the Federal Judicial Center's budget went from $300,000 to over $13 million in the same period.[101])

This lack of statistics on agency adjudication (and on agency rulemaking for that matter) makes it exceedingly difficult to assess agency procedural efficiency, personnel needs, or the need for proposed reforms such as alternative dispute resolution or the ALJ corps bills. Recently, for example, during consideration of the Fair Housing Act Amendments of 1989, a dispute arose over the relative efficiency of ALJ hearings versus federal district court enforcement. Both the Justice Department and civil rights groups asked Administrative Conference for its 10-year old data that remain the best available compendium.[102] There is an unquestionable need for these data; with the widespread availability of desktop computers and appropriate software, the benefits of such an effort should exceed the costs by an even larger ratio.

CHOICE OF FORUM FOR ADJUDICATION

Observers of the federal adjudication process may be surprised to read Article III of the Constitution, which provides that the "Judicial Power of the United States" shall be vested in courts whose judges enjoy tenure during good behavior and protection against reduction in salary.[103] Obviously, many "federal cases" are decided by adjudicators who are not the sort of "Article III" judges serving under that provision of the Constitution.

As Richard Fallon has admirably detailed,[104] the "article III literalism" position was doomed from the start. The first Congress assigned to Treasury Department officials disputes over veterans' benefits and customs duties. In 1828 the Supreme Court, through Chief Justice Marshall, held that Congress may create non-Article-III courts to adjudicate disputes in the federal territories.[105] These so-called legislative (or "Article I") courts (because they were created by the legislative branch) survive today in the territories, the District of Columbia, the military, or in highly specialized situations, such as the adjucation of claims against the United States.

The constitutionality of administrative agency adjudication was established a century later, when the Supreme Court upheld Congress's decision to vest responsibility for deciding cases under the Longshoremen and Harbor Workers' Compensation Act to an administrative agency (on the ground that "public rights" were at issue), so long as adequate review in an Article III court of the agency's decision exists.[106] Thus the foundation for the New Deal and the Administrative Procedure Act (APA) was laid.

The upshot of the Supreme Court's movement away from Article III literalism is that there is now a continuum of federal adjudicative forums. The continuum is arranged below according to the status of the adjudicator, which largely corresponds to the independence of the adjudicator and the formality of the adjudication.[107]

Article III Judges

The three-tiered federal judiciary currently includes 9 Supreme Court justices, 168 court of appeals judges organized into 13 circuits (one of which, the Court of Appeals for the Federal Circuit, has a somewhat specialized subject-matter jurisdiction), and 565 district court judges organized into 94 districts.[108] The specialized Court of International Trade (7 judges, 4 senior judges) is also an Article III tribunal.[109]

Article I Judges

The duties of judges on the various legislative courts have come to resemble closely those of the Article III judges. Judges on the U.S. Court of Federal Claims (16 judges, 2 senior judges), Tax Court (19 judges, 10 senior judges, 14 special trial judges), Court of Military Appeals (5 judges, 1 senior judge), and the new Court of Veterans Appeals (7 judges), have 15 year terms and can be removed only for cause. Although the possibility of reappointment may create some effect on independence, the terms are long and few judges have been denied reappointment. In other respects, the judges on these courts function as Article III judges.

Administrative Law Judges

As described above, there are approximately 1200 ALJs. It is easy for Congress to mandate the use of an ALJ to preside over agency hearings. Any statute that offers the opportunity for an "APA hearing" (or some variant thereof) or a "hearing on the record" (but not simply a "hearing") is deemed to require an ALJ (or agency head) hearing. There are probably more than 500 such statutes in the U.S. Code that so require, many of which contain more than one provision requiring APA hearings.[110]

Much ink has been spilled on the extent of ALJ independence. Suffice it to say that although one oftens hears about the perceptions among the bar that ALJs are not sufficiently independent (or are too imbued with the agency's mission) and one often hears grumbling from agency officials that ALJs are too independent, the reality is that they have decisional independence, they act like judges (many wear robes and are referred to as "your honor"), and agency officials are wary of any extrajudicial efforts to influence their decisions. Nevertheless, there have been increasing efforts to separate the adjudicative arm of the program from the policymaking arm, even more so than is now dictated by the separation of functions provisions in the APA.[111]

An early example of this was the 1947 Taft–Hartley Act's creation of an independent general counsel within the structure of the National Labor Relations Board.[112] The general counsel "prosecutes" the cases before the Board (and its ALJs). An even greater separation has been achieved by the so-called "split-enforcement" model in which the rulemaking and prosecuting agency seeks to enforce its rules before a separate, purely adjudicative commission with its own ALJs. Examples of this include the Department of Labor's Occupational Safety and Health Administration (OSHA) and Mine Safety and Health Administration (MSHA), which must seek enforcement by the independent Occupational Safety and Health Review Commission (OSHRC) and Federal Mine Safety and Health Review Commission (FMSHRC), respectively.[113] Another example is in the enforcement of federal aviation safety laws, where the independent National Transportation Safety Board (NTSB) adjudicates license revocation (and some civil money penalty cases) brought by the Department of Transportation's Federal Aviation Administration.[114] These OSHA–OSHRC and MSHA–FMSHRC models have not been free of controversy and, despite careful review of this approach, the Administrative Conference was unable to decide whether or when such a model was preferable to the traditional single-agency model.[115]

"Non-ALJ" Presiding Officers

The APA itself recognizes that many adjudications need not be heard by ALJs. Some types of adjudicatory programs are explicitly excepted from all of the APA's adjudication requirements. These include cases involving the selection or tenure of federal employees other than ALJs (now heard by Merit Systems Protection Board hearing officers), certification of worker representatives (now heard by NLRB regional office personnel), or the conduct of military or foreign affairs functions (there are many military and foreign service boards and panels).

The APA also allows for the possibility that another statute might designate other categories of boards or employees to preside over specific types of APA hearings. Thus the NRC's statute specifies that the Atomic Safety and Licensing Board Panel (made up of technical experts as well as lawyers) hears and decides nuclear power licensing cases using APA hearing procedures.

Perhaps the most non-ALJ adjudicators are used by agencies to preside over hearings that are not required by statute to be "on the record" or "under the APA." In those situations, the agency is free, within the bounds of due process, to fashion its procedures as it sees fit and to use any employee as presider. Some of these cases are presided over by statutorily designated officers who are equivalent to ALJs, such as immigration judges in the Department of Justice or the "administrative judges" on the various agency boards of contract appeals.[116] Other program areas use presiders appointed on an ad hoc basis. At this point the line between "formal" and "informal" adjudication begins to break down.

A recent Administrative Conference survey of federal agencies seeking information on programs that offer the opportunity for oral hearings presided over by non-ALJs turned up 2739 presiding officers.[117] Of these, 435 have no other duties and 1832 have other duties. Even if one subtracts the 1692 presiding officers involved with veterans benefits claims cases at the Department of Veterans Affairs, there are nearly as many non-ALJ presiders as ALJs.[118]

There is little uniformity among these presiders.[119] Other than members of boards of contract appeals (BCA) (who are paid more than ALJs), most non-ALJs are classified somewhere between GS-9 and GS-15 on the pay scale.[120] In most cases, they are simply hired like other federal employees (lawyers or nonlawyers), are subject to performance appraisals, and have no special protections against adverse personnel actions. Perhaps most important is that there is no real coordinated oversight of the needs or activities of this diverse group of hearing officers; unlike ALJs they have not even organized themselves. No one is assessing the independence of these adjudicators, the fairness or efficiency of their proceedings, or their appropriate place in the federal adjudicative system. They are now the real "invisible" judiciary.

Informal Adjudication

Even less visible are the less formal adjudications that occur throughout government with varying levels of formality. Many such decisions are reached with only a minimum of procedure, and without oral hearings. Such decisions include determinations to issue loans or grants, release information, conduct audits, approve plans, charge fees, and so on. It is impossible to catalog comprehensively these informal adjudications, and the APA provides little guidance to agencies that make these sorts of decisions. Paul Verkuil provided the sharpest focus on a slice of this pie when he examined 42 such programs in 4 departments.[121] He found a wide variety of procedural ingredients in these programs, although most made an effort to use an impartial decisionmaker.[122]

Because of the variety of informal processes, the drafters of the APA declined to set out procedures to govern them. A long-standing goal of some administrative reformers has been to amend the APA to add a section on informal adjudication procedures.[123] This has not occurred, despite increasing uncertainty as to what due process requires in varying situations and despite some constructive examples of such provisions in state APAs.[124]

Conclusion

It is hard to believe that Congress has created such a fragmented federal adjudicative system by design. Did members of Congress really stop and think when they placed the trials of numerous types of governmental disputes (e.g., federal tort claims, Freedom of Information Act appeals, Fair Labor Standards Act enforcement cases) in federal district court, others (e.g., Social Security benefit claims, unfair labor practice charges, or SEC civil penalty cases) before agency ALJs, and others (immigration cases, veterans benefits cases) before non-ALJ hearing officers?

What factors should be considered by Congress in allocating adjudicative responsibilities among Article III courts, Article I courts, ALJs, and non-ALJs? This is a macromanagement question of the first order. Public administrators, administrative lawyers, and political scientists must focus on this question in the coming decade, or many of the fine tuning and micromanagement initiatives discussed in this chapter will quickly become irrelevant.

A REFORM AGENDA

As suggested above, federal agency adjudication needs to be reexamined on both a macro and a micro level.

On the macro level, the current landscape needs to be remapped and reordered. Congress needs guidance as to how to allocate dispute resolution among Article III courts, Article I courts, and administrative agencies. Within the administrative agencies, Congress and agency heads need to be advised on when to choose to require administrative law judges or non-ALJ hearing officers, formal adjudication or informal adjudication, split-enforcement adjudication, or traditional single-agency adjudication. The Administrative Procedure Act's adjudication provisions—so painstakingly designed to reflect differences between types of cases—may need fortifying, clarifying, or revamping. The role of the administrative law judge in this system needs to be examined with special attention to the judicialization of the position (for better or worse) and to the fact that many important adjudicative programs are being channeled away from ALJs.[125] These fundamental issues should be at the top of the list of administrative law reformers. The Administrative Conference has begun a study of many of these issues.

More incremental issues also deserve attention. From a management point of view, reducing delay in administrative adjudication continues to be important. First and foremost, an adequate statistical collection and data analysis capability for agency cases need to be established. Once the bottlenecks are identified and the causes understood, more definitive suggestions can be made.

In the meantime, however, it is possible to suggest some areas of concern and identify some tentative recommendations:

Time limits and case tracking should be institutionalized at agencies.
Model or uniform rules of practice and procedure (including rules of evidence) should be explored.
ALJs should be given additional means for controlling hearings (including more power to reject duplicative evidence, and sanction frivolous or disruptive behavior).
Better mechanisms need to be developed for handling complaints against allegedly biased or abusive ALJs.
Recruitment of ALJs should be enhanced by eliminating veterans preference for that position.
Productivity guidelines should be arrived at consensually with each agency's ALJs.
Agencies with a few ALJs should experience with a pool (or "minicorps") of ALJs.
ALJs should have more opportunities for training and continuing legal education.
Telephone and video hearings should be explored.
Separation-of-functions rules should be loosened in nonaccusatory proceedings.
Agency discovery rules should be reexamined.
Agency heads should delegate more final decisional authority to ALJs.
Chief ALJs ought to be given more administrative power and responsibility.
The administrative process should be made more accessible to those who cannot—or choose not to—hire lawyers.

This is one observer's laundry list of future concerns for public administrators and lawyers concerned about federal agency adjudication. In closing, it should be noted that all of these micro issues (and even the macro ones) need to be considered in the context of our societal disillusionment with the litigation model and the concomitant movement toward alternative forms of dispute resolution. What is the role of adversarial hearings? When are they to be preferred and when are they necessary only as a last resort? When do we need a judge and when do we need a neutral dispute resolution specialist? Such questions point to a future agenda for public administrators and administrative lawyers: the role of alternative dispute resolution.

REFERENCES

1. Exec. Order No. 11,821, amended by Exec. Order No. 11,949 (President Ford); Exec. Order No. 12,044 (President Carter), Exec. Order Nos. 12,291, 12,498 (President Reagan).
2. Administrative Law Treatise (1970 Supplement) (§6.15); reaffirmed in 1 Administrative Law Treatise (2nd ed. 1978) (§6.1).
3. See Musolf, *Federal Examiners and the Conflict of Law and Administration* 35-46, Johns Hopkins Press (1953); reprinted by Greenwood Press, Westport, CT (1979).
4. See Scalia, Back to basics: making law without making rules, *Regulation,* July/Aug. 1981 at 25, 26.
5. See Lubbers, A unified corps of ALJs: A proposal to test the idea at the federal level, 65 *Judicature,* 266, 268 (Table 1) November 1981. In May of 1992, the total stood at 1185. See Table 1.
6. Idem at 269–270.
7. See Verkuil, The emerging concept of administrative procedure, 78 *Colum. L. Rev.* 258, 311–313 (1978) (noting criticism of the APA as overjudicialized).

8. *Federal Administrative Law Judge Hearings—Statistical Report for 1976–1978,* Administrative Conference of the U.S. (1980) (Introductory essays in that publication describe the data-gathering methods in detail.)
9. This has been the practice, for example, at the National Transportation Safety Board.
10. 5 U.S.C. §556(c)(5).
11. 5 U.S.C. §556(d).
12. Idem.
13. This point is well made in Verkuil, *supra* note 7, at 313–315.
14. See ACUS Recommendation 83-3, Agency structures for review of decisions of presiding officers under the Administrative Procedure Act, 1 CFR §305.83-3 (1992); Cass, Allocation of authority within bureaucracies: Empirical evidence and normative analysis, 66 *B.U.L. Rev.* 1 (1986).
15. 5 U.S.C. §557(b).
16. Idem.
17. 5 U.S.C. §706(2)(E). See *Universal Camera Corp. v. National Labor Relations Board,* 340 U.S. 474 (explaining the meaning of the substantial evidence test).
18. See Schuck and Elliot, To the Chevron station: An empirical study of federal administrative law, 1990 *Duke L.J.* 984 (study of judicial remands of agency cases).
19. See Estreicher and Revesz, Nonacquiescence by federal administrative agencies, 98 *Yale L.J.* 679 (1989).
20. 5 U.S.C. §§553(c), 554(a). On-the-record rulemaking (sometimes called formal rulemaking) is cumbersome and rarely required by statute.
21. 5 U.S.C. §556(b). The APA does, however, permit other employee boards to preside over "specified classes of proceedings" when so provided by statute. Idem.
22. 5 U.S.C. §§1104(a)(2).
23. 5 U.S.C. §5372 (1988), repealed by Pub. L. No. 101-509, Title I, §104(a)(1), Nov. 5, 1990, 104 Stat. 1445. See note 78, infra.
24. 5 U.S.C. §3105.
25. Idem.
26. 5 U.S.C. §554(d)(2).
27. 5 U.S.C. §§4301(2)(D), 5335(a)(5).
28. 5 U.S.C. §7521.
29. *Butz v. Economou,* 438 U.S. 478, 513 (1978).
30. Administrative law judges—Civil service, Senate Report 95–697, Legislative History of P.L. 95-251, 95th Cong., 1st Sess. 2 (1978), reprinted in 1978 *U.S. Code Cong. & Ad. News* 496, 497
31. *Administrative Law Judge Program Handbook,* U.S. Office of Personnel Management (Office of Administrative Law Judges) at 2 (May 1989). This is an excellent compendium of information on the ALJ program.
32. Idem at 5–6. The ALJ selection process is described in detail in P. Verkuil, D. Gifford, C. Koch, R. Pierce, & J. Lubbers, *The Federal Administrative Judiciary,* Report to the Administrative Conference of the U.S. (August 1992) chapter V.
33. See Office of Personnel Management, Announcement of revisions in administrative law judge examination, 55 *Fed. Reg.* 52340, 52341 (December 21, 1990) (citing those figures).
34. See *ALJ Program Handbook,* supra note 31, at 4.
35. ACUS Recommendation 92-7, The federal administrative judiciary, 1 C.F.R. §305.92-7 (1993).
36. 5 U.S.C. §556(c). Clauses 7 and 8 were added by the Administrative Dispute Resolution Act of 1990, Publ. L. 101-552.
37. ACUS Recommendation 74–1, Subpoena power in formal rulemaking and formal adjudication, 1 CFR §305.74-1 (1992).
38. ACUS Recommendation 90–4, Social Security disability program appeals process: Supplementary recommendation, 1 CFR §305.90–4 (1992).
39. See Pierce, Use of the Federal Rules of Evidence in federal agency adjudications, 39 *Admin. L. Rev.* 1 (1987).

40. Federal Rules of Evidence, Pub. L. 93-595, 88 Stat. 1726 (1975).
41. ACUS Recommendation 86-2, Use of the Federal Rules of Evidence in federal agency adjudications, 1 CFR 305.86-2 (1992), relying on Pierce, supra note 39.
42. Department of Labor final rule, 55 *Fed. Reg.* 13218 (April 9, 1990).
43. The Federal Bar Association has encouraged agencies to consider use of the Federal Rules, FBA Resolution 91-5, Administrative agency adoption of uniform rules of evidence patterned after Federal Rules of Evidence (April 13, 1991). The ABA has taken a similar position. See 60 U.S.L.W. 2492 (February 11, 1992) (reporting on action of ABA House of Delegates). Both bar associations based their effort in part on a study by Professor Michael Graham, Application of the rules of evidence in administrative agency formal adversarial adjudications: A new approach, *U. Ill. L. Rev.* 353 (1991).
44. See Levinson, Professional responsibility issues in administrative adjudication, 2 *BYU J. of Pub. L.* 219, 242-251 (1988).
45. See the SEC's debarment regulation, 17 CFR §201.2(e) (1992).
46. See Asimow, When the curtain falls: Separation of functions in the federal administrative agencies, 81 *Colum. L. Rev.* 759 (1981).
47. Idem at 763.
48. *Butz v. Economou,* 438 U.S. 478, 513-14 (1978) (dictum).
49. See Asimow, supra note 46, at 797-799.
50. Idem at 800.
51. See transcript of twenty-third plenary session of Administrative Conference of the U.S. 29-117 (December 11, 1981).
52. Rosenblum, Contexts and contents of "good cause" as criterion for removal of administrative law judges: Legal and policy factors, 6 *W. New Eng. L. Rev.* 593 (1984).
53. See Timony, Disciplinary proceedings against federal administrative law judges, 6 *W. New Eng. L. Rev.* 807 (1984).
54. See, e.g., Social Security administrative law judges: Survey and issue paper, Subcomm. on Social Security of the House Comm. on Ways and Means, 96th Cong. 1st Sess. (Comm. print 1979); The role of the administrative law judge in the Title II Social Security disability program, Report by the Subcomm. on Oversight of Government Management of the Senate Comm. on Governmental Affairs, 98th Cong., 1st Sess. (Committee Print 1983).
55. The agency's measures are described in the district court's opinion in *Association of Administrative Law Judges, Inc. v. Heckler,* 594 F. Supp. 1132 (D.D.C. 1984).
56. Idem at 1143.
57. *Nash v. Bowen,* 869 F.2d 675 (2nd Cir. 1989).
58. Idem at 686.
59. 19 M.S.P.R. 321 (1984). The description relies on Rosenblum, supra note 52, at 620-627.
60. See *Social Security Administration v. Balaban,* 33 M.S.P.R. 309, 314-316 (1987); *Social Security Administration v. Goodman,* 33 M.S.P.R. 325, 329-32 (1987). For a useful digest of MSPB decisions concerning ALJs see, Streb, The ALJ digest: A summary of statutes, regulations of MSPB and OPM and decisions of MSPB and the courts concerning disciplinary and other actions affecting administrative law judges." Office of Administrative Law Judge, MSPB, July 6, 1990.
61. Rosenblum, supra note 52, at 642.
62. ACUS Recommendation 86-7, Case management as a tool for improving agency adjudication, 1 CFR §305.86-7 (1992).
63. "Chief" status is conferred by (and may be revoked by) the agency head, although the higher pay status for chiefs may make removal an "adverse action" appealable to MSPB.
64. Administrative law process: Better management is needed, Comptroller General, Report to the Congress 48 (May 15, 1978) (FPCD-78-25).
65. *Study on Federal Regulation* (Volume IV, *Delay in the Regulatory Process*) Sen. Comm. on Governmental Affairs Committee Print 110-112, 95th Cong. 1st Sess. (July 1977).
66. ACUS Recommendation 92-7, supra note 35. See also the discussion in *The Federal Administrative Judiciary,* supra note 32, at Chapter VI (E).

67. See the Inspector General Act of 1978, Pub. L. 95–452, 92 Stat. 1101, 5 U.S.C. App. See also, *The Inspector General Act of 1978: A Ten Year Review,* Sixty-first Report by the House Comm. on Government Operations, House Report 100–1027, 100th Cong. 2nd Sess. (October 3, 1988).
68. *United States Navy-Marine Corps Court of Military Review v. Carlucci,* 26 M.J. 328 (C.M.A. 1988).
69. Idem at 337.
70. Idem.
71. See *In the Matter of Public Service Company of New Hampshire, et al. (Seabrook Station Unit 1 and 2),* Docket Nos. 50–443–OL, 50–444–OL, Memorandum from Administrative Law Judge Ivan W. Smith. (August 7, 1990).
72. S. 826 H.R. 3910, 102d Cong., 1st Sess. (1991). See generally Administrative law judge corps Act: Hearings on S. 594 Before the Subcomm. on Courts and Administrative Practice of the Senate Comm. on the Judiciary, 101st Cong., 1st Sess. (1989); Administrative law judge corps Act: Hearings on S. 1275 Before the Subcomm. on Administrative Practice and Procedure of the Senate Comm. on the Judiciary, 98th Cong., 1st Sess. (1983).
73. The states with "central panels" for all or some of their agency hearings include California, Colorado, Florida, Maryland, Massachusetts, Minnesota, Missouri, New Jersey, North Carolina, North Dakota, Pennsylvania, Tennessee, Washington, Wisconsin, and Wyoming. See Summary of Central Panel States' Activities for the 1991 Central Panel Conference (compiled from *The Central Panel,* Lutherville, MD), on file with author. New York City is also using a similar system, although the governor of New York vetoed a state-wide system in July, 1989.
74. See Hearings on S. 594, supra note 72. Testimony of witnesses from the National Conference of Administrative Law Judges, Federal Administrative Law Judges Conference, Association of [SSA] Administrative Law Judges and the American Bar Association in support of bill, and the Department of Justice, Social Security Administration, and the Forum of United States Administrative Law Judges opposing the bill.
75. Administrative law judge corps Act, Report of the Sen. Comm. on the Judiciary, 101st Cong., 2d Sess., Report 101–467 (September 19, 1990).
76. Lubbers, supra note 5, at 273–275.
77. The proposed experiment was described in Lubbers, Federal agency adjudications: Trying to see the forest and the trees, 31 *Fed. Bar News & J.* 383, 386 (November, 1984). The recent banking legislation, the Financial Institutions Reform, Recovery and Enforcement Act of 1989, required the five bank regulatory agencies, which had heretofore borrowed their ALJs from other agencies, to organize such a pool. Pub. L. 101–73 §916(1), 103 Stat. 183 (1989). The Office of Thrift Supervision currently employs two ALJs who serve all the bank regulatory agencies.
78. Pub. L. 101–509, Section 104; Stat. 1445–1446. See also, OPM interim ALJ pay regulations, 56 *Fed Reg.* 6208 (Feb. 14, 1991). The new pay scale substitutes for the former GS-15–18 scale a new set of 8 levels AL-1, AL-2, and AL-3 (A through F). AL-1 equals the basic pay for level IV of the executive schedule (the top of the senior executive service scale). AL-2 is 95% of that amount and AL-3(F), the lowest level, is 65% of that amount. Most ALJs are at the AL-3(E) or AL-3(F) levels. The rate increase for the former GS-15 judges (mostly Social Security judges) was proportionately higher.
79. Formerly known as the HHS Grant Appeals Board. See Cappalli, Model for case management: The grant appeals board, 1986 ACUS Recommendation and Reports 663.
80. ACUS Recommendation 86–7, Case management as a tool for improving agency adjudication, 1 CFR §305.86–7 (1992).
81. Pou and Jones, Agency time limits as a tool for reducing regulatory delay, 1986 ACUS Recommendations and Reports 835.
82. Executive Order 12778, 56 *Fed. Reg.* 55195 (October 25, 1991) §3.
83. ACUS Recommendation 70–4 (formerly No. 21) Discovery in agency adjudication, §1, Recommendations and Reports of the Administrative Conference of the United States (vol. 1) 38 (1970).
84. ACUS Recommendation 90–4, supra note 38, §2.
85. Idem.

86. 5 U.S.C. §556(c)(8).
87. Supra note 79.
88. Ruhlen, *Manual for Administrative Law Judges,* Administrative Conference of the U.S., (rev. ed. 1982) (1st ed. 1974). The third edition is being prepared for publication in 1993.
89. 29 CFR Part 18 (1990). DOL Chief ALJ Nahum Litt estimated the number of statutes covered, conversation with the author, April 1991. The Administrative Conference's proposed model rules are expected to be issued in 1993.
90. 7 CFR §1.130 (1992).
91. Financial Institutions Reform, Recovery and Enforcement Act of 1989, Pub. L. 101-73 §916 (2), 103 Stat. 183.
92. ACUS Recommendation 68-6, Delegation of final decisional authority subject to discretionary review by the agency. §2(a), 1 CFR §305.68-6 (1992).
93. Recently both the NRC and FCC have proposed elimination of their intermediate review boards. The FCC proposed elimination of its Review Board at 55 *Fed. Reg.* 28063, 28065 (July 9, 1990), but decided to retain it, 56 *Fed. Reg.* 787, 790 (January 9, 1991). The NRC did abolish its Atomic Safety and Licensing Appeal Panel, 56 *Fed. Reg.* 29403 (June 27, 1991).
94. ACUS Recommendation 68-6, supra note 92, §2(b).
95. Cf. the NLRB, SEC, and FTC.
96. Remarks before the twenty-third annual Rocky Mountain state-federal-provincial securities conference, Commissioner Mary L. Schapiro, page 8 (October 12, 1990).
97. *Study of Federal Regulation,* supra note 65, at 6.
98. See *Federal Administrative Law Judge Hearings—Statistical Report for 1976–1978,* supra note 8, at 1–6, for a fuller description of this history.
99. Study of Federal Regulation, supra note 65, at 151.
100. Idem at 152.
101. The Conference's figures come from the 1969 Annual Report of the Administrative Conference 1 ($250,000 budget for 1969) and the 1990 Annual Report of the Administrative Conference 29 ($1.865 million appropriations for 1990). The Federal Judicial Center's (FJC's) figures come from the Report of the Proceedings of the Judicial Conference of the United States for 1969 at 3 (Director of FJC reports 1969 appropriation of $300,000) and the *FY 1990 Budget of the United States,* Appendix 1-B8 ($13.17 million appropriation for 1990).
102. Supra note 8. Ultimately a compromise was reached which provides for administrative enforcement with Department of Housing and Urban Development (HUD) ALJs, but with the right of respondents to "remove" the case to federal district court. Pub. L. No. 100–430, §8(2), 102 Stat. 1629 (1988) (codified at 42 USC §3612).
103. Article III, Section 1.
104. Fallon, Of legislative courts, administrative agencies, and Article III, 104 *Harv. L. Rev.* 915 (1988).
105. *American Insurance Co. v. Carter,* 26 U.S. (1 Pet.) 511 (1828). Discussed in Fallon, supra note 104, at 921–923.
106. *Crowell v. Benson,* 285 U.S. 22 (1932). Discussed in Fallon, supra note 104, at 923–925.
107. See Bruff, Specialized courts in administrative law, 43 *Admin. L. Rev.* 329 (1991). In his comparison of federal adjudication, Professor Bruff pointed out, "The Constitution's focus on life tenure and salary stability as attributes of federal judges suggests that the constitutional stature of other adjudicators depends mostly on their job security" (at 342).
108. All statistics compiled from *1993 Judicial Staff Directory,* Staff Directories, Ltd., Mount Vernon, VA (1993). There were also 71 active senior circuit judges and 246 active district judges. Vacancies are not included.
109. There are also numerous magistrates, bankruptcy judges, and special masters who serve as "adjuncts" to federal district courts.
110. Pierce identified 280 separate evidentiary provisions in 1986. Of course, many more statutes are silent on that point, Pierce, supra note 39.

111. See text at notes 72–78, supra.
112. Act of June 23, 1947, c. 120, Title I, §101, 61 Stat. 139; 29 U.S.C. §153(d) 1988.
113. See Johnson, The split-enforcement model: Some conclusions from the OSHA and MSHA experiences, 39 *Admin. L. Rev.* 315 (1987).
114. See Fallon, Enforcing aviation safety regulations: A case for the split-enforcement model of agency adjudication, 4 *Admin. L. J.* 389 (1991); Perritt, Adjudication of civil penalties under the Federal Aviation Act, 1991 ACUS Recommendations and Reports 764.
115. ACUS Recommendation 86–4, The split-enforcement model for agency adjudication, 1 CFR §305.86–4 (1992). In 1991 ACUS recommended some modifications in the FAA-NTSB scheme but took care to say that its recommendation "is not to be read as a general endorsement of this model for other government programs." ACUS Recommendation 91–8, Adjudication of civil penalties under the Federal Aviation Act, 1 CFR §305.91–8 (1992).
116. See Robie and Morse, The federal executive branch adjudicator: Alive (and) well outside the Administrative Procedure Act? 33 *Fed. Bar News & J.* 133 (March 1986).
117. See Frye, Study of non-ALJ hearing programs, 44 *Admin. L. Rev.* 261 (1992).
118. Idem.
119. Idem.
120. See 5 U.S.C.A. §5372a(b) (1992). This BCA pay schedule, enacted in 1990 (Pub. L. No. 101–509) at the same time as the ALJ pay schedule, provides that rank and file members of BCAs are paid 94 percent of level IV of the executive schedule. Nonmanagement ALJs are paid from 65 to 90 percent of level IV, depending on seniority. This corresponds roughly to GS-15–17. See note 78, supra.
121. Verkuil, A study of informal adjudication procedures, 43 *U. Chi. L. Rev.* 739 (1976).
122. Idem at 760, n. 80 (finding that 38 of 42 programs so provided).
123. See Gardner, The procedures by which informal action is taken, 24 *Admin. L. Rev.* 155, 158–166 (1972) (containing a draft "Informal Procedure Act of 1980"). See also Levinson, Elements of the administrative process: Formal, semi-formal, and free-form models, 26 *Am. U. L. Rev.* 872 (1977).
124. See Model State Administrative Procedure Act, National Conference of Commissioners on Uniform State Laws (1981), providing for "conference adjudicative hearings" (Section 4–401) and "summary adjudicative hearings" (Section 4–502). The comments to sections 4–102 and 4–201 indicated the intent and derivation of these provisions.
125. Recently Congress has even authorized agency adjudication of civil money penalties with non-ALJ hearing officers. See, e.g., the Safe Drinking Water Act Amendments of 1986, 42 U.S.C. §300h-2 (1989 Supp.) and the Water Quality Act, 33 U.S.C. §1319(g) (1989 Supp.) (authorizing non-ALJs when penalty below $25,000). See Edles, Civil penalties receive new attention, 9 *Admin. L. Notes* 1 (Federal Bar Association) (April 1990).
126. ACUS Recommendation 88–5, Agency use of settlement judges, 1 CFR §305. 88–5 (1992).

BIBLIOGRAPHY

Books

Bernstein, Marver H., *Regulating Business by Independent Commission.* Princeton University Press, Princeton, NJ, 1955.

Burger, Paula, *Judges in Search of a Court: Characteristics, Functions and Perceptions of Federal Administrative Law Judges.* University Microfilms International, Ann Arbor, MI, 1984. (Ph.D. dissertation, Johns Hopkins University, 1984.)

Chamberlain, Joseph; Dowling, Noel; and Hays, Paul, *The Judicial Function in Federal Administrative Agencies,* The Commonwealth Fund, 1942; reprinted by Books for Libraries Press, Freeport, NY, 1970.

Cofer, Donna, Judges, *Bureaucrats and the Question of Independence: A Study of the Social Security Administration Hearing Process,* Greenwood Press, Westport, CT, 1985.

Dixon, Robert G., Jr., *Social Security Disability and Mass Justice: A Problem in Welfare Administration.* Praeger Publishers, New York, NY, 1973.

Mashaw, Jerry L. *Bureaucratic Justice: Managing Social Security Disability Claims.* New Haven: Yale University Press, New Haven, CT, 1983.

Mashaw, Jerry L., et al., *Social Security Hearings and Appeals,* Lexington Books, Lexington, MA, 1978.

Miller, Edward, *An Administrative Appraisal of the NLRB,* University of Pennsylvania, The Wharton School, Industrial Research Unit, Labor Relations and Public Policy Series No. 16, 1977.

Musolf, Lloyd D., *Federal Examiners and the Conflict of Law and Administration.* The Johns Hopkins University Studies in Historical and Political Science, Series LXX, Number 1, The Johns Hopkins Press, 1953; reprinted by Greenwood Press, Inc., Westport, CT, 1979.

Rich, Malcolm C., and Brucar, Wayne E., *The Central Panel System for Administrative Law Judges: A Survey of Seven States.* American Judicature Society; University Publications of America, Inc., Federick, MD, 1983.

Ruhlen, Merritt, *Manual for Administrative Law Judges,* rev. ed., Washington, DC: Government Printing Office, 1982. Prepared for the Administrative Conference of the United States.

Articles

Abrams, Norman, Administrative law judge systems: The California view, 20 *Admin. L. Rev.* 487 (1977).

Allen, William, Administrative actions, Paper delivered to [unidentified] Institute (November, 1981).

Ames, H. C., The hearing examiner and the Riss decision, 18 *ICC Prac. J.* 729 (1951).

Asimow, Michael, When the curtain falls: Separation of functions in the federal administrative agencies, 81 *Colum. L. Rev.* 759 (1981).

Auerbach, Carl A., Scope of authority of federal administrative agencies to delegate decision-making to hearing examiners, 48 *Minn. L. Rev.* 823 (1964).

Benkin, Isaac D., The shadow world of administrative law judges, 22 *Judges J.* 20 (Fall 1983).

Berg, Richard, Re-examining policy procedures: The choice between rulemaking and adjudication, 38 *Admin. L. Rev.* 149 (1986).

Bloomfield, David S., Disability claims under the Social Security Act: A practitioner's guide to administrative procedures, 6 *Cap. U.L. Rev.* 371 (1977).

Bok, Derek C., A flawed system, *Howard Magazine,* May–June 1983, p. 38.

Boyd, Robert R., A hearing examiner comments on the APA and the rule-making or adjudication controversy, 11 *Wm. & Mary L. Rev.* 424 (1969).

Caldwell, Louis G., A federal administrative court, 84 *U. Pa. L. Rev.* 970 (1936).

Caldwell, Louis G., The proposed federal administrative court: The arguments for its adoption, 36 *A.B.A.J.* 13 (1950).

Cary, William L., Why I oppose the divorce of the judicial function from federal regulatory agencies, 51 *A.B.A.J.* 33 (1965).

Cass, Ronald, Allocation of authority within bureaucracies: Empirical evidence and normative analysis, 66 *B.U.L. Rev.* 1 (1986).

Champagne, Anthony and Danube, Amos, An empirical analysis of decisions of administrative law judges in the Social Security disability programs, 64 *Geo. L.J.* 43 (1975).

Cleary, Timothy F., Some aspects of agency review of initial decisions of administrative law judges, 31 *Lab. L.J.* 531 (1980).

Comment, Social Security hearings for the disabled—Who decides: Trial examiners or administrative law judges? 69 *Nw. U.L. Rev.* 915 (1975).

Comment, Administrative law judges and the code of judicial conduct: A need for regulated ethics, 94 *Dickinson L. Rev.* 929 (1990).

Cramton, Roger C., A title change for federal hearing examiners? 'A rose by any other name . . .', 40 *Geo. Wash. L. Rev.* 918 (1972).
Cross, Hugh W, Statement to the President's Conference on Administrative Procedure concerning appointment and status of federal hearing officers, 22 *ICC Prac. J.* 120 (1954).
Davis, Frederick, Judicialization of administrative law: The trial-type hearing and the changing status of the hearing officer, 1977 *Duke L. J.* 389.
De Seife, Rudolphe J. A., A proposal for the establishment of an administrative court system, Washington Legal Foundation, Critical Legal Issues: Working Paper Series No. 16 (July 1987).
De Seife, Rudolphe J. A., Administrative law reform: A focus on the administrative law judge, 13 *Val. U.L. Rev.* 229 (1979).
Dixon, Robert G. Jr., The welfare state and mass justice: A warning from the Social Security disability program, 1972 *Duke L.J.* 681.
Dullea, Charles J., Development of the personnel program for administrative law judges, 25 *Admin. L. Rev.* 41 (1973).
Edles, Gary, The ICC hearing process: A cost-benefit approach to administrative agency alternative dispute resolution, 16 *Trans. L. J.* 99 (1987).
Etelson, Jesse, The new ALJ examination: A bright, shining lie redux, 43 *Admin. L. Rev.* 185 (1991).
Fallon, Richard, Enforcing aviation safety regulations: The case for a split-enforcement model of agency adjudication, 4 *Admin. L. J.* 389 (1991).
Fallon, Richard, Of legislative courts, administrative agencies and article III, 101 *Harv. L. Rev.* 915 (1988).
Fauver, William, An agenda for investigation: Should the APA be amended to provide standards for agency review of administrative trials? 1973 *Duke L. J.* 135.
Federal trial examiners seek to enjoin Civil Service Commission regulations, 19 *ICC Prac. J.* 369 (1952).
Freedman, James O., Review boards in the administrative process, 117 *U. Pa. L. Rev.* 546 (1969).
Friendly, Henry J., Some kind of hearing, 123 *U. Pa. L. Rev.* 1267 (1975).
Frye, John, Study of non-ALJ hearing programs, 44 *Admin. L. Rev.* 261 (1992).
Fuchs, Ralph F., The hearing examiner fiasco under the Administrative Procedure Act, 63 *Harv. L. Rev.* 737 (1950).
Fuchs, Ralph F., Hearing commissioners, 30 *N.Y.U.L. Rev.* 1342 (1955).
Fuchs, Ralph F., The hearing officer problem—symptom and symbol, 40 *Cornell L.Q.* 281 (1955).
Gardner, Warner, The procedures by which informal action is taken, 24 *Admin. L. Rev.* 155 (1972).
Gifford, Daniel, Adjudication in independent tribunals: The role of an alternative agency structure, 66 *Notre Dame L. Rev.* 965 (1991).
Gladstone, Arthur A., Commentary: The adjudication process in administrative law, 31 *Admin. L. Rev.* 237 (1979).
Graham, Michael, Application of the rules of evidence in administrative agency formal adversarial adjudications: A new approach, 1991 *U. Ill. L. Rev.* 353 (1991).
Hantman, Jack H., For an administrative court, 62 *A.B.A.J.* 360 (1976).
Harves, Duane, The 1981 Model State Administrative Procedure Act: The impact on central panel states, 6 *W. New Eng. L. Rev.* 661 (1984).
Harwood, Gerald, How necessary is the administrative law judge? 6 *W. New Eng. L. Rev.* 793 (1984).
Hayes, Social Security disability and the administrative law judges, 17 *A.F. L. Rev.* 73 (1975).
Hayes, Hearing examiner regulations promulgated under section 11 of the Administrative Procedure Act, 18 *ICC Prac. J.* 189 (1951).
Hayes, Hearing examiner status—A recurrent problem in administrative law, 1954 *Ind. L. J.* 86 (1954).
Hector, Louis J., Problems of the CAB and the independent regulatory commission, 69 *Yale L. J.* 931 (1960).
Hector, Louis J., The hidden judiciary and what it does, *U.S. News & World Report,* Nov. 1, 1982.
Holmes, John C., ALJ update: A review of the current role, status and demographics of the corps of administrative law judges, 38 *Fed. Bar News & J.* 202 (May 1991).

Horne, Brockman, Committee on hearing officers asks for help, 37 *J. of the Am. Judicature Soc.*, 182 (1954).

Improving the administrative process—time for a new APA? Proceedings of the National Conference on Federal Regulation: Roads to Reform, 32, *Admin. L. Rev.* 357 (1980).

Judging the judges—an outsize job—and getting bigger, *Time,* August 20, 1979, p. 49.

Joost, Robert and Battaglia, Nancy, The board for correction of military records of the Coast Guard: A unique dispute resolution mechanism, 41 *Admin. L. J.* 441 (1989).

Katcher, Monroe I., New York's elusive administrative law judge, 54 *N.Y. St.B. J.* 80 (1982).

Kauper, Karen, Protecting the independence of administrative law judges: A model administrative law judge corps statute, 18 *J. of Law Reform* 537 (1985).

Kinnane, Charles H., Administrative law: Federal trial examiners and the Ramspeck case, 4 *De Paul L. Rev.* 1 (1954).

Klement, Alice, 'Hidden judiciary' fights back, *Nat. L. J.,* September 24, 1979, p. 18.

Koch, Jr., Charles H. and Koplow, David A., The fourth bite at the apple: A study of the operation and utility of the Social Security Administration's Appeals Council, 17 *Fla. St. L. Rev.* 199 (1990).

Levant, Michael, A unified corps of administrative law judges—the transition from a concept to an eventual reality, 6 *W. New Eng. L. Rev.* 705 (1984).

Levinson, Harold, Elements of the administrative process: Formal, semi-formal and free-form models, 26 *Am. U. L. Rev.* 872 (1977).

Levinson, Harold, Professional responsibility issues in administrative adjudication, 2 *BYU J. of Pub. Law* 219 (1988).

Levinson, Harold, The proposed administrative law judge corps: An incomplete but important reform effort, 19 *New Eng. L. Rev.* 733 (1983–84).

Liebman, Ernst., Quality control for administrative law judges, 18 *Judges J.* 15 (1979).

Lindh, Frank, An examination of the proposed "closed record" administrative law judge hearing in the Social Security disability program, 6 *W. New Eng. L. Rev.* 745 (1984).

Litt, Nahum and Simon, Joseph, An administrative law judge corps: Its value and relation to the traditional justice system, 11 *Whittier L. Rev.* 569 (1989).

Lorch, Robert S., The administrative court idea before Congress, 20 *W. Pol. Q.* 65 (1967).

Lorch, Robert S., Administrative court via the independent hearing office, 51 *Judicature* 114 (1967).

Lorch, Robert S., Federal administrative court idea, 52 *A.B.A.J.* 635 (1966).

Lubbers, Jeffrey S., A unified corps of ALJs: A proposal to test the idea at the federal level, 68 *Judicature* 266 (1981).

Lubbers, Jeffrey S., Federal administrative law judges: A focus on our invisible judiciary, 31 *Admin. L. Rev.* 109 (1981).

Lubbers, Jeffrey S., Federal agency adjudications: Trying to see the forest and the trees, 33 *Fed. Bar News and J.* 388 (1984).

Lussier, Edward, The role of the Article I "trial judge", 6 *W. New Eng. L. Rev.* 775 (1984).

Macy, John W., Jr., The APA and the hearing examiner: Products of a viable political society, 27 *Fed. Bar J.* 351 (1967).

Mans, Thomas C., Selecting the 'Hidden Judiciary': How the merit process works in choosing administrative law judges, (2 Parts), 63 *Judicature* 60, 130 (1979).

Marquardt, Ronald G. and Wheat, Edward M., Case processing by administrative agencies: Administrative law judge perceptions vs. reality. Paper presented to Western Political Science Ass'n Convention (March 26, 1982).

Marquardt, Ronald G. and Wheat, Edward M., The developing concept of an administrative court, 33 *Admin. L.J.* 301 (1981).

Marquardt, Ronald G. and Wheat, Edward M., Hidden allocators: Administrative law judges and regulatory reform, 2 *L. & Pol'y Q.* 472 (1980).

Martin, Reforming asylum adjudication: On navigating the coast of Bohemia, 138 *U. Pa. L. Rev.* 1247 (1990).

Marzloff, George Ernest, Delay in review of initial decisions: The case for giving more finality to the findings of fact of the administrative law judge, 35 *Wash. & Lee L. Rev.* 393 (1978).

Miller, C. A., Federal trial examiners should not be subject to presidential appointment; Address, 21 *ICC Prac. J.* 4 (1953).

Miller, Edward B., The tangled path to an administrative judgeship, 25 *Lab. L.J.* 3 (1974).

Miller, John T., Jr., The Civil Service Commission's new hearing examiner recruitment program, 17 *Admin. L. Rev.* 104 (1964).

Miller, John T., Jr., Continuing forum for reform of administrative process, 27 *Admin. L. Rev.* 205 (1975).

Miller, John T., Jr., The education and development of administrative law judges, 25 *Admin. L. Rev.* 7 (1973).

Miller, John T., Jr., Hearing cases before several agencies—odyssey of an administrative judge—comment, 27 *Admin. L. Rev.* 218 (1975).

Miller, John T., Jr., The need for improvements in the hearing examiner recruitment program for the Civil Service Commission, 19 *Admin. L. Rev.* 319 (1967).

Miller, John T., Jr., The vice of selective certification in the appointment of hearing examiners, 20 *Admin. L. Rev.* 477 (1968).

Minor, Robert W., The administrative court—hear it comes again, 24 *ICC Prac. J.* 807 (1957).

Minor, Robert W., The administrative court: Variations on a theme, 19 *Ohio St. L.J.* 380 (1983).

Minow, Newton N., Suggestions for improvements in the administrative process, 15 *Admin. L. Rev.* 146 (1963).

Mogel, William A., The effect of a claim of privilege upon the subpoena power of an administrative law judge, 28 *Drake L. Rev.* 67 (1978–79).

Morse, Marvin, The administrative law judge—a new direction for the corps? 30 *Fed. Bar News & J.* 398 (1983).

Mosher, Lawrence, Here come the administrative law judges, *Nat. L.J.*, July 28, 1979, p. 1247.

Moss, Debra C., Judges under fire, 77 *A.B.A.J.* 56 (November 1991).

Musolf, Lloyd D., Independent hearing officers: The California experiment, 14 *W. Pol. Q.* 195 (1961).

Nathanson, Nathaniel L., The administrative court proposal, 57 *Va. L. Rev.* 996 (1971).

Nathanson, Nathaniel L., Proposals for an administrative appellate court, 25 *Admin. L. Rev.* 85 (1973).

Neslund, Nancy, Dispute resolution: A matrix of mechanisms, 1990 *J. of Dispute Resolution* 212 (1990).

Note, Administrative law judges, performance evaluation, and production standards: Judicial independence versus employee accountability, 54 *Geo. Wash. L. Rev.* 591 (1986).

Note, Veterans' preference in public employment: The history, constitutionality and effect on federal personnel practices of veterans' preference legislation, 44 *Geo. Wash. L. Rev.* 623 (1976).

Palmer, Victor, The evolving role of administrative law judges, 19 *New Eng. L. Rev.* 755 (1983–84).

Palmer, Victor, and Bernstein, Edwin, Establishing federal administrative law judges as an independent corps: The Heflin bill, 6 *W. New Eng. L. Rev.* 673 (1984).

Pfeiffer, Paul N., Hearing cases before several agencies—Odyssey of an Administrative Law Judge, 27 *Admin. L. Rev.* 217 (1975).

Pops, Gerald M., Judicalization of federal administrative law judges: Implications for policymaking, 81 *W. Va. L. Rev.* 169 (1979).

Reflections on the conduct of an administrative hearing, Panel Discussion, 20 *Admin. L. Rev.* 101 (1967).

Rhyne, Charles S., Developing the prestige of the hearing examiner, 47 *A.B.A.J.* 184 (1961).

Rich, Malcolm C., ed., The central panel system: A new framework for the use of administrative law judges, 65 *Judicature* 232 (1981).

Rich, Malcolm C., The central panel system and the decisionmaking independence of administrative law judges: Lessons for a proposed federal program, 6 *W. New Eng. L. Rev.* 643 (1984).

Robie, William and Morse, Marvin, The federal executive branch adjudicator: Alive (and) well outside the Administrative Procedure Act? 33 *Fed. Bar. News & J.* 133 (March 1986).

Rogers, James T. Trial examiners' impact on business grows, 21 *ICC Prac. J.* 187 (1953).

Rosenblum, Victor, Changing judicial perceptions of administrative decision-making and of the status of administrative law judges: Interrelations of case law with statutory and pragmatic factors in determining ALJ roles, 15 *Judges J.* 64 (1976).

Rosenblum, Victor, Contexts and contents of "for good cause" as criterion for removal of administrative law judges: Legal and policy factors, 6 *W. New Eng. L. Rev.* 593 (1984).

Rutledge, J. C., Administrative trial examiners: The anonymous matters, 30 *Wash. L. Rev.* 26 (1955).

Sahm, Henry S., The hearing examiner's roles in the federal administrative process, 20 *Fed. Bar. J.* 74 (1960).

Scalia, Antonin, The ALJ fiasco—a reprise, 47 *U. Chi. L. Rev.* 57 (1979).

Scalia, Antonin, The hearing examiner loan program, 1971 *Duke L.J.* 319.

Schapiro, Mary, Remarks before the twenty-third annual Rocky Mountain state-federal-provincial securities conference, Denver, Colorado, (October 12, 1990).

Segal, Bernard G., The administrative law judge: Thirty years of progress and the road ahead, 62 *A.B.A.J.* 1424 (1976).

Sharon, Amiel T., The measure of an administrative law judge, 19 *Judge J.* 20 (1980).

Sharon, Amiel and Pettibone, Craig, Merit selection of federal administrative law judges, 70 *Judicature* 216 (1987).

Simeone, Joseph J., The function, flexibility, and future of United States judges of the executive department, 44 *Admin. L. Rev.* 159 (1992).

Simon, Ruth, For ALJs, obscurity is ending, *Nat. L. J.,* June 6, 1983.

Skoler, Daniel L., The administrative judiciary: Change, challenge, and choices, 462 *The Annals* 34 (1982).

Skoler, Daniel L., The changing role of administrative law judges: Time to shift gears, 22 *Judges J.* 24 (1983).

Status of the trial examiner in administrative agencies, 26 *Harv. L. Rev.* 51 (1974).

Symposium: Administrative law judges, 6 *W. New Eng. L. Rev.* 587 (1984).

Symposium: Contemporary issues in administrative adjudication, 39 *U.C.L.A. L. Rev.* 1055 (1992).

Symposium: Review of administrative adjudication, 26 *Admin. L. Rev.* 51 (1974).

Thomas, Morgan, Tales from the forgotten judiciary, 63 *A.B.A.J.* 301 (1977).

Thomas, Morgan, The selection of federal hearing examiners: Pressure groups and the administrative process, 59 *Yale L.J.* 431 (1950).

Thomas, Morgan, The 350 hearing examiners: Chairman Wiley asks for open choice for witness, 33 *A.B.A.J.* 421 (1947).

Timony, James P., Disciplinary proceedings against federal administrative law judges, 6 *W. New Eng. L. Rev.* 807 (1984).

Tuggle, Kenneth H., Status of federal hearing examiners, 22 *ICC Prac. J.* 129 (1954).

Verkuil, Paul, A study of immigration procedures, 31 *UCLA L. Rev.* 1141 (1984).

Verkuil, Paul, A study of informal adjudication procedures, 43 *U. Chi. L. Rev.* 739 (1976).

Verkuil, Paul, The emerging concept of administrative procedure, 78 *Colum. L. Rev.* 258 (1978).

Von Rintelin, Victor A., Hearing examiner recruitment and the government lawyer, 35 *ICC Prac. J.* 7 (1967).

Wagner, Warren H., The future of the Interstate Commerce Commission and its examiners, 19 *ICC Prac. J.* 271 (1951).

Wald, Patricia, Some thoughts on beginning and ends: Court of Appeals review of administrative law judges' findings and opinions, 67 *Wash. U.L.Q.* 661 (1989).

Westwood, Howard C., Administrative proceedings: Techniques of presiding, 50 *A.B.A.J.* 659 (1964).

Woodall, Emery J., Appointment and compensation of federal hearing examiners, 10 *Fed. Bar J.* 391 (1949).

Zankel, Norman, A unified corps of federal administrative law judges is not needed, 6 *W. New Eng. L. Rev.* 723 (1984).

Zwerdling, Joseph, Reflections on the role of an administrative law judge, 25 *Admin. L. Rev.* 9 (1973).

Zwerdling, Joseph, The role and functions of federal hearing examiners, 400 *The Annals* 27 (1972).

Government Reports

Administrative Conference of the United States

Lester, Report on section II hearing examiners, to the Committee on Personnel, Administrative Conference of the U.S. (August 23, 1962).

Name change for hearing officers, Transcript of ACUS Plenary Session, October 22, 1969.

Park, Robert E., Several matters in regard to examiners and government attorneys: A report for the Committee on Personnel on its current recommendations. 1 ACUS 281 424 (1971).

Rosenblum, Victor G., The administrative law judge in the administrative process: Interrelations of case law with statutory and pragmatic factors in determining ALJ roles. Reprinted in Recent Studies Relevant to the Disability Hearings and Appeals Crisis. U.S. Congress. House Committee on Ways and Means. Subcommittee on Social Security. 94th Cong., 1st Sess., December 20, 1975, pp. 171-245.

Federal Administrative Law Judge Hearings—Statistical Report for 1975. Wash., D.C., U.S. Gov't Printing Office (1977).

Federal Administrative Law Judge Hearings—Statistical Report for 1976–1978. Wash., D.C., U.S. Gov't Printing Office (1980). (See especially Lubbers, *The Administrative Law Judge,* Chapter 1, p. 7.)

Capalli, Richard B., Model for case management: The Grant Appeals Board, 1986 ACUS Recommendations and Reports 663.

Pou, Charles and Jones, Charlotte, Agency time limits as a tool for reducing regulatory delay, 1986 ACUS Recommendations and Reports 835.

Administrative law judges: Should an independent corps be created? Transcript of ACUS Plenary Session, July 27, 1987.

Perritt, Henry, Adjudication of civil penalties under the Federal Aviation Act, 1991 ACUS Recommendations and Reports 764.

Frye, John, Study of non-ALJ hearing programs, Report to the Administrative Conference of the U.S. (August 1991). [Reprinted in 44 Admin. L. Rev. 261 (1992)]

Verkuil, Paul; Gifford, Daniel; Koch, Charles; Pierce, Richard; and Lubbers, Jeffrey; The federal administrative judiciary, Report to the Administrative Conference of the U.S. (August 1992).

ACUS Recommendations (Codified at 1 CFR §305)

Recommendation 68-6, Delegation of final decisional authority subject to discretionary review by the agency.

Recommendation 69-6, Compilation of statistics on administrative proceedings by federal departments and agencies.

Recommendation 69-9, Recruitment and selection of hearing examiners; continuing training for government attorneys and hearing examiners; creation of a center for continuing legal education in government.

Recommendation 72-6, Civil money penalties as a sanction.

Recommendation 74-1, Subpoena power in formal rulemaking and formal adjudication.

Recommendation 78-2, Procedures for determining Social Security claims.

Recommendation 78-3, Time limits on agency actions.

Recommendation 79-3, Agency assessment and mitigation of civil money penalties.

Recommendation 83-3, Agency structures for review of decisions of presiding officers under the Administrative Procedure Act.

Recommendation 86-2, Use of Federal Rules of Evidence in federal agency adjudications.

Recommendation 86-3, Agencies' use of alternative means of dispute resolution.

Recommendation 86-4, The split-enforcement model for agency adjudication.

Recommendation 86-7, Case management as a tool for improving agency adjudication.

Recommendation 87-12, Adjudication practices and procedures of the federal bank regulatory agencies.

Recommendation 88-5, Agency use of settlement judges.

Recommendation 90-1, Civil money penalties for federal aviation violations.

Recommendation 90-4, Social Security disability program appeals process: Supplementary recommendations.

Recommendation 91-8, Adjudication of civil penalties under the Federal Aviation Act.

Recommendation 92-7, The federal administrative judiciary.

Miscellaneous Government (and Related) Reports

American Bar Association. Judicial Administrative Division. Conference of Administrative Law Judges, Symposium on a unified corps of administrative law judges—how will it work, Washington, D.C., January 28, 1977.

Associated Staff Attorneys of the Office of Hearings and Appeals. National Treasury Employees Union, Social Security administrative law judges: The need to change the administrative law judge examination (September 1989).

Commission on Organization of the Executive Branch of the Government, Legal services and procedure, Report to the Congress, Recommendation No. 52 (March 1955).

Committee on Administrative Procedure Appointed by the Attorney General, Administrative procedure in government agencies, S. Doc. No. 8, 77th Cong., 1st Sess. (1941).

Development Dimensions International, Development of criteria and procedures for selection of administrative judge positions, Report to Department of the Army (January 31, 1981).

Federal Trial Examiners Conference, *The Case for Administrative Trial Judge.* Washington, D.C.: The Casillas Press, Inc., Washington, D.C., 1969.

Forum of U.S. Administrative Law Judges, Administrative law judges: A case study of recruitment and retention concerns, March 25, 1990, reprinted in Hearing to Consider S. 2274 before the Sen. Committee on Governmental Affairs, 101st Cong. 2d. Sess., S. Hrg.. 101-739 (March 21, 22 1990)

Government Law Center of Albany Law School, Art of administrative practice 1, (Contains training materials on prehearing management, role of ALJ in settlement, conducting hearings), Albany, NY (February 1991).

Government Law Center of Albany Law School, *Ethical Considerations in Administrative Adjudication,* Albany, NY (October 1990).

Horsky, Charles and Mahin, Amy, The operation of the Social Security Administration hearing and decisional machinery, Report to the Social Security Commission, Covington and Burling, (December 1968).

E. Kintner, R. Doyle, E. Reynolds, and Winings, L., Appointment and status of federal hearing officers, Report of Committee on Hearing Officers of the President's Conference on Administrative Procedure (August 10, 1954).

Lester, R., McElwain, J., Maloy, L., and Scharnikov, W., Appointment and status of federal hearing officers, Report to the President's Conference on Administrative Procedure (September 3, 1954).

Lewis, Floyd, The administrative law judge system, Congressional Research Service, American Law Division, (September 9, 1982).

Social Security Administration, *Operational Analysis of the Office of Hearings and Appeals* (SSA Publication 70-032) (Annually through September 30, 1986).

Social Security Administration, Key workload indicators, Office of Hearings and Appeals (FY 1988-present).

Streb, Paul, The ALJ digest: A summary of statutes, regulations of MSPB and OPM, and decisions of MSPB and the courts concerning disciplinary and other actions affecting administrative law judges, Administrative Law Judge, MSPB, (July 6, 1990).

United States Civil Service Commission

Report to the committee on hearing officers of the President's Conference on Administrative Procedure, U.S. Civil Service Commission, 1953.

Report of advisory committee for hearing examiners to United States Civil Service Commission, Office of Director, Office of Hearing Examiners, U.S. Civil Service Commission (July 2, 1963).

Material for the advisory committee on hearing examiners, U.S. Civil Service Commission (November 1967).
Park, Robert, Selective certification: A study of the arguments for and against, Paper submitted to the U.S. Civil Service Commission (September 11, 1968).
Report of the committee on the study of the utilization of administrative law judges. [The La Macchia Report] (July 30, 1974).
Final report of the advisory committee on administrative law judges (February 14, 1978).

United States Congress: House of Representatives

Background material on Social Security hearings and appeals, Subcommittee on Social Security, Committee on Ways and Means, Committee Print 94-79, 94th Cong., 1st Sess. (September 17, 1975).
Recent studies relevant to the disability hearings and appeals crisis, Subcommittee on Social Security, Committee on Ways and Means, 94th Cong., 1st Sess. (December 20, 1975).
Background material on H.R. 5723: Conversion of temporary Social Security ALJs, Subcommittee on Social Security, Committee on Ways and Means, Committee Print 95-16, 95th Cong., 1st Sess. (April 18, 1977).
Administrative law judges, Hearing before the Subcommittee on Civil Service of the Post Office and Civil Service Committee on H.R. 865 (change of job title and other matters), 95th Cong., 1st Sess., Committee Serial No. 95-15 (June 21, 1977).
Conversion of temporary administrative law judges. Report 95-617, to accompany H.R. 5723, 95th Cong., 1st Sess. (October 31, 1977).
Social Security administrative law judges: Survey and issue paper, Subcommittee on Social Security, Committee on Ways and Means, Committee Print 96-2, 96th Cong., 1 Sess. (January 27, 1979).
Regulatory Reform Act of 1979, Hearings before the Subcommittee on Administrative Law and Governmental Relations of the Committee on the Judiciary, Committee Serial No. 41, 96th Cong., 1st and 2d Sess. on H.R. 3263. Nov. 7, 13, 16, 29, Dec. 3, 5, 10, 1979; January 29, Feb. 1 and 5, 1980 (Parts 1 and 2).
Selection and oversight of administrative law judges, Hearings before the Committee on Post Office and Civil Service on H.R. 6768, 96th Cong., 2d Sess., Serial No. 96-79 (April 24, May 6, 1980).
Administrative law judge program of the Federal Trade Commission, Hearings before the Subcommittee on Investigations, House Comm. on Post Office and Civil Service, 96th Cong., 2d Sess., Serial No. 96-94 (June 17, 1980).
Administrative law judges, Report No. 96-1186, Committee on Post Office and Civil Service, H.R., 96th Cong., 2d Sess. (July 23, 1980).
Administrative law judge corps act, Hearing before the Subcommittee on Administrative Law and Governmental Relations, House Committee on the Judiciary on H.R. 1554 and H.R. 2726, 100th Cong., 2d Sess., Serial No. 57 (March 17, 1988).
Judicial independence of administrative law judges at the Social Security Administration, Hearing before the Subcommittee on Social Security of the Committee on Ways and Means, 101st Cong., 2d Sess., Committee Serial No. 101-117 (June 13, 1990).

United States Congress: Senate

Study on federal regulation, 5 vols.; Delay in the regulatory process, Committee on Governmental Affairs, Vol. IV, Prepared Pursuant to S. Res. 71, 95th Cong., 1st Sess., July 1977.
Increase in number of administrative law judge positions, Committee on Governmental Affairs Report to Accompany H.R. 6975, 95th Cong., 2d Sess., Rept. No. 95-697 (March 9, 1978).
Regulatory reform legislation, hearings before the Committee on Governmental Affairs on S. 262, S. 755, S. 445, S. 93, Committee on Governmental Affairs, pts. 1-2, 96th Cong., 1st Sess. (March-May 1979).
Hearings on S. 262 and S. 755, Subcommittee on Administrative Practice and Procedure, Committee on the Judiciary, 96th Cong. (July 1979).
Administrative law judge system, hearings, Subcommittee for Consumers, Committee on Commerce, Science, and Transportation, 96th Cong., 2d Sess. (September 4-5, 1980).

Reform of federal regulations, Joint Report of the Committee on Governmental Affairs and the Committee on the Judiciary, to accompany S. 262 (Oct. 30, 1980) (Parts 1 and 2).

Social Security disability reviews: The role of the administrative law judge, Hearing before the Subcommittee on Oversight of Government Management of the Committee on Governmental Affairs, 98th Cong., 1st Sess. (June 8, 1983).

Administrative law judge corps act, Hearings before the Subcommittee on Administrative Practice and Procedure, Committee on the Judiciary on S. 1275, 98th Cong., 1st Sess., Serial No. J-98-45 (June 23, September 20, 1983).

The role of the administrative law judge in the Title II Social Security disability insurance program, Report of the Subcommittee on Oversight of Government Management of the Committee on Governmental Affairs, 98th Cong., 1st Sess., Committee Print 98-111 (October 1983).

Administrative law judge corps act S. 673, Hearing before the Subcommittee on Administrative Practice and Procedure, Committee on the Judiciary, 99th Cong., 2d Sess., Committee Serial No. J-99-105 (May 13, 1986).

Administrative law judge corps act, Hearing before the Subcommittee on Courts and Administrative Practice, Committee on the Judiciary on S. 950, 100th Cong., 1st Sess., Committee Serial No. J-100-31 (June 21, 1987).

Administrative law judge corps act, Hearing before the Subcommittee on Courts and Administrative Practice, Committee on the Judiciary on S. 594, 101st Cong., 1st Sess., Serial No. J-101-22 (June 13, 1989).

Administrative law judge corps act, Committee on the Judiciary Report on S. 594, 101st Cong., 2d Sess., S. Rpt. 101-467 (September 19, 1990).

U.S. Department of Justice, The needs of the federal courts, Report of Committee on Revision of the Federal Judicial System (January 1977).

U.S. General Accounting Office

Social Security Administration needs to better manage the travel of its administrative law judges. Report of the Comptroller General of the United States, MWD-76-18 (December 5, 1975).

Administrative law process: Better management is needed, Report by the Comptroller General to the Congress. FPCD 78-25. (May 15, 1978).

Review of administrative law judge activities and the hearing process at the Federal Energy Regulatory Commission, G.A.O. Report to Hon. John D. Dingell, House of Representatives (February 13, 1979).

Management improvements in the administrative process: Much remains to be done, Report by the Comptroller General to the Congress. FPCD 79-44. (May 23, 1979).

Medicare claims: HCFA proposal to establish an administrative law judge unit, U.S. G.A.O. Briefing Report to Congressional Committees, GAO/HRD-88-84 BR (April 1988).

Administrative law judges: Appointment of women and Social Security Administrative staff attorneys, G.A.O. Report to Hon. Sander M. Levin, House of Representatives, GAO/GGD-89-5 (October 1988).

Social Security: Racial difference in diability decisions warrants further investigation, G.A.O. Report to the Ranking Minority Member, Special Committee on Aging, U.S. Senate, 6A0/HRD-92-56 (April 1992).

United States Office of Personnel Management

U.S. Office of Personnel Management, Administrative law judge. Announcement No. 318. (various editions).

Sharon, Amiel T., An investigation of reference ratings for applicants for administrative law judge. OPM Personnel Research Report 80-6 (May, 1980).

Sharon, Amiel T., Validation of the administrative law judge examination. OPM Personnel Research Report 80-15 (June 1980).

U.S. Office of Personnel Management, *Administrative Law Judge Program Handbook* (May 1989).

U.S. Attorney General Opinions

Administrative Procedure Act, promotion of hearing examiners, 41 Op. Att'y Gen. 74 (February 23, 1951).

Administrative Procedure Act, Promotion to chief hearing examiner at increased compensation, 42 Op. Att'y Gen. 289 (November 24, 1964).

Administrative Procedure Act—reprimand of administrative law judge, 43 Op. Att'y Gen., No. 9 (January 18, 1977).

12

Explaining Agency Decision-Making: The Federal Trade Commission and Antitrust Policy in the Reagan Era

Robert A. Katzmann *Georgetown University, The Governance Institute, and Brookings Institution, Washington, D.C.*

Several years ago, I sought in *Regulatory Bureaucracy: The Federal Trade Commission and Antitrust Policy*[1] to examine how an agency vested with considerable discretion chooses its caseload. That work detailed the reasons for the dramatic changes in antitrust policy from the reactive-conduct cases of the 1960s to the proactive-structural cases of the 1970s. Much influenced by the work of James Q. Wilson,[2] my approach was grounded in the view that the outcomes of governmental bodies can best be understood by examining the many factors, internal and external, that affect decision-making. Organizational arrangements have much to do with determining how power is distributed among participants in the decision-making process, the manner in which information is gathered, the types of data collected, the kinds of policy issues discussed, the choices made, and the ways in which decisions are implemented. The various professional norms and personal objectives of the actors (executives, managers, and operators) also shape decisions. Moreover, external forces (for example, the president, congressional committees, courts, and interest groups) may also influence agency behavior.

Regulatory Bureaucracy concluded that in the 1970s, the antitrust caseload of the Federal Trade Commission (FTC) was largely the product of the interaction between two bureaus and the five commissioners. These two bureaus, the Bureau of Competition (the lawyers' unit) and the Bureau of Economics (the economists' unit), were separate and coequal. The personnel of each had their own conception of the kinds of antitrust goals and cases the agency should pursue. One bureau competed with the other for commission approval of its viewpoint. It was clear from observing the competition between lawyers and economists that how the balance was struck between professionals with different norms and goals often significantly affected, and sometimes even determined, the definition of antitrust activity. The FTC acted within the parameters set by Congress, but the legislature did not control or determine its caseload in any simple sense. Agency leadership committed to change explained the FTC's shift in caseload in the 1970s more than congressional influence.[3]

In the years since the publication of *Regulatory Bureaucracy,* a challenge to its basic approach arose: the "congressional dominance" paradigm. This view, articulated by Barry

Weingast and Mark Moran, holds that Congress "controls" agency decision-making.[4] The preferences of congressional oversight committees in the early 1970s, according to this view, led the FTC to pursue an activist, antibusiness agenda. When those committees wanted a more probusiness, less vigorous agency, they were able to induce the commission to reverse policy direction. The "congressional dominance" conception, which became popular in the public choice literature of the 1980s, seemed to me and others to provide an inadequate account of FTC decision-making in the 1970s.[5] To suppose that the commission's caseload were simply determined by congressional preferences is to ignore a whole list of organizational factors that affect any agency's decisions: for instance, how power is distributed among decision-makers, their professional norms and objectives. It also ignored a list of factors specific to the FTC, such as the interaction between lawyers and economists, the value of precedents, and the role of commissioners.[6]

As the debate about which approach better explains agency decisionmaking raged in the 1980s, the FTC underwent yet another major change in policy direction. The commission altered its course again, redirecting its focus towards a narrow range of horizontal restraints, and towards activities that seek to promote competition among professions. The agency sought self-consciously to cut its budget drastically, significantly reduce its workforce, and alter its policy direction. On all counts, the agency succeeded. These developments seemed to provide another test for the "congressional dominance" approach. To that end, I returned to study the commission at the end of the Reagan era.[7] My investigation of FTC antitrust policy during the Reagan years only reinforces the conclusion that the congressional dominance view is incomplete. As this chapter describes, changes in antitrust policy were not the result of congressional pressure. Rather, the FTC took advantage of Congress's acquiescence in the agency's effort to cut the budget to change policy as it saw fit. The policy course of the FTC can be understood primarily in terms of any agency leadership that had not only a coherent view of what antitrust policy should be but also a strategy for bringing about change.

This chapter begins with some background about the FTC and antitrust policy in 1980, at the time of the election of Ronald Reagan. It moves to a discussion of the Reagan–Bush transition task force report on the FTC, and then to an account of the internal and external factors affecting the agency's decisions to bring cases in the 1980. That part includes analysis of the Bureau of Competition, the Bureau of Economics, the role of the commissions, Congress, and the courts.

THE FTC AND ANTITRUST POLICY IN 1980: THE COLLAPSE OF THE OLD CONSENSUS

Until the Reagan administration, antitrust policymakers took a broad view of their mandate. Enforcement decisions were guided by political and social concerns as well as economic ones, reflecting the statutory roots of the antitrust statutes. With respect to economic criteria, the FTC in the 1970s placed increasing emphasis on structural cases, which were intended to attack fundamental market imperfections that facilitate anticompetitive activity among the dominant firms in the industry. In fiscal 1978, for example, the commission allocated 59 percent of its antitrust budget to what have been described as structural programs in the energy, health care, transportation, chemical, and food industries. In 1973, the agency launched the *Exxon* case, a suit directed against the eight major oil companies, which consumed 12 to 14 percent of the antitrust budget alone in some years, before the action was dropped.

By 1980, changes in antitrust scholarship, legal thinking (discussed more fully below), procedural complexity, and economic context had altered the climate for antitrust.[8] As consequences of these changes, a consensus that had persisted for the better part of a century—on the allegedly harmful effects of economic concentration and the appropriateness of structural remedies—had come undone.

The most important element in this breakdown of consensus was a sharp challenge, mounted by the economists and law professors at the University of Chicago and elsewhere, to the conventional assumptions of antitrust analysis. Members of the so-called Chicago School argue that social and political objectives should not be factored into the setting of antitrust policy and priorities—and that statutes intended expressly to serve such purposes should be discarded.

In advocating a focus on economic considerations only, Chicago School analysts have advanced an increasingly influential view of marketplace dynamics. The standard conception had been that increases in concentration on the seller side of a market tend to yield increases in the elevation of prices above unit costs, reductions in competition, and restrictions of output. But according to the Chicago School, concentration in a market simply reflects the economies of scale available to producers; firms must be of a certain size in order to take advantage of these economies. If the largest sellers in the market make above-normal profits, those profits would be seen as the natural concomitants of greater efficiency; the largest firms are able to realize economies of scale more fully than their smaller competitors. Chicago School economists conclude that enforcement officials should proceed against horizontal restraints only in markets with very substantial barriers to entry—and that they ought to presume that most vertical restraints (for example, a firm's acquisition of its suppliers) are not anticompetitive. These changes in economic thinking, as will be described later, would, by 1980, begin to affect legal analysis as well.

To be sure, ideas matter. Changes in intellectual thinking can ultimately alter policy. Yet bureaucracies tend to have their own dynamic that resists change. In a law enforcement agency, dramatic examples of ambitious cases that did not realize their objectives can lead to a reassessment of policy. The mammoth structural antitrust suits of the 1960s and 1970s—for instance, those directed at the major oil companies, and the cereal manufacturres—were such examples. They took many years to develop and pursue. The frustrations of delay endemic to these cases, the procedural wrangling, and the difficulties of attracting and retaining first-rate attorneys to staff such lengthy proceedings all dampened the enthusiasm of enforcement officials for such prosecutions. Moreover, critics argued that during the protracted period between the filing of structural suits and their resolution, the market conditions in an industry could change so dramatically that the remedies originally sought might be inappropriate by the time they are granted. Even before James C. Miller, III, joined the commission in 1981, the agency had terminated the *Exxon* case against the oil companies.

Changes in America's economic circumstances also affected the climate for antitrust. By the late 1970s, the country was beset with a host of domestic economic problems: inflation, unemployment, and high interest rates. In such an environment it became harder to justify the allocation of resources to actions designed to further social goals. Moreover, concerns about the increasing rigors of international competition led conservatives and liberals alike to argue that domestic constraints on firm size and industry concentration weakened the ability of American companies to go toe-to-toe with foreign competitors in world markets.

By 1980, the changing world of antitrust enforcement affected perceptions in the business community and in Congress of the Federal Trade Commission. Hailed only 5 years before as a vigorous proponent of consumer welfare, the agency was under attack.[9] The FTC Improvements Act of 1980 prohibited the FTC from petitioning the commissioner of patents for cancellation of a registered trademark on the basis that the trademark had become the common descriptive name for an article or substance. Investigations of insurance companies were banned unless authorized by a vote of either the House or Senate Commerce Committees.

Barred as well were investigations of agricultural marketing orders or prosecutions of agricultural cooperatives exempt from the antitrust laws by the Capper–Volstead Act. The Softdrink Interbrand Competition Act of 1980 exempted soft drink bottlers' exclusive territorial franchises from antitrust challenge if there were competition from other soft drink brands.

The FTC had been involved in a wide range of matters in the 1970s touching economic life. But it had not defied the legislative will. Congress vested the agency with broad powers, without providing clear directives as to the meaning of the ambiguous statutes underyling FTC authority. The Commission was, therefore, forced to fill the vacuum. To the extent that legislature made policy pronouncements, the FTC was most responsive; that Congress should turn against the agency was thus all the more curious.

In part, the FTC's reputation suffered because of growing doubts about the agency's capacity to prosecute big structural antitrust cases. The targets of agency activities undertook sophisticated lobbying campaigns. In the 1970s members of Congress were apt to praise the lofty ideals of the FTC; as I have written elsewhere, once those ideals moved from symbolism to concrete actions, the legislators had to deal with well-financed groups affected by agency efforts.[10]

It is also probably true that the Commission's approach in the late 1970s made the business community apprehensive. For instance, Chairman Michael Pertschuk supported the idea that the agency's powers be used against large institutions that allegedly exercised undue social and political influence as well as market power. In contrast, previous commissions justified their objectives in noncontroversial terms: increasing economic competition and enhancing consumer benefit. The irony is that these activist Republican-led commissions initiated the big structural cases, as well as the controversial rule-making proceedings of the seventies. Yet critics thought those cases indicative of the Pertschuk leadership's hostility toward business.

The FTC was also attacked because many considered it to be the engine of overregulation. This perception was rooted in some controversial consumer protection proceedings having to do with children's advertising and funeral homes. In fact, long before it was fashionable, the agency recognized that much of economic regulation is excessive and called for greater reliance on market mechanisms. Thus, it championed airline deregulation. Its rule-making proceedings relating to eyeglass, hearing aid, and drug industries reduced or eliminated restraints on advertising, provided more information to consumers, and promoted competition.

Whatever the combination of circumstances, the commission's standing had suffered by the time Ronald Reagan was elected president in November, 1980. The very fact of the agency's ill-fortune provided an opportunity for the new administration.

THE REAGAN-BUSH TRANSITION TEAM AND THE FEDERAL TRADE COMMISSION

After the election, a transition team headed by James C. Miller, III, went to work.[11] The final report evaluated the agency's existing programs and provided a clear blueprint as to its future direction. What is remarkable is that the FTC of 1988 is very close to the transition team's design.

From the outset, the transition team rejected the social and political objectives of antitrust.

> We believe that in allocating its scarce resources to various programs and activities, the Commission should be guided by the effects of its actions on consumers, or more explicitly the effects on economic efficiency. Obviously, this means that a decision to take issue with a particular business practice transcends the question of legality. One must ask whether the probable effects of the agency's actions would be to improve the functioning

> of the economy, bring about greater efficiencies, and increase consumer welfare. One must also ask whether these resources might be better used in other areas, where the potential impact might be even greater.[12]

Determining that the FTC's role is to promote competition and foster consumer welfare, the transition team concluded that the Commission had "all too often mischaracterized certain business practices as anticompetitive, and in making such determinations," had "tended to ignore the effects these practices have in lowering costs of otherwise creating efficiencies that ultimately improve the well-being of consumers."

The transition task force analyzed the FTC's antitrust activity in terms of agreements among competing firms to restrain competition; monopoly behavior; mergers; distributional restraints between sellers and buyers; Robinson-Patman Act; and dual enforcement by the FTC and the Department of Justice.

As to agreements to restrain competition, the task force criticized the commission's "shared monopoly" cases (launched, ironically during the Nixon years), asserting that these industry-wide programs were basically flawed. Objecting to the "market concentration doctrine," the Reagan transition team contended that, at most, concentration is an extremely crude preliminary indication of the extent of competition. Monopoly cases, it asserted, suffered from acceptance of the view that increasing market shares was indicative of illegal behavior. In its prosecutions against so-called predatory pricing, the agency failed to take account of empirical studies, finding such activity to be "rare, perhaps even nonexistent," and theoretical objections that assert that the predator will likely incur disproportionately large losses relative to those borne by its victims.

With regard to mergers, the transition team attacked cases brought against vertical mergers (combinations among potential or actual producers and suppliers) and conglomerate mergers (combinations among firms not competing directly or not in the same chain of distribution), charging that such cases did not have anticompetitive effects. Also under fire were distributional restraints, for example, resale price maintenance cases (in which the manufacturer insists that dealers sell its products at or above a certain price) and vertical market division prosecutions (involving the provision of exclusive territories by the manufacturer to its distributors). In its analysis, the transition team claimed that most of these cases involve products "appearing to require the production of at least some information on the local level to aid consumers in making informed judgments." The principal effect of FTC orders in these cases was to "force manufacturers to use less efficient means of providing information to consumers and to reduce the total amount of information available."

Condemning the Robinson-Patman Act as tending to chill price competition, and to impede the efficient allocation of resources, the report looked with approval upon the Commission's diminished enforcement of the legislation.

As to dual enforcement of the antitrust laws, the transition team observed that "[m]any have questioned whether public antitrust enforcement should be shared by two agencies, or whether the FTC's activities should be consolidated in the DOJ [Department of Justice]." Noting that the "arguments on both sides of the issue are quite strong and have numerous facets, (eliminating 'duplication,' reducing uncertainty for the business community, maintaining 'competition' among enforcement agencies, maintaining an antitrust agency free of 'political' domination, et cetera)," the group recommended that the matter deserved "further study."[13] Some took the mere fact that the transition team would not dismiss the possibility of eliminating the FTC's antitrust jurisdiction as evidence that the administration would contemplate such a step upon assuming office. Indeed, there was a shared sense among supporters and opponents of the notion that the transition task force was floating a trial balloon; if, indeed, serious opposition developed to the idea of stripping the FTC of antitrust authority, the administration could abandon it. In fact, congressional opposition doomed any such possible move. For his part, James C. Miller, III, who headed the transition task force team, and would later become chairman of the commission, denied that the administration was committed to abolishing dual antitrust enforcement. "[F]urther study," he stated, meant just that, and nothing more.

Not only was the transition team critical of the substance of FTC antitrust policy, it was also convinced that the agency's budget was bloated. It recommended that the agency's budget be slashed by more than 30 percent over the first 2 fiscal years alone (fiscal years 1981 and 1982).[14]

As to policy direction, the transition task force suggested that the commission "concentrate its resources on those horizontal collusion cases where injury is great and where the market will be slow to respond." In shifting its focus to those cases, the agency should evaluate critically the status of shared monopoly, vertical merger, business practice, and conglomerate merger cases. Even as to horizontal cases, the Commission should be wary of actions brought principally on "structural" grounds, noting that concentration per se is neither a necessary nor sufficient condition for a decision to prosecute. With respect to Robinson–Patman cases, the task force concluded that "even judicious selection of Robinson–Patman cases would constitute an inefficient means of supporting this segment [small business] of the economy."[15] Rather, it would make better sense to eliminate other restraints on small business, such as regulatory impediments. In de-emphasizing litigation as a means of improving market conditions, the Commission should provide more guidance for businesses so that they will better know whether their behavior complies with the law.

As an important part of FTC antitrust activities, the task force recommended that the agency reinforce its economic analysis and reporting: "[t]he agency's economists should play a greater role in deciding which initiatives are brought before the Commission."[16] Noting that if agency's economists disagree with a proposed initiative of the Bureau of Competition, the only recourse was to object when the matter was formally presented, the task force urged that the Bureau of Economics have a part in determining which proposals come before the Commission. For example, it suggested that consideration be given to establishing a policy of joint approval by the Director of the Bureau of Economics and the other operating bureaus before proceeding. Indicative of the value placed on economic analysis, the task force suggested that steps be taken to integrate physically the Bureau of Economics with the rest of the agency. "[L]ines of communication are strained," the transition report stated, because "the Bureau of Economics is housed over a mile away from the rest of the agency."

The Bureau of Economics, the transition team continued, should analyze regulatory and market imperfections, emphasizing studies of the effects of government activities on the competitive marketplace. In so doing, the FTC should expand its program of intervening before other (especially) federal agencies. With regard to two of the Bureau of Economics's more expensive programs, the Line of Business and Quarterly Financial Report, the team urged that consideration be given to transferring the latter to the Department of Commerce, and terminating the former, if a review did not show substantial benefits.

Highlighting its view that the FTC needed a change in direction, the team recommended that the president appoint a new chair from outside the agency: one who "shares the president's basic philosophy, who has proven leadership abilities, who is committed to filling key staff positions with qualified persons who share a new vision for the agency, and whose appointment would signal to Congress and the general public that the agency will take a new direction."

With regard to Congress, the task force suggested that Congress, upon President Reagan's recommendation, eliminate the regional offices, charging that they are "difficult to manage and are repositories of the misguided initiatives" noted above. Moreover, Congress should terminate the intervenor funding program, observing that such support (usually to consumer groups) was warranted only when an agency's staff is "captured" by those who are regulated, or when it is the most efficient way of acquiring information. Neither condition, the task force concluded, obtained. Congress should also define the term "unfairness" contained in section 5 of the FTC Act in ways consistent with the original legislative intent. Such a measure was required because, in the task force's view, courts had provided the agency with powers "far too broad and beyond original Congressional intent." The commission, itself, should take steps to define the term on its own initiative; "complementary action by Congress would be even better."[17]

THE FTC AND ANTITRUST: 1981–1988

The transition report guided the Commission throughout the 1980s. In order to understand agency policy-making, I look first at the internal factors affecting the decision to prosecute in the Miller commission and the Oliver commission. I then consider the impact of external forces: the presidency, Congress, and the courts.

Internal Factors

The Miller Commission, 1981–1985

Changing personnel. Looking back on his tenure at the FTC, James Miller reviewed the transition report and concluded: "we achieved all of our objectives except for two: elimination of the regional offices, and a legislative change in section 5 of the FTC Act."[18] A clear management strategy was central to those successes.

Miller largely accomplished his purposes. A man well-schooled in the politics of regulation, Miller had been a senior staff economist for the Council of Economic Advisers, and Assistant Director for Government Operations and Research of the Council on Wage and Price Stability during the Ford administration. When the Republicans left the White House in January, 1977, Miller went to the American Enterprise Institute as codirector of the Center for Study of Government Regulation.

After the election of Ronald Reagan, Miller played a key role in the transition, and, as I have noted, he was "captain" of the team that produced the task force report for the new administration. In 1981, he became administrator for Information and Regulatory Affairs of the Office of Management and Budget (OMB), and executive director of the Presidential Task Force on Regulatory Relief. In those capacities, he was largely responsible for Executive Order 12,291, which sought to impose presidential control over the regulatory process, by centralizing authority in OMB to resolve tradeoffs among competing statutes and agencies.

During much of the first year of the Reagan presidency, while Miller was focusing on regulatory matters at OMB, FTC Commissioner David Clanton served as acting chairperson. Clanton was a Republican, but it was clear that the administration, true to the recommendation of the Miller task force, would name a new chairman from outside the agency. That indeed happened when President Reagan appointed Miller as FTC chairperson before the year was out.

In taking the helm of the FTC, Miller had obvious advantages that other agency heads seldom enjoy. Having served as the leader of the transition task force, he knew quite a lot about the organization's structure. Moreover, Miller had a strong sense of what the policy direction should be. The appointment of an economist to lead the commission—a traditionally lawyer-dominated organization—signaled that some changes would be made, or at least attempted.

To refashion the agency's agenda, Miller would have to have the support of two other commissioners (thus having a working majority of the commission). Soon he did, with the appointment of fellow economist George Douglas, and lawyer Terry Calvani. Douglas was a personal friend of Miller, and Calvani, a law professor at Vanderbilt, was sympathetic to the law and economics approach. The majority of Miller, Douglas, and Calvani left the two holdovers from the Carter commission—Patricia Bailey and Michael Pertschuk—in the lonely minority. Former chairperson Pertschuk would serve his term as commissioner until 1984, issuing dissents and producing reports critical of the Miller commission. It is perhaps worth stating the obvious: without the Douglas and Calvani appointments, Miller would have had a much more difficult task reshaping the commission's agenda. Miller played a role in the president's selection of the commissioners. He recognized that it was through the appointment process that the chair secures control of the agency, and, more broadly, that a president could further his own policy objectives if he appointed individuals who shared his perspectives.

That philosophy extended to the appointments of the key officials throughout the agency. To lead the Bureau of Economics, Miller appointed Robert Tollison, then an economist at Clemson University, and a proponent of public choice theory. Thomas Campbell, a young law professor at Stanford with a doctorate in economics, became the director of the Bureau of Competition. The appointment was perfectly suited to Miller's view that prosecutorial bent of the Bureau of Competition needed to be curbed. As I noted in *Regulatory Bureaucracy,* the director of the Bureau of Competition has typically been a practicing lawyer, who sought to bring big cases. Such a course would have the incidental effect of making her more attractive to the private bar, whose ranks she would someday rejoin.[19] That was not what Miller wanted. Rather, he sought someone who allied him- or herself with the law and economics school, and thus was sympathetic to reshaping antitrust policy. It made sense to choose an academic whose professional incentives were not to secure the approval of the private bar but of his or her law and economics school colleagues.

Miller's other major appointees tended to come from academia as well. Bruce Yandle, an economist from Clemson University, became the executive director. Wendy Gramm, an economist from Texas A & M, and friend of Miller's would succeed Tollison as director of the Bureau of Economics. Timothy Muris, a professor of law at the University of Miami School of Law, followed Campbell as director of the Bureau of Competition, upon the latter's return to academia in 1983.[20]

Muris deserves special mention because he was widely regarded as Miller's key lieutenant at the commission. In the mid-1970s, when in his midtwenties, Muris was assistant to the director of the Office of Policy Planning and Evaluation, Wesley Liebler, an advocate of the Chicago School. After leaving the agency in 1976, Muris was a Law and Economics Fellow at the University of Chicago, before joining the faculty at Miami as a teacher of law and economics. With the election of Ronald Reagan, Muris became a key member of the Reagan–Bush transition team for the Federal Trade Commission, and was named deputy counsel for the presidential task force on regulatory relief in 1981. Later that year, Muris moved to the FTC as director of the Bureau of Consumer Protection, a position he held until becoming director of the Bureau of Competition in 1983.

Organizational structure: The Bureau of Competition and the Bureau of Economics. With like-minded people to direct the various operating bureaus, Miller did little to change the organizational structure of the agency. The one exception was the Office of Policy Planning. The chair moved successfully to eliminate that office (headed by Robert Reich during the Pertschuk years). Miller's view was simple. The agency should be doing less rather than more. Having an office of policy planning served only to generate new initiatives, and thus was antithetical to the FTC agenda.

The Bureau of Competition retained the same decision-making processes as described in *Regulatory Bureaucracy.*[21] The bureau has two committees evaluating case projects, one for mergers, the other for the remainder of its cases. Almost all cases initiated in the bureau are evaluated at an early stage by either the evaluation committee or the merger screening committee. Both committees are advisory in nature; the bureau director or his or her designee makes the final decision. Evaluation and merger screening committee meetings include staff attorneys proposing a case, their supervisors, Evaluation Office attorneys, representatives of the Bureau of Economics, the Bureau Director, Deputy Directors, and are open to other interested Bureau of Competition staff members. The Merger Screening Committee meets weekly and the Evaluation Committee monthly.

Bureau of Competition attorneys are required to seek Evaluation Committee review before converting nonmerger initial phase investigations (usually limited to 100 hours) to full phase. That committee review begins when staff attorneys prepare and submit a memorandum summarizing the facts uncovered in initial phase investigation and the legal and economic theories on which a case might be built. Evaluation Office attorneys and the Bureau of Economics review these memoranda before the committee meets, normally preparing written summaries or comments on the matters to be examined. At the Evaluation Committee meeting, staff attorneys, Evaluation Office lawyers, and representatives from the Bureau of Economics offer comments and recommendations. The Evaluation Office summarizes discussions of each case, and the Bureau Director's Decisions are distributed to the staff attorneys in a short memorandum sometime after the meeting.

The FTC of the 1980s also retained a central feature of the organizational design of the 1970s: independence of the Bureau of Economics from the Bureau of Competition in the decision-making process. At the same time, the Miller commission sought to reinforce its view that economic analysis was more important than legal precedent in determining whether to undertake an investigation or issue a complaint. Faithful to the transition team's recommendation, the key personnel of the Bureau of Economics moved to the main building on Pennsylvania Avenue. The presence of two economists on the commission, one of whom was the chair, underscores the signal that economics would take precedence over legal doctrine.

The Commission eliminated in 1983 the permanent research staff in the Industry Analysis Division. Henceforth, economic studies, in keeping with a recommendation of the Grace Commission, would be geared toward continuing commission activities. In the past, the agency allowed its staff to pursue research studies bearing on microeconomic policy, which were not necessarily related to FTC proceedings. In addition, pursuant to the recommendation of the transition task force, the Commission in 1982 transferred the Quarterly Financial Report to the Department of Commerce. The agency also moved to cut drastically the controversial Line of Business program, consistent with the transition report.

I found particularly interesting the change in perspective of the Bureau of Competition leadership toward the Bureau of Economics. In the 1970s, the Bureau of Competition's view of the Bureau of Economics was strategic. It was important to take into account the economists' judgments about possible actions, not because they were necessarily right but because their opposition would make it more difficult to secure the commissioners' approval. Although legal doctrines had priority over economic ones in the commission of the 1970s, to the extent that economic analysis was assuming increasing importance, the Bureau of Competition had to be mindful of their counterparts. In the Bureau of Competition of the 1980s, the relationship was inspired far less by tactical concerns than by a shared view of antitrust policy. The bureau directors of Competition and Economics agreed that the primary determinant of whether a case should be pursued is whether it makes sense in terms of the principles of microeconomics (as understood by the Chicago School). They shared the opinion that governmental regulation is often counterproductive; the market should be allowed to work. In the exercise of its discretion, the Federal Trade Commission should ignore other criteria (political or social) at variance with the enhancement of consumer welfare. Lawsuits, they asserted, should be used to further those economic principles, as vehicles to set new precedents, and to reverse misguided ones.

The clashes between the Bureau of Competition and the Bureau of Economics, for the most part, were not over whether legal concerns should predominate over economic ones, but over whether microeconomic principles have been correctly applied. As one Bureau of Economics official stated:

> There are few things more frustrating than to argue with a bunch of lawyers who think they know more economics than we do. Our aggravation at times is only compounded when you add into the mix a few economist-commissioners who, though they've been away from the academic discipline for a long time, think they are better economists than we are.

FTC lawyers: The impact of new thinking about antitrust. However much the commissioners and the leadership of the Bureau of Competition and the Bureau of Economics might agree on how antitrust policy should be changed, they still, it is assumed, had to overcome opposition from the lawyers in the agency. After all, the Commission of the 1960s and 1970s was still a lawyer's agency. Most staff attorneys during those years looked to legal doctrine as their primary referent. Further, their objective was to secure as much trial experience as possible, and to make themselves attractive to the private bar (which they hoped to join after 3 or 4 years of government service). In short, they were prosecution-minded, and preferred the conduct cases to the more difficult structural cases.

In fact, the Miller commission did not have to be very concerned with accommodating disaffected attorneys eager for trial experience. The leadership deliberately sought to reduce the staff of the Bureau of Competition; the chair and the bureau director wanted attorneys to leave as part of their effort to lessen reliance on litigation. When attorneys left as a result of the usual turnover (lawyers serve on staff, on average, for 3.4 years), their positions were generally not filled. If a devotee of the Robinson-Patman Act left (and there were few by 1981), he or she was not replaced. To the extent that the commission recruited for staff attorney positions, they attracted people who shared the leadership's views about antitrust policy. As described in greater detail below, finding such individuals has become less difficult than in years past because of changes in legal thinking about antitrust.

All this is not to suggest that young recruits in the 1980s lost their desire to prosecute cases. Because of a reduction in staff and resources, the agency could pursue fewer cases; but there were enough "worthy" cases by the new standards to satisfy the lawyers' objective of securing trial experience.

Whether and how the quality of staff attorneys changed since the 1980s is hard to measure. The commission officials with whom I talked suggested that the widening disparity in salaries between the public and private sector had adversely affected recruitment. In the early 1970s, there was probably no more than a $5,000 to $10,000 difference between the starting salaries of New York and government attorneys (especially those in honors programs). For a young law school graduate, government service had the attraction of providing more responsibility than private practice. The tradeoff between money and more experience could tilt toward the latter, at least for the first few years in a lawyer's career. The 1970s were also a time when young attorneys, spurred on by the Naderite "public interest" movement, looked to government service as a means to pursue their ideals. But, as one Bureau of Competition official noted: "[by the mid 1980s] the *difference* between starting salaries in N.Y. firms and government offices . . . [was] as much as forty-five thousand dollars. We just don't stand a chance of getting the best talent, even for the first few years."

Important changes in how a growing segment of the legal profession approaches antitrust issues aided the FTC as it sought to alter the antitrust agenda.

Law school professors in general, and antitrust professors in specific, have traditionally used a pedagogical technique known as the case method. Course readings and classroom discussions have centered on past judicial opinions and their implications for the resolution of hypothetical cases. In antitrust courses, students have read, and reasoned from, judicial decisions that reflected the several types of values—political, social, and economic—underlying the major antitrust statutes, and they have become accustomed to thinking about antitrust issues from these several perspectives.

In recent years, however, the case method has been supplemented in most law schools by other approaches: lectures, interdisciplinary inquiries, simulations, and clinical training. Instruction in the fundamentals of microeconomic analysis has become a core component of most antitrust courses, and it is no exaggeration to say that in many classes the fundamental question antitrust students are adjured to focus on is not whether a particular judicial decision makes sense in terms of past cases, but whether it makes sense from the standpoint of economics. The political and social purposes of the antitrust laws are given less attention, and therefore less credence, than they were when the standard case method of training was employed. Thus, Robert Bork, a leading expositor of the Chicago perspective, has offered this assessment of the Robinson-Patman Act: "The Robinson-Patman Act is the *Fanny Hill* of antitrust—a statute no man should let his daughter read. Outright repeal, I think, is the only answer." Lawyers who have been trained to address antitrust issues from an economics perspectives are less apt than their predecessors to launch antitrust enforcement actions to serve noneconomic objectives.

The commissioners' criteria for determining whether to issue a complaint. As I explained in *Regulatory Bureaucracy,* in deciding whether to issue a complaint, commissioners must decide that there is reason to believe that the law has been violated and that commission action would be in the public interest.[22] Because the "public interest" is not defined in law or statute, a commissioner has the latitude to consider legal, economic, political, and other factors in reaching a decision—reflecting the diverse reasons that underly many of the antitrust statutes. The factors that commissioners considered in evaluating a complaint recommendation were the same, although there was a much heavier emphasis on economic principles as understood by the Chicago School. The judiciary, as will be described below, has been gradually changing antitrust doctrines to reflect new legal and economic thinking. That shift affected the commissioners' decision-making calculus as well.

The Miller commission and agency decision-making: A summation. In 1985, the commission leadership changed when James C. Miller, III, became the director of the Office of Management and Budget. Among the people he took with him were Timothy Muris, then director of the Bureau of Competition, and Wendy Gramm, the director of the Bureau of Economics. (Gramm, incidentally, became administrator of the Office of Information and Regulatory Analysis [OIRA], a position previously held by Miller and Christopher De Muth.)

In the nearly 4 years that Miller chaired the Commission, the agency had sharply shifted policy. Shared-monopoly cases were in the past. The Commission had terminated the *Kellogg* (cereal) case. The agency closed the door on prosecutions of vertical mergers, conglomerate mergers, structurally grounded horizontal mergers, and Robinson-Patman cases. In 1982, the Commission issued merger guidelines that signaled a more relaxed attitude toward horizontal restraints. During the Miller years, the commission approved what was then, at least, the largest merger in history, SoCal's $13 billion acquisition of Gulf. It also cleared the General Motors/Toyota joint venture.

As to those who criticized the commission's sharp drop in prosecutions, agency officials responded that figures are meaningful only if one accepts the premise that more enforcement actions (such as lawsuits) necessarily mean more effective law enforcement. To the contrary, Miller commission supporters contended that in any law enforcement activity the measure of success is not the number of prosecutions but the level of compliance with the law.

In changing direction, the commission brought suits, and intervened before state and local authorities, to promote competition with the professions and to seek removal of licensing requirements and regulations that unreasonably constrain market entry. It did this while sharply reducing its workforce, such that the competition mission in 1988 was some 40 percent less than it was when Ronald Reagan became president.

The Oliver Commission, 1986–1989. For about a year Terry Calvani served as the caretaker chair. In early 1986, President Reagan appointed and the Senate confirmed Daniel Oliver as the new FTC chair. Then serving as the general counsel of the Department of Agriculture, Oliver had previously held the same position in the Department of Education. A lawyer by training, Oliver had long been active in conservative politics, including a stint as director of research for James L. Buckley's successful 1970 senatorial campaign. Oliver's association with the Buckley family is a long one. In the early 1970s he was assistant to William Buckley at the *National Review,* and later became the magazine's executive director. Although he had no particular expertise in antitrust or consumer protection, Oliver did have some Wall Street experience.

For director of the bureau of competition, Oliver selected Jeffrey Zuckerman, a lawyer with a strong economics background. An experienced attorney, Zuckerman had served as special assistant to William Baxter, then assistant attorney general for antitrust, and later as staff director of the Equal Employment Opportunity Commission (EEOC). His application of economic principles to cases alleging gender discrimination led to the Senate Committee on Labor and Human Resources' rejection of his nomination in 1985 to be general counsel of the EEOC. In 1986, he joined the FTC.

For director of the Bureau of Economics, the new chair chose a careerist, David Sheffman. In so doing, he departed from the decade-old tradition of appointing an academic on leave from a university. Some economists believed that the bureau's ability to attract first-rate talent depended upon having a well-known scholar as bureau head, and that only such an individual would feel secure enough to challenge the Bureau of Competition and the commissioners. Others concluded that having a careerist would lend stability to the bureau.

Oliver continued the policies of the Miller commission. He looked to economists and economic analysis. As chair, Oliver was particularly spirited in using the agency to intervene before other governmental bodies in support of deregulation. He endorsed the view that the duties of the Post Office be turned over to the private sector.

The FTC's structure remained essentially the same, although Oliver restored a small Office of Policy Development to the organizational chart. The office was to advise the commission as to its future direction.

Oliver's management style differed sharply from Miller's. Miller put a premium on meeting with agency staff on a regular basis. Oliver was far more removed from the daily operations of the agency. Unlike Miller, he did not have the same opportunity to be involved in the selection of fellow commissioners. Although there was general agreement about the agency's continued policy direction, some concern has surfaced about the effect of the massive budget cuts. "At what point do we cut so close to the bone that we can't do anything?" one commissioner asked.

External Factors

Consideration of external factors that could affect agency action requires examination of the presidency, Congress, and the courts.

The Presidency. In early 1981, at the beginning of the Reagan presidency, OMB floated two trial balloons bearing on FTC activities, both considered in the administration's initial budget: one called for the closing of the 10 regional offices, and the other sought to eliminate the agency's antitrust activities (which the Department of Justice would be called upon to assume). These proposals reflected OMB director David Stockman's view that the FTC is "a passel of ideologues who are hostile to the business system, to the free enterprise system, and who sit down there and invent theories that justify more meddling and interference in the economy."[23] "If you eliminated the FTC, the world would never know the difference." Largely because of the opposition of congressional committees, as always loath to relinquish jurisdiction (but, as will be described below, acquiescent in the steady trend to cut the agency's budget), OMB quickly withdrew its proposal to eliminate antitrust and lost in its effort to close the regional offices.

It is in some sense artificial to view OMB as an external force seeking to impose change on the FTC in light of the former's close ties—almost blood ties—to the latter. OMB's proposals were consistent with the judgments of James C. Miller, III, the agency's administrator of the Office of Information and Regulatory Analysis—the man who was responsible for the transition task force report. When Miller became chair of the commission by the autumn of 1981, he did not leave behind his OMB contacts. Nor were his views lost on the OMB examiners. Both the OMB and the FTC agreed that the agency's budget should be drastically cut. Both moved in tandem to realize that end. In 1985, when Miller returned to OMB, he brought with him Wendy Gramm (the new OIRA administrator), Bryce Harlow (the new associated director for legislative affairs), John Carley (the new general counsel), and Timothy Muris (the new associate executive director for budget and legislation). All this served to tighten the identity of perspectives of the FTC and OMB. As one FTC official concerned with matters of budget and finance observed:

> In dealing with OMB, the typical case is for an agency to ask for a higher figure than it thinks it's going to get from OMB. At the FTC, we don't have to 'game' things out. We come in with a figure, and we usually get close to that figure. That is the measure of the closeness of our relationship with OMB.

Congress. In *Regulatory Bureaucracy,* I concluded that Congress did not determine the FTC's antitrust caseload, although it would occasionally show its dissatisfaction with particular actions or encourage agency officials to intensify their efforts in various areas.[24] Examination of the agency's internal dynamics best explained the decision to prosecute individual cases. Congress generally sanctioned FTC policy. The experience of the 1980s reinforces these findings. As an empirical matter, the congressional dominance view does not withstand scrutiny.

To be sure, congressional committees, mindful of preserving their formal jurisdiction over the FTC, rejected efforts to eliminate agency functions or structures. Thus, in the early months of the Reagan administration, before James C. Miller, III, became the FTC chair, congressional committees successfully joined with a united commission to oppose OMB's proposal to eliminate antitrust enforcement. Congressional committees also rejected Miller's attempts to close the 10 regional offices. In 1983, the Appropriations Committees of both houses of Congress determined that all 10 regional offices should remain open.

With respect to broad policy and, even more, with regard to particular cases, Congress largely allowed the FTC to pursue its agenda in the 1980s. The appropriations committees, consistent with FTC requests, steadily cut the agency's budget, although not as much as the FTC would have wanted. Still, 8 years into the Reagan administration, Congress had reduced the FTC's Bureau of Competition workforce by some 40 percent. Facilitating this downward trend was Congress's effort to satisfy Gramm–Rudman–Hollings targets. As a consequence, the FTC came to expect automatic across-the-board cuts. The continuing resolution, a mechanism Congress uses to wrap all of the 13 regular appropriations bills into a single passage, also reinforced the trend toward budget cuts. Those resolutions effectively required agencies to absorb pay raises in the context of their lowered budgets.

As problems of the deficit gain greater attention, the FTC, with its relatively small budget, received less scrutiny. Explained one agency official: "The same appropriations committees that look at us also look at the Department of State, Justice, Commerce and a whole host of other regulatory agencies. We're just a drop in the bucket." Commission Calvani put it this way: "In dollar terms, we're less than the wings of a B-1 bomber. So why should the appropriations committees bother with us?"

From time to time, the appropriations committees included language restricting particular agency activities. For instance, in 1984, after the FTC issued a complaint challenging municipal taxicab regulations, Congress adopted an appropriations measure forbidding the commission from using its fiscal year 1985 funds to prosecute antitrust suits against cities. The prohibition was removed not long thereafter. Such restrictions were the exception—however annoying they may have been to the Commission—rather than the rule.

Since October 31, 1982, the FTC has operated without reauthorization. The last measure authorizing commission activities expired on that date. In the House, the Energy and Commerce Committee reported, and the full chamber approved, reauthorization legislation in both the 98th and 99th Congresses, which failed to become law. On the Senate side, the Committee on Science, Commerce, and Transportation reported legislation that the full body did act upon in the 98th Congress; in the succeeding Congress, the Senate did act, but failed in conference to secure agreement needed for passage. A major stumbling block centered around efforts to restrict commission activities affecting professionals, such as lawyers and doctors, regulated by state governments. The American Bar Association and the American Medical Association, among other groups, fought to prevent the FTC from exercising jurisdiction over state-regulated professions.

For Chair Miller, congressional reauthorization was of top priority. It was important, he argued, for Congress to guide the agency affirmatively as to its course. For Chairman Oliver, the absence of reauthorization made no real difference. In the absence of authorizing legislation, the legislative committees sought to continue restrictions in the FTC Improvements Act of 1980 (the legislation that expired on October 31, 1982) in annual appropriation bills and continuing resolutions. Through such mechanisms, Congress maintained restrictions on agency prosecutions of agricultural cooperatives and federal credit unions.

As to oversight and investigations, the Subcommittee on Transportation, Tourism, and Hazardous Materials, chaired by James Florio (Democrat–New Jersey), of the House Committee on Energy and Commerce continued to monitor agency activities. John Dingell (Democrat–Michigan), the chair of the full committee, from time to time encouraged investigations of the agency. On the Senate side, in the years 1980 to 1986, oversight of the commission's antitrust activities was limited because Strom Thurmond, the chairman of the Judiciary Committee, eliminated the Subcommittee on Antitrust and Monopoly. That subcommittee, chaired in the 1970s by such aggressive overseers as Philip Hart (Democrat–Michigan) and Howard Metzenbaum (Democrat–Ohio), held many hearings to promote the strengthening of the antitrust laws. The rebirth of the subcommittee in 1987, upon the recapturing of Democratic control of the Senate, led to renewed activity. But those efforts in the late 1980s were directed more to general enforcement of antitrust laws than to specific cases. The Subcommittee on Consumer Protection of the Committee on Commerce, Science and Transportation sought to redirect resources from the agency's economics mission to the regional offices. Again, such a measure was geared more toward general policy than to specific cases.

Congress may occasionally make its preferences felt, and may impose restrictions on some activities. Yet the FTC remained largely free to set its own caseload. When chair Miller invited me to meet with him and his staff (all of the bureau directors were present), I asked them to what extent Congress "controlled the Commission." As one commission official put it: "The problem for us is to get Congress to say what it wants. The problem is that they seldom say anything." He continued that except for "bothersome congressional hearings, and occasionally stupid battles over whether we can promote competition among professions, we can do just about anything—or not do just about anything." Commented another "Congress doesn't want to make hard choices. . . . But from an enforcement perspective we benefit. We have the latitude to do what we want, until those rare, selective occasions when Congress says no."

In the course of another round of interviews in 1987 and 1988, another agency official observed: "Sure, a congressman might have us on the carpet. It's all for the benefit of particular constituents. After he chews us out, he satisfies his constituents, and things go on exactly as before." Noted one commissioner, "Congress enters our thoughts. You know that if you write something down on a scrap of paper, you better be careful . . . To say that Congress or its committees set our caseload is simplistic. I guess it's downright wrong." Said another agency decision-maker:

> Some call it arrogance, others aloofness. But I've been able to get along quite well, thank you, by having to do as little with the Hill as possible. . . . If we paid too much attention to Congress, would we be so insistent on preserving our program of intervening before state agencies to promote competition? If we were Congress's lackey, we would have caved in long ago.

The Courts. An external factor helpful to the FTC as it has sought to change direction has been the federal judiciary. As legal thinking has changed, so have court decisions. Recent law school graduates bring a law-and-economics background to their work as clerks to federal judges, and some of the most vigorous academic proponents of an economics-grounded understanding of antitrust—among them Robert Bork, Richard Posner, Ralph Winter, and Douglas Ginsburg—were appointed to the bench in the 1980s. Legal doctrines began to change, sanctioned by the Supreme Court, in ways that favor the economics approach. As early as 1974, the Supreme Court began to retreat from the structure–conduct–practice paradigm.[25] With respect to vertical restraints, the Supreme Court, relying on Bork, Posner, and Donald Turner, reversed the per se ban on nonprice vertical restraints it had established in *Schwinn.*[26] It became common to read judicial opinions citing the law and economics literature, particularly the treatise of Philip Areeda and Donald Turner. It may very well be that the kinds of cases brought in previous decades on political and social grounds would not survive today; indeed, the commission suffered defeats in federal courts in the late 1970s as doctrines began to change. All this served to relieve pressure on the FTC to initiate such actions.

CONCLUSION

In the 1980s the Federal Trade Commission underwent significant changes in policy direction. Gone were the structural shared-monopoly cases of the 1970s. No longer did the agency pursue cases based on traditional social and economic grounds. The Commission continued the downward enforcement trend of the Robinson-Patman Act. The agency strengthened its reliance on economic thinking (Chicago-style). The Commission cut its workforce by some 40 percent in the period 1981 to 1988 (from 531 work years in fiscal 1980 to 326 work years in fiscal 1989).[27] The impetus for these changes had mostly to do with the Commission itself. A vigorous leadership, a coherent management strategy, growing acceptance of new economics theories, and the evolution of legal thinking all were instrumental in the shift in antitrust policy-making. The agency used external forces—the presidency, Congress, and the courts—to its advantage.

All this reinforces the conclusion that we cannot understand agency decision-making solely by focusing on Congress as the determinant of FTC activity. The explanation lies instead in the full panoply of factors, external and internal, that affect organizational behavior.

REFERENCES

1. Robert A. Katzmann, *Regulatory Bureaucracy: The Federal Trade Commission and Antitrust Policy* (Cambridge, MA: MIT Press, 1980, paperback edition with new afterword, 1981) (hereinafter referred to as *Regulatory Bureaucracy*).
2. See, for example, James Q. Wilson, *Bureaucracy: What Government Agencies Do and Why They Do It* (New York: Basic Books, 1989).
3. For other accounts of the Federal Trade Commission during this period, see, for example, Kenneth Clarkson and Timothy Muris, eds., *The Federal Trade Commission Since 1970: Economic Regulation and Bureaucratic Behavior* (Cambridge: Cambridge University Press, 1981); William Kovacic, The Federal Trade Commission and congressional oversight of antitrust enforcement, 17 *Tulsa Law Journal* 587 (1982).
4. See, for example, Barry R. Weingast and Mark J. Moran, Bureaucratic discretion or congressional control? Regulatory policymaking by the Federal Trade Commission, *Journal of Political Economy* 91 (1983): 765–800; Randall L. Calvert, Mark J. Moran, and Barry Weingast, Congressional influence over policy making: The case of the FTC, in M. McCubbins and T. Sullivan, eds., *Congress: Structure and Policy* (Cambridge: Cambridge University Press, 1987); R. J. Mackay, J. C. Miller III, and B. Yandle, eds., *Public Choice & Regulation* (Stanford, CA: Hoover Institution, 1987).
5. See, e.g., Robert Katzmann, Letter to the editor, *Regulation Magazine,* Sept./Oct. 1982, pp. 4 and 56; Terry M. Moe, Congressional control of the bureaucracy: An assessment of the positive theory of "Congressional Dominance," *Legislative Studies Quarterly,* 12 (1987): 474–521; James Q. Wilson, note 2 supra, pp. 254–256; Timothy J. Muris Regulatory policymaking at the Federal Trade Commission: The extent of congressional control, *Journal of Political Economy* 94 (1986): 884–89.
6. FTC commissioners themselves agree on the importance of examining all of these factors. See, for example, Robert Pitofsky, Agency structure, case selection, and public policy: Antitrust enforcement at the FTC (a review of *Regulatory Bureaucracy*), 90 *Yale Law Journal* 726–40 (1981); Mary Gardiner Jones, Review of *Regulatory Bureaucracy,* in 15 *The Journal of Consumer Affairs* 175–178 (1981).
7. I undertook this examination at the invitation of James Q. Wilson to provide some assistance for his monumental work, *Bureaucracy*. I am grateful for that opportunity. With the wonderful aid of the FTC official Anna Davis, I was granted interviews throughout the agency in 1987 and 1988. I honor the pledge of confidentiality I gave to all those interviewed. Attributions are offered only in those circumstances in which remarks were made on the public record.

8. For a fine analysis of changes in antitrust policy, see Mark Allen Eisner, *Antitrust and the Triumph of Economics: Institutions, Expertise, & Policy Change* (Chapel Hill: The University of North Carolina Press, 1991); see also Robert Katzmann, The attenuation of antitrust, *Brookings Review,* summer 1984, pp. 23–27.
9. For an illuminating account, see Michael Pertschuk, *Revolt Against Regulation: The Rise and Pause of the Consumer Movement* (Berkeley: University of California Press, 1982), and Richard A. Harris and Sidney M. Milkis, *The Politics of Regulating Change: A Tale of Two Agencies* (Oxford: Oxford University Press, 1989).
10 *Regulatory Bureaucracy* (1981 edition), p. 214; Robert A. Katzmann, Capitol Hill's current attack against the FTC, *Wall Street Journal,* May 7, 1980.
11. In addition to Miller, the transition team consisted of Carol Crawford, Harry Diffendal, Jeffrey Eisenach, Kendall Fleeharty, Michael Horowitz, Kenneth Lazarus, Timothy Muris, Peter Pitsch, and Robert D. Tollison.
12. The introductory sections of the transition report were reprinted in the *Congressional Record*: 127 *Cong. Rec.* S10162–S10169 (daily ed. September 21, 1981). The Conclusions and Recommendations section is reprinted in *Antitrust and Trade Regulation Report,* No. 999, G-1–G-3, January 29, 1981 (hereinafter referred to as Conclusions and Recommendations).
13. Conclusions and Recommendations, G-3.
14. Conclusions and Recommendations, G-3.
15. Conclusions and Recommendations, G-1.
16. Conclusions and Recommendations, G-2.
17. Conclusions and Recommendations, G-3.
18. I am grateful to then-Chairman Miller for inviting me to have lunch with him and his bureau directors in the fall of 1984 and sharing their reflections with me. Miller describes his roles in James C. Miller III, *The Economist as Reformer: Revamping the FTC, 1981–1985* (Washington, D.C.: American Enterprise Institute, 1989).
19. *Regulatory Bureaucracy,* pp. 89–92.
20. Campbell would later be elected to the U.S.House of Representatives from California.
21. *Regulatory Bureaucracy,* pp. 15–26.
22. *Regulatory Bureaucracy,* pp. 96–108.
23. *Chicago Tribune,* February 23, 1981, p. A1.
24. *Regulatory Bureaucracy,* pp. 140–160.
25. *United States v. General Dynamics Corp.,* 415 U.S. 486 (1974).
26. See *Continental T.V. Inc. et al. v. GTE SYLVANIA, Inc.,* 433 U.S. 33 (1977).
27. An evaluation of the consequences of the shift in FTC policy can be found in American Bar Association, *Report of the American Bar Association Section of Antitrust Law, Special Committee to Study the Role of the Federal Trade Commission* (American Bar Association, 1989).

IV

RULES AND ENFORCEMENT

13

The Elements of Rule-Making

Cornelius M. Kerwin *The American University, Washington, D.C.*

Rule-making is the single most important function performed by agencies of government.

This assertion will be surprising to some and be dismissed as hyperbole by others. Such skepticism is understandable given the scant attention afforded rule-making in the mainstream literature of public administration. Inattention notwithstanding, the rationale for placing rule-making foremost among bureaucratic functions is substantial and compelling.

Rule-making is law-making. It is the exercise of our most basic constitutional power by administrative officials. In at least two ways it is more significant than the legislating done by Congress. First, the quantity of rules issued by agencies of the federal government each year dwarfs the output of congressional legislation. Compared to the thousands of proposed and final rules produced each year by agencies, the few hundred statutes enacted by Congress appear few. A simple quantitative comparison of statutes to rules is of limited value. Statutes often have far-reaching consequences while a given rule may be quite narrow in application. However, the cumulative effects of rule-making are broader and deeper than those of congressional legislation. It is the reach of rules and their relative influence on life in America that qualifies rule-making as the pre-eminent function of public administration.

Rules profoundly and ubiquitously affect the conduct and quality of life in this nation. Whether it is the factory owner who uses hazardous materials, a Social Security recipient concerned about the availability of health care, an airline mechanic attempting to repair a worn jet engine part, or any of the rest of us with our personal regulatory or entitlement issues, we turn to rules, and not their precursor statutes, for guidance about our rights and obligations. While it is certainly true that no rule can exist unless it is authorized by statute, few if any statutes can be implemented before rules are written. Put simply it is rules, not statutes, that tell us how to order our affairs.

Rule-making drives most of the other functions and activities performed by administrative agencies. It transforms the goals, objectives, mandates, and promises of statutes into the more precise standards and procedures needed to establish operating programs. Rule-making thus determines where and how large amounts of public resources, human and financial, will be spent. The contents of the rules also frequently require expenditures for compliance by both benefiting and regulated parties in the private sector. These compliance costs often dwarf the budgets of agencies administering the programs in question. Finally, the results of rule-making often trigger conflict that will be absorbed by the dispute resolution and adjudicatory processes of both agencies and courts. In short, rule-making provides the substantive and procedural content of public programs for which many other internal functions, bureaucratic and legal, provide support.

Our current dependence on rule-making is a more extreme version of a situation that has been with us for some time. In 1941, commenting on the reasons why rule-making was then an important element in the administrative process, a landmark study isolated two reasons why rulemaking had become so prominent: "(t)he increasing use by Congress of skeleton legislation" and "the expansion of the field of Federal control" (Committee on Administrative Procedure, 1941:98). Neither of these factors has diminished in importance over time. Legislation may be less skeletal but most laws still lack essential details, at least according to most serious observers of Congress. While at a slower pace than in previous periods, the reach of the federal government continues to grow. At this point, one is hard pressed to locate an area of contemporary life untouched by government; it is important to appreciate the role of rule-making in this vast enterprise.

Rule-making is much more than a mere by-product of governmental growth. On the contrary, it should be viewed as the device that allowed government to grow at the rate it did during the past half century. Without rule-making, congressional legislation would have to provide the massive detail needed in the design and implementation of public programs. Rule-making frees the Congress to respond broadly to the full range of public demands for action, secure in the knowledge that the lion's share of highly technical and frequently politically charged decisions about program operations would be made elsewhere. In this sense, rule-making is a fundamental element in our representative democracy because it allows Congress to deal, however superficially, with a much larger number of demands from constituents than would otherwise be the case. Rule-making is also a political appliance of great value to Congress. Faced with difficult political issues that divide powerful constituencies, it is often convenient, not to say prudent, to transfer responsibility for their resolution to the bureaucracy (Fiorina, 1982). Rulemaking allows Congress implicitly to promise satisfactory outcomes from this subsequent process without the risks attendant on actually making a decision.

Congress is not the only branch of government or political institution that finds rule-making attractive. While the enormous volume of rules severely challenges the capacity of a president to influence American domestic policy, rule-making also provides a president great opportunities if his efforts to channel and direct are properly managed (National Academy of Public Administration, 1987). Rule-making is an administrative action especially susceptible to judicial scrutiny. In their decisions in cases challenging rules, judges can affect a wide range of activities in programs administered by agencies (O'Leary, 1993). It is important to note, however, that rule-making is not favored by all judges (Scalia, 1981). Rule-making, with its frequently narrow focus and specialized, technical content would appear to be a process tailor-made for contemporary interest groups. Recent literature has noted the increasing specialization of interest groups (Scholzman and Tierney, 1986), and the attention they pay to decisions of administrative agencies (Lowi, 1987). For the bureaucrat, rule-making is a vehicle for the exercise of professional and policy judgments and for promoting regularity and predictability in subsequent program operations. Given the benefits it bestows on the major actors in our political and legal systems, rule-making is a device well suited to the realities of our contemporary public policy process.

As noted above, the literature on rule-making is curiously imbalanced. It has long been a prominent topic in law reviews and case books, where legal scholars have identified and attempted to resolve issues of central importance to both constitutional and administrative law. Rule-making has not, however, been granted comparable status or attention by scholars of public administration. This chapter will therefore examine themes that are both familiar and obscure. The traditional concerns of legal scholars—delegation of authority, procedural requirements, and judicial review of rule-making—will be covered. More attention will be paid to issues and topics that should be of deep concern to students of politics, public administration, and public policy. Among these are the management of rule-making, actual patterns of public participation in the development of rules, and the nonjudicial mechanisms of accountability. The goal of this chapter is to provide a broad overview of a crucial governmental function of concern to both the theory and practice of American government.

DEFINITION

The authoritative and most quoted definition of rule-making is found in the Administrative Procedure Act (APA) of 1946. It states in section 551, not surprisingly, that rule-making "means agency process for formulating, amending or repealing a rule." So, "rule" is the crucial term, and the APA defines it as:

> the whole or part of an agency statement of general or particular applicability and future effect designed to implement, interpret, or prescribe law or policy or describing the organization, procedure, or practice requirements of an agency . . . .

From this definition it appears that the key feature of a rule is its role in establishing the law, policy, or procedure that will guide future behavior and activities (O'Reilly, 1983:chapter 2). There are other fundamental instruments of administrative power to which rules are frequently contrasted. Orders, the products of agency adjudications, are usually characterized as the vehicle for applying existing legal rules and principles to individual controversies. Licenses are defined in the APA as an "agency permit, certificate, approval, registration, charter, membership, statutory exemption or other forms of permission." In fact, the lines that divide these fundamental tools of administrative agencies are often obscure (Breyer and Stewart, 1985:466–468). Both orders and licenses can contain requirements that define law or policy and have future effects. Rules, on the other hand, can be quite particular in their application and sometimes constitute "permission" to do something. The differentiation might be of little practical consequence except for the matter of procedure. The Administrative Procedure Act, and much subsequent law, contemplates different methods for writing rules, conducting adjudication, and issuing various types of licenses. Without doing violence to a copious literature devoted to the distinctions between rules and orders and the choice of appropriate procedure, suffice it to say that in certain circumstances the ability to differentiate rules from orders and licenses virtually disappears. In these cases the choice of procedural form is less a problem than it might first appear for, as we will see, in recent years the processes for writing rules and conducting adjudications have converged somewhat.

Rules are enormously varied in their content, length, applicability, and effective life. The Code of Federal Regulations stands in mute testimony to the vast scope of subject matter considered in the rule-making process. On a given day, the *Federal Register* might contain rules by the Federal Reserve System covering certain types of securities transactions, by the National Credit Union Administration covering "insurance and eligible obligations," by the National Aeronautics and Space Administration (NASA) governing the use of their research facilities by private parties, and the National Marine Fisheries Service to halt the fishing of a certain species in a given area, an "airworthiness directive" by the Federal Aviation Administration, an agricultural marketing order by the Agricultural Marketing Service, and a new source of performance standards for air pollution from the Environmental Protection Agency. Rules vary greatly in length. Some are only a few paragraphs, like a recent Coast Guard rule dealing with drawbridge operations on the Potomac River in the District of Columbia. Others literally fill hundreds of pages, like the 1990 regulation issued by the Department of Transportation dealing with hazardous materials. Their applicability is similarly varied. Some rules affect only a handful of individuals, organizations, or firms while others affect large segments of the population, such as Medicare beneficiaries, and sectors of the economy, such as banking or credit unions. Rules may have effect for remarkably short periods of time. Agricultural marketing orders that limit the amounts of certain commodities that can be shipped for sale are often in effect for a month or less. The Coast Guard has issued rules that are in effect for 1 hour, such as its temporary safety zone regulations that protect boaters from holiday fireworks displays.

An appreciation of the diversity in the substance and applicability of rules is an essential prerequisite to understanding the rule-making process. The subject matter of a rule, the issues it raises, and the segments of the public affected by its provisions have a profound effect on the methods used in its development. These relationships will be explained shortly.

BRIEF HISTORY

The history of rule-making is the history of American public policy. The first Congress turned its attention to the problems of unscrupulous practices of traders who dealt with Indian tribes. Congress enacted statutes that authorized the president to issue regulations governing the awarding and content of licenses issued to traders (Committee on Administrative Procedure, 1941:97). So it has gone since: Congress identifying areas for governmental intervention, setting objectives in statute, and directing administrative officials to "fill in the details" with rules and regulations. Over time we observe a steadily growing reliance on the rule-making process to carry out with greater detail and specificity the will of the people as it is expressed in legislation.

Much of the actual history of rule-making is lost. Until the establishment of the *Federal Register* there was no official repository of rules and regulations from which we can draw to chart the content and volume of rules issued by the federal government. Prior to that we must rely on what was captured, almost randomly, by a few historians, political scientists, and legal scholars who were the earliest students of the administrative process (Fuchs, 1938). Rather than attempt to construct what would at best be a fragmentary and speculative history, we will stick to what is at least somewhat better known. Thanks to a remarkable study conducted by the Attorney General's Committee on Administrative Procedure in the late 1930s, we have a strong starting point for an examination of the growth and diversification of rule-making over the past half century.

Completing their research in 1941, the Committee reported that it had found 51 agencies of the federal government whose activities "in a substantial way affect private interests by their power to make rules and regulations or by their power of adjudication in particular cases." While rule-making was conducted in virtually all of these government institutions, its importance to the operation of programs administered by the agency varied considerably. In some cases the volume of rules was substantial and rule-making was central to the agency's work; in others the subject matter of rules was confined to procedural matters and the agencies conducted their business using other administrative devices, notably various forms of adjudication.

The Committee found the Department of Interior, and agencies concerned with veterans' affairs, to be among the most prolific rule-makers, while the Interstate Commerce Commission, the Bureau of Marine Inspection and Navigation, and the Social Security Administration were busy as well. Other agencies were prominent less by the frequency of the rules than by the relative importance of those that they issued. The Federal Reserve Board and the Federal Deposit Insurance Corporation fall into this category. Still others with major regulatory powers, such as the Federal Trade Commission and the National Labor Relations Board, issued few significant rules, preferring to conduct their business on a case-by-case basis in quasijudicial adjudicatory proceedings.

From the end of World War II to the mid-1960s there were major developments in several types of public policy in which rule-making plays a major role. There was also considerable pleasure. Entitlement and benefit programs created during the New Deal diversified and expanded, and new programs were created (Dobelstein, 1990). These new social programs brought with them rule-making activities that defined the criteria for rights and obligations of both the intended beneficiaries and a variety of individual and institutional service providers. Regulatory programs grew as well. Notable among them are those dealing with domestic uses of nuclear power; regulation of safety in air, rail, and highway transportation; equal pay; and modest initiatives for air and water quality (Fritschler, 1984). Here the regulation restricted various kinds of private activities and set standards for state and local governments. A general expansion in the use of rule-making by government agencies was advocated during this period by a number of prominent academicians and practitioners and a major congressional task force in the mid-1950s. It was also favored by the federal courts. The Task Force on Legal Services and Procedures in its report to the Congress stated, "the primary methods which agencies should use to effectuate legislative provisions is the adoption of implementing rules . . ." (Cooper, 1983:98ff). By the early 1960s the judiciary was perceived to be more deferential to agency rules and rule-making than to other forms of administrative action (Shapiro, 1965:958–967). Academics and practitioners found rule-making a superior means of articulating policy, and for containing the growing power of administrative agencies several urged that it be used much more extensively (Davis, 1969).

The era that began in the 1960s and continues to this day deserves to be considered the most important in establishing the central importance of rule-making to our system of government. During these years what is generally termed an explosion of programs of social regulation occurred. By one count, during the period of 1969 to 1979 over 130 new regulatory laws were passed by Congress, including several landmarks in environmental protection, workplace safety and health, consumer protection, and employment equity (Lowi, 1987:298). While the volume of the new legislation would itself be significant, the programs of social regulation established during this period were peculiarly dependent on rulemaking. Lowi has noted that the delegations of the authority in these statutes were exceedingly broad (Lowi, 1987:296). Statutory language so vague leads to massive amounts of rule-making in order to create the substance needed for operational programs. Fritschler agrees, stating flatly that "social regulation (unlike economic regulation) proceeds by generalized rulemaking" (Fritschler, 1984:451).

Today, rule-making is continual. Daily, dozens of proposed and final rules appear in the *Federal Register* and the total for both types numbers in the thousands annually. The accumulated body of rules is staggering. The Code of Federal Regulations (CFR) is the official repository of rules currently in force. It now consists of 50 "titles" that correspond to broad areas of public policy (e.g., agriculture, housing, public health, transportation). Under each title are "chapters" that correspond to particular programs or issues within the broader policy areas (e.g., Agricultural Marketing Service, Office of Assistant Secretary for Community Planning and Development, Health Care Financing Administration, Federal Highway Administration). The Code has grown enormously since it first appeared in 1938. Then it filled 15 volumes; now it fills nearly 200. Individual titles have grown apace. Agriculture appeared in 1938 covering an impressive 1,200 pages but has swelled to nearly 11,000. Protection of the environment, which did not exist until the early 1970s is now approaching 9,000 pages in length.

The future almost certainly holds further growth and diversification. Major statutes of the early 1990s, such as the amendments to the Clean Air Act and the Americans with Disabilities Act, called upon agencies to issue hundreds of implementing regulations. Rule-making is simply an indispensable device that also happens to serve the interests of the major actors in our contemporary public policy system. Congress, the President, the judiciary, interest groups, and bureaucracies all find something appealing in rule-making. Because of its appeal and indispensability, rule-making will persist as a prime instrument of government. To be successful, however, a rule-making must overcome a number of potentially serious problems.

PROBLEMS OF RULE-MAKING

Constitutional Issues

The criticisms of rule-making are numerous. Most focus on operational shortcomings. One goes to the very heart of our constitutional democracy.

While long-settled as an issue in law, some critics persist in the view that delegations of authority from Congress to the agencies—the origins of all rule-making—constitute a dangerous and unjustified threat to constitutional democracy. Notable among these skeptics is Theodore Lowi, who argues that rule-making on the current scale is nothing less than a "derangement" of the Constitution (Lowi, 1987:299). He acknowledges that the delegation of some rule-making powers is unavoidable but that the current volume and importance of rule-making by administrative agencies is nothing less than an abrogation by Congress of its responsibility to write the law. While this critique still finds the occasional sympathetic ear among scholars and politicians, it has received little support among those with the authority to reverse the trend. Congress continues to authorize and sometimes compel rule-making and the judiciary remains a frequent, if occasionally uneasy, accomplice. In short, the constitutional critique, however sound, has had little impact on actual practice.

The Great Depression and the governmental response to it, the New Deal, initially brought the constitutional issues associated with rule-making to great prominence. The National Industry Recovery Act (NIRA) authorized a series of boards with wide-ranging powers over the various sectors of the economy. Rule-making was a key element in this regulatory strategy and the boards used the power frequently to set rates, production quotas, and codes of industry practice. When NIRA was successfully challenged as an unconstitutionally broad delegation of authority by Congress to the president, an important element in the plaintiffs' cases was the manner in which rule-making was being conducted. They argued that the lack of standards in the act led to the formulation of rules with little or no regard for the procedural rights of those affected and with contents that were alternatively arbitrary or clearly biased in favor of certain interests within a given industry (*Panama Refining Co. v. Ryan* [1935, 283 US 388]; *Schechter Poultry Corp. v. U.S.* [1935, 295 US 495]).

The decisions in the celebrated cases of *Panama* and *Schechter,* in which provisions of NIRA were actually overturned, stand as lonely monuments in the history of American administrative law. They are exceedingly rare instances of delegations of authority by Congress that were found to violate the Constitution because of their excessive breadth and lack of guiding standards. The New Deal was ultimately restored to constitutional health and rule-making under NIRA was revived. Challenges to delegations of authority on grounds similar to the arguments in *Panama* and *Schechter* have been mounted intermittently. Over time, however, it became clear that the judiciary would allow Congress considerable leeway when crafting legislation. The status of rule-making grew both conceptually and practically as a result of the Court's permissive view. Thirty-five years after the decisions in *Panama* and *Schechter* the judiciary explicitly established rule-making as the preferred remedy for vagueness in congressional grants of the authority. In that case (*Amalgamated Meat Cutters and Butcher Workmen v. Connolly* [1971, 337 F. Supp. 737]) the Court stated when an agency is the recipient of delegated authority in need of clarification and refinement, it falls to administrative officials to provide this basic guidance on statutory purpose and standards through rules.

Volume

It should be noted that the volume of rulemaking has been a concern for less abstract reasons as well. Certain programs have been cited for issuing too many rules and in some instances too few. Perhaps the most celebrated example of excessive rule-making is the case of the Occupational Safety and Health Administration (OSHA) in the early 1970s. In an apparent attempt to demonstrate its willingness to move aggressively, the then-new agency issued over 4,000 rules during the course of a few months. While most of these were borrowed from sets of voluntary standards adopted over a period of years by professional societies and associations, the response from the regulated community was swift and violently negative. In its rush to publish what it thought would be a comprehensive set of rules, OSHA had written into law a large number of standards that were simply obsolete or unsuited for a regulatory program (Viscusi, 1986). High-volume rule-making by the Environmental Protection Agency has also been criticized. For example, an internal agency study of the hazardous waste management program concluded, in a chapter titled "The Regulations Machine: Too Many, Too Fast," the Agency found that "[the program's] success in developing rules has been achieved at the expense of other important program objectives . . ." (U.S. Environmental Protection Agency, 1990: 31).

High-volume rule-making can be disruptive and difficult to manage for both the public and private sectors. The public employees who must write them and, to an even greater extent, those who must implement and enforce them can be put under considerable stress when the pace of rule-making is fast and the accumulated weight of rules is heavy. Those in the private sector who must comply with a steady stream of new or changing requirements will likewise face challenges as they attempt to remain informed and muster the resources to meet the requirements they contain. Furthermore, high-volume rule-making taxes the ability of those in the public and private sectors to participate in the process of regulation development. This can contribute to other, more serious, problems that are discussed below.

Too few rules can, on occasion, be a problem as well. Some agencies are known for their unwillingness to write rules, preferring instead to conduct their business on a case-by-case basis using quasijudicial techniques. Among the agencies cited most often in this regard is the National Labor Relations Board. It has resisted the entreaties of many external parties, including the federal bench, to establish operational principles through rule-making (Estreicher, 1985). Most agencies are cited for failing to issue rules that one or more external constituencies deem essential. This is a common complaint lodged against agencies administering programs of social regulation. While critics will often attribute a lack of rule-making to agency intransigence, ignorance, or dark political motives, a frequent cause of apparent inaction is the slow pace of rule-making, a problem discussed separately below.

Quality

However many rules an agency produces a reasonable expectation that they will, when issued, be of high quality. According to critics, this is too often not the case. A truly objective appraisal of the quality of a given rule is a formidable analytical task. Criteria are numerous. How well a rule reflects the intentions of the statute it seeks to implement is the ultimate qualitative issue. However, legislative intent is often obscure. The contribution that rules make to the success of public programs is also an important standard for evaluation. Here, the obstacles to measuring program performance and the number of variables other than rules that contribute to success and failure complicate the assessment of quality. We can adopt less ambitious measures of quality, namely the ease with which rules are implemented, complied with, and enforced. When taken from this perspective, it is evident from available literature that there are indeed problems.

Colin Diver has identified "incongruence," a lack of clarity and specificity, and excessive complexity as characteristics that impede the enforcement of rules (Diver, 1989:200). "Incongruence" is the failure of a rule to reflect or promote the goals of the statute it seeks to implement by "overinclusion" or "underinclusion" of regulated activity in a "rule's verbal formulation" (Diver, 1989:200–209). When rules are unclear or vague they are subject to multiple interpretations, leaving regulated entities free to fashion their own meanings of the rule's obscure language. The potential for partial or full noncompliance is great in these circumstances, so the task for government officials charged with monitoring behavior and enforcing the rule grows in magnitude and complexity. The enforcing officials are put at a disadvantage in at least two ways. First, they may be as confused as the regulated community about the meaning of the rule. Second, even if they understand the rule they may have a very difficult time convincing the regulated community, and the judges who will resolve the inevitable disputes that will arise, that their interpretation of the rule's content is correct and defensible.

Complexity puts the regulated community at a different sort of disadvantage. Those attempting to comply with the rule must struggle through multiple requirements that hinge on definitions of key terms that themselves are difficult to understand (U.S. Environmental Protection Agency, 1990:65–66). The applicability of the rule may itself turn on numerous exemptions, exceptions, and qualifications. According to at least one major study, this type of complexity hits smaller businesses and organizations especially hard, forcing them to turn to attorneys, accountants, and other compliance professionals to ensure that the organizations understand their obligations (Cole and Summers, 1981:121). This, in turn, translates into additional costs and an increased likelihood for conflict between the government and regulated entities.

Quality problems are particularly damaging because they undercut one of the most compelling rationales for extensive use of rule-making. The ability of agency experts to act as technical adjuncts to the Congress, to provide the expertise, insights, and experience that lead to programs that effectively and efficiently promote legislative goals, is central to any argument in support of rule-making. Failures of the sort mentioned above occur for a variety of reasons. Failure to reflect statutory goals, vagueness, and lack of clarity occur because rule-makers misunderstand statutory goals, fail to collect and use the best available information, cannot agree on approach or language, or simply neglect issues that emerge as crucial in program operations. Complexity can also be attributable to some of these root causes but it can also emerge when bureaucrats attempt to anticipate every possible situation that will confront the program and its administrators. Of course, Congress must share the blame when it writes legislation with goals and objectives that are themselves subject to multiple interpretations and opens the door, explicitly or implicitly, to possible exceptions and exemptions.

Delay

Even when rules are well written, and sometimes because they are, their issuance can be delayed. Observers in and out of government have identified the time it takes to write rules as a major problem (Kerwin and Furlong, 1992; Eisner, 1989). This is ample evidence that it deserves to be taken quite seriously. As early as 15 years ago one study found that government-wide it took, on average, nearly 2 years to issue rules (Committee on Government Affairs, 1977). A more recent study of rule-making by the Environmental Protection Agency found that on average it took approximately 4 years to complete a rulemaking (Kerwin and Furlong, 1992). All accounts—scholarly, practitioner, or popular—indicate that the problem is widespread and not confined to small number of agencies or a particular type of rule.

The consequences of delay are numerous and significant. The flow of benefits that Congress intended for the American people, or some segment of them, is retarded or stalled. Those who would gain from cleaner air, safer water, or more secure deposits in a savings and loan institution continue to suffer or be at risk (Kerwin and Furlong, 1992; McGarrity, 1992). Even those who would incur costs complying with the rules may also suffer losses. For example, regulated businesses will be reluctant to move into new areas or effect a number of internal changes until the rules governing the activity in question are clear. The government and the taxpayers who support it can be losers too when cost-saving rules are delayed, as has been reported in a number of instances.

The causes of delay are at least as numerous as its consequences (Eisner, 1989). Rules sometimes deal with complex subject matter and issues and it takes the responsible agency time to assemble the information needed for a full understanding of them (Bryner, 1987; Rothstein, 1985). Controversy attends the rule-making on a regular basis and its resolution takes time. Conflict is both internal to agencies and between them and affected external constituents or interests. Internal conflict has been attributed to the multiple professional and policy perspectives that characterize the different components of an agency now routinely in volved in writing rules of any consequence. Technical staff from the program office with primary jurisdiction over the subject matter of the rule, attorneys from both the office of general counsel and the enforcement staff, economists working in agency-wide policy planning and analysis offices, and representatives from other offices whose programs may be affected by the rule and field staff who will be charged with implementing it may be involved in the rule-making (Kerwin, 1992; McGarrity, 1991). The importance of these "workgroups" in contemporary rule-making will be discussed further below. Existing research indicates that the different priorities, professional training, and policy views of these different bureaucratic actors can lead to conflict in the rule-making process (West, 1988). Assuming the agency's leadership places some value on consensus, the resolution of this conflict can be time-consuming.

External conflict is a function of the benefits and costs the new rule may confer and impose on potentially affected parties. We will see subsequently that much has been done over the past 25 years to force agencies to identify the potential effects of new rules on certain interests and to give those affected ample opportunity to influence agency decision-making. Scholars have noted for some time the tendency among agencies to attempt to accommodate these interests (Stewart, 1975). When interests collide with one another, or when they take issue with a position those in the agency consider correct, conflict is inevitable and efforts to resolve it will add time to the rule-making.

Delay is also a by-product of increased procedural requirements. In a subsequent section we will observe the dramatic changes in the legal context of rule-making that have occurred since the landmark Administrative Procedure Act of 1946. Suffice it to say that these developments were generally not designed to make rule-making simpler and quicker (McGarrity, 1992; McCubbins, 1985).

Three other potential sources of delay merit a brief mention. Shortages of resources relative to statutory obligations are chronic in most regulatory agencies (Bryner, 1987). With fewer staff and dollars than needed to cover the full range of rule-making responsibilities, agencies ration what is available. The means used to set priorities will be covered below but too few resources mean that rules important to some must wait in line. When resources are ample, they may still be mismanaged. Rule-making is a complex organizational activity, requiring in many instances intimate knowledge of substantive and procedural requirements, careful planning, extensive communication, coordination of multiple parallel activities, and skillful leadership. When these are missing, delays in rule-making result. Finally, delay may simply be an agency tactic, used to avoid difficult or distasteful policy decisions (Barke, 1984).

The time spent in writing a rule is largely a function of its subject matter. As noted above, the substance of a rule determines to a considerable extent the procedural requirements the agency must satisfy during the course of rule-making. Furthermore, and perhaps more important, the subject matter determines the amount and intensity of interest in the rule-making by internal and external parties and the potential for conflict. If an agency seeks consensus, or even a rule that can be defended when written, these dimensions will add time to the rule-making task.

Participation

The openness of rule-making to public participation is also viewed as a problem. There are reservations about the opportunities afforded the public as well as the nature and form of participation when it does occur. Because of the central importance of public participation to rule-making, it is given special attention in two subsequent sections of this chapter. The problems associated with public participation will be briefly noted here.

Over the past five decades the opportunities for public participation in rule-making have expanded steadily. As we will note in the section devoted to rule-making procedures, the basic and minimalist approach to participation taken in the Administrative Procedure Act has been rendered effectively obsolete by a raft of statutes that provide additional direct and indirect openings for the public who wish to influence rule-making. However, the APA and other statutes allow agencies to sidestep public participation through a variety of exceptions for routine rules, exemptions for certain classes of regulations, and provisions for expedited rule-making in emergency situations. Recent research also suggests that agencies increasingly avoid rule-making altogether, preferring instead to issue "policy statements," "guidelines," and "interpretations" (Anthony, 1992). Critics charge that these devices are frequently indistinguishable from rules in content and effect and are used to avoid the procedural requirements associated with issuing rules, especially public participation.

Another dimension of the participation problem is the capacity of the public to take advantage of the opportunities in the law and offered by the agency. As noted above, rule-making appears suited to interest groups and firms with the sophistication to understand its importance and the resources to monitor its progress and influence its results. As we will note, available evidence suggests that these groups and firms are indeed heavily involved in rule-making and use a diversified set of tactics to get what they want from the process. By their own assessments, which will be noted below, they are successful in their efforts to exert influence. Critics alarmed by the growing power of interest groups will find little solace in a close examination of actual patterns of public participation in rule-making.

The problems of rule-making, if they are to be resolved at all, must be attended to during the process of developing regulations. That process has many elements, each of which will be discussed presently. The most fundamental element of this process consists of the legal requirements that must be met during the course of rule-making. It is to these we now turn.

THE RULE-MAKING PROCESS: LEGAL REQUIREMENTS

Two general types of law apply to rule-making. Substantive law, the content of statutes enacted by Congress, determines the goals and objectives that rules and subsequent implementation activities are expected to achieve. The substantive law associated with rule-making is vast, touching virtually every aspect of life in America. The second type of applicable law is procedural and it governs the manner in which agencies make decisions and the information they must consider as they develop regulations. While not approaching the scope of substantive law, the procedural law of rule-making is formidable and complex.

For much of our history rule-making procedure was virtually ignored in the statutes that transferred authority for writing law from Congress to agencies (Committee on Administrative Procedure, 1941:102). Over time, however, a variety of devices came to be used by agencies when they undertook to write rules. As we will discuss below, these correspond roughly to procedures still in place today. These devices were not universally employed, however. The lack of regularized procedure became increasingly controversial and figured prominently in the celebrated *Panama* and *Schechter* decisions discussed earlier.

Dissatisfaction with the irregularities and alleged injustices of rule-making procedure coalesced and led to passage of the Walter-Logan Act in 1939 (Rosenbloom, 1989:556). Strongly supported by elements of the legal profession, this statute would have transformed much of rule-making into the type of adversary proceedings normally associated with civil trials. It would have eliminated the informality that characterized most rule-making at the time and severely constrained the exercise of agency discretion. However, President Roosevelt vetoed the bill and further action on reform of rule-making was interrupted by World War II. The issue re-emerged shortly after the war when Congress enacted the Administrative Procedure Act. Unlike its predecessor, it was signed by President Truman and contained rule-making provisions very different from those found in the earlier legislation.

The basic rule-making provisions of the Administrative Procedure Act are found in section 553 and outline what has come to be known as "informal" or "notice and comment" rule-making. These elements are simple, designed to produce a flexible device for filling in the details of public programs not provided in legislation. The requirements are limited and they afford considerable discretion to agencies when writing rules. The agency must publish in the *Federal Register* a notice of the rule it is proposing to issue. This notice must include at least a description of the contents of the proposed rule, if not the actual language. The public is to be afforded an opportunity to provide comments on the proposal to the agency. Once these are considered, the agency, if it decides to proceed, publishes the final rule, also in the *Federal Register,* with a statement of "basis and purpose." As they came to be defined, "purpose" refers to the statutory provisions that authorized or mandated issuance of the rule and the "basis" to the agency's justification for choosing its particular content and form. The act also contained provisions for formal rule-making not unlike those proposed in the Walter-Logan bill, but they were reserved for those cases in which Congress specifically mandated the use of trial-type proceedings in authorizing legislation. This was and continues to be a relatively rare circumstance. Finally, the act made provision for judicial review of agency rule-making.

Since 1946, and particularly in the past three decades, Congress, presidents, and the courts have heavily supplemented these modest provisions of the APA. In many respects these efforts appear highly fragmented and incoherent, but close examination reveals that they have been driven by consistent legal and political theories.

Congress has used statutes with general applicability, such as the Paperwork Reduction Act and the National Environmental Protection Act, to alter rule-making procedures across the government. It has also inserted provisions in specific authorizing legislation to require additional procedures in individual agencies. Presidents have used executive orders to institute government-wide reform efforts. The decisions of judges in thousands of cases have affected the procedures used for individual rules. The applicability of these many legal instruments varies enormously, usually determined by the subject matter of the rule under development. The standard analysis is that these disparate efforts have combined to transform rule-making into a "hybrid" process (Cooper, 1983; Williams, 1975), possessing some elements normally associated with legislative deliberations and others found more often in adjudication. While this is certainly true, the growth in procedural requirements should also be viewed as a political response by the three branches to the growing dominance of rule-making as a mechanism for making policy and law.

Unable or unwilling to enact statutes with sufficient substantive detail, Congress imposes procedural requirements that confer special status on certain issues or interests affected by rule-making (McCubbins et al., 1987). This allows Congress to influence the process and to protect special interests without being held responsible for the content of individual rules (McCubbins, 1985; Fiorina, 1982). Surveying the vast rule-making machine that is the federal government, presidents have struggled to exert some measure of control in order to promote the policies initiatives that got them elected. Additional process, created by executive order, has been their preferred mechanism of influence (National Academy of Public Administration, 1987). The judiciary, having encouraged the growth of rulemaking, has assumed increasing responsibility for its performance. When deficiencies have been found, judicial remedies have frequently been procedural (O'Leary, 1993, Ch. 7) Heffron and McFeeley, 1983:311). To characterize what has happened to the rule-making process as "hybridization" is accurate but not sufficient. Viewed properly, the expansion and diversification of rulemaking procedure are testimony to a historic change in the way we govern ourselves. As Congress, presidents, and courts assert their authority and repeatedly tinker with the rule-making process, they reveal the difficulties they face in trying to influence or control the content of rules written by agencies. They are, in effect, competing for control of rule-making and struggling to direct bureaucratic rule-makers (McGarrity, 1992). It is an important example of what has come to be known as the "principal-agent" problem in organization theory and political economy (Mitnick, 1984).

Space does not permit a full discussion of the many procedural changes that have occurred since the Administrative Procedure Act became law in 1946. There are, however, basic underlying themes that bring some coherence to these many efforts to change the way rules are written. If we examine the various provisions of the Administrative Procedure Act, we find that they are based on three fundamental principles of democratic government: information, participation, and accountability. Virtually every law, executive order, and court decision that supplements the provisions of the APA, whether the intended target is rule-making across the government or a small number of rules in an obscure program, extend or elaborate on one or more of these three fundamental principles.

Under the provisions of the APA, information provided to the public in rule-making is limited to the proposed rule, or description thereof, and the final rule published by the agency in the *Federal Register* accompanied by the aforementioned statement of basis and purpose. The information requirements are limited. For example, the act is silent on the types of information an agency must develop during the course of rule-making. Since 1946 the information development and disclosure requirements that an agency may face for a given rule-making have changed dramatically. Examples include the "burden-hour" studies mandated by the Paperwork Reduction Act, the draft and final environmental impact statements of the National Environmental Policy Act, and small business impact assessments of the Regulatory Flexibility Act. Program-specific statutes such as these focus on particular issues and concerns across the government; authorizing statutes frequently impose special information requirements on a particular agency. These are very common in environmental and workplace safety statutes (Administrative Conference of the United States, 1984). These laws often mandate various forms of "risk assessment" or "risk analysis" to inform the rule-making process and share the common purpose of establishing a scientific basis for rules that limit pollution and exposures to hazardous substances or activities. Executive orders carry information requirements as well. By far the most important is E.O. 12291, which requires, among other things, a form of benefit/cost analysis for major regulations. Others call for analysis of federalism issues, impact on private property, and effects on the family. The courts have also been known to find the analytical support for a given rule insufficient and have ordered additional studies to be done.

Requiring additional information serves a number of purposes. It pushes agencies to develop a stronger basis for the rules it writes and to develop a better understanding of the effects they will have on the nation. As important is that better information, when it is made available by the agency, enables Congress, the president, judges, and the public to participate more effectively in the development of rules (McCubbins et al., 1987).

Participation has changed for reasons other than the availability of better information. Opportunities beyond the written comments called for in the APA have increased and diversified. We will discuss these additional opportunities more fully in the section of this chapter devoted to participation. Here it is important to note that written comment on the rule is only one of many ways the public attempts to influence the content of rules. Some of these additional mechanisms are required by legislation affecting all agencies, some by authorizing statutes that apply to a single agency or program, others have been ordered by the courts in individual cases, and still others have been developed by the agencies themselves. As we will see, opportunities to participate are determined by the subject matter, circumstances, and interests affected by the individual rule under development.

Mechanisms of accountability have been strengthened as well. This is also discussed in a separate section. It became common for Congress to go beyond the provisions of the Administrative Procedure Act and include more specific provisions for judicial review in the statutes that created regulatory programs. Accountability to the judiciary is now taken for granted. The ability of Congress to supervise the development of rules was once more robust than it is at present. The legislative veto allowed the Congress, and more often its committees and subcommittees, to reject rules developed by agencies. At its height, there were several hundred individual legislative veto provisions affecting a substantial portion of the rules that might be developed by federal agencies (Gazell and Pugh, 1985; Craig, 1983). Since the historic decision in the *Chadha* case, the legislative veto is no longer a force in rulemaking (*Immigration and Naturalization Service v. Chadha,* 462 U.S. 919 [1983]). Congress remains heavily involved, nevertheless, through both legislation and oversight activities of various sorts (Aberbach, 1990; Foreman, 1988).

The 1970s saw the rise of another form of accountability for rule-makers. Through executive orders and other directives, presidents, starting with Richard Nixon, attempted to exert control over the rule-making process. It started modestly as an effort to examine environmental regulations, but is now a multifaceted program to review and direct all rules from executive departments and agencies (Reagan, 1987:chapter 7). Special studies, various mandatory reviews of new rules, and retrospective analyses of existing regulations now enhance a president's ability to influence the course of rule-making. Presidents have been motivated by different concerns in their efforts to promote accountability to the White House. As we will see subsequently, Carter was driven by a general commitment to better public management and to regulatory reform; Reagan pursued a narrower policy of minimizing the effects of regulation on the private sector. All met with limited success and each contributed to a system of accountability now in place that is likely to last as long as rule-making itself.

To some this collection of legal requirements has combined to "ossify" rule-making through a dense web of mandatory analyses, serial consultations with the public, and reviews by judicial, legislative, and executive masters (McGarrity, 1992; Mashaw, 1992). Certainly, this can be the case for a given rule. However, most of these requirements are triggered only under certain circumstances and many allow for exemptions and emergency exceptions. For example, rules must involve the collection, retention, or reporting of information for the Paperwork Reduction Act to apply. Effects on smaller businesses activate the provisions of the Regulatory Flexibility Act. The executive order establishing Office of Management and Budget (OMB) review exempts a number of rule-making actions considered routine or relatively minor. Even the minimal provisions of the Administrative Procedure Act can be suspended in emergency situations or when the agency determines that their use is not "in the public interest." A cursory reading of the *Federal Register* on any given day will confirm that many rules are written without apparent concern for most of the potential requirements outlined above.

These many qualifications notwithstanding, the growth of legal requirements associated with the rulemaking process is highly significant. While minor rules may escape an agency after negotiating relatively few procedural steps, the most important rules almost certainly will not. The regulations that may affect major industries, sectors of the economy, or large numbers of people are the real targets of these procedural requirements. They are much less likely to be subject to exceptions and exemptions and much more likely to affect one or more of the major interests or concerns embodied in the requirements detailed above. For the most significant rules issued by agencies the rule-making process will be affected, often profoundly, by the varied information, participation, and accountability provisions found in general statutes, specific statutes, executive orders, and judicial decisions. These legal requirements must be observed for rule-making to be successful. Yet meeting the applicable legal requirements is only one dimension of the task confronting rule-making agencies. There are many others that require attention by those responsible for the management of rule-making. It is to the management task that we now turn.

MANAGEMENT OF RULE-MAKING

There are many reasons for there to be keen interest in the management of rule-making. As we have argued, it is a very important source of law and public policy. Management of the process allows political leaders to influence the development of rules and their contents. The performance of our public agencies in meeting their statutory obligations depends on the rules that undergird their programs. Senior officials in agencies may wish to manage rule-making in order to promote program objectives and to maintain effective working relationships with their external clienteles and constituencies. We noted above that rule-making may be beset by a number of potential problems. Management systems that supplement the rule-making procedures established in law are a means for dealing with some of these. Finally, rule-making is an activity that consumes budgets and the efforts of public officials at all levels of virtually all agencies. The amount of resources consumed during rule-making constitutes a significant share of some agencies' entire budget. Sound public administration demands that a function commanding this share of tax dollars be managed carefully.

Rule-making, in fact, is managed at three distinct levels. First, there are efforts to manage rule-making on a government-wide basis. Second, individual departments and agencies have developed and maintain systems to coordinate and direct rule-making. Finally, management occurs during the development of individual rules. These levels of management interact in a number of ways but each has distinct structures, processes, and goals.

White House Management

Efforts to manage rule-making government-wide are based in the White House and began during the Nixon administration. Contending with economic problems he attributed in part to government regulations, President Nixon instituted a "quality of life" review of a select group of new rules in an effort to gain some control over their substantive content (Reagan, 1987:163). The function was housed in the Office of Management and Budget. The Nixon program, although actually quite limited, can still be viewed as a precursor to more ambitious review programs that would follow. Subsequent presidents all built on the modest base, but the true architect of the key elements of the current system of presidential rule-making management was Jimmy Carter.

Midway through his presidency, Carter issued executive order 12044 as part of a far-reaching effort to improve government regulations. His program had a number of elements but those with enduring significance were the "Regulatory Council," requirements for regulatory analysis, the creation of a "Regulatory Analysis Review Group," and the oversight role created for the Office of Management and Budget. The Regulatory Council consisted of the heads of major federal regulatory agencies. Its charge was to develop a list of the rules under development that were most likely to have the greatest impact on the economy or other dimensions of our national life. It was also expected to take a more focused look on the overall effects of regulation on those parts of the economy in trouble or at risk. The goal of the regulatory analysis element of the executive order was to ensure that agencies systematically and rigorously considered all reasonable alternatives when developing rules. Carter's stated policy was that new regulations be cost-effective and operate efficiently. The Regulatory Analysis Review Group (RARG) existed to review the quality of regulatory analyses performed by government agencies. It was also expected that the RARG would function as a sounding board and clearinghouse for the views of other agencies on rules that affect more than one executive department or independent commission.

The Carter program anticipated the currently expansive role of the Office of Management and Budget in rule-making management. It was "responsible for watching agency regulatory actions" and was to "oversee the departments' and agencies' implementation of the

Administration's management reforms" (Executive Office of the President, 1979:7). In addition, OMB was expected to provide support for and work closely with both the Regulatory Council and the Regulatory Analysis Review Group. The Office of Management and Budget came to provide the organizational capability for promoting presidential influence over the development of rules. While its actual results were limited, the significance of the Carter program lies in the example it set and the models it provided subsequent presidents. Ronald Reagan came to Washington with a much more aggressive, focused, and simple approach to government regulation. He established a program that has attracted a great deal more attention from the professional and scholarly communities. On close examination, however, the various pieces of the Reagan approach were little more than refinements and alterations of those established by Carter.

Executive order 12291 came early in the Reagan presidency. It imposed a temporary moratorium on the issuance of new rules (an effort to frustrate Carter administration holdovers), and required review of all proposed and final rules by the Office of Management and Budget and mandatory regulatory analysis for all major regulations. Reagan also established the Vice President's Task Force on Regulatory Relief, in part to examine existing regulations, particularly those affecting troubled sectors of the economy. There are clear similarities between this and the earlier Regulatory Analysis Review Group. Review by the Office of Management and Budget under E.O. 12291 was a more aggressive and concentrated version of the role OMB was to play in the Carter program. Regulatory analysis was retained and the overall mission of the Vice President's Task Force's charge was similar to that of the old Regulatory Council.

President Bush tinkered a bit with the management system he inherited, but kept virtually all the major elements of the Reagan program intact. The major change was the creation of the Competitiveness Council, chaired by his vice president. Its role can best be described as a sort of super-OMB review. Rather than focusing on particular sectors of the economy, it has concentrated its scrutiny on individual rules, selected, some have argued, for their political salience as well as their economic impact (Triano and Watzman, 1991).

At this writing the Clinton program has been announced but not fully implemented. It involves continued OMB review of rules, but on a more selective basis and more open to public scrutiny. Benefit-cost analysis will still be used and more emphasis will be placed on regulatory negotiation, a device that will be discussed presently.

As it now stands, management of rulemaking from the White House is well developed and thoroughly institutionalized. Each president since Nixon has made a contribution to its development. The resulting program has been highly controversial. It has been challenged on the constitutional grounds that it violates separation of powers. It has been criticized as a backchannel for powerful, antiregulatory interests. These critiques have been largely unsuccessful. Criticisms and challenges notwithstanding, it is unlikely that any future president will abandon the effort to manage rule-making on a government-wide basis. Whether the goal is to ensure that appropriate policies are articulated in rules or simply responsible stewardship of public resources, the management of rule-making is a formidable weapon in any president's arsenal.

Agency-Based Management

It may seem strange but there is some evidence that systematic management of rule-making at the department and agency level is a more recent development than the various programs that have operated out of the White House. The Carter Administration surveyed the state of such programs and found "no coordinated management of regulatory decisionmaking existed in most agencies" (Executive Office of the President, 1979:7). In making this claim, the Carter White House was attempting to make a case for its own reforms but there is no scholarly evidence to refute the assessment. Fifteen years later, however, the situation is very different. Research has established that for those agencies with significant rule-making responsibilities, management systems, some quite sophisticated and elaborate, are firmly in place (Kerwin, 1992). These systems vary considerably across the federal government but they do have a number of common elements. Space prohibits extensive consideration of any one of them, but a brief survey will make the essential points.

Unlike what Carter found upon taking office in 1977, many agencies have procedures in place to set priorities and control the initiation of individual rule-makings. It is not uncommon to find high-level groups in place to approve or otherwise take cognizance of the start of rule-making projects. In many instances these groups serve more than one purpose. While they function as priority setters and gatekeepers, they also serve a representative function. Contemporary rule-making, even in smaller agencies, often affects the jurisdictions of multiple offices. Structures and procedures that regulate the initiation of rules can also serve to ensure that all offices with a legitimate interest in the outcome of a particular rule-making are informed that it is underway and given an opportunity to participate in its development. This often has the effect of transforming rule-making into a collective effort that engages representatives of several department or agency offices.

Once a rule-making is authorized, a number of other management and administrative functions are commonly performed. One particularly important element in a number of agencies and departments is the capacity for senior management or political leadership to provide direction to those who will actually be developing the rule. This may come through a formal structure like a "regulatory council" or be provided informally as noted below in greater detail; such a process represents more than just control over the policies embodied in the rule ultimately developed. Early and serious involvement of senior management can save time and money by avoiding conflict at a later stage in the rule-making process.

Because of legislative or judicial deadlines or the above-mentioned concern for delay, scheduling is a familiar element in agency rule-making management systems. Schedules can be established in a variety of ways by a variety of officials. Many agencies have established computerized rule tracking systems to support scheduling. These usually include the generic milestones that occur in a rule-making and any steps deemed particularly important to the department or agency in question. Some tracking systems note when the schedule for a rule has slipped, indicating the reasons why and new projected completion dates. These systems serve a number of purposes, but all reinforce the importance of timeliness in rule-making.

Surprisingly, and distressingly, budgeting has not emerged as a common element in agency-based rule-making management systems. Recent research has been unsuccessful in discerning how agencies marshall the resources, often considerable, needed to complete effectively and promptly those rule-making projects they have initiated. The key resources in any rule-making are people and information. The various ways that people are assigned to the development of rules will be discussed presently. As important to the development of a rule is the assembly and analysis of information. We do know that an agency in the process of writing a rule has several sources of information to draw upon. The significance of any one will be determined by the particular subject matter of the rule. Information available within the agency, that developed by contractors or advisory committees, academic and professional sources, and insights gained through public comment and other forms of participation are the general categories of information that will determine the contents of rules (Administrative Conference of the United States, 1984:101–102). Each of these sources requires at least some sort of administrative support and some may be heavily regulated, as is the case with contractors. Particularly important, because of the requirements of judicial review that will be considered subsequently is the information provided through public participation. Separate information management systems are often created to receive and retain the various inputs that arrive from the public. Agencies have also established procedures for the review and incorporation of this information into the rule under development.

Concurrence systems are in place in most agencies to ensure that a rule is acceptable to the major stakeholders, the senior management, and the political leadership of a given department or agency. Two types of systems have been identified (Emery, 1982). Lateral, or horizontal, concurrence mechanisms allow offices across a given agency to review a rule prior to its formal proposal or final publication. Representatives from these offices have often been involved in rule-making since the outset. Vertical concurrence systems move the rule up the management chain to the official with the ultimate authority to issue the regulation. Usually this is a political appointee. As we noted above, review of rules by the Office of Management and Budget is now mandatory and agencies have generally responded by centralizing the authority for maintaining liaison with OMB.

Given the range of functions that have evolved to direct, coordinate, and support rule-making, it should not be surprising that offices and staffs dedicated to rule-making management are present in many departments and agencies. They are engaged in a number of activities outlined above and serve as a focal point for monitoring, technical assistance of various sorts, and coordination. While frequently devoted to largely administrative activities, staff in these offices can also play a substantive role in the development of rules. On occasion they will perform one or more of the mandatory analyses that now must accompany a proposed rule and in some instances they participate in the actual drafting of the regulation. These offices may also provide support for the groups of senior officials that oversee the rule-making agendas and decision-making processes in a number of agencies. These "regulations councils," mentioned previously, were heavily promoted during the Carter years and are still operating in a number of departments and agencies.

Managing Individual Rule-Makings: The Workgroup

The elaborate management systems that operate out of the White House and at the level of the various departments and agencies exist to influence one or more aspects of individual rule-makings. The management of a rule-making increasingly depends on the ability to manage the collections of interests and offices in an agency affected by the regulation under development. Recent research has established that rules of any significance are written in a group setting (Kerwin, 1992; McGarrity, 1991; Bryner, 1987). The reasons for this approach to writing rules can be easily inferred from what was discussed above. A given rule can require the insights and expertise of numerous individuals in an agency and its content can affect the missions of a number of different offices. In addition to the office responsible for the program for which the rule is being developed, attorneys from the Office of General Counsel, policy analysts, staff from other programs that might be directly or indirectly affected, and those who will be charged with implementing and enforcing it have compelling reasons to be involved. Existing research suggests that the perspectives and priorities of staff from these various offices and functions will differ and conflict may result (West, 1988). Workgroups or task forces do not eliminate the conflict but they do provide a potentially effective mechanism for dealing with it when it occurs.

Rule-making by workgroups is the norm in most federal departments or agencies. They vary in size and formality but rarely are any but the most routine and simple rules written entirely by a single individual. There are a variety of mechanisms for assembling workgroups and some are quite structured. A number of departments and agencies consider the composition of workgroups sufficiently important use their regulatory councils to determine which offices will be represented (McGarrity, 1991). In other agencies, usually where rule-making is less prominent, individuals assigned the task of writing a regulation will simply seek out the expertise and help they need on an informal basis (Kerwin, 1992).

As the core units for the development of individual rules, workgroups present a number of interesting management issues. They are, in effect, temporary collections of individuals with differing responsibilities, perspectives, and objectives. With the exception of the workgroup leader, who is almost always from the office responsible for producing the rule, the members of the workgroup are likely to be performing their roles as an add-on to their normal job. Under such circumstances the management of workgroup operations is not an insignificant issue and is likely to have an effect on the ultimate success of the rule-making. Existing research suggests that the management of the workgroup has three critical dimensions: the workgroup leader, the workgroup members, and the integration of the workgroup with the senior management and political leadership of the agency or department (Kerwin, 1992).

The workgroup leader must perform a number of functions (Environmental Protection Agency, Office of Standards and Regulations, 1982). She must understand the goals and objectives of the rule that will be developed and be intimately familiar with the legal and administrative requirements that must be met during the course of the rulemaking. He must be able to communicate these to the workgroup and establish from the outset the roles and expectations of each workgroup member. The leader must also set the operating protocol for the workgroup. There is considerable variation in the roles performed by workgroup members. In some instances members serve merely as conduits to superiors in their respective offices: vehicles for consultation. In others they take a direct hand in developing some aspect or component of the rule. Whatever the model, these roles and responsibilities need to be communicated clearly so that there is no confusion or disagreement about what is expected of the members. Workgroups can operate in a number of ways. Some are characterized by frequent face-to-face meetings, others by teleconferencing, and still others by exchanges of paper. As with the expectations for workgroup members, any number of styles can be effective. What is important is that the manner in which the workgroup will conduct its business should be clear to everyone from the outset.

Workgroup leaders need to be alert to the performance of workgroup members, because they may have been selected by their respective offices carelessly or simply may lack the time and resources to perform well. In other instances they may bring to the workgroup goals and objectives of their own rather than the offices and senior officials they represent. Whatever the impairment, poor performance by workgroup members can not only slow the development of regulations but also damage the final product, as discussed below. Leaders must intervene in such circumstances and see that the necessary changes are made when members cannot or will not perform.

Workgroup leaders are most effective when they encourage members to criticize and disagree as early as possible in the rule development process. Early detection of disagreements maximizes the time available to resolve them in a mutually agreeable way. Furthermore, it prevents the so-called "late hit" from a senior official who raises a fundamental and serious objection to a rule at an advanced stage in its development. This is particularly debilitating since it threatens the value of the substantial efforts already invested by the workgroup and the offices they represent. Late hits have an inevitably corrosive and long-term effect on internal working relationships. Early recognition of a disagreement within a workgroup is no guarantee that a resolution can be found, so the workgroup leader needs to be sufficiently sophisticated and astute to realize when an impasse is at hand. Then the only recourse is to senior management to break the deadlock.

Because of the potential complexity of contemporary rule-making, the effective workgroup leader is a valuable resource in agencies and departments that issue numerous and important regulations. The requisite skills are those of any project manager—planning, analysis, communication, diplomacy, negotiation—with the added requirement of an appreciation for the intricate web of legal, administrative, and political factors that form the environment for contemporary rule-making.

Workgroup members must have the skills and experience needed in the workgroup, but they must have other characteristics and resources as well. As suggested above, they must be given the time and resources they need to do what is expected of them. As important, they must have access to the leadership of the office they represent and use it to determine the position they are expected to take on important issues that arise during the course of rule development. Members must be very clear about the extent of authority they enjoy to speak and negotiate for their management. Finally, members must subordinate their personal views to the policies and priorities of the office they represent. When they fail on any of these dimensions, members expose the rule to delays, unnecessary conflicts and, possibly, late hits.

Workgroups must be integrated with the agency or department's senior management in order to avoid conflict and wasted effort. Senior management must provide direction at the outset of the rule-making to ensure that the workgroup embarks on its task with a clear view of what is expected. During the course of the rule-making, the leader and members of the workgroup must have access to and direction from their superiors when an unanticipated issue arises or when a conflict occurs that cannot be resolved in the workgroup. It was noted that most agencies have concurrence systems that are activated when a draft or final rule is ready for review and sign-off. While these are important, they are no substitute for regular and close consultation between the workgroup and those they represent. When consultation is close, concurrence processes should work quickly and smoothly.

It is evident from this brief survey that rule-making is managed intensively. The White House has made a considerable investment in attempting to manage rule-making on a government-wide basis. At least since the Carter Administration, and likely well before, departments and agencies have been developing their own multifaceted and sophisticated systems for managing the development of rules. The complexity and reach of contemporary rule-making have stimulated the use of workgroups for the development of individual rules. While a potentially effective means for drawing upon available expertise and involving affected interests, workgroup operations must be supported by management systems and facilitated by management skills. The level of management associated with rule-making is an important indicator of its importance as a function of government. Another is the amount of attention it commands from those outside the agency or department where it occurs. It is to this dimension that we now turn.

PARTICIPATION IN RULE-MAKING

In granting the law-making power to government, the Constitution is explicit that it resides exclusively with the legislative branch. Congress, with the acquiescence of the federal judiciary, has delegated this power to a variety of departments, agencies, boards, and commissions. What cannot be avoided or obscured is that in these serial and increasingly broad delegations of legislative power is a profound contradiction of basic democratic principles. Congress is a representative institution whose members are elected by the American people; the link between representation and law-making is elemental in our constitutional system. When agencies write rules, as they do thousands of times each year, this link between the people and the laws they must obey is broken. A paradox exists. Law-making by elected representatives is at the base of our political system, but rule-making by unelected bureaucrats is indispensable to the design, implementation, and administration of the programs the American people have demanded from their government. The paradox has no real solution, only an accommodation. We have substituted public participation for elections as a means for ensuring responsiveness in rulemaking.

Participation by the public provides rule-making with its claim on constitutional legitimacy (Robinson, 1991; Harter, 1982). As a surrogate for the vote, it serves to allow the views of affected and interested people to be considered as a rule is developing. However, legitimacy is not the sole benefit that public participation confers on the rule-making process. As we will see, contemporary rule-making has created a symbiotic relationship between those affected by rules and those in agencies who conduct the rule-making. Those affected will have their lives changed in some way by the work done by the agency. In many instances the rule-makers are dependent on those who will be affected by what is being written to provide information and insights needed to complete the rule. Public participation serves what Glen Robinson has termed an "informing" function, vesting the rule with more authority and credibility than it might otherwise enjoy (Robinson, 1991:126–128). The quality of public participation thus affects both the abstract and pragmatic dimensions of rule-making. It determines to a considerable extent the compatibility of rule-making, fundamental constitutional principles, and democratic values. At the same time it provides vital information that increases the likelihood that a rule will actually accomplish the purpose for which it is intended.

The quality of participation is determined by the opportunities for involvement by the public provided by agencies that write rules and the extent to which members of the public take advantage of them. We know considerably more about the former than the latter, but it is evident that public participation in rule-making is a major dimension of our current political system.

There is no evidence that public participation was a significant factor in rule-making prior to this century. While it is reasonable to assume that there was some form of contact between those writing rules and those affected by them, there is no contemporaneous evidence that suggests whether or to what extent it actually happened (Committee on Administrative Procedure, 1941). The origins of systematic public participation can be traced to the early years of the twentieth century as more and more interests began to organize to influence government decision-making. Some have speculated that administrative officials came into contact with these groups in the course of their other duties and this led naturally to communication to obtain information from them when regulations were being developed (Committee on Administrative Procedure, 1941). Then legislators, previously inattentive to the matter of rule-making procedure in general and silent on public participation, began to call for consultations with professional and business groups. Early examples of such requirements can be found in statutes dealing with transportation and agriculture. Participation in rule-making grew rapidly thereafter.

By the late 1930s, when the Attorney General's Committee conducted its research, a wide variety of mechanisms were in place to solicit the views of the public on proposed rules. The committee identified in its report five types of public participation occurring in the agencies it studied. Informal consultations with affected or interested parties were still in use in a number of agencies. Conferences, a more structured form of information dissemination that are common today in academia, professional groups, and trade associations of various sorts, were used on occasion. Several agencies moved to semipermanent advisory committees with whom they would consult when developing rules. In at least one instance, the Fair Labor

Standards program in the Department of Labor, an advisory committee, actually developed the rule through a form of collective bargaining among different interests.

Hearings were also in use by the time the committee conducted its research. Mandated in certain statutes, the hearing took two forms. The first, legislative-type hearings, were conducted in manner not unlike those held by congressional committees. They differed from the conferences referred to above in that the exchange of information in legislative hearings tended to be more one-sided and restricted. Agency officials heard the views and collected data from the interests invited to attend and frequently withheld their own positions or revealed them indirectly through the questions they asked witnesses. Adversary hearings, on the other hand, were patterned after court trials and governed by formal rules of evidence and procedure. Those developing the rule for the agency assumed the role of a litigant and external interests, opposed in some way to the course of action being proposed, assumed a similar role in arguing before a disinterested judge or tribunal. The finding of the judicial officer would ultimately determine the content of the rule, if the parties failed to settle the matter prior to an official decision.

It is striking how little the basic mechanisms of public participation have changed since the committee did its work over 50 years ago. The remarkable growth in opportunities for the public to participate in rule-making that has since occurred is best seen as an effort to extend the availability of these devices to more people and more diverse interests. Little has been done, however, to change the basic ways the public become involved in rule-making.

Given the relatively rich variety of forms of public participation that were in place and the urge to reform that led to its passage, it may strike some as curious that the rule-making provisions of the Administrative Procedure Act are so spare. The "notice and comment" provisions of the act were intended as a minimum expectation; nothing in the act could be construed as prohibiting or inhibiting the other forms of participation in place at the time it was drafted. These provisions should be seen as promoting a fundamental level of equity, regularity, and predictability to rule-making and, perhaps, broadening the reach of agencies when they seek guidance or approval from the public. One thing is evident from the examples provided in the committee's report. Those who benefitted from the various forms of participation were well-organized and well-endowed interests, not the common person. While its notice and comment provisions did little to provide the unorganized with the capacity to participate, the act did establish a greater degree of openness and at least an opportunity for all interested to present views. These provisions served as foundation on which would later be built a massive statutory structure for public participation.

Two decades after enactment of the Administrative Procedure Act, a revolution in public participation was underway that would continue until the early 1980s. Its elements are too numerous and diverse for extensive review here. There were parallel movements. One demanded greater openness in government decision-making, and culminated in various "sunshine" laws; the Freedom of Information Act and the Federal Advisory Committee Act (Barry and Witcomb, 1981:chapter 10; Gellhorn et al., 1979:chapter 6). Another wing of the movement focused on the need for more direct and extensive participation in the operation of government programs. This led to a number of efforts to increase citizen participation in the decisions of administrative agencies, including rule-making (Paglin and Schor, 1977; Schuck, 1977).

It is of great importance to rule-making that the explosion of social regulation coincided with this revolution in public participation. The statutes that created dozens of new programs and institutions focused heavily on rule-making as a means for enhancing the role of affected parties in determining the course of regulatory policy. It was the rare statute that did not call for some additional form of participation beyond the minimum requirements of the APA.

Among the more popular provisions were extended periods of public comment; required disclosures to the public of agency studies and technical reports; mandatory legislative-type hearings; a few instances of formal, trial type hearings; and provisions for the public to "offer" rules to the government for consideration (Administrative Conference of the United States, 1984:66–71). Specific authorizing legislation was hardly the only source of support for enhanced public participation. General statutes, affecting all rule-making, provided direct or indirect means for public involvement. The National Environmental Policy Act, the Paperwork Reduction Act, and the Regulatory Flexibility Act provided the public lateral entry into rule-making by highlighting certain issues and interests and mandating that they receive special consideration. Certain segments of the public were given special access to rule-making through congressionally mandated and agency-based programs to subsidize their participation. In the mid-1970s, with Congressional blessing, programs were put in place in many agencies, including the Federal Trade Commission, the Consumer Product Safety Commission, and the Office of Pesticides and Toxic Substances in the Environmental Protection Agency (Paglin and Schor, 1977).

Congress was not alone in pushing greater involvement of the public in rulemaking. President Carter made public participation a major element in his efforts to reform the regulatory process. His efforts stressed better information on agencies' plans for rule-making, longer periods of public comment, and the use of "advance notice of proposed rulemaking" to engage affected and interested parties at the earliest stages of rule development. Carter's initiatives had broader effects. Agencies reported more extensive programs of outreach to the public, including aggressive advertising in mass media to invite involvement in specific rule-making, direct invitation to interested and affected parties, and increased use of public funds to facilitate participation by individuals and groups that would otherwise lack the resources to get involved (Executive Office of the President, 1979). It should be noted that the actual implementation of public funding programs was halting in some agencies (Rosenbaum, 1983:185–189).

The initiatives of the Carter years mark the high point of government efforts to increase public participation in rule-making. The Reagan administration took the position that direct public participation of the sort promoted by Carter and the Congress served to undercut the role of elected officials in guiding and overseeing rule-making (Berry et al., 1989) and other regulatory decisions. The Bush administration took a similar view. Although this skepticism and lack of support might halt or slow further growth, the range of opportunities for the public to become involved in rule-making is already enormous. The question is whether these opportunities are exploited, and by whom.

The movements to open the process of government decision-making and to increase and diversify opportunities for public participation influenced the rule-making process profoundly. Another development of enormous importance was the explosive rise of interest groups during the past 25 years. Whether the rise of interest groups was a cause or consequence of the participation revolution cannot be considered seriously here. It is important to understand how these groups attempt to influence the rule-making process and whether they are successful in these efforts. Research on interest group involvement in rule-making is neither extensive nor systematic. While there are a number of case studies of rule-making (some classics in the field) that shed some light on the behavior of interest groups, there is a paucity of work that attempts to deal with the issue more generally. A recent survey of Washington-based organizations attempted to learn more about interest group involvement in rule-making. The results, drawn from the responses of more than 170 organizations that answered the mailed questionnaire, do provide some insights into the rule-making strategies and tactics of interest groups (Kerwin, in progress).

More than three-quarters of the organizations responded that they were involved in rule-making and of these 90 percent reported that they considered this activity a medium or high priority. When asked to compare the importance of rule-making to other public policy activities the organization might engage in, over 60 percent of those who responded rated it as or more important than lobbying Congress, 67 percent rated it as or more important than contributing to political campaigns, and nearly 80 percent rated it as or more important than litigation. Interest groups use a variety of devices to monitor rule-making in the agencies. The survey results indicate that while the *Federal Register* is used by a majority on a regular basis, other means, including professional newsletters, informal contacts with professional colleagues, and informal contacts with agency personnel are also used quite frequently.

When interest groups get involved in rule-making they do so for a wide variety of reasons. The respondents in the survey were asked to consider the rule-makings they have attempted to influence and to estimate the percentage of time their involvement was due to a particular concern. A number of issues are common and persistent. Among these are the quality of information the agency is using as a basis for its rule, the quality of the agency's supporting analysis, the clarity of the rule, the time affected entities will have to comply with the rule's provisions, and the costs of compliance.

The means that groups use to influence rule-making are also varied. The most frequent are preparing written comments on proposed rules in response to a *Federal Register* notice, formation of coalitions with other organizations, and informal contacts with agency personnel both before and after the notice of proposed rule-making is issued. Also used, but less frequently, are mobilization of the organization's membership to influence the rule-making and participation in public hearings. The mechanisms least likely to be used are participation in advisory committees and petitions to initiate rule-making.

That a tactic to influence rule-making is used does not necessarily mean that it is effective in influencing the content of the rule. The organizations were asked to rank each form of participation on a scale that ranged from "least effective" to "most effective." The results are interesting and potentially quite important. Based on the frequency a given tactic was considered highly effective (a score of 4 or 5 on a five-point scale), the following rank order emerges: informal contact before the notice of proposed rule-making, coalition formation, written comments, informal contact after the notice of proposed rule-making, mobilizing the membership to influence the rule-making, participation in public hearings, advisory committee membership, and petitions to initiate rulemaking. It is striking that informal contacts figure so prominently in the tactics of the organizations surveyed, rivaling or surpassing in perceived effectiveness the forms that figured so prominently in the public participation revolution of the 1960s and 1970s.

Do interest groups get what they want from their participation in rule-making? Apparently so, at least according to this survey. When asked how successful they were, 77 percent of the organizations reported that they get what they want from rule-making 50 percent or more of the time they actively participate. A somewhat larger number stated that the agencies they worked with were responsive to their concerns 50 percent or more of the time they participated in rule-making.

What emerges from this survey, and from the available case studies, is a rule-making process in which interest groups are active and influential participants (Cheit, 1990; Fritschler, 1989). They use a variety of devices to remain informed about rules under development and a variety of tactics to influence their contents. It is evident that informal, extralegal devices play an important role in the relationships that develop between interest groups and agencies during the course of rule-making. It is also evident, however, that the devices established in law for public participation are themselves important and may in fact create the conditions in which less formal means of communication thrive. Interest groups are not the only institutions that take notice of rule-making and influence its course and results. Political and legal institutions external to rule-making agencies are intensely interested in their work.

ACCOUNTABILITY: THE REVIEW OF RULES BY CONGRESS, THE PRESIDENT, AND THE COURTS

Like participation, accountability takes on a special significance in rule-making. When unelected bureaucrats are engaged in the writing of law, accountability is an inevitable issue. The requirement of public participation is in itself no guarantee that departments and agencies will be true to the intent of the statutes that granted them the power to write rules and established the goals they were to achieve when doing so. Nor does it ensure that rule-makers will take cognizance of and heed the broader mandates of electoral majorities. Participation will not necessarily promote compliance with many legal obligations that attach to rule-making and require more than input from the public. If the bureaucrats who write rules are not directly accountable to voters, it is important that they be answerable to those who are elected and those in whom the protection of constitutional principles and legal mandates is entrusted. The roles of Congress, the president, and the judiciary in rule-making vary. Each employs very different mechanisms for reviewing rules, and each pursues different objectives. All, however, are deeply involved in the rule-making process.

Congressional Review

At one time the potential power Congress exerted over rule-making was more formidable than it is today. Armed with the legislative veto Congress could review, negate, and redirect the rules written in a large number of departments and agencies of the federal government. At its height, the legislative veto was a very popular device. Several hundred authorizing statutes empowered various elements of the Congress, ranging from both houses to single committees, to exercise this potentially lethal influence over the handiwork of rule-makers (Gazell and Pugh, 1985; Craig, 1983). The literature on congressional oversight of the executive branch has generally found it to be inconsistent both in frequency and effect. Research on the legislative veto indicates that it is true to this general form. However effective it once was, the legislative veto is no more. Since the decision of the Supreme Court in *Immigration and Naturalization Service v. Chadha* that found the veto provisions unconstitutional, Congress has had to resort to other means to ensure accountability in rule-making. The arsenal remains potent.

Congress always has at its disposal the powers to appropriate funds and confirm nominees to agency positions that exercise supervisory authority over rule-making. We noted in an earlier section the enormous increase in procedural requirements Congress has imposed on rule-making. It is important to note that Congress has also attempted to become more specific regarding the subject matter of rules in an effort to narrow the range of discretion of agency officials in the content of rules. Deadlines have become much more common in statutes that mandate the development of rules. A recent study found that over 600 deadlines were included in environmental statutes alone (Administrative Conference of the United States, 1991). Deadlines are controversial. Some consider them an essential counterweight to bureaucratic dysfunctions that lead to excessive delay in the issuance of rules. Others find them unrealistic, serving short-term political objectives rather than the long-term goals of the programs rules define. However determined, and whatever their underlying motives, deadlines, when combined with greater direction in statutes regarding the substance of rules, serve to structure the rule-making agendas of agencies. Each also gives external interests additional grounds to challenge the results of rule-making, or lack thereof, in court.

In addition to its efforts to direct the course of rule-making prospectively, Congress is also involved in reviewing results. The demise of the legislative veto did not end congressional inquiries into the performance of rule-makers. On the contrary, recent research confirms that the review of rules remains prominent among the various devices Congress uses to exercise oversight over the bureaucracy. In one study, based on extensive interviews with congressional decision-makers, review of rules ranked eighth among 14 oversight functions in terms of frequency with which it is used (Aberbach, 1990:135). In another, the author, commenting on the relative unimportance of the legislative veto, concluded that other, familiar oversight devices, such as those discussed above, were sufficiently effective to obviate the need to exercise the veto (Foreman, 1988:143).

It is certainly true that Congress acknowledges the importance of the powers it places in the hands of bureaucrats when it delegates rule-making authority. Congress has an impressive array of tools at its disposal to influence the course of rulemaking, both from the outset and after the fact. But, in efforts to maintain control the massive volume of law-making, serial delegations of authority set in motion by members of Congress face aggressive competition from the White House.

Presidential Review

An earlier section has reviewed the gradual development of a presidential capability to manage the rule-making process and influence its results. Through five administrations the structures and procedures of the White House program have developed and become more focused. It is important to underscore that White House efforts can properly be viewed as a form of accountability. The president, elected by the entire nation, has rightful claim to a mandate from the American people. No less than the Congress, the president has the obligation to see that this mandate is translated into policy and program. The White House rule-making management programs are designed to accomplish this objective.

Table 1 summarizes for 1989 key features of the review program administered by the Office of Management and Budget. It shows the number of rules reviewed according to agency and summarizes the actions taken.

It is worth noting that the volume of rules varies considerably by agency, as do the actions taken by OMB. In many instances the number of rules reviewed is small and number of rules altered in any significant way is also small. Of course, we cannot determine from Table 1 the relative importance of the rules affected by OMB review for their particular subject matter. It is evident, however, that the rules of some agencies have a different fate with OMB, with a substantial percentage altered, withdrawn, or returned for additional work.

This table demonstrates the size, scope, and significance of review by the Office of Management and Budget. The review function has been controversial and the target of several legal challenges by those who argued that it was an unconstitutional interference in the rule-making authorities granted to agencies and departments by Congress. In all but one relatively narrow instance, these challenges have failed. The National Academy of Public Administration concluded in a study of OMB review and related activities that, with certain qualifications and reforms, the president should retain this form of management control over rule-making (National Academy of Public Administration, 1987). One is hard pressed to find a plausible scenario that has a future president voluntarily ceding this powerful mechanism for influencing public policy and promoting bureaucratic accountability.

Table 1 Types of Actions Taken on Agency Rules by OMB During 1989

Agency	Total reviews	Consistent without change	Consistent with change	Withdrawn by agency	Returned for reconsideration	Returned, sent improperly	Suspended	Emergency	Statutory or judicial deadline
USDA	405	339	58	4	1	0	1	2	0
HHS	283	187	82	7	5	0	2	0	0
DOT	250	195	48	3	1	0	0	1	2
EPA	201	97	59	5	11	0	4	1	24
DOC	195	177	12	5	0	0	0	1	20
DOJ	100	87	6	2	0	1	0	2	2
DOI	97	82	11	2	2	0	0	0	0
VA	95	85	8	2	0	0	0	0	0
ED	82	51	26	4	0	0	1	0	0
HUD	78	27	30	14	3	0	3	0	1
GSA	61	46	10	3	2	0	0	0	0
DOL	60	22	33	0	2	0	2	0	1
OPM	53	43	5	2	2	0	0	0	1
TREAS	47	37	9	1	0	0	0	0	0
SBA	39	30	8	0	0	0	0	0	1
FEMA	29	16	10	3	0	0	0	0	0
RailroadRetirement Board	21	19	2	0	0	0	0	0	0
DOE	19	12	2	2	0	0	0	1	2
NASA	16	11	3	0	0	0	1	0	1
STATE	15	14	1	0	0	0	0	0	0
National Archives Records Administration	8	7	1	0	0	0	0	0	0
USIA	7	6	0	1	0	0	0	0	0
DOD	6	3	1	0	0	0	1	0	0
EEOC	5	4	1	0	0	0	0	0	0
NSF	5	5	0	0	0	0	0	0	0
USIDCA	4	3	1	0	0	0	0	0	0
Federal Mediation and Concilliation Service	3	2	1	0	0	0	0	0	0
Other Temporary Commissions	3	3	0	0	0	0	0	0	0
ACTION	2	2	0	0	0	0	0	0	0
ADF	2	2	0	0	0	0	0	0	0
IMS	2	2	0	0	0	0	0	0	0
PEACE	2	2	0	0	0	0	0	0	0
SSS	2	2	0	0	0	0	0	0	0
ATBCB	1	0	1	0	0	0	0	0	0
CCR	1	0	1	0	0	0	0	0	0
NEA	1	1	0	0	0	0	0	0	0
NEH	1	1	0	0	0	0	0	0	0
OMB	1	1	0	0	0	0	0	0	0
PBGC	1	1	0	0	0	0	0	0	0
Federal Acquisition Regulations	1	1	0	0	0	0	0	0	0
Federal Credit System Assistance Board	1	1	0	0	0	0	0	0	1
FHLBB	2	0	0	0	0	0	0	1	0
Inter-American Foundation	2	2	0	0	0	0	0	0	0
Office of Government Ethics	1	1	0	0	0	0	0	0	0
PCC	7	7	0	0	0	0	0	0	0
RTC	1	1	0	0	0	0	0	0	0
USTR	1	1	0	0	0	0	0	0	0
U.S. Office of Special Counsel	1	0	1	0	0	0	0	0	0
Total	2,220	1,638	431	61	29	1	15	9	36
Percentage of Total	100.0	73.8	19.4	2.7	1.3	0.1	0.7	0.4	16

Source: Regulatory Program of the United States Government: April 1, 1990–March 31, 1991. Executive Office of the President, Washington, D.C. P. 36

Review by the Office of Management and Budget of proposed and final rules is not the sole vehicle for accountability operating out of the White House. We noted earlier that President Reagan created the Vice President's Task Force on Regulatory Relief as part of his effort to roll back the presence of the federal government in the American economy. Included in its mission was the review of existing rules that were having a particularly deleterious effect on especially delicate sectors of the economy. For the period of its existence the task force devoted considerable attention to regulations affecting the automobile industry. Its record in achieving "relief" for the economy was apparently not sufficient, the next president decided that it was no longer needed.

President Bush, who headed the Task Force as vice president, reinstituted it in significantly modified form shortly after taking office in 1989. The new body, the Council on Competitiveness chaired by Vice President Quayle, would have supervisory authority over the entire OMB clearance function and independently review proposed rules that it deems especially significant. The council is different from the task force in that it is not limited to reviewing rules already on the books. Early in its tenure the council established itself as an aggressive and highly controversial agent for President Bush, reviewing and securing changes in a wide variety of important and visible rules. Most notable was the council's successful efforts to reverse an important rule proposed by the Environmental Protection Agency to implement a key provision of the 1990 amendments to the Clean Air Act. Critics charged that the council served as an agent of "regulated companies" and "exerts behind the scenes pressure to force agencies into compromising on environmental, health and safety initiatives" (Triano and Watzman, 1991:iii). President Clinton abolished the Council soon after taking office.

The president, unlike the diffuse system in place in Congress, now holds a funnel through which all rules of any significance must flow before they become law. The emergence and institutionalization of this capability are highly significant. The president now enjoys potentially unprecedented influence over the development of American law and public policy. The opportunity to review and influence the content of regulations is certainly less sweeping in its scope than the setting of the legislative agenda, the submission of a budget, or even the veto. Nevertheless, given the pace of the legislative process and the recent conflict between these branches (Thurber, 1991), an argument can be made that the small, incremental changes secured through the review of rules are more efficient and effective in the long run. One can only speculate on the "deterrent" effect that OMB exerts on rulemakers.

Judicial Review

A vast literature is devoted to judicial review of rules and the processes by which they are made. This aspect of rule-making has been studied the longest and is best understood. Every text in administrative law contains a chapter or section devoted to the topic. Three general issues dominate this body of scholarship. Much attention has been paid to the standards for granting judicial review. Another prominent theme in the literature is the scope of judicial inquiry once review is granted. Finally, some scholars have focused on the consequences of judicial review for the rule-making process.

Before granting review of rules issued by an agency, the court must be satisfied that the controversy in question and the persons bringing the case possess certain characteristics. Regarding the case, the courts will determine whether the issue in reviewable, that is, one the judiciary has the authority to hear. At least since the Administrative Procedure Act's general authorization, there has been a presumption in favor of review of important agency actions such as rule-making. Statutory preclusions of review are rare and can be circumvented when questions of constitutionality are raised. Beyond reviewability, the court will seek to ensure that the issue is "ripe" for review, a determination that hinges on whether the rule-making in question is final and that no additional agency action is contemplated or available to the parties bringing the case. The principles of finality and ripeness for review prevent premature judicial review and usurpation of legitimate administrative authority.

The parties bringing the case are of considerable interest to the court contemplating review of a rule. The principle at work here is "standing to sue" and seeks to ensure that there is indeed a case or controversy for the court to decide. Standing to sue administrative agencies was once difficult to obtain, but these obstacles were effectively swept away by the Administrative Procedure Act and subsequent judicial interpretations of it and related statutory provisions. In its section 702, the APA grants standing to those "suffering a legal wrong because of an agency action, or adversely affected or aggrieved. . . ." Since passage of the act the Supreme Court has interpreted these terms generously, granting standing to individuals and organizations whose claimed adverse effects are arguably intangible and whose linkage to agency rule-making is attenuated, at best. Of course, Congress has extended standing even more broadly by including "citizen suit" provisions in many regulatory statutes. While there is some evidence that the Rehnquist Court is beginning to take a more critical and restrictive approach to standing, the judiciary remains open to those with both minimal and creative definitions of adverse effects and who can map a plausible causal path between the rule and the harm they have or may suffer.

The Administrative Conference of the United States defines the scope of judicial review as "the standard by which a court will judge the validity of the agency action in review proceedings" (1991:320). Section 706 of the Administrative Procedure Act provides the starting point for consideration. It states:

> The reviewing court shall--
> (1) compel agency action unlawfully withheld or unreasonably delayed; and
> (2) hold unlawful and set aside agency action, findings, and conclusions found to be—
>   (a) arbitrary, capricious, an abuse of discretion, or otherwise not in accordance with law;
>   (b) contrary to constitutional right, power, privilege, or immunity;
>   (c) in excess of statutory jurisdiction, authority, or limitations, or short of statutory right;
>   (d) without observance of procedure required by law;
>   (e) unsupported by substantial evidence in a case subject to section 556 and 557 of this title or otherwise reviewed on the record of an agency hearing provided by statute; or
>   (f) unwarranted by the facts to the extent that the facts are subject to trial de novo by the reviewing court.

While each of these provisions is potentially important to rule-making, three deserve particular attention. The first, requiring courts to consider whether agency inaction is unlawful, has particular significance because of the volume of rule-making that can reasonably be expected from agencics. Sweeping delegations of authority and increasingly frequent statutory deadlines for the completion of rules have combined to expose numerous agencies to challenge for their alleged failure to undertake rule-makings or for conducting them in an excessively dilatory manner. Although courts have generally allowed agencies to set their own agendas for rule-making not expressly mandated in statute, this deference disappears when courts are persuaded that Congress has explicitly required issuance of a regulation, with or without an explicit deadline.

Section 706(2)(d) requires courts to act when rules are developed without benefit of proper procedure. As with the issue of agency inaction, patterns in contemporary legislation have increased the likelihood of challenge to rule-making on procedural grounds. As Congress increased the analytical and public participation requirements associated with rule-making, it was simultaneously providing new bases for lawsuits by those who believed that agencies were failing to meet these new responsibilities. Several of these statutes, notably the National Environmental Policy Act, the Paperwork Reduction Act, and the Federal Advisory Committee Act, establish procedural requirements at least as formidable as the original notice and comment provisions of the Administrative Procedure Act. In addition, these statutes potentially apply to the development of any rule not specifically exempted from their provisions. This means that an agency must frequently make a preliminary decision regarding the applicability of a given statute to a particular rule-making. These decisions are open to question as well.

The final provision to be considered is found in section 706(2)(a) and calls upon the courts to overturn rules that are found to be "arbitrary, capricious, an abuse of discretion, or otherwise not in accordance with law." The judiciary has struggled over the years to give meaning to these terms. Certainly, simple dictionary definitions of "arbitrary" and "capricious" would give enormous latitude to agencies, since few decisions would be so devoid of basis and purpose to merit such descriptions. "Abuse of discretion" is a phrase lacking any meaning without the context of the statute that an agency is entrusted with administering. This element in the scope of judicial review is crucially important, however, since it goes to the substance of rules and the quality of the information and judgment that contributed to their formation. The fundamental decision a court must make in measuring a rule against these standards is the extent to which it will defer to the agency writing the rule. At present, the standard of deference is by no means crystal clear. Supreme Court cases of the past two decades reflect the ambiguities in the judiciary's approach to reviewing the substance of rules.

In *Citizens to Preserve Overton Park v. Volpe* the Court concluded that agency rules would be closely examined during judicial review. In their decision they found the "arbitrary and capricious" standard to require an inquiry by the judges that was "searching and careful" and designed to determine "whether the (agency's) decision was based on a consideration of the relevant factors and whether there had been a clear error in judgment . . ." (Administrative Conference of the United States, 1991:324). However, the Court cautioned that judges were not to substitute their judgments for those of agencies. The *Overton Park* decision provided the courts with a broad mandate to review the substance of rules and the process by which they were developed. This basic approach, known as the "hard look" standard of review, has been reaffirmed on numerous occasions and further clarified. In 1984, for example, in *Motor Vehicle Manufacturers Association v. State Farm,* the Court stated that a rule should be voided by the judiciary "if the agency has relied on factors Congress has not intended it to consider, entirely failed to consider an important aspect of the problem, offered an explanation for its decision that runs counter to the evidence before it or is so implausible that it could not be ascribed to a difference in view or the product or agency expertise" (Administrative Conference of the United States, 1991:328). Phrases like "important aspect of the problem" and "counter to the evidence" have no intrinsic meaning; judges must define them in the context provided by the circumstance of each challenged rulemaking. In short, they must exercise discretion when reviewing decisions by agency personnel during the course of rulemaking. It has led one observer to conclude that cases like those noted above will "provide the framework for the seemingly never-ending dialogue on the shape of the partnership between courts and administrative agencies" (Mintz, 1990:371). It should be noted that a perspective on review different from that taken in *State Farm* can be found in the so-called *Chevron* decision, which is discussed at length by Schwartz in this volume's Chapter 9.

There is a great deal of evidence that judicial review has a substantial effect on the rule-making process or the content of rules. No agency with a substantial rule-making program escapes litigation and no agency is completely successful in answering these legal challenges. Judicial review can alter rule-making procedures across the entire government. The "hard look" standard of review discussed above forced agencies of all sorts to change in very fundamental ways the manner in which they conducted informal rule-making. One major impact was the development of the documentation, or record, that supported the rule that was written (Pedersen, 1975). Another was change in the way public comment and related input were considered and answered by rule-making agencies (Administrative Conference of the United States, 1991:271). We know from existing research and recent experience that judges have interpreted statutes in such a way that whole programs of rule-making, completely unanticipated by the responsible agency, were undertaken (Melnick, 1983).

Judicial review has had a particularly dramatic impact on the newer agencies of social regulation. The experience of the Environmental Protection Agency is instructive in this regard. Recent research has documented a wide variety of effects, including an increase in the power of certain offices and officials, internal redistributions of resources, loss of autonomy and discretion, and changes in the agency's policy and program priorities (O'Leary:1993:Chapter 7).

It is reasonable to expect, based on this scholarship, that decisions requiring the issuance or alteration of rules, especially when accompanied by a judicially imposed deadline, immediately become the top priority of the affected agency. This causes other organizational changes noted in studies of the effects of judicial review.

The impacts of review are both positive and negative. On the positive side, judicial review is a mechanism that forces an agency to meet its statutory responsibilities and correct its errors. In this regard, it is a powerful tool for accountability. It can also be a valuable aid to a program office struggling to meet these obligations with inadequate resources or attention from senior officials (O'Leary, 1993:160–162). The threat of a contempt of court citation can often do far more than memos and meetings to alter the internal distributions of personnel and money in a rulemaking agency. On the other hand, judicial review, by definition, deals with individual rules on a case-by-case basis. This has led some to argue that it has the potential to fragment rule-making and threaten the coherence of the programs that rules define. Others charge that judicial review often frustrates good scientific and technical analysis by imposing deadlines every bit as unrealistic as those by Congress on rule-makers. Although agencies have means of their own to deal with these negative effects, the arrival of an action-forcing judicial decision at a rule-making agency is bound to have a disruptive effect. These are effects that agencies have learned to live with and there is every indication that they will have to continue to adapt in the future.

Conclusion

Although it remains popular in some quarters to portray functions such as rule-making and the officials that perform them as irresponsible, unresponsive, and essentially out of control, this brief review of the mechanisms of accountability should leave the reader with a contrary impression. Indeed, the tools available to the constitutional branches have the potential to put rule-makers firmly under their control. There is competition between the branches for influence over rule-making. The potential of Congress, the president, and the courts is rarely fully realized, but the capabilities are there nonetheless. There is also ample evidence that they are used regularly to redirect and reform the substance and process of rule-making.

REFORMING RULEMAKING: THE PROMISE OF REGULATORY NEGOTIATION

We have been reforming rule-making for almost 100 years. Statutes enacted at the turn of the century required agencies to consult with external professional groups, ostensibly to improve the quality of the rules they produced. Since then there have been a number of legislative, executive, and judicial landmarks in this long effort to make rule-making all things to all people. In this section the focus is on a recent and much discussed reform of rule-making known as regulatory negotiation. Its roots can be traced to programs of rule-making that are well over 50 years old, but the proponents and practitioners of regulatory negotiation view it as a means for dealing with contemporary and serious problems.

Rule-making through the use of consensual processes can be traced back at least as far as the Fair Labor Standards Act of the 1930s (Committee on Administrative Procedure, 1941). As noted above, it contained provisions requiring that wages and other conditions be established in rules developed by committees that represented both management and labor as well as the agency. Contemporary regulatory negotiation differs from this and other earlier versions of the concept in that it contemplates negotiation among multiple parties that may or may not have a continuing relationship, such as those that exist between employees and employers, or the producers and sellers of agricultural products. Phillip Harter, a leading scholar and advocate of the use of this technique, views the quality of involvement by the interested parties as the crucial difference between it and conventional rulemaking. As he puts it, "parties participate directly and immediately in the decision. They share in its development and concur with it rather than 'participate' by submitting information . . ." (Harter, 1982:28).

Harter and other proponents of regulatory negotiation consider it a means of overcoming a number of the most significant problems that afflict rule-making. As we noted above, the development of important rules is often marked by conflict and delay. Information is frequently difficult to obtain and, once written, rules often prove difficult to implement because interested and affected parties do not know whether or how to comply, refuse to cooperate, or the rule itself is badly flawed. As a result, litigation has become, for some agencies, a normal step in the rule-making process.

Advocates for regulatory negotiation accept the fact that interests will disagree but substitute face-to-face communication for the indirect, antiseptic notice and comment process, the limited interchanges of public hearings, and the adversariness and information-distorting qualities of formal, trial-type proceedings. The quantity and quality of information available to the rule-making improve because those who possess it are at the table and sharing it with one another. For this reason the results are likely to be more accurate, realistic, and acceptable to the interested parties. Implementation, problems and litigation should decline and compliance should increase if those affected by the rule concur with the results of the regulatory negotiation. The legitimacy of the rule and the relationship between the agency and its external constituencies are enhanced (Harter, 1982).

Even the strongest proponents of regulatory negotiation realize that there are a number of potentially insurmountable obstacles that could prevent a regulatory negotiation from achieving these results. Harter identifies several. Some issues are simply nonnegotiable because they are determined by law or held too deeply by those affected. The interests affected by a prospective rule must be identified, and be willing and able to participate in the negotiation. They must also not be so numerous that the negotiation becomes unwieldly, or so hostile to one another that the animus prevents serious discussion. Explicit protocols for the conduct of the negotiation and decision rule about what will constitute consensus for the group must be agreed to, and must hold. Most regulatory negotiations will require an effective "convenor" who serves as a facilitator of the process and, depending on the circumstances, an intervenor. Finally, the agency responsible for the rule must be an active participant. Although the agency is legally constrained in its ability to delegate authority to negotiation groups (Susskind and McMahon, 1985), the expectation that the results will at least influence the content of the rule is fundamental to convincing interested parties to participate. These are substantial conditions but experience to date indicates that they can be met.

Regulatory negotiation has been and continues to be used in highly visible and potentially contentious rule-makings. A number of the most prominent rule-making agencies, including the Departments of Transportation, Agriculture, Interior, and Labor, the Environmental Protection Agency, and the Nuclear Regulatory Agency have used this device. The range of substantive rule-making issues to which it has been applied is impressive. The list includes flight time limitations for airline crews; nondiscrimination towards the handicapped in both air and surface travel; hazardous substances, such as pesticides, benzene, and asbestos; and financial assistance for children with special education needs (Pritzker and Dalton, 1990:chapter 10). Regulatory negotiation is currently being used to develop a number of important regulations that will implement the provisions of the 1990 amendments to the Clean Air Act.

A full evaluation of regulatory negotiation has not yet been done and will not be attempted here. There are instances of success and failure, but the available evidence suggests that regulatory negotiation can in fact accomplish some, if not all, of the ambitious goals outlined above. In a substantial number of well-documented cases the full range of affected parties has been successfully identified and agreed to negotiate. Actual negotiations have been structured and conducted in such a way that consensus was reached and the agreements became the bases for rules issued by the agency. It appears that litigation rates for negotiated rules are quite low. There is no hard evidence as yet on ease of implementation and compliance rates for negotiated rules.

The experience of the last decade highlights a number of problems that will confront regulatory negotiation in the future. The upfront investment for those engaged in the frequently intense and intensive sessions that characterize regulatory negotiation is greater than that for conventional rule-making. These costs include the time of key personnel, information collection, and travel (DR Forum, 1986). Although an obstacle to participation by all concerned, this is a particular problem for less well-funded organizations and raises again the question of public funding for involvement by those who otherwise lack the capacity to join the negotiation. Participation in regulatory negotiation may not always signal a desire for the rule-making to be successful. It can be manipulated by those seeking to extend the time it takes to produce the rule or to advocate positions that will ultimately make the rule difficult for the agency to work with. Some in the judiciary have made it plain that their reviews of the results of regulatory negotiation is likely to be just as searching as that for other forms of rule-making (Wald, 1985).

Despite these real and potential problems, regulatory negotiation has impressive support. The Administrative Conference of the United States is a longstanding proponent of the idea, a number of private organizations have been directly involved in negotiations, and the Congress has increasingly embraced it in both general and specific statutes. In 1990 it passed into law the Negotiated Rulemaking Act that established operating principles agencies were expected to observe when conducting regulatory negotiations. The act is generally supportive of the use of regulatory negotiation, instructs agencies on the criteria for selecting rules that will be developed in this way, and adopts provisions similar to the Federal Advisory Committee Act that govern the assembly and operations of negotiation committees. Congress has also required the use of negotiation in the development of rules in individual programs. Notable among recent provisions in authorizing statutes are those affecting rule-making in the Federal Aviation Administration, the Department of Education, and the Nuclear Regulatory Commission (Pritzker and Dalton, 1990:346–347).

As a concept, regulatory negotiation has much to commend it, but its ultimate success and long-term impact on rule-making are by no means certain. At this writing it appears that the Clinton administration has embraced it, but the operational problems it faces remain formidable. The most fundamental challenge is to overcome the tradition of adversariness that has characterized significant rule-making for so long. At a more pragmatic level, its legitimacy depends on locating and involving affected interests, its success depends on the conduct of the negotiations and the flexibility of those participating, and its credibility hinges on its results becoming law and surviving whatever judicial review occurs. Nevertheless, it stands among the most innovative and potentially significant changes in rule-making that have ever been attempted.

CONCLUSION

Whether or not one accepts my opening statement that rule-making is the most important function performed by agencies of government, one cannot dispute its central role in the definition of rights, obligations, and operational details of public programs. The subject matter of rule-making is enormously varied, spanning the full range of American law and public policy. Its crucial importance as an instrument of government is underscored by the amount of attention it commands from Congress, presidents, and the judiciary. Each of these branches, in their efforts to direct and review rule-making, are acknowledging implicitly the extent to which it influences their own roles in our constitutional system. We have seen that rule-making is managed as a government-wide program out of the White House, by each agency, commission, and department of government, and at the level of the individual role. Hence it is a major task for contemporary public management. It is also apparent that it has become a focal point of political activity for organizations, groups, and firms attempting to influence the content of law and public policy.

Proceeding from the assumption that the prominence and importance of rule-making as an instrument of government will not diminish, this chapter concludes with an entreaty to the fields of political science and public administration. Around rule-making have assembled all the major forces of contemporary politics and public management. Scholars of those disciplines must make an investment in the study of rule-making comparable to that made by students of the law. Legal scholars have made major contributions to our understanding of this process, but their perspective and concerns are different from those who study politics and the administration of public programs. Until its political, managerial, and policy dimensions are more completely explored, our understanding of rule-making will be incomplete. Political science and public administration will, as a result, fail to fully achieve their scholarly missions. And, if we believe in the link between research and practice, rule-making will not perform its crucial role as well as it otherwise might.

REFERENCES

Aberbach, Joel (1990). *Keeping a Watchful Eye: The Politics of Congressional Oversight,* Brookings Institution, Washington, D.C.

Administrative Conference of the United States (1991), 2nd edition. *A Guide to Federal Agency Rulemaking,* Washington, D.C.

Administrative Conference of the United States (1984) *A Guide to Federal Agency Rulemaking,* Washington, D.C.

Anthony, Robert A. (1992). Interpretive rules, policy statements, guidances, manuals and the like—should federal agencies use them to bind the public? *Duke University Law Review,* 14:1311-1384.

Barke, Richard (1984). Regulatory delay as political strategy, *Federal Administrative Agencies* (Howard Ball, ed.), Prentice-Hall, Englewood Cliffs, NJ, pp. 144-56.

Barry, Donald and Whitcomb, Howard (1981). *The Legal Foundations of Public Administration,* West Publishing, St. Paul, MN.

Berry, Jeffrey, Portney, Kent and Thomson, Ken (1989). Empowering and involving citizens, *Handbook of Public Administration* (James Perry, ed.), Jossey Bass, San Francisco.

Breyer, Stephen and Stewart, Richard (1985). *Administrative Law and Regulatory Policy,* Little Brown, Boston.

Bryner, Gary (1987). *Bureaucratic Discretion: Law and Policy in Federal Regulatory Agencies,* Pergamon Press, New York.

Cheit, Ross (1990). *Setting Safety Standards: Regulation in the Public and Private Sectors,* University of California Press, Berkeley, CA.

Cole, Roland and Summers, Paul (1981). *Complying with Government Requirements: The Cost to Small and Larger Businesses,* Battelle Human Affairs Research Centers, Seattle, WA.

Committee on Administrative Procedure (1941). *Administrative Procedure in Government Agencies,* Senate Document No. 8, 77th Congress.

Committee on Government Affairs (1977). *Study on Federal Regulation,* Senate Document, 95th Congress, 1st session.

Cooper, Phillip (1983). *Public Law and Administration,* Mayfield Publishing, Palo Alto, CA.

Craig, Barbara H. (1983). *The Legislative Veto: Congressional Control of Regulation,* Westview, Boulder, CO.

Davis, Kenneth Culp (1969). *Discretionary Justice: A Preliminary Inquiry,* University of Illinois Press, Chicago.

Diver, Colin (1989). Regulatory precision, *Making Regulatory Policy* (Keith Hankins and John Thomas, eds.). University of Pittsburgh Press, Pittsburgh, PA.

Dobelstein, Andrew (1990). *Social Welfare: Policy and Analysis,* Nelson-Hell, Chicago.

DR Forum, Regulatory negotiation: Four perspectives, *DR Forum,* National Institute for Dispute Resolution, January 1986:8.

Eisner, Neil (1989). Agency delay in informal rulemaking, *Administrative Law Journal,* 3:7 52.

Emery, Fred (1982). *Rulemaking as an Organizational Process,* Administrative Conference of the United States, Washington, D.C.

Estreicher, Samuel (1985). Policy oscillation at the Labor Board: A plea for rulemaking, *Administrative Law Review, 37*: 163.

Executive Office of the President (1979). *Improving Government Regulations: A Progress Report,* Office of Management and Budget.

Fiorinia, Morris (1982). Legislative choice of regulatory forms: Legal process or administrative process, *Public Choice, 39*: 33-66.

Foreman, Christopher (1988). *Signals from the Hill,* Yale University Press, New Haven, CT.

Fritschler, A. Lee (1989). *Smoking and Politics,* 4th edition, Prentice-Hall, Englewood Cliffs, NJ.

Fritschler, A. Lee (1984). The changing face of government regulation, *Federal Administrative Agencies* (Howard Ball, ed.). Prentice-Hall, Englewood Cliffs, NJ.

Fuchs, R. F. (1938). Procedure in administrative rulemaking, *Harvard Law Review, 52*: 259.

Gazell, James and Pugh, Darrell (1985). Voiding the legislative veto: Possible impacts for the administrative state, *Glendale Law Review, 7*: 1.

Gelhorn, Ernest, Byse, Clark and Strauss, Peter (1979). *Administrative Law: Cases and Comments,* Seventh edition, Foundation Press, Mineola, NY.

Harter, Phillip (1982). Negotiating regulations: A cure for the malaise, *Georgetown Law Review, 71*: 1, 28.

Heffron, Florence and McFeely, Neil (1983). *The Administrative Regulatory Process,* Longman, New York.
Kerwin, Cornelius (in progress). *Rulemaking: How Government Agencies Write Law and Make Policy.* Congressional Quarterly Press, Washington, D.C.
Kerwin, Cornelius (1992). The management of rulemaking, paper presented at the annual meeting of the American Society for Public Administration, Chicago, Illinois, April, 1992.
Kerwin, Cornelius and Furlong, Scott. Time and rulemaking: An empirical test of theory (1992), *Journal of Public Administration Research and Theory, 2*: 113.
Lowi, Theodore (1987). Two roads to serfdom: Liberalism, conservatism and administrative power, *American University Law Review, 36*: 295–322.
Magat, Wesley, Krupnick, Alan, and Harrington, Winston (1986). *Rules in the Making: A Statistical Analysis of Regultory Agency Behavior,* Resources for the Future, Washington, D.C.
Mashaw, Jerry. *Improving the Environment of Agency Rulemaking*, Report to the Administrative Conference of the United States, Washington, D.C., 1992.
McCubbins, Matthew, Noll, Roger, and Weingast, Barry (1897). Administrative procedures as instruments of political control, paper presented at the 1987 meeting of the Midwest Political Science Association, Chicago, Illinois, March, 1987.
McCubbins, Matthew (1985). The legislative design of regulatory structure, *American Journal of Political Science, 29*: 721–748.
McGarrity, Thomas (1992). Some thoughts on deossifying the rulemaking, *Duke University Law Review, 41.*
McGarrity, Thomas (1991). The internal structure of EPA rulemaking, *Law and Contemporary Problems, 54*: 57.
Melnick, Shep (1983). *Regulation and the Courts,* The Brookings Institution, Washington, D.C.
Mintz, Benjamin (1991). Consultants afterward, *A Guide to Federal Agency Rulemaking,* 2nd edition, Administrative Conference of the United States, Washington, D.C.
Mitnick, Barry M. (1984). Agency problems and political institutions, paper presented at the 1984 annual meeting of the Midwest Political Science Association, Chicago, Illinois.
National Academy of Public Administration (1987), *Presidential Management of Rulemaking,* Washington, D.C.
O'Leary, Rosemary (1993). *Environmental Change: Federal Courts and the EPA.* Philadelphia: Temple University Press, 1993.
O'Reilly, James T. (1983). *Administrative Rulemaking: Structuring, Opposing and Defending Federal Agency Regulations,* McGraw Hill, New York.
Paglin, Max and Schor, Edgar (1977). Regulatory responses to the development of public participation, *Public Administration Review,* March/April: 140–148.
Pedersen, William (1975–1976). Formal records and informal rulemaking, *Yale Law Journal, 85*: 38.
Pritzker, David and Dalton, Deborah eds. (1990). *Negotiated Rulemaking Sourcebook,* Administrative Conference of the United States, Washington, D.C.
Reagan, Michael (1987). *Regulation: The Politics of Policy,* Little Brown, Boston.
Robinson, Glen O. (1991). *American Bureaucracy,* University of Michigan Press, Ann Arbor.
Rosenbaum, Walter. The politics of public participation in hazardous waste management, *The Politics of Hazardous Waste Management* (James Lester and Ann O'Bowman, eds.) Duke University Press, Durham, North Carolina, 1983, pp. 176–195.
Rosenbloom, David H. (1989). Public law and regulation, *Handbook of Public Administration* (Jack Rabin, W. Bartley Hildreth and Gerald J. Miller, eds.). Marcel Dekker, New York, pp. 523–575.
Rothstein, Mark (1985). Substantive and procedural obstacles to OSHA rulemaking: Reproductive hazards as an example, *Boston College Environmental Affairs Law Review, 12*: 627.
Scalia, Antonin (1981). Back to basics: Making law without making rules, *Regulation,* July/August.
Scholzman, Kay and Tierney, John (1986). *Organized Interests and American Democracy,* Harper and Row, New York.
Schuck, Peter (1977). Public interest groups and the policy process, *Public Administration Review,* March/April: 132–140.

Shapiro, D. L. (1965). The choice of rulemaking or adjudication in the development of administrative policy, *Harvard Law Review, 78*: 785, 958–967.
Steward, Richard (1975). The reformation of American administrative law, *Harvard Law Review, 80*: 1667–1711.
Susskind, Lawrence and McMahon, Gerard (1985). The theory and practice of negotiated rulemaking, *Yale Journal of Regulation, 3*: 133.
Thurber, James A., ed. (1991). *Divided Government,* Congressional Quarterly Press, Washington, D.C.
Triano, Christine and Watzman, Nancy (1991). *All the Vice President's Men,* Office of Management and Budget, Washington, D.C., page iii.
U.S. Attorney General's Committee on Administrative Procedure (1941). *Administrative Procedure in Government Agencies,* Senate Document No. 8, 77th Congress, 1st session, pp. 97–98, 102.
U.S. Environmental Protection Agency (1990). *The Nation's Hazardous Waste Management Program at a Crossroads,* Washington, D.C.
U.S. Office of Standards and Regulations (1982). *Managing the Process,* Environmental Protection Agency, Washington, D.C.
Viscusi, W. Kip (1986). Reforming OSHA regulation of workplace risks, *Regulatory Reform: What Actually Happened* (Leonard Weiss and Michael Klass, eds.). Little Brown, Boston, 234–268.
Wald, Patricia (1985). Negotiation of environmental disputes: A new role for the courts, *Columbia Journal of Environmental Law, 10*: 1.
West, William (1988). The growth of internal conflict in administrative regulation, *Public Administrative Review, July/August*: 773–782.
Williams, Stephen (1975). Hybrid rulemaking under the Administrative Procedure Act: A legal and empirical analysis, *University of Chicago Law Review, 42*: 401.

Cases Cited

Citizens to Preserve Overton Park v. Volpe (1871, 401 U.S. 402).
Panama Refining Co. v. Ryan (1935, 283 U.S. 388).
Schechter Poultry Corp. v. U.S. (1935, 295 U.S. 495).
Amalgamated Meat Cutters and Butcher Workmen v. Conally (1971, 337 F. Supp 737).
Immigration and Naturalization Science v. Chadha (1983, 462 U.S. 919).
Motor Vehicle Manufacturers Association v. State Farm Mutual (1983, 463 U.S. 29).

14

Regulatory Enforcement

Robert A. Kagan *University of California at Berkeley, Berkeley, California*

Scan your newspaper, watch the news on television, peek into committee hearings at any American legislature, and, if you listen for the unarticulated subtext, you will probably hear a particularized version of this, our common prayer to the contemporary regulatory state:

> Protect us, O government, from harm! Protect us, surrounded as we are by the hazardous side effects of our economic endeavors and prized technologies. For we dwell in fear that we and our children might ingest or inhale invisible toxins. Agricultural chemicals, logging, auto exhausts, and construction projects threaten our remaining forests, marshes, and streams. Protect us, too, from deceitful promoters, discriminatory employers, and dangerous products and machines. In the name of human decency, O government, protect us from harm!

In technologically advanced, democratic societies, governments are inclined to answer these fervent prayers. They commission studies that analyze risks and highlight weaknesses in existing programs of protective regulation. They enact additional regulatory obligations and command regulatory agencies to enforce them. Secular prayers, like holy ones, however, are not always answered. Translating new regulatory laws into concrete, meaningful protective measures never is costless and rarely is easy. This chapter discusses what social scientists have discovered about the dilemmas of implementing protective regulation.

REGULATORY VARIABILITY

Underregulation and Overregulation

Some observers, noting the perennial gap between regulatory aspirations and appropriations for enforcement, conclude that most protective regulation is a manifestation of "symbolic politics" (Edelman, 1964). In this view, politicians appease the electorate by enacting well-publicized regulatory legislation, while subsequently starving enforcement agencies of the resources needed to implement the laws forcefully. Hence regulatory rules are empty symbols of governmental concern, but are never meant to, and hence never do, produce significant change at the ground level.

Examples that seem to support this "symbolic politics" theory are not difficult to find. American politicians have eagerly enacted very ambitious environmental laws, mandating sharp reductions in air and water pollution, cleanup and control of toxic wastes, and preservation of wetlands. With each new federal statute, Congress has heaped demanding new enforcement responsibilities on the Environmental Protection Agency (EPA), but without providing for corresponding increases in personnel, or has simply dumped enforcement duties on understaffed state and local agencies. Whereas antipollution laws have required industry to spend billions of dollars each year on abatement equipment, the same legislators have appropriated less than 1 percent of those amounts for governmental monitoring of air and water quality. This is hardly enough, some analysts argue, "to make the tedious and unending work of credible enforcement a bureaucratic reality" (Ackerman and Stewart, 1985: 1333; see also Russell, 1990, Crandall, 1984).

On the other hand, the "symbolic politics" theory rests on a utopian "full enforcement" standard. Few laws, from those against robbery and reckless driving to those against tax evasion and securities fraud, are fully enforced, largely because it is impossible to do so and still maintain the institutions of a free society. Although regulatory agencies generally lack the appropriations to ensure full enforcement, hardly any government body—the highway department, the Coast Guard, the Bureau of Prisons, and so on—is allocated sufficient funds to fulfill its statutory duties perfectly. The more ambitious the governmental program, the more it seeks to *change* social and economic behavior, the larger the shortfall is likely to be.

For these reasons, the degree of regulatory effectiveness (compared with the degree of mere "symbolism") is best viewed as a *variable.* Whereas some regulatory programs seem to accomplish little, others, despite "inadequate" appropriations, accomplish a great deal. Regulations to prevent anthrax in cattle herds virtually eradicated that deadly disease (Nash, 1964: 148, 238). The same is true with respect to laws designed to prevent the proliferation of illness-causing bacteria in dairy products, ensure the safety of blood products and electrical wiring systems, and (in Western Europe, Japan, and the United States) prevent meltdowns and serious radiation leaks from nuclear power plants. Despite considerable slippage in compliance (see Howe, 1991), environmental regulation has significantly reduced particulate matter, hydrocarbons, nitrogen oxide, lead and other pollutants in the air of Great Britain, Japan, Sweden, and the United States (OECD, 1985; Vogel, 1990a; Lundqvist, 1980; Portney, 1990; Sunstein, 1990:78). American civil rights laws, even if imperfectly complied with, have been enforced well enough to help open job markets to African-Americans, reducing the gap in average compensation for similarly educated employees of different races (NRC, 1989; Freeman, 1981; Shulman and Darby, 1989). Governmental regulation of underground coal mines helped to bring about dramatic reductions in fatalities in the United States (Lewis-Beck and Alford, 1980) and other countries (Braithwaite, 1985).

Indeed, a contrasting critique of regulation asserts not that it does too little but that it does too much, eroding economic efficiency and national competitiveness. This occurs, some scholars argue, because politicians bend to pressures from populist advocacy groups and enact unreasonably stringent regulatory laws (P. Weaver, 1978). Others root the cause in "rent-seeking" by business interests who pressure politicians to promulgate regulations that disadvantage certain business competitors (Stigler, 1975; Farber and Frickey, 1991). Some studies, in fact, show that political pressures lead legislators and regulators to exaggerate risks (Nichols and Zeckhauser, 1986). In many cases, regulators have imposed antipollution measures that are unnecessarily costly (Howe, 1991), benefiting some groups at great expense to others (Ackerman and Hassler, 1981; Leone, 1986).

As in the case of the "symbolic politics" theory, however, the economic inefficiency (or efficiency) of regulatory efforts is best viewed as a variable, not as a constant. Many regulations undoubtedly have extremely positive benefit-cost ratios. Academic critics tend to focus their studies on regulations that are questionable, not on those whose justifiability is so obvious as to require no research.

The interesting questions about the enforcement of protective regulation,[2] therefore, concern the *sources of variance* in regulatory agency behavior and social impact. Under what conditions is regulatory enforcement forceful and effective? When is it not? When is regulatory enforcement economically inefficient? When socially beneficial? What methods of enforcement contribute to effective and efficient results?

Legal Fidelity vs. Administrative Efficacy

The rule of law meshes uncomfortably with the tasks of the activist state. In order to regulate dangerous technologies, protect the environment, combat fraud, and attack discrimination, legislatures grant administrative agencies considerable powers of coercion. Regulatory enforcement officials can launch surprise inspections of factories and business records, impose fines, recall products, and halt expensive construction projects. But administrators are fallible. Their coercive powers can be used unfairly, arrogantly, and even corruptly. From a rule-of-law perspective, therefore, administrative officials should be closely constrained by objective legal rules, formal procedures, and review mechanisms. To ensure administrative diligence, statutes should articulate regulatory standards as judicially enforceable legal rights: to a safe workplace, equal opportunity, full disclosure, and so on. In sum, the standards to which regulatory administration must be held are equal treatment and fidelity to law.[3]

And there is the rub. To many political leaders and citizens, the primary social function of administration, as Philip Selznick has put it, is not to "discover the legal coordinates of a situation" in light of pre-established legal rules; rather it is "to get the work of society done," to refashion "human or other resources so that a particular outcome will be achieved" (Selznick, 1969: 14–16).[4] To do so, administrators must set priorities. Like battlefield medics forced to engage in triage, understaffed regulatory offices, instead of treating all cases equally, must work harder on some complaints than on others. In the administrative ideal, officials should have *discretion* to do what seems possible and desirable in the individual case, where particular factual uncertainties, economic constraints, and moral claims may not fit well into established legal categories. Strict legal enforcement often engenders legalistic defensiveness and costly court battles, not remediation. Effective regulation requires cooperative problem-solving, elicited by negotiation about the sensible application of legal rules (Scholz, 1984; Ayres and Braithwaite, 1991).

It is by no means clear, of course, that discretion and dialogue, as opposed to strict application of law, invariably improve regulatory effectiveness. The "morality of cooperation" (Selznick, 1969) presupposes integrity and wisdom on the part of administrators, as well as good faith on the part of individuals and organizations subject to administrative authority. Critics correctly point out that discretionary regulatory administration has often degenerated into intolerable laxity (Gunningham, 1987). Many advocacy organizations assert, therefore, that regulatory violations, with their risk of harm to innocent citizens, are a species of "white collar crime" and should be punished as such. If regulators are constrained to enforce strictly specifically worded regulations, it is argued, deterrence will be enhanced and administration will be more, not less, effective in "getting the work of society done." Beginning in the 1960s, many American regulatory laws, reflecting advocacy groups' mistrust of discretionary administration, specified strict implementation deadlines, detailed standards, and mandatory penalties, while empowering complainants and advocacy organizations to haul administrators into court for failing to adhere to statutory instructions (Bardach and Kagan, 1982:ch.2).

To other analysts, such a legalistic approach is as undesirable as discretionary regulation, if not more so.[5] It presupposes that most regulatory violations are the product of calculated evasion and that regulated enterprises respond only to the threat of legal sanctions; empirical studies suggest that neither assumption holds true (Kagan and Scholz, 1984; Braithwaite and Makkai, 1991).[6] Legalistic enforcement also presupposes that specifically worded regulations will be both wisely drafted and appropriate to the protean diversity of enforcement problems. Yet time and again, empirical studies indicate that regulatory rules tend to be *overinclusive.* Enacted in response to accidents that arise from the most dangerous conditions, regulations mandate precautionary measures that also apply to a wide variety of less dangerous conditions (Veljanovski, 1984; Bardach and Kagan, 1982: ch.3; Bacow, 1980; Vladeck, 1980). In moral terms, most regulatory rule violations, unlike embezzlement, bribery, fraud, and other intentional white collar crimes, are not committed surreptitiously, as ends in themselves, but occur through negligence, as side effects of legitimate, socially valuable business operations. Hence, although legal sanctions are often justified, especially when dealing with recalcitrant "bad apples," the appropriate response to most violations, many regulatory officials argue, should not be criminal punishment but reform-oriented "probation."[7]

As social scientists have turned their attention to regulatory administration, their research has reflected this tension between the rule of law and administrative efficacy. For some scholars, the primary research questions have concerned the regulators' "legal style." Do they routinely prosecute or issue corrective orders to detected violators, or do they negotiate with them about "coming into compliance?" Do they apply the law even-handedly, or do they favor the powerful?

Other students of regulation have focused on programmatic outcomes. They have asked whether particular regulatory programs are characterized by ineffective underregulation, or by wasteful, contentious overregulation, or by some happy medium. Recourse to concepts such as underregulation and overregulation reflects the conviction that regulatory effectiveness should be assessed not only in terms of ensuring "legal compliance" and also in terms of criteria such as economic efficiency or otherwise socially desirable results.

In surveying the existing body of research, only one thing seems fairly clear: reliable generalizations have been elusive. Legal style does not bear any single, invariable relationship to administrative effectiveness. Regulatory agencies come in many sizes and shapes, and they dwell in very different ecological niches. Some agencies administer laws that are well designed and generally accepted; others administer laws that are extremely costly to comply with, highly controversial, and trigger bitter resistance. Some agencies have potent, easily applied legal sanctions at their disposal; many do not. Some agencies are reasonably well funded and run by well-trained, highly professional administrators; others are drastically underfunded and run by uncommitted placeholders.

Because of this variability, scholars have proceeded primarily by conducting detailed case studies of individual agencies or of loosely matched pairs of agencies, over limited periods of time. However well executed, these studies have cast spotlights on only a handful of trees, if you will, in the murky, ever-growing, and incredibly diverse rainforest of regulatory programs. Thus the significant problems, from both a theoretical and policy perspective, still loom before us: to specify more carefully the conditions under which agencies adopt different "administrative styles", and what impact, under particular conditions, administrative style has on programmatic effectiveness, viewed in all its dimensions.

HOW DOES REGULATORY ENFORCEMENT VARY?

Researchers have discovered repeatedly that regulatory enforcement and decision-making styles vary, even across different offices that enforce the same law (Hutter, 1988; Shover et al., 1984; Scholz and Wei, 1986; Hedge et al., 1988; Church and Nakamura, 1993), across inspectors in the same office (Feinstein, 1989), and across individual cases (Kagan, 1978). Researchers have not been consistent, however, in articulating the dimensions along which regulatory enforcement style is seen to diverge.

One important dimension of regulatory behavior, which unfortunately has received little scholarly attention, concerns the level of administrative energy and responsiveness. Some regulatory agencies seek out violators and violations "proactively" (Reiss, 1984). They conduct frequent inspections, educate and encourage potential informants, and devote substantial resources to monitoring regulated entities. Other agencies are more "reactive," acting only when information flows into the office. When complaints do come in, some agencies respond rapidly, others slowly. After a violation is cited, a promise of remediation is received, or a permit is granted, some agencies reinspect the regulated firm regularly, others never follow up. In sum, agencies might be placed along a continuum extending from active/responsive to inactive/unresponsive.

More often, scholars have focused on the legal decision-making and penal style regulatory officials employ after they actually encounter regulated entities and spot potential violations. Using different terminologies, researchers have observed that some regulatory offices tend to be more "legalistic" or "sanction-oriented" than others, more devoted to a "deterrence" model or to a legally "coercive" style of regulation. At the other end of the continuum, some (indeed most) agencies are described as "conciliatory" or "accommodative," as more inclined to seek results via persuasion or cooperation rather than via legal coercion, as "consultants" rather than "cops."

There are, in fact, two activities embedded in such descriptions of "legal style." One concerns the way officials assess compliance or noncompliance with regulatory standards. Do officials interpret regulations stringently and apply them with bureaucratic literalness (i.e., legalistically)? Or are they more flexible, treating regulations as guidelines rather than as fixed obligations, taking the regulated enterprise's arguments into account in deciding what should be deemed legally acceptable behavior?

The second aspect of legal enforcement style concerns what officials do once they have decided that the regulated enterprise's actions constitute "violations." To pose the question simplistically, do officials punish the offender or do they negotiate about appropriate changes? "Legalistic" or "coercion-oriented" officials would respond to detected shortcomings by immediately issuing notices of violation, assessing files, shutting down operations until the violations are fixed, or flatly rejecting permit applications. "Conciliatory" or "cooperation-oriented" officials would give second (or third) chances to "come into compliance," give advice about how to comply, and agree to ignore violation A in return for faster action to correct violation B.[8]

Many regulatory officials claim that they strive for an intermediate or "flexible" style of rule-interpretation and enforcement: legalistic and tough in some cases, accommodative and helpful in others, depending on the reliability of the particular regulated enterprise and the seriousness of the risks at hand. Sanctions are imposed frequently enough to establish credibility of the threat, but usually are withheld as long as violators work hard at coming into compliance (Bardach and Kagan, 1982:ch.5). For example, most U.S. state agencies enforcing the federal Clean Air Act and Clean Water Act, writes Russell (1990:252), "claim to pursue a so-called voluntary compliance policy. . . . [N]o penalties are ordinarily levied for violations initially . . . [but only] to punish sources that . . . prove uncooperative."[9] British water pollution inspectors say the same (Hawkins, 1984). Nevertheless, although many agencies claim to be pursuing a flexible strategy, if one compares the frequency with which formal legal enforcement actions are taken in different agencies (Grabosky and Braithwaite, 1986; Bardach and Kagan, 1982) or in different offices of the same agency (Hutter, 1988), enforcement often can be characterized as leaning, on average, more toward the legalistic pole or toward the accommodative one.

As suggested by the second horizontal dimension in Figure 1, some agencies' enforcement style goes beyond reasonable "accommodation" or "conciliation" into a realm one might call "retreatism" (Kagan, 1978: 94). In this mode, officials avoid hard choices, backing down at the least sign of opposition, postponing decisions, or generating meaningless paperwork that creates only the appearance of regulatory enforcement. Regulatory officials can lapse into retreatism because they lack leadership, or time, or legal power to impose meaningful sanctions. Sometimes it occurs because officials are corrupt, or "captured" by regulated firms, or intimidated by political authorities sympathetic to the regulated industry. Occasionally, like whiskey control officers at the end of Prohibition, they genuinely believe the law they are assigned to enforce is meaningless or unjustified.

Whereas the legalistic-to-conciliatory (or retreatist) axis focuses on the strictness with which officials interpret legal standards and apply legal sanctions, regulatory enforcement sometimes is described in terms of regulatory outcomes. The most common approach focuses on fulfillment of the regulatory program's primary "police mission": reduction in pollution levels or accident rates, increases in racial integration, and so on. Researchers explicitly or implicitly posit a continuum, extending from the effective agency or enforcement program, which achieves significant concrete gains (according to the appropriate measures), to the ineffective agency, which does not.

Another way of characterizing outcomes, favored by many policy analysts, is based on the position that "effectiveness" alone provides too simple a standard of judgment. The social

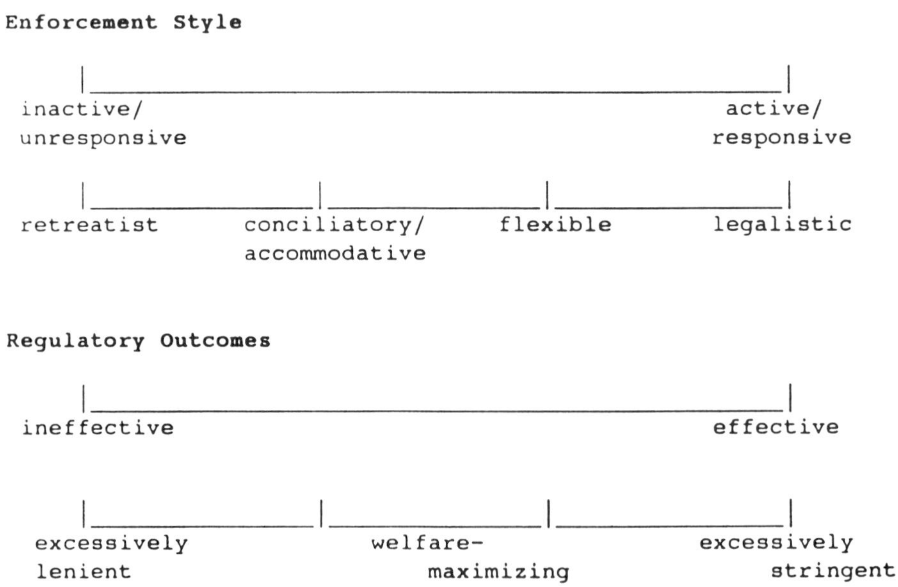

Figure 1 Four Dimensions of Regulatory Enforcement.

costs of achieving zero risk, no pollution, absolute safety, and proportional ethnic racial representation in all positions would be enormous, impinging on other social values. Responsible regulators, therefore, should be concerned about the opportunity costs of devoting human and economic resources to risk reduction, and regulatory enforcement should be described in terms of the economic efficiency of the outcomes of regulatory decisions and remedial orders.

From this perspective, as suggested by the fourth horizontal dimension on Figure 1, regulatory enforcement can be described as inefficient due to excessive strictness, as when an agency regularly demands protective measures whose compliance costs clearly exceed the resulting social benefits, or forbids practices which under the particular circumstances pose no serious risk of harm. At the other extreme, regulatory enforcement can lead to socially inefficient outcomes through underregulation. The excessively lenient agency repeatedly tolerates practices by regulated entities that risk imminent and serious harm, even when the costs of prevention would be moderate. Between these extremes lies "welfare-maximizing" enforcement, in which agency officials avoid both excessive leniency and excessive stringency, considering both costs and benefits in applying regulations and in formulating remedial requirements.

A regulatory agency's position on the outcome dimensions cannot always be extrapolated from its legal style or its level of activism. When we read that agency A brings prosecutions, recalls cars, or imposes fines more frequently than agency B, that does not tell us whether agency A is punishing "bad apples" for serious violations or whether it is building up a flashy record by bashing relatively "good apples" for trivial violations.[10] Knowing that an agency inspects each enterprise only once every 10 months and rarely brings prosecutions likewise does not indicate whether its officials are excessively passive and lenient or whether it faces an industry with a high compliance rate and can cure most violations by means of threat and negotiation. As suggested by Figure 2, the same legal style can produce a range of outcomes, measured in cost-benefit terms, depending on the degree of cooperativeness of the regulated entities and on the "goodness-of-fit" between the regulations and the seriousness of the hazards that enforcement officials encounter.

But it usually is very difficult to determine whether agency enforcement decisions produce economically efficient outcomes. Agencies gather no such data on a case-by-case, citation-by-citation basis. Regulatory officials often discuss whether a particular regulatory requirement "makes sense" under the circumstances, and make intuitive cost-benefit judgments about particular regulatory violations and permit conditions. That, indeed, is the essence of flexible

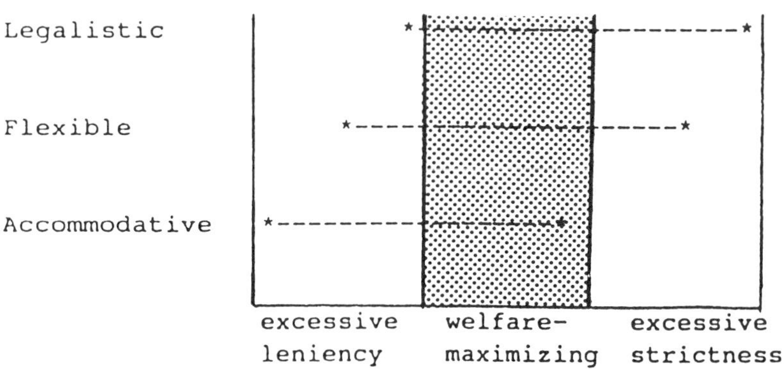

Figure 2 Enforcement Style and Economic Efficiency.

and cooperative legal enforcement styles. Yet determining whether enforcement officials make those judgments "correctly" requires in-depth analysis of particular decisions.[11] Most researchers, therefore, focus only on agencies' legal style, and sometimes, if systematic data exist, on regulatory effectiveness, defined without respect to economic efficiency concerns.

Scholz (1991a) provides an interesting effort to assess legal style from aggregate data and to relate it to regulatory effectiveness. Using detailed data on inspections, penalties, and workplace injury rates obtained from the U.S. Occupational Safety and Health Administration (OSHA), Scholz reasoned that an agency with a "flexible" enforcement style would concentrate formal legal sanctions on the minority of firms with a record of noncooperation or minimal compliance, and on "serious" rather than routine violations.[12] Comparing 34 state-level OSHA offices, Scholz calculated "serious violations" as a percentage of all citations issued by each agency, and the percentage of all penalties directed at serious violations. (OSHA regulations classify a violation as "serious" if it "substantially increases the possibility that an injury will occur" [Scholz, 1991:text at fn. 3].) He found that selective enforcement (by these measures) was significantly correlated with lower statewide injury rates, even after one controlled for frequency of inspection, economic conditions, state political climate, and other potential causal variables. John Braithwaite (1985) conducted a similar cross-national study of coal mine safety regulation. Using declines in worker mortality and injury rates as a measure of effectiveness, he was able to conclude that flexible enforcement, backed by a realistic threat of significant legal sanctions, was more effective than either legally toothless or legalistic, sanction-oriented methods.

It is unfortunate that most studies of environmental law enforcement, antidiscrimination law, and many other types of protective regulation have not been able to find and employ good outcome measures on which one might base a sensible assessment of the effectiveness of different enforcement styles, much less an assessment of where the enforcement program stands on the economic efficiency dimension.

WHY DO REGULATORY ENFORCEMENT STYLES DIFFER?

Why do regulatory agencies lean toward one enforcement style rather than toward another? The answer, as our review of the case study literature will make clear, is complicated. One wonders if it can ever be formulated with economy and precision. Perhaps the best that can be done at this stage is to organize the search for explanations as clearly as possible, differentiating carefully among different kinds of regulatory programs and types of explanatory factors.

Social scientists tend to offer two basic kinds of explanations. In one perspective, official action is shaped by the technical, economic, and legal problems the agency encounters. Regulatory officials, it is assumed, are like public-spirited carpenters. The laws they enforce provide the blueprint that sets forth their mission and define the tools they can use. Working within those constraints, the regulatory carpenters adapt the plans to the raw material with which they work: the hazards to be abated; the attitudes, capabilities, and economic resilience of regulated entities; the problems of detecting and preventing noncompliance; the unexpected disjunctions between the plans and what seems feasible in the particular situation. To understand enforcement style, therefore, one must look first of all to the "legal design" of the regulatory program: its substantive goals and standards, the powers it gives the agency, and the constraints it imposes on agency discretion. In addition, one must consider features of the "task environment" (Scholz and Wei, 1986) to which the regulatory administrator must adapt: the nature and seriousness of noncompliance, the characteristics of regulated enterprises, and the detectability of violations.

The second explanatory approach emphasizes the regulatory agency's "political environment." Regardless of the law and the regulators' notions of what would be best, it is assumed, regulators work within a charged political atmosphere. Interest groups attempt to control the agency's leadership. Officials who offend politically significant government officials or private organizations face public criticism, budgetary cutbacks, and replacement. Understanding variation in enforcement style, therefore, requires us to focus on the intensity and predominant direction of political pressures brought to bear on regulatory officials by political leaders, industry, proregulatory advocacy groups, and the news media.

Both the "legal/task environment" and the "political environment" explanations treat regulatory officials as fungible actors, responding to outside stimuli. In most social science studies, the political attitudes and personal characteristics of regulatory officials play no independent explanatory role; the agency's internal ethos, it is assumed, is shaped by the legal, social, and political winds that buffet the agency. Sprinkled through the case study literature, however, and pervading regulatory folklore, are signs that agency officials at all levels frequently have minds (and interests) of their own, and that intra-agency commitment and competence (or lack thereof) significantly affect regulatory enforcement style. Agency officials sometimes resist external political and economic pressures, or actively seek to influence their environment. In short, regulatory behavior can also be affected by variations in leadership and its effect on "agency culture."

All four sets of explanatory factors—regulatory legal design, the agency's social and economic task environment, its political environment, and its internal leadership—can simultaneously influence agency action. The intellectual problem is to analyze the relative weight of each under varying circumstances. As a preliminary step in that direction, the following subsections discuss each set of explanatory factors in turn.

REGULATORY LEGAL DESIGN

It may be true, as the legal realists said, that "rules don't decide cases. People do." Yet the cases regulatory officials get to deal with, and the choices they are forced to make, are powerfully shaped by the characteristics of the laws they are expected to implement. Those characteristics include (1) the ways that the authorizing legislation and the primary regulations define the agency's regulatory mission; (2) the powers the statute grants the regulators, the rights it accords regulated enterprises, and the rights it gives to advocates of strict regulation; and (3) the specificity with which the law prescribes the standards, procedures, and remedies to be employed in case-by-case administration.

Statutory Mission: Degree of Stringency

Common observation tells us that some regulatory laws are far more ambitious, or stringent, than others, demanding significant, costly, or controversial changes in existing patterns of human behavior. "Technology-forcing" regulations, for example, require regulated entities to develop and adopt novel measures, such as computerized braking systems for trucks (see Mashaw and Harfst, 1987), or "kneeling buses" to accommodate the physically handicapped (see Katzmann, 1986). Very stringent statutes, such as some U.S. Food and Drug Law and Clean Air Act provisions, adopt a "no risk" stance, ruling out any administrative-level accommodation to the degree of risk, compliance costs, or other competing values (Lave, 1981; Dwyer, 1990).[13]

At the less stringent end of the continuum, regulatory statutes demand only incremental changes in the plans or practices of most regulated entities. Many building code provisions, maintenance regulations for airliners, and pasteurization regulations governing milk product producers are included in this category. In these and many other industries, market pressures and exposure to private lawsuits threaten economic disaster to regulated firms that depart from prevalent safety standards; governmental regulations provide only an additional "fail-safe" layer of protection. Other regulatory statutes set forth ostensibly stringent standards but also command regulators to take compliance costs and other competing values into account in making specific enforcement decisions.

The relative stringency of legally defined regulatory standards influence—even if they do not control—the implementing agency's day-to-day actions. Agency Z, enforcing a law that more or less codifies accepted industry safety practices and authorizes severe sanctions only for deliberate or grossly negligent violations, is likely to bring few prosecutions.[14] Conversely, EPA enforces the very stringent "Superfund" law, which imposes liability (without fault) and complete clean-up responsibility on any firm whose chemical wastes ended up in an ill-maintained storage site, even if the disposal and maintenance practices used were not illegal at the time; not surprisingly, EPA's enforcement activities almost inevitably entail fierce legal contestation (Wilkerson and Church, 1989; Menell, 1991).[15] In terms of attitudes, officials in Workplace Safety Agency A may be more zealous than those in agency B. Yet if the regulation that agency A is instructed to enforce limits vinyl chloride fumes to a maximum of 25 ppm, while agency B's regulation demands reductions to 1 ppm, agency A cannot (and will not) punish a manufacturer whose fumes average 15 ppm, while agency B can. In an absolute sense, B's case-by-case determinations of what constitutes "compliance" are likely to be substantively more stringent.

On the other hand, the legally defined mission does not dictate an agency's "jurisprudential" style. Some EPA regional offices enforce CERCLA very legalistically, some in a more conciliatory manner (Church and Nakamura, 1993). Hypothetical Workplace Safety Agency B, enforcing a more stringent vinyl chloride standard than agency A, may adopt a flexible style, accepting 10 ppm for an interim period, because its officials think that 10 ppm would be optimal in the short run, and because insisting on 1 ppm would only trigger resistance.

Legal Powers, Legal Rights

Many regulatory laws prescribe protective standards for ongoing activity, enforced by the threat of ex post detection and sanctioning of violations. Traffic regulations as enforced by patrolling police officers provide an everyday model. So do regulations specifying workplace safety rules, housing maintenance standards for low-income apartments, and nondiscrimination rules for employers; these rules are enforced via after-the-fact (ex post) detection of violations by actual or potential victims (who complain to regulatory agencies) or by governmental inspectors. The threat of ex post legal sanctions against detected violations, it is hoped, will spur regulated enterprises toward ex ante compliance behaviors.[16]

In ex post programs, however, regulatory power is limited by the difficulty of monitoring scores, if not hundreds, of far-flung potential violators. Like highway patrol officers, there are never enough regulatory inspectors to detect all violations or recheck on compliance with remedial orders. Also, in many ex post programs, regulatory power is constrained by legal traditions drawn from criminal law, with its emphasis on due process for the accused and separation of law enforcement, prosecutorial, and adjudicatory powers. To bring a prosecution, regulators must persuade an independent prosecutor and then a judge that a legal penalty is justified. The regulated entity gains the protections—and the manifold opportunities for temporizing—provided by rules of notice, evidence, and appeal, not to mention the delays in getting to trial in overloaded court systems. In this legal structure, an agency enforcer must think twice about undergoing the expense, delay, and diversion of personnel associated with formal legal action.[17] It often seems wiser to work out a compromise providing some remedial action now.

In recognition of this dilemma, some statutes deliberately fortify ex post regulators' power. To facilitate detection, some laws require enterprises to maintain records of compliance-related actions (log books, emissions levels) or send periodic reports to the agency. Some agencies acquire summary powers to seize or recall hazardous products, halt dangerous operations, or impose fines, all without first seeking judicial authorization. Such an agency, enjoying more autonomy to act without delaying external review, gains bargaining power over regulated entities. To the same end, some statutes authorize large financial penalties that increase with each day of continued noncompliance, discouraging noncompliant businesses from seeking legal delays (Bardach and Kagan, 1982:ch.2).[18]

Regulatory enforcers' bargaining power is still stronger when laws provide for ex ante screening of regulated enterprises' proposed activities. No one, says the law, may build a new factory, market new pharmaceutical products or pesticides, or obtain a government contract or grant, without ex ante regulatory review of compliance with standards for environmental protection, safety, affirmative action, and so on. The primary sanction for failure to meet regulatory standards is quick and direct: denial of the initial application for a license, permit, grant, or contract.[19] When stringent ex post regulatory orders close down or financially constrain ongoing operations, the social costs of regulation are very visible and often controversial. Ex ante control agencies, in contrast, can more easily insist on strict legal compliance because the resulting costs and delays (e.g., lags in job creation, in availability of new products, in launching construction projects) are more diffuse and less visible (Bardach, 1989; Huber, 1983; Kagan, 1991a).[20] Braithwaite and Fisse (1987:226) observe:

> Health departments find it easier to control drug companies than food outlets, and find it much less necessary to resort to law enforcement to do so, because health departments . . . decide whether new drugs will be allowed on the market, and if so, with what promotional claims. . . . Organizational actors are more compliant with requests from actors who control vital resources (such as approvals and licenses). . . .

Another important statutory tool, although one infrequently granted directly to regulatory agencies, is the power to subsidize compliance, that is, to provide government grants, low-interest loans, or other financial benefits that, in effect, reduce the regulated enterprise's compliance costs. Thus the federal government, under the Clean Water Act, pays large proportions of governments' municipal costs of complying with antipollution regulations, and under other laws, picks up 50 percent of the costs local port authorities incur in complying with environmental regulations that govern harbor improvements and dredging (Kagan, 1990a:107). Subsidizing compliance presumably will reduce resistance, obviating the need to employ direct legal sanctions. Moreover, authority to suspend subsidies gives the agency a powerful sanction, one it can use without first having to go to court. Thus threats to withhold federal grants to local schools that were slow to integrate are often said to have greatly accelerated the dismantling of de jure racially segregated schools (Rosenberg, 1991). In many instances, however, regulatory authorities are reluctant to cut off subsidies. Federal regulators have shied away from withdrawing funding from local districts that fail to comply with regulations specifying use of federal aid for economically disadvantaged schools (Kagan, 1986) or from state highway departments that fail to institute the radical restrictions on motor vehicle use needed to attain clean air standards.

More generally, an agency's legal strength does not *dictate* its enforcement style. Greater legal powers *enable* an agency to increase use of legal sanctions. After the U.S. Congress authorized tougher criminal penalties in 1984 and again in 1987, regulatory officials sought and obtained much larger fines against corporate violators and more jail sentences for executives who violated environmental laws (Cohen, 1991; Vellen and Mayer, 1992). On the other hand, legally powerful agencies often regulate effectively with veiled threats alone, rarely having to resort to formal sanctions (Ayres and Braithwaite, 1992). When denial of a permit would cause existing businesses to close down, even agencies vested with strong legal powers may interpret permit conditions flexibly, grant variances, or "grandfather in" older regulated entities, as EPA did in enforcing federal laws imposing costly new standards on existing waste disposal sites (Wehling, 1987).[21]

Just as strong due process rights for regulated enterprises discourage an enforcement by prosecution, statutes that give citizen-complainants and advocacy groups rights to argue against or appeal lenient agency decisions encourage regulatory "toughness" or legalism.

In the ex ante Dutch legal regime for protecting employees against unjust dismissal, agencies processing employer applications to dismiss workers must make affirmative efforts to get the employees' side of the story (Knegt, 1989).

OSHA and implementing regulations give employees the right to stop work they think is dangerous until an OSHA inspector comes, and to accompany OSHA inspectors on their rounds (without losing pay); discrimination against workers who complain to OSHA is a serious offense. High rates of worker complaints are associated with more punitive enforcement styles (Scholz et al., 1991; Scholz and Wei, 1986).

Land use regulations sometime provide that neighbors, environmental groups, and specialized environmental agencies must be given notice of permit applications for local construction projects, together with rights to participate in zoning board hearings, to comment on impact statements, and to take land use agencies to court for insufficient deference to environmental values. These rights, case studies suggest, push the local land use agency toward a more legalistic, antidevelopment stance (Niemeijer, 1989; Coyle, 1988; Frieden, 1979; Sabatier and Mazmanian, 1983), and sometimes into deadening retreatism (Kagan, 1991).

In one striking case, American civil rights advocacy groups, bringing successive legal claims against the federal Office of Civil Rights, obtained judicial orders *compelling* the agency to adopt a more stringent and legalistic (and arguably counterproductive) enforcement policy (Rabkin, 1989).[22]

Specificity of Legal Rules and Remedies

In some regulatory programs, statutes and regulations stipulate in great detail the forms, plans, certifications, tests, and impact statements that must be filed to get a permit, and, once it is granted, the records to be kept, reports to be filed, and even the technologies to be used. Surveyors in New York's nursing home regulation program must fill out a 63 page protocol concerning structural requirements, records, and "negative outcome indicators" in the facilities they visit (Day and Klein, 1987). In the U.S. Mine Safety and Health program, regulations specify the precise frequency with which different categories of mines must be inspected, as well as the legal penalties or remedial orders that officials must impose on different categories of detected noncompliance (Braithwaite, 1985).[23]

A contrasting regulatory strategy assumes that detailed preventive rules cannot possibly anticipate and proscribe the inexhaustible variety of human heartlessness and negligence, and at the same time will often be harshly overinclusive. From this perspective, the appropriate strategy is to draft broadly worded statutes and regulations, laced with words such as "reasonable" and "so far as feasible," enabling regulatory officials to "custom tailor" regulatory requirements and penalties to particular enterprises and situations (Baar, 1986). In contrast with New York, this is the approach taken by British nursing home regulations (Day and Klein, 1987).

Many regulatory statutes, of course, seek a middle ground. Some call for specific, universal rules, but establish procedures for seeking variances, exceptions, or exemptions from higher-level officials. Some articulate regulatory objectives but "delegate the details" to government-supervised self-regulatory regimes. Under the U.S. Environmental Protection Agency's "bubble policy," instead of specifying control measures for each point source, the EPA allows petroleum refineries or large chemical plants to submit their own detailed plans for reducing pollution within an imaginary bubble enclosing their installations (see Levin, 1982). Meat-packing plants (see Grumbly, 1982) and large construction companies (see Rees, 1988) are authorized to devise their own purity or safety rules, tailored to their own operations, to be enforced by designated, in-house quality control officials or safety committees; agency officials receive regular reports and make spot checks, and are authorized to penalize enterprises for failing to follow their own rules.[24]

Specific rules and remedies are not necessarily associated with substantively stringent regulatory laws. Stringency and specificity vary independently.[25] Regulatory designs that specify standards and penalties in great detail likewise do not necessarily produce a legalistic enforcement style, even though they seem designed to. Enforcement officials in such programs sometimes bend detailed rules to fit their own vision of good regulation, adopting a flexible enforcement style (Day and Klein, 1987). Still, when legally prescribed standards and penalties are specific *and* complainants and advocacy groups can detect violations and exert pressure on the regulatory agency (features of the task environment and political environment discussed below), agencies are more vulnerable to criticism for lack of fidelity to law and legalistic enforcement is more likely. Where the standards and penalties are not carefully specified, conciliatory methods are more legitimate, legalistic enforcement is unlikely, and the possibility of excessive leniency is greater.

THE REGULATORY TASK ENVIRONMENT

Assume that regulatory enforcement officials strive to maximize social welfare as they see it, striking an intelligent balance between regulatory control and economic efficiency, between precaution and innovation. They seek to accomplish those goals through cooperation whenever possible, but through coercion when necessary, adapting their actions to the risks and compliance costs presented by case at hand, and to the character of the regulated enterprises they deal with. Agencies respond, in sum, to the interactions between the law's abstract demands and the concrete features of each agency's "task environment."

Striking support for this assumption is provided by Shover et al.'s (1984, 1986) study of the U.S. Office of Surface Mining (OSM). OSM enforced a stringent federal law[26] that requires coal companies to limit erosion during strip-mining operations and to restore the scarred land as far as possible. The statute specifically requires administrators to issue citations for every violation spotted and cessation-of-work orders for serious or repeat violations. Officials in OSM's Western Regional Office, however, adopted a conciliatory, cooperation-oriented enforcement style. During the period studied (1979 to 1981), they issued relatively few citations and very few cessation orders. Their counterparts in the eastern region, in contrast, saw themselves as deterrent-oriented cops. They issued many more citations and cessation orders—per inspector, per regulated enterprise, per ton of coal mined.

These differences in enforcement style seem to reflect rational responses to two differences in the regional offices' task environments: (1) the "visibility of violations" (and repeat violations), that is, the ability of officials to detect noncompliance or bad faith promptly; and (2) the capacity and willingness of regulated enterprises to comply with regulatory requirements. When violations are more visible and enterprises more willing to comply, it seems reasonable to expect, regulators can more sensibly adopt a cooperation-seeking enforcement style (Kagan and Skolnick, 1993).

When are those conditions likely to be present? Existing studies point to three task-environment features: the frequency of interaction between regulators and regulated enterprises, the size and sophistication of regulated firms, and the cost of compliance, viewed in terms of the economic resilience of regulated enterprises and the seriousness of the hazards to be controlled.

Frequency of Interaction and Visibility of Violations

OSM's western region officials policed the vast plains of Wyoming and Montana. Mining operations there were conducted by a handful of huge corporate enterprises. Each inspector was responsible for only 23 sites, on average, enabling him or her to visit each enterprise often. The eastern region covered the Appalachian Mountains, where mining operations were small and numerous. There was one inspector for every 111 firms; intervals between inspections undoubtedly were much longer than in the West.

Scholz's (1984) important game-theory analysis suggests why frequency of interaction affects enforcement style. In programs enforced by ex post monitoring, Scholz argues, rational regulators would adopt a "tit-for-tat" enforcement strategy. That is, they would apply regulatory requirements flexibly and suspend imposition of legal sanctions when they encounter first-time violations, but only so long as the regulated enterprise, in return, acts cooperatively. If a regulated enterprise tries to take advantage of the agency's cooperative stance, rational regulators would immediately turn "vengeful," imposing strong legal sanctions. In contrast, Scholz found, a uniformly legalistic and punitive approach is suboptimal because it often would be perceived as unreasonable and would provoke costly, compliance-reducing resistance. From this standpoint, it should not be surprising that most regulatory agencies employ a predominantly nonlegalistic enforcement style, and criminal enforcement is very uncommon.[27]

The tit-for-tat strategy, however, depends on prompt punishment of any betrayal of trust. That is most feasible when regulator and regulated firm interact frequently. If the inspector comes often, the regulated firm knows that breaking its promises to take corrective measures will be detected, increasing the likelihood of legal punishment for a "repeat violation" and related adverse publicity. When the inspector comes often, she learns the regulated enterprise's technologies, vulnerabilities, and resources; she can better evaluate risks and alternative ways of achieving regulatory goals. Firm-specific knowledge, based on frequent interaction, makes a flexible enforcement style more feasible.[28] (On the other hand, as Ayres and Braithwaite [1991] note, frequent interaction also creates the conditions under which enforcers are most likely to be "captured" by regulated enterprises.)

If the inspector comes infrequently, regulated entities can reasonably hope that violations will escape detection and that compliance cost can at least be delayed. The inspector has less knowledge of the conditions and the people he polices. A cooperative stance then is riskier. It becomes more rational for regulators, like the eastern region OSM inspectors, to adopt a deterrence-oriented style, imposing sanctions even on first-time violations. Thus Grabosky and Braithwaite (1986), in a multivariate analysis of 91 Australian regulatory agencies, found that infrequency of contact with regulated enterprises was strongly correlated with frequency of prosecution. Bridget Hutter (1989) found that British air pollution control enforcement officials, responsible for monitoring a relatively limited number of firms, prosecute violators far less often than British workplace safety inspectors, who visit a much larger number of firms more infrequently.[29] British health inspectors in urban areas resorted to formal enforcement more than their rural counterparts, who were better integrated into the community and had more time for reinspection and educational efforts (Hutter, 1988: 193–196).

In ex ante control programs, officials can compel repeated interaction with unknown or suspect enterprises simply by treating their initial applications strictly, requiring them to adjust their plans or conduct further tests until their good faith has been established. In subsequent applications, the same enterprises, if they have developed a reputation for reliability, can be dealt with less legalistically. Thus Niemeijer (1989) found that Dutch building code administrators often approve plans drawn by architects and contractors known to be reliable, even though some features may not comply strictly with the code, because officials have confidence that the building will conform to professional norms of construction.

Even if field inspectors cannot visit individual firms often, a functional substitute emerges when violations are visible to potential complainants who call enforcement officials. Thus where labor representatives participate in corporate safety programs, governmental inspectors can adopt a flexible enforcement style, knowing that workers will call the agency if the enterprise delays corrective action concerning serious violations (Bacow, 1980; Rees, 1988). When violations are less visible to complainants (as in the case of many kinds of air or ground-water pollution), or are visible only to vulnerable complainants (as in the case of nursing homes), enforcement officials find it harder to detect backsliding by regulated enterprises and a flexible enforcement style more readily deteriorates into excessive leniency.[30] And in general, the vigilance and capacity of potential complainants and advocacy organizations appear to be the most powerful influences on regulatory agency enforcement style (Scholz and Wei, 1986; Scholz et al., 1991; Sabatier and Mazmanian, 1983; Reich, 1992: 275–80).

Size and Sophistication of Regulated Enterprises

Western region OSM officials dealt with large corporate mining companies; their everyday interactions were with corporate environmental specialists who adopted a cooperative stance. Eastern region inspectors, who more frequently resorted to legal sanctions, dealt with much smaller, environmentally unsophisticated mining firms, which often adopted a noncooperative posture.

The pattern is a recurrent one. Regulating elephants is different from regulating foxes. It is harder for elephants to hide. Larger regulated enterprises, simply because of their prominence and potential for doing harm, can expect more frequent contact with regulatory officials (and proregulation advocacy groups). Partly because their violations are more visible, partly because they often are more concerned about maintaining a public image as responsible corporate citizens, larger enterprises are more likely to have a staff of in-house experts responsible for keeping the company out of trouble with regulatory officials. These corporate environmental engineers, safety experts, affirmative action officers, nurses, and auditors constitute a shadow regulatory bureaucracy, often supportive of the regulatory regime to which they owe their livelihood (Braithwaite and Fisse, 1987; Bardach and Kagan, 1982: ch.8). In dealing with them, legalistic rule-interpretation and sanctioning methods often seem counterproductive.

Eastern region OSM officials faced a very different task environment. They dealt with a population of smaller, entrepreneurial enterprises, few of which had full-time specialists in repairing the environmental effects of strip-mining. Their owners often were ignorant of the regulations and their rationale. Many were hostile to the agency on ideological grounds. This task environment suggested a deterrence-oriented enforcement style: hit them with penalties until they begin to invest in compliance programs. Grabosky and Braithwaite (1986) found that Australian regulatory agencies that dealt, on average, with smaller enterprises were more likely to resort to prosecution. Size of firm seems to operate as a rough proxy for "disposition to comply," which, in turn, affects enforcement style.

Of course, when regulatory concerns are generally well accepted (and supported by market pressures), smaller firms also may be sophisticated about regulatory standards and geared up for compliance. In health-related regulation of dairy farming, for example, legalistic enforcement seems to be rare and frowned upon (Frank and Lombness, 1988). Where small firms are represented by professionals in regulatory compliance, such as architects who help them apply for building permits, cooperative enforcement styles usually prevail (Niemeijer, 1989). On the other hand, where regulated firms are small and not geared up for compliance, the logical recourse to coercive enforcement may backfire. Dutch officials enforcing emissions taxes against large industrial firms established cooperative relationships that helped to reduce pollution sharply. In enforcing detailed controls on manure use against thousands of small, entrepreneurial firms, however, Dutch officials initially took a legalistic stance, but encountered such resistance that they ultimately were compelled to be more flexible, relaxing certain record-keeping and reporting rules (Huppes and Kagan, 1989). In sum, while size of firm, as a proxy for "disposition to comply," influences enforcement style, other task environment features affecting that disposition sometimes may be more important.

Cost of Compliance, Seriousness of Risks, and Economic Resilience of Regulated Entities

Why doesn't ambitious, stringent regulation always evoke a legalistic enforcement style? One reason arises from another crucial feature of regulatory task environment: cost of compliance with regulatory demands.

Consider again the U.S. strip-mine regulators, who employed a conciliatory style in the West and a legalistic style in the East. For large mining companies on the plains of Wyoming, land-restoration costs per ton of coal undoubtedly were far lower than the compliance costs demanded of smaller firms working the steep, forested hillsides of eastern Kentucky. When regulated enterprises see compliance as very costly, putting them at a disadvantage with their competitors (Leone, 1986), regulators presumably will encounter more noncompliance; sometimes this leads enforcers to adopt a legalistic enforcement style. Thus British local environmental health officials in urban areas with severe crowding and sanitation problems (that is, more and costlier-to-cure noncompliance) resort to formal prosecution more often than their counterparts in other regions (Hutter, 1989).

That strategy, however, is likely to work only up to a point. When compliance costs reach a level that threatens the economic viability of a regulated enterprise, department, or project, legalistic enforcement often becomes counterproductive. Environmental and occupational health regulators often pull back from strict enforcement if economically marginal employers in job-poor regions cannot absorb the costs of compliance and still make a profit on the operation (see Melnick, 1983; Gunningham, 1987). Thus Nichols (1991: 87–88) noted that regulators demanded less stringent emission limits for sulfur dioxide emissions from copper smelters in the American southwest than from electrical power plants. "[T]he smelters faced foreign competition and would probably close if they faced high [pollution control] costs. In contrast, regulated utilities could simply raise rates to cover the costs of stringent controls." In sum, the economic resilience of noncompliant regulated enterprises (their ability to absorb or pass on compliance costs), together with the social costs of closing down noncompliant firms,[31] is a crucial feature of the task environment, limiting the stringency and punitiveness of regulatory legal style (see also Kagan, 1978: ch. 4; Ould, 1986).

Reluctance to adopt regulatory methods that close down regulated enterprises is only an extreme example of taking compliance costs into account. Short of that extreme, enforcement officials are repeatedly called upon to gauge whether the imposition of additional compliance costs is "worth it" in terms of added public protection. The more stringent the regulatory legal mission and the more specific and dense the web of prophylactic rules, the more often such questions are raised. The answers are difficult. They require officials to make intuitive cost-benefit analyses, assessments of the economic resiliency of particular regulated enterprises, and of the seriousness of the risks posed by an accommodative decision in the case at hand. When mistakenly lenient cost-benefit analyses can result in imminent catastrophe, as in airline or coal mine safety regulation, one might expect special reluctance to make such judgments. In such cases, therefore, one might expect to see a legalistic style, as constrasted with situations in which mistaken leniency would result only in an incremental increase in nontoxic air pollution. Yet persistent refusal to make any cost-benefit judgments (which is a good definition of "legalism") can easily produce cooperation-depleting resistance, which is why many agencies, even in coal mine regulation (Braithwaite, 1985), prefer a flexible enforcement style.

THE POLITICAL ENVIRONMENT

Regulation is a political process. It emerges from political demands and political struggles, and is shaped by competing political ideas and theories. The features of a regulatory "legal design" (the first set of explanatory factors discussed earlier) often reflect the views of the winners in a political debate over how stringently an agency's legal mission should be stated, the powers it will have, the discretion administrators will be granted (Moe, 1989).[32] Such regulatory legal designs are shaped by many political factors, including national political culture, political party strength, interest group structure, legal doctrines concerning administrative power, and the vulnerability of the regulated industry to foreign competition (Vogel, 1986; Badaracco, 1985; Kagan, 1988:735–739; Katzenstein, 1988).

In discussing the relationship between a regulatory agency's "political environment" and its enforcement style, however, one can focus on a more limited set of political influences: those that impinge on frontline, day-by-day regulatory administration, *after* the basic regulatory laws and bureaucratic structures have been formulated. To argue that continuing political influences affect enforcement style requires a shift in the assumptions about regulatory behavior that governed the discussion in the preceding sections. We assumed earlier that regulatory officials seek to maximize the public welfare, and that their enforcement style reflects rational adaptation to the problems generated by the regulatory law and the task environment. Explanations based on the agency's political environment, however, shift the operative assumption from that of a "welfare-maximizing agency" to a "criticism-avoiding agency."[33] The underlying assumptions are as follows:

With varying degrees of intensity, interest groups and political leaders seek to affect agency behavior through the appointment of sympathetic administrators, manipulation of the news media, threats of budgetary restrictions, and appeals to the courts.

Regulatory officials seek to avoid political trouble in order to keep their jobs and maintain their agency's powers and budget.

Regulatory officials shape their enforcement style to avoid political trouble, adopting a legalistic style when they are most subject to criticism by political leaders or influential outsiders for real or suspected laxity, favoring a more accommodative style when those risks are not present or when they are subject to criticism for excessive strictness.

Among the variables that affect the balance of political pressures are the organization of interest groups and the preferences of political authorities.

Interest Group Pressures

A generation ago, focusing primarily on regulation of competition in the rail and air transportation industries, political scientists formulated the "capture theory." The idea was that repeated contact with representatives of a single industry, intensely interested in regulatory policy and appointments, would draw regulatory officials toward an "industry orientation," in which their view of the public interest coincided with that of the dominant firms in the regulated industry (Bernstein, 1955; Truman, 1953). A basic feature of those industry-stabilizing regulatory programs was that politically unorganized consumer interests rarely exerted pressure on the agency, counteracting industry influence.

The capture theory has collapsed as a general proposition (Quirk, 1981; Wilson, 1980). Even in economic regulation, increasing political participation by representatives of consumer groups often has pressured agencies to enact stringent policies, overriding industry objectives (Anderson, 1981). Reform-minded economic regulators have pushed cartelized industries out of the regulatory nest into a turbulent new competitive world (Derthick and Quirk, 1985). Contemporary protective regulatory agencies, moreover, often confront a more balanced pattern of interest group representation. Environmental protection and worker safety agencies regulate many industries, not one; they have little interest in favoring any particular group of firms, and strong incentives not to. In many protective regulatory programs, organizations advocating stringent regulation (labor unions, civil rights groups, environmental groups, neighborhood associations, and so on) actively monitor compliance and participate in rule-making and enforcement proceedings. In the United States, they take the agency to court over decisions they do not like, and influence selection of agency personnel (Wilson, 1989).

Case studies demonstrating that many protective regulatory agencies have not been "captured" do not eliminate the possibility of strong industry influence on agency decision-making. "Capture" simply becomes a variable rather than a constant. Political organization of relevant interest groups is definitely an important influence on regulatory enforcement. In a study of the 50 state and federal agencies that enforce the U.S. Occupational Safety and Health Act, Scholz and Wei (1986) found that the strongest influence on the frequency with which these agencies formally cited regulated firms and in the amount of fines they assessed was the strength of organized labor in the state, as indicated by the frequency of complaints to the agency about potential regulatory violations. Studies of land use regulation likewise indicate that active participation by politically organized environmental groups is associated with more stringent regulatory decisions (Sabatier and Mazmanian, 1979; Steele, 1987). Case studies of highly conciliatory enforcement styles, in which the agency declines to prosecute even serious violations, often involve programs or situations in which there are no politically organized complainants who can detect and protest official laxity (Frank and Lombness, 1988) or in which potential advocates of stringent regulation are weak and ineffective (Gunningham, 1987).

The precise relationship between proregulation interest group influence and regulatory enforcement style, however, is complicated. In the Netherlands, complaints by neighbors about building permits seem to drive officials toward a more legalistic style, but primarily as a way of defending their decisions, not as a way of being more responsive to substantive demands for more stringent regulation (Niemeijer, 1989). In the United States, strong pressure from organized labor seems to evoke a more legalistic enforcement style from OSHA, although not necessarily greater effectiveness.[34] In Sweden, however, where labor is politically far more influential, actually dominating the administrative regime for workplace safety regulation, legalistic enforcement is almost never necessary (Kelman, 1981). Legal design helps to explain the difference: Swedish law strengthens union safety stewards, mandating an in-house safety inspectorate with which employers must cooperate. The OSHA act, by giving workers power to complain to the agency and demand imposition of penalties (but not to participate in regulatory decision-making), encourages a legalistic enforcement style and legalistic resistance. When California law, like Sweden's, gave large employers incentives to establish strong labor–management safety committees, labor representatives acquired more power; they complained to OSHA less often, legal sanctions declined, and workplace injuries decreased (Rees, 1988).[35]

The Preferences of Political Authorities

In Western nations, administrative agencies are structured to enjoy a substantial degree of autonomy from political officials. Day to day administration, both in principle and to a substantial degree in practice, is immune to political intervention. Elected political officials have little interest in most regulatory programs. Nevertheless, with varying degrees of frequency and intensity, political authorities do affect some agencies' enforcement style: by appointing, or influencing the appointment of, higher agency officials; by expanding or contracting agency resources through the budget process; by legislative oversight hearings; and sometimes by telling agency officials how they would like particular regulatory matters of urgent political concern to be handled.

Regulatory officials usually are adept at reading the tenor of their political environment and at shaping enforcement methods accordingly (Frank and Lombness, 1988; Hutter, 1988). Scholz et al. (1991) compared OSHA enforcement activities in 30 counties in the state of New York (1976 to 1985) and found that OSHA inspectors imposed more penalties and larger penalties in counties whose legislative representatives were liberal Democrats. Under what circumstances, one might ask, is political influence most salient, pushing an agency's enforcement style away from a purely "rational" response to its legal mission and task environment? A number of influence-triggering events or situations might be noted.

Catastrophes and Scandals. Widely publicized catastrophes that fall within an agency's jurisdiction often trigger agency-changing political intervention. In the aftermath of a televised hotel fire, a death-dealing tunnel collapse, or a highly visible oil spill, political leaders often respond by holding hearings, replacing agency heads, and calling for new, more rigorously enforced regulations. A recent catastrophe is a reasonably good predictor of a more zealous, legalistic enforcement style, at least for a while. Scandals, including revelations of unpunished violations or regulatory incompetence, can have the same effect (Bardach and Kagan, 1982: ch.7).[36]

Economically Urgent Projects. On occasion, political authorities encourage agency officials to relax regulatory restrictions that impede a project the politicians (or their political allies) deem economically vital. A sense of urgency about development of off-shore oil wells in Great Britain generated political pressures to relax worker safety (Carson, 1982). In Dutch cities, time-consuming procedural rules concerning land use plans and building permits often are circumvented when municipal officials believe that a planned project is important to the community's economic health (see Niemeijer, 1989).

Much depends, however, on whether bending the rules is likely to spark political opposition and whether opponents have legal rights to appeal the agency's decision. In such cases, building and land use officials at least follow the form of the law, as in Niemeijer's account of a large project in Groningen. In the United States, where citizens have strong rights to appeal land use and licensing decisions in court, political authorities have often been stymied when they try to get agencies to relax environmental regulations concerning port dredging projects (Kagan, 1991a; National Research Council, 1985), off-shore oil drilling (Lester, 1991), waste disposal sites, or other large undertakings (O'Hare et al., 1983).

Political Controversy. A stringent regulatory program occasionally generates sustained political opposition, which political leaders try to defuse (or capitalize upon, depending on whether they are in or out of power) by pushing the agency to change its enforcement policy. For example,

In the late 1970s, amid repeated political attacks on OSHA's legalistic enforcement style (Levin, 1979), President Carter urged OSHA officials to reduce citations and small penalties for "nonserious" legal violations (Scholz, 1991: p.13). In 1980, President Reagan, elected after a campaign denouncing "excessive government regulation," appointed a new OSHA chief. OSHA's propensity to impose fines declined significantly (Scholz et al., 1991; Sigler and Murphy, 1988; Noble, 1986; Scholz and Wei, 1986).[37] The proportion of fines that employers contested dropped from 21 percent in 1979 to 3 percent in 1983 (Kniesner and Leeth, 1991:65).

Also in the late 1970s, surface coal mining companies and state regulatory officials vehemently attacked the federal Office of Surface Mining's stringent statutory interpretations and deterrence-oriented enforcement requirements. Influential members of Congress introduced a bill designed to weaken OSM's authority. The bill was not enacted, but in 1979 President Carter replaced the chief enforcement attorney in the Department of the Interior (OSM's parent agency) and OSM adopted a somewhat more conciliatory stance. After President Reagan's election in 1980, a new antiregulatory Secretary of the Interior, James Watt, replaced OSM's top leadership and promulgated new regulations shifting enforcement authority to state agencies. In addition, the regulations required inspectors to obtain high-level permission before issuing cessation of work orders or initiating prosecution (Shover et al., 1986).

In the late 1980s, after dramatic, political protests by patients with AIDS, Congress and the executive branch induced the FDA to relax regulations that had prevented distribution of experimental AIDS treatment drugs before they were fully tested for safety and efficacy (*Regulation,* 1988b).

A rapid shift toward accommodative enforcement can also stimulate political opposition by advocacy groups, disgruntled regulatory officials, and opposition politicians. In 1982 and 1983, congressional Democrats' aggressive oversight hearings, featuring allegations of undue laxity on the part of EPA officials, forced President Reagan to appoint new leaders who promised to enforce the law more vigorously. In consequence, administrative clean-up orders and referrals for criminal prosecution quickly increased to levels that exceeded those that prevailed during the Carter administration (Russell, 1990; Wood, 1988; Wood and Waterman, 1991). These events suggest that some regulatory issues have moved toward the center of the contemporary political stage, and that enforcement style will more often become a matter of political controversy and intervention.

Electoral Shifts in Political Leadership. Even in the absence of dramatic public controversy, agency enforcement style often changes following shifts in governmental control between conservative and liberal political parties. Sometimes such changes occur because new agency leaders are appointed (Wood and Waterman, 1991), and sometimes because existing agency officials feel greater or diminished political support for aggressive regulatory enforcement. Several studies note correlations between political party dominance and regulatory style. For example,

Hutter (1989) found that British environmental control officers working under an elected local council dominated by the Labour party prosecuted violators more often than officers in districts controlled by the Conservative Party.

In the United States, Scholz and Wei (1986), controlling for task-environment differences, found that state-run OSHA offices in states with Democratic governors and Democratic-controlled legislatures employed a more legalistic enforcement style than those in Republican states.[38]

The influence of electoral shifts is less predictable when political party control of government is divided, as not infrequently occurs in the United States. For example:

In the 1980s, EPA officials, operating under contradictory pressures from a Republican White House and a democratically controlled Congress, saw agency enforcement policies swing back and forth. In 1982, EPA enforcement actions against air and water pollutors declined rapidly, only to rise to a new high after 1986 (Wood, 1988).

A chief enforcement attorney appointed by President Reagan to the Equal Employment Opportunity Commission (EEOC) in 1981 sharply reduced the use of lawsuits against violators. Yet by mid-1983, after intense criticism by congressional Democrats, a new EEOC enforcement attorney had been appointed and litigation increased to levels equal to or exceeding Carter administration levels (Wood and Waterman, 1991: 807, 809).

In other regulatory programs (such as fair trade practices, motor vehicle safety, food and drug manufacturing practices), however, Reagan administration appointees succeeded in permanently reducing agency recourse to formal legal sanctions (Wood and Waterman, 1991). In those programs, interest groups seeking strict regulation were less well organized and influential in Congress than the environmental and civil rights groups that complained about Reagan's EPA and EEOC.

The influence of electoral shifts can be muted by the courts, at least in the United States, where the judiciary is uniquely active in supervising regulatory enforcement methods (Rabkin, 1989; Kagan, 1991b). When Democrats take over enforcement, regulated enterprises can delay and sometimes defeat stringent regulatory rulings by appealing to court, where they argue that the regulatory demands lack adequate legal authority or technical grounding (Dwyer, 1990; Mendeloff, 1987; Mashaw and Harfst, 1991), or that they are too insensitive to local economic needs (Melnick, 1983: ch. 7). Proregulatory advocacy groups, on the other hand, brought many successful court challenges against Reagan Administration regulatory agencies, arguing that the latter's efforts to soften or postpone enforcement measures violated the letter or spirit of legislation enacted by Democratic Congresses (Wenner, 1991; Shover et al., 1986: 156; Sunstein, 1983).

Moreover, local political influences can counteract the thrust of electoral changes at higher levels of government. For example:

Hedge et al. (1988) compared strip-mining law enforcement by state (West Virginia) and federal OSM officials. The state agency faced the same task environment as the eastern region OSM officials described by Shover et al. Yet state officials were less legalistic, writing fewer formal violation notices. Hedge et al. attributed those differences to the susceptibility of state agency leaders to local political pressure. Federal OSM officials, unlike their state counterparts, resisted local politicians' pressures for more flexible enforcement and instilled a more legalistic ethos in their staffs.[39]

Scholz et al. (1991a) found that federal officials also were susceptible to local political influence. According to OSHA data, even when Republican agency leaders in Washington favored a conciliatory enforcement style, where locally elected legislators (state and federal) were Democratic, the local OSHA offices adhered to more activist and legalistic enforcement methods than their counterparts in Republican-dominated counties.

All too little is known, however, about whether shifts in agency leaders and local political pressures have significant enforcement-style effects in countries that, unlike the United States, have strong traditions of bureaucratic government and in which political intervention by individual, entrepreneurial politicians is less common.

Budgetary Cutbacks. Most regulatory agencies feel chronically understaffed. Of course, as suggested earlier, most human institutions, from urban schools to machine maintenance departments in corporate factories, cannot afford to do everything they are supposed to, and complain about being short-changed when budgets are formulated. Nevertheless, it probably is true that when governments make budgets, highways, defense, and farm subsidies usually take political precedence over regulatory enforcement. At any time, as indicated in Table 1, political authorities' priorities leave some regulatory agencies with far lower inspector-to-site ratios than others, which affects frequency of inspection and hence enforcement style. In periods of retrenchment, simply by making across-the-board budget cuts, political authorities may force regulators to change their enforcement methods even more. Occasionally, however, political authorities consciously try to change controversial regulatory enforcement patterns through changes in budgetary allocations. Catastrophes or scandals, for example, sometimes induce political leaders to promise big increases in regulatory staffs. In the wake of the *Exxon Valdez* oil spill, the 1990 Pollution Prosecution Act quadrupled EPA's staff of special agents assigned to criminal investigation and criminal prosecutions soon increased (EPA 199). Complaints about regulatory overaggressiveness, on the other hand, led the Republican Reagan administration, stymied by Congress in its efforts to moderate regulatory statutes, to cut enforcement budgets in some agencies (*Regulation,* 1988b).

Table 1 Ratio of Inspectors to Sites to be Inspected, Circa 1980

Agency	Inspectors	Approximate No. Sites	Ratio
OSHA and state affiliates	3,300	5,000,000	1:1515
		335,000 high risk sites[40]	1:101
Cal-OSHA elevator unit	29	32,000 elevators/hoists, etc	1:1103
Bay Area Air Quality Control District	40	10,500 significant stationary sources	1:263
		1,700 establishments	
California Motor Safety Unit	14	3,560	1:254
FDA Food Mfg. and Storage	1,000	77,000	1:77
California Milk and Dairy	110	6,960	1:63
Mine Safety and Health Admin.	1,30	22,000	1:17
Nuclear Regulatory Commission	1,564	9,000	1:6

Source: Bardach and Kagan (1982:161).

The impact of budgetary cutbacks has not been well studied. In principle, if the ratio of regulators to regulated enterprises shrinks, inspectors cannot come as often and the agency might wish to compensate by adopting a more deterrence-oriented style. Within a year or two, the EPA adapted to 1982 budget cuts by increasing the volume of air pollution abatement orders it issued (Wood, 1988). Smaller budgets may, however, encourage some agencies to avoid costly legal contestation by adopting a more conciliatory style. If budget cuts and layoffs undercut morale, an agency may fade into a retreatist mode. If budget cuts leave prosecutors, administrative tribunals, and courts understaffed and backlogged, regulatory officials may come to feel that it is useless to seek formal legal sanctions, and, as did professional regulatory boards in California, adopt extremely conciliatory or retreatist styles (Hull, 1992). Between those extremes, budget cuts might spur agencies to target resources more accurately, adopting a tougher stance toward "bad apples" but a more cooperative approach to a majority of regulated firms. Financial cutbacks may lead some agencies to substitute lower-salaried "clerks" for more highly trained professionals, which limits their capacity to employ a consultative enforcement style. In sum, agency leaders have some options, and factors other than the cutback itself will be determinative.

Government as Regulated Entity. Political leaders' preferences also affect enforcement style when a government body is the regulated entity. It seems hardest for regulators to apply sanctions in such cases. In the United States, agencies responsible for enforcing regulations against local schools rarely use legal penalties, such as cutting off federal funds to noncompliant districts (Kagan, 1986). Pollution control regulators less often apply sanctions and tolerate more noncompliance by governmental entities, such as municipal water treatment plants, than by industrial sources (Ackerman et al., 1973; Fitzgerald et al., 1983; Russell, 1990). Dutch land use planning authorities are at their weakest, Niemeijer (1989) suggests, when the government seeks to build on municipally owned land.

This pattern may reflect the view that because government bodies serve the public, regulators should be cautious about forcing them to divert money away from other public services. Private entities, however, forced to spend money on regulatory compliance, also may have to reduce other socially useful expenditures. One suspects, therefore, that regulators' accommodative stance compared with governmental entities reflects the latters' greater capacity to make politically effective complaints about aggressive regulation. Again, however, systematic comparisons of regulating government vs. private entities remain too rare to permit any firm conclusion (see Bardach, 1989).

AGENCY LEADERSHIP

In 1981, following the inauguration of antiregulation President Ronald Reagan, the EPA *increased* its formal enforcement activity under the Clean Air and Water Acts, issuing antipollution abatement orders more often than it had under Democratic President Carter (Wood, 1988). Wood speculates that EPA officials did so in order to send regulated entities a message: notwithstanding Reagan's rhetoric, pollution control obligations remained in effect and the EPA would enforce them vigorously. This underlines a basic point: regulatory officials often have their own commitments and agendas. Backed by a committed intra-agency professional culture, or infused by particular notions of what must be done, they may be inclined to resist pressures from their political environment. At times, they try to reshape constraints imposed by their task environment. Some circumvent or seek to change their legal orders.

It is incorrect, in short, to suppose that "external" explanatory factors (the agency's legal mission and powers, its task environment, and its political environment) completely determine agency behavior. Moreover, the environment often sends mixed or conflicting signals, giving agency administrators several degrees of freedom. Within this space, regulatory enforcement style can be affected by different kinds of administrative leadership.

Outward-Directed Leadership

There have been few systematic studies of leadership in regulatory agencies. Not infrequently, regulatory officials are assumed to act like weathervanes, bending to every external political wind. A knowledgeable legal scholar (Latin, 1991:1673) writes, "Agency officials, like most human beings, prefer to avoid criticism and controversy whenever possible." Latin assumes that officials wish most of all to avoid conflict with regulated firms; hence they will guide agency policy and practice toward conciliatory enforcement methods, often resulting in undue leniency. In some political environments, however, agency officials may be more fearful of conflict with proregulation advocacy groups (who can take them to court or embarrass them in the news media), or with aggressive proregulation populists on congressional oversight committees; in such circumstances, a "weather vane" agency's enforcement methods are likely to be legalistic, and to err on the side of overregulation.

The underlying assumption of regulatory "reactiveness," however, clearly does not always hold. Like EPA during the first months of the Reagan administration, agencies sometimes take initiatives that seem to fly in the face of prevailing political winds. If some regulatory enforcement chiefs, to posit the extreme case, sit in their offices quashing any enforcement initiative that might ruffle politically important feathers, other top regulatory officials sally forth from their offices and try to change their environment. They lobby legislators, educate regulated entities, and hold press conferences. They speak at meetings of trade associations and consumer or environmental groups. If some agency chiefs are trouble-avoiding "careerists," Wilson (1980:374–382) points out, others are "politicians" who see their tenure as a stepping-stone to political visibility or electoral office, and eagerly court publicity-generating battles. Still others, Wilson argues, are "professionals," who try to adhere to analytically supported policies regardless of external political influences.[41]

As Wilson's notion of regulatory "professionals" implies, sometimes regulators' *ideas* matter. Articulate leaders who come to the job with carefully developed theories may set a new course, notwithstanding initial political opposition. For example:

Economists Alfred Kahn and Darius Gaskins, drawing on ideas developed in academia and endorsed by economists on regulatory agency staffs, led the Civil Aviation Board and the Interstate Commerce Commission, respectively, in radical new deregulatory directions, persuading reluctant members of Congress to override resistance from regulated firms, labor unions, and their political allies (Derthick and Quirk, 1985).

Another former academic, law professor William Baxter, upon being appointed to the Reagan Administration Justice Department, helped shift the intellectual basis and direction of antitrust law enforcement, despite opposition from the Democratic majority in Congress.

President Reagan's second and third EPA chiefs, William Ruckelshaus and Lee Thomas, more professional and politically astute than their predecessor, successfully reshaped the way certain health risks were analyzed and paved the way for wider political acceptance of economically flexible implementation methods (Landy et al., 1990: 245–278; Scott, 1988).

Often agency leaders work with pro- or antiregulation constituencies in an effort to change features of their task, political, or legal environment. They invite regulated entities to workshops on hazard identification or cost-effective compliance technologies, or coax trade associations to join in cooperative compliance programs (Bardach and Kagan, 1982: 177–178). In the early 1970s, California air pollution control agencies helped to organize and finance environmental advocacy groups (Sabatier, 1975). Scientists employed by the U.S. Forest Service sometimes leaked inside information to environmental advocacy groups, which in turn used the information to prepare lawsuits calling for more strongly conservationist agency decisions (Taylor, 1984). In the late 1970s, state strip-mine regulators, displeased when federal officials insisted that state agencies were legally obligated to adopt uniformly legalistic enforcement methods, joined with coal industry representatives to lobby for changes in the federal law, thereby convincing federal officials to adopt a more conciliatory posture (Shover et al., 1986: ch.8).

Of course, active attempts to reshape the regulatory environment do not always emerge. As noted earlier, some agency chiefs do cave in to political pressures for accommodative decisions, or feel bound to reflect the preferences of democratically elected political officials who appointed them, or control the agency's budget, or rewrite the laws that shape the agency's powers. Some agencies are so understaffed they can do little more than adapt to the demands generated by their task environment. In the American political system, where political power is extraordinarily fragmented and regulatory authority is subject to deep mistrust, even energetic and imaginative regulatory leaders can often be beaten back. Their opponents can fight novel regulatory initiatives in the courts, in a multiplicity of congressional subcommittees, in executive branch regulatory review offices, in other agencies with overlapping jurisdictions, and in the news media. In a political structure that gives interest groups incentives to appeal unwelcome policies to Congress or the courts (Kagan, 1991b), sometimes only the most dedicated and politically skillful regulatory leaders can succeed in winning compromise and cooperation from political opponents.

In sum, outward-looking regulatory leadership must be seen as a variable commodity. When the agency head's stance toward environmental constraints is accepting or reactive, enforcement style is more fully shaped by external pressures. When the agency head is more energetic and optimistic, his or her impact on enforcement style depends on the leader's political and legal attitudes, which can range, of course, from conservative to moderate to liberal, and from legalistic and deterrence-oriented to flexible and cooperation-oriented. Even then, the leader's influence can often be vitiated by appeals to a multiplicity of powerful institutions in the agency's political environment.

Internally Directed Leadership

In one common image, front-line regulatory enforcement officials are hard-to-manage "street-level bureaucrats," employing a variety of strategems to resist direction (Lipsky, 1980). Their day-to-day enforcement routines are shaped in part by their efforts to retain some autonomy and to manage their own workloads. When they have been recruited from particular backgrounds or professions, they may have policy views or preferred modes of action that tend to nullify those of political appointees in leadership positions. For example:

Staff lawyers often push for enforcement strategies that are more legalistic than those preferred by agency engineers, scientists or economists. Scholars have described this tendency in the U.S. EPA (Marcus, 1980: 288–294; Melnick, 1983: 259–260), Urban Mass Transit Administration (Katzmann, 1986:91–93), Federal Trade Commission (Katzmann, 1980; Clarkson and Muris, 1981; Rogowski, 1987), Justice Department (Weaver, 1980) and Highway Safety Agency (Mashaw and Harfst, 1991).

When trained foresters and civil engineers in the U.S. Forest Service and Corps of Engineers, imbued with a distinctive professional culture, were given new regulatory responsibilities, they tended to resist both internal and external pressures for strongly environmentally protective decisions (Taylor, 1984; Addison and Burns, 1991).

As Wilson (1989) summarizes some studies, senior bureaucrats in "activist" agencies (such as the EPA, the Consumer Product Safety Commission, and the Department of Health and Human Services), were significantly more liberal than the population at large and than their counterparts in departments such as Agriculture, Commerce, and Treasury.[42] When Republicans have been appointed to head such "liberal" agencies, the staff, at least in some cases, tended to resist directives to adopt more conservative interpretations of the law and more conciliatory enforcement styles (Rabkin, 1980; Wood and Waterman, 1991).

Internal agency culture, however, is not immutable. With varying degrees of energy and success, agency leaders attempt to control front-line officials and to inculcate a particular regulatory ethos. They can change recruitment patterns, intensify supervision, invest in intensive retraining, fire or transfer the recalcitrant. The methods chosen—and the ethos (or internal conflict and lowering of morale) that results—affect the agency's level of activism, its legal decision style, the efficiency of its operations, and the effectiveness with which top officials' enforcement policies are translated into the desired day-to-day decisions. Little systematic analysis currently exists concerning the leadership techniques and circumstances under which agency culture and enforcement styles are effectively transformed.

Controlling Discretion

An important sphere of internal leadership, related directly to issues of regulatory enforcement style, concerns the control of discretionary decision-making by "front-line" officials. Discretion is the key to the commonly advanced ideal of flexible enforcement. To many bureaucrats, regulated entities, advocacy groups, and political officials, however, "discretion" raises the specter of inconsistency, arbitrary treatment, bias, and corruption. When the law and external forces do not fully eliminate any choice, regulatory agency chiefs can approach the risk of misuse of discretion in a variety of ways.

The simplest approach, of course, is to forbid discretionary decision-making entirely, to create elaborate detailed manuals and instruct officials to "go by the book," and to institute review mechanisms that ensure that they do so. Careful records of each inspection or decision must be kept. Supervisors compare the volume of citations or remedial orders issued by different field inspectors, looking for deviations from the norm. Regulatory checklists and forms, dictating the kinds of information that must be considered and recorded, shield front-line officials from informal, face-to-face pleas for leniency by regulated enterprises.[43] The likely result, however, is legalistic decision-making, along with more resentment and political protest by regulated enterprises.

Another common approach is therefore to allow front-line officials some discretion, but to institute mechanisms designed to limit misuse. Many regulatory agencies adopt a system of rotating field enforcement officials from one assignment or area to another, in order to prevent them from becoming too friendly with or sympathetic to personnel in particular regulated entities. This practice, designed to prevent undue leniency, is often said to increase the level of legalistic decisions, since regulatory officials will then be unfamiliar with the technologies, risks, and trustworthiness of the entities they encounter and hence reluctant to make discretionary decisions (Bardach and Kagan, 1982:158).

Regulatory leaders can also manage discretion by recourse to selective recruitment and intensive training of personnel, although they face numerous obstacles in this regard. Unlike contemporary police forces, which rely on increasingly sophisticated academies to inculcate recruits with basic knowledge, skills, and, most importantly, a relatively professional ethos and sense of their proper social role, there are as yet no academies of regulatory enforcement (Kagan, 1984). Different agencies follow different patterns of recruitment. In some municipal agencies in the United States, such as those in charge of housing code enforcement, political patronage processes dominate the hiring process, and levels of professionalism tend to be low. In many agencies, budgetary constraints hold salaries at comparatively low levels, and it is difficult to recruit and retain ambitious, capable officials, while civil service restrictions make it difficult to fire the indifferent ones. Levels of budgetary restraint vary, however, and in some agencies regulatory leaders can make a difference.

By recruiting officials with some experience in the regulated industry, for example, agency heads build up a staff that has more confidence about making discretionary judgments and is more likely to avoid legalism and engage in flexible enforcement. Recruiting officials with university training in environmental protection, industrial hygiene, public health, and so on seems to enhance the likelihood that officials will have high levels of commitment and eagerness to take on the "bad apples," but also will reject regulated entities' arguments for flexibility based on economic considerations (Hawkins, 1984: ch.3; Bardach and Kagan, 1982: 154–156).

As in police work (Muir, 1977), the most important factor in controlling discretionary enforcement may be day-to-day interactions among enforcement officials, and particularly interactions with supervisors. Through discussion of "hard cases" with fellow enforcement officials and experienced supervisors, regulators learn informal norms concerning the interpretation of regulations (Kagan, 1978: ch.6), methods of identifying and dealing with untrustworthy enterprises, cost-effective compliance methods to convey to regulated firms, and, most importantly, a confidence-building sense of priorities and esprit des corps (Blau, 1955). By designing office routines to encompass such interaction, regulatory leaders can combat tendencies toward excessive legalism and excessive leniency, while encouraging flexible enforcement.

Targeting Enforcement

Most regulatory enforcement activity is, in retrospect, a waste of time, or close to it. Customs inspectors check thousands of forms and packages to find the few importers or travelers who really might be engaged in smuggling. Officials in all sorts of regulatory agencies process scores of permit applications and reams of mandatory compliance reports, most of which raise no significant problems. The fact that all this activity may have significant deterrence effects, that compliance would be worse if it did not occur, does not undercut the point: looking for needles in haystacks may be necessary, especially if the needles are very dangerous, but it is an inefficient process. The more efficiently a regulatory agency can focus its scarce monitoring, analytic, and sanctioning resources on the "bad apples," where its surveillance and interventions have the greatest value added, the more effective its enforcement efforts are likely to be.

Efficient targeting and deployment of enforcement resources also affect enforcement style. Flexible enforcement requires judgment, and hence takes time and knowledge. When an agency does not target enforcement efforts efficiently, its forces are spread thin and must deal with each case or inspection more cursorily. They might do so legalistically, or in a ritualistic, "retreatist" manner, or in an accommodative, "wave them through" style, but each of these methods risks missing the "needle" when it is really present. When regulatory officials do target and deploy enforcement resources more efficiently, therefore, they are more likely to approach the commonly held goal of flexible enforcement.

Thus enforcement style may vary when agency leaders can institute or take advantage of extensive data analysis concerning the regulated industry. As Scholz (1991b) has pointed out, an interesting model is provided by the Internal Revenue Service's analysis of a specially designed sample of intensive audits, yielding a formula for efficient targeting of future audits. OSHA uses an annual survey of accident rates, compiled by the Bureau of Labor Statistics, to establish priorities for workplace safety inspections (Scholz, 1991b: 13).

For most regulatory agencies, however, reliable measures of where the worst problems are likely to be found do not exist, and attempts to develop a data base from self-reporting by regulated firms can founder because of the firms' incentives to understate problems. Efficient targeting requires an experience-based type of judgment, based on constant efforts to pool and discuss the information that passes through the net of individual enforcement officials as well as on statistical sources. It rests, therefore, on a program-specific kind of administrative leadership.

For the most part, regulatory agencies have not invested heavily in new kinds of data-gathering or surveillance technologies. The development of environmental monitoring, for rapid identification of dangerous "hot spots," for example, has lagged far behind the promulgation of new regulatory obligations. Yet technological developments in monitoring will gradually occur, and those agencies whose officials take the lead in seeking funding for and using new data sources are likely to be able to adopt better-targeted, and hence more flexible, enforcement methods.

CONCLUSION

Explaining why agencies favor one implementation style rather than another, we have seen, is extraordinarily complicated. A large number of variables seem important. These include the character of the law to be enforced, the agency's task environment, its political environment, and the capacities and attitudes of agency leaders. Table 2 summarizes these factors.

A definitive explanation of regulatory enforcement, therefore, requires a complex, multivariate model. Moreover, the enumerated independent variables interact. The effect of one is contingent on the strength and direction of others, suggesting complicated propositions such as:

If an agency has (1) strong *ex ante* legal powers, and (2) a stringently stated regulatory legal mission, and (3) a task environment characterized by political pressures for proregulation advocates, *then* its enforcement style is likely to be (4) legalistic and (5) substantively stringent, *unless* (6) its decisions arouse substantial political controversy, or (7) threaten to stop economically or socially urgent projects, and (8) conservative political authorities (or a strong conservative agency chief) are in power.

If an agency has (1) only *ex post* enforcement powers, and (2) enforces stringent regulations in (3) an industry characterized by low economic resiliency, and (4) proregulation groups are weak or unable to monitor violations and pressure the agency for action, *then* a (5) conciliatory (or retreatist) enforcement and (6) excessively lenient decisions are likely, *unless* (7) there has been a recent catastrophe or scandal.

To take all the relevant variables into account, the number and complexity of such statements (or equations) in a full-dress model would be very large indeed.

Moreover, a fully developed model would have to impute appropriate *weights* to each factor. Scholz and Wei (1986) assign causative weights to a number of nicely specified task-environment and political-environment factors, but they have done so only for different offices of one agency: OSHA. It is impossible to know without additional, similarly designed studies whether the same pattern holds for agencies that, compared to OSHA, have less stringently

Table 2 Factors Affecting Regulatory Enforcement Style

- Legal design factors
  - Stringency of regulatory mission
  - Legal powers
    - Ex ante/ex post controls
    - Potency and immediacy of sanctions
    - Legal rights of regulated
    - Legal rights of complainants
  - Specificity of legal standards and penalties
- Task environment factors
  - Visibility of violations
    - Frequency of interaction with regulated entities
    - Visibility of violations to complainants
  - Regulated entities' willingness to comply
    - Size and/or sophistication of regulated entities
    - Cost of compliance/economic resilience
  - Seriousness of risks to be prevented
- Political Environment Factors
  - Strength and aggressiveness of proregulation interests
  - Preferences of political authorities, as influenced by:
    - Recent catastrophes or scandals
    - Economically urgent projects subject to regulation
    - Political controversy over enforcement style
    - Electoral shifts/changes in regulatory leadership
    - Budget cutbacks
    - Resistance by regulated governmental entities
- Leadership factors
  - Reactive vs. strong-minded regulatory leaders. If strong:
    - Leaders' policy beliefs
    - Beliefs concerning enforcement style
  - Degree of staff professionalism

and specifically worded legal designs, or programs in which violations are less visible to individuals and groups positioned to complain, or agencies in countries where regulatory bureaucracies are better shielded from political influence. In addition, studies that rely on regression analysis of quantitative data, however useful, generally are limited to rather simple measures of regulatory enforcement style, such as frequency of prosecution or other enforcement actions. These are not informative with respect to policy-oriented descriptions of enforcement style, such as the incidence of excessive leniency or excessive stringency.

Perhaps the most perplexing problem in developing a systematic analysis of regulatory enforcement arises from the fluidity of the regulatory task and political environment, and the ensuing adaptive behavior by agencies. Recurrent and unpredictable fluctuations in the profitability and resilience of regulated enterprises, stemming from changes in the marketplace and national economic policies, can diminish regulated enterprises' disposition and ability to comply, in response to which agencies change their approach from year to year, firm to firm (McKenzie and Shughart, 1987). Catastrophes occur virtually unpredictably; the resulting "crackdown" is sometimes short-lived, especially if budgetary resources are not expanded; sometimes lasting, if the agency acquires new legal powers. The incidence and targets of agency-changing scandals shift according to fashions in investigative journalism. The political party in power and its attentiveness to regulatory decisions both are subject to sudden change. Regulatory requirements that evoke resistance today become institutionalized tomorrow, as attitudes change, preventive technologies become cheaper, and established enterprises gain a comparative advantage through cost-effective compliance techniques. While compliance is increasing with respect to old regulation #1, the same regulated enterprises might bitterly resent new regulation #26. New regulations, which are as inevitable as the tides, are constantly changing most agencies' task and political environments.

Perfect models of regulatory behavior, therefore, are not likely to be forthcoming. Yet that is not the only end of scholarship. Scholars can continue to make a contribution to the continuing political debate about how regulation should be designed and implemented, and about the conditions under which regulation is effective and responsive. They can do so by detailed, empirical analyses and comparisons of regulatory problems, decision methods, and outcomes, pointing to the sources of variation in decision methods and outcomes in particular kinds of programs.

Beyond that, it is not too much to hope for a more sustained dialogue between regulatory scholars and regulatory practitioners. Aggressive protective regulation is only a generation or two old. Regulatory administrations have remained fragmented, each addressing its own problems, in its own political, economic, and technological context. The idea of regulatory administration as a profession, sustained by a developing body of practical knowledge and ethical principles, has barely been born. Yet as regulators increasingly are asked to cooperate across national boundaries, and as policy-makers seek their advice about "what works" under different circumstances, the perceived need for a knowledge-based regulatory professionalism is likely to grow. With more sustained scholarly attention to the relevant issues, that need will be better met.

NOTES

1. This chapter is a substantially revised version of Kagan, "Editor's Introduction: Understanding Regulatory Enforcement." 11 Law & Policy 89–119 (1989).
2. A distinction often is drawn between "economic" regulation—governmental efforts to stabilize or control markets by regulatory market entry, prices, or wages—and "protective" or "social" regulation, designed to deter or control specific practices, products or processes that endanger human health and safety, degrade the environment, or violate norms of equal opportunity and fair treatment. This chapter's focus is on protective regulation.
3. As Hutter (1988:9) observes, when regulatory officials "do come into contact with other legal institutions, such as the legal profession and the courts, agency activities will be judged in light of the formal law."
4. For example, Selznick argues: "A judge becomes an administrator when his objective is to reform a criminal, avert a strike, or abate a nuisance. For then his aim is not justice but accomplishment, not fairness but therapy" (id. at 16).
5. For a spirited debate, see Pearce and Tombs, 1990, 1991; Hawkins, 1990, 1991.
6. In a rare (and imaginative) empirical examination of perceived deterrence in a regulatory context, Braithwaite and Makkai (1991) found that Australian nursing homes whose directors believed that enforcement officials probably would detect and severely punish regulatory violations did not have higher (or lower) compliance rates than facilities that were less concerned about detection and legal sanctions. Differences in compliance rates were associated, rather, with such variables as age and size of the facility, the level of disability of nursing home residents, and managerial autonomy (which may relate to motivation and morale).
7. In practical terms, criminal prosecution, with its high burden of proof, ties up agency officials in extended investigations and court proceedings, and still entails significant possibilities of an em-

barrassing legal defeat (Hawkins, 1989). With large corporate offenders, criminal penalties large enough to have a significant deterrent effect would impose losses on innocent people (e.g., laid-off employees), so that judges are loathe to impose them (Coffee, 1981:400–407). Hence many influential commentators suggest that even criminal penalties should have a reform-oriented, probationary quality (Coffee, 1981; Stone, 1975; Braithwaite, 1989:ch.9).

8. In principle (and sometimes in practice) a regulatory agency may be "accommodative" in deciding what should be considered legal noncompliance and what should be permitted, and at the same time be "legalistic" in imposing sanctions or issuing corrective orders in reaction to shortcomings it deems legally impermissible. Or vice versa.
9. For an excellent, detailed account of water pollution enforcement in Great Britain, with comparable findings, see Hawkins, 1984.
10. For a useful effort to assess the policy significance of different approaches to motor vehicle recalls, see Tobin and Fizgerald (1986).
11. The possibility of regulatory misjudgment is always present. A compliance measure regulators think unnecessarily costly may turn out to have been necessary to prevent a serious accident or environmental harm. A costly protective measure officials think necessary really may be unnecessary or excessively costly under the particular circumstances. Hence Figure 2 indicates that even a flexible enforcement style, in which officials attempt to be equally alert to both kinds of errors, sometimes leads to excessive leniency and sometimes to excessive stringency. Legalistic enforcement can be explained in terms of the desire to minimize the likelihood of errors of excessive leniency, and conciliatory enforcement suggests a greater concern about avoiding errors of excessive strictness.
12. A high rate of legal citations and penalties alone, Scholz argued, could indicate either an indiscriminately legalistic policy or, if noncompliance and resistance were rampant, a sensibly flexible, welfare-maximizing enforcement policy. A low citation and penalty rate could be consistent with either a flexible, welfare-maximizing style or an excessively lenient one.
13. The Delaney clause of the U.S. pure food laws, for example, bans any food additive that is linked to cancer in laboratory animals, without regard to the product's degree of risk or benefits to humans. Until recently, U.S. Food and Drug Administration regulations, in their zeal to protect against adverse side effects, required an extensive third round of controlled clinical studies of new drugs, although such tests rarely contradicted the results of earlier trials, while adding 2 more years of delay in getting efficacious drugs to dying or suffering patients (*Regulation,* 1988a).
14. U.S. Food and Drug Administration (FDA) "good manufacturing practice" regulations governing manufacture of intravenous solutions and blood products basically codify industry safety norms. The FDA interprets and applies those very demanding regulations legalistically, precisely because everyone agrees that the law deals with serious hazards, but for the same reason it rarely is compelled to prosecute violations (Bardach and Kagan, 1982: 83).
15. The authorizing statute for the federal Superfund program is the Comprehensive Environmental Response, Compensation, and Liability Act (CERCLA), enacted in 1980, revised in 1986 (42 U.S.C. sec. 9601-9657). Litigation costs in implementing CERCLA have been estimated to amount to 22 to 44 percent of total waste-cite clean-up costs (Menell, 1991: 108).
16. For useful analyses of such *ex ante* and *ex post* design issues in regulatory programs, see Bardach (1989) and Reiss (1984). My use of the terms *ex ante* versus *ex post* refers to *modes of regulatory implementation*: (1) prescreening of planned products and activities, as opposed to (2) field inspection or compliant-based investigation of continuing or past activities. This usage may be idiosyncratic. Some scholars have used the term *ex ante* to describe all forms of regulation by governmentally prescribed prophylactic standards that try to prevent accidents or other harms before they occur, whether those standards are enforced by prior permit and licensing procedures or by field inspections. In that context, *ex post* controls refer to standards that operate by the imposition of monetary penalties after the fact of injury or harm, as a result of civil lawsuits for damages or workers' compensation claims (Wittman, 1977).
17. For an indication of the costs of criminal prosecution, see DiMento, 1986: ch.1.

18. A recent move to enhance enforcement power in *ex post* control systems entails the U.S. Racketeer Influenced or Controlled Organization Act (RICO), which authorizes enforcement officials to seize the assets of enterprises accused of a variety of law violations, before the charges have been proved in court. Aimed primarily at organized-crime-controlled enterprises, it has been used by the Securities and Exchange Commission against securities and investment banking firms accused of insider trading.
19. Of course, licensing agencies usually also have ex post sanctions at their disposal, such as suspending or revoking an operating license.
20. Regulated entities denied permits usually can appeal to court or another tribunal, but in an ex ante program the cost of delay pending judicial decision rests upon them—rather than on the agency (and the intended beneficiaries of regulatory protection), as in ex post control programs.
21. Similarly, the claims of patients with acquired immunodeficiency syndrome (AIDS) that FDA premarketing testing requirements for new drugs have slowed access to potentially helpful treatments have forced the FDA to relax its traditionally stringent rule interpretations (Vogel, 1990b; *Regulation,* 1988b).
22. For a similar account of how advocacy groups used the courts to force state air pollution control agencies to make more stringent enforcement decisions (and with similar questionable effects), see Melnick, 1983: ch.6. Conversely, Melnick shows how polluters in many cases appealed to local courts, which in turn compelled environmental agencies to back off from strict enforcement, probably with excessively lenient results (Melnick, 1983: ch.7).
23. Such highly specific legal designs have been reported primarily in the United States (see Vogel, 1986). They reflect a certain mistrust of the capacity of regulatory officials, if allowed discretion, to deal sternly with local regulated enterprises. In addition, they reflect regulated enterprises' demands for guarantees of competitive parity throughout a large area. As a consequence, the growth of multinational regulatory regimes in the European Community (Rehbinder and Stewart, 1988) probably will increase pressures for highly specified regulatory laws in other countries as well.
24. Regulation by means of tradable emissions permits or taxation represents another kind of compromise (Dwyer, 1992). In the Dutch system of charges against industrial emissions to surface waters, officials set very specific tax levels per unit of pollution and enforcement officials are expected to follow uniform rules in monitoring emissions and collecting taxes. Some sensitivity to contextual variation is preserved, however, because each regulated enterprise decides for itself what control technologies would be cost-effective (Huppes and Kagan, 1989).
25. American groups seeking stringent or controversial policies often desire specific rules and remedies, telling regulated enterprises and front-line enforcement officials alike precisely what must be done and what the legal penalties will be for noncompliance. However, some ambitious environmental control programs, such as Great Britain's water pollution program, decentralize decision-making, relying on local water pollution control officials to tighten standards on a gradual, affordance schedule, tailoring abatement requirements to each site on the basis of intuitive cost-benefit calculations (Hawkins, 1984). When the range of problems and appropriate remedies is well understood, governmental regulations may be quite specific (as in the case of dairy product plants, canneries, and building construction codes) but not very stringent, in the sense that they do not require substantial and costly changes in the regulated industry.
26. The Surface Mining Control and Reclamation Act of 1977.
27. In remarks before the National Research Council's Committee on Law and Justice (December, 1990), the chief of EPA's Office of Criminal Enforcement observed that even after substantial increases in staffing in his office, fewer than 2 percent of EPA "enforcement cases" are handled as criminal matters; about 90 percent are dealt with via administrative methods, and about 8 percent result in legal action seeking civil penalties.
28. Specialization of enforcement officials, either by professional training in the technology and economics of the regulated industry or by regular assignment of individual officials to particular kinds of problems or firms, may serve as a partial substitute for the "knowledge-enhancing" aspect of frequent contact between regulators and particular firms. Specialization, by increasing officials' self-confidence in judging hazards and suggesting cures, often is associated with a more flexible

enforcement style (Hedge et al., 1988). Niemeijer's (1989) portrait of Dutch building permit officials provides another example.

29. When British air pollution officials did mount legal prosecutions, Hutter (1989) points out, the defendants often were "cable burners"—"fly-by-night" operations that may not even be in business when the inspector comes back again to check on compliance. For similar reasons, British workplace safety inspectors are more inclined to use legal sanctions in dealing with transitory construction sites than with permanent, easily "revisitable" chemical factories (Hawkins, 1989:374).
30. Where violations are not visible to complainants, the possibility of regulatory corruption also increases. Most reported examples of corruption involve agencies like building code inspectors checking in-progress construction projects or in-plant meat inspectors (see Schuck, 1972). Such agencies have strong *ex ante* powers to order very costly halts in operating or planned projects and have task environments in which violations, if ignored by officials, cannot be spotted by likely complainants in the near future. The fixed place of business of most regulated enterprises, however, and the continuing, readily observable nature of many regulatory violations, seem to make corruption less likely than one might expect, given the stakes for regulated enterprises (see Kagan, 1984).
31. Thus nursing home regulators become reluctant to revoke the license of noncompliance facilities if government funding for impoverished patients is inadequate and there is a shortage of "good" facilities in the community (Vladeck, 1980).
32. In an insightful article, Moe (1989) argued that American regulatory bureaucracies are shaped by structural features of the American political system: a central bureaucracy that in comparative terms is weak and politically responsive; legislatures that are very responsible to interest-group pressures; and a constitutional system that allows (or encourages) election of legislative and executive branch leaders from different political parties. In this structure, interest groups seeking regulatory legislation fear that their political opponents will sooner or later gain control of the administrative apparatus. Hence groups seek regulatory rules and structures that "lock in" the substantive policies they desire, or allow them to challenge administrators who seek to change those policies. One example is business interests' successful demand that OSHA (which they expected would be dominated by organized labor) be legally checked by a separate, independent appeal board, to which business could appeal OSHA citations, thereby moderating the impact of legalistic enforcement.
33. One might argue that politics inevitably pervades any effort to make "apolitical" regulatory decisions that maximize public welfare, and indeed makes such a concept meaningless. In one sense, this is undeniable. Thus a decision whether to adopt conservative or looser estimates of the risk posed by a chemical (Nichols and Zeckhauser, 1986), or how heavily to weigh risks against the economic and opportunity costs of a stringent decision, ultimately comes down to questions of value, and hence often is influenced by the decision-maker's political attitudes. Nevertheless, I believe it is useful to differentiate between (1) choices based on the decision-maker's sense of what is "best" (acknowledging that the choice may be influenced by his or her political views), and (2) choices based on overt political pressures from external sources or from political superiors that push the decision-maker to deviate from his or her own "public-spirited" assessment of what would best serve the public interest. In discussing political pressures in the text, I mean to refer to pressures of the second type.
34. In the 1970s, labor's pressure for sanction-oriented OSHA enforcement generated a considerable amount of resistance from employers, who contested legally the frequent fines and mounted political attacks on the agency (Kelman, 1981; Levin, 1979; Bardach and Kagan, 1982: ch.4). Using OSHA data from 34 states over the 1976 to 1985 period, Scholz (1991a) found that heavy organized labor pressure, measured by complaint rates, seemed to increase the number of OSHA inspections, citations, and penalties, but resulted in less effectiveness (measured by reductions in injury rates) than that achieved by state agencies. Operating under less labor pressure, state agencies were free to employ a more flexible, carefully targeted use of legal penalties.
35. On the advantages of more corporatist, less legalistic ways of enabling proregulation interests to affect regulatory decision-making, see also Ayres and Braithwaite, 1991; and Badaracco, 1986.
36. Understanding when, and for what kinds of agencies, catastrophes and scandals are most likely to

occur, has not been a subject of serious study. Scandals, one might suspect, are largely a product of the characteristics of investigative journalism in a community. In some regulatory programs the gap between aspiration and control is almost always wide—for example, quality of care in nursing homes, safety in dangerous workplaces, air pollution control, fire safety regulation in slums, clean ups of hazardous waste disposal sites—and a clever journalist can write a good exposé almost at will. Catastrophes are almost by definition harder to predict, although some calculations, and correlations with regulatory enforcement practices, probably could be made.

37. It is by no means clear that the reduction in legalistic enforcement by OSHA had a deleterious effect on workplace accident rates, which are sensitive to changes in factors other than enforcement, such as the age and turnover of the work force, union policies (Bacow, 1980), increases in the generosity of workers' compensation systems (Kniesner and Leeth, 1991), the targeting of inspections, and the intraorganizational dynamics of corporate safety programs. Under vigorous enforcement in the 1970s, the positive effects seem to have been limited (Viscusi, 1986; but see Scholz and Gray, 1990; Gray and Scholz, 1993). Alternative, nonlegalistic approaches apparently have considerable promise (Rees, 1988).
38. Scholz et al. (1991: 835) attribute this result to the overall political climate and level of support agency officials receive from locally elected politicians, noting that "participant observation yields little evidence of direct case-by-case influence by politicians on OSHA enforcement." See also Headrick, 1990.
39. Despite similarities among individual inspectors in training and years of experience (both of which, by themselves, were associated with a more flexible enforcement style), OSM inspectors had a more negative view of coal operators than state agency inspectors and were more supportive of the stringent regulations.
40. High-risk sites are fixed establishments that had rates of lost workdays due to injury above the relevant industry average. Of those, only 125,000 had more than 20 employees (Bardach and Kagan, 1982:162).
41. Wilson's (1980) typology of regulatory leaders—careerists, politicians, and professionals—might be compared with bureaucratic typologies carved out by Downs (1967: 88) (climbers, conservers, zealots, advocates, and statesmen) and by Heclo (1977: 148–153) (program bureaucrats, staff bureaucrats, reformers, and institutionalists). None of these accounts provides any empirical evidence for the prevalence of different types in different agencies, or sets forth methods for classifying particular officials.
42. Summarizing the findings of Rothman and Lichter (1983), Wilson (1989:66) writes: "In the activist agencies, bureaucrats were more likely than their counterparts in traditional agencies to say that women and blacks should get preference in hiring, that poor people are the victims of circumstances, and that U.S. foreign policy has aimed at protecting business." According to Aberbach and Rockman's (1976) study of federal bureaucrats during the Nixon administration, over 90 percent of Democrats in activist agencies were "on the left," compared with only 25 percent of Democrats in "traditional" agencies (Wilson, 1989:66).
43. When regulated entities' applications appear to regulatory officials only in the form of written files, thereby excluding informal face-to-face interaction, legalistic and substantively stringent decision-making, some studies indicate, is much more common (Kagan, 1978: 152–154). For similar results in a nonregulatory bureaucratic context, see Mashaw (1983).

REFERENCES

Aberbach, Joel D. and Bert A. Rockman (1976) Clashing beliefs within the Executive Branch: The Nixon administration. *American Political Science Review* 70: 446–68.

Ackerman, Bruce A., Susan Rose-Ackerman, James W. Sawyer, Jr., and D. W. Henderson (1973). *The Uncertain Search for Environmental Quality*. New York: Free Press.

Ackerman, Bruce, A. and William T. Hassler (1981) *Clean Coal/Dirty Air*. New Haven: Yale University Press.

Ackerman, Bruce A. and Richard B. Stewart (1985) Comment: Enforcing environmental law. *Stanford Law Review* 37: 1333.

Addison, Thomas and Timothy Burns (1991) The Army Corps of Engineers and nationwide permit 26: Wetlands protection of swamp reclamation? *Ecology Law Quarterly* 18:619–669.

Anderson, Douglas (1981) *Regulatory Politics and Electric Utilities*. Boston: Auburn House.

Ayres, Ian and John Braithwaite (1992) *Responsive Regulation*. New York: Oxford University Press.

Ayres, Ian and John Braithwaite (1991) Tripartism: Regulatory capture and empowerment. *Law & Social Inquiry* 16:435–496.

Baar, Ellen (1986) Redesigning regulation: Insights from down under. Paper presented 2nd Annual Meeting Canadian Law and Society Association, Winnepeg, June 5.

Bacow, Lawrence S. (1980) *Bargaining for Job Safety and Health*. Cambridge: MIT Press.

Badaracco, Joseph L. (1985) *Loading The Dice: A Five Country Study of Vinyl Chloride Regulation*. Boston: Harvard Business School Press.

Bardach, Eugene (1989) Social regulation as a generic policy instrument, in L. Salamon, ed., *Beyond Privatization: The Tools of Government Action*. Washington: Urban Institute Press.

Bardach, Eugene and Robert A. Kagan (1982) *Going By The Book: The Problem of Regulatory Unreasonableness*. Philadelphia: Temple University Press. A Twentieth Century Fund Report.

Bernstein, Marver (1955) *Regulating Business by Independent Commission*. Princeton: Princeton University Press.

Blau, Peter (1955) *The Dynamics of Bureaucracy*. Chicago: University of Chicago Press.

Braithwaite, John (1985). *To Punish or Persuade: Enforcement of Coal Mine Safety*. Albany, NY: SUNY Press.

Braithwaite, John (1989) *Crime, Shame and Reintegration*. Cambridge: Cambridge University Press.

Braithwaite, John and Brent Fisse (1987) Self-regulation and the control of private crime. In C. Shearing & P. Stenning, eds., *Private Policing*. pp. 221–246.

Braithwaite, John and Toni Makkai (1991) Testing an expected utility model of corporate deterrence. *Law & Society Review* 25:7–40.

Braithwaite, John, John Walker, and Peter Grabosky (1987) An enforcement taxonomy of regulatory agencies, *Law and Policy* 9:323–350.

Carson, W. G. (1982) *The Other Price of Britain's Oil: Safety and Control in the North Sea*. Oxford: Martin Robertson.

Church, Thomas and Robert Nakamura (1993) *Cleaning Up the Mess: Implementation Strategies in Superfund*. Washington, D.C.: Brookings Institution.

Clarkson, Kenneth W. and Timothy Muris (1981) *The Federal Trade Commission Since 1970*. Cambridge: Cambridge University Press.

Coffee, John C., Jr. (1981) No soul to damn, no body to kick: An unscandalized inquiry into the problem of corporate punishment. *Michigan Law Review* 74:386–459.

Cohen, Mark A. (1991) Corporate crime and punishment: An update on sentencing practice in the federal courts, 1988–1990. *Boston University Law Review,* 71:247–280.

Coyle, Dennis J. (1988). The Balkans by the bay. *The Public Interest* 91:67.

Crandall, M. S. (1984) The political economy of clean air: Practical restraints on White House review. in V. K. Smith, ed., *Environmental Policy Under Reagan's Executive Order 205* (Washington, D.C.: Resources for the Future.

Day, Patricia and Rudolf Klein (1987) The regulation of nursing homes: A comparative perspective. *The Milbank Quarterly* 65:303–347.

Derthick, Martha and Paul J. Quirk (1985) *The Politics of Deregulation*. Washington, D.C.: Brookings Institution.

DiMento, Joseph F. (1986) *Environmental Law and American Business: Dilemmas of Compliance*. New York: Plenum Press.

Downs, Anthony (1967) *Inside Bureaucracy*. Boston: Little Brown.

Dwyer, John P. (1992) The use of market incentives in controlling air pollution: California's marketable permits program. *Ecology Law Quarterly* 20:103

Dwyer, John P. (1990) The pathology of symbolic legislation. *Ecology Law Quarterly* 17:233–316.

Edelman, Murray (1964) *The Symbolic Uses of Politics.* Urbana, IL: University of Illinois Press.

Farber, Daniel and Philip Frickey (1991) *Law and Public Choice.* Chicago: University of Chicago Press.

Feinstein, Jonathan (1989) The safety regulation of U.S. nuclear power plants: Violations, inspections, and abnormal occurrences. *Journal of Political Economy* 97:115–154.

Fitzgerald, Michael R., Stephen Rechichar, Robert Durant and Larry Thomas (1983) *Intra-Government Regulation and The Public Interest: Air Pollution Control in the Tennessee Valley.* Knoxville, TN: University of Tennessee, Bureau of Public Administration.

Frank, Nancy and Michael Lombness (1988) Gaining regulatory compliance: Law enforcement and power in an interactionist perspective. *Administration & Society* 20:71–91.

Freeman, Richard (1981) Black economic progress after 1964: Who has gained and why? in Sherwin Rosen, ed., *Studies in Labor Markets.*

Frieden, Bernard J. (1979) The new regulation comes to surburbia. *The Public Interest* 55:15–27.

Friedman, Lawrence M. (1985) *Total Justice.* New York: Russell Sage Foundation.

Grabosky, Peter and John Braithwaite (1986) *Of Manners Gentle: Enforcement Strategies of Australian Business Regulatory Agencies.* Melbourne: Oxford University Press.

Gray, Wayne and John T. Scholz (1993) Does regulatory enforcement work? A panel analysis of OSHA enforcement. *Law & Society Review* 27:177–213.

Grumbly, Thomas P. (1982) Self-regulation: Private vice and public virtue revisited in E. Bardach and R. A. Kagan, eds., *Social Regulation: Strategies for Reform.* San Francisco: Institute for Contemporary Studies.

Gunningham, Neil (1987) Negotiated noncompliance: A case study of regulatory failure. *Law & Policy* 9:69–91.

Hawkins, Keith (1984) *Environment and Enforcement: Regulation and the Social Definition of Deviance.* Oxford: Oxford University Press.

Hawkins, Keith (1989) 'FATCATS' and prosecution in a regulatory agency: A footnote on the social construction of risk. *Law & Policy* 11:370–391.

Hawkins, Keith (1990) Compliance strategy, prosecution policy, and Aunt Sally: A comment on Pearce and Tombs. *British Journal of Criminology* 30:444–466.

Hawkins, Keith (1991) Enforcing regulation: More of the same from Pearce and Tombs. *British Journal of Criminology* 31:427–430.

Heclo, Hugh (1977) *A Government of Strangers: Executive Politics in Washington.* Washington, D.C.: The Brookings Institution.

Headrick, Barbara (1990). Incentives and influence: OSHA inspectors in urban areas. Ph.D. dissertation, SUNY-Stony Brook.

Hedge, David M., Donald Menzel and George Williams (1988) Regulatory attitudes and behavior: The case of surface mining regulation. *Western Political Quarterly* 41:323–340.

Howe, Charles W. (1991) An evaluation of U.S. air and water policies. *Environment,* Sept. 1991, pp. 10–15, 34–36.

Huber, Peter (1983) Exorcists vs. gatekeepers in risk regulation. *Regulation* Nov./Dec: 23–32.

Hull, Tupper (1992) Regulatory boards mired in red tape. *San Francisco Examiner,* February 16, p. A1.

Huppes, Gjalt and Robert A. Kagan (1989) Market-oriented regulation of environmental problems in the Netherlands. *Law & Policy* 11:215–239.

Hutter, Bridget (1988) *The Reasonable Arm of The Law? The Law Enforcement Procedures of Environmental Health Officials.* Oxford: Clarendon Press.

Hutter, Bridget (1989) Variations in regulatory enforcement styles. *Law & Policy* 11:153–174.

Jasanoff, Sheila (1986) *Risk Management and Political Culture.* New York: Russell Sage Foundation.

Kagan, Robert A. (1978) *Regulatory Justice: Implementing A Wage Price Freeze.* New York: Russell Sage Foundation.

Kagan, Robert A. (1984) On regulatory inspectorates and police, in K. Hawkins and J. Thomas, eds., *Enforcing Regulation.* Boston: Kluwer-Nijhoff.

Kagan, Robert A. (1986) Regulating business, regulating schools, in D. Kirp and D. Jensen, eds., *School Days, Rule Days: The Regulation and Legalization of Public Schools.* Philadelphia: Falmer Press.

Kagan, Robert A. (1988) What makes Uncle Sammy sue? *Law & Society Review* 21:718–742.
Kagan, Robert A. (1989) Editor's introduction: Understanding regulatory enforcement. *Law & Policy* 11:89–119.
Kagan, Robert A. (1990) *Patterns of Port Development: Government, Intermodal Transportation, and Innovation in the United States, China, and Hong Kong*. Berkeley: Institute of Transportation Studies.
Kagan, Robert A. (1991a) The dredging dilemma: Economic development and environmental protection in Oakland Harbor. *Coastal Management* 19:313–341.
Kagan, Robert A. (1991b) Adversarial legalism and American government. *Journal of Policy Analysis & Management* 10:369–406.
Kagan, Robert A. and John T. Scholz (1984) The "criminology of the corporation" and regulatory enforcement strategies, in Keith Hawkins and John Thomas, eds., *Enforcing Regulation*. Boston: Kluwer-Nijhoff.
Kagan, Robert A. and Jerome H. Skolnick (1993) Banning smoking: compliance without enforcement, in Robert Rabin and Stephen Sugarman, eds., *Smoking Policy: Law, Politics, and Culture* New York: Oxford University Press.
Katzenstein, Peter (1988) *Small States in World Markets: Industrial Policy in Europe*. Ithaca, NY: Cornell University Press.
Katzmann, Robert A. (1986) *Institutional Disability: The Saga of Transportation Policy for the Disabled*. Washington: Brookings Institution.
Katzmann, Robert A. (1980) *Regulatory Bureaucracy: The Federal Trade Commission and Antitrust Policy*. Cambridge, MA: MIT Press.
Kelman, Steven (1981) *Regulating America, Regulating Sweden: A Comparative Study of Occupational Safety and Health Policy*. Cambridge, MA: MIT Press.
Knegt, Robert (1989) Regulating dismissal from employment: Administrative and judicial procedures in the Netherlands. *Law & Policy* 11:175–188.
Kniesner, Thomas and John Leeth (1991) Improving worker safety. *Regulation* Fall:64–70.
Landy, Marc K., Marc J. Roberts, and Stephen R. Thomas (1990) *The Environmental Protection Agency: Asking the Wrong Questions*. New York: Oxford University Press.
Latin, Howard (1991) Regulatory enforcement, administrative incentives, and the new Clean Air Act. *Environmental Law* 21:1647–1720.
Lave, Lester B. (1981) *The Strategy of Social Regulation: Decision Frameworks for Policy*. Washington: Brookings Institution.
Leone, Robert (1986) *Who Profits? Winners, Losers, and Government Regulation* New York: Basic Books.
Lester, Charles (1991) *The Search for Dialogue in the Administrative State: The Politics, Policy, and Law of Offshore Oil Development*. Ph.D Dissertation, University of California, Berkeley
Levin, Michael (1982) Getting there: Implementing the bubble policy, in E. Bardach and R. A. Kagan, eds., *Social Regulation: Strategies for Reform*. San Francisco: Institute for Contemporary Studies.
Levin, Michael (1979) Politics and Polarity: The Limits of OSHA Reform. *Regulation* Nov/Dec: 33–39.
Lewis-Beck, Michael and John R. Alford (1980) Can government regulate safety? The coal mine example. *American Political Science Review* 74:745–755.
Lipsky, Michael (1980). *Street-Level Bureaucracy*. New York: Russell Sage Foundation.
Lundqvist, Lennart (1980) *The Tortoise and The Hare: Clean Air Policies in the United States and Sweden*. Ann Arbor: University of Michigan Press.
Marcus, Alfred (1980) Environmental protection agency in J. Q. Wilson, ed., *The Policitcs of Regulation*. New York: Basic Books.
Mashaw, Jerry L. (1983) *Bureacratic Justice: Managing Social Security Disability Claims*. New Haven, CT: Yale University Press.
Mashaw, Jerry and Daniel Harfst (1987) Regulation and legal culture: The case of motor vehicle safety. *Yale Journal on Regulation* 4:257–316.
Mashaw, Jerry and Daniel Harfst (1991) *The Struggle for Auto Safety*. Cambridge: Harvard University Press.

McKenzie, Richard B. and William F. Shughart II (1987) Deregulation and air travel safety. *Regulation* 3/4:42–47.

Melnick, R. Shep (1983) *Regulation and The Courts: The Case of The Clean Air Act.* Washington, D.C.: The Brookings Institution.

Mendeloff, John (1987) *The Dilemma of Rulemaking for Toxic Substances.* Cambridge, MA: MIT Press.

Menell, Peter (1991) The limitations of legal institutions for addressing environmental risks. *Journal of Economic Perspectives* 5:93–113.

Moe, Terry (1989) The politics of bureaucratic structure, in John Chubb & Paul Peterson, eds., *Can Government Govern?* Washington: Brookings Institution.

Muir, William K., Jr. (1977) *Police: Streetcorner Politicians.* Chicago: University of Chicago Press.

Nash, Gerald (1964) *State Government and Economic Development: A History of Administrative Policies in California, 1849–1933.* Berkeley: Institute of Governmental Studies.

National Research Council (1985) *Dredging Coastal Ports: An Assessment of the Issues.* Washington, D.C.: National Academy Press.

NRC (1989) *A Common Destiny: Blacks and American Society.* Washington, D.C.: National Academy Press.

Nichols, Albert L. (1991) Comparing risk standards: The superiority of a benefit-cost approach. *Regulation* Fall:85–94.

Nichols, Albert L. and Richard J. Zeckhauser (1986) The perils of prudence: How conservative risk assessments distort regulation. *Regulation* Nov/Dec:13–24.

Niemeijer, Bert (1989) Urban land-use and building control in the Netherlands: Flexible decisions in a rigid system. *Law & Policy* 11:121–152.

Noble, Charles (1986) *Liberalism at Work: The Rise and Fall of OSHA.* Philadelphia: Temple University Press.

OECD (1985) *The State of the Environment,* 1985. Paris: OECD.

O'Hare, Michael, Lawrence Bacow, and Debra Sanderson (1983) *Facility Siting and Public Opposition.* New York: Van Nostrand Reinhold.

Ould, Patricia (1986) The housing code in action: A comparison of three cities. Paper presented at annual meeting of the Law and Society Association, Chicago.

Pearce, F. and S. Tombs (1990). Ideology, hegemony and empiricism: Compliance theories of regulation. *British Journal of Criminology* 30:423–443.

Pearce, F. and S. Tombs (1991) Policing corporate 'skid rows': A reply to Keith Hawkins. *British Journal of Criminology* 31 (4).

Portney, Paul R. (1990) Air pollution policy, in Portney, ed., *Public Policy for Environmental Protection.* Washington, D.C.: Resources for the Future.

Quirk, Paul J. (1981) *Industry Influence in Federal Regulatory Agencies.* Princeton: Princeton University Press.

Rabkin, Jeremy (1980) Office of civil rights, in J. Q. Wilson, ed., *The Politics of Regulation.* New York: Basic Books.

Rabkin, Jeremy (1989) *Judicial Compulsions: How Public Law Distorts Public Policy.* New York: Basic Books.

Regulation (1988a) Dying for drugs. 3:9–11.

Regulation (1988b) The iceberg's tip. 3:12.

Rehbinder, Eckard and Richard Stewart (1988) *Environmental Protection Policy: Legal Integration in the United States and the European Community.* New York: Walter de Gruyter.

Rees, Joseph (1988) *Reforming The Workplace: A Study of Self-Regulation in Occupational Safety.* Philadelphia: University of Pennsylvania Press.

Reich, Peter L. (1992) Greening the ghetto: A theory of environmental race discrimination. *University of Kansas Law Review* 41: 271–314.

Reiss, Albert J., Jr. (1984) Selecting strategies of social control over organizational life, in K. Hawkins and J. Thomas, eds., *Enforcing Regulation.* Boston: Kluwer-Nijhoff.

Rogowski, Robert A. (1987) The pyrrhic victories of section 7: A political economy approach, in R.

J. Mackay, J. C. Miller III, and B. Yandle, eds., *Public Choice and Regulation: A View from Inside the Federal Trade Commission.* Stanford, CA: Hoover Institution Press, pp. 220–239.

Rosenberg, Gerald N. (1991) *The Hollow Hope: Can Courts Bring About Social Change?* Chicago: University of Chicago Press.

Rothman, Stanley and S. Robert Lichter (1983) How liberal are bureaucrats? *Regulation* Nov/Dec:18.

Russell, C. S. (1990) Monitoring and enforcement, in Paul Portney, ed., *Public Policies for Environmental Protection.* Washington, D.C.: Resources for the Future.

Sabatier, Paul (1975) Social movements and regulatory agencies: Toward a more adequate—and less pessimistic—theory of clientele capture. *Policy Science* 6:301.

Sabatier, Paul and Daniel Mazmanian (1983) *Can Regulation Work? The Implementation of the 1972 California Coastline Initiative.* New York: Plenum.

Scholz, John T. (1984) Cooperation, deterrence, and the ecology of regulatory enforcement. *Law and Society Review* 18:601–646.

Scholz, John T. (1991a) Cooperative regulatory enforcement and the politics of administrative effectiveness. *American Political Science Review* 85:115–136.

Scholz, John T. (1991b) Managing regulatory enforcement in the United States. Paper presented at Symposium on the Organization of Administration of Major Regulating Functions in Government Agencies, American University, Washington, D.C., May 16.

Scholz, John T., Jim Twombly, and Barbara Headrick (1991) Street level political controls over federal bureaucracy. *American Political Science Review* 85:829–850.

Scholz, John T. and Wayne B. Gray (1990) OSHA enforcement and workplace injuries: A behavioral approach to risk assessment. *Journal of Risk & Uncertainty* 3:283–305.

Scholz, John T. and Feng Heng Wei (1986) Regulatory enforcement in a federalist system. *American Political Science Review* 80:1249–1270.

Schuck, Peter (1972) The curious case of the indicted meat inspectors. *Harper's*, September, pp. 81–82.

Scott, Esther (1988) Managing environmental risk: The case of Asarco, in Robert B. Reich, ed., *Public Management in a Democratic Society.* Englewood Cliffs, NJ: Prentice-Hall.

Selznick, Philip (1969) *Law, Society, and Industrial Justice.* New York: Russell Sage Foundation.

Shover, Neil, Donald A. Clelland, and John Lynxwiler (1986) *Enforcement or Negotiation: Constructing a Regulatory Bureaucracy.* Albany, NY: State University of New York Press.

Shover, Neil, Donald A. Clelland and John Lynxwiler (1984) Regional variation in regulatory law enforcement: The Surface Mining Control and Reclamation Act, in Keith Hawkins and John Thomas, eds., *Enforcing Regulation.* Boston: Kluwer-Nijhoff.

Shulman, Steven and William Darby (1989) *The Question of Discrimination.* Middletown, CT: Wesleyan University Press

Sigler, Jay A. and Joseph E. Murphy (1988) *Interactive Corporate Compliance: An Alternative to Regulatory Compulsion.* New York: Quorum Books.

Steele, Eric H. (1987) Community participation and the function of rules: The case of urban zoning boards. *Law & Policy* 9:279–304.

Stigler, George (1975) *The Citizen and the State.* Chicago: University of Chicago Press.

Stone, Christopher D. (1975) *Where the Law Ends: Social Control of Corporate Behavior.* New York: Harper & Row.

Sunstein, Cass R. (1990) *After the Rights Revolution: Reconceiving the Regulatory State.* Cambridge, MA: Harvard University Press.

Sunstein, Cass R. (1983) Deregulation and the hard-look doctrine. *Supreme Court Review* 1983:177.

Taylor, Serge (1984) *Making Bureaucracies Think: The Environmental Impact Strategy of Administrative Reform.* Stanford, CA: Stanford University Press.

Tobin, Richard J. and Roy Fitzgerald (1986) Assessing the consequences of corporate discretion on regulatory compliance: The case of motor vehicle safety in Canada. *Law & Policy* 8:59–76.

Truman, David (1953) *The Governmental Process.* New York: Alfred Knopf.

Veljanovski, Cento (1984) The economics of regulatory enforcement, in Keith Hawkins and John Thomas, eds., *Enforcing Regulation.* Boston: Kluwer-Nijhoff.

Viscusi, W. Kip (1986) Reforming OSHA regulation of workplace risks, in L. Weiss and M. Klass, eds., *Regulatory Reform: What Actually Happened.* Boston: Little, Brown.

Vladeck, Bruce (1980) *Unloving Care: The Nursing Home Tragedy.* New York: Basic Books.

Vogel, David (1990a) Environmental policy in Europe and Japan, in Norman Vig and Michael Kraft, eds., *Environmental Policy in the 1990s.* Washington, D.C.: Congressional Quarterly Press.

Vogel, David (1990b) When consumers oppose consumer protection: The politics of regulatory backlash. *Journal of Public Policy* 10:449–470.

Vogel, David (1986) *National Styles of Regulation.* Ithaca, NY: Cornell University Press.

Weaver, Paul H. (1978) Regulation, social policy, and class conflict. *The Public Interest* Winter.

Weaver, Suzanne (1980) Antitrust division of the Department of Justice, in J. Q. Wilson, ed., *The Politics of Regulation.* New York: Basic Books.

Wehling, Carol (1987) RCRA permitting. *Natural Resources and Environment* 2:27.

Wenner, Lettie M. (1991) Environmental policy in the courts, in Norman Vig & Michael Kraft, eds., *Environmental Policy in the 1990s.* Washington, D.C.: Congressional Quarterly Press.

Wilkerson, William R. and Thomas W. Church (1989) The gorilla in the closet: Joint and several liability and the cleanup of toxic waste sites. *Law & Policy* 11:425–449.

Wilson, James Q. (1980) *The Politics of Regulation.* New York: Basic Books.

Wilson, James Q. (1989) *Bureaucracy: What Government Agencies Do and Why They Do It.* New York: Basic Books.

Wittman, Donald (1977) Prior regulation versus ex post liability: The choice between input and output monitoring. *Journal of Legal Studies* 6:193–211.

Wood, B. Dan (1988) Principals, bureaucrats, and responsiveness in clean air enforcement. *American Political Science Review* 82:213–234.

Wood, B. Dan and Richard W. Waterman (1991) The dynamics of political control of the bureaucracy. *American Political Science Review* 85:801–828.

Yellen, David and Carl J. Mayer (1992) Coordinating sanctions for corporte misconduct: Civil or criminal punishment? *American Criminal Law Review* 29:961–1024.

15

Managing Regulatory Enforcement in the United States

John T. Scholz *State University of New York at Stony Brook, Stony Brook, New York*

The history of regulatory policies in America goes back to the beginning of the country. Regulatory enforcement in its current form, however, really goes back only a few decades. Although enforcement was always a necessary part of any attempt to regulate behavior, until recently there were a relatively small number of enforcement officials. The last several decades have witnessed a dramatic growth in the number of inspectors hired by the public and private sectors to enforce regulations of all sorts. As a consequence, systematic knowledge about how enforcement agencies should and actually do behave is relatively underdeveloped. The primary purpose of this chapter is to integrate and interpret the scattered literature that has studied enforcement and enforcement agencies from the perspective of regulatory managers and policymakers. What do we know about enforcement behavior? What can be done to improve its efficiency? And how can we improve the scientific basis for managing agencies and setting enforcement policies?

Many basic enforcement functions and problems share common features across all agencies at the local, state, and national level, and even across national boundaries. We will begin by discussing the fundamental tasks of monitoring and prosecution that are associated with deterring noncompliance, surveying various solutions to common technical problems. Then we will consider alternative enforcement strategies that add educational and persuasive components to deterrence basics, in recognition of the range of motivating factors involved in compliance behavior. A primary theme in this discussion is the need for discretion to adopt enforcement tactics that are appropriate for given situations facing the agency.

Although the basic tactics and strategies of enforcement are universal, the organizational and political setting of enforcement agencies can dramatically alter the choice and effectiveness of appropriate tactics and strategies. As a consequence, the discussion is broadened first to

This chapter was originally prepared for presentation at Managing Regulation, a Symposium on the Organization and Administration of Major Regulating Functions in Government Agencies, sponsored by The American University, School of Public Affairs, Washington, D.C., May 16, 1991.

consider management techniques and organizational factors that shape the available enforcement tools agency leaders can employ. Given the potential importance of discretion for effective enforcement, we will emphasize the primary threats of "capture" and corruption that inevitably arise when field officers have discretion. We will also consider managerial control techniques that maintain reasonable limits on the threats. Finally, we will broaden the discussion to include the critically important political culture in which agencies operate. In many ways, this political environment poses the most difficult challenges to enforcement agency leadership. The American political system was not designed to produce efficient government agencies. The fragmentation of power, mistrust of governmental police powers, antagonistic relationships between competing regulatory interests, and adversarial use of the legal system all create major impediments to the development of reasonable enforcement policies. Although we ignore these problems in the initial sections on enforcement tactics and strategies, we return in the third section to discuss the constraints that arise in the broader political context. The discussion will conclude by focusing on the broader role of enforcement activities in the political system.

Several caveats should be mentioned initially. First, the scope of this project does not include discussions of alternative policy methods to achieve goals currently pursued using "command and control" regulations and enforcement. Such discussions are important, but have already received appropriate attention elsewhere. The discussions also tend to leave out the kind of management decisions that provide the primary concern in this chapter. In fact, discussions of the regulatory alternative of utilizing taxes to provide appropriate incentives seldom consider the range of enforcement problems encountered in collecting taxes. Yet enforcement problems are so important to the Internal Revenue Service (IRS)—the largest tax collection agency in the United States—that we include examples from the IRS in our discussions.

A second caveat is that most of the examples come from descriptions by agency officials, and are not accompanied by any systematic evaluation about their effectiveness. I draw on 10 years of discussions with managers from many federal and state agencies, although most examples will come from the Occupational Safety and Health Administration (OSHA) and the IRS, the two federal agencies I know most extensively. Surprisingly few of the techniques have been systematically evaluated for their impact on compliance, and even fewer of these evaluations are available outside the agency. Most evaluation studies published in journals have focused on the most general level of whether enforcement makes any difference, rather than on the question of which approaches are most effective in eliciting desired behavior. Thus the scientific basis for discussing the effectiveness of alternative enforcement techniques is woefully inadequate for the broad range of enforcement activities that provide the backbone of most regulatory agencies.

This leads to one of the primary conclusions of this chapter: research and policy development need to become a more commonly utilized tool of management. Innovative enforcement techniques and policies should be introduced as field experiments in a manner that would provide some evaluation about their effectiveness. The advantages of greater utilization of practical evaluation techniques would be further increased by establishing routine interchanges to share techniques, ideas, and experiences across enforcement agencies. Some suggestions will be made for how these can be established.

I have tried in this discussion to provide a basic framework for considering any specific enforcement problem. The framework covers a range of alternative enforcement, management, and political concerns that might provide important contributions to an innovative solution to the problem. By going through this checklist, one might develop alternative approaches that are not immediately apparent to those most knowledgeable about the problem. The examples provided are meant to stimulate ideas for comparable solutions for the problem under consideration. With practice, it is easy to apply the techniques discussed here to any given problem. While many may be impractical with undesirable side effects, some may be developed into the kind of innovative approach that is essential to developing efficient and effective enforcement policies.

ENFORCEMENT TECHNIQUES: TACTICS AND STRATEGIES

If the only goal of enforcement were to coerce as much compliance with existing rules as possible, deterrence techniques aimed at finding and punishing noncompliers might be the only ones needed by regulatory agencies. Given sufficient resources and a free hand to use the most effective deterrence techniques, an agency could most likely produce almost any desired level of compliance.

However, enforcement is never so simple. The primary goal in most regulatory enforcement is not obtaining a given level of compliance, but gaining a desirable level of statutory policy goals (e.g., worker or consumer safety and health) in an efficient manner. Furthermore, techniques for obtaining policy goals are constrained not only by the need for regulations and enforcement that encourage efficiency on the part of regulated firms and other entities but also by the need for enforcement techniques that are both efficient and within the rather ambiguous limits on government coercive powers set by the political system.

Such constraints have encouraged the development of "voluntary compliance" as the primary enforcement philosophy of federal regulatory agencies. This philosophy takes on many forms, but essentially recognizes the need for educational and persuasive techniques to complement the coercive, deterrence-oriented techniques at the core of most enforcement programs.

To clarify the basic components of the voluntary compliance approach, we will consider three distinctive strategies and enforcement tactics associated with each. Each strategy is most effective for a different set of enforcement problems, as discussed by Kagan and Scholz (1984). To develop an effective enforcement program, each agency must develop the particular blend of strategies and tactics appropriate for the agency's enforcement problems.

The *deterrence strategy* is the most familiar and best understood of the three. This approach is based on the assumption that regulated entities are amoral, and will not obey regulations unless given an incentive to do so. The deterrence strategy uses coercive means to provide incentives by punishing all firms that are found to be noncompliant. The basic tactics include methods of monitoring firms to detect noncompliance and imposing penalties sufficient to deter future noncompliance.

The *educational strategy* assumes that at least some noncompliance stems from the difficulty certain firms have with understanding regulations and implementing effective internal controls to prevent noncompliance (see Stone, 1975). Although fines and punishment may force incompetent firms to focus more clearly on regulatory duties, they may also further distract firms or provide only temporary cures for recurrent problems. Basic tactics for the educational strategy consist of methods to provide compliance information in usable forms and to establish organizational routines necessary to ensure future compliance. They do not shy away from coercion, but use it to focus attention rather than to punish noncompliers.

The *persuasive* or *cooperative strategy* assumes that firms perceive enforcement agencies as one of several important actors that the firm must deal with over the long haul. Furthermore, it assumes that firms develop principles to govern their relationships with all actors. Thus a firm may forgo short-term temptations to cheat on an agency that cannot easily monitor its activities in order to establish a more cooperative long-term relationship with the agency and with others in its environment. Tactics for this persuasive strategy include techniques to convince firms in the agency's jurisdiction that it is in their long-term best interest to comply. Such techniques include methods of negotiating compliance requirements sensitive to the particular characteristics of the firm, avoiding unnecessary short-term confrontations as long as the agency's long-term goals are being fulfilled.

The primary advantage of this strategy is that successful relationships can minimize monitoring and prosecution costs on the part of the agency while reducing the inefficiencies associated with legalistic enforcement of uniform rules. The firm can trade greater progress in areas where goal attainment is cheaper in return for less progress in legally mandated areas where the costs are out of line with the benefits. Flexibility in enforcement can potentially compensate for the inherent inefficiency of uniform regulations when applied to heterogeneous settings.

However, flexibility can only develop after a credible deterrence threat has been established. Since the educational and persuasive strategies both depend in part on deterrence, we will begin the discussion with a review of alternative tactics of the deterrence strategy.

Improving Deterrence

Most of the routine work of enforcement is involved in the process of finding and penalizing violations of statutes and regulations that the agency is responsible for enforcing (Diver, 1980; Hawkins, 1984). Inspectors must decide which firms to inspect and what to look for during inspections. They must apply abstract regulations to concrete situations and decide whether a violation exists, and whether it is worth citing.

Once the inspector writes out a citation, the process of adjudicating and penalizing begins. Agencies can control only part of this process. The firm must be formally charged with a violation, and various formal or informal forms of negotiation over penalties begin. Many federal agencies immediately propose a fine, based on an established penalty policy. In general, administrative appeals are allowed within the agency. Contested citations can then be appealed to special administrative courts. The federal and state courts form the final level of appeal, used primarily in landmark cases or where criminal penalties rather than civil penalties are being sought by the agency.

According to deterrence theory, the effectiveness of this process in deterring noncompliance will be determined by its success in finding violations and imposing penalties sufficient to deter future noncompliance. The greater the proportion of violations that are detected and the higher the penalty imposed, the greater the incentive for a firm to comply. Deterrence takes into consideration the dual impact of enforcement actions. I will follow the convention in the research literature of referring to the impact of an enforcement action on future compliance of the firm as *specific deterrence,* and the generalized effect of the enforcement action on other firms as *general deterrence.* Both forms of deterrence have been studied extensively in criminal settings.

Although studies of police behavior have conceptualized a range of alternative enforcement techniques and compiled systematic empirical evidence about differential effectiveness, regulatory enforcement studies have focused primarily on the very basic deterrence question of whether enforcement activities in general (primarily inspections, citations, and penalties) are related to increased compliance and the accomplishment of policy goals (Bartel and Thomas, 1985; Cook and Gautschi, 1981; Downing and Hanf, 1983, Feinstein, 1989; Gray and Jones, 1989, 1990; Gray and Schulz, 1992; McCaffrey, 1983; Mendeloff, 1979; Smith, 1979; Viscusi, 1979, 1986). With few exceptions (Bardach and Kagan, 1982; Scholz, 1984b; Sigler and Murphy, 1988), theory development has been left at a level of generality that is of little direct relevance to the choices made by enforcement officials.

Instead of reviewing the general literature, in this section we will discuss two different approaches to improving deterrence by increasing the agency's ability to detect and penalize violations. The first approach enhances deterrence through improvements in the efficient allocation of resources. The second approach considers techniques and procedures that can be applied under certain circumstances to enhance the effectiveness of finding and penalizing violators.

Efficient Allocation of Enforcement Resources

Unlike firms in the private sector that invest heavily in analyzing and utilizing cost-effective methods of production, public sector enforcement agencies are provided with little research funding to evaluate the effectiveness of their main product—enforcement—in achieving enforcement goals. In most agencies, improvements in enforcement effectiveness can begin with careful evaluation of the effectiveness of existing patterns of allocation of enforcement resources. The best studies may require considerable thought, expensive data-gathering operations, and complex analyses, but even relatively simple evaluations using existing enforcement data can frequently suggest ways in which a simple shift of existing enforcement resources from one activity to another can increase the agency's deterrence capability.

Such evaluations can help enforcement agencies to allocate inspection time among competing priorities. For example, how much time should inspectors focus on the worst firms vs. the marginal compliers and the best firms? How intensive should inspections be? Should inspectors spend a small amount of time per firm in order to monitor a broad number of firms, or should they intensively monitor a small number of firms? When violations are found, how much additional time should inspectors spend to impose large penalties on the violator? Is the size of penalty sufficiently important to offset the additional time required?

Gray and Scholz (1991) evaluate OSHA enforcement relating to the two allocational choices reflected in these questions: one relating to the nature of the firm and the other to the intensity of the inspection. Their initial analysis confirms that inspections of larger plants take considerably longer than inspections of small plants, although the difference is less than expected given the larger number of employees and more complex operations in larger plants. They also found considerable difference in the time taken for different classes of inspections, with inspections limited to checking records taking half the time of normal inspections. Penalties also increased the length of time required for inspections. The purpose of the evaluation is to determine the relative impact of an hour of inspection time in each of these activities.

The primary argument developed here is a straightforward application of economic principles: enforcement resources should be allocated in a manner that produces the highest level of goal attainment with available resources. Shifting resources from activities with lower productivity to those with higher productivity will result in greater deterrence impact without an increase in enforcement resources. Which activities are most productive is far from self-evident, however, given our current state of knowledge about compliance. Until the knowledge base becomes more adequate for providing general guidelines for enforcement policy decisions, evaluations can at least indicate the relative effectiveness for enforcement activities of the evaluated agency.

For example, the Gray and Scholz (1991) evaluation confirmed the finding of previous studies that additional OSHA enforcement would prevent more injuries in large (over 500 employees) and particularly in midsize firms (250 to 500 employees) than in small firms (under 250 employees). A 1 percent increase in inspection hours would reduce total injuries by 296 if focused on midsize firms and 249 in large firms, compared with only 100 in small firms. Each 10 hour increase in inspection time would prevent 4.6 injuries if focused on midsize firms but only 1.5 injuries if focused on small firms. Since the figures are the same for decreases as increases in enforcement, each 10 hours shifted from small to large firms will produce an increase of 1.5 plus a decrease of 4.6, or a net decrease of about 3 injuries without any additional resources. The benefit of shifting inspection resources from large to midsize firms is less significant, since the difference in that case is relatively small.

These figures include both general and specific deterrence effects, although the general deterrence effect is much more important than the specific deterrence effect. Firms appear to have a considerable capability for monitoring enforcement risks among similar firms, and therefore they rely less on their own history of enforcement than on their knowledge of the record of other comparable firms (Scholz and Gray, 1990). Of equal interest, specific deterrence accounts for a declining proportion of deterrence effects as the size of the firm increases, dropping from 15 percent for small firms to 9 percent for midsize firms and less than 2 percent for large firms. These differences support the general belief that the amount of managerial effort available for monitoring the regulatory environment increases exponentially with the size of the firm. They suggest that OSHA enforcement has a greater impact on midsize and larger firms, primarily because these firms are more aware of OSHA's general enforcement activities.

The evaluation also found evidence that very short and very long inspections were less productive per hour than intermediate-length inspections. Inspections that only looked at a plant's injury records had no impact on injury rates, and the longer inspections associated with penalties greater than $500 were found to have no greater impact on injury rates than the shorter inspections associated with penalties less than $500. A different means of evaluation estimated that a 10 percent increase in the number of penalties would decrease injuries by 1.6 percent, while a 10 percent increase in the amount of penalty would decrease injuries by only 0.9 percent (Scholz and Gray, 1990). In short, spending a moderate amount of time per inspection appears to be most productive. The time required to produce higher penalties does not, on average, increase the effectiveness of the inspection. We will consider why this might be so in the discussion of penalties below.

How far should resources be shifted to gain the greatest enforcement efficiency? Given the large difference found in the analysis of plant size, one would suspect that a reasonably large shift would be called for. On the other hand, all evaluation studies must be considered in the broader agency context. All studies are dependent on the quality of available data and the assumptions required for analysis, and the results are valid only for marginal shifts of inspection activities.

For example, the OSHA study was based on plant-level injury and inspection data for an extensive data set of almost 7,000 firms over a 7-year period. However, the data set consisted primarily of larger, more frequently inspected plants that were included in the Bureau of Labor Statistics surveys. To establish policy for the broader population of firms in OSHA's jurisdiction, the differences between the sample and population need to be considered.

Furthermore, the figures noted above are based on current patterns of enforcement allocations. If large shifts were made that increased enforcement for midsized firms while dramatically reducing enforcement focused on smaller firms, deterrence for small firms might become completely ineffective. Likewise, if all inspections produced only trivial penalties, these penalties might lose their current ability to induce compliance. As a final point, the evaluation was not designed to look at the effect of very large penalties, since very few penalties exceeded

$5,000. A different research design would be required to evaluate the impact of large penalties such as those involved in OSHA's "megapenalties." In short, changing enforcement allocations will change productivity, so that evaluation studies are most valid for moderately small adjustments in the kinds of allocation they were designed to evaluate. Evaluation should be thought of as a continuing management process to guide reallocations of resources over multiyear periods. Once general evaluations have established general allocational guidelines, more focused evaluations of specific problem areas utilizing more detailed categories of activities can be used to guide management decisions at the field level. Single-evaluation studies cannot provide reliable allocation policies suitable in all jurisdictions and all problem areas the agency faces.

Of course, efficiency is not the only important criterion for allocating enforcement resources. Is an injury or illness prevented in a safe environment worth the same to society as one prevented in a dangerous one? Even if they are worth the same, should equity concerns override efficiency concerns when the potential victims are poorer, less informed, or less able to choose the level of risk they are willing to face? All of these questions at the heart of the rule-making process are involved in enforcement policies as well, and cannot be brushed aside by exclusive reliance on efficiency studies. However, the primary problem at this time for most enforcement agencies is that efficiency questions are being ignored because of the lack of the kind of systematic analysis presented here. Established organizational procedures and equity concerns articulated by active interest groups tend to overshadow efficiency concerns, in part because agency leaders and managers have little systematic evidence to justify allocational decisions on efficiency grounds.

The primary point of this discussion has been to suggest that evaluation studies should become an integral part of enforcement management, a point elaborated in a National Academy of Science study of IRS enforcement (Roth et al., 1989). Informational technologies and management information systems now provide greater access to relevant data that could be developed into resources for systematic evaluation of enforcement productivity. Program changes provide excellent opportunities to utilize field experimentation in order to estimate the effectiveness of new procedures in securing compliance (Boruch, 1989). What is needed is greater concern with productivity on the part of agency leaders and oversight committees, and a willingness to devote sufficient resources to develop the agency's ability to evaluate productivity of its enforcement activities.

Techniques to Increase Deterrence

The primary consideration in the previous section was how to allocate resources among the agency's current activities. In this section we consider tactics for increasing deterrence that might not yet be in the agency's standard repertoire of enforcement activities. We will begin by considering techniques for improving the detection of violations, including tactics for targeting inspections and for making violations more visible through better rules, information-reporting systems, and structural changes in industrial procedures. Then we will consider techniques to increase the impact of penalties. The examples discussed below may not be relevant to a given agency's enforcement tasks, and probably represent a very partial cataloguing of tactics already in use by various enforcement agencies. The point in discussing what some agencies have done is primarily to stimulate the process of thinking creatively about the range of potential tactics for increasing the detectability of violations and the impact of penalties.

Targeting Tactics. An efficient inspection program requires tactics that increase the likelihood that an inspector will visit firms with the highest likelihood of having violations, and will be there when violations are most likely to occur. Experienced supervisors develop a sense of where the trouble spots are in their districts, and when troubles are likely to occur. Good information systems allow the supervisor and inspector to view the past enforcement record of a firm to determine when the last inspection took place, whether past violations justify a thorough inspection, and what areas may require special attention. It is unfortunate that political constraints and legal concerns have unduly restricted the ability of some agencies to utilize fully information about past violations in formal targeting systems, forcing supervisors to rely on memory and word of mouth among inspectors to gain an impression of a given firm. Utilizing experienced enforcers to schedule inspections rather than to inspect may not be an efficient use of this valuable resource. Furthermore, overreliance on past experience may focus enforcement on an unduly small number of older problems while ignoring fewer problems that may be less visible but of greater concern to the agency.

Agencies have developed several innovative tactics to aid supervisors in assigning appropriate inspection targets. The most interesting tactics analyze specific information bases to determine compliance problem areas in a manner that will allow problem areas to be targeted for most inspections. The IRS has perhaps the most elaborate and successful targeting program based in information developed in the Taxpayer Compliance Measurement Program (TCMP). To help determine which of over 100 million individual tax returns to audit, the IRS audits approximately 50,000 returns every 3 years. These audits differ from ordinary enforcement audits in two very important ways that differentiate this targeting scheme from the evaluation studies discussed previously. First, the audits are very thorough in order to detect as much noncompliance as possible, even though the added length is inefficient for detecting violations in comparison with normal audits. Second, the sample is carefully randomized to ensure that results for the sample will accurately reflect national levels of compliance for various audit classes and line items on the tax return. Again, random selection is less efficient from an enforcement viewpoint, but essential to produce the information base necessary for more efficient targeting of normal audits.

In addition to describing the pattern of compliance problems, the TCMP program also provides the basis for selecting particular returns to be audited. The TCMP audits can be used to predict the likelihood that an audit would result in a substantial tax increase, based on the pattern of income and deductions reported on the return. Returns with profiles associated with a higher likelihood of tax increase are selected to be processed for audit.

OSHA inspections also are partially determined by a comparable data base that reports workplace injury rates for various industries. The Bureau of Labor Statistics provides this data based on an annual survey of a stratified sample of firms. OSHA then determines national priorities for inspections in various industries to ensure that a large proportion of inspections will occur in the most dangerous industries. Although these industries may not necessarily have the greatest number of violations, they are the industries with the greatest problems for OSHA's statutory mandate.

Both examples indicate how data can be used to enhance the likelihood that inspectors are looking at appropriate targets, particularly for agencies with larger numbers of targets than can be readily inspected. Some limitations of information-based targeting are also apparent in these examples. First, it is difficult to obtain data in a timely manner. TCMP surveys are done only every 3 years because of the costs, and the size and complexity of the analysis further ensure that current audit selections are based on data from several years ago. Second, tests in the 1960s indicated that TCMP-based audit selections were not significantly better than the previous method of screening by experienced auditors. The primary benefit of the computer-based system was to provide a cheaper, less labor-intensive method of targeting.

Third, the data may not be provided in a form most useful for targeting inspections. OSHA's national priority industries may not be the most dangerous industries in a given enforcement district. This is generally true when the enforcement agency must rely on a different agency with different priorities for data-gathering, as is the case with OSHA and the Bureau of Labor Statistics (BLS). As we shall discuss later, political problems provide considerable constraints in developing targeting systems that could otherwise provide substantial improvements in enforcement efficiency. The costs and complexity of such systems make them difficult to establish, and political difficulties that occurred when OSHA selected a small number of specific industries for enforcement emphasis indicate the dangers in using certain categorizations for targeting.

On balance, however, targeting systems based on analyses of compliance problems can provide a solid foundation for enforcement programs, as has been the case with the IRS. The same advances in computer technology and management information systems that make evaluation studies more feasible than before also increase the feasibility of developing automated targeting systems to aid supervisors in effectively targeting inspections.

Using Information-Reporting and Informants. The methods discussed so far depend on the agency to generate information to allocate detection resources efficiently and select appropriate targets for monitoring activities. However, agencies can also utilize information generated by the regulated firm or "third parties" knowledgeable about the firm to improve enforcement efficiency. As we will see, techniques that rely on others have the advantage of providing a broader base of information at relatively low costs, which may allow the agency to utilize better scarce monitoring resources. Of course, processing the information can become very burdensome, and ensuring the accuracy of the information also may require considerable resources when the information-provider has strong incentives to misinform the agency.

Consider first the use of information provided by the regulated firms. Such information is readily gathered when permits and licenses are required for doing business or running different processes. At a minimum, such systems provide a basic list of firms to be monitored. This may sound trivial, but just getting such a list and locating firms in an agency's jurisdiction is frequently not easy, particularly for small, mobile, transient firms such as those found in the construction industry. For example, OSHA has a pilot program in which inspectors devote a day to driving through their districts just to locate worksites (primarily construction sites) that the agency does not have records for. For the IRS, one major enforcement problem involves individuals who do not file returns and are therefore not on the primary data system. Nonfilers are estimated to account for about 10 percent of all tax noncompliance. Particularly in such situations, cooperation between local agencies providing business licenses and other specialized agencies responsible for regulating different functions of the businesses could improve the ability of specialized agencies to develop more adequate enforcement programs without imposing greater paperwork burden on the businesses.

Licenses and permits can also be used to provide more specific information relevant to regulation. Pollution enforcement in particular can be aided in tracing the source when high levels of pollutant are found in a river, if the agency's permit system can generate a list of potential sources of the given pollutant. Inventories of hazardous waste products provide agencies with information that can be used to prioritize sites to be monitored according to the relative volume and risk associated with each product.

In addition to information supplied on a regular basis for licenses and permits, agencies may require firms to report certain important kinds of incidents. For example, the Nuclear Regulatory Commission (NRC) requires reports of malfunctioning systems in nuclear plants, the Environmental Protection Agency (EPA) requires plants to report when breakdowns result in emissions exceeding standards, and OSHA requires direct reports of workplace accidents that result in deaths. These reports serve two distinct purposes. The first is to provide information about specific plants that may be developing patterns of problems requiring special attention from the agency. The second is to provide a continuous monitor of potential new problems when unfamiliar events begin to develop into patterns of unanticipated problems.

Information reports can provide an important foundation for monitoring regulated activities of firms in the agency's jurisdiction. Since firms themselves would generally need the kind of information required by the agency to ensure their own level of compliance, the information burden need not impose unnecessary costs on the firm. Even if agencies are not equipped to utilize the information fully, the fact that the information is at least used selectively can be an important factor in ensuring that firms themselves will be concerned about the aspects of their behavior reflected in the information they are required to report. Some minimal level of perceived enforcement use is critical to maintain a credible deterrence effect from informational reports.

The more an information-reporting system is used for enforcement purposes, however, the greater the incentive to report false information. For example, OSHA requires all workplaces to maintain reports about work-related injuries. Inspectors look at the logs to determine the areas within a plant that had the most injuries, which could provide important clues about the most dangerous areas within the plant. When OSHA initiated a "records-check" program in which plants with injury rates below a pre-established industry target would not be inspected, plant management had a powerful incentive to reduce injuries reported on the OSHA log. Ruser and Smith (1989) found that states with records-check programs systematically reported fewer injuries, suggesting that plants really did report fewer injuries when doing so decreased their chance of getting inspected.

Since information-reporting systems are of little use unless the information is accurate, enforcement resources must be devoted to preserving the accuracy of information that is reported. OSHA responded to underreporting of injuries by imposing very large penalties on firms not complying with record-keeping requirements, even though such "technical" violations did not directly endanger workers. The IRS provides the most extreme example of the use of self-reported information, since a firm's taxes are determined by the information reported annually on the tax form. Firms have considerable incentive to cheat, so the IRS employs most of its enforcement resources to ensure the accuracy of information reports. If regulations are ambiguous and complex, however, enforcement breaks down since it is difficult to differentiate and punish intentional misreporting from honest disagreement in interpreting reporting requirements.

Other innovative monitoring systems might be developed to increase the ability of inspectors to cover more territory in the time available. Mail and telephone inquiries to obtain information from regulated firms could be developed as an extension of actual sites visits that now make up the bulk of regulatory inspection programs. For example, the IRS used to rely primarily on field visits by auditors to gather information on location. The last three decades have witnessed a dramatic shift in the area of individual income tax enforcement from field to office audits; now the individual brings information to IRS offices, saving considerable travel time for inspectors. More recently, the percentage of returns audited each year has dropped from over 6 percent in the early 1970s to around 1 percent today, as mail contact has become the primary mode for monitoring individual returns. Inquiries about possible violations uncovered in the information reporting program (discussed below) are mailed to millions of taxpayers each year. Although such mail contacts provide much less opportunity than field visits to discover false or misleading reporting, they can be performed much more cheaply through automation. There have been suggestions that the IRS experiment with telephone audits as a further alternative to office audits, based on the positive experience insurance companies have had in using telephone contacts to settle routine claims involving small amounts. Few of these techniques have yet been developed or adapted to monitoring problems in the regulatory arena, so the potential remains unknown.

In some cases, structural changes in related government programs could produce considerable improvement in the information available for enforcement. The clearest example of structural impediments to usable information relates to OSHA enforcement. State agencies that regulate compensation paid for job-related injuries and illnesses and the federal Bureau of Labor Statistics both could develop powerful information bases for enforcement, but neither has much incentive to do so. Past attempts to provide a more integrated and uniform information system have faltered over political and institutional disputes.

In sum, information-reporting systems provide no quick, costless solution, but may provide effective and economical alternative methods of monitoring in situations where information relevant to regulated behavior is relatively accessible for the firm to report, the agency has the capability to analyze and act on the information, and incentives to provide misinformation can be sufficiently countered.

Information reports from other parties who know about the actions of the regulated firm suffer less from a clear motivation to provide misinformation. The IRS, for example, uses third-party reporting of income and expenditure items as the backbone of its enforcement system for individual income tax. Sophisticated programs are used to compare the taxpayer's return with information filed about the taxpayer by employers, banks, brokerage firms, and others. These programs generate millions of notices to taxpayers requiring explanations about discrepancies. With the expansion of computer capabilities during the past decade, they have replaced audits as the primary source of contacts for monitoring returns. Compliance studies inevitably find that tax items for which such third-party reporting is available have considerably higher levels of compliance than tax items without such reporting systems.

Of course, programs of this scope require major resources to develop and maintain. Several billion information returns filed by third parties each year must be processed and analyzed to provide the level of comprehensiveness that makes for an effective program. Costs to the third parties required to provide the information are a constant source of dispute. However, less exhaustive programs can also be developed to make use of alternative sources of information. Requiring documentation of certain sorts of transactions will establish a "paper trail" that investigators could follow to prosecute violations, even if the information is not reported to the agency. For example, documenting the flow of radioactive or other hazardous products would provide investigators information about the hazardous products entering and leaving a particular plant. Knowing that discrepancies might have to be accounted for would make firms more sensitive to the need for a clear control policy.

To date, regulatory agencies have used third-party information primarily from informants reporting illegal behavior. For example, workers aware of violations of OSHA regulations have been given statutory rights to file complaints with OSHA. OSHA inspectors can then know not only which plant to inspect, but where to look within the plant for a reported violation. Consumers, residents, and competitive businesses could potentially provide a large army of volunteer inspectors that the agency could use to enhance its ability to find violations.

On the other hand, Bardach and Kagan (1982: 166–172) have discussed several problems that may arise when poorly informed, self-interested complainants are allowed to redirect a program's enforcement resources into relatively low priority targets. A common problem is that political pressures rather than enforcement effectiveness guide the response to complaints.

To minimize these problems, Bardach and Kagan suggest several important features that need to be developed. Appropriate screening devices are required that obtain sufficient information from complainants to establish the relative priority of the inspection; that provide alternative responses such as letters and telephone calls for lower-priority targets; that redirect inappropriate complaints to appropriate alternatives, such as the Better Business Bureau; and that utilize less-skilled inspectors for the kind of low-complexity violations frequently associated with complaints. As an alternative, special training can be given to concerned community groups or workers to do more sophisticated monitoring (e.g., of water pollution, exposure to workplace chemicals) that the agency would not have time to do. Packaging laws requiring labels and instructions for use on hazardous materials make it easier for workplace informants to know when hazardous products are being used improperly. Complaints from more knowledgeable sources (such as a firm's competitors) can likewise be encouraged through informal contacts. In the processed food industry, for example, competitors are constantly monitoring the products of their competition with highly sophisticated analyses, which may detect violations the regulatory agency is unlikely to uncover.

Third parties can also be incorporated more directly into the monitoring process. The OSHA statute, for example, allows a worker representative to accompany the OSHA compliance officer on the plant's inspection. The worker can point out hazardous work conditions that are of concern to the workers. In experimental programs, worker-management committees in relatively safe plants have been delegated inspection authority in lieu of an OSHA inspector. Then OSHA is only responsible for monitoring the effectiveness of the committee, rather than directly monitoring safety in the plant. The Securities and Exchange Commission (SEC) has further developed this strategy by relying on private agents to scrutinize the books of publicly owned companies. The accounting profession both provides the personnel and develops standards for the routine monitoring of public corporations, which allows the SEC to focus its resources on trouble spots.

The possibilities for "privatizing" routine monitoring operations are considerable, given the large number of private inspectors used by insurance companies, trade associations, purchasing departments, and so on. For example, Food and Drug Administration (FDA) drug approval routinely relies on analyses and experiments performed by independent laboratories. OSHA could contract with insurance companies to perform routine inspections and certify compliance of the plants it covers under workers' compensation insurance. The IRS could develop a program to allow the professional preparers (who file over 50 percent of individual returns and almost all business returns) similarly to certify compliance of the tax return.

Again, privatization of routine inspections is not costless. In each situation, the agency must provide appropriate incentives to ensure that satisfactory inspections and analyses do take place. Private inspectors could be licensed, and some proportion of the firms inspected by the private inspectors could be reinspected. Unacceptable levels of violations could result in penalties for the private inspector and loss of license. The potential advantage of such second-tier inspections over direct inspections is enormous. Compared to the task of overseeing 100 million taxpayers, the task of overseeing the approximately 200,000 professional tax preparers is much more manageable. Yet the problems of providing sufficient incentives to private inspectors while maintaining control over the process would also require considerable creativity.

Making Violations More Visible. Enforcement agencies can also improve their ability to detect violations by making violations more visible to their information-gathering systems

(Kagan, 1989). These techniques include requirements for automatic monitoring devices, rule-making strategies focusing on processes rather than outcomes, and structural changes to minimize opportunities to hide violations. One straightforward technique provides the clearest example of how violations can be made visible. Many standards specify that automatic monitoring devices be installed for processes prone to exceed standards. For example, recording thermometers can be require to ensure that refrigerator temperatures have been maintained within proper ranges, obviating the need for health inspectors to be present to check the thermometer at all hours of the night. Recording tachometers can likewise be matched with freight delivery logs to ensure that truck safety regulations have not been violated. This technique essentially extends the other techniques discussed above that require the regulated firm to provide information, with many of the same problems of costs to the firm and incentives to distort reported information. Whenever automatic monitoring equipment is relatively inexpensive and tamperproof, such equipment can provide greater evidence to the inspector about a plant's behavior.

The use of rule-making to make violations more visible is more complex, particularly since rules provide several different functions that are seldom compatible. The basic idea behind this technique is straightforward: make sure when rules are promulgated that violations of these rules are both clear and readily observable. Consider rules promulgated to ensure that canned foods are not contaminated. Standards could simply specify upper limits for the levels of contaminants and toxic substances found in canned goods. However, enforcement would then require extensive and expensive sampling to test products continuously for violations, which would still be difficult to detect if they were sporadic in nature and fell between the sampling framework of the monitoring process.

As a consequence, regulations for most food and drug processing have taken a different strategy of regulating "good manufacturing practices" during the production process. Although the outcome is important, it is much easier for an inspector to observe aspects of the manufacturing process likely to lead to contamination than actually to find the contamination in the final product. Dirty, leaking equipment above food-processing vats, infrequent cleaning of the assembly line, improper use of equipment processing both toxic and edible products are all potential sources of contamination that are relatively visible to a trained inspector. Finding the resultant contamination in a warehouse of the finished product would take a longer time and require sophisticated equipment.

In many areas, rules governing the design of equipment or standard procedures can be written to make violations more visible to a trained inspector with little additional equipment. Most of OSHA's regulations to reduce workplace injuries involve the specification of safety features for various machines. Such rules have the added advantage of being visible to other interested parties as well; machinery designed to meet OSHA standards is likely to say so on the equipment and in advertising.

Rules that make violations more visible inevitably compromise the other functions of rule-making. By governing process rather than output, such rules are biased against innovative processes not acceptable under current rules that might actually produce more desirable outputs. If such rules are enforced legalistically with no concern for the underlying purposes of the rules, they can lead to "technical violations" that will do little to achieve the regulatory goals (Bardach and Kagan, 1982). In its early years, OSHA's inexperienced inspectors tended to focus on easily visible violations (the height of fire extinguishers, lack of ground even in unused electric outlets), which seriously hurt the credibility of the agency. Furthermore, the simplicity required for rules that promote the visibility of violations frequently conflict with the complexity required for efficient engineering solutions. Technical specialists generally want to differentiate many situations or provide many exceptions. Yet each added complexity reduces the ease of enforcement and particularly of prosecution. It is necessary to balance optimal flexibility with practical enforcement needs at the rule-making stage. As will be discussed in the section on persuasive strategies, it is also important to adopt flexible enforcement strategies that can counteract some of the costs associated with process-oriented rules.

Structural changes not directly related to the regulated behavior can occasionally be introduced to improve the visibility of violations, although these changes tend to involve drastic measures that are politically infeasible. One clear example in a different arena is the proposal that would eliminate large-denomination dollar bills in order to make the transfer of illegal drug money more difficult. Drug enforcers (and tax collectors) can more easily detect noncash transfers of money, and carrying large amounts of cash in small denomination bills would be impractical. Regulatory examples are not readily available, although one could imagine hypothetical possibilities. Most agencies, for example, have the greatest enforcement difficulty with the smallest, most transient businesses. Licensing laws could be redesigned to make new companies themselves more visible, and possibly to ensure some minimal levels of competence in the regulatory requirements applicable in their line of business.

Increasing the Impact of Penalties. The rapid development of administrative penalties in the last two decades has provided a powerful and more flexible tool to be used in conjunction with criminal penalties that had traditionally been available to agencies. Strategies to use administrative and criminal penalties are limited by statutory constraints as well as by procedural requirements imposed by courts and relevant administrative review institutions. Yet the biggest constraint to the efficient use of penalties may be in our limited knowledge of the role of penalties in enforcement strategies. Most deterrence models assume that higher penalties deter more violations. The optimal penalty in these models is one with an expected value slightly higher than the benefit gained from noncompliance, which would therefore remove the incentive not to comply with the law. Expected value theory assumes that for risk-neutral firms, doubling the penalty would have the same effect as doubling the probability of imposing the penalty. The implication for enforcement is clear: resources should be allocated to enforcement activities so as to maximize the combined probability and amount of penalty (that is, the expected value).

Sensible as this model seems, this simple conclusion does not appear to capture what really goes on in compliance decisions. Empirical studies of deterrence have found that the frequency rather than the amount of penalties appears to be more significantly related to compliance (Nagin, 1978; Lempert, 1982). A number of studies suggest that there are penalty thresholds—increases above certain threshold do not appear to increase compliance (Klepper and Nagin, 1989; Gray and Scholz, 1991). Finally, numerous laboratory experiments have demonstrated that predictions based on expected utility theory do not correspond to actual decisionmaking under risk. Consequently, enforcement policies based on the simple model are not likely to be very efficient.

Unfortunately, there are no alternative models that provide equally clear and compelling advice about penalization strategies. Until a more systematic understanding of penalties develops, several speculations might provide useful suggestions for possible reforms in penalties.

Indirect sanctions. One well-known aspect of legally imposed sanctions is that they are frequently less important than other consequences of being caught and punished. In criminology, it is the loss of friendship and peer approval that occurs when someone is found guilty that provides a greater deterrent than the legal penalty for most citizens. This is why criminal sanctions for executives—particularly jail sentences—provide such a powerful device for controlling corporate misconduct (Stone, 1975). For punishing corporations directly, the monetary value of most regulatory penalties may be insignificant compared to the organizational resources required to deal with the legal implications of the violation, the potential damage to the corporate image that may accompany a conviction, and liability exposure for future injuries related to the penalized violation.

These indirect sanctions can provide considerable leverage, particularly against corporations whose markets depend on their reputation. The threat of prosecution is frequently enough to convince food and drug manufacturers or securities firms to recall a product voluntarily or desist from questionable practices. Of course, such market-oriented threats need to be used with caution, since mistaken allegations are likely to cause irreparable damage to the accused corporation. Other means of leveraging an agency's formal sanctions through publicizing violations and providing information supportive of private liability suits may increase the agency's generally meager armory of penalties to tackle those chronic noncompliers who ignore agency penalties.

Publicity and targeting penalties. Enforcement officials are also aware of the importance of publicizing penalties to increase their general deterrence effect on other firms not subjected to penalties. Large penalties affecting well-known firms tend to gain the attention of both the general public and trade associations in related industries. They therefore play an important role in the commencement of new enforcement campaigns, in which a well-known noncompliant corporation will be singled out for full prosecution. The point of this costly prosecution is not really to show the size of penalty others firms can expect, since the agency would not have the resources for many such prosecutions. The point is rather that the agency is serious about enforcing a given law, and that the courts will back up the agency's authority and interpretation of the law.

The importance of showcase prosecutions for routine enforcement is less clear. As IRS officials put it, the question is whether to prosecute well-known celebrities or the common person on the street. Does the added publicity that accompanies successful prosecution of a celebrity increase deterrence for the average citizen? Or does the average citizen assume that the IRS will only prosecute the rich and famous, and therefore that he or she is likely to be prosecuted? Furthermore, does publicity that the rich and famous cheat actually increase the incentive for average citizens to cheat? Both the prosecutorial costs and potential negative effects on compliance need to be considered in deciding on appropriate targets for prosecution.

Penalty targeting strategies need to consider the communication aspects of administrative penalties as well. Some administrative penalties are large enough to gain as much attention as criminal prosecutions, like OSHA's carefully targeted "megapenalties" imposed on auto manufacturers, chemical plants, and meatpackers or the SEC penalties imposed on brokerage houses. Even more mundane penalties could be targeted with the communication process in mind to increase deterrence. A number of studies have found that firms in an industry appear to know and respond to changes in OSHA enforcement in their industry (Viscusi, 1985; Scholz and Gray, 1991), even though the median penalties in each industry are below $500. On the other hand, Richardson and colleagues (1983: 141ff) noted that many British water pollution enforcers thought that firms had very little idea about the risks of prosecution, and tended universally to overestimate the likelihood of prosecution. We know very little about how firms learn about enforcement risks. For example, gossip at trade associations may be driven by the number of firms that were penalized rather than the size of penalties imposed. If this is true, agencies should maximize the number of firms it penalizes rather than the total amount of penalty. This advice is consistent with the results of the evaluation study noted above. On the other hand, penalties below a certain level may be too insignificant to even be discussed, which would then set minimum levels for penalties to effect general deterrence.

Beyond Deterrence: Educational Strategy

The deterrence-oriented techniques discussed above provide the core activities of most regulatory agencies. However, no enforcement agency relies exclusively on the coercive power of deterrence. Several studies of enforcement agencies reveal that persuasion and educational activities play at least as great a role as monitoring and prosecutorial activities in most regulatory enforcement agencies (Shover et al., 1983; Bardach and Kagan, 1982; Hawkins and Thomas, 1984; Kagan and Scholz, 1984), particularly in U.S. agencies prior to the 1960s and outside the United States (Kelman, 1981; Hawkins, 1984; Braithwaite, 1985; Grabosky and Braithwaite, 1986).

Why should enforcement agencies undertake educational and persuasive activities? Apart from the political incentives to do so (to be discussed later), agencies provide these noncoercive services because they can enhance compliance. Although they can never fully replace coercive tactics, they supplement them in ways that enhance the overall enforcement efficiency of the agency. We will begin with a discussion of techniques associated with the educational strategy.

Deterrence theory itself provides a justification for educational enforcement activities, since the deterrent effect of coercive enforcement is dependent on the costs of compliance. To the extent that the agency can lower compliance costs, its enforcement efforts should, even in theory, increase the willingness of firms to comply.

Education and New Regulations. An educational strategy is most obviously required when new laws or regulations are enacted. In such situations, firms must become aware of requirements affecting their operations, devise working routines that comply, and develop mechanisms to ensure that the routines are followed consistently. All three stages could require considerable time, effort, and resources before successful compliance could be achieved.

At minimum, the agency has some obligation to provide clear guidelines for what the new regulations require firms to do. As a practical manner, minimizing the learning costs and stimulating the development of detailed compliance guidelines can minimize impediments to compliance with new laws. The development of appropriate methods of compliance is a public good in the sense that once someone has developed the knowledge, it costs no more to have others use it. Like other public goods, there is a reasonable argument that the public interest is best served by using public funds to develop basic compliance procedures and making these available to regulated firms.

OSHA reported the following activities to assist firms in complying with the Hazard Communication Standard, which provide a useful illustration of the range of educational techniques that can be applied when new standards are issued:

1. Compiled list of consultants and commercially available materials to help employers manage chemical inventories, prepare and maintain labels and required information, provide training programs, and so on.
2. Published and distributed over 250,000 copies of *Chemical Hazard Communication,* a book describing the requirements of the standard, as well as distributing almost 300,000 copies of the standard itself.
3. Designated a hazard communication coordinator in each regional office to work with trade and professional organizations in organizing and participating in seminars and workshops about the standard.
4. Funded the development of expertise in unions and employer organizations through educational and training grants on hazard communication and other subjects.

5. Provided an appendix to a proposed modification of the standard that provides a step-by-step approach to simplify compliance activities.
6. Developed a compliance kit with samples of compliance checklists, a hazard communication program, and a training program.

Education and Compliance Systems. Some educational tactics are based on the assumption that firms do not always act "rationally." In this view, a certain amount of noncompliance is due to incompetence and ignorance rather than cost calculations. "Bad-housekeeping" is frequently seen by compliance officers as a primary cause of noncompliance. An environmental enforcement office in England described a typical case as one in which the waste disposal plant "was poorly operated, there was no one with direct responsibility, utensils were left dirty, toxic materials were stored with insufficient care, shortcuts were taken with no regard for their effluent implications . . ." (Richardson et al., 1982:126).

Given the complexity involved in compliance with regulations, some firms appear to be incapable of complying even when it is in their own best interest to do so (Stone 1975; Kagan and Scholz, 1984; Scholz, 1984a,b). Of course, high levels of punishment will *eventually* either focus the firm's attention on the agency's regulations or drive it out of business—there is nothing like the prospect of a hanging to focus the mind, as the saying goes. Whatever capability a firm has to comply is more likely to be applied first to the regulations of agencies that can cause the firm the most problems. Yet the costs and potential consequences of penalties sufficient to induce eventual compliance may be unnecessarily high. In the interim, society must bear the consequences of such inadvertent noncompliance, which may be quite high if loss of life or irreversible contamination of the environment takes place.

As a consequence, educational techniques focus on the need for firms to develop managerial systems capable of ensuring the maintenance of compliance with existing regulations and the timely implementation of compliance programs to deal with new regulations. As management attention focuses on different problems facing the firm, established routines tend to erode if they do not have systems constantly to check on them and keep them in place. Management battling a hostile takeover bid is likely to ignore safety concerns on their agenda. Even on the shop floor, production demands to meet deadlines cause normal precautions and important housekeeping procedures to be ignored. In such situations, an enforcement program focused on the development and maintenance of compliance systems could be more effective than one focused primarily on detecting and punishing violations. Violations are difficult to catch if the inspector does not appear at the right time, and are the symptoms rather than the cause of the problem.

Compliance management in large corporations. During the past decade, larger corporations have developed a range of managerial systems and techniques to monitor and manage compliance problems across the diversity of plants in the organization and regulations affecting them. For most corporations, the idea of a compliance program is limited to the issuance of a written compliance policy by senior management, an educational program including guidebooks and presentations, and arrangements for legal counsel to be available to key decision-makers (Sigler and Murphy, 1988). However, some corporations have developed extensive programs in certain regulatory areas that demonstrate the potential ability of such programs to ensure compliance.

The degree of sophistication is perhaps greatest for corporate compliance programs focused on antitrust laws. Sigler and Murphy attribute this development to the severity of antitrust enforcement that actually sent senior managers to prison. They observe that in this area "compliance has developed into a business of its own" (Sigler and Murphy, 1988: 57), complete with prepackaged training programs employing sophisticated video presentations for specific subareas of the antitrust laws. This development emphasizes the importance of effective deterrence to motivate educational efforts for large firms.

Several agencies have played an active role in the development of compliance systems. The Federal Communications Commission required the regional telephone companies that replaced American Telephone and Telegraph (AT&T) to submit plans for compliance programs to ensure the required separation of portions of their business. Substantial self-audit programs were developed that included sophisticated training and control systems to prevent, for example, the transfer of restricted information between different parts of the company (Sigler and Murphy, 1988; Rees, 1988). The U.S. Sentencing Commission has provided a more general incentive in the new corporate criminal sentencing guidelines, which propose that criminal penalties can be reduced if a company has made credible efforts to prevent criminal behavior on the part of its employees through the implementation of comprehensive compliance programs.

Environmental regulations include many requirements for companies to provide information through licensing, permits, and required inventories of emission points and hazardous wastes. Corporations have been encouraged to utilize "environmental audits" that will provide management with a broad perspective on the corporation's environmental strengths and weaknesses, playing a comparable role in the environmental arena to financial audits in the financial arena. At minimum, these requirements attempt to ensure that management is aware of the kinds of problems that exist on the plant floor, which supervisors may be less willing to report without such informational requirements (Stone, 1975).

OSHA has developed a voluntary compliance program aimed at encouraging safety planning mechanisms that go beyond systems for gathering compliance-related information (Sigler and Murphy, 1988: 155). Corporations that meet program standards are certified for given sites, which are then subjected to very limited surveillance by OSHA. The minimal requirements include a continuing management control system that includes self-inspections, accident inspections, and a system for tracking employee hazard reports. If OSHA's on-site review team recommends certification, the company is publicly recognized as a model. Although the idea seems appealing, only 18 sites were approved in the first 4 years of the program, indicating the limited commitment to making the program more viable.

A range of other activities has also been suggested for ensuring the competence of compliance systems in larger corporations. At minimum, agencies can strengthen the position of compliance professionals within the corporation by assisting in the development of appropriate professional standards (similar to the third-party strategy described above) and by working more closely with these professionals. More extreme suggestions call for placing outside directors responsible for compliance on corporate boards. For chronic noncompliers, Stone (1975) has suggested that outside managers be empowered to oversee specific abatement programs.

Compliance management in small businesses. The problem of ignorance and incompetence is even greater in smaller companies, and requires different educational techniques to bring about desired results. Smaller companies may lack managerial resources to monitor new regulatory requirements and financial resources to abate known violations. Short-term survival is frequently more pressing than compliance, regardless of the potential enforcement threat. Furthermore, the difficulty in monitoring thousands of small firms, the sentiment to protect small firms from fines, and the potential political disruptions from closing down small firms all reduce the effectiveness of the deterrence-oriented strategy.

As a result, the educational strategy may be the most viable for small firms. Many of the techniques discussed above to deal with new regulations are most appropriate for smaller firms who rely on the agency to provide information on compliance requirements, since larger, more established firms can hire consultants or in-house staff to provide advice geared to their specific circumstances. For example, OSHA gives the highest priority to small businesses that request on-site consultation to provide advice to how to comply with OSHA standards. The program sent nonenforcement inspectors to over 35,000 worksites annually in the mid-1980s.

In addition to providing assistance for small businesses who seek help, educational programs could also supplement punitive strategies for firm found in violation of particular regulations. Driver education programs provide an instructive example. As part of the penalty for breaking traffic laws, courts may impose the requirement that the driver participate in a registered driver education program. Some regulatory agencies will informally negotiate with small businesses found in violation to forgo penalties if the business hires a consultant to devise a workable compliance program or installs a better control system.

More formal programs could be devised to subsidize the development of compliance programs, training materials, and workshops geared to the particular problems of specific kinds of small businesses, and to link these programs with deterrence-oriented programs in ways discussed below.

Whether the government or the private sector should pay for the development of compliance knowledge does not have an easy answer, particularly since government efforts can easily produce impractical materials of little use to firms. In the case of small businesses, the argument is that subsidizing these costs as part of a combined enforcement program may be more cost-effective than adding the same amount of money to standard deterrence-oriented techniques to enhance compliance.

Beyond Deterrence: Persuasive Strategy

Just as the educational strategy can enhance the effectiveness of basic deterrence-oriented techniques in the situations described in the previous section, so also can the persuasive strategy improve enforcement effectiveness in other situations. The inherent economic inefficiency of the regulations being enforced and the costs of monitoring and prosecution make persuasive enforcement attractive. The enforcement agency can reduce legalistic enforcement in order to persuade the regulated firm to do things beyond minimal legal requirements that will fulfill the policy objective, in OSHA's case to reduce industrial injury and illness rates. Thus the persuasive strategy emphasizes the need for flexibility to reduce the undesirable and counterproductive consequences that occur when legal rules are enforced with no consideration of mitigating circumstances.

To understand fully the basis of the persuasive strategy, we need to digress briefly to consider the fundamental problems of using rule enforcement to obtain policy goals. The problems all stem from the inescapable truth that rules are a clumsy method of imposing the behavioral changes required to secure improvements in health, safety, economic security, and the other goals of regulatory policies. (However, as Churchill said of democracy, they may still be less bad than any other policy tool.) These problems can be summarized as problems of heterogeneity, knowledge, complexity, and enforceability:

Heterogeneity: Given the diversity of situations in which any given problem arises, there are generally a range of solutions that are more efficient in one situation than in another. Machine guards designed to protect unskilled workers using table saws in lumberyards are likely to be entirely too cumbersome for experienced cabinetmakers using comparable equipment.

Knowledge: It is difficult for rule-makers to envision all concrete circumstances a rule will cover, the best rules for each situation, and even the relative importance and frequency of circumstances requiring different solutions.

Complexity: Even if optimal rules for each situation could be designed, the resulting rules would likely be too complex for regulated firms to understand: what is gained in engineering efficiency may be lost in comprehension. Consider the income tax code, which has grown to commanding volumes in attempts to classify clearly many heterogeneous situations. Most of us have personal experience with such complexity problems in filling out our income tax returns. *Money* magazine finds enough complex issues each year that 50 experienced tax professionals will find 50 very different amounts of tax due for its model taxpayer profile.

Enforceability: Rules that solve the above problems may be completely without effect if they are unenforceable. The most efficient solution to a problem may not produce observable behavior that could be monitored with available monitoring resources to determine whether violations take place. As a consequence, rules need to sacrifice efficiency in order to gain visibility and enforceability, as discussed above.

Because of this tentative connection between rules and efficient solutions to the goals of regulations, full compliance with rules is seldom an appropriate goal of regulatory enforcement. The deterrence-oriented strategy is not only constrained by the inevitable inefficiencies in rules but also tends to exaggerate the inefficiencies in order to increase enforceability. The persuasive strategy, on the other hand, attempts to maximize goal achievement rather than compliance. It utilizes rule enforcement as only the beginning tool to achieve regulatory goals.

The persuasive strategy assumes that desired behavioral changes will only occur if they reflect the self-interest of the firm, just as the deterrence strategy does. The primary difference between the two strategies is that persuasive techniques appeal to a broader range of motivations than deterrence techniques, particularly the firm's concerns over its long-term relationships with the agency and other organizations such as unions, suppliers, purchasers, and the general public.

Persuasion begins with a solid enforcement program. As many enforcement officials have observed, a strong voluntary compliance program has to hit hard at the bad apples to keep them from spoiling the good ones who "comply voluntarily." The agency presents firms with a choice: behave reasonably and we will enforce regulations flexibly, or behave badly and we will enforce regulations as stringently as possible. To the extent that the reasonable level of compliance acceptable to the agency is no worse than the stringent enforcement outcomes, compliance is in the firm's long-run self interest.

The persuasive strategy requires the agency to use maximal enforcement with firms that have established a record of poor compliance in the past, and flexible enforcement with firms with an established record of compliance. By being vengeful, this strategy discourages poor compliance. By being forgiving of firms once they have begun to comply, it encourages firms to join the ranks of compliant firms.

The real power of this strategy occurs over time, as the agency persuades more and more firms to cooperate. The agency can then focus more of its limited prosecutorial resources on the fewer and fewer bad firms, thereby increasing penalties and the incentives of firms to cooperate. Given greater incentives, the agency can insist on higher levels of performance by cooperative firms as the regulation becomes more accepted by the business community. As regulations become reflected in the standards of organizational routines and of acceptable business practices, relatively little enforcement action is needed to maintain compliance (Lane, 1977).

Another evolutionary advantage of the persuasive strategy is that it preserves greater communication between agency and firms, enabling the agency to gain early warnings on new problems that develop as technological developments and organizational routines interact in unforeseen and potentially dangerous ways. For example, when toxic substances began to be transported more routinely in tanker trucks, the established techniques for cleanup after tanker accidents produced disasterous results. When a local fire department followed established routines by washing material spilled in an accident onto the side of the road in order to open the road to rush-hour traffic, the resultant contamination of soil with a highly toxic chemical seriously increased the damage to the environment and ensuing cleanup costs.

Persuasion at such times may reduce the need for rules, as long as there is a credible threat that the rules will be promulgated and enforced if the consensual arrangement breaks down. In this case, the California highway patrol (CHP) was in a position to bring together the range of concerned parties from transportation companies and the teamsters union to local police, fire, and health departments to work out new procedures for such situations. The persuasive force to gain cooperation from these groups arose because of the fallback that the CHP would issue and enforce regulations if the interested parties could not arrive at a consensual arrangement.

The potential evolution of cooperation is limited by several factors. First, there must be sufficient flexibility in enforcement and sufficient inefficiency in the rules to allow both the firm and the agency to be better off if they cooperate with each other. Second, firms must be sufficiently interested in their long-run relationship with the agency to forgo the short-term temptation to take advantage of the agency's flexible enforcement. This generally means that the persuasive strategy will be most likely to induce cooperation with those firms that interact more frequently with the agency. Third, the agency must be able to tell good firms from bad ones. The more mistakes the agency makes in prosecuting good firms or failing to prosecute bad ones, the less the incentive to cooperate. Finally, the less organized resistance offered by firms acting together, the more likely that cooperation can evolve. The extent of organization among firms thus provides a limit to the level of cooperative compliance an agency can insist on relative to the base deterrence level of compliance. If the agency seeks too high a level of compliance, organized resistance is more likely to occur.

Before considering specific persuasive techniques, it may be useful to compare the pattern of enforcement under a persuasive and a deterrence strategy. The use of educational and persuasive techniques alone does not ensure the combination of vengefulness and forgivingness of a persuasive strategy, since persuasion and education are sometimes employed by agencies simply because they have no power to do otherwise (Grabosky and Braithwaite, 1986). The clearest mark of the persuasive strategy is the concentration of enforcement activities on fewer firms, resulting in fewer penalties per inspection than would be the case for the deterrence strategy. As noted above, these larger penalties are generally less efficient from a strict deterrence perspective, since the longer inspection required to document and prosecute them suffers from diminishing returns. Thus the deterrence-maximizing strategy leads to a relatively large number of small and moderate penalties, while the persuasive strategy requires a greater number of larger penalties.

Cooperative strategies should therefore lead to higher percentages of serious citations and higher percentages of penalties imposed for serious violations, larger penalties per citation, a greater number of shorter inspections with no citations (after all, you have to make sure that the cooperators are still cooperating), a high percentage of fines imposed on a small percentage of firms, and so on (Scholz, 1984b). Although evidence supporting the effectiveness of the persuasive strategy is far from conclusive, at least one study found that OSHA enforcement was more likely to have the desired impact on injury rates in enforcement districts with more concentrated enforcement, once levels of enforcement were controlled for (Scholz, 1991).

Persuasive Techniques for Inspectors. The inspector provides a critical link in persuasive strategies, since it is at this level that the agency must differentiate between cooperative firms and clearly noncompliant ones. The characteristics of the persuasive inspector have been described in greater detail elsewhere, and will only be summarized here. Bardach and Kagan (1982) emphasize that persuasiveness of the good inspector can be enhanced by responding to the concerns of the firms, by offering information on cost-saving compliance, and by trading forbearance on petty violations for meaningful compliance on more serious violations.

Richardson et al. (1982) describe the different stages of an inspector's relationship with a regulated firm. Initially inspectors portray themselves as reasonable and experienced individuals making reasonable demands on the firm. They place great importance on appearing to be authoritative and expert, and less importance on friendliness, which could raise suspicions of corruption. Inspectors found it particularly useful to begin in parts of a plant where noncompliance could cause considerable damage, where they could emphasize the objectives behind regulations and the moral responsibility of industry to take appropriate precautions.

If violations and problems were identified, the problem-solving stage begins (Richardson et al., 1982). They found that inspectors were most persuasive when they could aid in problem-solving by proposing concrete steps to be taken to abate the violation. Stressing potential benefits from such actions was helpful, as was a willingness to help in minimizing costs when doing so would not result in greater hazards. If the firm remained recalcitrant, the inspector would gradually increase the frequency and length of inspections, with the implicit threat of taking action if violations were not abated. Citing violations and imposing fines were the last resort when previous techniques failed to gain compliance.

The appropriate sequence of steps will vary with characteristics of the agency and regulated firms, but the combination of reasonableness and vengefulness is critical to the persuasive strategy. Inspectors need sufficient substantive knowledge not only to recognize violations but also to impress firms, assist in problem-solving, and recognize when a firm is not cooperating. They also need skills in persuasive interactions. Enforcement agencies may do well to emulate the training that insurance companies provide for their inspectors, which includes training in skills of persuasion. In some insurance companies, the job description emphasizes this motivational aspect of their job rather than the technical one of analyzing hazards and engineering appropriate solutions. Enforcement officials also need to be trained and encouraged to practice motivational skills appropriate for their tasks.

Persuasive Techniques for Supervisors. Just as the inspector provides the critical link in developing cooperative relationships with individual firms, so does the area supervisor provide the link with the various industrial and organizational sectors of firms within the supervisor's jurisdiction. The supervisor needs to ensure that inspectors are focusing on the worst problems in the area. They need to defend the discretionary decisions of the inspector against a broad range of possible complainants. To do so, they must be reasonably sure that inspectors are behaving consistently. This requires considerable attention to the problem of assisting the inspection staff in clarifying acceptable standards of compliance across the range of situations encountered in each industry.

In addition to supervising the inspectorate, the supervisor generally plays an important role in negotiating fines and abatement schedules in the most difficult cases. Supervisors are aware of the difficult balance in such negotiations between supporting the citations and fines proposed by their inspectors and creating a cooperative link with the firms involved. One variation of the persuasive strategy involves the good-cop bad-cop choice. When the inspector's relationship with the firm calls for stringent enforcement, the supervisor may be able to encourage the firm to become cooperative by reducing technical penalties in return for meaningful abatement on the part of the firm. Of course, this strategy may discourage future cooperation of other firms with the inspector once they know that the supervisor will routinely reduce penalties and offer a better deal.

Finally, area supervisors play a more "political" role in relationships with other organizations and leaders concerned with the regulatory problem within their jurisdiction. Managing the local image of the agency is important not only for long-term political concerns but also for immediate cooperation of regulated firms and regulatory supporters with the agency's inspectors. Supervisors must project this kind of image that will gain the support of the community for everyday inspections as well as for tactics to be used in tackling high-priority enforcement problems. To a large extent, this is accomplished through the agency's willingness to meet with organizations in the community concerned with the agency's activities. Cooperation with firms in an industry may be gained more readily by threatening the most blatant violators individually, but cooperating fully with local trade organizations in working out specific interpretations of regulations that meet the local organization's primary objections. The supervisor who can establish trust with a few organizations is in a stronger position to negotiate with other more recalcitrant organizations. The supervisor who can also establish a local consensus among regulated firms and regulatory advocates about appropriate priorities is more likely to have the flexibility required to utilize the most effective enforcement techniques to tackle high-priority problems. Of course, establishing such consensus in the contentious American context requires considerable skill and good fortune, including the presence of at least some local allies.

Managing the agency's public image also requires appropriate choices of enforcement strategies in line with community sentiments. This sometimes requires choosing targets for prosecution that will dramatize a problem, as when a community suffers from an accidental toxic discharge in its water supply. "Just deserts" rather than deterrence may then be the primary goal in determining penalties. At other times, a prosecution may be dropped because of mitigating circumstances that gained sympathy in the community, as occurred in Britain after one offender suffered a prolonged labor dispute (Richardson et al., 1982). The sentiment against undue government coercion is particularly strong in America, which requires supervisors to use the most intrusive deterrence tactics sparingly, only in situations in which firms are clearly violating important regulations.

Formalizing Persuasion in Programs. Agency leaders are primarily responsible for establishing appropriate incentives and organizational abilities to allow both inspectors and supervisors to develop effective persuasive strategies. General managerial techniques to induce appropriate incentives and capabilities will be discussed in the next section. In addition, leadership can attempt to formalize various aspects of persuasive strategies. There have been few successful attempts to do so to date, primarily because of the problem of political support discussed in the last section of this chapter. Yet the programs discussed here provide some examples of the kinds of persuasive techniques that can be formally introduced into enforcement programs.

Most educational and information programs discussed above attempt to provide positive incentives for compliance, particularly recognition of the "good citizen" role of cooperative firms. OSHA's voluntary compliance program, for example, is sometimes referred to as the "star program" because it provides star designation to participating plants that earn the highest rating. OSHA helps to publicize the leading role of the plant in their industry's safety and health efforts through various techniques, including a public ceremony at the plant involving OSHA's top leadership to announce the award. These plants are encouraged to fly special flags at corporate headquarters and use the star designation on corporate stationery. At the EPA, firms are encouraged to undertake voluntary environmental audits, and given recognition for their efforts.

Reciprocity provides another positive incentive to comply. When the agency appears more willing to help the regulated firm, the firm will be more likely to respond positively to agency demands. The IRS, for example, has in the past several years emphasized the importance of "customer service" to counteract the growing frustration facing taxpayers who could not find anyone in the organization with the authority to resolve their problem. To establish a more reciprocal relationship of cooperation, the IRS has increased the availability of taxpayer assistance, created problem resolution officers to take care of taxpayer problems involving multiple functions in the IRS, and moved toward individual case responsibility to ensure that the first officer contacted by a taxpayer would be responsible for resolving the problem for the taxpayer.

An IRS research conference in November, 1990 focused on other positive incentives the IRS could use, ranging from moral appeals and amnesty programs to lotteries providing prizes for those who were audited and found to be honest. The conference emphasized that compliance would be most enhanced by enforcement programs appearing to be tough but fair, and noted that programs offering positive incentives could backfire if not used with caution. For example, an amnesty program that would forgive penalties for past violators who voluntarily reported their violations and paid the taxes and interest may actually be perceived as unfair by taxpayers who have obeyed the law all along. Amnesty programs made most sense in situations where lax enforcement was being dramatically increased. "Forgiving" past noncompliers provided a greater incentive for them to move to the higher level of compliance expected by enforcers in the future.

Combining Enforcement Strategies

Most of the literature on deterrence, educational, and persuasive strategies attempts to characterize the primary strategy used by an agency, implicitly assuming that agencies pursue only one primary strategy. Agencies themselves frequently segregate different strategies into separate divisions within the agency. OSHA's consultants are functionally separated from enforcement compliance officers, even though they look for the same signs and violations. The IRS division of taxpayer services that provides educational programs and direct assistance to taxpayers is organizationally separate from the enforcement division. Even though this separation of strategies may be useful from a managerial point of view, as will be considered in the next section, it limits the ability to combine techniques from all three strategies into an effective program to tackle specific compliance problems.

Educational and persuasive techniques are most important as methods of enhancing the basic deterrence-oriented activities of the agencies, as has been emphasized in the above discussions. To be effective, there needs to be considerable coordination across strategies. For example, a deterrence strategy to scare a particular set of noncompliant firms into compliance can completely negate an educational strategy to help these firms if animosity prevents firms from utilizing the agency's educational services. An educational strategy that provides loopholes to avoid prosecution can likewise undermine the deterrence strategy. Only a coordinated program can combine the benefits rather than the deficits of both strategies.

We have already discussed educational techniques to enhance the efficiency of deterrence actions in the case of new regulations. For established enforcement programs, efficiency gains arise from combining strategies to deal with specific enforcement problems that routine activities cannot solve. Agencies generally uncover a succession of such problems either during routine enforcement activities or through programs designed to discover such problems. These problems may simply be recurrent problems that the agency has previously ignored due to lack of resources. They may also be new or growing problems arising from changing economic and technological circumstances or from the discovery of clever ways of evading regulations.

As an example of programs designed for special problems, the district offices of the IRS criminal investigation division focus on fraudulent tax practices found to be widespread in their area among a given occupational group (e.g., catfish farmers, shellfish fishermen, nurses, and so on). They have been successful in dramatically reducing the problem by analyzing the nature of the problem, defining acceptable standards of compliance, and developing a few "showcase" prosecutions to deliver the threat to those who continued the old practices.

Special programs utilizing combined strategies are most likely to make a strong impact on enforcement problems involving a clearly defined, homogeneous set of firms operating in clear violation of existing standards. The larger the diversity of firms and compliance problems involved, the more difficult it is to develop a unified strategy. Given an appropriate problem, several elements are generally involved. First, the nature of the violation needs to be analyzed to find appropriate techniques to make the violations more readily detectible and prosecutable. At the same time, standards of compliance need to be established that balance the intent of the regulation with the agency's ability to enforce that intent.

Depending on the willingness of the firms and trade associations involved to cooperate in this development, prosecutions seeking large fines are likely to be necessary to publicize the agency's intent and ability to enforce the regulation. The evolution of a successful solution can be accelerated by working simultaneously with cooperative firms in developing appropriate compliance standards. To the extent that there are other agencies or concerned groups (unions, consumer, or environmental groups) with an interest in the problem, the agency may help play a catalytic role in developing mutually acceptable compliance standards that reflect the main concerns of other interested groups. Coopting other groups could considerably strengthen the firm's willingness to comply if these groups add their activities to the support of the compliance program. Of course, attempting to coopt contentious groups may simply stall progress and lead firms to an organized resistance.

As standards are developed, educational techniques can be employed to encourage other firms as they become more willing to implement compliance programs. The agency at this point becomes a conduit for developing and spreading knowledge about cost-saving ways of achieving compliance. Private consultants and specialized businesses would be ideal to take over this function once the agency has reached an acceptable level of compliance in the area. Successful pilot programs eventually expand beyond the initially limited geographical focus to other regions experiencing the same problem, eventually becoming absorbed into the agency's continuing routine enforcement program.

The primary benefit of pilot programs employing combined strategies is in solving particularly difficult compliance problems for which routine enforcement activities are ineffective. This contribution will most enhance productivity if such programs are well targeted at important problems. Thus agencies with the best ability to foresee growing problems will be best able to utilize focused pilot programs. The IRS, for example, devotes considerable resources to analyzing developing trends in patterns of noncompliance. They utilize quantitative analyses of demographic and enforcement data as well as more qualitative analyses based on puzzling patterns reported in some enforcement districts. For example, one program has involved upper management in an attempt to anticipate developments likely to affect compliance levels by the end of the decade (e.g., the increase in minority and foreign populations with declining levels of language and mathematical skills) and to formulate strategies to deal with them (educational outreach programs using trained interpreters in predominantly non-English-speaking neighborhoods).

Although few agencies have sufficient resources for such long-range projections, most could systematically utilize existing information to prioritize various targets for pilot enforcement projects. For example, investigations of accidents, particularly those that result in deaths, provide a useful tool for investigating the kind of possible violations associated with such undesirable outcomes. Recurring patterns can become targets for special pilot programs.

Developing this managerial capability and suitable pilot project teams can benefit the agency beyond the solution of a particular problem. Pilot programs become a source of innovation that could be applied to existing enforcement problems in other areas. They expose both management and operating personnel to a problem-oriented approach to compliance, require them to become familiar with alternative strategies, and provide experience in the success of different techniques under a range of conditions. Coordinating the prosecutorial, educational, and persuasive components of pilot programs is a challenge that can sharpen managerial skills. The program's effectiveness is clearly limited by the resources the agency is willing to commit, but successful coordination of the component strategies can considerably enhance the productivity of these resources both in the pilot project and in subsequent enforcement assignments.

MANAGING THE ENFORCEMENT AGENCY: CONTROLLING DISCRETION

This discussion has so far considered the potential efficiency gains associated with the three enforcement strategies and their respective enforcement techniques. Yet these techniques require certain organizational capabilities to be performed successfully. For the most part, the required capabilities are relatively straightforward, and are too diverse and technical to be considered in this general discussion. One critical feature of effective enforcement programs, however, is particularly important to discuss because of its broad ramifications for the organization of an agency.

It can be argued that the most critical problem facing the leaders of an administrative agency is the problem of controlling enforcement discretion. The problem becomes most public when inspectors are accused of corruption. The more important and less obvious problem arises when agencies respond to fears of corruption by minimizing the discretion given to inspectors. Many of the major benefits of educational and persuasive strategies depend on the ability to choose the most appropriate tactic for a given enforcement situation. As a consequence, an agency that controls the problem of corruption by standardizing procedures and minimizing discretion loses most of the potential benefits of combined enforcement strategies.

However, there are no clear solutions to the problem of discretion. Too little control over the behavior of inspectors invites corruption, while too much control ensures an inefficient enforcement program. Furthermore, control techniques that are appropriate in one circumstance are not appropriate in others. For example, rotating inspectors between different assignments (to reduce the familiarity that breeds corruption) may be possible where inspection sites are reasonably similar. However, rotation would be counterproductive if inspectors unfamiliar with unique characteristics at each site could be more easily duped by noncompliant firms. Requiring inspectors to cite every violation they see (as OSHA is required to do by statute) may be appropriate where rules are closely related to regulatory objectives, but such stringency is misplaced when rules are more loosely related to objectives (as is true of OSHA rules).

The following discussion of managerial techniques to control discretion therefore attempts only to provide an outline of the kinds of control mechanisms available that lead to minimal adverse effects on efficiency. We will first discuss the need for discretion and the resultant problems, then consider the range of controls to counter such problems.

Causes and Consequences of Field Office Discretion

Field office discretion arises from the generic problem of interpreting national regulations under a diversity of changing local conditions (Bardach and Kagan, 1982; Diver, 1980; Hawkins, 1984). Observers of regulatory enforcement consistently comment on the broad discretion that each inspector must deal with in determining how closely to scrutinize a given establishment, whether observed conditions constitute a violation, and whether a violation is intentional and should be cited or "accidental" and should be dealt with informally (Hawkins, 1984; Kagan, 1989). Discretion leads to considerable variation in the way different inspectors (Feinstein, 1989) and field offices (Hedge et al., 1988; Shover et al., 1984; Hutter, 1988) enforce the same law, and even to variation in the way similar cases are treated in the same office (Kagan, 1978).

Field office discretion may develop in directions undesired by agency leaders and their political superiors for three reasons: field offices do not know what the national headquarters wants, they cannot do what it wants, or they refuse to do what it wants (Kaufman, 1973). These themes have been developed concretely in several studies. In the first case, internal bureaucratic factors such as local decision rules, operating procedures, and personal interests of bureaucrats fill the vacuum when central guidelines are ambiguous (Lipsky, 1980). In the second case, resources required by the field office to complete statutory tasks may be controlled by local groups, who can exchange resources for more favorable interpretations of central guidelines (Selznick, 1966; Pressman and Wildavsky, 1973). As noted in organization theory (Scott, 1987; Pfeffer and Salancik, 1978), local influences will increase in importance as resources obtained from the central environment (budgets, authorized procedures) decrease in importance in comparison to resources obtained from the local environment (cooperation, local assistance).

In the third case, local bureaucrats may sympathize with local groups and share interpretations of policy guidelines favorable to those groups (Blau, 1963; Kaufman, 1960). As Kaufman (1960: 87) noted in a slightly different context: "The customs and standards of the groups [inspectors] work with, the values and attitudes and pressures of the communities in which they reside, and the preferences and prejudices they bring with them from their extra-organizational experiences and associations may lead them in a variety of directions." This congruence in outlook with local interest groups may be particularly problematic for regulatory enforcement officials: they spend much of their time in contact with businesses they regulate; they frequently share similarities of professional outlook with their counterparts in firms; and they face considerable psychological pressure to reduce the confrontational nature of their daily contacts with the businesses they inspect (Kelman, 1981; Blau, 1963; but see Quirk, 1981).

Control Strategies of National Offices

Of course, agencies may counteract local influences with a range of techniques and strategies, which include procedures for controlling and "pre-forming" decisions, detecting and discouraging deviation, and developing the will and capacity of field officers to conform to central guidelines (Kaufman, 1960). OSHA and all federal agencies employ similar techniques to reduce local influences on field office discretion.

Controlling Inspection Decisions. Enforcement activities in particular are governed by thick manuals of required procedures developed in response to judicial demands for due process and consistent treatment (Pierce et al., 1985). Compliance officers spend much of their time documenting completed inspections in a manner that justifies their actions according to official guidelines. Enforcement procedures are probably more completely specified than most other agency activities not only because of stringent administrative law requirements governing enforcement procedures in all regulatory agencies but also because enforcement decisions of most agencies can be appealed to administrative review commissions set up to monitor enforcement activities.

The agency shapes enforcement procedures through the forms the inspector is required to file. Filling out such forms becomes one of the primary activities of inspectors, and reports based on these forms provide the basis for monitoring enforcement activities. The discretion necessary for educational and persuasive techniques implies that the inspector faces a range of choices. Forms can help channel necessary discretion in desired directions if the forms reflect the reasoning process a good inspector should follow in determining what to do. For example, forms could allow an inspector to cite violations but suspend penalties if designated conditions were met. Or the forms could make provisions for inspectors or their supervisors to allow a variance for specified violations in return for other designated actions to meet the desired regulatory goals. The primary goal is to make the use of discretion visible to those in the agency responsible for guiding its use.

The limitations in using standard routines and forms to control discretion are well known. Just as regulations can seldom specify the exact behavior desired of regulated firms, so also can organizational rules and forms seldom capture the exact behavior desired of inspectors and their supervisors. Subordinates unable or unwilling to use discretion to enhance persuasion cannot be forced to do so with rules and forms, and can indeed use rules to reduce the ability of supervisors to control their behavior. Adequate rules and forms can facilitate, not necessitate, the use of efficient enforcement techniques.

Detecting Improper Use of Discretion. Communication and computer technology has considerably increased the information available to monitor and detect deviations from normal patterns of field office and even individual officer behavior. Management information systems are routinely used that can record all enforcement activities and analyze patterns of enforcement in many ways. Most agency headquarters are awash with information about field office activities, although the interest and ability of central leaders to make sense out of this mass of information is less than certain, as Kaufman (1973) noted of the six federal agencies he studied even before the current explosion of information.

With current technologies, monitoring techniques can be developed to provide considerably greater flexibility to inspectors and field office supervisors. Previous systems were limited to comparing the average performance of a given inspector or field office with performances of comparable inspectors and offices. Deviations from standard performance would be most visible, and require justification that would not be evident in the data. However, if forms were developed that provide justifications for a range of alternative actions, analysis could then focus on the nature of the justifications and the range of actions taken by inspectors or their supervisors, as would be more appropriate for persuasive and educational strategies.

As Kaufman (1973) found in other agencies, it is likely that enforcement agency leadership will continue to rely on other monitoring devices as well, such as personal inspections, investigations, and, in particular, the "web of personal contacts" throughout the agency that provides informal sources of information about field office problems. In addition, efficiency evaluations and pilot projects discussed above could also provide information about weaknesses in existing enforcement routines.

Kaufman also notes that agency leadership seldom uses the information available to them, in part because of disincentives for agency leaders to know how discretion is being used: ignorance of inappropriate behavior may be better than knowledge if it can save the agency leader from responsibility or if the leader is relatively helpless to alter the behavior in any case. Both of these problems are exacerbated by the political context of enforcement agencies, as we will discuss in the next section. These disincentives to create more effective monitoring systems are a particular difficulty in improving the efficiency of enforcement agencies, since the discretion necessary for flexible enforcement strategies is unlikely to be acceptable to regulatory policy supporters without sufficient means for control. Greater discretion means greater political problems for the agency leadership unless accompanied by better methods of control that do not expose agency leadership to greater risks.

Developing Good Inspectors. The ideal way to control discretion is to have inspectors who are willing and capable of making the kinds of decisions and tradeoffs necessary for effective enforcement. Recruitment, training, and supervision provide the primary techniques by which agencies attempt to shape common beliefs about appropriate enforcement behavior, build loyalty to the goals of the agency, and develop necessary technical skills. These techniques become especially important to an agency pursuing an efficient combined strategy of enforcement, particularly since the educational and persuasive strategies require a broader range of skills and a deeper commitment to the goals of the agency than a more standard deterrence strategy.

Recruitment. Recruitment can enhance the ability of the agency to pursue a combined strategy by emphasizing knowledge about the regulated area rather than enforcement experience. In addition to seeking individuals with appropriate knowledge bases, agencies can encourage the development of professional training programs to produce appropriately trained individuals. The growth of industrial hygiene as a profession has been aided by OSHA regulations, which increased the demand for trained hygienists by both OSHA and regulated industries. Working closely with professional associations to shape professional training can improve the pool of trained applicants.

A common problem facing all agencies is the general lack of knowledge about enforcement among potential recruits. Some have had prior law enforcement experience, although such experience generally emphasizes deterrence techniques to the detriment of educational and enforcement ones. One solution may be for enforcement agencies to work together on a common curriculum on basic enforcement. There are several ways to encourage the development of a basic curriculum. A small number of colleges or professional schools could be selected to develop such programs, with the expectation that graduates would be recruited by specified agencies. This curriculum should be available as a part of specialized studies in areas such as environmental studies, industrial hygiene, and so on. Incentives such as fellowships may initially be required to get good applicants, with the provision that recipients spend a specified number of years after graduation in the agency providing the fellowship.

As an alternative (or in addition), an enforcement academy could be established specifically to train individuals interested in enforcement careers. The academy would have the greatest impact if it combined basic professional training with a broad range of educational and research activities such as training and workshops for middle managers, seminars and workshops for agency leaders, and research and evaluation programs undertaken in cooperation with various agencies. The broader benefits of this proposal are discussed in the final section of this chapter. In terms of recruitment, the benefit is to expose trainees to an environment that is intellectually stimulating and dedicated to the improvement of enforcement.

Recruiting inspectors with the most appropriate personality traits is a more difficult task. As Muir (1977) noted of the "good cop," the good inspector needs to be able to be tough and confrontational when the situation requires, but also needs to be reasonable and willing to listen in appropriate situations. Experienced supervisors probably have developed a good sense of which inspectors are likely to be able to operate in both modes. Some of this knowledge might be systematized for the recruitment process by the development of tests that can differentiate personalities that can operate conditionally in both tough and flexible modes from those prone to be too tough or too lenient all the time. Such a test, if successful, would be useful across all enforcement agencies.

Training. Training has two primary functions: to provide specialized skills, and to develop values and attitudes supportive of the goals of the agency. Given the low salary scales and civil service restrictions that most agencies have to deal with, training has become increasingly necessary just to ensure minimal competence in essential technical knowledge. Rapid turnover of employees also discourages a large investment in training. For agencies to make substantial progress in improving enforcement efficiency, however, the role of training needs to be expanded. As emphasized above, persuasive and educational strategies require inspectors with the technical and enforcement knowledge to utilize discretion appropriately.

Each agency now provides its own training programs, which cover important technical and legal aspects of the job. I have not found any training programs that improve the use of persuasive skills, although these are frequently a part of the training of inspectors employed in the private sector to ensure compliance with the corporate or insurer's policy. Most agencies provide an apprenticeship period in which the persuasive skills of an experienced inspector can be directly observed by the trainee, at least to the extent that the experienced inspector has and uses persuasive skills. It is also unclear how well training increases the understanding of the relationship between rule enforcement and regulatory objectives.

To the extent that agencies move in the direction of coordinated strategies, these missing components need to be included in training programs. There may be economies of scale for agencies to develop combined programs or training resources and facilities to provide these missing components, since the basic techniques are common across agencies. To do so, agencies would have to agree on the general philosophy of enforcement to be reflected in the training program. In the past decade the private sector has become aware of the importance of "corporate culture" for the success of corporations. An appropriate "enforcement culture" is equally important for efficient enforcement, and training is one factor that can be used to shape that culture.

Supervision. The primary force for shaping the enforcement culture of the inspector, however, must come from the constant interactions involved in supervision and in office routines overseen by supervisors. Blau (1963) observed long ago that enforcement agencies in particular require some sense of "esprit de corps" to provide sufficient psychological support for inspectors who spend much of their time in the field in potentially confrontational situations. Without some sense of commitment to agency goals or camaraderie with fellow inspectors and supervisors, the natural inclination to avoid confrontation would diminish the inspector's effectiveness. Supervisors can assist this process by defending good inspectors against outside criticisms (even when a quiet rebuke is necessary), upholding the legitimacy of the agency in the eyes of the community, and justifying decisions in terms of the general goals of the agency. In short, the supervisor must be a leader.

Encouraging commitment is a difficult task, but supervising an effective combined strategy requires consistency as well as commitment. Inspectors must use appropriate techniques for different situations, and they must do so in a way that is consistent for all inspectors in an office. Manuals and training programs can provide some general guidelines, but experience in the field is what shapes the way inspectors interpret what they see and how they respond. Given the critical role of discretion in efficient enforcement, a primary function of supervision is thus to ensure that all inspectors working in the same program share a common framework of experience and interpretation. For example, as inspectors experience emerging problems likely to affect others, the case could be discussed in a staff meeting. Supervisors can use such discussions to clarify the justifications for alternative possible actions. Supervisors at times must impose their interpretation of a given situation and recommendation for action on reluctant inspectors, yet the policy is more likely to be followed if there is general agreement on the reasons behind the given action. In an efficient program, the supervisor must become an effective educator, encouraging inspectors to understand the broader picture of enforcement.

For supervisors to function as educators, they also need to be exposed to the broader experience of the agency and the justifications for various procedural requirements. Regular meetings to discuss policy changes, specific workshops to help formulate agency responses to broader problems, acting assignments on special programs in other areas, occasional assignments in the national office, and other means of exposing supervisors to broader issues affecting the agency can all be used to help educate the supervisor. These activities become increasingly important as the supervisor is required to understand and apply a greater range of responses to particular problems. As a consequence, promotion decisions for supervisors should increasingly encourage the diversity of experience required for efficient enforcement programs.

In short, the kind of enforcement policy described in the first section requires a system of supervision that reflects the characteristics of persuasive and educational enforcement strategies. The supervisor is only partly a cop who monitors inspectors and punishes those who disobey agency policies. The supervisor must also persuade and educate inspectors, and be willing to learn from them. Organizational procedures provide the same role within the agency as regulations do in the broader context of regulation: clumsy but necessary bases for action. From inspector through supervisor to top management, adherence to strict policy guidelines is tempered by concern for the goals the agency pursues and a willingness to adopt new procedures when existing ones seem counterproductive.

Of course, the essence of good management is to make decisions appropriate for the immediate organizational context rather than for some ideal situation. The discussion in this section focused on changes in management that could potentially increase the efficiency of enforcement, provided that the political context approved and encouraged the combined strategy discussed in this chapter's first section. The extent to which they are appropriate for an agency's setting depends on the broader political context in which the agency operates.

POLITICAL CONTEXT: CONSTRAINT, RESPONSIVENESS, AND LEADERSHIP

The greatest source of administrative inefficiency in federal enforcement agencies stems not from lack of enforcement knowledge or management resource, but from a political system and political culture that value efficiency less than protection against state power. As de Tocqueville observed of America over a century ago, we prefer a weak, corrupted, politically passive bureaucracy to a strong, efficient, and politically powerful one. The accelerated growth of government policies intervening in a broad range of areas previously left to private means has not increased concern with efficiency. If anything, the problems stemming from the fragmentation of political power and lack of policy consensus among contentious interest groups have increased administrative inefficiencies (Kagan, 1990; Seidman, 1980).

The low value placed on administrative efficiency in our system is demonstrated by the history of most regulatory policies. Moe (1989) has documented the success of business interests opposing regulation in weakening regulatory agencies through statutory features that divide important functions among separate and competing agencies, limit access to information necessary for enforcement, impose cumbersome administrative procedures on rule-making and enforcement procedures, and provide multiple points at which agency decisions can be challenged. The courts have also encouraged contentious interest groups to mount challenges to agency procedures and decisions, limiting the flexibility of agencies and drastically slowing their ability to resolve issues (Kagan, 1990).

Even supporters of regulatory policies have limited the ability of the agency to develop effective enforcement strategies (Scholz, 1991); the concern that agency discretion will lead to capture by business interests has prompted supporters to require agencies to pursue stringent deterrence-oriented strategies, to respond to all complaints, and to open the enforcement process to a broad range of actors with differing interests. As Moe (1989) argues, groups anticipate that their current ascendancy in the legislative process is only temporary, and that their opponents will soon get their turn in power. Thus, instead of selecting an administrative structure that would most effectively deliver the desired service, policy advocates prefer structures that lock in benefits even after the opposition has taken control of the administration. What appears to be a perverse choice of structure from a narrow public administration perspective becomes more sensible when viewed from the broader perspective of the political control game.

It is important to note that these inefficiencies arise from deep-seated features of the political system designed to protect individuals and minorities against government coercion. They arise from the fundamental belief in the American political culture that citizens have the right to organize in order to pursue their individual political interests, but that the primary purpose of government is to protect the rights of citizens against the tyranny of majority interests. They are inextricably set in the fragmentation of power reflected in the federalist system; the divisions between legislative, executive, and judicial powers; the separate policy domains of federal agencies; and the multiple access points. Nor are politically induced administrative inefficiencies unique to regulatory agencies, as two decades of literature on implementation failures has amply demonstrated.

In short, inefficiencies arising from the political system are not just idiosyncracies of the system, but are the indirect costs of pursuing other values. Just pointing out the inefficiencies caused by political interventions will not make them go away. Nor should they provide agencies with an excuse for more avoidable forms of inefficiency. Management needs to function within the constraints of the political system, not just give in to them. Efficiency should be seen not in a technical sense, but in the sense of achieving the best politically feasible utilization of available resources to accomplish the most feasible statutory goals. The following discussion provides a brief example of how the political environment hampers managerial controls, and then considers the role enforcement managers can play by working within the constraints of the system. The need for political reforms to achieve more stable consensus on policy matters will be discussed briefly, but our primary concern is with the role management can play in mitigating the inevitable inefficiencies in regulatory enforcement.

Political Fragmentation and Polarization Limit Central Controls over Discretion

Consider the constraints that the political system place on the efficiency of OSHA's enforcement policy. A critical limitation on OSHA's control of field office activities derives from the polarized central political environment in which it must survive. From the beginning, business, labor, and their respective allies clashed on many issues directly relevant to enforcement (Noble, 1986; Moe, 1989). Labor won the critical battle to place OSHA within the Department of Labor rather than Commerce, and also won the right of workers to file complaints alleging OSHA violations in their plant. As a consequence, OSHA's level of enforcement was strongly influenced by the willingness of workers in a given area to file such complaints (Scholz and Wei, 1986; Headrick, 1990). However, business won the battle over the independence of the review commission, which allowed businesses to influence the level of enforcement by threatening to appeal more citations; appeals could reduce the level of enforcement by diverting inspection resources to these judicial proceedings (Headrick, 1990).

Political polarization has continued to plague OSHA's national office. OSHA's oversight committees have been used as extreme examples of partisan committees (Fenno, 1973) that produce much confrontation, occasional truces, and little consensus. As a consequence, OSHA officials note with some frustration that they are probably enforcing at the appropriate level when both business and labor are upset with them. Although political conflict encourages the profusion of formal procedures that bureaucrats can use to protect themselves, it also undermines the national office's willingness and ability to provide clear, unambiguous signals to field offices about how vigorously to pursue formal procedures.

Changes in presidential administration have further weakened central controls over field offices. Carter's administration attempted to shift enforcement priorities to the most hazardous plants and most serious violations, while Reagan's administration emphasized consultation and tried to minimize enforcement. These contrasting views led to changes in signals from the central office, and undoubtedly exacerbated the usual divergence in beliefs among field officials about how stringently to enforce regulations (Noble, 1986; Kelman, 1981). Budget cuts and morale problems under the Reagan administration further exacerbated general civil service problems of hiring and maintaining qualified compliance officers. These changes have most affected the ability of OSHA's national office to shape common beliefs and loyalties among compliance officers, leaving them less loyal to some clear set of agency goals and more open to influences from the communities in which they live and work.

In summary, enforcement activities inevitably leave considerable discretion to field offices to determine how vigorously regulations should be enforced. National offices have powerful techniques for channeling discretion in directions preferred by the central political institutions. However, for OSHA, local influences have been enhanced by statutory provisions for local participation, which provide business and labor groups with enforcement resources important to field offices. Furthermore, the polarized, dynamic political environment has led to reluctance and inability of the central office to provide field offices with clear, legitimate guidelines for desired levels of enforcement. OSHA's procedural guidelines and monitoring system provide powerful standardizing and integrating influences, but the problematic political environment has worked against the development of standardized beliefs and values among field officials about the appropriate level of enforcement.

Politics and Management

Managing a regulatory agency obviously requires more than the technical skills of designing efficient enforcement programs and devising appropriate organizational routines. Regulatory policies generally arise out of conflict, and seldom emerge with a clear consensus about how to change the behavior of some powerful economic interest. Legislators like to grab the bull by its tail and give it a good yank, and then hand it to an agency to control. What should we expect of agency management in such situations?

Perhaps the most important skill of the public manager is the ability to grasp opportunities at hand to achieve some progress toward significant goals within the constraints of the moment. As Barnard (1938) noted for both private and public organizations, the primary function of the executive is to provide direction and build consensus among all parties interested in the agency that can overcome the inevitable conflict of views among interests competing for attention and influence over the organization.

Yet how can public management derive a viable consensus about agency goals and enforcement strategies in the contentious political climate of the 1990s? There is little that scientific inquiry can do to provide a clear, foolproof path for administrators to follow in any given historical moment. Kaufman (1956) has provided a useful catalogue of three different doctrines on public administration that have emerged as the most creative force shaping agencies in different periods of history. Each doctrine suggests a different emphasis in the direction an enforcement agency would evolve, and each suggests a different mix of enforcement techniques and organizational control strategies. Kaufman referred to the three doctrines of public administration as neutral competence, responsiveness, and executive leadership.

The doctrine of *neutral competence* views the function of the agency to be the efficient implementation of goals determined by political authorities. It assumes that broad consensus exists over agency goals. The task of the agency is thus to provide the technical expertise required to bring about these goals in the most efficient manner, as was emphasized in the initial discussion about the techniques of enforcement. This doctrine was perhaps most clearly reflected in the design of the independent regulatory commissions during the 1930s, which were to be insulated from political pressures in order to function as a competent body of professionals. It is probably the least relevant doctrine in terms of the current evolution of regulatory agencies.

The doctrine of *responsiveness* reflects the view that agencies need to respond to the problems of groups affected by the agency, and not simply to pursue abstract goals in the most efficient way. Expertise is therefore less important in the design of the agency than methods to ensure that the agency responds to the changing situations and preferences of their clientele as well as the changing balance of political power between advocates and opponents of new policies. Responsiveness imposes efficiency costs on the agency, since it requires changes and adaptation of basic organizational routines to accommodate a more complex, dynamic environment.

As the tasks given to government agencies have expanded, so also has the concern with responsiveness as an antidote to the seemingly all-powerful and indifferent agency. Many of the social regulatory agencies created in the past two decades include features that allow clients to participate more directly in decision processes. Such features were also fashioned to prevent the "capture" of experts by businesses by requiring agencies to respond to client demands. The demand for protection against bureaucratic excesses continues to be a powerful theme in national politics, one that is particularly sensitive to the coercive powers at the heart of enforcement programs.

The doctrine of *executive leadership* recognizes the need for innovative leadership to overcome conflicting, competing demands that frustrate all parties interested in a policy arena. This doctrine is particularly strong in response to a single, overpowering problem. Wartime agencies obviously evolve under this influence, with centralized controls and coordination mechanisms providing the favored means of cutting through fragmented administrative arrangements that cannot efficiently achieve the single most important goal. The attempts of the Carter and Reagan administrations to increase regulatory attention to economic efficiency provide recent examples of reforms under the doctrine of executive leadership.

Given the general discontent among all contending parties in most regulatory arenas, it appears likely that the doctrine of executive leadership may remain a dominant concern in each specialized policy arena. As groups become increasingly dissatisfied with a fragmented system that gives everyone the ability to frustrate others but almost no one the ability to achieve desired results, political concerns may focus on ways of devising alternative structures to provide the kind of stable consensus more consistent with efficient achievement of regulatory goals.

In my view, the greatest contribution that agency management can make to this process may be to

1. Create efficient enforcement programs that combine the advantages of deterrence, educational, and persuasive strategies
2. Develop control mechanisms that can ensure policy advocates that educational and persuasive strategies will not lead the agencies to favor regulated firms at the expense of regulatory goals
3. Educate and persuade concerned interests and political leaders about the nature of enforcement programs and the need for stability and consensus to provide efficient and effective regulatory policies

Agency leadership must bear a major part in such an effort, but creativity and leadership at all levels of the agency are necessary to develop appropriate programs and change the perceptions of others at all levels of the political process.

The first point is the most critical, since clearer demonstrations about the advantages of mixed strategies are necessary to convince skeptics that there is more than deterrence to enforcement. The task of devising successful programs falls most heavily on inspectors and their immediate supervisors.

The second point is necessary in order to gain the support of regulatory advocates and policy beneficiaries. Without this support, the discretion necessary for efficient enforcement will be hampered by clumsy constraints meant to protect against undue business influence. To reassure policy supporters, mechanisms must be developed to ensure that inspectors are making appropriate use of discretion. These mechanisms will inevitably rely heavily on supervisory techniques to maintain consistency. For examples, supervisors will meet frequently with inspectors to discuss how to handle problem cases, and supervisors from various areas will meet together for similar discussions. Forms and monitoring systems also need to provide warnings and assurances that discretion is being used to support policies, as well as to monitor compliance and goal success in ways that can be related to the enforcement program. As an alternative, methods of coopting beneficiaries and regulated firms into local oversight committees might provide the necessary reassurances, but only if consensus rather than confrontation could be developed. Development of adequate controls falls heavily on middle managers, who must bear the risks involved in increasing discretion at the field office level. Agency leadership must be willing to share this risk and encourage such developments.

The third point could potentially bring the greatest long-run gains for enforcement efficiency by providing the consensus on appropriate goals and techniques that could allow agencies to concentrate on technical efficiency. Agencies can play a leading role in educating policy advocates about what can realistically be achieved given the competing values and constraints on enforcement resources that come with our political system. The appearances of agency officials at conferences and trade talks at both local and national levels provide appropriate occasions for explaining the advantages and requirements of combined enforcement strategies. Convincing businesses about the advantages of educational and persuasive techniques is probably relatively easy; convincing policy advocates and beneficiaries to approve the needed flexibility and discretion required to combine strategies efficiently is more difficult.

A Modest Proposal

The extent to which agency leadership can change the political climate of enforcement is unclear, particularly given the fragmented nature of our political system. Yet the political and efficiency costs of conceiving enforcement in narrow deterrence terms and in seeking maximal advantage of political power are becoming clear.

An appropriate goal for those concerned with reforming enforcement may be to develop a new consensus supporting the flexibility necessary for serious attempts at combined enforcement programs. The old consensus that provided many common features to regulatory agencies for the past two decades has enhanced deterrence at the cost of enforcement discretion, and continues to limit the development of enforcement strategies. Most of the examples of innovative programs provided in the first section have remained extremely limited because of the difficulty in gaining the support of both regulated firms and regulatory beneficiaries over appropriate terms of the program. Only when both sides understand the mutual benefits in devising combined enforcement strategies will the agency be willing and able to create efficient enforcement programs.

A critical step in working toward a consensus is to consolidate the lessons about enforcement that have been learned over the past two decades. I propose a series of steps leading eventually to a modest form of enforcement academy to provide a center for the development and dissemination of knowledge about enforcement problems across different policy arenas and agency jurisdictions. The initial steps would be to share knowledge and experience by bringing together officials working with similar kinds of enforcement problems (e.g., approaches taken by different agencies to enforcement targeted at small businesses). Working groups could be expanded to include policy-makers and representatives of business, union, and other interested parties in seminars focusing on specific enforcement techniques or particular enforcement problems. The advantage of such settings is to get groups to think more broadly about alternative possibilities rather than about their specific policy interest. It may be particularly fruitful to develop informal cross-agency workshops to help in the initial design of special projects.

Eventually, a series of evaluation studies should be introduced to provide a more systematic basis of knowledge in support of combined enforcement programs. A core of experts familiar with enforcement problems can be gathered to assist agencies in designing and implementing their own studies and to help make the results of evaluation studies available to other agencies and to the broader policy community.

The working groups and evaluations should eventually provide the foundation for specialized enforcement training programs appropriate for the different levels from inspectors to top management. This training would supplement the substantive training inspectors need in their specialized regulatory areas, and would focus on the range of skills needed for the enforcement aspect of the job. It would impart knowledge about the techniques associated with the deterrence, educational, and persuasive strategies necessary for the "good inspector," as discussed above. The training for supervisors would encourage creative approaches to specific problems that take advantage of the most appropriate techniques of all strategies. Seminars for middle and top-level managers would emphasize techniques to manage the external environment of the agency as well as organizational alternatives to provide adequate control mechanisms and managerial incentives to encourage the development of efficient enforcement.

The appropriate institutional form for this development depends on the interest and willingness of agencies, political oversight committees, and private foundations to support and nurture such developments. This chapter has attempted to raise some of the main issues that need to be developed. I have noted throughout, however, the surprising lack of a common knowledge base and institutionalized mechanisms for sharing knowledge across agencies and policy-makers. Many of the ideas are admittedly speculative. I hope that they will ring true enough to encourage others to continue the dialogue and explore common interests in developing an enforcement academy.

CONCLUSION

Enforcement problems are here to stay. After a decade of determined assault against regulation and regulatory agencies by very popular and powerful presidents, it seems clear that enforcement will remain an essential part of regulatory policies for some time to come. In democracies such as ours, few people will publicly endorse the general idea of coercion and call for more enforcement, particularly when enforcement is focused on businesses and local governments rather than criminal and drug dealers. Whether or not one supports the current form of regulations and regulatory enforcement, it is time to recognize that enforcement agencies are a permanent part of the political landscape. As the proverb has it, if you can't beat them, join them. Instead of battling to increase or decrease the deterrence capabilities of agencies, all sides may be better off cooperating to reduce harmful inefficiencies associated with the narrow deterrence mode of enforcement. Enforcement officials cannot bring this about by themselves, but they can help in the evolution toward more efficient enforcement by systematizing and integrating the knowledge we have accumulated in separate policy arenas and educating all participants about the mutual advantages of alternative enforcement strategies.

REFERENCES

Ayres, Ian and John Braithwate. 1992. Responsive Regulation: transcending the Deregulation Debate. New York: Oxford University Press.

Bardach, Eugene, and Robert A. Kagan. 1982. *Going by the Book: The Problem of Regulatory Unreasonableness.* Philadelphia: Temple University Press.

Bardach, Eugene. 1977. *The Implementation Game.* Cambridge: MIT Press.

Barnard, Chester. (1938). *Functions of the Executive.* Cambridge: Harvard University Press.

Bartel, Ann and Lacy G. Thomas. (1985). Direct and indirect effects of OSHA regulation, *Journal of Law and Economics* 28, 1–26.

Becker, Gary S. (1968). Crime and punishment: An economic approach, *Journal of Political Economy* 76, 169–217.

Blau, Peter. 1963. *The Dynamics of Bureaucracy.* Chicago: The University of Chicago Press.

Braithwaite, John. 1985. *To Punish or Persuade: Enforcement of Coal Mine Safety.* Albany: State University of New York Press.

Boruch, Robert F. 1989. Experimental and quasi-experimental designs in taxpayer compliance research, in Roth, J. A., J. T. Scholz, and A. D. White (eds.), *Taxpayer Compliance*. Philadelphia: University of Pennsylvania Press. Pp. 339–379.

Casey, Jeffrey and John T. Scholz, (1991). Boundary effects of vague risk information on taxpayer decisions, *Organizational Behavior and Human Decision Processes* 50:360–394.

Centaur Associates. 1985 *The Impact of Osha Enforcement Activities*. Report submitted to the Occupational Safety and Health Administration, January 16, 1985.

Cheit, Ross E. 1991. *Setting Safety Standards: Regulation in the Public and Private Sectors*. Berkeley: University of California.

Cook, William N. and Frederick H. Gautschi, III. (1981). OSHA, Plant Safety Programs, and Injury Reduction, *Industrial Relations* 20:245–257.

Diver, Colin. 1980. A theory of regulatory enforcement, *Public Policy* 28: 257–99.

Downing, Paul B. and Kenneth Hanf (eds.). (1983). *International Comparisons of Pollution Enforcement*. Boston: Kluwer-Nijhoff Publishing.

Erlich, Isaac. (1973). Participation in illegitimate activities: A theoretical and empirical investigation, *Journal of Political Economy* 81: 521–565.

Feinstein, Jonathan S. 1989. The safety regulation of U.S. nuclear power plants: Violations, inspections, and abnormal occurrences, *Journal of Political Economy* 97:115–154.

Fenno, Richard F. 1973. *Congressmen in Committees*. Boston: Little, Brown.

Gellhorn, Ernest (1973). Adverse publicity by administrative agencies. *Harvard Law Review* 86:1437-1440.

Gormley, William, John Hoadley, and Charles Williams. 1983. Potential responsiveness in the bureaucracy: Views of public utility regulation. *American Political Science Review* 77:704–717.

Gormley, William T. 1983. *The Politics of Public Utilities Regulation*. Pittsburgh: Pittsburgh University Press.

Grabosky, Peter and John Braithwaite. 1986. *Of Manners Gentle: Enforcement Strategies of Australian Business Regulatory Agencies*. Oxford: Oxford University Press.

Graetz, Michael J., Jennifer F. Reinganum, and Louis J. Wilde. 1986. The tax compliance game: Toward an interactive theory of law enforcement. *Journal of Law, Economics and Organization* 2:1–32.

Gray, Wayne B. and Carol Adaire Jones. (1989). Longitudinal patterns of compliance with OSHA health and safety regulations in the manufacturing sector, *Journal of Human Resources* 26:623–653.

Gray, Wayne B. and Carol Adaire Jones. (1990). Are OSHA health inspections effective? A longitudinal study in the manufacturing sector, *Review of Economics and Statistics* 73:504–8.

Gray, Wayne B. and John T. Sholz. 1991. Analyzing the equity and efficiency of OSHA enforcement. *Law and Policy* 13:185–214.

Gray, Wayne B. and John T. Scholz. 1992. Does regulatory enforcement work? A panel analysis of OSHA enfocement. *Law and Society Review* 27:177–213.

Greenberg, J. 1984. Avoiding tax avoidance: A (repeated) game-theoretic approach. *Journal of Economic Theory* 32:1–13.

Gricar, Barbara Gray. 1983. A preliminary theory of compliance with OSHA regulation, *Research in Corporate Social Performance and Policy* 5:121–141.

Hawkins, Keith. 1984. *Environment and Enforcement: Regulation and the Social Definition of Deviance*. Oxford: Oxford University Press.

Hawkins, Keith and John M. Thomas, eds. 1984. *Enforcing Regulation*. Boston: Kluwer-Nijhoff.

Headrick, Barbara. 1990. Federal enforcement in urban areas. Doctoral dissertation, State University of New York at Stony Brook.

Hedge, David, D. Menzel and G. Williams. 1988. Regulatory attitudes and behavior: The case of surface mining. *Western Political Quarterly* 41:323–340.

Huntington, Samuel P. 1952. The marasmus of the ICC: The commission, the railroads, and the public interest. *Yale Law Journal* 51:467–509.

Hutter, B. 1988. *The Reasonable Arm of the Law? The Law Enforcement Procedures of Environmental Health Officers*. Oxford: Clarendon Press.

Kagan, Robert A. 1978. *Regulatory Justice: Implementing a Wage-Price Freeze*. New York: Russell Sage Foundation.

Kagan, Robert A. 1990. Adversarial legalism and American government. Paper presented at the annual meeting of the Law and Society Association, Berkeley, CA.

Kagan, Robert A. 1989. Editor's introduction: Understanding regulatory enforcement. *Law and Politics* 11:89–119.

Kagan, Robert A. and John T. Scholz. 1984. The 'criminology' of the corporation and regulatory enforcement strategies. In Keith Hawkins and John M. Thomas, eds., *Enforcing Regulation*. Boston: Kluwer-Nijhoff.

Kaufman, Herbert. 1960. *The Forest Ranger*. Baltimore: Johns Hopkins University Press.

Kaufman, Herbert. 1973. *Administrative Feedback*. Washington: Brookings Institution.

Kelman, Steven. 1981. *Regulating America, Regulating Sweden*. Cambridge: MIT Press.

Klepper, Steven and Daniel Nagin. (1989). Tax compliance and perceptions of the risks of detection and criminal prosecution," *Law and Society Review* 23, 209–240.

Lane, Robert. 1977. Why businessmen violate the law, in Gilbert Geis and Robert Meier (eds), *White Collar Crime*. New York: Free Press.

Lempert, Richard. (1982). Organizing for deterrence, *Law and Society Review* 16, 513–568.

Lipsky, Michael. 1980. *Street-Level Bureaucracy*. New York: Russell Sage Foundation.

Marlow, Michael. 1981. The impact of different government units in the regulation of the workplace environment. *Public Choice* 37:349–356.

Marlow, Michael L. 1982. The economics of enforcement: The case of OSHA. *Journal of Economics and Business* 34:165–171.

Marvel, Mary K. 1982. Implementation and safety regulation: Variations in federal and state administration under OSHA, *Administration and Society* 14:15–33.

McCaffrey, David. 1982. *OSHA and the Politics of Health Regulation*. New York: Plenum Press.

McCaffrey, David. 1983. An assessment of OSHA's recent effects on injury rates, *Journal of Human Resources* 18:131–146.

McCubbins, Mathew D. 1985. The legislative design of regulatory structure, *American Journal of Political Science* 29:721–748.

McCubbins, Matthew D., and Thomas Schwartz. 1979. Congressional oversight overlooked: Police patrols versus fire alarms, *American Journal of Political Science* 28:165–79.

Mendeloff, John. 1979. *Regulating Safety: An Economic and Political Analysis of Occupational Safety and Health Policy*. Cambridge, MA: MIT Press.

Moe, Terry M. 1982. Regulatory performance and presidential administration, *American Journal of Politics* 26:197–224.

Moe, Terry M. 1984. The new economics of organization, *American Journal of Political Science* 28:739–777.

Moe, Terry M. 1985. Control and feedback in economic regulation: The case of the NLRB, *American Political Science Review* 79:1094–1116.

Moe, Terry M. 1989. The politics of bureaucratic structure, in John Chubb and Paul Peterson, eds., *Can Government Govern*. Washington, D.C.: Brookings Institution.

Muir, William K. 1977. *Police: Streetcorner Politicians*. Chicago: University of Chicago Press.

Nagin, Daniel. (1978). General deterrence: A review of the empirical evidence, in Al Blumstein, J. Cohen, and Daniel Nagin (eds.), *Deterrence and Incapacitation: Estimating the Effect of Criminal Sanctions on Crime Rates*. Washington, D.C.: National Academy of Sciences.

Noble, Charles. 1986. *Liberalism at Work: The Rise and Fall of OSHA*. Philadelphia: Temple University Press.

Nonet, Phillipe and Phillip Selznick. 1978. *Law and Society in Transition: Toward Responsive Law*. New York: Harper Colophon Books.

Pfeffer, Jeffrey, and Gerald Salancik. 1978. *The External Control of Organizations*. New York: Harper and Row.

Pierce, Richard J., Sidney A. Shapiro and Paul R. Verkuil. 1985. *Administrative Law and Process*. Mineola, NY: Foundation Press.

Pressman, Jeffrey and Aaron Wildavsky. 1973. *Implementation.* Berkeley: University of California Press.

Quirk, Paul. 1981. *Industry Influence in Federal Regulatory Agencies.* Princeton: Princeton University Press.

Rees, Joseph. 1988. *Reforming the Workplace: A Study of Self-Regulating in Occupational Safety.* Philadelphia: University of Pennsylvania Press.

Richardson, Genevra, Anthony Ogus and Paul Burrows. 1982. *Policing Pollution: a Study of Regulation and Enforcement.* New York: Oxford University Press.

Roth, J. A., Scholz, J. T., and Witte, A. D. (1989). *Taxpayer Compliance: An Agenda for Research.* Philadelphia: University of Pennsylvania Press.

Ruser, John W. and Robert S. Smith. (1988). The effect of OSHA records check inspections on reported occupational injuries in manufacturing establishments, *Journal of Risk and Uncertainty,* 1:415–435.

Sabatier, Paul. 1988. An advocacy coalition framework for policy change and the role of policy-oriented learning therein, *Policy Sciences* 21:129–168.

Scholz, John T. 1984a. Cooperation, deterrence, and the ecology of regulatory enforcement, *Law and Society Review* 18:601–646.

Scholz, John T. 1984b. Voluntary compliance and regulatory enforcement, *Law and Policy* 6:385–404.

Scholz, John T. 1984c. Reliability, responsiveness, and regulatory policy, *Public Administrative Review* 44:145–153.

Scholz, John T. 1989. Federal vs. state regulation: Does it matter? in Malcolm Feeley and Harry Scheiber, eds., *Power Divided: Essays on the Theory and Practice of Federalism.* Berkeley: Institute of Governmental Studies.

Scholz, John T. 1991. Cooperative enforcement and the politics of administrative efficiency, *American Political Science Review* 85:115–136.

Scholz, John T. and Wayne B. Gray. 1990. A behavioral approach to compliance: OSHA enforcement's impact on workplace accidents, *Journal of Risk and Uncertainty* 3:283–305.

Scholz, John T., Jim Twombly, and Barbara Headrick. 1991. Street-level political controls over federal bureaucracy, *American Political Science Review* 85:829–850.

Scholz, John T. and Feng Heng Wei. 1986. Regulatory enforcement in a federalist system, *American Political Science Review* 80:1249–1270.

Scott, W. Richard. 1987. *Organizations: Rational, Natural, and Open Systems,* second edition. Englewood Cliffs, NJ: Prentice-Hall.

Seidman, Harold. 1980. *Politics, Position, and Power.* New York: Oxford University Press.

Selznick, Phillip. 1966. *T.V.A. and the Grass Roots.* New York: Harper and Row.

Shover, Neil, J. Lynxwiler, S. Groce, and D. Clelland. 1984. Regional variation in regulatory law enforcement: The Surface Mining Control and Reclamation Act of 1977. In *Enforcing Regulation.* K. Hawkins and J. M. Thomas, eds. Boston: Kluwer-Nijhoff Publishing, 1984.

Shover, Neil, John Lynxwiler, and Donald Clelland. (1983). *Developing a Regulatory Bureaucracy: The Office of Surface Mining Reclamation and Enforcement.* Washington, D.C.: National Institute of Justice.

Sigler, Jay A. and Joseph E. Murphy. 1988. *Interactive Corporate Compliance: An Alternative to Regulatory Compulsion.* New York: Quorum Books.

Silbey, Susan. 1984. The consequences of responsive regulation. In Keith Hawkins and John Thomas, eds. *Enforcing Regulation.* Boston: Kluwer-Nijhoff Publishing, 1984, pp. 145–168.

Smith, Robert S. 1986. Greasing the squeaky wheel: The relative productivity of OSHA complaint inspections, *Industrial and Labor Relations Review* 40:35–47.

Smith, Robert S. 1979. The impact of OSHA inspections on manufacturing injury rates, *Journal of Human Resources* 14:145–170.

Stone, Christopher D. 1975. *Where the Law Ends: Social Control of Corporate Behavior.* New York: Harper and Row.

Thompson, Frank J. and Michael J. Scicchitano. 1985. State implementation effort and federal regulatory policy: The case of occupational safety and health, *Journal of Politics* 47:687–703.

U.S. General Accounting Office. 1979. *How Effective are OSHA's Complaint Procedures?* Comptroller General's Report to Congress HRD-79-48.

Viscusi, W. Kip. 1986. The impact of occupational safety and health regulation, 1973–1983, *Rand Journal of Economics.*

Viscusi, W. Kip. 1979. The impact of occupational safety and health regulation, *Bell Journal of Economics* 10:117–140.

Williams, Bruce A. and Albert R. Matheny. 1984. Testing theories of social regulation: Hazardous waste regulation in the American states, *Journal of Politics* 46:428–458.

Wood, B. Dan. 1988. Principals, bureaucrats, and responsiveness in clean air enforcement, *American Political Science Review* 82:213–237.

V

TRANSPARENCY AND THE ADMINISTRATIVE STATE

16

Federal Information Policy and Administrative Law

Robert G. Vaughn *The American University, Washington, D.C.*

The perception that federal information provisions form an isolated and perhaps idiosyncratic body of law obscures many aspects of federal information law and policy. Moreover, this perception has impeded reform of federal information law and hidden important considerations for the future of such provisions. This chapter briefly explains some of the reasons for the perception of uniqueness but then explores how federal information provisions relate to the theoretical structure of administrative law. The chapter finally discusses the implications of this relationship for specific proposals regarding information provisions and for the future of federal information policy. In so doing, the chapter emphasizes the federal Freedom of Information Act (FOIA) but draws as well on examples and experience with other information provisions.

A number of factors may account for the perception of the uniqueness of federal information law. Information provisions, such as the FOIA, usually of government-wide scope, do not relate directly to the regulatory responsibilities of agencies as do, for example, many of the other provisions of the Administrative Procedure Act. Information provisions may seem directed primarily at an issue of governmental administration. Perhaps more important, debate has focused on the specifics of information laws, a focus that emphasizes the insularity of the field. Moreover, information provisions deviate in many significant ways from basic administrative law doctrines. These doctrinal deviations act to segregate public information laws. The Freedom of Information Act provides some examples.

The federal Freedom of Information Act established that government documents and records were public unless the government could properly claim one of nine exemptions. The act regulated public access and evidenced congressional concern with agency information practices and agency secrecy (1974 Source Book). This concern motivated exceptions from existing doctrines.

The FOIA created a number of exceptions to doctrines in administrative law. The act relied upon judicial enforcement initiated by requesters.[1] Although administrative law normally requires deference to the judgments of administrative agencies and directs review based on the administrative record, the FOIA provides that review of agency actions allegedly violating the FOIA is to be de novo.[2] A district court can create its own factual record and decide based on its own interpretation of the statute, whether or not the agency had violated the act.[3] This deviation from administrative doctrine reflected the importance that Congress attached to judicial enforcement.

An aggrieved party cannot normally seek judicial review until all agency remedies have been sought and denied. This doctrine of the exhaustion of administrative remedies reduces the need for judicial intervention by relying on agency correction of errors and by discouraging affected parties from pursuing redress in the courts. Amendments to the FOIA permit a requester to seek judicial review when an agency fails to respond within time limits established by the amendments.[4] This limitation of the doctrine of the exhaustion of administrative remedies restricts the role of agency decision-making.

Prior to the FOIA, a requester of government information could be required to articulate reasons for seeking the information that justified access (O'Reilly, 1979). Through this requirement agencies imposed "need to know" standards that significantly limited access to agency records. The need to know standard encouraged agencies to balance the interests of the requester in the documents against the reasons articulated by the agency for denying access. This standard, combined with agency discretion in its application, resulted in the denial of many requests. Under the FOIA, Congress required disclosure of documents and records unless the documents fell under one of the exemptions to the act.[5] The requester is not required to give any reason for seeking the documents and the burden is upon the agency to establish that the law permits withholding of the documents. These aspects of the act articulate a standard of "any person" access by which the motives of the requester or the requester's use of the information became irrelevant. Essentially all requesters are placed in the same group. Any-person access and allocation of the burden of persuasion to the agencies demonstrated a bias in favor of disclosure.

These deviations from traditional administrative law doctrines give the FOIA, and other information laws, a uniqueness that isolates them from the body of administrative law. An examination of the reasons for these deviations, however, shows that these provisions fit easily into the theoretical structure of administrative law. The isolation of information laws benefits analysis by creating a body of law that can be separately evaluated. The isolation retards analysis by minimizing the ways in which these information provisions are embedded in administrative law.

In exploring the relationship of information provisions to the theoretical structure of administrative law, this chapter relies on the ideals of administrative law used by Professor Thomas Sargentich to organize proposals for administrative reform (Sargentich, 1984). Although a brief summary does not capture the detail and subtlety of his analytical scheme, a summary can provide sufficient explanation to show how information policy reflects not specialized but general debates about administrative law.

THE THREE IDEALS OF ADMINISTRATIVE LAW

Professor Sargentich articulates three competing ideals of administrative law: the rule of law ideal, the public purposes ideal, and the democratic process ideal. These ideals reflect differing viewpoints regarding the appropriate character and scope of administrative law. According to Professor Sargentich, these ideals conflict with each other and constantly struggle for dominance in administrative law (Sargentich, 1984). Moreover, each ideal presents a core embodiment of its view, but one that conflicts with the practical realities of administrative practice. Therefore, each ideal has an alternative expression more acceptable to reality but less true to the underlying ideal. Each ideal is also accompanied by a methodology of decision-making (Sargentich, 1991). A review of these three ideals, their core embodiments and alternative expressions, and methodologies permit placement of information laws in the context of administrative law theory.

This chapter discusses how federal information laws, particularly the FOIA, rely upon each of these ideals. After discussing each of these ideals, the chapter explores how the weaknesses and contradictions in each ideal have influenced the application and development of federal information policy. The inconsistencies and failures of information policy relate directly to the contradictions and weaknesses of these ideals. Although the future of federal information laws requires specific changes and modifications in those laws, that future also requires recognition of the inconsistencies in administrative theory that information policy reflects.

Rule of Law Ideal

The rule of law ideal requires that administrative action rest upon positive law, preferably statutes (Sargentich, 1984). This ideal draws on contract theories of the state that require the consent of the governed. Therefore, the core embodiment of the rule of law ideal is formalism: that all exercises of public power must be guided by legal rules. This emphasis on legal rules is inconsistent with the immense discretion held by administrative officials and leads to the alternative expression of proceduralism. Proceduralism protects the individual from abuse of government power by requiring that administrative officials follow certain procedures before acting. Proceduralism, however, does not ultimately restrict discretion because it does not address the ability of administrative officials to act on the basis of vague, unarticulated powers that permit a number of substantive choices. The rule of law ideal relies on judicial reasoning as a principal methodology (Sargentich, 1991). This methodology manifests the importance of restrictions on the exercise of power by the application of specific legal rules.

Information provisions, particularly the FOIA, rest in part on justifications relying on the rule of law ideal. Reliance on the rule of law ideal is reflected not only in the justifications for several information provisions but also in their specific content. For example, central to the rule of law ideal is the application of existing and known standards. One of the most common justifications for the FOIA asserted that public access was necessary in order to avoid secret law (O'Reilly, 1979). Congress believed that agencies applied standards and procedures to the resolution of administrative disputes that were unknown to the parties. The availability of the applicable standards of decision stands as a central underpinning of the rule of law; without knowledge of the rules, it is impossible to believe that rules serve to limit administrative authority. Therefore, the FOIA requires that agencies make available to the public, without request, final opinions and orders in the adjudication of cases, statements of policy and interpretations adopted by the agency that have not been published in the *Federal Register,* and staff manuals and instructions that "affect a member of the public."[6] The Privacy Act likewise requires that agencies publish information regarding the character and scope of records maintained by the agency.[7]

Open meeting provisions, such as the Sunshine in Government Act[8] and the Federal Advisory Committee Act[9] also relate to the rule of law ideal. These provisions generally do not permit the public to participate in agency proceedings but do require that decisions be made in public proceedings. Although this openness helps to ensure that agency standards are known to the public, the concern regarding secret law seems subsidiary to ensuring that decision-makers follow the applicable rules. The Federal Advisory Committee Act particularly reflects this concern because of the fear that nongovernmental employees may improperly influence the application of administrative rules (Paladino, 1991). The emphasis on the control of abuse contained in these provisions as well in the FOIA presuppose pre-existing and specific standards against which the behavior of government officials may be judged.

Congress placed enforcement of the FOIA in the courts. This placement uses the principal methodology of the rule of law ideal, judicial reasoning, as the technique for enforcement of the act. Other information provisions, including the Privacy Act, and the Sunshine in Government Act, likewise rely on judicial enforcement.[10] This model of enforcement, of course, assumes the applicability of the rule of law ideal.

The concept of any-person access also implements the rule of law ideal. The genesis for the concept of any-person access rested on the congressional desire to remove agency discretion. Agencies must treat all requesters similarly; agencies could not evaluate the purposes or motives of requesters.

As will be examined below, failures in judicial enforcement of the act reflect the weaknesses in formalism, the core embodiment of the rule of law ideal. In particular, the substantial agency discretion that remains in the application of information laws illustrates the limits of formalism. With these information provisions, proceduralism is an inadequate substitute. In paradoxical fashion, the reliance on formalism has actually increased agency, and judicial, discretion and thereby weakened information policy relying on the rule of law ideal.

Public Purposes Ideal

The public purposes ideal stresses the role of administrative agencies in accomplishing important public goals (Sargentich, 1984). The ideal draws on the importance attached to the affirmative tasks of government in policy-making and in administration. Therefore, the core embodiment is instrumentalism, "by which is meant the familiar notion that the significant worth of a policy inheres in its success as an instrument of the public good" (Sargentich, 1984). This instrumentalism focuses on carrying out the public purposes of an agency's enabling legislation or choosing between alternatives based on agency judgments regarding the public good, as in cost-benefit analysis. By focusing on rational analysis, instrumentalism leads to ever-expanding analytical schemes that inescapably become vague and devoid of substantive content. Indeed, such an approach can eventually become the guise for political manipulation. These weaknesses lead to an attempt to achieve the public good through the market and private decision-making rather than principally through administrative agencies. This alternative expression, however, disavows a central role for the administrative process. The public purposes ideal relies on expertise as its principal methodology (Sargentich, 1991). The methodology manifests the ideal's reliance on technical judgments to achieve the public good.

Information provisions, particularly the FOIA, rest also upon the public purposes ideal. Although not central to justifications for the FOIA, the improvement of agency decision-making procedures emerged as one of the arguments for the act and for other open government provisions (O'Reilly, 1979; McGarity and Shapiro, 1980). This justification was often paired with, but differs significantly from, the argument that these provisions control abuse. Information provisions encourage better articulation of the rationale for decisions and, by making these rationales available, the premises as well as the techniques of analysis can be challenged and refined by others. This argument, as does instrumentalism, sees administrative decisions as almost scientific in character.

The instrumentalist vision of agency behavior, however, conflicts in important ways with the concept of openness underlying information provisions. The exemption to the FOIA protecting agency deliberations illustrates this conflict.[11] The deliberative process exemption rests on the need of bureaucratic organizations for secrecy. An agency needs secrecy to canvass all alternative courses of action that could be selected based on the application of rational criteria to the particular circumstances. It is assumed that governmental deliberations need to be frank, addressing rational criteria without yielding to existing political or social pressures.

This instrumentalist vision of agency behavior justifies considerable secrecy. In this sense, the deliberative process exemption exalts bureaucratic efficiency above the competing interest of openness and represents the incompatibility of instrumentalism with publicity that stands at the center of the rule of law ideal and with participation and oversight central to the democratic process ideal. These aspects of instrumentalism help explain why information policy turned first to the alternative expression of the public purposes ideal: use of private decision-making to determine the public good.

From the inception of the FOIA, Congress was aware that information acquired through the FOIA would be used for a variety of purposes other than evaluating the conduct of government officials (Hearings, 1965). Critics of the act have emphasized the acquisition of much information for commercial or business purposes (Scalia, 1982) while proponents have noted the amount of health and safety information provided to consumers by information provisions (Hendricks, 1982). By 1974, Congress, at least, perceived the clearinghouse function of the FOIA as a central one (Source Book, 1974). This clearinghouse function, by providing information to commercial enterprises and to consumers, uses the market and private decision-making to accomplish the public good and principally views agencies as sources of the relevant information. This perception of the FOIA represents the alternative expression of the public purposes ideal.

The FOIA did not address the management of government documents and records. The FOIA did not require that documents be created or indeed even if they be maintained.[12] To many the failure of the FOIA to cover information management issues reduced its effectiveness (Source Book, 1974). Subsequent legislation, such as the Federal Privacy Act, did resolve issues regarding the acquisition, maintenance, and use of records.[13] More recent legislation, such as the Computer Matching Act[14] and the Computer Security Act,[15] address in detail the management of federal records. In the Privacy Act and these recent information provisions, federal information policy has focused much more on expertise in the management of information and records. This focus on expertise highlights the methodology of the public purposes ideal.

Commentators have noted that federal information policy lacks consistency and coherence (ABA Commemorative Conference, 1991). Information provisions contain differing, often conflicting, judgments, regarding similar information and considerable discrepancy in the treatment of information related issues exists among federal agencies (Vaughn, 1991). Implicit in these comments is the perception that unification of policy requires resolution of the issues in information policy under rational criteria. In addition, these comments contain the suggestion that more centralized administrative direction is required. These implications mirror tenets of the public purposes ideal.

Federal agencies increasingly keep documents and records in electronic form. This change in technology has generated recommendations that require modifying the role of government agencies by making these agencies responsible for developing an information policy, including dissemination of information, consistent with the regulatory goals of the agency (Perritt, 1989). In some instances, an agency might wish to rely principally on the private market to accomplish its information dissemination goals. In making these judgments, the most widely known proposal offers to the agencies cost-benefit analysis (Perritt, 1989). These proposals reflect instrumentalism, the core embodiment of the public purposes ideal.

As will be examined below, recent developments in federal information policy confront the core embodiment of the public purposes ideal: instrumentalism. These developments suggest a change in emphasis from the market-based alternative to the core embodiment. Partly because of the perceived isolation of public information law, discussion of the future has focused on specific proposals for change. Thus far, the discussion has generally ignored the consequences of aligning federal information policy around instrumentalism. The contradictions and weaknesses of instrumentalism permit an examination of the future from the perspective of administrative theory rather than from an analysis of specific proposals.

Democratic Process Ideal

The democratic process ideal rests on a participatory and representative decision-making process in which agency officials consider the views of those affected by administrative decisions (Sargentich, 1984). This ideal sees the administrative process as primarily a political one and as its core embodiment relies on public participation in that process. Because public participation conflicts with the bureaucratic structure of administrative decision and challenges the principle that public employees are politically neutral actors (a principle basic to the modern civil service), the ideal offers an alternative expression of oversight by politically responsible officials. This alternative expression, of course, abandons direct public participation central to the ideal. The methodology of this ideal is politics (Sargentich, 1991): the process of balancing and compromising affected interests. This methodology manifests the judgment that the administrative process is a political one.

The rhetoric of federal information law has been strongly antibureaucratic. The passage of the FOIA in 1966 followed years of hearings documenting bureaucratic abuse and arrogance in the administration of the information provision of the Administrative Procedure Act (ABA Commemorative Conference, 1991). The 1974 amendments to the FOIA expressed congressional anger at the administration of the act (Source Book, 1974). These amendments included the first provision that permitted a federal official to be held personally accountable for the arbitrary and capricious withholding of information.[16] Likewise, the Federal Privacy Act followed extensive hearings by Senator Sam Ervin's Constitutional Rights Subcommittee regarding invasions of individual privacy by the federal bureaucracy (Legislative History of Privacy Act, 1974). The Sunshine in Government Act (Government-in-the Sunshine Source Book, 1976) and the Federal Advisory Committee (Federal Advisory Committee Act and Source Book, 1978) reflected similar suspicions about the bureaucracy. The legislative history of federal information law is replete with calls to alter the practices of the bureaucracy and to return government to the people. This rhetoric shares with the democratic process ideal's core embodiment of participation a basic inconsistency with bureaucratic organization and function.

Information provisions also directly relate to the core concept of participation. Citizens must be armed with information to participate directly in the administrative process. Rights of participation such as standing to appear and the right to intervene in proceedings mean little without a right to information. The sense that citizens are the ultimate repositories of political power requiring information to be effective is aptly summarized by Madison's quote, one that often prefaces discussions of the FOIA. "A popular government without popular information or the means of acquiring it, is but a prologue to a farce or a tragedy or perhaps both" (Source Book, 1974).

As Professor Sargentich's analysis, however, would predict, federal information policy has not turned to the core embodiment of public participation (Sargentich, 1984). Information provisions do not provide persons with any right to participate in the administrative process. For example, although the Sunshine in Government Act and the Federal Advisory Committee Act require that certain meetings be open to the public, these provisions do not give members of the public any right to speak at these meetings or to participate otherwise. Document and record laws, like the FOIA, do not purport to permit public participation in agency processes or in any agency decision. One could argue that persons who obtain information either through documents and records or by observing directly an administrative proceeding could use that information to identify any rights of participation and to make those rights more meaningful. Still, it is not public information provisions that provide the right of participation.

Public information law relies more on the alternative expression of the democratic process ideal: oversight by politically responsible officials. The FOIA permits persons who obtain information about government decisions to respond to those decisions politically. When citizens are aware of the actions of the bureaucracy and understand the justifications for those actions, citizens can oppose or support those actions through the political means available to them. The right of political participation, however, requires knowledge of the need to act and information to frame arguments and objections. In this sense, the view that the FOIA is a statutory enactment of a right to information that empowers the First Amendment right of free speech captures nicely the concept of political oversight.

Federal information provisions also sought to equalize information resources. The express aim of these provisions is to give citizens and agencies a rough equality of relevant information as a basis for political conflict regarding bureaucratic actions. These provisions also contain an implicit goal: to equalize informational resources between interest groups who contend in political arenas. Information provisions tend to give less highly organized interests information to battle with more highly organized interests, particularly regarding administrative action affecting both groups. In this context, the disputes regarding the rights of submitters of information to the government address the ability of all groups to use the methodology of the democratic process ideal: political conflict.

As will be examined below, the practical difficulties confronting the users of public information laws, particularly the FOIA, reduce the ability of these provisions to implement even the alternative expression of the democratic process ideal. It is ironic that the strong antibureaucratic character of information provisions may have provoked a reaction beyond that justified by the effects of these provisions. Also, the conflicts emerging between categories of requesters and between requesters and submitters raise issues of "information equity" that directly concern the effectiveness of political oversight of bureaucratic action.

APPLICATION OF THE THREE IDEALS IN INFORMATION POLICY

Rule of Law Ideal

Despite reliance on the rule of law ideal, Congress was unable to eliminate administrative discretion from the FIOA and other information laws and the courts have failed in some significant ways in structuring and controlling the exercise of this discretion. The FOIA provides some examples.

Although the FOIA adopts the principle that government records are public, the act gives agencies considerable discretion in applying the nine exemptions that permit agencies to withhold requested documents.[17] These exemptions incorporate interests of the government and of private parties that justify protection. The discretion of agencies is substantial in that with most of the exemptions an agency may decide to release the records even though the records are covered by one of the exemptions.[18] It is not surprising, given the breadth of the exemptions and the discretion entailed, that the bulk of litigation under the act concerns interpretations of the exemptions.

Interpretation of the exemptions goes directly to the heart of agency discretion and tests the ability of the FOIA to rely on the specific legal rules as limitations. As Professor

Sargentich's general analysis would suggest (Sargentich, 1984), courts have often failed to limit agency discretion. Two examples illustrate the judicial failure to structure discretion: first, the courts' interpretation of the exemption for records classified for purposes of national security; second, the courts' general approach to interpretation of the exemptions.

The first exemption, enacted as part of the FOIA in 1966, concerned national security documents and records and exempted documents "specifically required by executive order to be kept secret in the interest of national defense or foreign policy." The structure of the exemptions and subsequent legislative history suggest that Congress sought to limit the discretion of federal agencies in claiming this exemption (Source Book, 1974). As with the act in general, Congress relied on judicial review to implement this limitation.

In 1973, Representative Patsy Mink, among others, requested information regarding a pending underground nuclear test in Alaska. The Environmental Protection Agency refused to release the documents, claiming that as classified documents they fell under the exemption.

The United States Supreme Court ruled that courts could not examine the propriety of executive agencies' classification decisions.[19] If appropriate government officials informed a federal court that requested documents were classified, a court must of necessity yield to that determination and conclude that the exemption applied.[20] Therefore, in camera review of documents was not permissible and the provision of the FOIA that mandated release of nonexempt portions of documents that could be segregated did not apply.[21]

The Supreme Court rested its ruling on interpretations of the legislative history of the exemption but emphasized the discretion granted to officials dealing with national security information.[22] The Court also asserted that federal judges lacked the experience and expertise to evaluate the decisions of appropriate government officials and that deference was required to executive classification actions.[23]

This ruling effectively eliminated judicial review of executive classification decisions. The rule of law ideal, underlying the FOIA, failed once again to control the reality of administrative discretion.

In the 1974 amendments to the FOIA, Congress expressly rejected the Supreme Court's interpretation of the exemption. Congress recognized that the Supreme Court's interpretation undermined the basic structure of the act relying on judicial review. The rejection of the Supreme Court's interpretation was reflected both in the congressional deliberations and in the text of the amendment. Several members of Congress reasserted the importance of de novo review, including in camera inspection, as a means of limiting executive discretion (Source Book, 1974). The language of the exemption was altered to require that documents and records falling under the exemption must be "in fact properly classified."

In vetoing the 1974 amendments, President Ford gave as one of the reasons, the change in the (b)(1) exemption (Source Book, 1974). Congress overrode the veto, thus, enacting the amendments and through the (b)(1) exemption reaffirming judicial review as a mechanism for limiting administrative discretion. Even under the revised version, however, the executive retained the authority to establish the criteria for classification.[24]

Subsequent interpretation of the exemption reminds us of the weaknesses of formalism, the core embodiment of the rule of law ideal. Through a number of devices, federal courts have routinely refused to implement the 1974 amendment to the (b)(1) exemption. Courts have relied heavily upon agency affidavits describing withheld information as properly classified under the relevant classification order and relegated in camera inspection to a limited role in enforcing the requirement of proper classification.[25] Moreover, agency affidavits are often viewed only by judges depriving attorneys for requesters of even a limited ability to argue regarding the propriety of the classification.[26] The combination of these techniques has undermined the concept of the de novo review and reflects continuing judicial concern about the courts' lack of experience and expertise.[27]

To an extent, Congress has also yielded to a similar concern about judicial review of executive discretion. Amendments to other legislation have effectively eliminated application of the FOIA to a significant portion of records of the Central Intelligence Agency.[28]

Although the national security exemption concerns extremely sensitive documents regarding which broad discretion would be expected, the interpretation of the (b)(1) exemption illustrates the problem of discretion that plagues application of all of the exemptions. The approach to interpretation of the other exemptions demonstrates the commonality of the problem. In fact, interpretation of the FOIA shows that unquestioning reliance on formalism not only can be ineffective in limiting discretion but also can be harmful to information policy.

Courts recognized early that the discretion embodied in the exemptions threatened the more specific rules requiring access. Therefore, the Supreme Court articulated an approach to interpretation of the exemptions that required that the exemptions be narrowly interpreted.[29] Commentators noted, however, that the Supreme Court often adopted the broader rather than the more narrow interpretation, while reciting the canon of narrow interpretation of the exemptions (Moon, 1985). Recently Justice Scalia, not himself a supporter of the FOIA (Scalia, 1982), expressly challenged the commitment of the Court to the canon of narrow interpretation of the exemptions.[30] He argued that if the canon were to be meaningful, it must mean, at least, that the Court would choose the most narrow reading permitted by the language of the exemption.[31] Justice Scalia demonstrated how, in the case before it, the Court had abandoned this canon of interpretation.[32]

The Court's opinion reflects instead an approach in which the Court balances the governmental or private interests to be protected by the particular exemption against the policy or purpose of access to government documents.[33] As a practical matter, the Court has articulated interests to be served by an exemption and used these interests rather than the canon of narrow construction as the primary guide to interpretation. Of course, this approach emphasizes the interests in withholding.

The attempts of Congress to limit discretion through any-person access have sharpened the focus on the interests in withholding and weakened the importance of access embodied in any-person access. In establishing the concept of any-person access, Congress sought to limit agency discretion in evaluating the reasons for access and thereby to establish the principle that government documents and records are public. In so doing, however, the law removed from inquiry the interests justifying disclosure. As a result, debate and litigation assumed the reasons for access but emphasized the reasons for withholding. This emphasis on the interests supporting withholding has given them a concreteness and detail often not given to the interests supporting disclosure. When combined with the Supreme Court's balancing approach, the unintended result of any-person access, an important aspect of formalism, has been to elevate the interests in withholding and gradually to expand the scope of administrative discretion.

It is not surprising, given the failure of the FOIA to guarantee access by limiting discretion, that a good deal of the FOIA, particularly amendments to the original act, focus on procedures as a method of ensuring access. Illustrative of this proceduralism are the 1974 and 1986 amendments to the act. A good portion, perhaps the most substantial portion, of the 1974 amendments concerned procedures including time limits for agency response,[34] provisions for administrative appeals,[35] and criteria for charging fees for complying with requests.[36] Also, portions of the 1986 amendments addressed issues regarding fees and fee waivers.[37]

These procedural rules have not been particularly effective even on their own terms. Many of the procedures, such as those regarding appeals and fees, have not been easy to apply or to interpret. These procedures have not significantly reduced agency discretion nor ensured that the rules regarding access would be clearly applied.

Perhaps a more telling indictment of proceduralism's reliance on rules lies in the lack of any serious attempt to enforce the 10 day limit on an agency response to an FOIA request. Neither the agencies nor the courts have applied this clear and unambiguous procedural rule. The principal justification for the refusal asserts that the lack of agency resources prevents agencies from complying with the rule. Good faith processing of requests has replaced the specific time limits established by Congress. This justification for failure to comply with the rule also rejects a clear congressional judgment because included in the rule must have been a congressional direction to agencies to allocate existing resources so that the directive could be satisfied. That the rule addresses the possibility of limited extensions in particular circumstances emphasizes that the justification rejects congressional judgments. Lack of compliance with a clear procedural rule challenges the underpinnings of the rule of law ideal.

The analysis above risks the conclusion that the FOIA has failed to open government documents and records to the public. This conclusion would ignore the many accomplishments of the law, including the availability of significant amounts of important information and the alteration of agency behavior and expectations. The analysis above does demonstrate the weaknesses of formalism when confronting agency discretion and the failure of proceduralism to substitute adequately. These weaknesses suggest the limits of formalism and caution that reliance on it may lead to frustration and damage to the goals of the FOIA. The analysis above also suggests the limitations of the rule of law ideal and directs attention to those strains of federal information policy that rely on other ideals of administrative law.

Public Purposes Ideal

Given the compromises inherent in the application of the rule of law ideal and experience demonstrating the weaknesses of formalism and the limits of proceduralism, federal information policy has turned to aspects of the public purposes ideal. The increasing prominence of the clearinghouse function of the FOIA exemplifies this change in orientation.

Although the clearinghouse function of the FOIA was implicit in the act, the 1974 Amendments marked recognition of this function. As discussed above, this clearinghouse function represents the alternative expression of the public purposes ideal: use of the market in making decisions regarding the public good. Many experts now believe that all has been accomplished that can be with the present structure of the FOIA and that the future now requires greater use of the clearinghouse function (ABA Commemorative Conference, 1991). Indeed, these prognostications, implicitly recognize the limits of the rule of law ideal and, without specifically articulating that judgment, seek salvation in another ideal.

The clearinghouse function represents the alternative expression of the public purposes ideal. Reliance on the market to establish the public good reduces the role and function of federal agencies. Two recent developments, however, point to the core embodiment of the public purposes ideal: instrumentalism. These two developments, an emphasis on information management and the electronic dissemination of information, share much with instrumentalism.

The FOIA, itself, did not address information management issues. As early as 1974, however, Senator Sasser commented on the lack of uniform standards, training, or administration of the FOIA. He called for more centralized standards and procedures for managing information (Source Book, 1974).

Subsequent legislation focused more specifically on information management issues. The Federal Privacy Act regulated how agencies could acquire, maintain, and use some specific types of records.[38] The Federal Paperwork Reduction Act, the Computer Security Act,[39] and the Computer Matching Act also addressed issues of information management. The Computer Security Act[40] and the Computer Matching Act[41] directed specific management procedures. Legislation and administrative practice have increasingly perceived information policy as involving issues of management relying on agency experience and expertise in administration.

Senator Sasser's assertion of the lack of uniformity in federal information policy has become more and more obvious. The passage of a number of information-related provisions has created conflicts between these provisions, has illustrated the lack of a coherent information policy, and has highlighted inconsistencies within specific information statutes.

The passage of the Federal Privacy Act generated an energetic and never completely resolved debate regarding the relationship between the Privacy Act and the FOIA (O'Reilly, 1979). Although the courts and Congress have attempted to reconcile these conflicts, some commentators do not believe that the reconciliation has been successful (O'Reilly, 1979). In addition, more general conflicts between policies of privacy and access are in a perpetual tension that cannot be resolved simply by modifications in the Privacy Act and in the FOIA.

Other information provisions embody different, often conflicting, decisions regarding access to the same or similar information. Two examples illustrate the inconsistencies. First, the whistle-blower protection provisions permit employees, in some circumstances, to release documents that fall within one of the exemptions even if an agency has decided to withhold the documents under the FOIA.[42] Therefore, these laws contain conflicting judgments regarding the role of agencies in determining information policy.

Second, the Consumer Product Safety Act restricts the access of certain health and safety information that would otherwise be available under the FOIA and restricts the discretion to release information that agency officials would enjoy under the FOIA (Zollers and Barry, 1991). The two laws reach differing conclusions regarding the weight to be given to manufacturer interests in withholding. As a result, different federal agencies possessing similar documents regarding health and safety issues are bound by conflicting standards (Zollers and Barry, 1991).

Similar inconsistencies can be found in the administration of the FOIA among federal agencies. Agencies treat similar records differently. Agency regulations can vary, agencies present differing interpretations of the law, and treat similar documents and records differently (Vaughn, 1991). Moreover, both Congress and the executive lack information regarding significant issues of administration of the act that makes difficult additional comparison of administration among the agencies.

The emphasis on information management and the recognition of the lack of coherent government-wide information policies suggest the need for greater centralization of administration. Many see the future of the FOIA more closely tied to agency expertise in management and administration. These suggestions implicitly require greater agency determinations of policy based on criteria developed by them.

Indeed, during the 1980s, the Office of Management and Budget's Office of Information and Regulatory Affairs used the Paperwork Reduction Act as authority for its review of agency paperwork requests and regulatory proposals (Funk, 1987). The experience with the Paperwork Reduction Act exemplifies how the desire for rational criteria in information management supports more centralized administrative direction.

Another recent development has led to more specific proposals relating federal information policy to agency management and to the agencies' determination of policy. These proposals explicitly rely on agency determination of the public good and appeal directly to instrumentalism.

Federal agencies, increasingly, store, retrieve, and disseminate information through electronic means. This change in technology required some interpretations of the FOIA including the meaning of the term record, of when a new document is being created, and of the application of fee provisions. This change in technology also permitted a reassessment of the role of agencies in information policy.

A study conducted for the Administrative Conference of the United States by Professor Henry Perritt, leading to recommendations of the Conference, addressed both the issues of interpretation and of the role of agencies in setting information policy. The study resolved the interpretative issues in favor of application of the FOIA to electronically held records (Perritt, 1989).

The study and recommendations also asserted that the change in technology for maintaining and disseminating records permitted an alteration in the ways in which agencies assessed their roles in information policy (Perritt, 1989). Given the potential for dissemination of electronically held records, the Administrative Conference recommendations identified varying levels of dissemination ranging from "access," in which agencies simply turn over electronic data for further processing; to "disclosure," in which agencies make records available electronically to persons in public reading rooms; to "dissemination," in which agencies take an active role in making electronically held records available to the public in user-friendly form (Perritt, 1989). Agencies could decide, based on their own assessment of their missions, to choose among the varying approaches, perhaps adopting different approaches for different types of records.

The recommendations also noted that agencies should decide whether to disseminate information themselves by creating the menus and other programming to make electronically held information widely available or by relying on private companies to accomplish the same goal. Once again, an agency was to determine which approach best served the public good.

This reliance on agency expertise in determining the public good reflects the tenets of instrumentalism. In part, agencies could determine the public good by looking to their own mission statements. The recommendations, however, pointed to cost-benefit analysis in determining the appropriate level of access and in deciding whether to rely on agency resources or on private enterprise (Perritt, 1989).

These recent developments, pointing directly to instrumentalism, seek to alter the orientation of federal information policy. By giving agencies a greater role in policy, proponents hope to improve the administration and efficiency of information policy. These proposals also seek to identify agency interests with requester interests and to create incentives for much broader public access to government information (ABA Commemorative Conference, 1991). Proponents speak of point-of-purchase information for consumers and access to a wide range of government data bases by any person having a modem.

These proposals, although important and perhaps supportable, have failed to consider the limitations of instrumentalism. Even in these proposals, which articulate the costs and benefits to be considered, cost-benefit analysis remains vague and open-ended. Professor Sargentich's analysis would predict that instrumentalism will fail to accomplish the goals of reformers because instrumentalism will permit agency determination of the public good under increasingly vague general standards. At best these will fail to guide agency decisions and at worst will provide the justifications for political actions that may undercut the goals of the reform (Sargentich, 1984). These proposals also ignore the strong tension between an instrumentalist vision of agency behavior and the commitment to openness underlying public information provisions.

Democratic Process Ideal

Although federal information provisions rely on oversight, the alternative expression of the democratic process ideal—the practical difficulties confronting the users of public information laws, particularly the FOIA—reduce the ability of these provisions to provide information that permit citizens to challenge bureaucratic action politically. The FOIA provides several examples.

Users of the FOIA face delays that limit the usefulness of the FOIA. A number of studies have identified delay as a principal impediment to the proper functioning of the Act (ABA Commemorative Conference, 1991; Alternate Dispute Resolution Hearings, 1987). Delay occurs at all stages in the process of seeking information, including response to the initial request and administrative and judicial review (Alternate Dispute Resolution Hearings, 1987). Requesters can wait many months to receive an agency response and delays of years in completing the administrative and judicial process are not unknown. The time limits of the act have become largely irrelevant in the administration of the law, in part because the courts are unable to police these limits effectively. Courts are unwilling to act because delay will accompany judicial action, particularly if an agency is processing requests in good faith. Therefore, cases appear in which requesters asked to be moved to the head of the agency queue.[43]

Delay discourages many requesters. As important, delay makes information law less useful in providing a basis for political oversight of agency decisions. If requesters must wait months or even years for relevant information, administrative decisions and actions may have already been implemented before groups possess sufficient information to challenge them.

Delay results in part from a lack of resources. The allocation of resources, however, rests with the agencies and the administration of information laws can be seen as an irritant disconnected from more specific agency missions. Not uncommonly, FOIA officers serve part-time or are the newest attorneys in an agency counsel's office.

Delay can also reflect hostility toward requesters and toward the goals of the FOIA. For example, an examination of FOIA court decisions from 1980 to 1984 discovered dozens of opinions in which federal judges admonished federal officials for administration of the law (Vaughn, 1984). Studies of the Sunshine in Government Act (Common Cause, 1977, 1978) and the Federal Advisory Committee Act (Paladino, 1991) also suggest agency noncompliance with the requirements of these laws. This hostility, in part, may represent the reaction of government officials to the antibureaucratic rhetoric of information provisions.

Requesters also lack sufficient knowledge to ensure that provisions like the FOIA will provide the basis for political oversight of bureaucratic action. To be effective, information must be acquired when it is useful. Before requesters can seek documents, they must be aware of the existence of the records. Bureaucratic action could proceed to a point where resistance or reversal would be difficult before a potential requester would learn of the need to acquire information. Requesters lack knowledge of when to request information.

Requesters also lack knowledge of the character or description of the records that they seek (Alternate Dispute Resolution Hearings, 1987). This lack of knowledge impedes requests and administrative appeals, as well as judicial review of administrative action. Requesters can often make only the most general requests and are unable to evaluate agency responses or to respond to agency arguments that documents are exempt. Although the courts have developed procedures to address the inability of requesters to address agency arguments,[44] these procedures are not completely effective and do not apply to the administrative process. Requesters are left at a considerable disadvantage in the use of information provisions as a means to accomplish political oversight.

Many requesters are discouraged by the costs of requests. The costs of requests are more likely to screen individual requesters or requesters representing groups that lack substantial economic resources.

Congress addressed these concerns in the 1974 amendments by providing attorney fees for requesters and by permitting agencies to waive or reduce fees.[45] In 1986 Congress modified the fee waiver provisions, responding in part to restrictive interpretations of the 1974 provisions.[46]

These congressional attempts, while useful, have not eliminated the difficulties for many requesters. The attorney fees provisions does not apply to the administrative process and the grant of attorney fees is not automatic;[47] in addition, determination of the amount of attorney fees can itself be the source of some controversy.[48] Judicial interpretations of the 1986 changes in the fee waiver provisions do not represent a dramatic break from restrictive interpretations of the previous provisions.[49]

The attorney fee and fee waiver provisions represent the first congressional attempts to differentiate between categories of requesters. The legislative history of the attorney fees provisions differentiated public interest and media requesters from others and suggested that requesters with a commercial interest would rarely be entitled to attorney fees (Source Book, 1974). The 1986 amendments to the fee waiver provision set out three categories of requesters regarding the cost of requests that could appropriately be charged against them.[50] Once again, the most substantial charges were permitted against commercial requesters.

Although these provisions reflect many goals, they demonstrate some concern with "information equity." Commercial interests are more likely to have the resources and, in some instances, the relationship with agency personnel to acquire information. Less wealthy or well organized groups are disadvantaged. The attorney fees and fee waiver provisions help to redress the imbalance in resources.

Some recent proposals place more emphasis on differentiating groups of requesters. For example, different categories of requesters could enjoy different procedures or perhaps different avenues for relief from denials. Experience with the fee waiver provisions suggests that this approach falters because of the difficulty in defining groups or types of requesters. For example, trade associations of large economic interests could create newsletters that might qualify as media requesters.[51]

The debate regarding the rights of submitters of information, however, portends rules and procedures likely to impede "information equity." Much of the literature on this debate sees the principal conflict as between privacy and access, balancing the interests of submitters against the interests of those seeking the information (O'Reilly, 1979).

This debate can also be viewed as an important one regarding "information equity," an equality of access necessary if all interests are able to use political oversight as a method of controlling bureaucratic behavior. Aside from issues of the personal privacy of individuals protected by a specific exemption,[52] the interests of submitters are normally those of commercial interests who desire, for a variety of reasons, to protect information submitted to the government. Although requesters may themselves be large economic or commercial enterprises, many requesters are individuals or smaller, less well organized, interest groups. Particularly in areas regarding public health and safety, requesters are more likely to be individuals or representatives of more diverse groups. Therefore, the debate at one level addresses whether all groups affected by administrative action will possess the information resources necessary to seek political redress of that action.

The procedural and substantive rights granted to submitters reduce "information equity" and the effectiveness of political oversight for many interests. An executive order issued by President Reagan imposes procedural requirements that delay response to requesters and focus agency decision-making on the interests of submitters (Executive Order 12,600, 1987). Some statutory provisions, such as the Consumer Product Safety Act, elevate the interests of submitters above those of requesters (Zollers and Barry, 1991).

Federal information laws, particularly the FOIA, rely on the alternative expression of the democratic process ideal. The practical difficulties confronting users of these laws have significantly reduced the effectiveness of them in permitting political oversight of bureaucratic action.

CONCLUSION

Although perceived as an isolated body of law, federal information provisions are firmly embedded in administrative theory. An application of Professor Sargentich's analytical model demonstrates that information provisions draw on all aspects of the three ideals for the administrative process. The reliance of information policy on each of these ideals ties information policy to administrative theory. Conflicts regarding information policy inescapably participate in major debates about theories of administrative legitimacy and decision-making.

An examination of the weaknesses of the core embodiments of two of the ideals illuminates issues in information policy in a new light and permits examination of them from a new perspective. For example, uncritical use of formalism to control administrative discretion can lead only to frustration and perhaps to damage to information policy; attempts to alter the role of agencies in forming information policy by aligning information policy around instrumentalism ignore the weaknesses of instrumentalism and invite a failure easily predicted from the perspective of administrative theory. In addition, application of the alternative expression of the democratic process ideal—political oversight—provides an important basis for examining the effectiveness of information provisions.

Because the three ideals of administrative law of necessity conflict with one another, recognition of how information laws use these three ideals is crucial to the future. Recognition of the relationships between information policy and administrative theory prevents the repetition of common errors, illuminates choices previously hidden, reminds us of the limits of these approaches, and identifies the compromises and frustrations that cannot be avoided. Placement of information policy in the context of administrative theory promises significant advantages for information law and policy.

NOTES

1. 5 U.S.C. § 552(a)(4)(D).
2. *Idem.*
3. *Idem.*
4. *Idem* § 552(a)(b)(A).
5. *Idem* § 552(a)(3).
6. *Idem* § 552(a)(2)(C).
7. *Idem* § 552a(2)(5).
8. *Idem* § 552 b.
9. *Idem* App. II.
10. *Idem* §§ 5522, 5526.
11. *Idem* § 552(b)(5). The exemption exempts information falling under common law privileges from discovery enjoyed by the government. The primary privilege, however, has been the deliberative process privilege.
12. *Kissinger v. Reporters Committee for Freedom of the Press,* 445 U.S. 136 (1980); *Forsham v. Harris,* 445 U.S. 169 (1980).
13. 5 U.S.C. § 552 a(d)(e).
14. P.L. 100-903 is an amendment to the Privacy Act.
15. P.L. 100-235.
16. 5 U.S.C. § 552(4)(F).
17. 5 U.S.C. § 552 (b).
18. *Chrysler Corp. v. Brown,* 441 U.S. 281 (1979). The Privacy Act eliminates agency discretion

regarding documents falling under the (b)(6) exemption protecting against clearly unwarranted invasions of personal privacy, and the Trade Secrets Act reduces agency discretion regarding the release of certain business records.

19. *Environmental Protection Agency v. Mink,* 410 U.S. 73 (1973).
20. 410 U.S. at 95.
21. 410 U.S. at 84.
22. 410 U.S. at 83-84, 95.
23. 410 U.S. at 95.
24. 5 U.S.C. § 552 (b)(1).
25. See, for example, *Weisman v. CIA,* 565 F.2d 692 (D.C. Cir. 1977); *Stein v. Dept. of Justice,* 662 F.2d 1245 (7th Cir. 1981); *Hoch v. CIA,* 593 F. Supp. 675 (D.D.C. 1984); *Branch v. FBI,* 658 F. Supp. 204 (D.D.C. 1987); *Hayden v. NSA,* 608 F.2d 1386, 1387 (D.C. Cir. 1974). Some courts have placed less emphasis on agency affidavits, e.g., *Ray v. Turner,* 587 F.2d 1187 (D.C. Cir. 1978).
26. *Phillippi v. CIA,* 546 F.2d 1009 (D.C. Cir. 1976); *Hayden v. NSA,* 608 F.2d 1381 (D.C. Cir. 1979); *Schlesinger v. CIA,* 591 F. Supp. 60 (D.D.C. 1984) (plaintiff's counsel excluded from in camera review); *Weberman v. NSA,* 507 F. Supp. 117 (S.D.N.Y. 1981).
27. *Weismann v. CIA,* 565 F.2d 692, 697 (D.C. Cir. 1977); *Stein v. Dept. of Justice,* 662 F.2d 1245, 1254 (7th Cir. 1981).
28. 50 U.S.C. § 431 (exemption of "operational" files of the CIA from FOIA requirements to search for records and to review them).
29. *Department of the Air Force v. Rose,* 425 U.S. 352 (1976); *FBI v. Abramson,* 456 U.S. 615 (1982); *United States Department of Justice v. Julian,* 486 U.S. 1 (1988).
30. *John Doe Agency v. John Doe Corp.,* 110 S. Ct. 471, 480-481 (1989).
31. 110 S. Ct. at 480.
32. 110 S. Ct. at 480-481.
33. *U.S. Department of Justice v. Reporters Committee for Freedom of the Press,* 109 S. Ct. 1468 (1989).
34. 5 U.S.C. § 552 (a)(6)(A)(i).
35. *Idem* § 552 (a)(6)(A)(ii).
36. *Idem* § 552 (a)(4)(A).
37. *Idem.*
38. *Idem* § 552 a(e).
39. 44 U.S.C. § 3501.
40. P.L. 100-235.
41. P.L. 100-503.
42. 5 U.S.C. § 2602 (b)(8) permits the disclosure of certain information if its release is not prohibited by law. The exemptions to the FOIA are generally not prohibitions against disclosure but only authorizations to disclose because agencies have discretion to release documents that fall under one of the exemptions.
43. See, for example, *Exner v. FBI,* 443 F. Supp. 1349 (S.D. Cal. 1978).
44. *Vaughn v. Rosen,* 484 F.2d 820 (D.C. Cir. 1973), cert. denied, 415 U.S. 977 (1974) establishes requirements that agencies provide an itemized index of withheld records describing the document and the reasons for the withholding.
45. 5 U.S.C. § 552 (a)(4)(A), (E).
46. Anti-Drug Abuse Act of 1986, P.L. 99-570, title I, subtitle N, §§ 1801-1804.
47. The Court retains discretion to award fees to a "prevailing" requester.
48. *Consumers Union v. Board of the Federal Reserve System,* 410 F. Supp. 63 64 (D.D.C. 1976) (fair market value test).
49. Compare *Larson v. CIA,* 664 F. Supp. 15 (D.D.C. 1987) (district court applied pre-Reform Act standard) with *Larson v. CIA,* 843 F.2d 1481 (D.C. Cir. 1988) (court of appeals applied post-Reform Act Standard). Compare *Blakey v. CIA,* 549 F. Supp. 362 (D.D.C. 1982) with *Fitzgibbon*

v. CIA, 724 F. Supp. 1048 (D.D.C. 1989) (release of information already available in public reference room).

50. 5 U.S.C. § 552 (a)(4)(ii) (commercial use requesters, educational nonscientific institutions, and news media requesters and all other requesters).
51. E.g., *National Security Archive v. Department of Defense,* 881 F.2d 1381, 1386-1387 (D.C. Cir. 1989) broadly defines "representative of the news media."
52. 5 U.S.C. § 552 (b)(6).

REFERENCES

Articles

Funk, W. (1987). The Paperwork Reduction Act: Paperwork reduction meets administrative law, *Harv. J. on Legis.* 24:1.

McGarity, T.O. and Shapiro, S.A. (1980) The trade secrecy status of health and safety information: Reforming agency disclosure policies, *Harv. L. Rev.* 93:837.

Moon, J. (1985). The Freedom of Information Act: A fundamental contradiction (comment), *Am. Univ. L. Rev.* 34:1157.

Paladino, M. (1991). The Federal Advisory Committee Act: An analysis of an obscure statute (comment), *Admin. L. J.,* 5:279.

Perritt, H. (1989). Electronic acquisition and release of federal agency information: Analysis of recommendations adopted by the Administrative Conference of the United States, *Admin. L. Rev.* 41:253.

Sargentich, T.O. (1984). The reform of the American administrative process: The contemporary debate, *Wisc. L. Rev.* 385.

Sargentich, T.O. (1991). The future of administrative law (review of Edley: Administrative law: Rethinking judicial control of bureaucracy), *Harv. L. Rev.* 104:769.

Scalia, A. (1982). The Freedom of Information Act has no clothes, *Regulation* (Mar./Apr.): 14.

Vaughn, R. G. (1984). Administrative alternatives and the Federal Freedom of Information Act, *Ohio State L. J.,* 45:185.

Vaughn, R. G. (1991). Consumer access to product safety information and the future of the Freedom of Information Act, *Admin. L. J.,* 5:673.

Zollers, F. and Barry, D. (1991). A regulation in search of a rationale: An empirical study of Consumer Product Safety Act section 6(b) and its effect on information disclosure under the Freedom of Information Act, *Admin. L. Rev.* 43:455.

Books

Hendricks, E. (1982). *Former Secrets: Government Records Made Public Through the Freedom of Information Act.* Campaign for Political Rights, Washington, D.C.

O'Reilly, J. (1979). *Federal Information Disclosure.* Shepard's, New York.

OTHER

Alternate dispute resolution proposals, hearings before a subcommittee of the Committee on Government Operations, House of Representatives, 100th Cong., 1st Sess. (1987).

American Bar Association, Conference Commemorating the 25th Anniversary of the Freedom of Information Act, May 21, 1991, Washington, D.C.

Common Cause, Agency compliance with the Government in the Sunshine Act (1978).

Common Cause, Shadows over the sunshine act: A study of federal agency compliance (1977).

Executive Order No. 12,600, 52 *Fed. Reg.* 23781 (1987).

Federal Advisory Committee Act (Public Law 92-463) and source book: Legislative history, texts and other documents, Subcommittee on Energy, Nuclear Proliferation, and Federal Services of the Committee on Governmental Affairs, United States Senate, 95th Cong., 2d Sess., July 1978.

Freedom of Information Act and Amendments of 1974 (P.L. 93-502), Source Book: Legislative history, text and other documents, Comm. on Government Operations, U.S. House of Representatives, Comm. on the Judiciary, United States Senate, 94th Cong., 1st Sess. (1974).

Government-in-the-Sunshine Source Book: Legislative history, texts, and other documents, Committees on Government Operations, U.S. Senate and House of Representatives, 94th Cong., 2d Sess. (1976).

Hearings on S. 1160, S. 1136 and S. 1768 before Senate Comm. on Judiciary, 89th Cong., 1st Sess. 365-503 (1965) (Appendix I: Agency comments on S. 1160, S. 1136 and S. 1768).

Legislative History of the Privacy Act of 1974, S. 3418 (Pub. L. 93-579): Source book on privacy, Joint Committee Print of Senate and House Committees on Government Operations, 94th Cong., 2d Sess. (1976).

17

Regulatory Bias and Conflict of Interest Regulation

Robert Roberts *James Madison University, Harrisonburg, Virginia*

Early in 1989, President Bush appointed Dan Quayle to head the new President's Council on Competitiveness (Fly, 1989: 37). Throughout the term of the Bush administration, the council moved to block federal regulations the council believed would make it more costly for small and large businesses to operate. The council publicly supported weakening antitrust laws, limiting the tort liability of American business, narrowing the definition of wetlands, using regulations to limit the impact of the 1990 Clean Air Act Amendments on business and industry, and the easing of restrictions on bioengineering (Duffy, 1991: 25).

The council, in brief, saw itself as a spokesperson for those inside and outside of government who saw unreasonable government regulation as a major threat to the international competitiveness of the country. Critics of the activities of the council, during the 1992 presidential campaign, pointed to its activities as evidence of the power of special interests to manipulate the federal regulatory process.

When Representative Henry Waxman, chair of the House Subcommittee Health and the Environment, accused Allan Hubbard, Director of the Council, and Vice President Dan Quayle of financial conflicts of interest (*Chemical Marketing Reporter,* Dec. 16, 1991: 22), the accusations raised further doubts regarding the objectivity of the council. Waxman reported that Allan B. Hubbard owned stock in chemical and utility companies that stood to benefit if Hubbard's recommendations for watering down Clean Air Act regulations were adopted. Even though White House lawyers ruled that Hubbard had done nothing wrong, Hubbard agreed to place his assets into a blind trust and gave "1000 shares of PSI Resources, Inc., a utility holding company, to charity" (Magnusson, 1991: 39).

Waxman also criticized the vice president for being involved in the dropping of a proposed Environmental Protection Agency (EPA) trash recycling rule because he held "a sizeable block of shares in a family newspaper company that would have suffered under the proposed rule" (Ichniowski, 1991: 7). These disclosures, however, received little media attention and did little to deter the council from pursuing its antiregulation agenda.

Democratic frustration with the Competitiveness Council, by the summer of 1992, led to accelerated congressional efforts to cut off funds to the council and to make its behavior a partisan political issue. The effort was more symbolic than substantive since "the council spent only $86,000 for salaries of two Quayle aides" and that cutting off funds would not prevent the Bush White House from detailing other administration personnel to meet the personnel demands of the council (Cooper, 1992: A6).

Bill Clinton, throughout the 1992 presidential campaign, stressed the need to take steps to reign in the power of special interest to influence the formulation and implementation of public policy. If history is any predictor of future performance, President Clinton will find it necessary to support the enactment of new conflict of interest rules in order to demonstrate his commitment to high ethical standards in government.

It is the principle thesis of this chapter that conflict of interest regulation cannot prevent regulatory bias. Modern conflict of interest regulation, to the contrary, makes it much more difficult for critics of regulatory bias to discredit the activities of regulators by raising conflict of interest allegations. Furthermore, it argues that instead of enacting even more stringent conflict of interest rules to protect the regulatory process from special interests, policy-makers must rely upon traditional political means, such as the appointment process, to protect the objectivity of the regulatory process.

MATURING OF CONFLICT OF INTEREST REGULATION AND THE ADMINISTRATIVE STATE: AN OVERVIEW

Modern conflict of interest regulation, to a large extent, has become the principal weapon of critics of regulatory bias. When new instances of perceived regulatory bias appear, such as the Council on Competitiveness, proposals for even tighter conflict of interest rules surface. Faced with calls for action, presidents and Congress find it necessary to support further fine-tuning of the rules while recognizing that those affected by regulatory policy will find a way to get their views heard by the regulators or prevent regulators from pursuing their own regulatory philosophy or biases.

Era of the Rogue: 1850–1887

Besides transforming the national economy, the 19th century industrial revolution brought with it an unprecedented centralization of economic power in the hands of a small number of industrialists. History documents the fact that the "robber barons" had few reservations about using their economic power to purchase preferential treatment from local, state, and federal executive and legislative officials.

The growth of the late 19th century populist movement was the direct consequence of heightened concern that unregulated private economy power threatened to undermine the long-term survival of the nation's democratic institutions. Unprecedented levels of public corruption persuaded good government reformers that representative political institutions were easy pickings for special interests.

Reformers came to regard the independent regulatory agency as the way to permit regulatory expertise to operate unfettered by the corrupting influences of representative government (Warren, 1982: 30). The establishment of the Interstate Commerce Commission in 1887 symbolized the victory of reformers who had argued "that Congress no longer had the time, patience, or special talents to regulate all of the vital activities necessary to preserve social order and prosperity in American society" (Warren, 1982: 30). The unwavering confidence of reformers in the personal integrity of administrative experts helps to explain the almost total absence of concern over regulatory bias threatening the legitimacy of the administrative process.

Ethics and Regulatory Expertise: 1887–1946

The success of the Interstate Commerce Commission opened the door for the proliferation of federal and state regulatory commissions. Instead of developing into adversarial watchdogs of regulated industries, state and federal regulatory agencies evolved into partners of regulated industries. In return for submitting to the directives of the regulators, regulated industries received protection from competition and guaranteed rates of return on investment.

Coinciding with the birth of independent regulatory agencies, the civil service reform movement provided regulatory reformers additional reason to believe that the new regulatory agencies could find individuals who would place the public interest before personal interest.

Felix Frankfurter, writing to Learned Hand in 1912, argued that for government regulations to be effective they should be patterned after the British model (Freedman, 1978: 45). That model, Frankfurter said, relied upon

> a highly trained and disinterested permanent service, charged with the task of administering the broad policies formulated by Parliament and of putting at the disposal of government that ascertainable body of knowledge in which the choice of policies must be based.

The views of Felix Frankfurter to a very large extent mirror those of modern administrative law scholars who historically have questioned the effectiveness of conflict of interest prohibitions as a means of preventing regulatory bias. "From Confucius and Plato," comments administrative law scholar Kenneth Warren, "to more modern democratic theorists such as Thomas Jefferson, the thinking has been that a person's inner attitudes toward governance, not conflict of interest or other similar statutes, provide the best guidance for proper conduct" (Warren, 1982: 206). Civil service reformers, as explained by civil service reform historian Frederick Mosher, sought "to make active politics once more attractive to men of self-respect and high aspirations" (Mosher, 1968: 65).

Despite the open hostility of business and industry to many New Deal programs, proponents of the explosion in New Deal regulatory activities and the explosion in federal regulatory activities, surprisingly, expressed few fears that special interests might successfully "capture" regulatory agencies (Freedman, 1978, 44–45). Criticism of the administrative process focused on violations of fundamental principals of fairness and due process, not conflicts of interest.

Because the new generation of regulatory agencies exercised extensive investigatory, prosecutorial, and adjudicatory authority, administrative law experts grew increasingly concerned over the growth of unaccountable federal agencies. Instead of restructuring regulatory agencies to conform to separation of powers principles, a consensus developed on the need for the enactment of uniform rules of procedures to increase the accountability of regulatory agencies (Robinson, 1980: 34–35).

Supporters of the Administrative Procedure Act of 1946 believed that its provisions would help to reign in the excesses of federal regulatory agencies (Freedman, 1978:139–189). The act, however, contained few provisions dealing with influence peddling or conflicts of interests. The act did prohibit "ex parte contacts between the prosecuting staff and trial examiners . . . in adjudicatory procedures" (Robinson, 1980: 35). The act, however, failed to address other more persuasive forms of influence peddling (Warren, 1982: 206–214). The act, of particular interest, did not include a definition of administrative bias (Freedman, 1978: 193).

Conflicts of Interest and the Ideologies of Regulation: 1946–1989

The drafters of the Administrative Procedure Act of 1946 greatly underestimated the impact of regulatory polarization on the legitimacy of the administrative process. The years following World War II saw the Republican critics become much more vigorous in their criticism of the impact of government regulation on private enterprise. Influence peddling scandals after World War II involving members of the Truman Administration raised serious doubts in the public mind regarding the integrity and impartiality of the caretakers of the administrative state (Roberts, 1988: 37–42).

The same period saw supporters of aggressive government regulation become much more concerned about the quality of special interests to exert undue influence on government decision-makers. Instead of accepting the argument that the Administrative Procedure Act provided adequate safeguards against regulatory bias, a new generation of good government reformers advocated new conflict of interest restrictions directed at protecting public confidence in the impartiality of government decision-making (Roberts, 1988: 42).

The issuance, in 1951, of a report entitled *Proposals for Improvement of Ethical Standards in the Federal Government,* by a Senate subcommittee headed by Senator Douglas of Illinois, provided reformers with a conflict of interest reform agenda. The report advocated the amendment of the Administrative Procedure Act to construct a wall of conflict of interest restraints around federal officials.

The subcommittee specifically supported the summary dismissal of federal employees for (1) engaging in business transactions related to the performance of officials responsibilities, (2) accepting gifts or favors from individuals or organizations having dealings with their agency, (3) discussing future employment with a person or organization having dealings with the employee's agency, (4) divulging confidential information to unauthorized individuals, and federal officials and employees who (5) "[became] unduly involved . . . through frequent luncheons, dinner parties, or other expense social engagement with persons outside the government with whom they do official business" (U.S. Senate, Committee, 1951:2).

The Douglas subcommittee proposed to bar former government officials from lobbying their former employers for 1 year after leaving office, regardless of whether they had any involvement with the matter while serving in the government. The Douglas report, finally, supported public financial disclosure for high-level federal officials in all three branches of the federal government.

Despite the fact that Congress did not enact any of the proposed reforms during the 1950s, good government reformers became fixated on external conflict of interest restraints as the way to protect public confidence in the impartiality of big government. Without tighter conflict of interest rules, critics of big government would face a much easier time convincing the public that effective big government was impossible because of the strong likelihood that public officials would use their public positions for personal gain.

The 1960 presidential election began a period in which Democratic candidates for president and Democratic presidents came to regard conflict of interest regulation as essential to maintaining public confidence in big government. The Kennedy White House moved aggressively to tighten conflict of interest rules and regulations through the issuance of a series of executive orders and the revision of criminal conflict of interest laws (Roberts, 1988: 73–93).

As subsequent administrations would find out, the Kennedy White House found that implementation of conflict of interest rules had a serious bureaucratic downside. The years following World War II found federal agencies relying more and more heavily upon part-time consultants or experts to assist federal agencies with increasingly complex scientific and technical problems. Federal agencies maintained that unduly strict conflict of interest rules would make it extremely difficult to recruit experts because consulting contracts or service on advisory committees might force them to forgo lucrative private employment with companies having dealings with the government (Perkins, 1963: 1123).

Acceptance of the theory that conflict of interest rules must be balanced against their impact upon the manpower needs of federal agencies forced the Kennedy administration and subsequent presidents to accept a swiss cheese approach to conflict of interest regulation. The Kennedy White House, for example, helped to persuade Congress to exempt from key criminal conflict of interest rules "special" or "intermittent employees" or provide for administrative waivers of conflict of interest rules (Perkins, 1963: 1123).

The swiss cheese approach to conflict of interest regulation, however, made it much more difficult to enforce conflict of interest rules and familiarize full-time and part-time employees with the complexities of modern conflict of interest regulations. This situation helps to explain why the "conflict of interest bark has been historically much greater than its bite" (Warren, 1982: 205).

The late 1960s and early 1970s saw popularization of the view that regulated firms and industries had captured federal regulatory agencies. Supporters of this theory argued that regulatory agencies recruited key personnel from regulated industries and many officials working for regulatory agencies did the bidding of regulated industries because they hoped to work for regulated companies after leaving government service (Gerlach, 1991:405; Lanouette, 1977:1796).

The development of the theory of regulatory capture represented a turning point in the evolution of conflict of interest regulation. Conflict of interest regulation became much more than a way to protect the political legitimacy of big government but a way to wrest the control of government from the corrupting influence of big business. The issuance of a series of General Accounting Office reports during the mid-1970s criticizing the conflict of interest programs of federal regulatory agencies provided advocates of regulatory capture with hard evidence that many federal regulatory agencies regarded conflict of interest regulation as a nuisance rather than a high-priority item (United States House, Committee on Interstate Commerce). The Watergate scandal, finally, provided conflict of interest reformers a golden opportunity to push an extensive conflict of interest reform agenda.

Running as a Washington outsider committed to cleaning up Washington, candidate Jimmy Carter embraced the theory of regulatory capture and the view that conflict of interest reform provided the means for controlling special interest influence in Washington. President Carter, consequently, proposed a series of conflict of interest reforms directed at controlling influence peddling by special interests. The list included (1) public financial disclosure for high-level officials in the three branches of the federal government, (2) strict rules for the establishment of blind trusts, (3) procedures for the appointment of independent special prosecutors to investigate allegations of criminal conduct by high-level federal officials, (4) the establishment of an Office of Government Ethics, and (5) tighter rules on the postemployment lobbying activities of former federal officials. The period culminated with the passage of the Ethics in Government Act, which enacted a large part of the conflict of interest reform agenda (Roberts, 1988: 161–170).

The victory of the conflict of interest reform movement proved short-lived. The 1980 landslide election of Ronald Reagan ushered in a period of outright hostility to government regulation and conflict of interest regulation. It also ushered in a period that saw countless numbers of Reagan administration officials accused of conflict of interest violations (Roberts, 1988: 171–181; Austin, 1988:6).

The Reagan administration placed much of the blame for their predicament on misuse of the appearance of impropriety rule issued in the early 1960s by the Kennedy administration and made a key part of federal standard of conduct regulations by the Johnson administration in 1965 (Morgan, 1992: 599). Critics of the Reagan administration found the appearance standard an effective weapon to raise serious questions regarding the attitude of Reagan administration officials towards standard of conduct rules. (Brownstein, 1985:639)

The Reagan administration throughout the 1980s did little to hide the fact that it intended to reduce the regulatory burden on American business. The Reagan administration, moreover, saw nothing improper about working closely with regulated industries on the drafting of regulations that directly affected their interests (Cohen, 1983:122; Huntley, 1986:27). The Reagan White House, however, greatly underestimated the impact of public integrity scandals on public support for their regulatory agenda. The scandals helped to reinforce widely held views that special interests received preferential treatment from government policy makers. This view only served to increase public hostility to traditional political institutions (Garment, 1987:10).

SYMBOLIC LEGITIMACY AND THE REGULATORY STATE: 1989–1992

The 1992 defeat of George Bush and the series of ethics, lobbying, and campaign finance reforms put forward by President Clinton makes it easy to forget that the Bush White House succeeded in shifting the focus of ethics reform from the executive branch to Congress and greatly reduced the number of administration officials accused of conflict of interest violations.

Upon assuming the presidency, President Bush directed all members of his administration to avoid even the appearance of impropriety in the performance of their official duties (Morgan, 1992: 600). The Bush administration, however, had no intention of endorsing a conflict of interest reform agenda that took as a given that special interests had captured federal regulatory agencies. The Bush White House, instead, focused its efforts on tightening congressional ethics rules while loosening some rules on executive branch personnel.

On January 25, 1989, President Bush created an eight-member President's Commission on Federal Ethics Law Reform. President Bush gave the commission the mandate of reforming federal ethics rules to meet four general objectives. First, "ethical standards for public servants must be exacting enough to ensure that the officials act with the utmost integrity and live up to the public's confidence in them." Second, "standards must be fair, they must be objective and consistent with common sense." Third, "the standards must be equitable all across the three branches of the federal government." Fourth, "we cannot afford to have unreasonably restrictive requirements that discourage able citizens from entering public service" (President's Commision, 1989:Fact Sheet, p. 1)

These directives left little doubt that the Bush White House wanted to tame the conflict of interest monster without bringing the wrath of Congress, good government groups, and the media down on its neck. The Bush White House proved remarkably successful in implementing its reform agenda.

The President's Ethics Commission issued its report on March 9, 1989. The most significant recommendation was to extend to members of Congress a number of conflict of interest statutes that only applied to executive branch officers and employees. The commission specifically recommended requiring members of Congress to comply with (1) self-dealing prohibitions, (2) bans on accepting honoraria, (3) and lobbying prohibitions applying to former government employees. The commission also recommended that Congress allow officials forced to divest themselves of financial holdings to deter capital gains taxes and liberalize rules governing the acceptance of things of value from nonpublic sources (President's Commission, 1989).

On April 12, 1989, President Bush revoked President Johnson's standard of conduct, executive order (Executive Order 11,222) and replaced it with his own executive order establishing principles of ethical conduct for government officers and employees (Executive order 12,674). The Bush White House decided to issue the order to demonstrate its commitment to ethics in government, even though the order made few substantive changes in standard of conduct rules. President Bush became the first Republican president to issue an executive order regarding standards of conduct.

The order, however, did make a significant but little noticed change in the federal "appearance of impropriety" rule. The new order directed all federal employees to "endeavor to avoid any actions creating the appearance that they are violating the law or the ethical standards promulgated pursuant to this order" (Executive Order 12,674 sec. 101 n). By replacing "shall" with "endeavor" the White House significantly increased the "aspirational" character of the appearance standard. The new appearance standard, in other words, tied violations of the appearance standards to specific legal or standard of conduct rules.

The passage of the Ethics in Government Reform Act of 1989 (P.L. 101-194) proved to be the capstone on the Bush administration's effort to redirect the federal ethics program from the executive branch to Congress and to loosen conflict of interest regulations in order to make it easier to recruit and retain full-time and intermittent employees. The Bush White House made masterful use of the fact that ethics scandals involving Congress put great pressure on Congress to subject itself to tighter ethics rules and of the fact that Congress badly wanted President Bush to sign on to a pay increase for members of Congress.

The key features of the 1989 Ethics Reform Act included (1) prohibiting members of Congress and all federal officials from accepting honoraria, (2) extending some postemployment lobbying rules to former members of Congress and their staff, (3) barring former senior members of the executive branch from lobbying high-level officials in all federal agencies, (4) permitting federal officials forced to divest themselves of financial holdings for conflict of interest reasons to defer capital gains taxes, (5) permitting each branch of government to establish its own gift acceptance policies, and (6) giving all federal agencies the authority to accept travel reimbursement from nonpublic sources (Roberts and Doss, 1992, 260).

Probably the most interesting provision of the Ethics Reform Act is an amendment to section 208 of title 18, United States Code. The statute prohibits full-time and intermittent federal employees from taking action with respect to any particular matter in which they have a financial interest. Opinions issued by the Justice Department broadly construed the scope of the self-dealing disqualification rule, which meant that section 208 prohibited part-time members of federal advisory committees from making recommendations that might affect their financial interests. A member of a federal advisory committee employed by a university, for example, must disqualify himself or herself from taking any action with respect to any matter involving the university that employed the member of the advisory board on a full-time basis (Nuszkiewicz, 1992: 957–960).

Federal agencies, through much of the 1980s, lobbied Congress and the Reagan and Bush administrations to exempt special government employees serving on advisory committees from the provision of section 208. Because of strong resistance from the democratically controlled Congress, federal agencies were forced to settle for the authority to grant section 208 waivers on a case-by-case basis. The Ethics Reform Act, consequently, granted federal agencies the authority to grant advisory committee members waivers if the appointing authority certified in writing "that the need for the individual's services outweighs the potential for a conflict of interest created by the financial interest involved."

On August 7, 1992, the Office of Government Ethics issued a final rule that established uniform standards of ethical conduct for officers and employees of the executive branch of the federal government (5 CFR 2635). Taking up some 61 pages in the *Federal Register,* the rules provide federal employees with a detailed road map of how to comply with conflict of interest rules and regulations.

Like corporations across the country that adopted strict ethics codes during the 1980s, the Bush White House recognized that it was in its best interest to take conflict of interest regulation seriously. The Bush White House, however, misjudged the depth of commitment to the theory of regulatory capture by supporters of aggressive conflict of interest regulation. Improved enforcement and management of the conflict of interest regulation did not silence critics who believed that special interests exerted too much influence on government policymaking.

In the 1992 presidential campaign Ross Perot blamed much of the "mess in Washington" on former government officials who took lucrative positions as the paid lobbyists of foreign governments and other special interests. In the third debate, both Ross Perot and Bill Clinton vigorously attacked former officials who took positions as lobbyists for foreign governments. President Bush, on the other hand, rejected calls for tighter postemployment restraints and stressed the point that former officials of his administration had complied with all applicable laws and regulations. Nothing better demonstrates the vast gulf that separates political views regarding the role of conflict of interest regulation in protecting public confidence in government.

FUNDAMENTAL PRINCIPLES OF CONFLICT OF INTEREST REGULATION

Despite the fact that conflict of interest rules are not formerly part of the Administrative Procedure Act, the last four decades have seen the development of fundamental principles of conflict of interest regulation directed at maintaining public confidence in the impartiality of the administrative process.

Conflicting Financial Interests: The Disqualification Rule

One of the fundamental tenets of modern conflict of interest regulation is that public officials should not take action with respect to matters in which they, or a member of their immediate family or a business associate, have a financial interest. Supporters of disqualification for conflicting financial interest argue that when public officials take action with respect to matters in which they have a financial interest, the public will question the motives behind the decision.

Section 208 of title 18, the federal conflicting financial interest rule, prohibits members of the executive branch

> from participating personally and substantially in an official capacity in any particular matter in which, to his knowledge, he or any person whose interests are imputed to him under this statute has a financial interest, if the particular matter will have a direct and predictable effect on that interest (5 CFR 2635.402).

Besides upholding the general section 208 disqualification rule, federal agencies have the authority to prohibit employees from acquiring or holding financial interests that "would cause a reasonable person to question the impartiality and objectivity with which agency programs are administered" (5 CFR 2635.403).

Federal employees use (1) disqualification, (2) divestiture, (3) blind trusts, and (4) administrative waivers to resolve conflicting financial interest problems. Disqualification has become the most common remedy because it does not force the employee to divest himself or herself of a financial interest or go through the costly process of setting up a blind trust.

Divestiture and the establishment of blind trusts have historically been the least favored remedies for conflicting financial interest. Besides disrupting long-term investment plans, the tax consequences of divestiture deter officials from making it the preferred remedy. The Ethics in Government Reform Act of 1989, at the strong urging of the Bush White House, included a nonrecognition of gain provision (Sec. 1043, Internal Revenue code). If the president or director of the Office of Government Ethics certifies that divestiture of specific property is "reasonably necessary to comply with any Federal conflict of interest statute, regulation or executive order," the employee may roll over the gain into another investment without paying taxes on the gain.

The final method for resolving self-dealing problems is the waiver process. The Ethics Reform Act of 1989 gives individuals responsible for the appointment of federal officials expanded authority to grant individual officers and employees conflicting financial interest waivers upon a finding by the appointing authority that the conflicting financial interest "is not so substantial as to be deemed likely to affect the integrity of the services which the Government may expect from such officer or employee." The Ethics Reform Act, as noted, makes these waivers available to members of federal advisory committees (section 208(b)(3) of title 18 U.S.C.).

Acceptance of Things of Value from Nonpublic Sources

The second tenet of modern conflict of interest regulation is that public servants should not accept things of value from nonpublic sources for the performance of official acts or from sources with a direct interest in actions taken by the official. Supporters of strict rules against public officials accepting things of value from nonpublic sources argue that such conduct seriously erodes public confidence in the loyalty and impartiality of public servants. Public servants, they argue, should receive nothing more than their salaries in relation to the performance of official duties.

The practical realities of modern public administration have led local, state, and federal employers to develop flexible gift-acceptance rules in order to permit some nonpublic sources to assist public agencies and their employees in the performance of official duties. This situation helps to explain why enforcement of gift-acceptance rules has become the most difficult area of federal conflict of interest regulation.

Federal law and regulation at present require federal employees to comply with (1) the illegal gratuity official acts statute (18 U.S.C. 201 (c)(1)(B); (2) the supplementation of salary prohibition (18 U.S.C. 209(a); (3) the prohibited source gift acceptance prohibition (5 C.F.R. 2635.203); (d) and, for procurement officials, 41 U.S.C. 423(b)(2). It is beyond the scope of this chapter to detail the workings of the major gift-acceptance provisions of federal law. It is important to note that the Bush White House succeeded in relaxing extremely tight nonfederal source gift acceptance rules.

First, federal regulations permit federal employees to accept (1) certain gifts of $20 or less, (2) gifts based on personal relationships, (3) certain discounts and similar benefits, (4) awards and honorary degrees, (5) gifts based on outside business or employment relationships, (6) gifts to Hatch Act-exempt employees from political organizations, (7) gifts provided to federal employees as part of widely attended gathering or speaking engagements, and (8) social invitations from persons other than prohibited sources (5 CFR 2635.204).

Second, the Ethics in Government Reform Act of 1989 gives all federal agencies the authority to accept travel, subsistence, and related expenses from nonpublic sources (41 CFR part 304-1). One should not underestimate the significance of the enactment of government-wide gift acceptance authority. Federal agencies now have the authority to make widespread use of nonpublic funds to assist them in the performance of official duties.

Third, and most significant, the Ethics in Government Reform Act places in the hands of the Office of Government Ethics and Ethics Committees in both houses of Congress the authority to issue regulations that have the force of law regarding the acceptance of gifts. Instead of having to go to Congress to obtain statutory approval to exempt certain gifts from the illegal gratuity or salary supplementation prohibitions, the Office of Government Ethics and congressional ethics committees have the authority to establish their own gift acceptance rules (5 CFR 2635.202 (a)).

Incompatible Outside Activities

The third principle of modern conflict of interest regulation, and the one with the longest historical tradition, is that outside activities of public employees should not conflict with the performance of their official duties. Long before the recent preoccupation with conflicts of interest, many government agencies prohibited rank and file government employees from moonlighting or holding second jobs. Congress, during the mid-1800s, prohibited federal employees from accepting compensation for prosecuting claims against the United States (Roberts, 1988: 9–10).

First, sections 203 and 205 of title 18 of the United States Code prohibit federal employees from representing for compensation or without compensation private parties in federal proceedings. The public policy argument for this prohibition is that federal employees should not work against the interests of the United States while on the federal payroll.

Prior to 1962, the in-service representation bar applied to all federal employees. Congress, in 1962, exempted special or intermittent federal employees from the representation prohibition. Federal agencies, particularly the Department of Defense, heavily lobbied the White House and Congress for the exception, because many experts refused to take part-time advisory and consulting positions on the grounds that the representation bars interfered with their full-time employment opportunities (Roberts, 1988: 100–101).

Second, federal administrative regulations direct federal employees "not to engage in outside employment or any other outside activity that conflicts with his duties" (5 CFR 2635.802). The regulations, however, require agency ethics officials to undertake a case-by-case review to determine whether outside employment activities conflict with the performance of officials duties. Equally significant is that the regulations gave agencies independent authority to require employees to obtain "prior approval before engaging in outside employment or activities" (5 CFR 2635.803).

Third, the Ethics in Government Reform Act of 1978 dramatically expanded the scope of bans on honoraria. Since the early 1960s, administrative regulations prohibited executive branch officials from accepting payment for teaching or speaking within the province of the employee's official duties. Members of Congress, however, frequently supplemented their income by accepting tens of thousands of dollars in honoraria.

Instead of establishing separate rules for members of Congress and executive branch officials and employees, Congress and the Bush White House agreed to put in place a blanket ban on officials in all three branches of government from accepting honoraria for giving speeches or writing articles, regardless of the subject matter of the article or the speech.

The enactment of the across-the-board honorarium ban sent shock waves through the federal work force. Federal employee unions argued that the ban violated the first amendment and due process rights of federal employees. The Office of Government Ethics attempted to defuse the controversy by issuing regulations narrowly construing the scope of the honoraria ban as applied to the outside activities of federal employees.

The regulations, for example, exempt from the prohibition compensation received by federal officials for teaching a course requiring multiple presentations by the employee, if the course is offered as part of (1) an institution of higher education, (2) a covered elementary school, or (3) covered secondary school (5 CFR 2635.807). The regulations, however, did not end litigation designed to overturn the constitutionality of banning payments for non-job-related teaching, speaking, and writing by rank and file federal employees.

If restrictions on in-service representation, outside employment, and acceptance of honoraria were not enough, high-level federal officials must also comply with outside earned income limitations. Noncareer federal employees who are paid at the rate of basic pay for level II of the executive schedule may not receive outside earned income that exceeds 15 percent of their annual salary. Even more significant is that the outside earned income limits for covered noncareer employees prohibit them from receiving "any compensation for practicing a profession which involves a fiduciary relationship; serving as an officer or member of a board of any association, corporation or other entity" (5 CFR 2635.804).

Besides the outside earned income limitation of the Ethics in Government Reform Act of 1989, President Bush's executive order on standards of conduct prohibits "presidential appointees from receiving any outside earned income for outside employment, or for any other outside activity performed during that presidential appointment" (5 CFR 2635.804(a)).

Supporters of outside earned income limitations argue that they are necessary to prevent high-level officials from becoming involved in conflict of interest controversies. Critics, however, point out that the outside earned income ban penalizes those who choose government service but who have limited financial resources.

Misuse of Nonpublic Information

The fourth principle of modern conflict of interest regulation is that public officials should not use nonpublic information for financial gain.

Bureaucratic considerations led the Johnson White House, in 1965, to broaden the definition of the misuse of public information to prohibit use of official information "for the purpose of furthering a private interest." White House documents indicate that the Johnson White House intentionally used broad language to punish federal employees for the use of inside government information, even when the employee did not use the information to further a personal financial interest (Roberts, 1988: 118).

Regulations implementing President Bush's executive order prohibit all federal employees

> (1) from engaging in a financial transaction using nonpublic information . . . (2) nor allow the improper use of nonpublic information to further his own private interest or that of another, whether through advice or recommendation, or by knowing unauthorized disclosure (5 CFR 2635.703).

The regulations state that any employee of the Army Corps of Engineers who is also actively involved with an environmental group violates the prohibition if he or she gives to a newspaper nonpublic information about long-range plans of the Corps of Engineers to build a particular dam (5 CFR 2635.703).

Postemployment Lobbying by Former Federal Employees

The fifth and most controversial principle of modern conflict of interest regulation is that restrictions should be placed on former government officials lobbying the government on behalf of private parties (Darley, 1991:302). Supporters of postemployment lobbying bans argue that former officials (1) may make improper use of inside information to help private clients, (2) that they may receive preferential treatment from friends inside the government, (3) and that those inside the government may try to curry favor with possible outside employers to increase their opportunities for lucrative employment outside of the government.

Critics of postemployment bans argue that the bans actually do little to stop lobbying and may deter individuals with badly needed expertise from entering the government. A number of different postemployment lobbying bans now apply to (1) all former federal employees, (2) former senior officials, (3) former very senior officials, and (4) former members of Congress and former congressional staff.

It is important to note that most of the postemployment bans enacted as part of the Ethics in Government Reform Act of 1989 apply to activities in which former officials try to influence federal officials directly. Most of the federal postemployment laws do not prohibit former federal officials from quarterbacking: providing clients with advice on how to lobby federal officials or insights into how the policy-making process operates in various federal agencies and departments.

First, section 207(a)(1) establishes a lifetime ban on all former federal employees representing any other person with respect to matters in which they participated personally and substantially as a government employee. Congress enacted the so-called "switching sides" prohibition to prevent former employees from using inside information and government contacts to obtain preferential treatment on matters pending before the government.

Second, section 207(a)(2) establishes a ban for 2 years after government service on the part of all former government employees for representing any person in a matter the former employee knew or reasonably should have known was "actually pending under his or her official responsibility as such officer or employee within a period of 1 year before the termination of his or her service or employment with the United States or the District of Columbia." Congress enacted the so-called 2 year official responsibility cooling off period to prevent former employees from marketing to private client their ability to represent them with respect to general matters pending before the government.

Third, section 207(c)(1) establishes a general 1 year no contact ban for former high-level federal officials. The 1 year cooling off period prohibits covered individuals from seeking official action through any communication or appearance from anyone working for the department or agency the former official previously worked for. The ban, however, does not apply to special government employees who work for fewer than 60 days for the agency in the year preceding their departure.

Fourth, section 207(d) establishes a broader 1 year no contact ban for former senior officials of the Executive Branch. Former Cabinet members, for example, may not request official action from anyone in their former department or from high-level presidential appointees in any other federal agency or department. Congress included this provision in the Ethics in Government Reform Act of 1989 to deal with the perceived problem of high-profile administration officials leaving government and attempting to influence high-level officials throughout the government. Members of Congress pointed to the lobbying activities of Michael Deaver and Lyn Nofziger, former high-level Reagan White House officials, as justification for the new 1 year contact ban for former very senior officials (Gerlach, 1991: 401).

Fifth, section 207(e) prohibits former members of Congress for 1 year from "knowingly making, with the intent to influence, any communication with or appearance before: a current member of Congress, a current officer of Congress, or employee of either house of Congress" (Gerlach, 1991: 418). The provision also restricts personal staffs of congressional members, for 1 year after leaving government, "from contacting the member for whom they worked or any employee of that member" (Gerlach, 1991: 419). The provision also applies a similar 1 year restriction on employees of "the joint, standing and select committees of Congress" and of leadership staff of Congress.

Sixth, section 207(b)(1) establishes a 1 year prohibition on former federal employees and former members of Congress who personally and substantially participated in any trade or treaty negotiation on behalf of the United States "from knowingly representing, aiding or advising any other person (except the United States) concerning such ongoing trade or treaty negotiation for a period of one year after his or her service or employment with the United States terminates."

Congress passed the provision in response to intense criticism of former trade negotiators who left federal agencies to become lobbyists for foreign governments and foreign companies or organizations. In contrast to other postemployment restrictions, Section 207(b) prohibits behind-the-scenes quarterbacking as well as direct communication with government officials.

CONCLUSION

Shortly after the election, President-elect Clinton announced that he planned to tighten ethics rules significantly for members of his transition and executive branch employees. The president-elect announced his intention to increase the length of the 1 year no contact ban to 5 years and to impose a lifetime lobbying ban on former trade negotiators. On September 30, 1993, President Clinton issued an executive order making substantial changes in federal rule-making procedures. The order severely restricts the authority of the Office of Management and Budget to intervene or modify regulations issued by federal agencies and departments. The order, equally significant, "requires that communications of White House and OMB staff with outside interests concerning regulations be made in writing and placed in a public file" (Barr, 1993: A22). The Clinton White House issued the order to deal with the perceived problem of special interests exercising too much influence in rule-making by federal agencies and departments.

The decision of President Clinton to tighten ethics rules for members of his administration and his rule-making executive order demonstrates how external restraints have come to dominate measures to guarantee administrative legitimacy and the lack of confidence in internal safeguards as a means to preserve public confidence in government.

Supporters of the Administrative Procedure Act believed that it would significantly increase the accountability of federal agencies. The drafters, however, could not have anticipated the importance that conflict of interest regulation would assume in the battle to protect the legitimacy of the administrative state. Although conflict of interest regulation may help to prevent individual government officials from using their public positions for personal financial gain, little evidence exists that it stops regulators or other public officials from pursuing specific regulatory agendas. The election of Bill Clinton, not conflict of interest regulations, sealed the fate of President Bush's Council on Competitiveness.

Despite continuing criticism from administrative law scholars, who question the effectiveness of conflict of interest regulation as a means of dealing with regulatory bias, a reversal of the trend toward tighter and tighter conflict of interest rules does not seem likely. Conflict of interest regulation has become the cornerstone of efforts to deal with regulatory bias, whether or not it works. Modern conflict of interest regulation has helped to rebuild public confidence in government, but there is little evidence that it provides an effective remedy for regulatory bias.

REFERENCES

Austin, Ian. (1988). The president's rogues, *MacLean's, 101*: 6.

Bar, Stephen. (1993). Clinton tightens access to rule-making: President seeks to oust special interests from review of regulations. *The Washington Post*, October 1, A22

Brownstein, Ronald. (1985). Agency ethics officers fear Meese ruling could weaken conflict laws, *National Journal, 14*: 639.

Cohen, Robert M. (1983). Reagan's cost control 'bloodhounds' are hounded by charges of conflicts, *National Journal, 15*: 122.

Cooper, Kenneth. (July 2, 1992). Divided House bars fund for Quayle Competitiveness Council, *The Washington Post,* A6.

Darley, Roger. (1991). Personal conflict of interest digest, *Public Contract Law Journal, 20*: 302.

Duffy, Michael. (November 4, 1991). Need friends in high places? *Time,* p. 25.

Executive Order 11, 222. (May 8, 1965). Prescribing standards of ethical conduct for government officers and employees.

Executive Order 12, 624 (April 12, 1989). Principles of ethical conduct for government employees and officials.

Fly, Richard. (February 27, 1989). Introducing Dan Quayle, competitiveness czar, *Business Week,* p. 37.

Freedman, James O. (1978). *Crisis and Legitimacy: The Administrative Process and American Government.* Harvard University Press, Cambridge.

Garment, Suzanne. (1987). Political imperfections: Scandal time in Washington, *Public Opinion,* 10: 10.

Gerlach, Wendy. (1991). Amendment of the post-employment laws, *Arizona Law Review, 33*: 401.

Huntley, Steve. (May 12, 1986). 'Revolving door' furor, *U.S. News & World Report, 100*: 27.

Lanouette, William. (November 19, 1977). The revolving door: It's tricky to stop it, *National Journal, 9*: 1796.

Magnusson, Paul. (December 23, 1991). Quayle's pet project is looking more like a liability, *Business Week,* p. 39.

Morgan, Peter W. (1992). The appearance of propriety: Ethics reform and the Blifil paradoxes, *Stanford Law Review, 44*: 563.

Mosher, Frederick. (1968). *Democracy and Public Service,* Oxford University Press, New York.

Nuszkiewicz, Michelle. (1992). Twenty years of the Federal Advisory Committee Act: It's time for some changes, *Southern California Law Review, 76*: 1123.

Perkins, Roswell. (1963). The new federal conflict-of-interest law, *Harvard Law Review, 76*: 1123.

President's Commission on Federal Ethics Law Reform. (1989). *To Serve With Honor: Report and Recommendations to the President,* Washington, D.C.

Quayle council repeals attack on role in regulatory agencies (December 16, 1991). *Chemical Marketing Reporter,* p. 22.

Roberts, Robert. (1988). *White House Ethics: The Politics of Federal Conflict of Interest Regulation,* Greenwood Press, Westport, CT.

Roberts, Robert and Doss, Marion. (1992). Private hospitality and public service, *Public Administration Review,* 52: 260–269.

Robinson, Glen O. (1980). *The Administrative Process,* West Publishing Company, St. Paul.

Seib, Gerald F. (July 16, 1987). GOP's legacy. *Wall Street Journal,* 1B.

Standards of Ethical Conduct for Employees of the Executive Branch, Office of Government Ethics, final rule, Friday, August 7, 1992, *Federal Register,* 35006–35067.

United States House Committee on Interstate Commerce, *Conflict of Interest in Regulatory Agencies:* hearings, May 23–June 2, 1977. Washington, D.C.

U.S. Senate, Committee on Labor and Public Welfare, Report of the Subcommittee on Labor and Public Welfare on Ethical Standards in Government, 82d Cong: 1st Sess., 1951, p. 2

Warren, Kenneth F. (1982). *Administrative Law: In the American Political System,* West Publishing Co., St. Paul.

VI

FRONTIERS

18

Discretion

Martin Shapiro *University of California at Berkeley, Berkeley, California*

Discretion is a phenomenon that lies in the tension between two imperatives of governance. One is the imperative that officials possess the flexibility to meet particular situations that do not easily fall within the application of known, preexisting general rules. They are granted discretion in order to achieve public purposes effectively. This imperative can be seen as one of efficiency or justice, or both. A state's foreign policy, for instance, might be unsuccessful if all of its actions were governed by known rules and so could be completely anticipated by other states. Beyond efficiency, discretion may serve justice in the Platonic sense by dealing with situations in which the application of a general rule to a particular situation leads to less than perfect results. The second imperative is that of the rule of law. Particularly where the interests of individuals are involved, we believe that official decisions ought to be governed by preexisting rules or at least justifiable in terms of such rules. Thus discretion, at least as a legal concept, is always to be seen as bounded discretion, that is, a certain flexibility or choice within limits set by law.

Beyond boundedness, legal discretion is also subject to another more subtle criterion suggested by one of the common meanings of the word. A person of "discretion" is a wise or prudent person who shapes his or her responses carefully in the light of past developments, current circumstances, and future goals. An official wielding discretion is judged not only on the flexibility and lawfulness but on the wisdom or prudence of his or her decisions.

In theory, the term discretion might be applied to legislative as well as executive and judicial bodies. In constitutional law we might say that the legislature has the discretion to make whatever laws it pleases within the limits set by the Constitution. In general, however, discretion is treated in its administrative and judicial aspects, although one of the major forms of administrative and judicial discretion is the power to make law.

In the narrowest view, administrative discretion exists when a statute specifically authorizes an official to make certain specified choices entirely free of any legal restraints. For instance, some civil service statutes allow a public employer to choose any one among the three applicants scoring highest on qualification examinations. The statute contains absolutely no criteria or instructions for choosing among the three. Even here, however, discretion is relative. For other statutes forbid the public employer to engage in racial or gender discrimination in making this otherwise free choice. This narrowest view of discretion is sometimes summed up as administrative choice when there is "no law to apply." As the example above shows, however, it is extremely rare that there is no law to apply at all.

A somewhat broader view of discretion is suggested by the Administrative Procedure Act (APA), which establishes procedural requirements and judicial review for administrative adjudication and rule-making but provides neither procedures nor judicial review for "discretion." Any decision of government that is not adjudication or rule-making might then be considered discretion. That even this discretion is not entirely unconstrained is suggested by the APA's proclamation that government decisions in general are subject to judicial review under an arbitrary and capricious, abuse of discretion standard even after the same statute has proclaimed discretion to be non reviewable. Moreover many government decisions that are neither adjudication nor rule making are nevertheless so highly constrained by the statutes authorizing them that they can hardly be labelled discretionary. Discretion is some unclearly bounded subset of this large range of "informal action."

Finally, at its broadest, administrative discretion encompasses every situation where the law does not clearly impose a single correct choice on administrators but instead allows or requires them to choose among a number of alternatives based on policy considerations. In that broadest sense, elements of discretion inhere in almost all administrative decisions given the inherent and often purposeful uncertainties of statutory commands and the complex world to which those commands must be applied.

SUPERVISING MECHANISMS

Because legal discretion is a power of bounded choice granted to administrators and judges to make prudent decisions serving public purposes, legal systems devote greater attention to describing mechanisms for supervising and evaluating it than they do to describing its actual practice. There is a broad spectrum of such mechanisms to match the wide range of kinds of discretion. At one extreme, the vast discretion granted to chief executives to conduct the foreign policy of a nation may be checked only by the need to maintain a parliamentary majority or win the next election. Some systems incorporate other, intermediate, political checks such as the question period in the British Parliament, or the capacity of legislative committees to oversee executive departments. At the other extreme, the discretion of a lowest rank civil servant to accept an application form for government benefits may be governed by numerous laws and rules and by four or five levels of administrative supervisors and judges. One family of checks are those involving record-making, publication, and giving reasons that allow subsequent public scrutiny of discretionary decisions. Another is consultation requirements that ensure that various voices are heard before a discretionary decision is made. Informal or formal, oral or written, inquisitorial or adversarial hearings may be required before decision or at appeal. Thus much of the law of discretion is procedural, specifying just what administrators wielding discretion must do before, during, and after their decisions.

Often these procedural requirements are interwoven with substantive ones. Thus both administrative and judicial review proceedings may look not only to whether the decision-maker followed correct procedures but also to the substantive wisdom and/or lawfulness of the decision. In nearly all nations such review will examine questions of law, that is, whether the decision is within the bounds of choice established by the legislation granting discretion and whether it is otherwise in accord with statutory law. Various legal systems vary enormously in the levels and the degree to which reviewers may also question the policy, wisdom, or prudence of the initial decision, but some elements of substantive or merits review inhere in most legal systems.

In most English-speaking nations administrative decisions are subject to judicial review for abuse of discretion, which is commonly measured by whether officials have (1) considered something they should not have considered, (2) not considered something they should have considered, (3) given improper weight to something they should have considered, or (4) decided without sufficient evidence. These criteria suggest both that a court may not substitute its own judgment on what the right decision would be for that of the official exercising discretion and that the official decision-maker is subject to a check on the basic fairness and reasonableness of the way he or she went about making the decision. Civil law concepts of détournement du pouvoir are comparable. As their very wording suggests, they treat discretion as power, but they establish a regime of judicial supervision of even such power to ensure that it has been exercised for the public purposes it was intended to achieve and in a fundamentally fair way.

Indeed in many legal systems there is an endemic pressure to inject more law into discretion and whittle away at its boundaries. The United States Supreme Court holds that even when a statute specifically assigns a matter to agency discretion, courts may review its decisions unless "there is no law to apply." British courts, confronted by a tradition in which Parliament grants broad discretion to administrative agencies and tribunals and seeks to shield them entirely from judicial review, nonetheless have discovered that they must reverse administrative decisions for "clear error of law on the face of the record." European administrative courts have similarly held that even administrative decisions solely within the discretion of the ministries are void if they are in conflict with law.

Discretion frequently is granted by statute to administrative officers to decide highly particularized questions about government's treatment of individuals. Particularly in modern, industrialized, regulatory, welfare states, government officers must make millions of decisions about individual entitlements to various government benefits and about whether or not individuals and organizations have or have not violated some law or rule and, if they have, what to do about it. Here the potential conflict between flexibility and the rule of law can be seen most clearly. The rule of law requires that such decisions be made according to relatively fixed, known, preexisting legal rules, rather than at the discretion of officials. Yet in a number of situations a pure rule of law solution is either impractical or impossible. Among these are situations in which the administrative agency must distribute a scarce resource of which there is not enough to supply all those legally entitled to receive it, for instance, only 1,000 public housing units are available for 10,000 legally qualified families. Another is high-volume low-level decisions in which the costs of controlling discretion outweigh the benefits and yet it is undesirable to eliminate the discretion. It may be deemed undesirable to require parking officers to ticket every illegally parked vehicle. Yet it may be impossible to maintain a record of, let alone audit, every one of the officer's decisions *not* to ticket. A third frequently encountered situation is one in which an official must make many decisions involving subtle and complex assessments of human characteristics. The official, choosing among two job applicants with equal formal qualifications, the prosecutor deciding whether to charge as an accomplice the close friend to whose house a robber went immediately after the crime, and the social worker deciding whether a family is suitable for the placement of a foster child are examples. Here the decision rests on an experiential and prudential "feel" for the human condition that does not seem to be subsumable under rules and in which following rules will lead to a less good result than discretion would.

In all of these situations there is a general tendency to narrow the boundaries of discretion over time, partly by substituting rules for discretion and partly by introducing various devices that permit at least postauditing of the prudence of the decisions reached. Thus the making of unemployment, disability, pension, general assistance, and family grant payments tends in most countries over time to move to a very extensive and complex regime of strict rules that replace official discretion concerning who is or is not entitled to payments. This occurs even though it is recognized that individual and family conditions vary so infinitely that rules can never fully capture them. The pattern is invariably one in which abuses of discretion accumulate, either through favoritism to friends, relatives, coreligionists, and so on, or through petty spite, malice, or laziness. Rules are incrementally introduced to eliminate such aberrations. As rules accumulate, there are complaints of red tape and injustice done through rigid application. The response is not usually the elimination of rules but their amendment to make those that are punitive more and more underinclusive and those that are beneficial more and more overinclusive, so that individual suffering will be reduced. However, this occurs at the cost of increasing the number of incorrect decisions, from the government's point of view.

In addition to procedural requirements and the substitution of rules for discretion, there is a wide array of other devices for confining discretion. One not normally noted in legal analysis is of particular importance. Many of those wielding discretion hold their official positions by virtue of various professional qualifications. Both consciously and unconsciously their discretion is limited by the canons of professional practice with which they have been imbued. Government engineers may have the authority to choose among alternative bridge designs, but they will not choose a design that their training indicates is unsafe. Where large numbers of small, low-visibility discretionary decisions are involved, such as decisions to arrest, postauditing by statistical analysis may identify patterns of unwise or unlawful decision-making that can be attacked by organizational changes of various sorts, even if past individual injustices cannot be corrected.

Often the most powerful check on administrative discretion is budgetary control both by superior administrators and by the legislature and its committees. Such oversight through budgetary hearings and staff analysis may track the course of particular discretionary decisions or the pattern of such decisions. It can reward or punish past discretionary choices and direct or prevent future ones through channelling the life blood of bureaucracy: money. Such a check on judicial discretion is not usually available, however, because of fears of compromising the independence of the judiciary.

Budgetary control may either seek to control discretion in advance or serve as a postaudit device. Statutory control may operate in both ways as well. A statute granting discretion to administrators may seek, to a greater or lesser degree, to bound that discretion in advance. Indeed the Supreme Court has from time to time toyed with the idea that a statute that does not sufficiently bound the discretion it grants to the executive branch violates the constitutional separation of powers requirement. Yet in reality American statutes range from bounding discretion only by principles of policy so vague and sweeping that they could justify almost any discretionary administrative decision to provisions so minutely detailed that the discretion granted by the statute with one hand is withdrawn by the other. Other legal systems go as far or further. Many allow executive action "when it shall appear to the minister" or that the minister is "satisfied" or "the minister has concluded" that a given state of facts exist or that it would serve the public interest to take the actions chosen. Such "subjectivity" clauses in statutes require only that the minister have achieved a certain internal state of mind before acting. They serve more as a moral than a legal restraint on ministerial conduct. They may, however, restrain discretion by placing clear responsibility for decision on a politically accountable leader rather than a faceless bureaucracy.

Statutes are also a significant postaudit device for both administrators and judges. When administrators exercise discretion under a statute, the legislation may subsequently be amended to indicate that they did not act as the legislature intended, or at least that they are forbidden to act in future as they have acted in past. Statutes may correct judicial discretion based on statutory interpretation in the same way and without perceived threat to judicial independence.

Ultimately, of course, in democratic regimes, elections are the central pre- and postaudit of administrative, and sometimes of judicial, discretion. The voters may choose for office those whom they most trust to wield discretion and throw out of office those that have failed that trust. Traditional theories of prospective elections that conceive voters as choosing for office those whose policy proposals they approve have been followed by theories of retrospective elections. These perceive voters as essentially punishing past conduct in office rather than choosing future conduct. These theories in turn have been supplemented by current "competence" theories that see voters as choosing among current candidates on the basis of predictions about the candidates' general competence to run government rather than preferences among their specific policy proposals.

APPEAL

Of course the postaudit device most familiar to legal analysts is appeal. Elaborate chains of internal agency appeal very typically appear where low-level officials must make masses of decisions that affect individuals and depend upon high personalized and thus highly discretionary findings. Some appeal within agencies from lower to higher, and particularly to political agency head, exists nearly everywhere. In some instances these devices allow someone other than the initial decision-maker to make a second decision de novo. In other instances the initial discretionary decision may be reversed only for errors of procedural or substantive law or for clear prejudice or unreasonableness. Many statutory arrangements that place responsibility for decision in the minister, or in the "commissioners" of a multiheaded agency, are in fact appeals procedures in which actual decisions are made lower down but must be passed to the top for final approval. Because in theory the top of an agency is always responsible for what goes on below, such special, specific vesting of decision-making in the top typically is a way of saying that the top ought to review these particular decisions more carefully and more de novo than it does other decisions.

Appeal beyond the agencies to the courts is a widely practiced and widely varying post hoc control of administrative discretion. When administrative agencies are asked to act like courts, that is, engage in highly particularized decisions about who is legally entitled to or best qualified or most deserving of some benefit or punishment, ultimately they are driven to act like courts, substituting rules and precedents for unfettered personal judgment. And as the agencies are required to act more and more like courts, it comes to seem natural to set real courts to watch them. Sometimes the process is reversed. Courts are set to review agencies. Courts are most comfortable reviewing other courts. So courts set to review agencies will tend to force the agencies to act more and more like courts, or more precisely like the trial courts that appeals courts are accustomed to reviewing. Under this pressure the agencies will adopt quasijudicial procedures and in turn their quasijudicial behavior will make it appear natural that they should be reviewed by real and higher courts.

On the other hand, strong arguments are often made against judicial review of agency discretion. Where review of masses of individual claims is at issue, both the money costs and the time costs of delay, and the lesser competence of appellate courts than the persons who initially investigate them to deal with the primary facts, counsels against extensive review. Questions of relative competence also arise acutely when it is proposed to set courts to review complex technological decisions made by agencies that have accumulated technical expert that the courts have not. Where courts are institutionally wedded to complex regimes of procedural and substantive rights, the issue may be whether, in certain areas of public decision, interests in expediency ought to overcome those rights. Judicial review of certain kinds of security or emergency decisions may be precluded for this reason. On the contrary, judicial review may be introduced to ensure that rights are not overriden on the plea of emergency.

Finally, and most centrally in modern bureaucratic states, judicial review becomes a difficult question when "policy" discretion is at issue. Where administrative discretion is essentially policy discretion, judicial review inevitably is, to some degree, policy review, even when it is thickly disguised as procedural review and/or statutory interpretation. If judicial review shifts policy discretion from administrators to judges, of what use is it? Do we cure the problems of administrative discretion by adding judicial discretion, by setting judicial discretion wielders to watch administrative discretion wielders? This is Plato's classic problem of who guards the guardians.

Like most classic problems, it is unlikely to be solved in the abstract. Questions will immediately arise as to just who the administrators are, just who the judges are, just what the policies are, and what the institutional setting is. It is in the area of administrative rule-making that these questions become most pressing.

ADMINISTRATIVE RULE-MAKING

Where an administrative agency has been assigned not the discretion to make particularized decisions about individuals but the discretion to make laws, or rules, or policies of broad effect on the society as a whole, we usually expect them to act not like a court but like a legislature and "promulgate a rule." Some statutes providing for administrative rule-making also provide for judicial review, some are silent, and some specifically exclude review. Even where review is not excluded, there is often little or nothing on which a court may base an invalidation of a rule because the ministry's findings of fact are taken as final and the law delegating rule-making discretion contains no legal norms against which the rule can be tested. In some systems executive supplementary law-making is reviewed by a committee of the legislature itself and/or is said to be limited by such devices as collective cabinet responsibility, parliamentary inquiry and the possibility of withdrawal of confidence by the parliament. Such devices are, for the most part, illusory but may place some limits on the most extreme abuses of rule-making discretion.

The prevalence of legislative delegation of rule-making power to administrators and the enormous power it vests in executive officials has led to a growing judicial and public restiveness since the 1950s. Much of the movement toward judicially enforceable constitutional individual rights to be seen worldwide is directed as much against executive abuses of rule-making authority as against abuses of legislative power. From a position in the 1950s in which nearly all national courts deferred almost entirely to administrative "expertise" in rule-making, the courts of a number of countries, most notably the United States, have moved to a far more aggressive review of rule making often backed by new or amended statutes providing for greater review. Courts still universally profess to defer to the executive's "policy" judgments. However, more and more often they find devices for treating more of the rule-making process as involving questions of law on which the judges are the ultimate experts or questions of fact about which the executive must at least show that it has made sufficient inquiry.

The attempt to control discretion while purportedly leaving "political" or "policy" choice unfettered has largely taken the form of piling up procedural requirements. The effort is less to place legal limits on executive discretion than to make executive decision-making processes more "transparent," that is, more subject to public scrutiny and public response both before and after decisions are made. One, not entirely happy, result is that those wielding discretion are much more subject to pressure from a much wider range of interest groups than they once were. Most notable in the United States, but also in Great Britain and in Europe, such discretionary rule-making more often gives rise to litigation than it once did. As procedural requirements mount, it becomes easier to show that the administrative agency has made a procedural error. The degree to which the courts of any given nation have been using procedural objections as smoke screens behind which to strike down rules in which their real objections are on policy grounds is a perennial subject of debate. It is argued that more active review defeats the very purpose of rule-making, which is to make quicker, more flexible, more detailed government response than a legislature can make by statute. In the United States rule-making has taken on so many of the trappings of an adversary, judicial proceeding and is subject to such detailed and prolonged judicial review that many observers believe that it has become almost as cumbersome as the legislative process. It is not so much that the ultimate policy discretion of the rule makers has been severely cut back as that the costs of wielding that discretion in a nonconsensual way have been enormously increased. Such tendencies likewise exist in all systems that attempt to increase public supervision of executive discretion by procedural requirements designed to increase transparency.

In the nations moving from one-party socialist systems to party competition and mixed economies, rule of law and transparency are of particular concern. Such states typically have histories of secret decision-making and the wielding of party discretion to override even the laws and rules enacted by party dominated government. Enormous revivals of administrative law, usually based on European models, are now underway in such countries designed to increase administrative obedience to law, transparency, and review of discretionary action. As the power of centralized rule-making by the commission increases in the European Community, interest also increases in the introduction of more procedural devices and more active judicial review to increase the transparency and reduce the discretionary component of Community rule-making.

DISCRETION IN PLANNING

Lying between the millions of discretionary decisions of "small" individual claims and the discretion to make general rules lie a host of government discretionary decisions about large, but particular, matters. Many of these are "planning" decisions, for instance, where an airport should be built or a highway routed. Many others involve government financial and economic activities, such as interest rates or government borrowing or the business strategies of a government-owned firm or industry. There is the desire, on the one hand, to vest unfettered "management" discretion in government because the decisions involve such a mixture of uncertain and rapidly changing facts, uncontrollable outside forces, and pure policy considerations that they do not seem to be suitable for rule-bound decision-making at all. On the other hand, these decisions have so much potential for adversely affecting individual interests that it seems undesirable to leave them entirely to the discretion of a handful of government officials.

The revival of interest in constitutional property rights in the United States, including the concern for "regulatory takings," the worldwide disillusionment with socialist planning, the countervailing interest in "industrial policy," and concerns about adversary legalism are now generating acute concerns about discretion in planning. Of course any distinction between planning and regulatory discretion is somewhat artificial because webs of environmental, health and safety, and financial regulation are now so thick that they impinge on planning at every turn. The general picture often portrayed is one in which the mix of planning, regulation, and subsidy practiced by European and Japanese governments in close and largely confidential relations with enterprises and unions is to be contrasted with arms-length, very public, often adversarial and litigation-prone processes in the United States. The European style is said to be rapid and efficient, because it avoids confrontation, encourages cooperation, and inspires voluntary compliance. The American style is said to lead to planning failure and delayed implementation, particularly because complex, highly legalized procedures, and opportunities for multiple and overlapping administrative and judicial review encourage confrontation and resistance. Put somewhat differently, the European style is one of maximum discretion wielded with low visibility by a small elite of government and private managers and technicians; the American style is one of highly pluralist, transparent, and heavily rule-bound discretion.

Nevertheless American planning has also been criticized for granting excessive discretion to government planners. The problem is most openly observed in urban land use planning, but is found in many other areas as well. The typical system has become one in which draconian rules are legislated and/or unbridled discretion is vested in planning authorities to block private development. The unbridled discretion is either in the open form of broad authorizations to the planning agency to protect the public interest, or in sets of procedures and permissions so detailed and complex that no developer can get through them without the good will of the administrators. Actual development then depends upon waivers and exceptions granted by government to the excessive substantive and procedural demands that government has made. Planning then becomes bargaining between government and all other interested parties about how much those who wish to go forward must pay in the form of "mitigation" or "amenities." Precisely because the legal form of these negotiations is that one party is asking to be allowed to "break" the law, and the government has the lawful authority but no legal obligation to allow the party to do so, the government has absolute discretion as to what price it exacts from the party subject to planning. Any restraints on the discretion of the government agency are economic and political, not legal. That is, the planning agency may be threatened by political action such as a legislated change in its planning authority or by the withdrawal of development plans and subsequent economic loss to the city, but it is legally free to extort from the developer whatever it can get for granting waivers and exemptions it is under no obligation to grant.

The problems inherent in such waiver and exception planning are further exacerbated by any attempt to limit such discretion by judicial review. Precisely because the acts of government are formally characterized as ones that deviate from the law on the books, those who wish to engage in court challenges to the government's refusal to grant an exception find themselves on weak legal ground. Once a bargain is struck, however, no matter how advantageous to others than the prospective developer, all those who would have wished to extract an even higher price for the waivers and exceptions granted are in a strong position to sue, precisely because what is granted is not the law but an exception to the law and thus legally suspect.

One counter to both the wide discretion granted by such waiver and exception planning and the subsequent litigational leverage of those opposing enterprise is reassertion of the property rights of those being planned over. So here we encounter a classic dialectic between private rights and government discretion. Another response is to simplify planning procedures and rewrite planning statutes to create legal entitlement to develop rather than laws against development with waiver and exception clauses. Yet the discretion to waive or grant exceptions to legal rules would seem to be essential at least to some degree in all regimes of planning. At least a catch-22 is involved. Planning statutes may vest nearly total discretion in the planners bounded by only few and vague general rules. In such instances the planner need not be granted discretion to waive rules, because there are no rules. Because there are no rules, however, the planner has too much general discretion. If, however, that general discretion is bounded by many detailed rules, planning cannot proceed efficiently unless the planner is granted discretion to waive the rules. The discretion to waive is itself a form of discretion that it is particularly difficult to protect from abuse.

The American response has largely been to make exception-granting a more and more transparent, pluralist participatory process, to limit or validate discretion by making it a more and more public act. This approach has its own costs. As more groups with more pay off-demands participate, the costs of waivers go up. The potential for postbargaining litigation increases as more parties challenge whatever final bargain did not give them all of what they wanted. As the number of players and the stakes rise, each development scheme for which particular waivers are needed is treated more and more as a separate planning event. The very ad hoc nature of all exception and waiver schemes is thus further exaggerated, so that whatever comprehensive quality the planning regime was supposed to have becomes further diluted. On the other hand, it may well be argued that it is precisely the public opening up of the waiver process that ensures that the waiver will not be treated as an ad hoc, highly particularized matter because various participating groups will bring broader community-wide concerns to the process.

The administrative law of waivers and exception is best developed where the exception involves highly individualized interests of relatively little consequence to the community at large. In such instances the multiplication of procedural rules and layers of review is a common response. Little real progress has been made, however, in developing legal devices for ensuring against the potential for abuse of discretion inherent in exception and waiver planning regimes. For better or worse, larger political and economic forces currently are the major restraint on that kind of planning discretion.

INFORMAL ACTION AND THE DISCRETION TO BARGAIN

Some planning decisions, including some waiver or exception decisions, are made through a relatively formal hearing process. Many are made without formalities, either in the routine work of officials at their desks or in internal conferences. Many more are made in negotiations with developers, neighborhood groups, and others. In this sense, the land use planning process is a microcosm of government decision-making as a whole. Most of what government does it does by "informal action," that is, by a host of successive, interlocking decisions made without formal procedures or record in the course of day-to-day business. A substantial share of government decision-making is now done in informal negotiating settings in which bargains are struck between government and those whom it regulates, or services, or who service it. Of course most business dealings are by such essentially private negotiation, and that fact has never put them beyond the reach of judicial review. Contract, tort, patent, and dozens of other areas of private and criminal law, as well as civil rights, labor, and other bodies of public law, bear on such negotiations and provide for judicial supervision through regular lawsuits between the parties. When government is a party, it is, with some exceptions for sovereign immunity, subject to the same kind of Diceyian supervision. Disputes between a private individual and government are submitted to settlement by a regular court under regular law as if the government were itself a private party. This approach is precisely that which 19th century English liberals viewed as the essence of the rule of law and attainable without any special body of administrative proceedings.

Today, however, there is increasing pressure to bring even these informal actions of government under some kind of supervision beyond that provided by the potential for ordinary lawsuits. Freedom of information and sunshine statutes are designed to provide more public observation of the total stream of government decisions. Where government acts by negotiation with multiple competing private interests, the move to negotiate is itself a move toward greater public observation. Much government negotiation, however, is either with a single party or a small number of mutually supporting groups. Such negotiation may often appear to be a kind of conspiracy or capture, greatly in need of public ventilation. Yet such negotiation often depends on confidentiality for success. Bargaining or negotiation often represents the most extreme case of government discretion in which officials even have the discretion to negotiation away the full enforcement of the law. Plea bargaining is perhaps the most dramatic example. All sorts of regulatory negotiation, however, including environmental negotiation, include discretionary reductions in legal obligation in return for some level of voluntary compliance.

One fairly obvious and frequent move to limit such discretion is to increase the responsibility of higher executives for such bargains, requiring them to approve bargains struck by their subordinates. Routine discretion-supervising devices, such as administrative appeal followed by appeal to the courts, are difficult in such situations. For if one of the parties to a bargain, having gained some concessions and given others in the course of agreeing to it, is then free to file administrative appeals against the concessions he or she gave, the whole bargaining process may become inoperable. The move toward environmental mediation and negotiation to avoid cumbersome rule-making and administrative adjudication procedures, and many similar moves, ran into grave difficulties because appeal is both an expected mode of supervising the discretion wielded by government in such negotiations and potentially destructive of the whole process.

Particularly where the mere public observability of government decisions is not enough or is inappropriate, or formalized administrative decision and appeals processes are viewed as too cumbersome and/or adversary and so replaced by more informal bargaining processes, it is hard to know how to supervise government discretion. This difficulty constitutes a major reason why contemporary regulatory strategies turn increasingly toward economic incentives implemented through markets. For instance, a market in pollution permits substitutes an open, publicly observable mode of granting permission to break the law a little as a substitute for official discretion in granting waivers or bargaining compliance.

The most obvious tool for checking informal action and bargaining discretion by government administrators is, of course, political responsibility. Elected or politically appointed higher executives, parliamentary question periods, congressional hearings, and various postauditing institutions such as the General Accounting Office designed to bring information about administrative decisions to legislatures and political executives are the central and essential tools of bringing administrative discretion under public control. This centrality of political control must be especially emphasized. Too often the search for legal control of discretion becomes frantic and counterproductive because it conceives itself as either the only or the necessarily best mode of controlling discretion. The result may be an unrelenting pressure to introduce formalized, courtlike proceedings and courts themselves into more and more phases of government decision-making. There are frequent complaints today that a climate of "adversary legalism" is strangling the regulatory sphere of American government, creating inflexibility and inertia at huge costs both to economic development and protection of the public. These charges are countered by claims that higher levels of legalization have resulted in more open, more correct, better reasoned, and more responsible discretionary decisions by government than would have been achieved otherwise. No matter how the balance between these claims is struck, however, it seems unlikely that turning every discretionary decision of government into a trial decided by a judge is the ultimate solution to the problem of discretion.

Nevertheless, tendencies in that direction are sufficient that no account of administrative discretion would be complete without a consideration of judicial discretion.

JUDICIAL DISCRETION

In spite of the judges' claim that they are only ensuring that administrative decisions lie within the statutory rules that bound the range of discretionary choice, it is obvious that ultimately those who place the final stamp of judicial approval on discretion must themselves be wielding some discretion. To some degree the reviewing judge must do for a second time the same discretionary weighing of costs, benefits, and values that the administrator wielding discretion first did. Some element of judicial discretion to review the merits of discretionary decisions always inheres in an abuse of discretion or détournement de pouvoir standard of judicial review. Similar elements of policy discretion are also often hidden behind procedural and jurisdictional review. Judges are more likely to find procedural errors and jurisdictional excesses in administrative decisions that appear to them wildly imprudent on the merits than in those in which they believe discretion to have been wielded soundly. Judicial review of administrative interpretation of statutes also contains major elements of discretion. Many judicial decisions holding that an administrative act fails for "clear error of law" really arise in situations where a statute allows a discretionary choice of interpretations and a court believes that an agency has made a poor choice.

In one of its aspects, the issue of judicial discretion is but a fact of the issue of judicial law-making. Although many judges and a few legal scholars persist in the view that judges only "discover" or "interpret" rather than "make" law, the phenomenon of judicial law-making is widely recognized. If judges make law, they wield discretion, in the sense of the power of choice, over what law to make. Ultimately all interpretation (including statutory interpretation) involves the power to choose between contending meanings.

STATUTORY INTERPRETATION

The renewed interest in statutory interpretation that seized the American legal world in the late 1980s is a direct response to the changing character of judicial review of the rule-making discretion vested in administrative agencies. In the 1960s, 1970s, and 1980s the courts of appeal dramatically increased their supervision of agency rule-making. At first this increase took the form of demands for more elaborately pluralistic rule-making procedures and then for more reasoned elaboration of agency decisions. Although largely characterized by the judges as procedural review, the substantive character of much of this review peeped through. Moreover, Congress switched from a statutory style that granted extremely broad rule-making power to the agencies to one in which agency rule-making was much more vigorously and precisely subordinated to the substantive demands of the statutes. Judicial review of rules for "lawfulness" thus became substantive review because the statutes themselves were more substantive. Whether or not an agency rule was in accord with the statutes authorizing rule-making depended upon what the statute's substantive demands were. What the statute's substantive demands really were was a matter of statutory interpretation. Thus courts that had earlier disguised their substantive disagreements with agency policy choices as quibbles over the agencies' procedures now could cast their policy disagreements as disagreements over statutory interpretation. The extent to which courts grant agencies unfettered policy discretion in rule-making is the extent to which courts defer to agency interpretation of the statute under which the rule is made.

The American experience of divided government escalates the concern for statutory interpretation. The situation is frequently one in which an agency of a Republican administration is "interpreting" a statute passed by Democratic congressional votes. Two alternative visions of this situation are available. In one, when a statute authorizes an agency to make rules, the statute is establishing a range of discretion, within which a number of alternative rules might be chosen. The agency is essentially engaging in a task of law-making discretion. Within the range established by the statute, the agency may choose A, B, or C. Its choice of A, B, or C may legitimately be determined by whether it is an agency of a Republican or a Democratic administration. Indeed, by granting rule-making authority to choose among alternatives within boundaries, the statute-maker is acknowledging that within those boundaries the rule may change as the policy preferences of the agency change. In this view, it is perfectly proper for an agency to say that the last administration chose rule A because it was Democratic; we choose rule B because we are Republican. So long as our choice is within the statutory boundaries, rule A is not legally right and rule B legally wrong, just because Rule A got there first.

Most rule-making constitutes decision under conditions of uncertainty in which the uncertainties are resolved in one direction or another in large part on the basis of policy preferences. If science tells us that it is completely uncertain whether the risk of cancer from a given chemical is 0 percent or 5 percent and uncertain whether the economic gain from use of the chemical is $0 or $5, Republicans are entitled to choose risk 0% and $5 and Democrats risk 5 percent and $0, with Republicans then writing a rule permitting the chemical and Democrats a rule forbidding it. As long as the science remains the same, no better reason than "we are Democrats, they are Republicans" ought to be necessary for changing the rule as the election results change.

On the other hand, a statute authorizing rule-making may be viewed as having a single precise, even if not precisely stated, substantive goal in mind rather than as creating a range of discretion with boundaries. The statute is then viewed as commanding not "you may choose either A, B, or C, so long as you do not choose F, G, or H;" rather, it may be seen as saying "we authorize the rule maker to choose and only to choose that rule that best implements the substance of this statute." The rule-maker, strictly speaking, is granted no discretion. Instead it is commanded to choose precisely the rule that the legislation envisions. There is a single right rule, and it is the statutory duty of the agency to find it. Once it is found, if the agency subsequently wants to change it, it may not say "We used our discretion before in a Democratic way; now we want to use it in a Republican way." Instead it must say either "Now we have discovered that the rule we wrote before was wrong" or, "Now we have discovered that circumstances have so changed that the purpose of the statute can only be achieved by a new and different rule."

In one view a reviewing court is asking whether the agency has breached the bounds of its discretion. In the other view the court is asking "Did the agency reach the single best rule to fit the statute?" Both questions, of course, require some statutory interpretation. Yet under one view the agency loses only if it has bootstrapped itself beyond the powers granted it by the statute. In the other, the agency loses if it has not discerned exactly what the statute wanted and done it. Of course, in the real world some statutes may in fact grant agencies bounded discretion, and others may indeed have wanted the agency to come up with the single correct rule to achieve the statutory purpose, which, for some reason or other, the statute-giver could not precisely formulate but believed could be found.

Currently, then, the subjects of administrative law and statutory interpretation are inextricably entwined and come down to the question of whether statutes that grant rule-making authority grant discretion or command that agencies find the single right rule. Questions of whether courts should defer to agency statutory interpretation or are themselves responsible for determining what the law means come down to the same issue of discretion. Ultimately the question being asked is whether agencies are to be treated as little legislatures—free to change their laws as their policy preferences change—or as little courts—free to change their laws only when they can argue persuasively that their old legal decisions were wrong or have become wrong due to new circumstances. Both academic authorities and courts currently are in considerable disarray over these questions.

JUDICIAL DISCRETION AND ADMINISTRATIVE DISCRETION

Whether in the arena of statutory interpretation or other arenas of procedural and substantive review, the employment of courts to check administrative discretion invokes the classic question of who guards the guardians. No matter how often repeated, the assertion that reviewing judges only decide whether administrative discretion was wielded according to law or not is misleading. Judicial supervision of administrative discretion inevitably checks the discretion of administrators by subjecting them, to some degree, to the discretion of judges. The cost to the people or to the legislature of setting the judges to watch the administrators is an increase in the discretion of judges. Given that judges are less subject to direct electoral or legislative control than are administrators, transferring some measure of discretion from administrators to judges would not appear, on its face, to be a good idea. If the only justification for the transfer is the mistaken belief that all it entails is a substitution of law for discretion rather than of judicial discretion for administrative discretion, we ought not to be enthusiastic about markedly increasing judicial review of administrative discretion.

A number of justifications for active review have been offered beyond that of the simple substitution of law for discretion. These justifications rest on a comparison of the merits of administrators and judges as decision-makers. Administrative discretion is discretion bounded by law, so expertise in law is essential to defining the limits of administrative discretion. Judges can plausibly claim a greater expertise in law than administrators. Furthermore, administrators may have a self-interest in pushing on the legal boundaries of their discretion. Judges are more neutral policers of these boundaries, or, perhaps, they are faithful watchdogs of the legislature in keeping administrators within the bounds set by legislation.

These conventional arguments have been supplemented with newer claims that account for much of the relative appeal of judicial discretion over administrative discretion. We are in the midst of a grave distrust of administrative expertise. Administrative agencies may be "captured" by special interests. Administrators necessarily suffer from professional deformation. That is, precisely because each is expert at some particular subject area or technology, he or she has a special interest in his or her own concerns or programs which, by definition, disturbs any ability to make disinterested decisions in that area. The people who have devoted their lives to developing agricultural irrigation programs cannot possibly be the best people to decide how much water goes to farmers and how much to cities. Agencies that operate programs are prone to pragmatic invasions of individual interests or rights in order to achieve overall programmatic goals. Agencies that possess technical knowledge are prone to disguise what are really discretionary and thus debatable policy judgments as unassailable "scientific" findings. Technocrats, by that very status, are not democrats and pose the threat of elite, mandarin rule. Finally, particularly in an age of divided government, administrative agencies may yield to immediate political pressures at the cost of faithful obedience to the statutes that direct their discretion.

The judge may appear to be the ideal corrective to technocratic government gone awry. Judges are neither technological experts nor program operators. Thus they bring to bear general, lay, that is to say, democratic, perspectives. They are relatively insulated from immediate political pressures. Because they regulate the whole range of interests, they are not so subject to capture by any one. They are, by definition, neutral and independent. If they suffer from any professional deformation, it is toward an overemphasis on law. Given that we are seeking to bind administrative discretion by law, this deformation helps rather than hinders the cause. The process of litigation can have certain advantages over that of administration for deliberating seriously over basic questions of value and for testing factual assertions, policy proposals, and predictions about the future state of things emanating from self-interested sources. Thus some degree of substitution of judicial discretion for administrative discretion is, first of all, ameliorated by the judge's dedication to law and, just as importantly, is the substitution of a better and, even ultimately, more democratic discretion.

The various responses are too obvious to detain us long here. The institutional neutrality and independence of judges must be balanced against actual selection methods and persons selected. Expertise in law may be as professionally deforming as other expertise. Far from offering an especially good mode of deliberation, litigation from adversarial stances may distort fact finding and encourage excessive and rigid claims. Judicial dedication to law easily becomes conflation of what the judge thinks best and what the law demands.

The paradox of judicial discretion to counter administrative discretion cannot be solved. It usually leads instead to the conclusion that judges ought to counter administrative discretion with their own, but not too much. Much of administrative law doctrine consists of verbal formula, such as "arbitrary and capricious," "abuse of discretion," "hard look," "reasoned elaboration" designed to, but inevitably failing to, capture precisely how much judicial discretion is enough.

DISCRETION AND EFFECTIVE DECISION-MAKING

The relation of law to discretion may be viewed in the light of modern political and organizational theories of decision-making and long-standing traditions of prudence. By the turn of the 20th century the Western world had experienced a vast exhilaration of the spirit of science. Science and its attendant technologies promised marvelous human control over nature and thus improvement in the human condition. Social sciences were announced that might emulate the physical and biological sciences. Among them was the science of public administration, or administrative science. Initially largely oriented to questions of how policies chosen by others might be rationally, precisely, and correctly carried out by administrators, this movement soon came to claim that many areas of government activity were purely technical rather than political in character and could be conducted on a purely scientific, objective, neutral, nonpartisan basis by experts. In countries subject to Roman law this new claim for science resonated with the older claim of Roman law itself to be a neutral, universal legal science common to all Europeans and the concept of a nonpartisan, neutral, legally expert civil service that had stemmed from that claim. In England the new science was consonant with civil service traditions. In the United States it led to massive civil service reform designed to create the kind of government services that Europe already enjoyed.

By the 1930s technocracy (scientific rule by expert administrators) was a significant aspect of Western democracies, of both Fascism and Communism, and of Socialist aspirations, as in the "scientific socialism" of the Fabians. From the perspective of nonbelieving outsiders, the administrative science movement was merely the wholesale transfer of policy-making discretion from the citizens and their elected legislators to political executives and their administrative subordinates. From the point of view of believers, the issue of discretion was not involved, because most decisions of government were purely technical and involved not discretion but scientific inquiry designed to achieve correct solutions. If there is a single right answer, there is no discretion.

This scientific stance has later been labeled *synopticism* by decision theorists. Synoptic decision strategies require that all relevant facts be gathered, all values or goals be clearly prioritized, all alternative policies be fully assessed, and the policy chosen that achieves the maximum satisfaction of the most important goals at the least cost. Central economic planning, indeed the whole vogue for planning of the pre- and post-World War II periods, was the epitome of synopticism.

By the 1960s many severe doubts about synopticism began to arise and a rival theory of decision-making appeared, often labeled "incrementalism." The incrementalists argued that the ideal of synopticism was not, could not, and indeed should not be met in real-world decision-making. Synopticism, they argued, imposed unacceptably and unattainably high costs on the decision process. Acquiring all the facts relevant to a given decision in modern, complex societies would involve enormous costs in money, time, and resources. In diverse societies, getting a completely agreed and prioritized list of values or goals was impossible. The costs of imagining and considering all alternatives would be as high as considering all facts, even if the human imagination were good enough to think of all alternatives. In short, fully "rational" "scientific" decision-making was either impossible or too costly. Incrementalism recovers the enormous role of discretion in policy-making which had been obscured by notions of scientific decision-making. For the incremental decision-maker chooses only a few facts, values, and alternatives to consider and he or she chooses among a number of small-step policy changes, none of which is even supposed to be "correct" in any absolute sense.

Incremental theory has recently come under critical scrutiny from two directions, both of which emphasize discretion even more than does incrementalism. On the one hand, critics of incrementalism have charged that it is excessively wedded to the status quo and to small change when often larger and more continuous change is needed. If decision-makers are to consider larger as well as smaller changes and to consider change even when things are not going too badly, they will have more discretion not less. On the other hand, critics have argued that incrementalism overestimates its own potential for rationality. In reality the small change—feedback—further small change low-risk cycle may be a comforting illusion. It is so difficult to imagine what the next state of the world will be like that all policy decisions are large policy gambles. Sticking to the status quo and/or small changes may entail risks as large as large changes seem to entail. This point is most obvious in foreign policy decision-making. Of course if all policies are policy gambles because the world is so unpredictable, those who wager the stakes necessarily have great discretion.

Thus theories of organizational decision-making have thrown up two models of limitations on discretion: incrementalism and synopticism. The former emphasizes that those who wield discretion must and should limit themselves to small changes. The latter, in theory at least, eliminates discretion entirely by predicating a single correct answer to every policy question. If there is a single correct answer, there is no discretion to choose among answers. It now appears clear, however, that synopticism is usually both impossibly expensive and impossible to achieve and that the small steps of incrementalism do not necessarily guarantee success. The attempt to replace administrative discretion with a set of strict legal rules and procedures that has reached a pinnacle in the United States has likewise come under increasing attack. Such an attempt may only transfer policy discretion from administrators to judges and may render decision-making slow, cumbersome, and adversarial when the world's problems demand more rapid, efficient, and cooperative action. Increasingly there are calls for less law and more negotiation and mediation, which inevitably means more discretion vested in the negotiators. There is also a growing appeal, particularly in environmental policy, for a more European approach that uses detailed statutory rules less, vests more discretion in political executives, and operates by a less rule-bound, less public style of discretionary bargaining among government, business, and labor executives. Although both the American and European literatures of administrative law have always emphasized rule over discretion, the general literature of administration has always stressed executive "leadership," which implies great discretion.

The growing appeal of discretionary bargaining in the United States is matched by the growing appeal of legal limits on discretion in Eastern Europe. As long as obeisance continued to the claim of the Communist Party that it made scientifically correct decisions, the issue of discretion disappeared as it does under models of synopticism in the West. Once the Communist claim to scientific correctness dissolved, it became clearer that the Party's claim to unconstrained political authority was a claim to total, unbounded discretion. Eastern European states are now in the process of rebuilding legal regimes to limit government discretion. The growth of constitutional judicial review in Western Europe and the growing European interest in employing administrative law as a vehicle for human rights are movements in the same direction. Whether English courts and the administrative courts of Western Europe, and especially France, have retained their relatively passive stance toward administrative discretion or have actually become more intrusive in their review of administrative action remains in question. Certainly there is great interest in various incentive systems designed to substitute decentralized, private market-driven choices for the discretionary choices of administration.

DISCRETION AS MORAL CHOICE

Recent movements in moral and political philosophy suggest that further uncertainties about discretion are now arising. Utilitarianism defines the good solely in terms of the preferences of individuals. Pluralist political theory and decision theory more generally turn this ethics into a practical standard for collective decision making. A government decision is good if it satisfies the preferences of the participating interests or interest groups, that is, if it gives each enough of what it wants to get it to accept the outcome. There is then no substantive standard of goodness for government decisions. The only standard is procedural. If all groups have participated in a decision and each (or most, or a majority) have given some modicum of consent to it, it is a good decision. Administration is then a kind of coat-holding for the group strugglers. Administrative discretion is the capacity to keep throwing proposed outcomes to the groups until they find one on which to settle.

Utilitarianism is now being challenged by various ethical movements that assert that the good is more and different than the sum of individual preferences and that the good, or at least the better, can be identified by deliberative processes that enlist not merely the particular interests or preferences of the participants but their critical moral senses. Such moral discourse will yield substantively better public policies. The duty of the administrator is to foster and participate in public deliberation.

In some senses the movement toward deliberation is a movement in reaction to pluralism and back toward synopticism. The incremental decision-maker stopped as soon as he or she satisficed. His or her decisions were not good or bad or even better or worse. They were simply whatever decision quieted things down among the contending groups. The deliberator is seeking the single, best decision in a world in which some decisions are intrinsically better or worse, no matter what the initial self-perceived preferences of the participants in decision making. In this deliberative world, it is not clear that there is any room for discretion. The deliberator has no choice but to reach the best decision. If discretion remains, it must be a kind of authority to make prudential guesses as to what would be best when the deliberators cannot arrive at a very certain conclusion about what would be best.

Such a view of discretion perhaps returns us to its basic appeal. Except at the height of realism, no one supposed that either administrative or judicial discretion entailed decision-makers doing whatever struck their fancy. The word discretion always had certain overtones of caution, prudence, and modesty about one's own infallibility. We wanted discretion, not indiscretion. Current optimism about the search for substantive good may, or may not, be misplaced, but it serves to reenforce this older belief that discretion ought to be something more and other than the mere power to do whatever one pleased within the boundaries set by law. Certainly American judicial review standards that have transmutted "arbitrary and capricious" from a lunacy test for administrators into a demand for reasoned and ultimately for substantively good decisions reflect the growing attraction of the view that discretion is not merely the freedom to act but the freedom to act well. If the substantive side of discretion is emphasized, however, strong movements are necessarily inspired again to bring discretion under more and more rules. For, if we can know the good, why not announce it in rules rather than trust to administrators to find it?

Thus the tension between rule and discretion is a permanent feature of policy-making and management because the real world confronts decision-makers with many situations in which single correct answers are not attainable and choice among uncertain alternatives is unavoidable. In such situations, discretion is inevitable, prudence is desirable, the ultimate aim is the discovery of the good and some bounds or limitations or discretions are deemed essential by those believing in democracy and/or opposing arbitrary government. The decades immediately preceding and following World War II were marked by a great fascination with "leadership," with its implications of broad discretion. Subsequent decades have seen a vast proliferation of constitutional and administrative law rules, and an increasing judicial activism aimed at limiting the discretion of political executives and bureaucrats. Yet the continuing demand that government act dynamically in response to economic, environmental, and security problems leaves open the question of how many limits we are willing to place on discretion.

REFERENCES

Kenneth Culp Davis, *Discretionary Justice,* University of Louisiana Press, Baton Rouge, 1969.

Yehizhel Dror, *Policymaking Under Adversity,* New York, 1986.

Serio Galeotte, *The Judicial Control of Public Authorities in England and Italy,* London, 1954.

C. J. Hamson, *Executive Discretion and Judicial Control,* London, 1954.

Martin Shapiro, Administrative discretion: The next stage, *Yale Law Journal,* 1983, 92: 1487–1522.

Martin Shapiro, *Who Guards the Guardians,* University of Georgia Press, Athens, GA, 1988.

Roger Vidal, L'évolution du détournement de pouvoir dans la jurisprudence administrative, *Revue du Droit Public et de la Science Politique,* 1952, 275–316.

James Q. Wilson, *Bureaucracy: What Government Agencies Do and Why They Do It,* Basic Books, New York, 1989.

19

Administrative Democracy

Gerald E. Frug *Harvard Law School, Cambridge, Massachusetts*

The conviction that the bureaucratic form of organization is indispensable has long co-existed with the doubts that have been expressed about its desirability. Max Weber, the foremost theorist of bureaucracy, asserted that "the choice is only that between bureaucracy and dilettantism in the field of administration,"[1] even though he also eloquently expressed his own anguish about the triumph of bureaucratic rationalism:

> [O]f this last stage of cultural development it might well truly be said: "Specialists without spirit, sensualists without heart; this nullity imagines that it has attained a level of civilization never before achieved."[2]

Of these two conflicting messages, the dominant ingredient has generally been the sense of inevitability: whether we like it or not, the overall message suggests, bureaucracy is here to stay.[3] As a result, debates about the legitimacy of bureaucracy (debates in which I have participated)[4] have for many people a rather unreal quality. Why debate the inevitable? In this chapter, therefore, I intend to put aside the issue of the desirability of the bureaucratic form of organization in order to focus instead on the possibility of changing it.

In recent years, some elements of the picture of a modern, nonbureaucratic world—or at least of a modern, less bureaucratic world—have begun to be described. One ingredient in this sketch (at the moment it is still only a sketch) involves the internal transformation of the primary locus of bureaucracy, the workplace. Life at work, a large literature has begun to argue, can be made much less hierarchical and much more democratic than normally is the practice today.[5] A second ingredient consists of reducing the size and reorganizing the structure of economic enterprise. The development of the large-scale corporation and its organization into a vehicle for mass production has been revealed as a historical choice rather than an economic necessity;[6] even today, it is argued, the hierarchical style of mass production could efficiently be replaced by much smaller, technologically sophisticated, highly flexible forms of economic organization.[7] A third ingredient involves reducing the extent of governmental regulation of (at least some of) these economic enterprises. By doing so, one can eliminate parts of the public bureaucracy that have been created in order to control the power exercised by private bureaucracy.[8] Other ingredients in this sketch include transforming the bureaucratic structure of the educational system[9] and attacking the influence of bureaucracy on the structure of family life.[10]

One major part of the picture of a postbureaucratic society, however, has not yet been adequately developed: the possibility of creating a more democratic administrative state. This omission is perhaps due to the power of the link between our conceptions of bureaucracy and of government, as well as to the pervasiveness of the notion that creating a truly democratic society requires the state to wither away. Instead of discussing the transformation of the administrative state, proponents of democracy have largely focused on eliminating it. Public policy, according to this vision, can be formulated through the direct participation of the public at large. It has become increasingly recognized, however, that even in a fully democratic society some form of governmental structure will continue to exist and must continue to be taken seriously.[11] The difficulty of inserting democratic forms into the public bureaucracy, therefore, must squarely be faced: How can one run a modern state without full-blown bureaucratic structures? Even if decentralization to nonbureaucratic forms were possible for (at least parts of) the activity of the private marketplace, is it not naive and impractical to suggest that, in our complex modern society, day-to-day government administration could be run democratically? This chapter addresses this aspect of the effort to replace bureaucratic forms of social organization with more democratic forms. To be sure, it too presents no more than a sketch. Indeed, any specific suggestions outlined below may well ultimately have to be replaced with others found, through experimentation, to be preferable. I will have accomplished my objective here, however, if I can shift the debate from the question of whether alternatives to bureaucracy are possible to the problem of identifying the best way to reform governmental institutions.

In attempting here to describe democratic forms of government administration, I do not draw such a sharp dichotomy between the concepts of bureaucracy and democracy that only a "purely democratic" government becomes acceptable. On the contrary, I argue that there are a wide variety of possible ways to organize the government and that these forms of organization often share characteristics normally associated with both the terms "bureaucracy" and "democracy." Bureaucracy is traditionally defined as an organization composed of a clearly defined hierarchy of offices filled with employees who are appointed because of their technical qualifications; bureaucratic employees are thought to engage in a kind of activity that is clearly distinguishable from politics (in Max Weber's words, they are "entirely separated from ownership of the means of administration").[12] Democracy, by contrast, is defined not in terms of hierarchy or technical qualifications but in terms of the equality of its members, not as a form of top-down control but as vehicle for popular control, not as a means of separating administration from politics but as a political form of organization. No pure example of either bureaucracy or democracy has ever existed, however, and the task of making the current structure of governmental organization more democratic does not require a pure form to be invented. "Administrative democracy" is not the opposite of bureaucracy but a form of organization continually engaged in expanding—sometimes step-by-step, sometimes dramatically—the role of democratic institutions within government administration. My argument for administrative democracy thus consists of a demonstration that it is possible to increase substantially the extent to which the organization of the government can be built on characteristics normally associated with democracy. Many of my suggestions are based on aspects of government administration (such as citizen advisory boards, public hearings, and juries) that currently nurture notions of equality, popular control, and politics in government decision-making. Indeed, the complicated mixture of bureaucracy and democracy that exists within the government today itself undermines the assertion that the "bureaucratic" form of organization is necessary or inevitable.

I discuss below five different aspects of the project of fostering administrative democracy. Four of these involve suggestions for making governmental institutions more democratic: the transformation of the internal organization of the government to promote workplace democracy; the creation of more effective public control of government administration; decentralization of political power; and the insertion of a democratic voice into the agencies of the national government that remain after decentralization has taken place. The bulk of this chapter thus seeks to answer the contention that bureaucracy is indispensable by describing democratic mechanisms that could, if we so desired, be incorporated into the government. The fifth section, however, discusses not a change in government institutions but the limited way we think about the possibility of such a change. This final section is devoted to a discussion of modern bureaucratic consciousness. One of the reasons that bureaucracy seems inevitable is the prevalent distrust of democracy, which has been nurtured by the process of accommodating ourselves to the bureaucratic institutions within which we work and live.

WORKPLACE DEMOCRACY

The first element of administrative democracy involves the application to the public sector of the ideas about workplace democracy that have been developed in the context of the private sector. With rare exceptions,[13] the literature on workplace democracy has not focused on the possibility of fostering worker control in a government setting. The failure to do so may be attributable to the emphasis that proponents of workplace democracy have placed on making workers fully self-governing. According to the standard literature, one of the requirements of a workplace democracy is the collective exercise by workers of all power previously allocated to property owners and management; under this view, workers have to be able to decide all policy issues faced by their workplace themselves.[14] Such a conception is plainly inapplicable to government. Employees of the government are not collectively entitled to make governmental decisions by themselves.[15] On the contrary, the traditional assumption is that government employees have no role whatsoever in making public policy. Their job is simply to execute the policy decisions made by democratically elected officials or by citizens generally; indeed, a layer of politically appointed administrators is normally given the job of seeing that they do. Thus even proposals that have concentrated specifically on adding a democratic voice to government administration have assumed that such a voice would be that of outsiders—members of the public at large—while government employees themselves would continue to be organized bureaucratically.[16]

Meaningful administrative democracy, however, must start with establishing a democratic organization for government employees. One cannot attack the bureaucratic form if one leaves the internal organization of government intact: democratization requires transforming the hierarchical structure of individual government offices into vehicles for collective decision-making about the management of the office's day-to-day activities. Such a change is important not only for the empowerment of those inside the government[17] but also for the potential effects such a changed workplace could have on the relationship between government employees and the recipients of government services.[18] This effort to foster organizational democracy within the government need not undermine the extent of the government's accountability to the electorate. Indeed, the creation of a participatory workplace could even enhance the exercise of political control over government administration. The bureaucratic form may exacerbate the difficulties of establishing political control over government employees by fueling employee resentment over the lack of respect accorded government workers and government work. The role of government employees is denigrated when they are portrayed simply as the means (perhaps even as impediments) to the accomplishment of ends determined by others.[19] Thus it is possible, as Michael Smith claims, that workplace democracy "may serve to increase . . . [political] accountability and responsiveness to the extent that it succeeds in infusing each member of the organizational polity with an increased sense of moral responsibility for his or her public choices."[20] At the minimum, the relationship between the advent of workplace democracy and political control is indeterminate; there is no reason to believe that responsiveness would necessarily deteriorate.

The kinds of decisions that government employees would be entitled to make in a worker-controlled government setting need to be determined through a political process (a process discussed in the next section). Possible examples of such decisions include those that Yugoslavian law delegated to collective decision-making by governmental employees: allocation of lump-sum budget appropriations to specific tasks, the internal organization of the office, the establishment of a salary scale, the nature of professional training, and the improvement of working conditions.[21] Those who believe in the necessity of bureaucracy may well object to this (or any other) list because they believe decisions on matters such as these cannot be made democratically. When people these days claim that the bureaucratic form of decision-making is necessary, it is hard to know exactly what form of organization they have in mind. Early proponents of bureaucracy thought the Weberian model of bureaucracy was indispensable for prompt, efficient, and responsive decision-making.[22] According to this model, organizational efficiency requires a hierarchically organized chain of command, with lower-level employees applying, in an impersonal, standardized fashion, policies articulated by their superiors. In recent decades, however, this version of bureaucracy has been subject to a vast literature of critique. Critics have asserted not only that the model fails to capture how bureaucracy actually works[23] but also that attempts to make it work are counterproductive. Efforts to impose such a model produce not efficiency but a "bureaucratic vicious circle": they lead to alienation, resistance, and organizational conflict that, when sought to be corrected by stricter bureaucratic controls, induce even greater bureaucratic malfunctioning.[24] Thus many organizational theorists contend that bureaucratic efficiency requires abandonment of the Weberian model of bureaucracy and its replacement with a system that relies on widespread worker involvement in organizational decision-making.[25] Even within the literature of bureaucratic theory, in short, there is considerable debate over the extent of worker participation necessary for proper organizational functioning.

Defenders of workplace democracy seek to increase the level of worker participation beyond that now envisioned in a bureaucratic setting. They tend to consider the current extent of worker participation a form of worker cooptation rather than worker control.[26] Yet the exact form of workplace democracy that might be established in the different settings within the public sector has to be worked out in practice; it certainly cannot be specified in advance in a chapter such as this. The literature on workplace democracy suggests a wide variety of mechanisms for increasing the extent of worker control of organizational decision-making: workers can make their own decisions by vote or consensus; they can elect an executive committee that is given considerable authority or elect one that remains subject to strict control by the group as a whole; they can select managers from their own ranks or hire them from the outside.[27] As with any of the ingredients of administrative democracy discussed here, one can adopt a gradualist approach of step-by-step reform (thereby risking the charge that nothing is really being changed) or a sudden, dramatic increase in the extent of organizational democracy (thereby risking the charge that the plan is utopian and unworkable). Choosing a specific course of action within such a spectrum is a matter of strategy. However, given the successes of a vast array of diverse organizational forms—ranging from 19th century American utopian communities[28] to the network of worker-controlled cooperatives in Mondragon, Spain[29] to the American plywood industry in the Pacific Northwest[30]—workplace democracy cannot be dismissed as impossible.

RELATIONSHIP BETWEEN POLITICAL DEMOCRACY AND ORGANIZATIONAL DEMOCRACY

To construct a relationship between the public at large and government employees that promotes administrative democracy, one cannot rely on bureaucratic theory. Modern bureaucratic theory embraces two contradictory conceptions of such a relationship: one is that political decision-makers establish the policies that the government workforce implements (the "formalist" model) and the other is that government employees legitimately make many decisions themselves because they, unlike the legislature or the general public, have the time, knowledge, and experience necessary for proper decision-making (the "expertise model").[31] Neither of these conceptions, however, offers a way to control the actions of government employees;[32] indeed, their failure do so is one of the justifications for increasing the level of democratic control of the government. Government employees will never be merely instruments for the execution of policies decided by others, but their discretionary judgments are not rendered innocuous by the expertise on which they purport to be based. Of course, effective political control of the government is not easily achieved. The issue here, however, is whether democratic forms exist that are plausible alternatives to the inadequate attempts to accomplish such an objective through bureaucratic controls.

The classic method of establishing democratic control over those to whom power is delegated is through a town meeting or assembly. All citizens (more accurately, those who attend the meeting) gather in one place, question their agents about their performance of assigned tasks, and make whatever policy decisions are needed to deal with the problems raised by the discussion. If the agents convince the assembly of the correctness of their policies, they are given deference; if they are not convincing, they are instructed to act differently (or perhaps even discharged). Government employees are thus neither assumed to be following instructions nor assumed to be experts whose views ought to prevail; the extent of deference and control is worked out on a case-to-case basis in the course of the discussion in the meeting and, sometimes, after a popular vote. To democratic theorists, face-to-face discussions are essential both for democratic decision-making and for control over those to whom power has been delegated. Only through discussion can employees and the public at large state their own views and hear opposing arguments about the meaning of the governing rules (both legal and customary) and the appropriate role of expertise; only through discussion can they resolve conflict over alternative courses of action.[33]

Most proponents of democratic control of government decision-making seem to have accepted the proposition that it would be hopelessly naive and romantic to expect that town meetings of this kind could take place in modern society. As a result, they have sought to find ways to approximate the structure of the town meeting by inserting some form of democratic involvement into bureaucratic decision-making. Their principal methods of doing so have been to include representatives of interest-groups in the decision-making process. They have expanded interest-group representatives' ability to appear before agencies, increased their access to agency information, and added them to citizen advisory boards within the government.[34] Even under these initiatives, however, the role of the public has been limited to giving advice; government decisions have remained the responsibility of government employees.

One way to foster administrative democracy, therefore, might be to strengthen these existing attempts to establish democratic control of the government.[35] For example, the number, membership, and power of citizen advisory committees[36] could be expanded so that these committees could engage in government decision-making. One form this effort might take would be to create administrative boards of directors, altering the European notion of codetermination[37] from a practice of joint decision-making by workers and management to a practice of joint decision-making by workers and members of the public. A model for such a board of directors can be found in the structure of the governing board of the Caja Laboral Popular (CLP), the central financial institution and major unifying ingredient in the network of worker-owned companies in Mondragon. One-third of the CLP board is selected democratically by the workers in the bank, and the remaining two-thirds is selected by the cooperatives whose interests the bank purports to serve.[38] Administrative agencies could similarly be managed by boards of directors consisting of a majority of representatives of the public and a minority of representatives of the agency's employees. It is important both that members of the public be able to control the board's decision-making and that government employees be ensured a voice in board decision-making.

To adopt such a structure in a government agency, one would not have to alter the relationship that currently exists between the government bureaucracy and the legislature. The government bureaucracy is not only the mechanism for implementing laws adopted by the legislature but it also has broad discretion to make its own decisions within the legislative mandate. This divided message of legislative control and legislative delegation could govern the newly constituted board of directors in the same way that it now governs the government bureaucracy. The difference would be that the interpretation of the message would be made not simply by government employees but through a democratic discussion between government employees and representatives of the public; whatever decisions are entrusted to the state would be made by a democratically constituted board of directors.[39]

The creation of such a board would, however, significantly change the role of the politically appointed administrators who have the job of managing the full-time government workforce as representatives of the public. Under bureaucratic theory, these political appointees are the central figures linking civil service employees and the desires of the public. If democratically elected worker-representatives and members of the public constituted an agency's board of directors, the importance of politically appointed administrators would be considerably diminished. An administrator's effectiveness would come to depend on her or his ability to bring the two sets of representatives together. The task of "managing" the government to serve the public interest would become more than a job description;[40] it would describe a process of face-to-face discussion with both the government workers and members of the public. Indeed, the more the board of directors gained the power of decision rather than simply the opportunity to offer advice—and the more it became representative of the public at large—the closer it would approach a "town meeting" model of decision-making on direct discussion between members of the public and government employees.

A major problem with adopting such a codetermination structure for administrative democracy is the difficulty of finding an acceptable method of selecting public representatives. If representation on the boards of directors is based on a theory of interest-group pluralism, as the other efforts designed to democratize the bureaucracy have been, the codetermination idea is likely to be frustrated by the problems with interest-group pluralist theory that have troubled these earlier initiatives.[41] Uncertainty about whether the interest groups that participate in the bureaucratic process represent the public interest have led even defenders of interest-group representation to oscillate between a desire to defer to collective decisions made by these groups (in order to promote democracy) and a desire to limit the groups' influence on bureaucratic decision-making (in order to avoid "capture" of the government by special interests).[42] This kind of ambivalence will be even stronger if the powers exercised by the interest-group representatives are increased in the way I have suggested. The ambivalence is unavoidable, however, as long as one continues to rely on group representatives rather than the public as a whole to articulate the public interest.

A more radical strategy, therefore, would supplement (or replace) such a plan with mechanisms that allow the public at large to debate the recommendations of government employees and to reject them when they think it appropriate. It is not clear to me why many people seem to think that such a scheme is impossible. The reason cannot be that the general public is unable to make governmental decisions directly; the initiative and referendum, after all, are standard parts of American public life.[43] Moreover, once it is recognized that administrative democracy envisions decentralization of power, it is clear that decision-making by the general public can be made not only by vote but also in a direct face-to-face discussion with other citizens and with government employees. Governance by assembly has recurred throughout history, not only in ancient Athens but even today in town meetings,[44] workplace democracies,[45] and the kibbutz.[46] In democratic Athens, a very complex society—made up, one should note, of an estimated 40,000 citizens—was governed in a time of great stress by a system in which every citizen was entitled to vote on questions of governance in regularly scheduled assemblies that met more than 40 times a year.[47] Government officials routinely appeared before the public assembly to be questioned and, sometimes, overruled by the populace; no government official had the power to decide an issue in a way not controllable by the popular assembly.[48] There are, of course, thousands of distinctions between our society and that of ancient Athens, and many people seize on one or more of these distinctions (such as the supposed greater homogeneity or greater leisure time or lesser complexity of their world compared to ours[49]) to "prove" that full-scale democratic assemblies have now become impossible. However, arguments of this kind seems to me less a product of a defensible social theory than the product of pervasive, albeit inconsistent, fears of democracy. One fear is that such an assembly will serve no useful purpose because ultimately experts will be able to control the decisions.[50] An opposite fear is that assemblies actually will make decisions and therefore lead to mob rule. Neither the prospect that experts will retain too much power nor the prospect that they will retain too little is inevitable. Although either fear could be realized, it is also possible that any new assembly, like others before it, could find a way to obtain the advantage of expertise without being overawed by it.

The critical question, in my view, is not whether a system of popular governance is possible in modern society but how to implement it. Although in some cities the remnants of town meetings still exist and could be reinvigorated, in most cities new institutional structures would have to be created. One such structure might be built on the current practice of holding public hearings prior to bureaucratic decision-making. Public hearings are now advertised as open to the public and are designed to permit all interested citizens to participate in the administrative process. Of course, at present these hearings are well within the expertise model of decision-making: they are intended to inform government experts, not to control them. One could, however, begin to certify to a public hearing the power to *decide* a specific issue. The issue selected would no doubt depend on the level of confidence in the democratic process; cautious reformers would more likely be affected by the fear that the meetings would be poorly attended or stacked by interest groups than would those more willing to experiment with democratic forms. Yet since even now a vote on governmental issues is possible in an initiative or referendum, these meetings might well turn out to be preferable; after all, they would allow public discussion of opposing sides, consultation with government officials, and an opportunity to find compromise solutions.[51] No doubt, given the current level of inexperience with public decision-making, a period of experimentation with any form of democratic decision-making would be essential. Reinvigorated public hearings could not be organized to decide the full range of administrative matters overnight. Even a beginning of such a process, however, would create—for many people for the first time in their lives—the experience of democratic decision-making: the experience of collectively deciding with members of their community (including strangers) issues of public policy. It would also introduce government officials to the practice (and not just the formal invocation) of popular control. Reinvigorated public hearings could thus serve as vehicles to help rethink and improve upon mechanisms to foster administrative democracy.

There is, to be sure, an intermediate position between an interest-group pluralist and a fully democratic model of the relationship between political democracy and organizational democracy. One could create a citizen group of (say) 100 people to serve for a stated period of time as public representatives in an administrative agency; the groups would have to be chosen by lot, rather than by election or through interest group representation, to ensure that their members were a microcosm of the public at large rather than chosen because of who they are.[52] Once constituted, the group would be authorized to meet with the agency's employees, discuss the issues facing the agency, and, after the discussion, debate and decide how to proceed. The more rapid the turnover of this citizen group and the greater the number of agencies whose policies were governed by this process, the more widespread the experience of democratic self-governance would become. One can envision this process as an expanded and modified form of the jury: as with jury service, citizens would be expected to devote a portion of their time to public policy decision-making.[53] Moreover, like jurors, these public representative would have the job of applying legal rules, and judges might well retain the authority that they currently exercise in reviewing administrative decisions to ensure that they keep within this mandate. Of course, for many people, this form of democratic control of administrative decision-making would raise the same fears of democracy as the proposal to change the nature of public hearings; for others, it is an unhappy compromise because only a limited portion of the public would be involved. One could easily debate the proposal's desirability, but it certainly would be possible to implement it.

DECENTRALIZATION

Both workplace democracy and effective democratic control of the government require decentralization of power. As long as one imagines the task of creating administrative democracy in terms of democratizing (say) the United States Department of Health and Human Services,[54] it remains (at least to me) inconceivable. If, however, economic power can be decentralized (as proponents of economic democracy argue is desirable as well as possible),[55] a significant amount of political power could be decentralized as well. The need for a nationwide public bureaucracy to oversee nationwide (and worldwide) private bureaucracies has, after all, been one of the principal reasons for creating and sustaining the centralization of public power.[56] Moreover, it is not necessary to take an extremist view that *all* power needs to be decentralized; I describe below measures that can increase the level of democracy at the national level as long as the scope of national power is limited. It is important, however, that significant power be decentralized to units small enough to make popular participation in government decision-making feasible; in my view, this requires decentralization to cities and towns and not just to states.[57]

One major impediment to the decentralization of political power in the United States has been a frequently expressed preference for centralized power over decentralized power; many people consider the national government to be more fairly administered and to attract better-qualified employees than state or local governments.[58] Rather than discuss the long-standing controversy over the comparative desirability of centralization and decentralization[59] here, however, I shall concentrate on the second major impediment to decentralization: the notion that decentralization, even if it were desirable, is impossible. Solving problems with a regional or national impact requires centralization, it is often said, because individual localities cannot effectively deal with them.

The argument that decentralization is impossible is based on an assumed link between decentralization and local selfishness. Decentralization is often defined as a mechanism for allowing people to create for themselves the kind of community they want to live in.[60] Since this notion of local self-governance permits local self-protection, the amount of self-governance that seems tolerable diminishes as the nation appears more and more interdependent. Because local decision-making often affects neighboring localities, the sphere of local control has to be limited to matters that are "purely local" in character.[61] Otherwise, a community could protect itself at the expense of its neighbors. There is a growing recognition, however, that virtually every local decision (whether dealing with the environment or sewage disposal or crime control or transportation) has external effects on outsiders. As a result, specifying a kind of decision that local citizens can be allowed to make by themselves has become increasingly hard to do, and finding a mechanism to solve interlocal problems has taken precedence over the need to promote local control. One way to deal with interlocal problems is centralization: increasing the authority not only of the national legislature but of the federal bureaucracy.

To decentralize political power, institutional mechanisms have to be created that can deal with the external effects of local decision-making without relying on a nationwide bureaucracy. The way to create these mechanisms, and to operate them, is through interlocal cooperation. Interlocal cooperation cannot be achieved, however, if the argument for decentralization remains linked with local selfishness.[62] The chances of interlocal cooperation are undermined by individual cities' attempts to advance themselves at the expense of their neighbors. The goal of decentralization needs to be understood not in terms of local self-protection but in terms of the ability of localities to participate, along with other communities, in governmental decision-making: the ability to replace centralized, bureaucratic power with democratic forms of governance. Decentralization allows local governments to solve their problems together rather than empowering a higher level of government to do so. The success of efforts to decentralize, however, depends on establishing *between* cities the kind of democratic relationship that the proposals described above for workplace democracy and for the political control of government employees[63] contemplate *within* cities. Indeed, these internal transformations of local governmental bureaucracies are likely to be prerequisites to interlocal cooperation. The possibility of interlocal cooperation has to be built on experience with democracy (the educational experience of resolving conflict over public policy) gained on the local level.[64] Interlocal cooperation is a strategy that can be adopted by *democracies,* not a strategy that can be adopted by anyone. Of course, even under the strongest interlocal alliance, some interlocal conflict is likely to seem unresolvable; the temptation to seek a solution to conflict from a higher level of authority will not easily go away. Proponents of decentralization have to learn, however, that to the extent they cede power to a centralized government because of localities' failure to agree among themselves, they will be subject to centralized control. The only way to avoid being subject to this control is interlocal government.

Very few mechanisms for interlocal cooperation now exist in the United States. The principal current vehicle for interlocal cooperation is the national legislature: congressional action involves a process of compromise and agreement between people elected by local constituencies.[65] Yet congressional decision-making cannot adequately deal with the problems that face the administrative state; on the contrary, the inability of Congress to solve these problems is one of the traditional arguments advanced for the growth of the federal bureaucracy. The task of building administrative democracy thus requires the rejection of the standard bifurcation between interlocal compromise (made by legislatures) and bureaucratic decision-making (made by government officials); a multitude of mechanisms for interlocal cooperation need to be built within the government itself.

One way to do so is to create regional agencies empowered to deal with specific interlocal problems (such as the environment, health care, or transportation). Even today, a version of these agencies exists in the form of regional public authorities and special districts. The powers currently allocated to these agencies, however, are often very limited; decentralization would involve giving them much of the power now exercised by the state and federal governments. Moreover, these agencies, now run as bureaucracies, need to be transformed into vehicles for interlocal cooperation. They need to be managed by a democratically constituted board of directors, one consisting, perhaps, of a majority of representatives of the local communities and a minority of representatives of the agency's (democratically organized) employees. By organizing the board in this way, its decisions could be based on a process similar to that of local government agencies: the decisions would be the product of a discussion that includes people from the affected area and full-time government employees. Moreover, by choosing representatives of local communities rather than representatives of interest groups as the public members of the board, one can ensure that the public members are connected (through election, by being city officials, or through public hearings) to forms of democratic organization on a local level.[66] This connection between public representatives and the local community is designed in part to ensure their representativeness; although direct public participation at every level of government decision-making is not necessary for administrative democracy, the term "public representative" has to be more than a formal designation. The connection with the local community has another benefit as well: the greater the engagement between the locality's representatives and their constituencies, the greater the number of people who understand the process of, and the need for, interlocal agreement and compromise.

Not every interlocal problem needs to be solved by the creation of a regional government entity. Some problems can be handled by local governments directly as long as there is sufficient interlocal consultation to permit them to exchange information, identify interlocal conflicts, and coordinate appropriate local action. The extent to which problems can be resolved by informal processes depends on the success of the effort to create an understanding of the need for interlocal cooperation. Sometimes cooperative efforts will require regional entities empowered to enforce decisions against recalcitrant localities; sometimes permanent structures with a full-time staff but without coercive power (like trade associations) will be sufficient; sometimes a regional conference will be all that is needed.

One informal vehicle for interlocal cooperation that can be adopted by local governments is a variant of what is popularly called "adhocracy."[67] Proponents of adhocracy envision the postbureaucratic organization as a series of task forces (ad hoc organizations) created to solve specific problems and disbanded after the task is completed. In the words of Warren Bennis:

> The social structure of organizations of the future will have some unique characteristics. The key word will be "temporary"; there will be adaptive, rapidly changing *temporary systems*. These will be organized around *problems-to-be-solved*. The problems will be solved by groups of relative *strangers* who represent a set of diverse professional skills. The groups will be conducted on *organic* rather than mechanical models; they will evolve in response to the problem rather than programmed role expectations. The function of the "executive" thus becomes *coordinator*, or "linking pin" between various project groups. He must be a man [sic] who can speak the diverse languages of research and who can relay information and mediate among groups. *People will be differentiated not vertically according to rank and role but flexibly according to skill and professional training.*[68]

Although Professor Bennis defends adhocracy as a triumph of democracy over bureaucracy,[69] his version of the idea remains, as the excerpt quoted illustrates, quite professional in character. It need not be so. Experts and the lay public could be integrated within these ad hoc organizations as they would be in the more permanent forms of interlocal organization. Indeed, the temporary character of ad hoc organizations would enable local government employees and members of the public to participate more easily in these organizations than in permanent organizations. The frequency of turnover and the short-term nature of service would also have the advantage of engaging a variety of different people in interlocal decision-making and, thereby, broadening the base of experience with interlocal cooperation.

I have described interlocal cooperation in this section as being regional in scope; I have selected the word *regional* because of the uncertainty of the area to which it refers. The size of a region appropriate for an interlocal alliance will vary not only with the problem to be addressed but also with the experience of interlocal cooperation gained over time. Assemblies of several hundred (even thousands)[70] of representatives could well be workable, and forms of interlocal efforts might be expanded to deal with problems more and more national in scope. I assume that some problems will be too large to be handled by interlocal cooperation and that some federal agencies will therefore survive even after the process of decentralization has run its course. Yet it would be a mistake to set one's sights too low on the possible range of interlocal agreement. Efforts to decentralize power are clearly never easy, but significant power has been successfully decentralized in the past[71] and it could be done again.

ADMINISTRATIVE DEMOCRACY AT THE NATIONAL LEVEL

Decentralization of power is essential to the promotion of administrative democracy, but it is not sufficient. Democratic forms also have to be created within the national government. One way to do so would be to assign to Congress the role of inserting a democratic voice into national administrative decision-making. Members of Congress could either participate in administrative decisions directly or reserve the power to veto those decisions with which they disagree. The possibility of implementing this idea, however, has largely been undermined, at least in the United States, by a series of Supreme Court decisions interpreting the Constitution to require a radical separation between legislative and executive functions. The Court's rejection, for example, of the legislative veto in *INS v. Chadha* stripped Congress of an innovative way to combine democratic and bureaucratic forms.[72]

Yet Congress is neither the only nor the best instrument for democratic involvement in federal decision-making. Individual members of Congress were not selected to be representative of the nation as a whole, and they could easily use their influence to promote their own agendas rather than to voice objections that Congress, as a collective body, would consider appropriate.[73] These defects in congressional involvement in administrative decision-making need not be remedied, as is now so often suggested, by rejecting public involvement in administrative decision-making in favor of a bureaucratic vision of greater executive control.[74] Congressional oversight could be replaced with oversight by the general public. Many of the ideas suggested above for the local levels (boards of directors consisting of members of the public and government employees, expanded public hearings, citizen groups chosen by lot, and ad hoc task forces) could be incorporated into administrative decision-making at the national level.

Of course, adding these elements to the structure of the federal government will not ensure democratic control of its actions. The idea of "public" representation in government becomes more and more of an abstraction as the opportunity for widespread participation diminishes; democratic structures incorporated into the national government need to be regularly reconnected with local democracy to make their claimed "democratic" nature credible.[75] Bob Reich describes one method of accomplishing this objective that was adopted by the United States Environmental Protection Agency (EPA), the agency empowered to promulgate national standards for emission of hazardous air pollutants.[76] In 1983, the EPA had to decide whether American Smelting and Refining Company (Asarco), a major employer in the Tacoma, Washington, area, was within the statutory margin of safety for its emission of inorganic arsenic, a cancer-producing pollutant. Defining the required "margin of safety" was complex: the pollutant was admittedly a health hazard, but excessive controls would lead to the closure of the plant and thereby injure the area's economy.

> William Ruckelshaus, then Administrator of the EPA, decided that the citizens of the Tacoma area ought to wrestle with the problem. Accordingly, Ruckelshaus flew to Tacoma to announce a series of three public workshops to be held during the summer of 1983. Their purpose was to acquaint residents with the details of the pollution problem, help them prepare for subsequent formal hearings, and enable them to deliberate about what should be done. Two of the workshops were held in a local public high school in Tacoma; they attracted environmental groups, local citizen organizations, and a large number of smelter workers. The third workshop took place on Vashon Island, a residential area where the winds of Puget Sound carried many of Asarco's emissions; most of the attendees at this workshop were island homeowners. EPA officials began each workshop by explaining how the agency had estimated health risks from the factory and the likely effects of different levels of pollution control. They then divided the audience into three groups, and had agency officials and staff circulate among the groups to facilitate a more informal discussion.[77]

The EPA's effort was highly controversial,[78] but it suggests one way to involve the local public in a federal agency's decision-making. Although the public's role as envisioned by the EPA was simply advisory, even this role could well be influential, particularly if the federal agency itself were managed (as the EPA was not) by a board of directors consisting of a majority of public representatives. Moreover, there is no reason to assume that a public debate of this kind would be appropriate only in cases in which the effects of the decision were limited to a particular locality. Federal agencies could select representative localities, or pick localities by lot, to help resolve issues of national policy. Juries, after all, are selected in a way that allows a random sample of the population to engage in public decision-making.

The public could be incorporated into federal decision-making in another way as well. Many federal agencies (including the EPA) are now organized into district offices managed by a national headquarters in a top-down organizational structure, with little or no public involvement at any level of decision-making. District offices do not have to be operated in this hierarchical manner; they could instead become the vehicles for allowing public participation in federal agency decision-making. Each district office could, like local governments, include members of the public in its organizational structure, and the individual offices could be connected with each other in a manner analogous to the intercity links described above. Regularly scheduled interdistrict discussions, involving both public and employee representatives from district offices, could focus on agency policy and problems of implementation. As this structure developed, the power relationship between top officials in the central office and the people involved at the district level would begin to change: top officials would have to take seriously ideas developed on an interdistrict basis rather than simply treating district employees as means to national ends. Moreover, as with other democratic forms discussed earlier, there is no reason to assume that such a structure would transform an efficient organization into one that is unmanageable. On the contrary, worker and public involvement in decision-making might both improve national policies and help ensure that they have the support necessary to be implemented.[79]

Even if initiatives of this kind were successful, some federal agencies would remain for which public hearings and district reorganization would not seem feasible. Consider, for example, the Department of Defense or the Federal Bureau of Investigation. Operation of these agencies requires a level of secrecy that makes public scrutiny difficult, and their need for urgent action makes streamlined decision-making essential. It does not follow, however, that there is no role for the public within even these agencies. Civilian control of the military (and the police) is an essential ingredient in American democracy, and the definition of "civilians" need not be limited to government employees. Citizens have a role in investigating police abuse on the national as well as on the local level.[80] Moreover, as advocates of the nuclear freeze have argued, issues of national defense require public involvement and debate; attempting to resolve defense issues solely in the language of scientific expertise distorts public policy decision-making.[81] Of course, the members of the public involved in these agencies would have to be selected in a way that ensures both their representativeness and their discretion,[82] and not every issue would be amenable to public review. Like efforts to implement workplace democracy in agencies as large as these, experimentation will be required. But a detailed analysis of agency functioning could find a role for the public in these agencies if the analysis were performed by people adequately sympathetic to democracy.

No matter how many of these kinds of innovations are put into place at the national level, the major national contribution to administrative democracy is still likely to be the process of decentralization. To ensure that this process has adequate momentum, Congress should institute periodic reexaminations of the list of subjects thought absolutely essential for national rather than regional or local attention. Every kind of government action, even national defense, has components that can be handled on a regional or local basis.[83] Determining what is national and what is local in scope is a political choice, one that requires reevaluation as information about and experience with decentralization are developed.

BUREAUCRATIC CONSCIOUSNESS

As I hope I have demonstrated, there are a great many ways to increase democratic institutional mechanisms within our current system of government. How fast these changes could be made is a legitimate subject of debate. Implementing them would certainly transform the government bureaucracy. "Democracy" might not replace "bureaucracy," but the claim that bureaucratic form of government is inevitable would surely no longer seem credible.

What prevents us from making these changes? The answer, in my view, does not lie in our inability to create the necessary institutional mechanisms. Suggestions, like those made above, could be implemented if we wanted to do so. Nor does the answer lie in the charge that a government that included so many democratic institutions "wouldn't work." There is no uncontroversial definition of what "working" means. Indeed, there is an equally common charge that bureaucracy doesn't "work" either. Bureaucracy is the modern symbol not only of efficiency (as Weber suggested)[84] but of incompetence—hence the powerfully negative associations with the word "bureaucrat" and the prevalence of the popular belief that public sector employees do not put much effort into their jobs. The notion of a smoothly operating bureaucracy is as much of a utopian fantasy as that of a smoothly operating democracy. Why do we adopt a definition of "what works" that highlights the problems with democracy and minimizes the equally serious (although very different) problems with bureaucracy? Why do we accept the goals of one system and try to make the best of it and largely reject the promise offered by the other?

The answer, I think, lies in our distrust of democracy. If my suggestions of workplace democracy, popular control of the government, or decentralization are labeled "impossible," it is likely to be because it is so widely believed that people cannot govern themselves. Even if the size of an entity is small (as in a workplace or small town), even if the level of general education is high (as in most industrialized countries), even if solving the problem in question plainly requires the kind of judgment expertise cannot possibly provide (as is true for most policy-making), democracy is commonly thought not to be an option. People are too lazy (or too busy), it is said; they will not participate. People are too stupid; they will not know what to do. Meetings will go on forever; no decisions will ever be made. Anyway, people *want* to have experts make decisions for them; they do not even *want* democracy. These antidemocratic sentiments, like countless others, are endlessly repeated, although they are rarely based on empirical evidence or a theoretical explanation of the reasons for different levels of popular participation.[85] They are also not likely to be based on personal experience. They are often voiced by people who have had no personal experience whatsoever engaging in collective decision-making on an issue of public policy. These sentiments do not reflect an insight into "human nature," as is often claimed; they are, instead, a reflection of antidemocratic prejudice.

Antidemocratic prejudice shares many of the ingredients classically associated with other kinds of prejudice: the objects of prejudice are often depicted as lazy, ignorant, and appropriately kept in their place.[86] Moreover, the assertions of antidemocratic prejudice mistake the nature of democracy. There is no single mode of decision, called "democracy," that specifies how much participation is required, how much time people need to spend in meetings, or the role of expertise in decision-making; there are countless ways to organize democratic forms of governance. The notion of democracy surely does not require everyone to decide everything in one big meeting.[87] None of the suggestions offered above, for example, requires limitless participation or endless meetings. The amount of participation required depends on the democratic mechanism chosen, and people have found many ways to organize discussions to budget people's time. It is wrong simply to assume that democratic participation will take more time than, say, bureaucratic infighting.

Moreover, democracy and expertise are not mutually inconsistent. Every form of government, whether democratic or authoritarian, has to obtain the benefit of knowledge and specialization. Expert knowledge plainly contributes to political decision-making; it is just no substitute for it. Hanna Pitkin and Sara Shumer have articulated why this is so:

> First off, stupidity knows no class. Maybe most people are foolish, but foolishness is found in all social strata. Education removes some kind of ignorance, but may entrench or instill others. The cure is not to exclude some but to include as diverse a range of perspectives and experience as possible in political deliberation. Second, expertise cannot solve political problems. Contemporary politics is indeed full of technically complex topics, about which even the educated feel horribly ignorant. But on every politically significant issue of this kind, the "experts" are divided; that is part of what makes the issue political. Though we may also feel at a loss to choose between them, leaving it to the experts is no solution at all. Finally, while various kinds of knowledge can be profoundly useful in political decisions, knowledge alone is never enough. The political question is what we are to *do;* knowledge can only tell us how things are, how they work, while a political resolution always depends on what we, as a community, want and think right. And those questions have no technical answer; they require collective deliberation and decision. The experts must become a part of, not an alternative to, the democratic political process.[88]

Democratic systems, when they are successful, learn how to accommodate expertise: they neither automatically reject it nor automatically defer to it. At present, judges and politicians are the people with the most experience with this kind of engagement with experts; administrative democracy is an attempt to expand this kind of experience to the public at large.

Antidemocratic prejudice thrives in an environment in which experience with democracy is rare; it is recreated and reinforced in the process of accommodating oneself to bureaucracy. Democratic theorists often insist that the experience of democracy creates a different kind of person: a different way of relating to others and even of being oneself.[89] The experience of bureaucracy nurtures a particular kind of person as well; it too fosters ways of relating to others and ways of being oneself. To survive in a world filled with bureaucratic institutions, we learn to defend our own assertion of expertise and our own deference to it. We assure ourselves that our power is legitimate, and that our powerlessness is legitimate as well. "Other people cannot be involved in our decisions," we claim; "they don't even want to be involved. We can't be involved in their decisions either." Decision-making is thus allocated into a hierarchy of specialties, each filled with people chosen because of their technical competence. Indeed, people often treat the problem of choosing between democratic and bureaucratic forms of organization in this way. The issue is posed as a question that calls for a cost-benefit analysis or the correct allocation of different kinds of talent. To approach the issue in this way is the equivalent in thought of the bureaucratic form of organization: it calls for the application of expertise not politics, for an objective answer rather than discussion and compromise. Only under this approach could the question of whether democracy is impossible be understood as answerable in an academic conference without the participation of anyone but scholars.

This kind of bureaucratic consciousness is a major impediment to fostering administrative democracy; it makes it hard to take the prospects of democracy seriously. Combatting it is thus as important as institution building in overcoming the felt necessity of bureaucracy. Indeed, combatting it is part of the process of institution-building. Suspicions about democracy, nurtured by the experience of bureaucracy, cannot be overcome simply as a matter of thought. They need to be confronted through experience with democracy. This is not to suggest that democratic experience is or will ever be unproblematic; neither democracy nor bureaucracy can be embraced in utopian terms. In building different kinds of institutions, we learn to confront different kinds of problems and, in this way, create a different sense of self. The end result of such a process cannot be known in advance; it depends on the institutions we build and how we learn to live with them. If this is so, how do we decide what institutions to build? How do we decide if administrative democracy is a good idea? There are certainly many ways to answer these questions. Surely one possible way to do so is to create democratic forms of organization that are empowered to analyze, debate, and decide them.

NOTES

1. M. Weber, *Economy and Society,* 223 (G. Roth & C. Wittich eds. 1978).
2. M. Weber, *The Protestant Ethic and the Spirit of Capitalism,* 182 (T. Parsons trans. 1958).
3. The classic statement of this position is by Robert Michels in R. Michels, *Political Parties* (1911). See also, e.g., Gouldner, *Metaphysical pathos and the theory of bureaucracy,* in A. Etzioni, *Complex Organizations,* 82 (1961) ("Wrapping themselves in the shrouds of nineteenth century political economy, some social scientists appear to be bent on resurrecting the dismal science. Instead of telling men how bureaucracy might be mitigated, they insist that it is inevitable."); E. Jacques, *A General Theory of Bureaucracy,* 141 (1976) ("Social systems cannot endure in the way the bureaucratic system has endured if they are not closely attuned to man's nature").
4. See, e.g., K. Ferguson, *The Feminist Case Against Bureaucracy* (1984); G. Frug, The ideology of bureaucracy in American law, 97 *Harv. L. Rev.* 1276 (1984); M. Foucault, *The Birth of the Clinic* (A. Smith trans., 1975); H. Braverman, *Labor and Monopoly Capital* (1974). For a related analysis of the impact on technology on human existence, see M. Heidegger, *The Question Concerning Technology and Other Essays,* 3–35 (W. Lovitt trans., 1977).

5. See, e.g., E. Greenberg, *Workplace Democracy: The Political Effects of Participation* (1986); R. Dahl, *A Preface to Economic Democracy* (1985); R. Russell, *Sharing Ownership in the Workplace* (1985); C. Gunn, *Workers' Self-Management in the United States* (1984); P. Brannen, *Authority and Participation in Industry* (1983); J. Simmons & W. Mares, *Working Together* (1983); D. Jones & J. Svejnar (eds.), *Participatory and Self-Managed Firms* (1982); F. Lindenfeld & J. Rothschild-Whitt (eds.), *Workplace Democracy and Social Change* (1982); R. Mason, *Participatory and Workplace Democracy* (1982); M. Carnoy & D. Shearer, *Economic Democracy: The Challenge of the 1980's* (1980); J. Witte, *Democracy, Authority and Alienation in Work: Workers' Participation in an American Corporation* (1980); D. Zwerdling, *Workplace Democracy* (1980); B. Horvat, M. Markovic & R. Supek, *Self-Governing Socialism* (1975); M. Poole, *Workers' Participation in Industry* (1975); and J. Vanek, *Self-Management: Economic Liberation of Man* (1975).
6. See, e.g., Sabel & Zeitlin, Historical alternatives to mass production, *Past and Present,* no. 108 (1985), pp. 133–176; W. Sewall, *Work and Revolution in France: The Language of Labor from the Old Regime to 1848* (1980); R. Edwards, *Contested Terrain* (1979); D. Montgomery, *Workers' Control in America* (1979); D. Noble, *America by Design* (1977); A. Chandler, *The Visible Hand: The Managerial Revolution in American Business* (1977); A. Dawley, *Class and Community: The Industrial Revolution in Lynn* (1976); and H. Braverman, supra note 4.
7. See, e.g., R. Unger, *False Necessity,* 180–195, 480–508 (1987); L. Hirschhorn, *Beyond Mechanization: Work and Technology in a Postindustrial Age* (1984); M. Piore & C. Sabel, *The Second Industrial Divide: Possibilities for Prosperity* (1984).
8. See, e.g., Breyer, *Regulation and Its Reform* (1982); a bibliography is collected in at pp. 382–385.
9. See, e.g., E. Duckworth, *Inventing Density* (1986); H. Levin, Education and organizational democracy in C. Crouch & F. Heller (eds.), *Organizational Democracy and Political Processes,* 227 (1983); F. Lindenfeld, Problems of power in a free school, in F. Lindenfeld & J. Rothschild-Whitt, supra note 5, at 257; I. Illich, *Deschooling Society* (1970).
10. See, e.g., K. Ferguson, supra note 4, at 46–59; M. Foucault, *The History of Sexuality,* Vol. 1 (1980).
11. See, e.g., Evans, Rueschemeyer & Skocpol, *Bringing the State Back In* (1985).
12. M. Weber, supra note 1, at 220–21; see also 2 idem at 956–958.
13. See, e.g., Cvitan, Self-management in Yugoslav government administration, in C. Crouch & F. Heller, supra note 9, at 531; M. P. Smith, Barriers to organizational democracy in public administration, 8 *Administration and Society* 275 (1976); Garson, Self-management in the public sector (unpublished paper prepared for the International Conference on Self-Management, Cornell University, 1975); Meade, "Participative" administration—emerging reality or wishful thinking? in D. Waldo (ed.), *Public Administration in a Time of Turbulence* 169 (1971).
14. See, e.g., Gunn, supra note 5, at 34; Vanek, supra note 5, at 33.
15. To be sure, employees of a private corporation are not collectively entitled to make corporate decisions by themselves either. To treat them as if were so entitled vests them with the Blackstonian version of the rights of property owners: "that sole and despotic dominion which one man claims and exercises over the external things of the world, in total exclusion of the right of any other individual in the universe." 2 Blackstone, *Commentaries* *2. This extreme view of the prerogatives of property owners has never been the law for sole proprietors, however, and it could never be the law for collective proprietors. Thus defenders of workplace democracy in the private sector also need to confront (as by-and-large they have not) the kind of intergroup problems that so clearly need to be addressed by defenders of workplace democracy in the public sector.
16. See, e.g., Stewart, The reformation of American administrative law, 88 *Harv. L. Rev.* 1667, 1760–1802 (1975); Waldo, Development of the theory of democratic administration, 46 *Am. Pol. Sci. Rev.* 85 (1952).
17. For general statements of the goals of workplace democracy, see, e.g., Mason, supra note 5, at 25–57; Pateman, A contribution to the political theory of organizational democracy, in G. Garson & M. Smith (eds.), *Organizational Democracy* 9 (1975).
18. See Ferguson, supra note 4, at 123–53 (The client as second sex); Simon, Legality, bureaucracy and class in the welfare system, 92 *Yale L. J.* 1198 (1983).

19. See Ferguson, supra note 4, at 83–122 (The bureaucrat as second sex).
20. Smith, supra note 13, at 282; see also Garson, supra note 13, at 24–26.
21. See Cvitan, supra note 13.
22. M. Weber, supra note 1, at 956–1003; R. Michels, supra note 3. See generally, G. Frug, supra note 4, at 1297–1300.
23. See, e.g., M. Lipsky, *Street-Level Bureaucracy* (1980); G. Allison, *Essence of Decision* (1971); J. March & H. Simon, *Organizations* (1958).
24. M. Crozier, *The Bureaucratic Phenomenon* 193–94 (1964); see also P. Blau & M. Meyer, *Bureaucracy in Modern Society* 142–150 (3d. ed. 1987).
25. See, e.g., P. Blau & M. Meyer, supra note 24; R. Blake & J. Mouton, *The New Managerial Grid* (1978); H. Leavitt, *Managerial Psychology* (1978); R. Likert, *The Human Organization: Its Management and Value* (1967); W. Bennis, *Changing Organizations* (1966); C. Argyris, *Integrating the Individual and the Organization* (1964); R. Likert, *New Patterns of Management* (1961); T. Burns & G. Stalker, *The Management of Innovation* (1961); D. McGregor, *The Human Side of Enterprise* (1960). See generally, G. Frug, supra note 4, at 1318–22; Meyer, *Participative Decision Making: An Analysis and Review* (1970).
26. For a critique of employee stock ownership plans on these grounds, see J. Blasi, *Employee Ownership: Revolution or Ripoff* (1988).
27. See works cited in note 5, supra.
28. R. Kanter, *Commitment and Community* (1972).
29. H. Thomas & C. Logan, *Mondragon: An Economic Analysis* (1982); Oakeshott, Spain: The Mondragon enterprises, in F. Stephen (ed.), *The Performance of Labor-Managed Firms* 122 (1982); H. Thomas, The performance of the Mondragon cooperatives in Spain, in D. Jones & J. Svejnar, supra note 5, at 129; Johnson & Whyte, The Mondragon system of worker production cooperatives, in F. Lindenfeld & J. Rothschild-Whitt, supra note 5, at 177.
30. E. Greenberg, supra note 5.
31. See generally, G. Frug, supra note 4, at 1297–1334.
32. Some defenders of establishing workplace democracy in the public sector have sought to defend their attack on the bureaucratic form within the government by embracing the formalist model: no matter how the workplace is organized, they suggest, government employees "operate within constraints set by higher levels of democratic governance." Garson, supra note 13, at 22; Smith, supra note 13, at 283.
33. For an analysis of role of discussion in democratic politics, see B. Barber, *Strong Democracy* 163–212 (1984).
34. See, e.g., Reich, The law of the planned society, 75 *Yale L. J.* 1227 (1966). For an analysis, see Sunstein, Interest groups in American public law, 38 *Stan. L. Rev.* 29 (1985); Sargentich, The reform of the American administrative process, 1984 *Wisc. L. Rev.* 385, 425–38; Stewart, supra note 16.
35. For an illuminating discussion of a way to accomplish this objective not discussed in this essay—one than emphasizes the involvement of the government's clients in formulating public policy decisions—see J. Handler, *The Conditions of Discretion* (1986).
36. See generally, The Federal Advisory Committee Act, 10 *Harv. J. of Legis.* 217 (1973).
37. See generally, Summers, Worker participation in Sweden and the United States: Some comparisons from an American perspective, 133 *U. Pa. L. Rev.* 175 (1984); Hopt, New ways in corporate governance: European experiments with labor representation on corporate boards, 82 *Mich. L. Rev.* 1338 (1984).
38. Oakeshott, supra note 29, at 130.
39. The goal of administrative democracy is to change bureaucracy, not the principle of the separation of powers. Nevertheless, altering government bureaucracy is likely to affect society generally and thus will ultimately have an impact on the other parts of the governmental system. The different nature of the government will affect legislative decision-making, and these legislative changes will themselves modify the operation of the government. The same sort of feedback effects are also likely to occur between the executive branch and the courts, even though, as with the legis-

lature, no initial change in the role of courts would have to be made to foster administrative democracy.

40. The perennial conflict between short-term political appointees and civil service employees cannot adequately be rationalized by bureaucratic theory. Neither seeing civil service employees as effectively constrained by political managers (the formalist version) nor portraying them as exercising the kind of objective expertise to which politicians can legitimately defer on day-to-day matters of administration (the expertise version) adequately acknowledges the difficulties faced by political managers who attempt to control government employees. See G. Chase & E. Reveal, *How to Manage in the Public Sector* (1983).
41. See Stewart, supra note 16; T. Lowi, *The End of Liberalism* (1966).
42. See G. Frug, supra note 4, at 1370–72.
43. See generally, D. Magleby, *Direct Legislation* (1984); Ranney (ed.), *The Referendum Device* (1981); Sirico, The constitutionality of the initiative and referendum, 65 *Iowa L. Rev.* 637 (1980).
44. See J. Mansbridge, *Beyond Adversary Democracy* (1980).
45. See works cited in note 29, supra.
46. See Y. Criden & S. Gelb, *The Kibbutz Experience* 37–57 (1974).
47. See M. I. Finley, *Democracy Ancient and Modern* 51 (1985); M. I. Finley, *Politics in the Ancient World* 73–74 (1983). See generally, V. Ehrenberg, *The Greek State* (1969); A. H. M. Jones, *Athenian Democracy* (1957).
48. "Not even Pericles had such power. While his influence was at its height, he could hope for continual approval of his policies, expressed in the people's vote in the Assembly, but his proposals were submitted to the Assembly week in and week out, alternative views were before them, and the Assembly always could, and on occasion did, abandon him and his politics. The *decision* was theirs, not his or any other leader's; recognition of the need for leadership was not accompanied by a surrender of the power of decision. And he knew it. It was not mere tactical politeness that led him to use the following words (as we are told) in 431 B.C. when he proposed rejection of a Spartan ultimatum and therefore a vote for war: 'I see that on this occasion I must give you exactly the same advice as I have given in the past, and I call upon those of you who are persuaded to give your support to these resolutions which we are making all together.' " Finley, *Democracy Ancient and Modern,* at 24–5 (citing Thucydides).
49. The majority of Athenian citizens were not rich landowners supported by slaves but small farmers, craftsmen, or laborers, and the class conflict between these citizens and those with wealth (as well as among the farmers and craftsmen and shopkeepers) was intense. See Ehrenberg, supra note 47, at 88–102; Jones, supra note 47, at 75–96. Moreover, the notion that our society is complex and theirs was not is very puzzlng. Consider how complex it must have been to govern a city with a population of several hundred thousand people (the estimated population including those excluded from citizenship, such as women, metics, and slaves, as well as citizens) without the aid not only of computers or telephones or xerox machines but much more that we now consider indispensable. In their world, it was necessary "to tell time without watches, to cross rivers without bridges, and seas without a compass . . . to study poetry without books, geography without maps, and politics without newspapers." Zimmern, *The Greek Commonwealth* 215 (1961).
50. The classic modern example is a shareholder democracy. See, e.g., A. Berle and G. Means, *The Modern Corporation and Private Property* (1932). For a general statement of the inevitability of expert control, see Michels, supra note 3.
51. For a critique of the initiative and referendum on the grounds that they lack these qualities of a public meeting, see Bell, The referendum: Democracy's barrier to racial equality, 54 *Wash. L. Rev.* 1 (1978).
52. The classic definition of democracy emphasized selection by lot; selecting people by elections or appointment, it was thought, led not to democracy but to oligarchy. See Jones, supra note 47, at 100–107. See also J. Norwich, *A History of Venice* 166 (1982), describing the use of selection by lot in Venice "to ensure that the supreme office of the state should not fall, either directly or indirectly, into ambitious or unscrupulous hands." For a general analysis of and argument for democracy by lottery, see Amar, Choosing representatives by lottery voting, 93 *Yale L. J.* 1283 (1984).

53. Of course, such a system would have to establish a method of dealing with excuses and exemptions from service, a problem that has plagued the jury system. As experience with the jury has demonstrated, the greater the loopholes, the less representative the public process.
54. As of April 23, 1988, the Department of Health and Human Services had 123,418 employees, according to a personal conversation, on July 1, 1988, with the Press Office of the Department (to which I was referred by the Office of Public Affairs to which, in turn, I had been referred by the Office of Public Information).
55. See notes 6 and 7, supra.
56. See, e.g., M. Keller, *Affairs of State* 409–438 (1977); cf. G. Kolko, *The Triumph of Conservatism* (1963), arguing that centralization of public power was designed to protect large-scale private power, not to regulate it.
57. See generally, G. Frug, The city as a legal concept, 93 *Harv. L. Rev.* 1057 (1980); Dahl, The city in the future of democracy, 51 *Am. Pol. Sci. Rev.* 953 (1967).
58. Such a position was expounded in its classic form by James Madison in Federalist X. See *The Federalist Papers* (B. Wright ed. 1961).
59. See, e.g., Madison, supra note 58, and the antifederalists' response to Madison, found in *The Anti-Federalist: Writings by the Opponents of the Constitution* (H. Storing and M. Dry eds. (1985); see also, H. Storing, *What The Anti-Federalists Were For* (1981). Selections from both sides of the debate over the virtues and defects of the United States Constitution (and, consequently, of centralization) have been collected in *The American Constitution: For and Against* (J. R. Pole ed. 1987). See also de Tocqueville, *Democracy in America* (F. Bowen ed. 1863); G. Frug, supra note 57.
60. See, e.g., H. Arkes, *The Philosopher in The City* 320–26 (1981); R. Nozick, *Anarchy, State and Utopia* 297-331 (1974).
61. This information has severely limited the power of cities to exercise home rule as a matter of state constitutional law. See G. Frug, *Local Government Law* 87–127, 156–191 (1988).
62. The argument in this paragraph is a condensed version of one made at some length in G. Frug, Empowering cities in a federal system, 19 *Urban Lawyer* 553 (1987).
63. See sections 1 and 2, supra.
64. See, e.g., works cited in notes 17 and 33, supra; see also Rayman, Collective organization and the national state: The kibbutz model, in F. Fischer & C. Sirianni, *Critical Studies in Organization and Bureaucracy* 406 (1984).
65. For an articulation of the importance of this aspect of the structure of Congress, see *Garcia v. San Antonio Metropolitan Transit Authority*, 469 U.S. 528 (1985).
66. As a matter of constitutional law, choosing representatives from local communities is likely to invoke the requirement of one person, one vote. See *Avery v. Midland County,* 390 U.S. 474 (1968). Thus it will be difficult to allocate representation on the basis of local democratic units rather than on the basis of population. One might try to ensure that the representatives are not considered "elected"; only elected officials are governed by the one person, one vote requirement: *Sailors v. Board of Education,* 367 U.S. 107 (1967). As an alternative, the public representatives might be chosen by lot in order to create a microcosm of the regional population. Choosing the best way to organize the boards of directors will, in short, require a legal as well as a political strategy.
67. The concept was formulated by the organizational theorist Warren Bennis. See W. Bennis, *Changing Organizations* (1966); W. Bennis, *Organizational Development: Its Nature, Organization, and Prospects* (1969). It was popularized as "adhocracy" by Alvin Toffler in A. Toffler, *Future Shock* 112–135 (1970). For further elaboration of the idea, see, e.g., H. Mintzberg & McHugh, Strategy formation in adhocracy, 30 *Admin. Sci. Q.* 160 (1985); H. Mintzberg, *Structure in Fives: Designing Effective Organizations* 253–281 (1983).
68. W. Bennis, *Changing Organizations* 12 (1968).
69. *Idem* at 16.
70. See text at note 47, supra; Dahl, supra note 57.
71. Zuckerman, *Peaceable Kingdoms* 10–45 (1970).
72. *INS v. Chadha,* 462 U.S. 919 (1983); see also *Bowsher v. Synar,* 106 S. Ct. 3181 (1986).

73. See Bruff & Gellhorn, Congressional control of administrative regulation: A study of legislative vetoes, 90 *Harv. L. Rev.* 7 (1977).
74. See, e.g., Symposium on administrative law, presidential oversight of regulatory decisionmaking, 36 *Am. Univ. L. Rev.* 443–599 (1987).
75. See J. Dewey, *The Public and Its Problems* 143–219 (1927).
76. Reich, Public administration and public deliberation: An interpretive essay, 94 *Yale L. J.* 1617, 1632–1641 (1985). See also, Reich, Policy making in a democracy, in R. Reich (ed.), *The Power of Public Ideas* 123–156 (1988).
77. Reich, Public administration and public deliberation: An interpretive essay, 94 *Yale L. J.* 1617, 1633 (1985).
78. Id. at 1634. The plant closed for other reasons even before regulations were promulgated.
79. See text at note 25, supra.
80. See, E. Ostrom & G. Whitaker, Community control and governmental responsiveness: The case of police in black neighborhoods, in W. Hawley & D. Rogers (eds.), *Improving the Quality of Urban Management* 303 (1974).
81. L. Cohn, Sex and death in the rational world of defense intellectuals, 12 *Signs* 687 (1987).
82. Perhaps mayors and governors should be empowered to appoint the public representatives, subject to whatever security clearance is appropriate.
83. For one argument for local initiative in the defense area, see G. Sharp, *Making Europe Unconquerable: The Potential of Civilian-Based Deterrence and Defense* (1985).
84. See note 1, supra.
85. The available evidence is, at worst, mixed: empirical work has found elements of success and failure in both existing democratic and bureaucratic forms. See notes 25 and 28–30, supra. For an attempt to offer a theoretical explanation of the level of popular participation, see J. Gaventa, *Power and Powerlessness* (1980).
86. See Crenshaw, Race, reform, and retrenchment: Transformation and legitimation in antidiscrimination law, 101 *Harv. L. Rev.* 1331, 1373 (1988).
87. Cf. Walzer, A day in the life of a socialist citizen in M. Walzer, *Radical Principles* 128 (1980).
88. H. Pitkin and S. Shumer, On participation, 2 *Democracy* 43, 52 (1982).
89. See, e.g., Pateman, *Participation and Democratic Theory* (1970).

20

Bureaucracy and the Public: Observations and Reflections from Field Research

Richard D. Schwartz *Syracuse University, Syracuse, New York*

This chapter differs in orientation from most of the chapters in this *Handbook*. Instead of dealing in detail with aspects of the administrative structure, it asks broad questions about the relationship between agencies and the public.

Experience with government leads many citizens to question how well the administrative agencies serve the needs and meet the criteria of a democratic society. Until recently, these concerns have received little attention from professional public administrators or from scholars in the field.

Getting administrators or scholars to think about major alternatives to our present system of governance is not an easy task. The system described by Dwight Waldo as *The Administrative State* has become so central a part of our political life that we tend to dismiss any discussion of major alternatives. There are several reasons, nevertheless, that justify such a discussion at this time.

First, there is the discontent that our population has shown in its attitude toward bureaucracy. The strength of this concern has been demonstrated in the appeal to the electorate of candidates who won election to the presidency, Jimmy Carter and Ronald Reagan, and of two third-party candidates, George Wallace and Ross Perot, who ran surprisingly strong campaigns on the issue of governance.

All of these political figures tapped in one way or another the discontent of the electorate over the way the country has been governed. Their solutions differed widely, but the problem they addressed was essentially the same: all ran against Washington. None has succeeded in providing a resolution of this problem, which remains high on the agenda of what the country must cope with.

Second, a new administration has been installed after a campaign that promised change as its major theme. It is clear from the early moves of the Clinton administration that the changes proposed in the campaign are likely to involve a greater use of the federal government's powers to accomplish economic and social goals. If its efforts are to succeed, the basic vehicles of our executive branch, the administrative agencies, must be given a thorough checkup. They may require a tuneup, a major repair, or even a new design.

Third, there are signs that alternative models of governance are emerging, not only as blueprints but also as functioning models that merit attention. Following the ideas of Peter Drucker, Osborne and Gaebler have chronicled in *Reinventing Government* the effects of administrators at state and local levels to change in fundamental ways the ways in which governments get things done.

To accomplish major changes rapidly will require a concerted effort. The established practices of bureaucracy have been entrenched in ways that resist examination and change. Together these add up to a steady state that effectively resists change, or even serious discussion of change. If you can't get under the hood, to borrow a phrase from Ross Perot, how can you expect to fix the car?

My belief that major change in governmental method is needed and possible comes from several experiences involving local, state, and federal agencies. At the federal level, I have worked in one capacity or another with the Department of Justice, the Department of Transportation, the National Science Foundation, the National Endowment for the Humanities, the Internal Revenue Service, the U.S. Information Agency, and the Environmental Protection Agency. I have not been employed by any of them, but have consulted with all of them. I also served as consultant for the American Bar Association on a major project that appraised the Delivery Systems Study of the Legal Services Corporation.

From these experiences, I did not generate systematic data on how the agencies operate. I mention them primarily to say that I am no stranger to the world of government. Yet it is worth noting that in all of those contacts, I saw nothing to contradict the impressions that I report in this chapter, which are derived from one particular research project.[1] On the whole, I came away from the consulting work with the impression that something generic in the agencies needed fixing.

Let me make clear that this essay is not intended as an attack on those who run the agencies or those who work for them. Agency officials are often at least as frustrated as the general public with the way in which the agencies run. Many have dedicated themselves to public service in the belief that they are doing something important for the society. They are, but they could be doing it better. It is the system they have received that leads to their frustration and to the disappointing results that often flow from agency action.

That system is a compound of ideas and practices that reinforce each other. In this chapter, I want to spend some time on the theory of bureaucracy as it relates to democratic governance and then deal with practices that protect the agency from scrutiny, favor rigidity, and limit effective feedback.

In brief, my thesis is that since the beginning of this century, we have come to believe that bureaucracies as described by Max Weber are the "ideal type," the only way of rationally governing a complex society. Proceeding on that assumption, we have granted enormous discretion to the agencies, which is justified on the theory that the agencies alone possess the expertise to carry out the policies adopted by Congress for execution by the executive.

With this rationale, the agencies have developed their own characteristic mode of working. It includes the Weberian features of hierarchy (orders from above, obedience from below), specified tasks, promotion within the ranks, and so forth. However, it has also come to include as working principles three characteristics that help to explain its difficulties. These are called by different terms, depending on who is describing them.

In the agency's perspective, these characteristics are confidentiality, uniformity, and objectivity. Viewed critically from the outside, these same characteristics can be described as secrecy, rigidity, and ignorance.

Agencies can justify existing patterns by reference to the uses these characteristics fulfill. Confidentiality is needed because the agencies often deal with sensitive matters. If their records were available indiscriminately to the public, the result might be embarrassing to clients. Second, uniformity of policy (similar cases treated similarly) is necessary for fairness and to avoid favoritism. Finally, the agency must base its policy on technical expertise, avoiding influence by extraneous political considerations.

These same characteristics may be described differently by those outside who are affected by the work of the agencies. First, to an outsider the agency's work is not clearly understood. The scope of the agency's duties remains unknown. What is perceived is an experience: waiting in line, being investigated, given or being denied a benefit.

Second, the citizen does not usually understand the individual result, much less how this compares with actions taken by the agency in comparable circumstances. Without adequate information about the policy, the individual client cannot readily understand its application in his or her case. Bureaucratic decisions seem inappropriate, frustrating, unfair to the outsider. Satisfactory explanations are rarely given, perhaps because it is difficult for officials to be patient and not patronizing in typical relationships between "street-level bureaucrats" and their clients.

Finally, the agency rarely if ever receives and uses systematic information about the impact it makes. Feedback of honest reactions helps to steer an organization toward its objectives. In principle, at least, such feedback is available to the corporation in the form of consumer decisions. The situation is characteristically different in dealing with agencies.

As Hirschman points out, in a competitive market the consumer can express displeasure with the product or service by exiting and going to another provider. In dealing with government, exit is not so easy. Instead, voice is the major way in which citizens' views can be conveyed. The mechanisms by which citizen input is sought (e.g., congressional hearings, notice and comment under the rule-making procedures of the Administrative Procedure Act) have, at best, had limited effects on agency structure and practice.

These arrangements for voicing reactions to the agencies are so indirect that their sounds are muted or distorted by the time they reach bureaucratic ears. The channels are rarely direct, but pass instead through voting machines or interest-group lobbying. The noise/signal ratio is so high that the message rarely gets through. Even if it does, it must compete with more powerful voices than those of individual citizens.

All of this suggests a tension between bureaucracy and democracy. The ideology of democracy requires that government be not only of the people and for the people but also by the people. Can those ideals be reconciled with a bureaucratic style of governance?

The conflict between bureaucratic governance and democratic ideals was foreshadowed at the beginning of the 20th century by the German sociologist Max Weber. In the course of outlining the model or "ideal type" of bureaucratic agencies, Weber suggests some sources of "irrationality" that may be exacerbated within a democratic polity. Among these, two are particularly noteworthy: bureaucratic softheartedness and political interference. These sources of tension must be understood in the context of Weber's model, which in this setting requires only a brief summary.

WEBER ON BUREAUCRACY AND DEMOCRACY

The classic conception of bureaucracy advanced by Weber emphasizes the efficiency of government organized by bureaus. Bureaucratic government is the only way in his view to achieve "formal rationality." Formal rationality means to Weber that the unit is well organized. He leaves little doubt as to how well he thinks such a unit works in modern societies, at least relative to any available alternative. On this matter he is emphatic and categorical: nothing can match it.

> [I]t would be sheer illusion to think for a moment that continuous administration can be carried out in any field except by means of officials working in offices . . . the needs of mass administration make it to-day completely indispensable. The choice is only that between bureaucracy and dilletantism in the field of administration. (Weber, p. 223)

Formal rationality does not mean to Weber that bureaucratic agencies will always be "substantively rational," that is, achieve their goals. Usually, but not always. Why then might a formally rational organization fail to achieve its goals? Weber suggests two possible sources of substantive failure that merit particular attention, one internal to the agency and one external.

The first mechanism that may detract from formal rationality, Weber tells us, is found within the organization. It is "the tendency of officials to treat their function from what is substantively a utilitarian point of view in the interest of those under their authority" (p. 226). In other words, officials wanting to help individual people might therefore interfere with the uniformity and predictability that formal rationality requires.[2]

In that event, formal rationality may be rescued and substantive rationality advanced, says Weber, by "the enactment of formal regulatory measures [which] generally express . . . this utilitarian tendency." Yet Weber leaves little doubt that this regulatory utilitarianism represents a threat to formalism. With what sounds to me like a sigh, he promises to treat these regrettable problems under the "theory of 'democracy'," (*idem*), a commitment that he left largely unfulfilled.

A more significant source of bureaucratic failure, according to Weber, comes from outside the agency. In order to function properly the agency must be given clear and unambiguous goals. In a democracy, he tells us, this requirement is not likely to be met. In this passage, Weber describes the problems posed by democracy for economic life and, we may assume, the process by which it is regulated:

> The presence of elective officials is a source of disturbance to formally rational economic life. This is true in the first place because such officials are primarily elected according to party affiliations and not according to technical competence. Secondly, the risks of recall or of failure of re-election make it impossible to pursue a strictly objective course of decision and administration, without regard to such consequences. (Weber, p. 270)

In other words, Weber is saying that the elective principle that lies at the heart of democratic governance can explain the inefficiency of bureaucracy. If that proposition were true, and if nothing could be done about it, the growth of bureaucracy could lead to trouble. One might anticipate an effort to limit the scope and growth of bureaucracy lest it threaten democracy and/or an effort to diminish the capacity of democratic institutions to impinge on bureaucracy.

There is another possibility, however, that ought to be explored. Let us suppose that Weber is right in seeing a basic tension between democracy and bureaucracy. The tension might be contained, so that the two systems could coexist and even be mutually supportive. If that could be accomplished, bureaucracy might support the democratic principle rather than undercutting it.

Weber never seriously entertained the possibility that governance could be more efficient if more democratic. While granting that there were nonbureaucratic organizations (such as "collegial representative bodies, parliamentary committees, soviets, honorary officers, lay judges, and what not") they do not constitute for him a realistic alternative to bureaucracy (Weber p. 223).

WEBER COULD BE WRONG

However, the stability of modern societies may well require a relaxation of the "formal rationality" of the bureaucratic form. This need has been apparent in our own society, where the failure of government to deliver needed services has become part of the folk wisdom. In a joke that made the rounds several years ago, the question was asked, "What are the three most frequently told lies?" To which these answers were given:

1. I gave at the office.
2. The check is in the mail.
3. I'm from the government and I'm here to help you.

What makes this a joke, one hardly needs to explain, is that most people do not perceive government officials as "here to help."

One response to dissatisfaction with bureaucracy takes the form of efforts to control administrative discretion. In a detailed study of these efforts, Stewart pointed out as early as 1975 the difficulties in doing so by the use of the courts or the legislature. Lowi also emphasized the growing power and discretion of the agencies in his book, *The End of Liberalism* (1978). Both studies imply that these developments have not been accompanied by a corresponding capacity of the agencies to accomplish their appointed tasks.

Stewart also examines the possibility that greater reliance on market mechanisms might become a way of disciplining the agencies. In 1975 he saw little reason for optimism that this approach would improve the performance of the agencies. Reliance on markets did find support in subsequent years: in the deregulation programs initiated during the Carter years and continued during the Reagan and Bush administrations that followed. The results are held up to detailed examination in some of the chapters in this handbook, notably those by Frug and Dempsey.

Emerging in current thinking is a mixed use of government and the market. As described by Osborne and Gaebler, this approach would diminish the role of government as a source of service, leaving that to a competitive field in which private agencies would compete with each other and government would concentrate on the steering functions: setting the objectives and evaluating the adequacy with which they were met. This approach does not rule out government agencies as competitors, but insists that there be independent and comparative evaluation of performance according to criteria set by the political process.

Whether such an approach will improve the performance of agencies at the national level remains to be seen. It is worth noting that the examples they have chosen come almost entirely from local and state government. While these are useful as demonstrations—potential harbingers of what might be done in the federal system—the dominant concentration of governmental power is found in Washington. Administration at the state and local level is deeply affected by the cooptative power, guidance, and example of the federal government.

Even if there were a shift toward state and local government, as some analysts have been suggesting (Rivlin, 1992), the conflict between bureaucratic administration and democratic governance would continue to require attention. Such a shift could contribute in several ways toward resolving the bureaucracy–democracy problem.

Solutions can be tried out more readily in smaller units, because the burden of persuasion for experimentation may be more easily overcome. Among a large number of units, we can expect more variations in the will to try something new. Governmental reform might well begin at the grass roots.

If the solutions require fuller public participation, as I believe they often do, that may be more easily and fully obtained at the local level. Facilitated by interstate and interlocal comparisons, demonstration projects and quasiexperiments can help to locate promising designs that can be adopted with modifications by other local and state governments.

Local-level experimentation can be enhanced by an inclination at the top to foster new approaches to governance. Because of a growing perception that governance reform is needed, opportunities for experimental efforts may be greater in the coming decade than at any time since the New Deal. Given the Clinton administration's emphasis on change, we may expect substantial efforts in this direction. However, such efforts require an analysis of the problem, as well as a procedure for envisioning and trying out alternatives.

To lay the foundation for major administrative change, we may need to expand the inquiry beyond its current boundaries. With few exceptions (such as those by Osborne and Gaebler, Rivlin), discussions of reform are limited by the prevailing assumption that the basic outlines of administrative agencies are inevitable. That premise cannot easily be countered, for several reasons.

First, we have not had clearly before us a sharply defined alternative to the prevailing system. For a society to take seriously a major change in its mode of governance, it must either find itself in deep distress, or it must believe in the plausibility of a clear alternative. Neither has been the case until very recently. Even now, there is a widespread tendency to assume the inevitability of prevailing governmental ways. Accordingly, we tend to react lethargically to bureaucracy as an inevitable condition, rather than as a problem to be solved.

Second, we lack the conditions for developing, testing, and implementing alternatives to prevailing modes of governance. Alternatives may be suggested, but they are not easily carried out. Where a task is to be done, the command-and-control model tends to be employed. It has some dependable virtues: people can be counted on to be visibly doing the task to which they are assigned. Experimental alternatives, not very clearly defined at the outset, are likely to seem less promising. They may, in consequence, not get a fair try.

Third, there is a tendency to judge performance by formal, rather than substantive, outcomes. It is easy enough to count the cases processed; not so easy to measure the satisfaction and adjustment of those whose cases have been processed. Nor is this problem necessarily overcome by legislative oversight. Blau describes, in his *Dynamics of Bureaucracy,* how legislative demands on a job-placement agency for success led to more numerous, but more temporary, placements. That dynamic observed by Blau in a rare field study conducted decades ago continues in force. Quantitative "evidence" of good performance does not necessarily mean actual success.

Finally, the agency activities are difficult to study. As a result, there is little knowledge outside the agency of how they operate. There tends to develop a kind of bureaucratic obscurity. To the outsider, at least, there is generally a scarcity of solid, detailed information about the functioning of the agency. Freedom of information and sunshine laws, reflecting an impulse toward openness, are only a beginning.

The dearth of information about the actual working of the agencies is attributable in large measure to the difficulty of access experienced by those outside the agencies: citizens, scholars, and even elected officials. In general, governmental agencies are not open for inspection. There are all kinds of reasons for this, some of them meritorious. Yet the consequence is a prevailing obscurity that cloaks the agencies from public view and from the kind of analysis that could lead to fundamental change.

One might well ask why this practice has occurred. It does not appear as a prominent feature of the model described by Weber, although he discussed it in an interesting passage (pp. 993–994). In some cases, the reasons for secrecy on certain matters are obvious (e.g., military secrets) and/or may, as in the tax code, be required by law. Yet other agencies show a propensity toward secrecy whether or not authorized by legislation to do so. It is a good example of the culture of bureaucracy, generated perhaps by the structure of the agency, its place in the governmental system, and its relation to the larger society. At all events, this feature contributes to the alienation of citizens by leaving them puzzled about their treatment and unable to find adequate answers to their questions.

BUREAUCRACY IN ACTION

Governmental bureaucracies have tended to shield their operations from detailed public scrutiny. This practice is often justified in terms of the legitimate interest of privacy for individuals whose case records have been processed by the agency. In addition, the rule of confidentiality serves to protect the agency from public scrutiny. Protecting the agency may be the more compelling of the two.

As a result, it is difficult for the ordinary citizen or community to obtain the kind of information that would permit them to understand or intelligently participate in the agency's decision process. Information available to the agency personnel but not to the public tends to be used to further policies favored by the agency. Justification for policies is often given in terms of technical expertise of the bureau, compared with the lack of expertise on the part of citizens.

The significance of the knowledge discrepancy becomes particularly clear when one examines programs explicitly designed to involve and inform citizens. An effort of this kind was undertaken by the Environmental Protection Agency (EPA) in regulations calling for public participation in the planning of waste-water treatment facilities under the Clean Water Act. The program was conceived under the aegis of EPA Administrator William D. Ruckelshaus when he headed the Agency during the period 1970–1973. It was put into practice in the late 1970s under Jimmy Carter and continued into the early years of Ronald Reagan's first term.

The regulations issued to secure informed public participation (40 Code of Federal Regulations 25, 35) were extremely detailed. They were supposed to be invoked in every community where large-scale construction was under consideration or where it appeared likely that public controversy might result. They called for a Citizens Advisory Committee (CAC) of 12 to 20 members drawn in approximately equal numbers from four categories: politicians, business people, environmentalists, and impartial citizens. This group, working on a volunteer basis, was to be convened and oriented by the state environmental agency. It was also to be advised by a professional consulting engineer, paid for by state and federal funds, about the optional plans for handling waste water treatment.

Researching the way these rules were put into practice made clear that the conception of the agency and its programs is very different in the agency offices than it is in the perspective of citizens at the local level. The difference in knowledge and point of view was enormous. The state agencies to whom EPA delegated this program varied in their manner of implementation, but each developed for itself a standardized approach within the framework supplied by the EPA.

Under delegation agreements between EPA and the states, public participation under the Clean Water Act became the responsibility of certain officials. Some states designated the program as the responsibility of an established branch of the agency (e.g., an Office of Water Resources). Others developed a special office to coordinate citizen participation. Some states handled the entire program from a central office while others used a regional structure. What they had in common was a clearly organized program in which each official had a specific assignment of duties and an obligation to record the way in which they were carried out.

The usual way of describing such a program is from a "top down" perspective. One could begin with the organization chart and the internal operating rules of an agency. Another approach is to examine the enabling legislation in which Congress (or another legislative body) authorizes and instructs the agency to proceed. Yet another perspective comes from the judicial side, especially those decisions of the appellate courts that seek to adjudicate disputes over the authority and procedures of the agency.

All of these approaches can be useful in describing how an administrative agency works, as seen by those who make decisions in our government. However, that approach leaves out the view from below, of those who are affected by the agency's actions. The agencies themselves seem to have no systematic way of gathering such information. They know about the legislature, whence their authority derives. They know about their top administrators and follow their decisions very carefully. They know about the courts, which may constrain their freedom of action, but they do not seem to know in any depth how they are perceived by the people they are supposed to regulate and serve.

To understand the discontent with bureaucracy it is important to look at bureaucracy from below: from the perspective of ordinary citizens who do not regularly come into contact with governmental offices. Here are some of the things that members of Citizens Advisory Committees told us when we asked them to describe the agency that sponsored and guided their committee.

> The way things are going today, people really don't trust the government, the EPA. Industry doesn't trust the EPA for different reasons. People are always feeling that government is going to set standards that are too high and it could affect them and they should be part of the decision making process and understand what goes on, and really get their understanding of what's happening. I think it would take some of the fear out of some of the problems that we're seeing now.

A participant from another community suggested the value of local citizen participation conducted without detailed monitoring by the agency:

> How do you tell when the process is really a bona fide one or just a charade? You probably have to monitor the thing from beginning to end before you really know that. So [the state environmental agency] if they wanted to enforce it on a community without a commitment to it, they'd probably have to go out to every meeting and require some kind of a regular reporting so that they could monitor whether the thing actually worked or not. But I don't think they actually intend to do that. So I think it actually depends on the commitment at the local level.

Both of these comments suggest the possibility of governmental enforcement, while expressing the hope that local action will be given greater sway in the actual decision process. This was a widespread theme. Was the concern over enforcement justified by the orientation of the agency? Sometimes yes and sometimes no. For the citizens, there was little chance of knowing for sure.

To understand the concerns of citizens, as expressed in these comments, one must look inside the administrative agency. While access is generally difficult, some agencies permit outside observers into the process. The view from within helps to explain the uncertainties among citizens outside the agency. As will be seen, the agency has a dynamic of its own, a kind of "formal rationality" that greatly affects the functioning of the agency and helps to explain how it is understood and why it is so often misunderstood.

The state agency described here is a large and complex unit. Its operations are run from offices in the state capital, but it carries out its work through a series of regional offices that have responsibility for implementing regulations in the geographical area they cover. To implement its program of public participation, the state developed a civil service specialty called public participation specialist (PPS). Each region has at least one PPS, as they came to be known. In addition to the regional specialists, there are six who hold the same title in the state office.

The atmosphere in the state office is remarkably different from that in the regions. The central staff had responsibility for planning the implementation of the program. When a Citizens Advisory Committee was brought together it sent a person to give orientation to the committee. In these presentations, the regional PPS usually deferred to the person from the central office.

Meetings were held in the central office at least twice a year that were attended by the regional PPS. These were usually conducted as information and orientation meetings. Characteristically they were addressed by the commissioner, the executive deputy commissioner, the assistant commissioner for public information, some specialists in technical engineering subjects, and public relations persons.

In these early meetings, the central office PPS played a key role. They were closer to the source of authority, having regular access to the executive deputy commissioner, and other key persons in the department. While they held the same formal rank as the regional PPS, they showed in many ways the significance of their proximity to the source of power.

When the program became operational in 1980, the task of implementation was assigned to the central staff. Under the direction of the officer in charge of public information, they instituted a program of training for all PPS. This was done in a 3 day seminar that was prepared and conducted by Hans and Annemarie Bleiker, of the Institute for Participation Planning of Laramie, Wyoming.

The Bleiker course, as it was called, was self-described as "citizen participation by objectives" using the management terms of the time that had been popularized in Washington by Robert McNamara. The course was described as "a tried and proven, practical method for developing broad public acceptance of plans, projects, programs, that are inherently controversial and unpopular." The training manual carried the title of *Citizen Participation Handbook: For Public Officials and Other Professionals Serving the Public.* The course promised that, "in just three to four days you can learn what took us and other MIT researchers 18 years to learn," namely, how to implement projects that are unpopular.

The flavor of the Bleiker approach is reflected in another course, described as an advanced version that assumes a knowledge of "CP-by-Objectives." This one is called Proposition 31 (Or: How to Reverse the Proposition 13 Mood for Projects, Programs, Bond Issues, and Agencies that are Vital). This four-day seminar is described as a supercondensed version of a four-semester graduate course on the augmentation/meta process, "A planning process that simultaneously develops technical solutions for a given problem and the 'Informed Consent' from those interests who might want to stop the implementation of any of the solutions."

Publicity for the advanced course suggests that it was intended for the really difficult problems that might arise in "serving the public." In a brochure advertising it, the "Proposition 31" course is described as "concentrat[ing] on how to avoid the 50+ errors that are frequently made in public-sector planning projects . . . and that usually lead to a great big controversy instead of an integrated program, policy, or plan."

The same brochure goes on to appeal to the interest of the individual administrator. It is designed, "to make you more effective and successful" and, in words that seem designed to comfort the harassed public servant, "especially if you and your agency deal with the very skeptical, cynical public that's characterized by the 'Proposition 13 Mood.' "

These courses were used by the agency to train regional and central public participation specialists in carrying out their assignments in helping to administer the Clean Water Act. The objective of the act—building and rebuilding water treatment plants in localities across the country—was clearly intended to "serve the public." Yet the technique for doing so, as suggested in the Bleiker approach, seemed to add "whether it likes it or not."

This kind of language should not by itself cast the public participation program of the agency in an unfavorable light. After all, the brochure might have been written by an enthusiastic publicity person seeking to attract maximum participation in the course. One must look beyond the publicity to the way in which the courses entered into the activity of the agency.

At one time or another, virtually every public participation specialist in the agency took the basic Bleiker course. It provided a common experience and some language with which to discuss the technique of handling public participation. The program was intended for a group of employees, and group discounts were offered, on the premise that it worked more successfully when taken as a team by employees of a given agency.

Whether it created a common orientation toward the task is quite a different matter. Explanations covered a wide range. To the regional PPSs, the Bleiker course provided some useful pointers to think about as they undertook to guide the public participation process. For administrators in the central office, it came closer to the description in the brochure. In fact, one supervisor outdid the brochure. Asked what the public participation course was all about, he replied, "It's just a way of identifying and dealing with your enemies."

This orientation suggests a defensive attitude that certainly was present in the agency. However, that attitude was tempered to some extent by the orientation of the regional specialists. Left to their work in the field, they developed their own style based more on their own background and personality than on a single set of rules or procedures. Even in meeting the requirements of standard reporting, they showed considerable variation. More marked variation showed up in the ways different PPS dealt with citizens in the local communities.

In the field data, these differences become quite clear. The regional PPS themselves came from a variety of backgrounds and they interpreted their roles quite differently. This feature of the program contributed to the variations that are found in the different cases studied. However, the degree of variation was limited by certain standard practices imposed by the central agency.

The strain between uniformity and diversity is not unique to the program studied here. Lipsky observes this tension in the work of field officials whom he denotes as "street-level bureaucrats." In describing a variety of public officials, he identifies a universal tension between dealing with clients as individuals (taking into account the distinctive nature of their situation) and applying a uniform set of rules handed down from above.

Lipsky believes that the tension now leads to erratic and ineffective administration. His solution: either move toward a far more efficient control system that ensures genuine uniformity, or provide discretion at the street level combined with the kind of professionalism that would make it possible for agency employees to perceive the needs of their clients more clearly and respond flexibly to provide an optimal outcome. Lipsky clearly would choose the individualized approach as preferable.

The same kind of analysis can be applied to this program, except that the community rather than the individual is the client. That fact complicates the task of the official enormously, for he or she must deal with diverse personalities brought together to search for a consensus. Moreover the communities in the program vary widely in their history, culture, and structure. These differences might well make any single formula unlikely to succeed for all.

Pending detailed study and reporting of the public participation process, no one can fully anticipate the kinds of variations that exist. Enough has been seen to date, however, to suggest the need for an approach that takes into account community variations within a larger framework of rules. To insist on business representation in a predominantly agricultural community, for example, can reduce the chances of effectively representing the interests of the farmers in a Citizens Advisory Committee. In another community, the volunteer fire department turns out to be the real center of political power, not the formally elected officials.

A possible way to deal with such diversity is to provide communities with the opportunity to select or develop their own modes of public participation and to report, along with the results, the methods used. Systematic analysis of that kind of information might then be used to advise other communities as they select or devise their own ways of bringing the public in. An approach of that kind has rarely been tried, perhaps because of the implicit assumption that experts in the agencies are supposed to know the right way to proceed. That assumption rests on the premise that there is a single right way and that the experts know what it is.

My guess is that the tension between bureaucracy and democracy is a serious problem, but one that can be dealt with. To do so, I think we must be aware of the tension, and find ways of identifying it better than we now do. We must also try to learn where the bureaucratic model can usefully be employed and where it cannot; how in the latter cases we can create alternative modes of organization that work better than classic bureaucracy to achieve our substantive ends.

Such inquiries are surely appropriate in a democratic society. The fundamental principle of democracy provides that government will be not only *of* the people but also *by* the people. When we see agents of government seeking to identify the enemy in a "cynical" public, something would seem to have been lost from the original understanding. We must therefore try to understand what the lost element is and how it can be restored.

Might it be possible to develop governmental forms that include the people in a larger role in their own governance? If so, could that kind of inclusion increase the likelihood that the outcomes would also more nearly meet popular needs, thus fulfilling the goal of government *for* the people as well.

It may prove easier to identify what has been lost. I think it is the composition of differences, the art of creative compromise, that has lost its vitality in our political life. This loss is especially evident among ordinary citizens, whose experience rarely includes a chance to learn through experience how to compose their differences and work responsibly toward policy consensus.

However, enough of it remains to be able to identify the motive and the ability. The Public Participation Program attracted people who had a drive toward responsible civic interaction. Their dedication to the ends of responsible governance was, on the whole, remarkable. Whether their efforts succeeded was quite another question.

They were brought together under the aegis of an agency rule promulgated in Washington. Here was an instance in which government sought to elicit advice from the grassroots. That demonstrated an impulse in the EPA to encourage local-level participation processes.

The implementation, however, revealed many aspects of bureaucracy that frustrated the original intention. Some of these were evident from the very beginning of the research; others emerged in time. The barriers to effective citizen participation resulting from bureaudynamics (to coin a term) warrant close scrutiny. On the whole, they were not included in Max Weber's ideal type.

WHAT WEBER LEFT OUT

Weber's model of bureaucracy left out a number of features that tend to characterize bureaucratic organizations. Those of particular interest for us are the features that impinge on the functioning of a democratic society. Among these, I want at this point particularly to mention obscurity, inflexibility, and selective ignorance.

These are unpleasant-sounding words, and I did earnestly consider alternatives that would seem less negative. In the end, I felt it better to avoid euphemistic synonyms, lest I fail to make my meaning clear. After all, to risk obscurity in discussing obscurity can hardly be helpful.

I repeat that these observations are not meant as an attack on those who are employed in bureaucratic work. Many administrative officials take very seriously the obligation of serving the public interest in their work. Sometimes they succeed. To do so, however, they characteristically must face a set of conditions that discourage the continued maintenance of an altruistic orientation.

Michael Lipsky makes this point emphatically in *Street-Level Bureaucracy*. People often enter these jobs (e.g., as teachers, police, or social workers) with a motive for service. But this quickly declines in most public-service work, he observes, as workers find themselves unable to serve clients' needs while meeting the requirements of the agency.

Many conditions of bureaucratic work militate against an effective altruistic, service-oriented relation to the client. Among the conditions Lipsky cites are large case loads and mass processing of clients, tight control of agency resources, the need to control client behavior, and the requirement that one's actions in relation to clients will be reviewed by other administrators and judged by the adequacy with which they meet preestablished requirements (Lipsky, pp. 73–74).

The consequence of these conditions is that administrative workers, especially in the lower ranks, must limit their inclination to advocate the needs of their client or risk failure to meet the criteria of the agency. This leads many "street-level bureaucrats" to give up the service orientation that often brought them to the job.

My own observation suggests, contrary to the Lipsky view, that service orientation often remains, but that it is translated from service to the individual client into a more generalized orientation. In the work I observed, the regional public participation specialists were faced with huge work loads that required far more knowledge of particular circumstances than they could possibly manage to obtain from the sources and by the methods available to them.

Faced with that situation, they reacted to these difficulties by interpreting their task more narrowly, in line with the conception promulgated from the central headquarters. Over time, indeed fairly quickly, they adopted a basic orientation toward the requirements of the job that came from headquarters.

This is not to say that they lost interest in the cases that were their primary responsibility. Some showed a remarkable concern for the communities they worked in. It does mean that their work was carried out within the constraints imposed by higher authority, and that authority embodied some features, quite important for the actual operation of the agency, that Weber hardly mentioned.

Obscurity

The first of these little-noticed characteristics is the obscurity of bureaucratic operations. Agencies differ, of course, in their contacts with ordinary citizens. Where the nature of work requires direct contact with nonemployees, the contact with the agency is likely to be highly specific and well controlled. As a result, the client learns primarily about one case (his or hers) and is rarely informed of the general scope of the agency.

Where individual contact is not required, the agency is likely to be even less well understood by the public. Information concerning the functioning of the agency is generally handled by the public relations officers of the agency. Legislative committees do exercise oversight, by getting reports and hearing testimony, but these sources tend to be highly general except in the rare instance of a scandal.

In recent years, some concern has developed regarding the content of agency files. This concern gained impetus during a period of unrest, when the federal government was said to be keeping secret files that assertedly contained much unverified information that could be used to deprive people of privileges or to impose penalties. As a result, Congress devised a statute requiring that agencies divulge requested information unless it was specifically privileged. Many states followed the lead of the Freedom of Information Act with comparable statutes of their own.

Did such statutes reflect a general tendency on the part of agencies to keep information confidential? If so, why would that be the case? And what would be the consequence for relations between the agency and the public?

In general, it seems that administrative agencies control information as a regular practice. The inquiring outsider may be informed of some aspect of the work of the agency, provided that the relevant information has already been generated and approved for release. Where such information is not already available, the response tends to be less forthcoming.

Certain kinds of information are explicitly subject to control. That would be true, by definition, of classified materials. Recognizing this as a legitimate governmental need, the Congress has moved to regulate the maintenance of what it has decided are legitimate governmental secrets.

Some kinds of information are likewise kept confidential to protect the privacy of citizens. Thus tax records of individuals may not be revealed to people outside the Internal Revenue Service except in specified circumstances.

Beyond these specific areas, there arises the issue of general policy. Agencies might take one of two positions: a presumption against or a presumption for disclosure. Do agencies tend to ask the question, Why should this information be made available? or the opposite question, Why should this information not be made available?

The failure to supply requested information may partly result from the extra work that would be required to meet the request. Since agency personnel tend to be overworked, an additional request may be seen as adding work that is unnecessary. In addition, the response may generate questions concerning its purpose. How will the requested information be used, by whom, for what purpose?

Other factors being equal, the disinclination to supply information reflects the defensiveness of the agency. When an agency has been under attack, one of its characteristic defenses is to increase its supply of selected information, while decreasing free access by outsiders. Those responses can be characteristic of the agency as a whole, or of a particular segment. Sometimes confidentiality is invoked on behalf of the agency by a particular individual whose actual motive—rationalized by agency interest or public good—is to protect his or her own interest.

An example of resistance to the release of information occurred at an early stage in this research. In the course of exploring the feasibility of the project, I asked my research assistant to check with the headquarters of the agency to determine how many construction grant cases they had processed. The assistant came back to report that there were 300 to 500 cases and that he would be welcome to look into the files.

The report pleased me for two reasons: first, because I was surprised to learn of the scope of this kind of work and second, because I was pleased to discover that the information would be accessible. As a result, I called to confirm the report and to make preliminary arrangements for studying the records.

In response to a phone call, the person my assistant had contacted said that I would have to check with his supervisor to confirm the availability of the records. On doing so, I was told that these records were not available for public inspection. When I asked why not, I was told it was agency policy. Could anything be done to alter that, to permit me to proceed with my study? The response, without hesitation: "File a freedom of information request." That procedure, I was told, would take at least 6 months.

Distressed at the prospect of a long delay, I decided to try a more direct approach. Asking for advice from politically well-placed people, I came into contact with a person widely known as "the governor's man for this part of the state." Using the name of a mutual friend, I told him my story and asked whether he could do anything about it. That request led immediately to a phone call to the commissioner of the agency, an interview in the commissioner's office, a referral to the executive deputy commissioner, an interview there, and a similar contact with the deputy commissioner for public information.

In the interviews, I gave the rationale of the study. In discussing my reasons for the study, I started by stating my civic concern for effective action to clean up the environment. I also gave academic reasons for the study: to learn whether public participation can help generate consensus at the local level on environmental policy issues. I also emphasized that the study was not intended to embarrass or expose anyone, that I was anything but an investigative journalist.

Also mentioned rather casually in both conversations was the name of an official in the governor's office. I had dropped in to see my old friend George Billetdoux before coming to the agency headquarters. George turned out to have become the governor's second in command, with responsibility for overseeing and coordinating the administration of all the state agencies. I was pleased to learn that the commissioner and the executive deputy commissioner knew George well and considered him an excellent administrator, always helpful in meeting the needs of the agency.

These methods produced positive results. They seem to have worked because my contacts enabled me to get quickly to the top of the organization. Once there, I was able to reassure the officials that my study would not harm them or the agency, and that it might have some positive value. Against that, I suppose they considered some negative consequences that could result, given my contacts, from an arbitrary decision to delay access.

Compare this organizational response with the one I faced originally. At first, my student got a positive response from a lower-middle level PPS. When I followed that up, the initial response had to be confirmed by a second official, the immediate superior of the first. His negative reaction ("File a freedom of information form") could have been appealed to the deputy commissioner for public information. The whole process took on the appearance of a defense in depth.

Most citizens would not have ventured this far into the inner realm of an administrative agency. Records of one's own case tend to be confidential; records of other cases even more so; and the procedures that are applied to a range of cases lie beyond the reach of ordinary citizens. While freedom of information laws provide access to some people after delay and sifting, ordinary citizens continue to find the work of the agencies obscure.

The success I had in gaining the agency's cooperation was an exception. Most people would not try and those who did would likely have encountered the kind of responses I initially encountered. By that time discouragement or lack of interest would inhibit further inquiry. Left alone for the most part, the agency remains obscure, its initiatives only partially understood by the public, its purposes unclear, its usefulness doubted.

Action and Mission

The agency's obscurity is not necessarily diminished, and may indeed be enhanced, by its methods of operation. Administrative agencies tend, as Weber pointed out, to be limited in their objectives. Our administrative agencies use the term *mission* to describe their responsibilities. Policies adopted by the agency tend to be related to that mission. Relating policy to mission provides a justification for the agency's action: internally to the staff, and externally to the legislature, the executive, and the courts. Whether goal-oriented action has the same effect for the public affected by its actions is another question.

I was given complete access to all written records relating to the work of the Citizens Advisory Committees. The manner in which that permission was granted throws some light on the significance of mission for the agency.

The records, as it turned out, were not available at the central headquarters, but were kept instead at regional offices. Accordingly, the Executive Deputy Commissioner sent a memo to the following officials: executive staff, division directors, regional directors and other appropriate staff. A copy of the document was sent to the commissioner.

The memo effectively opened the files to me and my research staff. For the study of governmental administration, it is an instructive document. After identifying me by my academic affiliation, the memo gives the topic of the study. It then provides a rationale for opening the files, namely, that the study "can provide valuable information and insights that will contribute to the work of the department." This conclusion was reached, the memo says, by the top two officers of the Department, "the Commissioner and I" after "[h]aving discussed this project with Professor Schwartz."

The memo goes on to develop the rationale in some additional detail, as follows:

> As a possible product of this study, we hope to learn how and when citizen participation can better serve its intended purposes. The research is designed to discover, by looking at a series of cases, how the process actually works.

These sentences are followed immediately, within the same paragraph, by a "request" "To this end, we request that you be as helpful as you can to Professor Schwartz and his staff." And then a reiteration of the rationale:

> With your cooperation, we hope to derive from the study knowledge that will help us to do a better job in meeting the needs of our citizens by involving them effectively in the process of environmental planning.

This first half of the memo seems designed to serve two main purposes: to assert the authority behind the "request," and to give the rationale for doing so.

The authority comes from the two top-ranking officials of the agency, who have made a discretionary decision based on conversations held by each of them with the professor. Their joint action in making the "request" gives it maximum authority within the agency. Coming from the top, as it does, this memo, whatever term is used to describe it, constitutes an order.

On the basis of subsequent experience, it seems clear that this order did have the intended effect—almost miraculously—of opening the files. It was received by officials in all the top administrative posts at the agency's headquarters and in the regional offices. Through both channels, it was delivered to the public participation specialists (undoubtedly included as addressees under the category "other appropriate staff") whose files were the principal subject of the memo.

What it meant to the regional PPSs was that they had the go-ahead to make their files available for this purpose. If they had been so inclined, the memo assured them that they could do so without hesitation. If they were not so inclined, the memo told them that they must do so whether they liked it or not. The concluding line of the memo made this even clearer. It said, "If you believe that you cannot assist Professor Schwartz in his efforts, for any reason, please let me know immediately."

The rationale for the request serves a variety of purposes. Heavy if not exclusive emphasis is placed on the potential value of this research for the agency to "contribute to the work of the department."

This serves to affirm that the order (as I shall call it) falls within the scope of the administrators' responsibility. As the top officers, they clearly are charged with the obligation to run the department efficiently. Little in the memo goes beyond that duty.

One sentence does suggest a wider objective, in its assertion of the hope that the resultant knowledge "will help us to do a better job in meeting the needs of our citizens by involving them effectively in the processes of environmental planning." While this phrase begins with an emphasis on the agency's responsibility to "do a better job," it goes on to cite the external outcome of "meeting the needs of our citizens by involving them effectively in the process of environmental planning." There are two possible interpretations of this interesting sentence.

First, it could mean that citizen involvement is a means to the end of "meeting the [environmental] needs of our citizens." In that event, the agency would be continuing to focus on its limited task of improving the environment, aided now by the technique of bringing citizens in. What would be the purpose of bringing them in? To discover what they felt their needs to be; to get their ideas as to how these needs could best be met; to determine which among alternative plans would be most acceptable to the community; or even to locate the source of opposition in a "very skeptical, cynical public." Any or all of these might turn out to be interpretations of citizen participation when seen as a means to the end of "doing a better job."

A second interpretation would see citizen involvement as a means to the end of "meeting the [political] needs of our citizens" to have a say in determining how their environmental needs ought to be met. Is that a plausible interpretation? Its plausibility depends (as the deconstructionists have been pointing out) on who is doing the interpreting.

If one asks how this statement was meant by the executive deputy commissioner who drafted it, it seems quite plausible that he intended both meanings. He could well have intended to meet both the environmental and the political needs of the citizens. He was a lawyer who had served in the post for many years, through Republican and Democratic administrations. He was widely respected in the legislature, other agencies of state government, and in the governor's office. Within the agency, he was respected and liked throughout the ranks, with a reputation for clarity and fairness that helped the agency to function effectively.

As a person, he clearly welcomed a program of public participation for both reasons: to do the environmental job better and to give citizens a say in the shaping of the agency's projects. On the other hand, he also accepted the governmental framework that limited the agency's mission. This agency, like all other administrative agencies, has a clearly specified mandate. The task of this agency, as specified in the statute establishing it, was to protect the environment. The legislation makes no mention of the agency's responsibility to meet political needs, implement citizens rights of participation, or anything of the kind.

If the executive deputy commissioner did want to deliver participation for its political value, whence would he derive the authority? In a general sense, he might find warrant for doing so in the Declaration of Independence or in the Preamble to the Constitution. But such general ideas would hardly merit the term "authorization." If he decided to implement such a program, using agency funds to do so, he would likely feel obliged to point to some specific directive in the statute or in a regulation, if not also in a budgetary allocation for the purpose.

Authority for the program of public participation did derive from the federal regulation (40 CFR 125,135) that specified the requirement of public participation in the planning and, to some extent, in the construction phase of facilities to be built under the Clean Water Act. This regulation was not explicitly invoked in these circumstances.

Characteristically, the federal regulation was interpreted in its significance for carrying out the task of the agency. In the choice between the broad and narrow goals, the agency tended to emphasize the narrow, task-oriented objective. Public participation was generally construed throughout the agency as a requirement of the federal government that the state had undertaken under its delegation agreement with the EPA.

In accepting that responsibility, the agency undertook to follow the regulations to the letter. As a result, the agency developed, in cooperation with the state civil service office, a new specialty, that of public participation specialist. The responsibility of those specialists, as stated in their job description, was to carry out the mission of the agency. Public participation was merely a means to that end.

One can understand the tendency of government agencies to make narrow interpretations of their mission. If the objective had been twofold (to protect the environment *and* to foster participatory democracy), administrative responsibility might have become more complex. A single goal is easier to administer than a double one. In pursuing that goal, it is always possible to specify the kind of actions that must be undertaken in working toward that goal. To work simultaneously toward two goals, however, carries the danger of disagreement, confusion, and ultimately an abandonment of the program.

The problem posed by multiple goals for a mission-oriented agency is described in detail by Daniel Patrick Moynihan in his book, *Maximum Feasible Misunderstanding*. There he describes the three different interpretations that were given by legislators and administrators in Washington to the phrase "maximum feasible participation." His account certainly suggests that the program was hampered from the start by the ambiguity of the phrase and the three different interpretations given to it by proponents, administrators, and citizens. As a result, the War on Poverty experienced great difficulty in carrying out a program whose purposes were never clearly set forth.

To say that a single mission helps to organize the work of an administrative agency is important but insufficient. As Howard Odum, an early student of social problems used to say, "That's true, what else is true?" In this case, the additional important truth derives from the way in which the participatory program was understood by the people who formed the CACs. They were not at all clear about the source, structure, or rationale of the program.

For the most part, they started with the account given to them by the orienting officer of the agency. He left them with a largely technical impression of their task. His visit to each CAC typically occurred at the first session of the CAC. On the occasion of that first meeting, he gave a standard talk that stressed the requirement of regular meetings and laid out the task of the group: to recommend one of alternative possibilities that would be presented to the group by the engineering consultant.

The person who gave the orientating talk rarely reappeared at subsequent CAC meetings. His specialized task was to come from the capital headquarters, stay briefly in the region, and provide a lecture that was intended to tell the CAC how to do its job.

This orientation was also intended to introduce the regional public participation specialist and, if available, the consulting engineer. While the orienting official met only at the beginning, the other two were regularly available. The consulting engineer typically attended every meeting, and the regional PPS was kept apprised by regular reports and phone conversations of the progress of the Citizens Advisory Committee.

The single appearance of the orienting officer left the CACs somewhat baffled. Some of this puzzlement may have resulted from the nature of his performance. The person who gave these talks (let me call him Frank Orient) presented a great deal of information in a relatively short session. It was absorbed with difficulty by many of Frank's listeners.

Those who came to the session, newly selected as members of the CAC, comprised a diverse set of people. They differed in their knowledge of waste-water treatment techniques, in their educational background, in their occupation, and in the source of their interest. A group might include a shopkeeper, a college-educated environmentalist, the supervisor of the existing treatment plant, the clerk of the Board of Selectmen, and so on.

To bring such a group to a common level of knowledge would have been a difficult task even for an unusually skilled teacher. Frank happened to fall short of that standard. He lacked the capacity, noteworthy in some of the other public participation specialists, to sense the range of his audience and to provide information designed to reach as many of them as possible.

This difficulty may have arisen because of Frank's distinctive history and characteristics. He had played a major role in establishing the public participation program in the state. He had been involved in drafting the delegation agreement between the state agency and EPA, and he became a major advocate within the agency for full implementation of the program. Frank believed strongly in the importance of the program. He brought to this task a conviction that citizen participation, as he conceived it, would without question facilitate the reconstruction of water treatment plants throughout the state.

My first encounter with Frank impressed me with the strength of that conviction. Of all the state agency people I met, he alone told me bluntly that my proposed study was unnecessary. There was no need, he said, to redo research that had already been done. He was certain that public participation was a successful program. I was reminded of an interview in Washington with a former EPA official who was equally certain that "it just doesn't work." Neither could provide me with systematic feedback. Both tried to discourage the study.

Frank did not supply me with references to back his belief. Instead, he referred me to the Bleikers. After contacting them and reading their materials, I concluded that they had not undertaken any systematic research on this form of public participation. When I reported that to Frank when next we met, he reiterated his position that the necessary research had been done and that the program had been tested and found successful.

What can be learned from this incident? Certainly not that this attitude on Frank's part was typical. In the course of the study, I met and worked with many public participation specialists, in the regions and at headquarters, who were far less convinced about the method and far more flexible than Frank. If someone of that sort had been assigned his role, the orientation lectures might well have been done differently and I almost certainly would not have been met with so bluntly negative an attitude toward the proposed research.

What can be seen in this account is a bit of evidence regarding the kind of attitude and performance that was at least permissible in the work of this administrative agency. Frank's conduct in giving the lectures was premised on the assumption that a standard orientation would suffice to get the CACs started. As far as I could determine, he made no effort to vary his presentation according to the state of knowledge, diversity, number, need, or preference of his audience. That he did this regularly throughout the state did not run counter to any rule, instruction, or procedure that he received from the agency.

The other point to notice is that his performance was not subject to evaluation *from below*. His supervisors in the agency would surely have known if he had not come to the meetings that had been scheduled for him. However, they lacked a method by which they could be apprised of the reaction of his audience. They had no systematic method of studying the impact of his performance on the success or failure of the public participation program.

In principle, such information might have been gathered, for example, by evaluation questionnaires. In practice it was not. Generally speaking, such information is not regularly or systematically gathered from below, that is, from the clientele who are supposed to be served at the "street level" by agency personnel.

In this case, it would not be expected to come from the regional PPSs either, although they were quite aware of the problem. To have reported through official channels that Frank's presentation started a program badly would have been a risky action for a regional CPS, given the greater access to power of the PPS in the central office. In the circumstances, one might expect the regional specialists who accompanied Frank to be discreet, rather than to report their misgivings to officials at a higher level. They were.

Neither was there feedback on this matter to higher agency officials from members of the CACs. Their orientation session was a single experience, not sufficiently disturbing to lead them to complain. When they mentioned this part of their experience, as many did in our interviews, they usually shrugged it off as typical of "the government."

Even if they were antagonized or turned off by Frank's presentation, there was no regular channel through which to register their concerns. The easier course was simply to forget it and get on with the job. Some initial members dropped out at that stage for a variety of reasons, one of which was the orientation lecture. Most stayed on, and undertook to perform the advisory role. Their capacity to do so, however, had started at a disadvantage.

In initiating its public participation program, the agency was proceeding in a typical manner. It developed a general method by which to accomplish its task. The method consisted of analyzing the tasks that needed to be done, assigning them to an individual or group who specialized in doing those tasks, checking to see whether the required performance had occurred, and going on to the next task.

Characteristic of this approach is its generality. The orientation given to the CACs was a standard one. The person who provided it was convinced that it was the best possible mode of initiating the process. Alternatives were not systematically explored; if anything, deviations from the standard orientation were avoided if possible.

Some variations were built into the process. For example, the regulations made a distinction between two types of public participation: full and basic. Full participation required a Citizens Advisory Committee and basic did not. Full participation required two public meetings and a more formal public hearing, while basic required only one public hearing.

The decision as to which kind of public participation was to be required depended, under the rules, on the magnitude of the project and the probability of community conflict over the outcome. This variation constituted an attempt to fit the program to certain characteristics of the community. It illustrates an attempt at flexibility, within a larger frame of standardization.

Once this decision was made, the selected method was supposed to be followed with precision. Each regional public participation specialist was responsible for approving the program plan. They proceeded with their work in varying ways and these differences in style were significant in determining the outcomes. Some of the specialists were constantly in touch with the process; others confined themselves to initial approval, after which they depended on written reports.

In the early stages, all of the specialists were active. Determining full or basic participation was a decision set forth by the regulation; it was recommended at the regional level and recorded at central headquarters. This decision was made in consultation with local officials, in particular the head of the "lead agency" or a person designated by the head. The lead agency could consist of the water authority, village board, board of public works, or the like. Approval of the public participation plan by the agency was one of the requirements that must be completed before state and federal funds were made available in support of the planning process. This feature showed attention to local variation.

How this approach worked will be addressed in detail elsewhere. If the agency was not set up to provide for its own feedback, it was at least willing to open its process to scrutiny by someone from outside. An external look has certain advantages over an internal process.

The outsider may not know as much as people within, but that can be overcome with their cooperation. After the doors were open, I received remarkable cooperation from virtually everyone in the agency. Regional participation specialists gave us hours of their time going over each individual case in the sample we selected. While some preferred us to choose the most "interesting" cases rather than the most typical, they willingly told us everything they could about those we chose.

Equally cooperative were the CAC members and other knowledgeable people we interviewed. Each of them added something of importance to our information about a particular community. Their central motive for doing so was clear. They had spent a substantial amount of time trying to contribute to the needs of their community. They were being asked whether and how they felt they had succeeded and, if not completely, what had impeded their effort to do so.

Many of them saw beyond the borders of their community and well beyond the environmental task on which they were engaged. Their commitment and common sense stands out in the interviews as an encouraging reminder of the availability among American citizens of a base of civic responsibility on which democratic government ultimately depends.

Officials of the agency and participating citizens have tried to make citizen participation work effectively within the frame of agency policy. If and to the extent they have succeeded, the lessons deserve to be recorded to guide comparable future efforts. If and to the extent they have failed, we must try to understand why, and draw out the implications for the reform of administrative governance in America.

Without a detailed account of experience in each of the several communities studied, such inferences would necessarily be shallow. This essay is intended primarily as an introduction to detailed reporting. Until that is done, no conclusions are justified.

CONCLUSIONS

What does emerge from this research is a series of questions. What is the evidence of obscurity, rigidity, and rejection of feedback in the conduct of the agency? Are these regularly experienced by citizens in their contacts with the agency? If there are variations in these regards, under what circumstances do they occur, and with what results? How might they be alleviated? How might a community and an agency develop alternative measures for minimizing these characteristics?

These questions seem appropriate in light of the tensions that otherwise develop between bureaucracy and democratic governance. Before that gap becomes uncomfortably broad, we should be asking why the gap exists and what can be done about it. It is fortunate that the conditions for investigating these problems exist in a society committed to the principle of openness.

Some first steps in this direction would be to provide our agencies with better means than they now have for self-study. Such self-study should be conducted by independent researchers. If we can require auditing oversight by independent agencies (Office of Management and Budget, Congressional Budget Office), we ought to be able to do something comparable in other spheres.

Such research should be carried out with a broad mandate to study the agency as it actually relates to the people it is supposed to serve. What is needed goes beyond the usual corporate-type efficiency study. Closer to the mark is the kind of ethnographic method used by Peter Blau in *Dynamics of Bureaucracy.*

The research that is needed must also deal with the clients and communities that are affected by the agency's actions. We need to understand not only what the agencies do or do not do, and why. We also need to know in detail how the agency actions are perceived, understood, and reacted to by those who are affected.

On the basis of such research, we should be better able to devise a variety of innovations aimed at securing better connections between agencies and citizens. The research itself should contribute to this end, not only by identifying the needs but also by turning up instances that suggest promising alternatives. Examples emerge readily, once one begins to inquire in detail how a given program worked or failed, what approach a particular "street-level bureaucrat" took that led to increased effectiveness. Findings of the latter kind could encourage administrators to appreciate the value of benign variations in locating better ways of meeting public needs.

On the basis of research already available, James Q. Wilson documents the existence of variations in administrative organizations. His book *Bureaucracy* provides a data-rich panorama of diversity in the organization and functioning of governmental agencies. One conclusion is that they sometimes work very well and sometimes very badly. Wilson does not attempt to explain why, although he suggests that bureaucratic malfunctioning has something to do with the separation of powers built into our form of government.

Although Wilson describes his approach as "bottom up," he focuses his analysis on the offices and work places of the agencies. I think we need to go one step further to include in a systematic way the people whose lives are affected by the agencies. It is their interaction with bureaucratic agencies of government that is of greatest concern, and detailed knowledge of that interaction seems vital if we are to reexamine seriously the tensions between bureaucracy and democracy.

Of particular interest is research that seeks information on community reactions to bureaucratic regulation. Our society has operated on an individualistic model to such an extent that the community dimension tends to be underemphasized. Yet many programs are implemented in ways that affect communities, not just individuals. If government is to restore its partnership with citizens, it must find ways of relating to the community dimension when that is appropriate.

That dimension seems to me particularly important because the polity, taken as a whole, has done little to encourage and much to discourage community. Social scientists have contributed to this tendency by the heavy use of aggregated individual responses in national samples. If government were more responsive to community, it might thereby foster a sense of the community as a significant entity.

Many governmental programs could be more effective if tailored to the needs and orientations of local communities. The study referred to above, of public participation in the planning of water treatment facilities, is a case in point. By bringing citizens together to represent different interests, the agency set out on a path that would help to develop a community response to various policy alternatives. That effort illustrates a method for encouraging community response.

How well it worked is a story still to be told. We need to know whether a common voice emerged, whether it represented the community, how it related to established political institutions, how sound were its recommendations, and whether those recommendations were taken seriously by the agency.

The method in its conception showed promise of fostering a community response. As a potential, its importance for our civic culture is very great in that it promised voice to the citizens. That voice was not a series of isolated speakers, but a composite. Properly fostered such voices could become, in Carl Sandburg's phrase, "a hallelujah chorus forever changing its star soloists." Is there any conceivable way in which government can lead such a chorus, or at least provide a proper auditorium?

NOTES

1. The research on Citizens Advisory Committees was supported by grants from the Ford Foundation, The American Bar Foundation, and the Environmental Protection Agency. I am grateful to Donald T. Campbell and Arnold S. Feldman for their helpful suggestions.
2. An earlier translation emphasizes the rule-utilitarian point more clearly:

> There is another tendency, which is apparently in contradiction to [formalism], a contradiction which is in part genuine. It is the tendency of officials to treat their official function from what is substantively a utilitarian point of view in the interest of the welfare of those under their authority. But this utilitarian tendency is generally expressed in the enactment of corresponding regulatory measures which themselves have a formal character and tend to be treated in a formalistic spirit. (Parsons, p. 340).

REFERENCES

Blau, Peter M., *The Dynamics of Bureaucracy.* Chicago: University of Chicago Press, 1955.

Bleiker, Hans and Annemarie, *Citizen Participation Handbook.* Laramie, NY: Institute for Participatory Planning, 1978.

Drucker, Peter F. *Innovation and Entrepreneurship: Practice and Principles.* New York: Harper & Row, 1985.

Harris, Richard A. and Sidney M. Milkis, *The Politics of Regulatory Change.* New York: Oxford University Press, 1989.

Hirschman, Albert O., *Exit, Voice, and Loyalty: Responses to Declines in Firms, Organizations, and States.* Cambridge: Harvard University Press, 1970.

Lipsky, Michael, *Street-Level Bureaucracy: Dilemmas of the Individual in Public Service.* New York: Russell Sage Foundation, 1980.

Lowi, Theodore J., *The End of Liberalism: The Second Republic of the United States,* 2d ed. New York: W. W. Norton, 1979.

Marini, Frank, ed., *Toward a New Public Administration: The Minnowbrook Perspective.* Scranton: Chandler, 1971.

Moynihan, Daniel Patrick, *Maximum Feasible Misunderstanding.* New York: Free Press, 1970.

Osborne, David and Ted Gaebler, *Reinventing Government: How the Entrepreneurial Spirit is Transforming the Public Sector.* Reading, MA: Addison-Wesley, 1992.

Parsons, Talcott, ed., *Max Weber: The Theory of Social and Economic Organization* (Henderson & Parsons, trans.). New York: Oxford University Press, 1947.

Rivlin, Alice M., *Reviving the American Dream: The Economy, the States and the Federal Government.* Washington, D.C.: Brookings Institution, 1992.

Stewart, Richard B., The reform of American administrative law. 88 *Harvard Law Review* 1667 (1975).

Waldo, Dwight, *The Administrative State: A Study of the Political Theory of American Public Administration,* 2d ed. New York: Holmes & Meier, 1984.

Weber, Max, *Economy and Society: An Outline of Interpretive Sociology,* Vols. I & II. Guenther Roth and Claus Wittich, eds. Berkeley: University of California Press, 1978.

Wilson, James Q., *Bureaucracy: What Government Agencies Do and Why They Do It.* New York: Basic Books, 1989.

Index

The index was prepared by Annie Chang, Washington, D.C.